Methods in Dialectology

Multilingual Matters

Afrikaner Dissidents
  JOHA LOUW-POTGIETER
Aspects of Bilingualism in Wales
  COLIN BAKER
Australian Multiculturalism
  LOIS FOSTER and DAVID STOCKLEY
Bilingualism and the Individual
  A. HOLMEN, E. HANSEN, J. GIMBEL and J. JØRGENSEN (eds.)
Bilingualism in Society and School
  J. JØRGENSEN, E. HANSEN, A. HOLMEN and J. GIMBEL (eds.)
Code-Mixing and Code Choice
  JOHN GIBBONS
Communication and Cross-Cultural Adaptation
  YOUNG YUN KIM
Communication and Simulation
  D. CROOKALL and D. SAUNDERS (eds.)
Conversation: An Interdisciplinary Perspective
  D. ROGER and P. BULL (eds.)
Cultural Studies in Foreign Language Education
  MICHAEL BYRAM
Evaluating Bilingual Education
  MERRILL SWAIN and SHARON LAPKIN
The Interdisciplinary Study of Urban Bilingualism in Brussels
  E. WITTE and H. BAETENS BEARDSMORE (eds.)
Key Issues in Bilingualism and Bilingual Education
  COLIN BAKER
Language Acquisition of a Bilingual Child
  ALVINO FANTINI
Language Attitudes Among Arabic-French Bilinguals in Morocco
  ABDELÂLI BENTAHILA
Language and Ethnic Identity
  WILLIAM GUDYKUNST (ed.)
Language and Ethnicity in Minority Sociolinguistic Perspective
  JOSHUA FISHMAN
Language in Geographic Context
  COLIN WILLIAMS (ed.)
Minority Education: From Shame to Struggle
  T. SKUTNABB-KANGAS and J. CUMMINS (eds.)
Minority Education and Ethnic Survival
  MICHAEL BYRAM
Minority Language Conference: Celtic Papers
  G. MacEOIN, A. AHLQVIST, D. O'hAODHA (eds.)
Minority Language Conference: General Papers
  G. MacEOIN, A. AHLQVIST, D. O'hAODHA (eds.)
Neurotic and Psychotic Language Behaviour
  R. WODAK and P. Van De CRAEN (eds.)
Perspectives on Marital Interaction
  P. NOLLER and M. A. FITZPARICK (eds.)
Talk and Social Organisation
  G. BUTTON and J. R. E. LEE (eds.)
The Use of Welsh: A Contribution to Sociolinguistics
  MARTIN J. BALL (ed.)

Please contact us for the latest book information:
Multilingual Matters,
Bank House, 8a Hill Road, Clevedon, Avon BS21 7HH, England.

MULTILINGUAL MATTERS 48
Series Editor: Derrick Sharp

Methods in Dialectology

Proceedings of the Sixth International Conference held at the
University College of North Wales, 3rd—7th August 1987

Edited by

Alan R. Thomas

MULTILINGUAL MATTERS LTD
Clevedon · Philadelphia

British Library Cataloguing in Publication Data

Methods in dialectology: Proceedings of the
sixth international conference held at the
University College of North Wales, 3rd —
7th August 1987 — (Multilingual Matters: 48).
1. Dialectology
I. Title
417' .2

ISBN 1-85359-022-3

Multilingual Matters Ltd
Bank House, 8a Hill Road,
Clevedon, Avon BS21 7HH,   &   242 Cherry Street,
England.   Philadelphia, PA 19106-1906
                                      USA.

Copyright © 1988 Alan R. Thomas and individual contributors.
All rights reserved. No part of this work may be reproduced in any form or by any means
without permission in writing from the publisher.

Printed and bound in Great Britain by Short Run Press, Exeter.

Preface

The Sixth International Conference on Methods in Dialectology was hosted by the Department of Linguistics in the University College of North Wales, 3-7 August, 1987. The meeting was held jointly with that of the Summer meeting of the American Dialect Society. This volume contains a substantial selection of the papers presented.

The papers are wide-ranging in their coverage, with a satisfying leaning towards the practical matters of survey and field-work methodology, to the application of statistical techniques in analysis of data, and to computational methodology in the presentation of results, particularly in atlas form.

The conference was designed to reflect the currect concerns of dialectologists, as they exploit these methodological tools in the twin contexts of insights which derive from sociology via sociolinguistics, and their awareness of the interplay between synchronic variation and linguistic change. The papers in this volume combine all these aspects of variation study, though the mix varies with individual authors' concern.

In all, these Proceedings mirror the wide range of interests which characterise the practice of Dialectology as a research discipline, and well illustrate the dilemma of the pedant who seeks an inviolate line of demarkation between 'dialectology' and 'sociolinguistics'. The defining criterion for dialectology, perhaps, is its central concern with variation in the spatial parameter, and with diffusion through space and time, in addition to refinement of the data by an enhanced awareness of the significance of factors of communal social structure.

I read this set of papers as a celebration of those who, while working a 'face' (to use a Welsh mining idiom) which involves the collection, storage and analysis of vast amounts of data, are equally concerned with issues of methodology which are at the forefront of research in the study of language use.

I would like to record the thanks of the Conference Steering Committee to the Department of Linguistics at the University College of North Wales for substantial financial support; to the College for a grant towards the cost of the Conference Dinner; and to the British Academy and the American Dialect Society for contributions to the travel costs of the two featured speakers, Professor Wolfgang Viereck, University of Bamberg, and Professor William A. Kretzschmar Jr., University of Wisconsin at Whitewater.

Alan R. Thomas,
Department of Linguistics,
University College of North Wales,
Bangor.

Contents

PREFACE v

Introduction
Martin J. Ball 1

Discourse Variation and the Study of Communicative Competence
Gary R. Butler 11

Ma'am and Sir: Modes of Mitigation and Politeness in the Southern United States
Marvin K.L. Ching 20

Some Innovative Linguistic and Procedural Solutions, Relative to Sea Island Creole, in General; Some Aspects of the Sea Island Creole Verbal Auxiliary in Particular
Irma Aloyce Ewing Cunningham 46

Canadian Urban Survey Methodology: A Summary of Research Techniques and Results
Gaelan Dodds de Wolf and Erika Hasebe-Ludt 55

Linguistic Variation and Welsh Mutations in Children
Wynford Bellin 67

Stylistic Variation in Nova Scotia Acadian French
Karin Flikeid 79

Commercial Television as a Source of Language Data
Timothy C. Frazer 89

The Construction of a Rural Sociolinguistic Corpus: The Prince Edward Island Study
Ruth King and Robert Ryan 95

Written Records of Spoken Language: How Reliable Are They?
Natalie Maynor 109

Diachronic Interlinguistic Contact as Reflected in the Typological Structure of Today's Acadian Fishermen's Terminology
Rose Mary Babitch 121

Verb Analysis of the Linguistic Atlas of the North Central States: A Case Study in Preliminary Analysis of a Large Data Set
Michael D. Linn and Ronald R. Regal 138

Terminology vs Jargon: Canadian Hockey Talk
James Arthurs 155

Slander and Defamation as a Source for Historical Dialectology
G.M. Awbery 164

Beyond Linguistic Divergence in Black American English: Competing Norms of Linguistic Prestige and Variation
John Baugh 175

Uses of Dual Scaling in Social Dialectology: Multidimensional Analysis of Vowel Variation
Wladyslaw Cichocki 187

Computers and the American Linguistic Atlas
William A. Kretzschmar Jr. 200

The Limits of Chi Square
Lawrence M. Davis 225

The Quantitative Paradigm and the Study of Literacy: A New Initiative in Variation Studies
Rick Evans 241

Log-Linear Statistical Models: Explaining the Dynamics of Dialect Diffusion
Dennis Girard and Donald Larmouth 251

Research on Mural Sprayscripts (Graffiti)
Urs Dürmüller 278

Linguistics and Dialectology: Controlling Strange Data
Robert B. Hausmann 285

Acoustic Comparative Study of Contradictory /a:/ and /æ/ between Maine Dialect and General American
Tsuneko Ikemiya 306

Focus of Change in American Folk Speech
Frederic G. Cassidy 326

Sex-Linked Differences Among Atlas Informants: Irregular Verbs
Virginia G. McDavid 333

Eavesdropping and the Analysis of Everyday Verbal Exchange
Graham McGregor 362

Methods in the Study of Dialect Perceptions
Dennis R. Preston 373

Informants' Response Ratings in the *Survey of English Dialects*
Edgar W. Schneider 396

Accent and Identity
Gary Neal Underwood 406

A Method for Discovering Historical Language Variation
Jacob Bennett 428

The Study of Linguistic Change in the Study of Vancouver English
Robert J. Gregg 434

Approximation of the Standard: A Form of Variability in Bilingual Speech
Miklos Kontra and Maria Gosy 442

A Microsociolinguistic Study of the Dialect of Ayr
Ronald K.S. Macaulay 456

Ransacking Linguistic Survey Data with a Number Cruncher
Michael I. Miller 464

The Roots of Appalachian English
Michael Montgomery 480

The Dialectology of Scots: The Use of Dramatic Texts
John M. Kirk 492

Locating Minority Language Informants: A Network Approach to Fieldwork
Peter Wynn Thomas 510

The Computerisation and Quantification of Linguistic Data: Dialectometrical Methods
Wolfgang Viereck 524

Linguistic Atlasses of German: A Survey of Computer-Aided Projects
Werner H. Veith 551

Caught in the Web of Change
Joan H. Hall 557

Creative Linguistic Databases from Machine-Readable Dialect Texts
Ossi Ihalainen 569

The Automatic Computation of Linguistic Maps with the aid of Cluster Analysis
Bernhard Kelle 585

Managing Phrasal Data with a Microcomputer Generated Concordance
Richard A Spears 600

Aitken's Context in Northumberland, Cumberland and Durham: A Computer-Assisted Analysis of Material from the Survey of English and Dialects (SED)
Beat Glauser 611

The Verisimilitude of the Gullah Dialect in Francis Griswold's *A Sea Island Lady*
Mailande Cheney Sledge 625

The Historical Present as Evidence of Black/White Convergence/Divergence
Ronald R. Butters 637

Acquisition of Phonological Variants
J.K. Chambers 650

Dialects as Stepping Stones to a Language
Einar Haugen 666

Variation in the Plural Reflexive in Spoken English: Preliminary Evidence for Merger
John J. Staczek 674

Linguistic Variation in the Non-Stratified Context
Sandra Clark 684

Investigating Performance and Competence in Variation Studies: Adapting Techniques from Speech Pathology

MARTIN J. BALL
Polytechnic of Wales

INTRODUCTION

Dialectology and, more recently, sociolinguistics have been concerned almost as much with matters of methodology as with the analysis and interpretation of data. Perhaps this is natural in any social science, where the matter under investigation is less easily controlled than in natural sciences. Perhaps the methodological concern mostly under discussion in studies of linguistic variation is that of data collection.

Techniques of data collection have developed from the early postal questionnaires to the recent developments in group interviews through exploiting social networks (see Milroy, 1980). However, whichever technique is adopted, the problem remains of ensuring sufficient examples of the linguistic feature under investigation in the sample collected. In earlier work, single examples of lexical items or phonological variables were considered sufficient. However, recent work in sociolinguistics has demonstrated the inherent variability of the individual speaker's linguistic repertoire, and this has led to a recognition of the need to gain larger sized samples, through the use of the extended interview, for example Labov (1966).

Whatever techniques have been suggested however, all face the problem highlighted by Wolfram and Fasold (1974, p56): "even in quite extended interview situations, we may not get all the linguistic data for which we are looking", and they conclude that some of the unobtained data may be crucial for an adequate linguistic statement.

A more recent problem that has recently come into focus (Ball, 1985a) is that of investigating the status of linguistic variables in speakers' competences. By this is meant that linguistic features that may superficially seem equally variable may in fact have different statuses in the competence of speakers. This is an area which is particularly difficult to investigate, as is the case in most aspects of psycholinguistics.

In this chapter I intend to look at two procedures which have been adapted from techniques used in speech pathology. The first is a method of collecting data in dialect studies, and the second a way of investigating the competence of speakers. In this way I hope to show that dialectologists can gain by looking outside their discipline to other areas of linguistic research which also are concerned with the collection and investigation of natural speech samples.

Clinical linguistics is that area of study that intersects linguistics proper and speech-language pathology, i.e. the linguistic study of non-normal speech and language. Speech and language disorders may have a variety of aetiologies, but in their investigation an adequate data sample is essential. The dangers of basing a diagnosis and treatment regime on an inadequate analysis are obvious (see discussion for example in Crystal, Fletcher and Garman, 1976, and Müller, Munro and Code, 1981). Therefore a whole range of data collection techniques and linguistic tests and profiles have been developed within clinical linguistics: a resource that the dialectologist may well wish to tap.

THE REPORTER'S TEST

I mentioned earlier the problem involved in guaranteeing that a particular variable or set of variables occurs in a data sample. This problem can of course be surmounted by direct questioning of informants, or through the use of written stimuli (reading passages, word lists, etc). However, the disadvantage here is that such techniques are most likely to produce a formal style in the informants responses. While it is often important to know what happens in formalising environments, we usually still wish to gain examples of an informal style as well. Another problem is that some variables are particularly difficult to show in writing, in that the written form may automatically trigger a particular variant.

It appears from the preceding discussion, then, that what is needed is a data collection technique which has a high predictive power in terms of which variables will occur in a sample, but does not rely on writing and avoids formalising the style used by the subjects. One such potential method appeared to be a technique used in the assessment of aphasics: *The Reporter's Test*. This test was designed by DeRenzi and Ferrari (1978) to investigate the expressive abilities of aphasics, and is based on the earlier *Token Test* (DeRenzi and Vignolo, 1962, DeRenzi and Faglioni, 1978) which in turn investigates the comprehension abilities of aphasics. The token test utilises a set of coloured circles and squares (some large, some small); the investigator reads a list of instructions to the subject, who has to respond by touching or moving the relevant token(s). The instructions increase in complexity from "touch a circle ..." to "put the red circle between the yellow square and the green square ..." and so forth (DeRenzi and Faglioni, 1978, p43-44).

The reporter's test is derived from the token test by a simple reversal of the roles of the investigator and the subject. Here, the

investigator touches and moves the tokens, while the subject has to say what is happening. The following is the recommended initial instruction to the subject from the investigator:
> Imagine that a person is sitting beside you, but is prevented from seeing what I am doing by a curtain ... Your task is to describe what I am doing as carefully as possible, so that this person would be able to repeat exactly my performance on another set of tokens. (DeRenzi and Faglioni, 1978, p281)

How useful such a procedure might be in the study of aphasics is beyond the scope of this chapter (see discussion in Müller, Munro and Code, 1981), but it appeared to me that it could well solve a problem that confronted me while undertaking research into the use of initial consonant mutation in Welsh dialects.

Welsh, in common with the other Celtic languages, has a system of initial consonant mutation: that is to say, that in certain environments, certain word initial consonants change. What is unusual is the fact that these changes are not triggered by phonological environments, but by morphosyntactic ones. There are three sets of mutations: *Soft Mutation* converts fortis stops and liquids to lenis, lenis stops to lenis fricatives (though /g/ → ∅), and /m/ → /v/. *Nasal Mutation* converts fortis and lenis stops to homorganic fortis and lenis nasals, and *Aspirate Mutation* converts fortis stops to homorganic fortis fricatives.

The triggering environments for the mutations are many and various. For example, feminine singular nouns undergo soft mutation after the article: *cath, y gath*, 'cat, the cat'. The direct object of an inflected verb undergoes soft mutation: *gwelodd cath*, 'a cat saw' as opposed to *gwelodd gath*, 'he saw a cat'. Other triggers of the various mutations include prepositions, conjunctions, personal pronouns and non-normal word-order.

The mutations are recognised in the writing system and overtly recognised by native speakers as marks of correctness. They are taught in schools, and at times can become matters for public discussion by language purists in the media. In many environments, if the mutations were not triggered, this would be deemed a non-native form. However, in certain cases (particularly with the aspirate and nasal mutations) considerable insecurity exists as to which is the 'correct' form.

Previous studies of Welsh dialects (reviewed in Ball, 1984) have noted patterns of non-usage or partial usage of both the aspirate and nasal mutations, but no systematic attempts at quantifying these patterns had been attempted. However, the acquisition of an adequate data sample was a severe problem in this respect. Most of the triggers for the aspirate mutation occur relatively seldom, and unlike the other mutations, only three consonants are mutatable. These problems are not so apparent with the nasal mutation, but here only two major triggers are found.

The use of written material to ensure adequate examples of the potential triggering environments, apart from the disadvantage of the formalising effect noted above, is not available to a study of mutation phenomena. The reason for this is that the power of the writing system is such that if the mutation is shown it would almost always lead to it being used in speech, whereas if it is ommitted the mutation is likely to be left out (even though the subject may well comment on its absence). An investigation showing these results is reported in Ball (1981, 1984). It appeared to me therefore that new techniques had to be tried out in this case.

In an initial study (see also Ball, 1986a, b) a series of different techniques was utilised to investigate the use of the aspirate mutation, but in this pilot study only one, relatively common, trigger was included: following *a*, 'and'. As well as the aspirate mutation variable (variants were usage/non-usage of the mutation, being the standard/non-standard versions respectively), a more traditional phonological variable was investigated for comparison purposes: (h), whose variants were /h/ and Ø, again standard versus non-standard.

The techniques included the formal interview and casual styles as defined by Labov (1966), and for (h) only, reading passage, word list and minimal pair styles. The new techniques were as follows:
1 translating sentences from English: a) spoken stimulus, b) written stimulus
2 sentences including pictures of the mutatable word
3 prose passage including pictures of the mutatable word
4 description of items in a composite picture
5 memory test - recalling items from a composite picture
6 a reporter's test (for this study a test was designed containing tokens and actions linked by 'and')

For the purpose of the study, four literate, educated south Walian speakers were used as subjects.

The results of this initial study are shown in Table 1 below. As will be seen from the table, there is considerable variation between the techniques, and between the two different types of variable. Reasons for this variation are discussed fully in Ball (1981, 1984). However, it will be seen that for both (h) and (AM) (i.e. Aspirate Mutation), the reporter's test has provided an adequate sample, and indeed a fairly informal speech style in comparison with the formal and casual interview styles. An explanation for this informal style appears to be that subjects are concentrating so hard on the non-linguistic task in hand that they temporarily suspend the monitoring of their own speech that normally occurs in data collection (see Labov, 1966, on the similar effect of the shoelace test).

This initial study had of course to be followed by others to ensure that these results could be found with other variables too. Accordingly a study of the pronunciation of a set of personal possessive pronouns was undertaken.

Table 1. *Percentages of non-standard variants for both variables and all techniques*

	(h) N	(h) %	(AM) N	(AM) %
Casual	21	14	5	100
Formal	43	11	9	34
Prose	54	4	--	--
Word Lst	44	3	--	--
Min Pairs	27	0	--	--
1a	--	-	15	0
1b	24	4	17	12
2	16	0	36	6
3	4	25	18	0
4	9	0	22	37
5	6	0	12	9
6	9	11	52	52

The possessive pronouns of Welsh (with the exception of *dy*, 'thy') have the interesting characteristic of two separate pronunciations, whose usage seems to depend on style. The variation in the case of *ei*, 'his, her', *ein*, 'our', *eich*, 'your' and *eu*, 'their' is due to a relatively recent spelling pronunciation, which has caused the introduction of a diphthong. In the case of *fy*, 'my', the variation is older and revolves around whether the initial /v/ is pronounced.

A series of data elicitation techniques was used in this study, as reported in Ball (1985b, 1986b), but of interest to us here is the fact that a reporter's test was designed to gain data on pronoun usage. In order to aid analysis, and indeed the construction of the reporter's test, the pronouns were allocated to three groups according to their basic phonological make-up: *fy*, *ei/eu*, and *eich/ein*. The reporter's test was used along with casual and formal interview styles (as defined by Labov, 1966), a prose passage, a set of sentences, and a set of sentences containing blanks for the words to be tested. For the purposes of this investigation, six literate, educated south Walian speakers were used.

Table 2 shows the results of this investigation, and it will be seen that in all cases the figures for the reporter's test are almost identical with those for casual style, but that in all cases more actual tokens occurred. Indeed, the *eich/ein* form did not occur in the interview styles, demonstrating the predictive power of this technique.

Table 2. *Pronoun Variables:*
Percentage of non-standard variants

	fy		ei/eu		eich/ein		total	
	N	%	N	%	N	%	N	%
Casual	4	100	10	100	0	-	14	100
Formal	26	73	16	94	0	-	42	81
Prose	12	25	31	68	24	67	67	60
Blanks	13	54	23	83	24	67	60	70
Sentences	12	0	24	67	24	67	60	53
Rep test	24	92	30	97	39	100	93	97

It would appear, then, that the reporter's test could well provide a useful addition to the range of data collection techniques available to the dialectologist. However, we have not got here a panacea for all our ills! The test will be effective for investigating phonological variables, as a sufficient variety of lexical items will be predictable with the use of a bit of ingenuity. It is a different matter with regard to syntactic or lexical studies - I am at a loss to think of a convinving reporter's test that could predict the wide range of lexical items needed for a study of dialect vocabulary.

In other research I have carried out, reporter's tests were designed to investigate the usage of aspirate and nasal mutation in virtually all their trigger envirnoments in speakers from the Swansea Valley and from Anglesey. In most cases, the results found above were repeated, in that the test had high predictive power, and produced generally casual speech. These results are reported in Ball (1984, and forthcoming).

AN ERROR RECOGNITION TEST

Whatever results are obtained in studies of linguistic variation, the researcher cannot be sure whether variable usage of a feature is somehow a stable part of the speaker's competence, or whether it is the result of uncertainty, and part of an ongoing linguistic change. The major study of mutations referred to immediately above found similar results for the usage of the nasal mutation and for the aspirate mutation in many environments, but speakers' reports seemed to indicate that these two mutations were not viewed in the same way. This section describes an attempt to investigate this difference.

Sentence imitation tasks have often been used in clinical linguistics and psycholinguistics to investigate a subject's sense of grammaticality, or linguistic competence. Gleitman, Gleitman and Shipley (1972) describe such a task for looking at children's development of grammatical competence, and in the context of Welsh mutations, Bellin (1976, 1984) undertook a comparable study of children's Welsh. However, as Wolfram and Fasold (1974) point out, such tests have their drawbacks, particularly with adults, who may be able to imitate a short utterance, whether or not it is part of their competence. To avoid this drawback, I constructed an error recognition test as a variant of the imitation task.

This test required recording a list of sentences, some containing errors, some correct. Amongst the errors were non-standard usages of the mutations under investigation. These non-standard usages varied from those recorded as occurring naturally in informal speech, to variants markedly deviant from any known usage. The tape would then be played to subjects who would be asked to note any errors that they heard, and to specify what those errors were (Stenson, 1987, has used a similar technique in investigating Irish).

It is argued that speakers who seldom use the standard variant of a particular variable would be less likely to note the 'error' of non-standard usage. If the standard variant is used often, or the standard and non-standard variants have significant and set stylistic roles, it would be expected that the subject would readily note the 'error' of non-standard usage. The narrowing of concentration required in a task like this, coupled with the knowledge that errors were likely, would seem to suggest that, as long as the subjects had access within their linguistic repertoires to the standard usage of the mutations, such a test would yield high scores of error recognition throughout. This, then, implies that a low score could point to features not well established in a speaker's competence. An error recognition test is therefore a test of competence not performance.

Ball (1985a) gives full details of how an error recognition test was constructed to study both the nasal and aspirate mutations, and also to a lesser extent, the soft mutation. Six triggering environments were investigated for the aspirate mutation, three for the nasal mutation. Only a couple of soft mutation environments were included, as diversions. Thirty-two sentences were recorded and presented to eight subjects, all first language Welsh speakers in the age-range 30-40. All had some knowledge of standard Welsh. The results of the test are presented in Table 3. For the aspirate mutation, the trigger *ei*, 'her' is presented separately, for both in production and in this test it consistently scores higher than the others in terms of standard usage.

Table 3 *Percentage Errors Recognised in Test*

Error type	% recognised
AM→radical	56
ei→radical	100
AM→SM	50
NM→rad/SM	88
SM→radical radical→SM	81

The results in this table do certainly show a difference in the ability to spot errors involving AM, and other errors. The high score for the *ei* trigger is partly explainable by the semantic load carried by the mutation in this instance, as *ei*+SM means 'his', and *eu*+radical (i.e. no mutation) is pronounced the same and means 'their'.

This error recognition test suggests that AM and NM are treated separately in terms of competence and performance by this group of speakers. Although superficially they are both variables in the sociolinguist's definition, it is clear that NM is displaying static variability, whereas AM is being subjected to language change.

CONCLUSION

Dialectology has developed greatly over the years, and can be expected to continue doing so. Arguably nowhere has this development been greater than in data collection methodology. In this chapter I have attempted to outline two techniques borrowed from the fields of clinical linguistics and psycholinguistics in the hope that my experience may profit others working in the area. I do not claim they are revolutionary, nor that they will solve all our problems. However, an ability to look outwards to the work of fellow linguists is surely to be desired, and I look forward to hearing of other such 'borrowings'.

References

Ball, M. J. (1981) Data collection techniques for a sociolinguistic study of the Welsh mutation system. *Cardiff Working Papers in Welsh Linguistics*, **1**, 10-18.

Ball, M. J. (1984) *Sociolinguistic Aspects of the Welsh Mutation System*. Unpublished Ph.D. thesis, University of Wales.

Ball, M. J. (1985a) An error recognition test as a measure of linguistic competence: an example from Welsh. *Journal of Psycholinguistic Research*, **14**, 399-407.

Ball, M. J. (1985b) Phonological variation in the personal pronouns of Welsh. *Cardiff Working Papers in Welsh Linguistics*, **4**, 25-30.

Ball, M. J. (1986a) Exploring stylistic variation in the aspirate mutation of Welsh. *Etudes Celtiques*, **23**, 255-64.

Ball, M. J. (1986b) The reporter's test as a sociolinguistic tool. *Language in Society*, **15**, 375-86.

Ball, M. J. (ed) (forthcoming) *The Use of Welsh*. Clevedon: Multilingual Matters.

Bellin, W. (1976) *Psycholinguistics and Language Learning*. Unpublished D.Phil thesis, University of Reading.

Bellin, W. (1984) Welsh phonology in acquisition. In M. J. Ball and G. E. Jones (eds), *Welsh Phonology. Selected Readings*. Cardiff: University of Wales Press.

Crystal, D., Fletcher, P. and Garman, M. (1976) *The Grammatical Analysis of Language Disability*. London: Edward Arnold.

DeRenzi, E. and Faglioni, D. (1978) Normative data and screening power of a shortened version of the token test. *Cortex*, **14**, 41-49.

DeRenzi, E. and Ferrari, C. (1978) The reporter's test: a sensitive test to detect expressive disturbance in aphasics. *Cortex*, **14**, 279-93.

DeRenzi, E. and Vignolo, L. (1962) The token test: a sensitive test to detect receptive disturbance in aphasics. *Brain*, **85**, 665-78.

Gleitman, L., Gleitman, H. and Shipley, E. (1972) The emergence of the child as a grammarian. *Cognition*, **1**, 137-64.

Labov, W. (1966) *The Social Stratification of English in New York City*. Washington D.C.: Center for Applied Linguistics.

Milroy, L. (1980) *Language and Social Networks*. Oxford: Basil Blackwell.

Müller, D., Munro, S. and Code, C. (1981) *Language Assessment for Remediation*. London: Croom Helm.

Stenson, N. (1987) Initial mutation of loanwords: some Irish evidence. Paper presented at the *Eighth International Congress of Celtic Studies*, Swansea.

Wolfram, W. and Fasold, R. (1974) *The Study of Social Dialects in American English*. Englewood Cliffs, N.J.: Prentice-Hall.

Discourse Variation and the Study of Communicative Competence

GARY R. BUTLER
York University, Canada

Introduction

The study of local and regional variation in linguistic phenomena has most commonly focussed on manifest expression at the level of the word, or at the very most, at the level of the sentential utterance. The main concern of such studies has been such features as pronunciation, the choice of lexical items and variation in the meaning of similar items, and the syntactic constructions characterising different regional, social, and ethnic varieties of a language. What has not been addressed to anywhere near the same extent is variation at the level beyond the sentence; that is, at the level of discourse. It is the aim of the present paper to present some of the possible applications of the variationist perspective to the study of naturally occurring discourse, and to outline the methodologies which might be employed in such investigation.

The analysis of sequences or oral utterances as they occur in natural contexts has become increasingly important in the study of the social and cultural role of language in human societies. In the early 1960s, a method of inquiry known as the ethnography of speaking/communication combined both linguistic and anthropological perspectives in an effort to understand the nature, structure, and function of discrete communicative events (e.g. Hymes, 1962; Gumperz & Hymes, 1966; Bauman & Sherzer, 1974; Saville-Troike, 1982). Advances in this field were paralleled in the area of speech act analysis, where what was said with words was distinguished from what was socially performed by speaking (e.g. Austin, 1962; Searle, 1969). Conversational analysis extended this practice, expanding the analytic framework to encompass the alternation of speech acts during the course of turn-taking in conversation (e.g. Sacks, Schegloff & Jefferson, 1974). And discourse analysis, a term often applied as a general rubric covering any or all of these approaches, examined the relationship between the complementary communicative processes of encoding/decoding and implicature/inference. While the labels attached to these various approaches tend to overlap to some greater or lesser extent, all

---

*The research upon which this paper is based initially was funded by means of a Social Sciences and Humanities Research Council of Canada Postdoctoral Fellowship, and is to continue under a Canada Research Fellowship, jointly funded by the SSHRCC and York University (Canada).

such studies have one essential characteristic in common, this being a concern with linguistic phenomena as communicative strategies transcending the level of the single sentence or utterance and deriving their essential meaning from the interactive context.

Implicit in most, if not all such studies, is the recognition of the influence of social variables upon the context of communication and, subsequently, upon the speakers' ultimate choice of which discursive strategies are available to them for the accomplishment of their communicative intentions. The speakers' interactional behaviour is thus viewed as reflective of a set of communicative constraints and options which are recognized by and adhered to by their speech community, and which together define the parameters of acceptable communicative behaviour. As Gumperz notes:

> Social rules, therefore, are much like linguistic rules, they determine the actor's choice among culturally available modes of action or strategies in accordance with the constraints provided by communicative intent, setting, and identity relationships (Gumperz, 1972: 16).

These so-called "social rules" obviously are among those components of communicative competence acquired by the members of a particular speech community during the socialization process, whereby the individual speaker learns what he or she needs to know to communicate successfully and to perform appropriately among their fellows. As such, different social groups, be they defined regionally, socially, or ethnically, should possess somewhat different considerations as to what constitutes the parameters of acceptability of communicative behaviour, and these parameters include both what constitutes formal modes of expression and the social constraints governing their realization in context. These rules, sometimes referred to as linguistic codes, are seen as conditioning "the individual's perception of his and his interlocutor's social role" (Gumperz, 1972: 16). During the course of communicative interaction, perception of identity relationships come to bear, and the ultimate situated meaning of language form and content ultimately "reflects speakers attitudes to each other, and to their topics" (Hymes, 1972: 37).

Hence, from the perspective of ethnographically-oriented discourse analysis, at least two levels of variation in communicative behaviour may be differentiated. The first involves variation in what is considered acceptable performance and appropriate behaviour for individuals of different social statuses within the same speech community, what I shall refer to here as 'intra-cultural variation.' The second level on which variation in discursive behaviour may be analyzed is at the inter- or cross-cultural level, whereby differences in what constitutes the normative communicative behaviour expected of and deemed appropriate to similar social categories of individuals in two or more different speech communities are examined. The following sections will deal with each of these in turn.

Intra-Cultural Variation in Communicative Behaviour: The L'Anse-à-Canards Study

In 1979, I embarked on a doctoral research project to investigate the supernatural belief tradition of L'Anse-à-Canards, a small rural fishing community located on the isolated Port-au-Port Peninsula of Newfoundland's west coast. The aim of the project was to ascertain the content of the tradition, and to determine the expressive forms which served as vehicles for the communication of this cognitive domain. Equally important, however, was to analyze the communicative contexts within which such natural expression of supernatural propositions took place, and to determine the social function and cultural significance of communication involving such propositions. Field research was conducted over the course of the next six years, during which time I spent a total of eleven months in residence in the community. A corpus consisting of over ninety hours of sound recordings, collected both in natural contexts and by way of informal interview, and a total of some two hundred pages of ethnographic field notes was collected.

The project, which for practical reasons to be discussed below was restricted primarily to male residents, quickly found its focus in the variation which characterised this particular tradition in this community of less than two hundred individuals divided into 32 households and representing just 7 extended families. Not too surprisingly, and indeed as was anticipated from the start of the project, the various residents displayed varying degrees of knowledge of their community culture's supernatural belief tradition. Much more interesting, however, was the lack of correspondence between individuals' knowledge of specific conversational narratives and their actual attitude towards performing those narratives. It soon became apparent that some characteristic of the narratives other than supernatural belief content was conditioning the individual's willingness to perform, and that this feature was related to some aspect of communicative propriety. On a number of interview occasions, the informant would hesitate about recounting specific stories with which they were obviously quite familiar, and, visibly uncomfortable, would suggest that I go and talk with another individual who could enlighten me about the incident in question. This other individual was in all cases either the central figure in the experience narrative, or a close family member. Such chance occurrences suggested that a certain principle of proprietory rights concerning certain narratives was at work, and this became clear upon an examination and analysis of the data base collected. Of the 99 narratives collected dealing with living members of the community, fully 82 recount the experiences of the speaker/narrator or of a member of his immediate family, while just 17 examples concerned the experiences of unrelated residents. An additional 42 narratives dealing with experiences of "unknown others" were also collected. Of the total of 141 narratives, then, a mere 12% duplicated the personal or family narratives of "known others" (Butler, 1985). This pattern is in keeping with the principle of "prominence" as outlined by Pickering in his discussion of discursive frameworks, and corresponds to Callow's treatment of the same subject (Pickering, 1980; Callow, 1974).

A basic conclusion drawn from this and other data used in this particular study is that narrative performance is in part determined by the existing pattern of social relationships, and that performance serves to reaffirm and strengthen the social relationships existing among participants in a communicative event involving such narrative expression. In fact, it might not be an over-generalization to conclude that narrative performance not only reflects protagonist-narrator relationships, but relationships from the social system as well.

What is imminently clear from this particular example is that the evaluation of one's data relies as much on what was not collected as on what was collected. Conventional studies of traditional discourse genres by anthropologists and folklorists have tended to base their findings upon examples collected from those informant-specialists who possess both the ability and authority to perform examples of the traditional discourse genre under investigation. Had I not investigated possible reasons for non-performance (or 0-performance), the relevance of the findings to the communicative competence of the L'Anse-à-Canards speech community would have remained hidden. By considering a broad representative sampling of most segments of the male population, it was possible to determine "the nature and distribution of norms of interaction to be found within the community, insofar as these organize social interaction" (Bauman & Sherzer, 1974: 7).

The above-discussed example of intra-cultural variation in the narrative performance among male residents of L'Anse-à-Canards stems from the differentiation, according to ethnographically derived regularities, of a body of structurally similar expressive forms into sub-categories reflecting real distinctions perceived to exist by the society investigated. Certainly, other features of discursive interaction might as easily be examined, such as the effect of social variables of age, sex, kinship and peer-group networks, and social rank on narrative competence. Moreover, one could analyze, in a manner analogous to research on code-switching and registers, the manner in which different combinations of participant-types influence the contextual discursive behaviour of the individual, to discover whether or not formal and interactional 'registers' of traditional discourse genre-performance exist, and, if they do, what their differential characteristics are. Obviously, such research, particularly that dealing with rank, networks and other such socially determined variables, requires a considerable base of ethnographic information if the study of intra-cultural variation within a single speech community is to be successful.

Inter-Cultural Analysis of Variation in Discourse: The Three-Community Acadian Study

The preceding discussion outlines some of the potential approaches and possible orientations related to the conduct of an ethnography of communication for a single speech community. The strengths of the technique have been proven over the course of several decades involving numerous individual studies. However, the weaknesses of single community studies in the determination of general principles of communicative behaviour are clear. The most obvious drawback, and that potentially most painful to the researcher, is the limitations imposed on extrapolation by the relativeness of all conclusions derived from the analysis of the data base. The variability of communicative forms, modes, and functions and their degree of conjunction with variables discerned within the social system may reflect regional or local conditions. As well, the observed discursive performance may be a function of principles of communicative competence particular to the community under study, and certainly, such will be the case in some instances. However, it is impossible to differentiate with full confidence the general from the community-specific solely on the basis of the study of a single community; rather, an analytic framework must be found which will allow the application of a rigidly controlled methodology to several communities.

Obviously, a crucial phase in setting up a research project of this type involves the selection of those communities which are to serve as the study's focus. Since the objectives of such a study are similar to those of scholars dealing with dialectal variation characterizing a single language, the communities chosen must be clearly identifiable as culturally related, but have experienced sufficient isolation from one another for the effect of local conditions of context to have exerted a differentiating influence upon the communicative behaviour of the members of these community cultures. This is the essential concept underlying the three-community Acadian study soon to begin.

In 1987, I will commence work on the research project entitled "A Study of Folk Discourse Processes in Three Acadian Communities" under the joint funding of the Social Sciences and Humanities Research Council of Canada and York University (Canada). The project is to be conducted over a period of five years, and will attempt to establish a comparative ethnography of communication (or "ethnology of communication") based on data collected and analyzed separately for each of three rural communities in the Canadian Atlantic Provinces. The communities where research is to be conducted were chosen because of their similar historical, cultural and linguistic antecedents. All three communities--L'Anse-à-Canards in Newfoundland; Chéticamp on Cape Breton Island, Nova Scotia; and Abram's Village in Prince Edward Island--were established in large part by Acadian French settlers during the period between the start of the eighteenth and the end of the nineteenth century. And while each speech community displays some linguistic features not found in the others, the language of all three is recognizable as the linguistic variety known as Acadian French (King, 1983; King & Ryan, 1987a & b). Equally important is the fact that, despite the related social history uniting the inhabitants of these villages, the three communities have been effectively isolated from one another, and have experienced quite different local conditions, for well over a century. The result is a triad of distinct community cultures which meet the requirements for general control and local variation required for the proposed research project.

The fieldwork required for the collection of sociocultural data for the construction of community profiles (Arensberg & Kimball, 1965) and the compilation of a representative base of communicative data will be conducted over the course of the project's first three years. Data collection will involve the use of informant-collectors native to each community, and both male and female collectors representing a range of ages and family units will be employed. There are a number of reasons for this. First, since the collector will be involved as a participant/interactant during the collection of data through both formal interview and natural contexts, it is important to consider the collectors themselves as variables affecting the communicative situation. An attempt will be made to render observable the effect of their socially defined identity by having different collectors perform identical fieldwork with the same informants at different times. Certainly, this will not eliminate the effect of the observer's paradox, but should provide some interesting comparative field data. An additional control will be my own fieldwork between 1987 and 1990, during which time I hope to spend at least six weeks to two months in each of the three communities. Preliminary analysis of collected data will be conducted parallel to collection, so that required or desirable alterations or modifications may be introduced when recognized, and at as early a stage in the project as possible.

A second obvious consideration is also related to the question of collector identity, and involves the need for access to peer-group networks delineated on the basis of age, sex, and family. In the previously-discussed L'Anse-à-Canards study, my own collection activities were restricted in this patriarchal society by virtue of my male-ness, which excluded me from participant/observation in a whole range of female-oriented activities. Again, this may be at least partially remedied by the proposed use of a heterogeneous team of informant-collectors. Not to be overlooked is the need to avoid identifying the research project too strongly with any particular family or group, which could lead to the subjectivization of informant response to the project cum project.

The data concerning communicative performance to be collected will be of a number of kinds, the most important of which may be referred to as Textual (including both generic and conversational modes of expression), Ideational/Conceptual, Behavioural, Contextual, Discursive, and Social/Interactional. Some of the specific material to be collected include the following:

1) A variety of traditional discourse genre texts (i.e. experience narratives, anecdotes, proverbs, jokes), collected by fieldworkers by means of informal elicitation interviews. These texts would constitute the informants reconstruction, or 'report,' of naturally performed generic texts. [Textual]

2) The descriptive reports of the communicative situation perceived as the normal setting for the performance of these genres, and of the communicative event per se as an interactional phenomenon. This will include informant evaluations of the appropriate and expected behaviour in those contexts which they would associate ideally with each element in a set of social role categories.[Contextual;Ideational/Conceptual;Social/Interactional]

3) A series of recordings collected during the course of actual social interaction within the settings and contexts ideally associated by informants in (2) with certain discursive behaviour. [Textual; Contextual; Behavioural; Discursive; Social/Interactional]

4) A series of recordings of naturally occurring conversation involving various combinations of social role

categories outside the communicative events outlined in (2) and (3). In some instances, the topic of conversation will be controlled or directed by the informant-collector, while in other cases, the conversation will be left to the spontaneity of the participants. [Discursive; Textual; Behavioural; Contextual]

5) In follow-up fieldwork, an adaptation of the "eavesdropper" technique of interview (McGregor, 1985: 288-89) will be used. A series of texts defined according to local taxonomy by the members of one community in the study will be played for informants in another without prior explanatory comment from the fieldworker, and their reaction to the text will be elicited. In some cases, a text will be placed in a context described by the fieldworker, and the listener's evaluation of what was transpiring, and of the appropriateness of the performance, will be elicited. [Ideational/Conceptual]

6) The informant-collector will be asked to make a written record of any reference to a variety of predetermined topics he or she encounters during the course of their collection; this will provide information concerning the relative use of encoding/decoding and implicature/inference in natural conversational discourse, and will make possible the analysis of the role of shared cultural knowledge during the course of everyday interaction. [Discursive]

In addition to the above data relating to discursive performance and to the differentiation of ideal as opposed to real parameters of social interaction, a considerable body of information concerning local conditions of context and culture will be accumulated. This information concerning the social framework (e.g. networks, kinship and marriage patterns, history, community world view and cognitive map, etc.) will represent the general context relative to which the community is defined as a system, as opposed to the particularistic contexts within which actual communicative behaviour occurs.

Concluding Remarks

At this preliminary stage of research, it is extremely difficult to anticipate the type and degree of variation in qualitative and quantitative data which will be revealed by the Acadian project. Certainly, each speech community will display internal variation in the communicative competence of its residents, and the study's intensive breadth and depth collection methodology will reveal this, as it did for the L'Anse-à-Canards study herein described. It cannot be known whether or not and to what degree inter-cultural variation will be significant, but it is almost inconceivable that all three communities would possess identical form and content criteria for the performance of acceptable texts, let alone identical social criteria for appropriate communicative interaction involving traditional genres of discourse. Doubtless, there will be many similarities among the significant communicative situations, events, and acts encountered, as well as in the discursive modes which organize them and in the formal genres and utterance types which constitute their content; such similarities are, after all, the basis for the system of genre classification which has permitted past cross-cultural analyses of texts by ethnographers and anthropologists alike. What remains to be determined whether or not these manifest and latent similarities reflect identical cognitive considerations, or stem merely from the constraints upon what communicative strategies and expressive forms are possible within a given speech community. This can be accomplished not through a comparison of isolated and unrelated ethnographic studies, but through the application of an analytic and methodological framework which incorporates from the outset a comparativist perspective.

References

Arensberg, Conrad M. & Solon T. Kimball (1965) *Culture and Community*. New York: Harcourt, Brace & World.

Austin, J.L. (1962) *How To Do Things With Words*. Oxford: Oxford University Press.

Bauman, Richard and Joel Sherzer (eds.)(1974) *Explorations in the Ethnography of Speaking*. London: Cambridge University Press.

Brown, Gillian and George Yule (1983) *Discourse Analysis*. London: Cambridge University Press.

Butler, Gary R. (1984) "Folklore and the Analysis of Folk Discourse: Cultural Connotation and Oral Tradition in Communicative Events." In Susan Ehrlich et. al., eds. *Toronto Working Papers in Linguistics*, Vol. V, pp. 32-50.

Butler, Gary R. (1985) *Supernatural Folk Belief Expression in a French-Newfoundland Community: A Study of Expressive Form, Communicative Process, and Social Function in L'Anse-a -Canards*. St. John's: Memorial University of Newfoundland.

Callow, Kathleen (1974) *Discourse Considerations*. Grand Rapids: Zondervan.

Corsaro, W.A. (1985) "Sociological Approaches to Discourse Analysis." In Teun van Dijk, ed. *Handbook of Discourse Analysis*, vol. 1. London: Academic Press.

Grice, H.P. (1975) "Logic and Conversation." In P. Cole and J.L. Morgan eds. *Syntax and Semantics*. New York: Academic Press, pp. 41-58.

Gumperz, J.J. (1978) "Dialect and Conversational Inference in Urban Communications." Language in Society, 7(1978), 393-409.

Gumperz, J.J. and Dell Hymes (1964) "Introduction: Toward Ethnographies of Communication." American Anthropologist, 66:6, Part 2 (1964), 1-34.

King, Ruth (1983) Variation and Change in Newfoundland French: A Sociolinguistic Study of Clitic Pronouns. St. John's: Memorial University of Newfoundland.

King, Ruth and R. Ryan (1987a) "Dialect Contact vs. Dialect Isolation: Nasal Vowels in Atlantic Canada Acadian French." Paper presented at the XIVth International Congress of Linguistics, Berlin, August 10-16, 1987.

----------------------(1987b) "La phonologie des parlers acadiens de l'Ile du Prince Edouard." In Papers of the Tenth Annual Meeting of the Atlantic Provinces Linguistic Association. A.M. Kinloch et. al., eds. Fredericton: University of New Brunswick, pp. 95-108.

Kreckel, M. (1981) Communicative Acts and Shared Knowledge in Natural Discourse. London: Academic Press.

Leech, G.N. (1983) Principles of Pragmatics. London: Academic Press.

McGregor, Graham (1985) " 'Lissnty mi tokenty yi': A Look at Linguistic Variation from the Listener's Point of View." Methods V, 285-98.

Pickering, Wilbur (1980) A Framework for Discourse Analysis. Arlington: University of Texas at Arlington.

Saville-Troike, Muriel (1982) The Ethnography of Communication. Oxford: Basil Blackwell.

Sacks, H., Schegloff, E.A. & Jefferson, G. (1974) "A Simplist Systematics for the Organisation of Turn-taking for Conversations." Language, 50, 696-735.

Searle, J. (1969) Speech Acts. Cambridge: Cambridge University Press.

Ma'am and Sir: Modes of Mitigation and Politeness in the Southern United States

MARTIN K.L. CHING
Memphis State University

A Yankee visitor to the South usually notices a high degree of politeness to which he/she is not usually accustomed. Southerners' use of Ma'am and Sir and Yes/No, Ma'am, and Yes/No,Sir, is uncommon to norms in the northern United States.

To determine 1) who says Ma'am and Sir and Yes/No, Ma'am, and Yes/No,Sir; 2) the situations when these modes of mitigation and politeness are used in the Southern United States, and 3) the way the data should be interpreted—I used a written questionnaire with objective questions which could be computer-scored and analyzed and which ended with a free-response section encouraging written comments to clarify informants' objective answers. The variables tested included age, sex, race, educational status, and political and religious orientations.

Oral in-depth interviews of 31 individuals largely from Memphis State University proved helpful in constructing the questionnaire and in interpreting the data with caution. Interviewees included Black maids and both Black and White persons in these categories: graduate and undergraduate students, faculty members, and secretaries. The oral in-depth interviews and the free-response section of the questionnaire also uncovered information which could not possibly be elicited by objective questions on a questionnaire. Moreover, because of the time limitations during a class period to answer the questionnaire, the interviews provided information not asked on the questionnaire. The objective data of the questionnaire largely confirmed some of the interviewees' intuitions concerning the use of the deferential terms in specific contexts. But the free response section of the questionnaire was also helpful in interpreting the results of the data, because it solicited informants' comments on why some items on the questionnaire caused problems or were ambiguous to informants. The free response section also gave a chance to elicit comments on uses not tested by the questionnaire.

When presented with a questionnaire whose instructions included the promise to preserve complete anonymity because the informants' names were not to be indicated on the computer answer sheet and because the researcher was interested only in group totals, the informants were willing to shade in not only their grade or educational status and sex, but also sensitive information, such as religious and political orientations, race, and age. The informants used for this study are 640 Southerners, Memphis State University students and faculty who spent 15 or more of their first 18 years of their life in the South—namely from from the area of the United States listed below:

Alabama
Arkansas
Florida--<u>Northern part down to Orlando</u>
Georgia
Kentucky
Louisiana
Mississippi
Missouri--<u>The Bootheel part</u>
North Carolina
South Carolina
Tennessee
Texas
Virginia

Informants on the questionnaire used these terms of deference the most with 4 groups: 1) Older Persons, 2) Ministers/Clergy, 3) Employers/Supervisors, and 4) Police Officers. The first two groups are persons normally accorded respect, perhaps often with genuine affection; the last two, often because of the power of hiring and firing or the fear of punishment because of a violation, according to the oral in-depth interviews and the written comments on the questionnaire.

Age of addressee played an important factor. Those in the 18-29 age group were the most likely to use these terms, with nonusers of these terms more likely in the 40s, but, after the dip in the curve, the 50-year-olds seemed to pick up the use of the terms. There were not enough 60-year-olds, however, for comparison purposes for that age group.

The composite group total for all 640 Southerners is as follows for the question on whether the informant used <u>Ma'am</u> and <u>Sir</u> with Older Persons:

Figures and Charts for My Paper:

<u>Ma'am</u> and <u>Sir</u>: Modes of Mitigation and Politeness in the Southern United States

Address to Older Persons: Composite Total

Answer	Percent	Frequency
Older persons of only the same race	4.6	29
Older persons of both races	88.2	552
Do not use at all	7.2	45

Missing cases: 14

Figure 1

Age variation, however, shows a great decline with those using the terms in the 40s and a resurgence with those in the 50s, as indicated in Fig. 2 below. On all charts, the corresponding frequency, when indicated by parentheses, is shown under a percentage figure; when a chi square (x^2) test of independence is performed and is statistically significant at the .05 level of significance, the results are cited.

Address to Older Persons: Age Breakdown

Answer	18-29	30s	40s	50s	60s
Older persons of only the same race	3.5% (18)	3.7% (2)	16.2% (6)	17.6% (3)	
Older persons of both races	90.2% (461)	87.0% (47)	62.2% (23)	82.4% (14)	100.0% (2)
Do not use at all	6.3% (32)	9.3% (5)	21.6% (8)		

Missing cases = 19

Statistical analysis resulted in a significant X^2 value of 34.437 ($p < .0001$).

Fig. 2

The 40s show a definite dip in percentage of frequency of use with a concomitant growth in nonuse of the deferential terms. Perhaps the fact that accounts for this pattern is that the 40s is the rebellious generation of the 1960s now grown up. This pattern of the drop in the 40s also holds true for whether the informants used the deferential terms with their Instructors, Parents, Grandparents, Doctors/Dentists, Nurses, Employers/Supervisors, and Ministers/Clergy, questions whose answers proved to be significant at the .05 level of significance when a X^2 test was performed. This decline, however, though most precipitous with the 40s, was progressively quick in the 30-year age group for some questions more than others. The 30-year-olds sharply declined in using the terms for questions on address to Instructors, Doctors/Dentists, and Nurses. But there is a definite need to use these terms when one is younger, especially in the 18-29 age group.

However, as some oral in-depth interviews indicate, distinction between sex of parents and between sex of grandparents was made, often depending upon degree of intimacy and the expectation of the addresser. For example, a person who feels close to her father may not use the proper deferential term; the same person who has a strict mother demanding the terms of address will accede to her mother's request. The results in the data indicate that 7% of the informants make such a sex differentiation:

Address to Parents

Answer	Percentage	Frequency
To both parents	48.9%	313
To Mother only	4.2%	27
To Father only	2.8%	18
Childhood only	31.4%	201
Nonuse	12.7%	81

Fig. 3   Missing cases: 0

The data also show that 31% consider the use of the terms a childhood phenomenon only. After a child grows up, according to oral interviewees, he/she feels closer and more equal to his/her parents. Thus, the use of the terms may be discontinued.

Besides age of addresser and age of addressee making a difference upon whether the terms are used, the religious orientation of the addresser proved to be statistically significant in whether Male Instructors, Doctors/Dentists, Nurses, Employers/Supervisors, and Ministers/Clergy were addressed with the deferential terms. In every case, those who indicated that they were agnostic or atheistic in religious orientation seemed to use the deferential terms much less; those who were affiliated with a church scored the highest in use; and those who had no affiliation with a church but who believed in a supreme power closely followed the pattern of those who were affiliated with a church, though to a lesser degree. Although there were individuals who used the terms of deference, it is always the Agnostic or Atheistic group which uses the terms the least. Examine the data for these charts below for evidence of this definite pattern.

Address to Male Instructors: Relgious Orientation

Answer	Church-Affiliated	Agnostic/Atheist	Non-Church Affiliated, but Belief in a Supreme Power
Yes:	61.2% (285)	36.0% (9)	55.6% (50)
No:	38.8% (181)	64.0% (16)	44.4% (40)

Missing cases = 59

Statistical analysis resulted in a significant X^2 value of 6.807 ($p < .03$).

Fig. 4

Address to Doctors/Dentists: Religious Orientation

Answer	Church-Affiliated	Agnostic/Atheist	Non-Church Affiliated, but Belief in a Supreme Power
Yes:	73.4% (361)	36.4% (12)	64.3% (63)
No:	26.6% (131)	63.6% (21)	35.7% (35)

Missing cases = 17

Statistical analysis resulted in a significant X^2 value of 21.963 ($p < .0001$).

Fig. 5

Address to Nurses

Answer	Church-Affiliated	Agnostic/Atheist	Non-Church Affiliated, but Belief in a Supreme Power
Yes:	66.9% (329)	39.4% (13)	61.2% (60)
No:	33.1% (163)	60.6% (20)	38.8% (38)

Missing cases = 17

Statistical analysis resulted in a significant X^2 value of 10.754 ($p<.005$).

Fig. 6

Address to Employers/Supervisors

Answer	Church-Affiliated	Agnostic/Atheist	Non-Church Affiliated, but Belief in a Supreme Power
Yes:	82.4% (406)	63.6% (21)	77.6% (76)
No:	17.6% (87)	36.4% (12)	22.4% (22)

Missing cases = 16

Statistical analysis resulted in a significant X^2 value of 7.627 ($p<.02$).

Fig. 7

Address to Ministers/Clergy

Answer	Church-Affiliated	Agnostic/Atheist	Non-Church Affiliated, but Belief in a Supreme Power
Yes:	86.8% (426)	54.5% (18)	82.7% (81)
No:	13.2% (65)	45.5% (15)	17.3% (17)

Missing cases = 18

Statistical analysis resulted in a significant X^2 value of 24.653 ($p<.0001$).

Fig. 8

Note that although the Agnostic and Atheistic category scored lower than the other two categories for all groups addressed, the Agnostic and Atheistic category followed the trend of using the terms most with Employers/Supervisors (63.6%) and Ministers/Clergy (54.5%), the two groups which the other categories addressed with high scores. The Agnostic and Atheistic category even fell below 50% in addressing Male Instructors (36%), Doctors/Dentists (36.4%), and Nurses (39.4%). The results indicate that the more unconventional, free-spirited group does not believe as much in holding on to conventional values and practices of decorum, but will use the terms for pragmatic expediency--i.e., with Employers/Supervisors--and perhaps for grace in preventing awkward social situations--i.e., with Ministers/Clergy-- since most of society does use the terms with this latter category.

A caveat on the interpretation of the statistics above, however, comes from the free written comments about Doctors/Dentists and Ministers/Clergy. Instead of saying Yes/No, Sir, a few persons said they could show respect by using "Yes/No, doctor," or "Yes/No, Father." This alternative way of giving respect might have lowered the number of positive responses for the two categories, because the informants stated they alternated between methods.

That conservatives hold more to established values may also be seen in the subgroup which was old enough to vote in the last presidential election. Of those who voted in the last presidential election, Reagan voters clearly outstripped the Mondale voters and the voters who voted for some candidate other than Reagan or Mondale in using the deferential terms, as the charts below indicate:

Address to Female Instructors

Answer	Reagan	Mondale	Other
Yes:	72.6%	49.0%	41.2%
	(135)	(48)	(14)
No:	27.4%	51.0%	58.8%
	(51)	(50)	(20)

318 cases

Statistical analysis resulted in a significant X^2 value of 22.136 (p<.0001).

Fig. 9

Address to Male Instructors

Answer	Reagan	Mondale	Other
Yes:	69.6%	40.8%	42.9%
	(126)	(40)	(15)
No:	30.4%	59.2%	57.1%
	(55)	(58)	(20)

314 cases

Statistical analysis resulted in a significant X^2 value of 25.121 (p<.0001).

Fig. 10

Don't Use Terms with Police Officer When Informant Is Confronted for a Possible Violation

Answer	Reagan	Mondale	Other
True:	12.8%	26.3%	15.4%
	(25)	(30)	(6)
False:	87.2%	73.7%	84.6%
	(170)	(84)	(33)

348 cases

Statistical analysis resulted in a significant X^2 value of 9.203 (p<.01).

Fig. 11

Address to Doctors/Dentists

Answer	Reagan	Mondale	Other
Yes:	72.7%	58.6%	55.0%
	(144)	(68)	(22)
No:	27.3%	41.4%	45.0%
	(54)	(48)	(18)

354 cases

Statistical analysis resulted in a significant X^2 value of 8.976 ($p<.01$).

Fig. 12

Address to Employers/Supervisors

Answer	Reagan	Mondale	Other
Yes:	84.4%	69.0%	72.5%
	(168)	(80)	(29)
No:	15.6%	31.0%	27.5%
	(31)	(36)	(11)

355 cases

Statistical analysis resulted in a significant X^2 value of 11.016 ($p<.004$).

Fig. 13

Moreover, it was also Reagan voters who led in having received instruction in the home to use these terms of address:

Parental Instruction to Use Deferential Terms to Parents

Answer	Reagan	Mondale	Other
Instructed to address Parents at home:	60.5% (115)	42.9% (48)	52.5% (21)
Instructed to only address Parents outside the home when in the presence of people:	6.3% (12)	4.5% (5)	5.0% (2)
Not instructed to address Parents:	33.2% (63)	52.7% (59)	42.5% (17)

342 cases

Statistical analysis resulted in a significant X^2 value of 11.208 ($p<.024$).

Fig. 14

The reason that the second option--i.e., parental admonition to address parents outside the home only when in the presence of people--appeared on the questionnaire is that one informant of the the oral in-depth interviews stated that his parents did not require him to use the terms in the home but only outside the home when in the presence of others for fear that outsiders would think their child was not well trained. The questionnaire confirms the fact that some persons do indeed receive such parental admonition.

One must use caution, however, in interpretating the data. As one written comment indicated, lack of home instruction for the informant did not necessarily mean lack of use. This informant stated that one caught on to the use of terms from the community by osmosis.

Besides age, religious orientation, and political orientation, race proved an interesting variable. Many times, Blacks followed the trend of the composite total, but at a lesser rate; at other times, the difference between Blacks and Whites was dramatic. For example, in address to Doctors/Dentists, Employers/Supervisors, and Police Officers, the Blacks followed a similar curve to Whites, with a positive response, but at a lesser rate, as the charts below indicate:

Address to Doctors/Dentists

Answer	Black	White
Yes:	61.3%	72.2%
	(98)	(314)
No:	38.8%	27.8%
	(62)	(121)

Missing cases = 45

Statistical analysis resulted in a signficant X^2 test of 6.063 ($p<.01$).

Fig. 15

Address to Employees/Supervisors

Answer	Black	White
Yes:	71.3%	83.9%
	(114)	(366)
No:	28.8%	16.1%
	(46)	(70)

Missing cases = 1

Statistical analysis resulted in a significant X^2 value of 11.238 ($p<.001$).

Fig. 16

Address to Police Officers upon a Possible Violation: Race, Sex, and Age Do Not Matter

Answer	Black	White
True:	74.1%	87.3%
	(117)	(379)
False:	25.9%	12.7%
	(41)	(55)

Missing cases = 48

Statistical analysis resulted in a significant x^2 value of 14.066 (p<.0002).

Fig. 17

But sometimes a positive response for Blacks resulted in a percentage of only 50% or less as compared to Whites, who scored higher, as illustrated in the charts below, for address to female and male instructors:

Address to Female Instructors

Answer	Black	White
Yes:	50.3%	66.1%
	(78)	(265)
No:	49.7%	33.9%
	(77)	(136)

Missing cases = 84 (Note: Faculty not taking courses did not answer this question.)

Statistical analysis resulted in a significant x^2 value of 11.095 (p<.001).

Fig. 18

Methods in Dialectology   31

Address to Male Instructors

Answer	Black	White
Yes:	45.5%	65.3%
	(70)	(260)
No:	54.5%	34.7%
	(84)	(138)

Missing cases = 88 (Note: Faculty not taking courses did not answer this question.)

Statistical analysis resulted in a significant X^2 value of 17.42 (p<.0001).

Fig. 19

At other times, the difference was even more dramatic, especially in these areas: 1) parental instruction to use deferential terms at home; 2) the age when one is old enough to be called by the deferential terms; 3) address to Ministers/Clergy by informants' age, as seen in the charts below:

Parental Instruction to Use Deferential Terms to Parents

Answer	Black	White
Instructed to address Parents at home:	34.0% (53)	57.0% (237)
Instructed to only address Parents outside the home when in the presence of people:	3.2% (5)	5.5% (23)
Not instructed to address Parents:	62.8% (98)	37.5% (156)

Missing cases = 68

Statistical analysis resulted in a significant X^2 value of 29.467 (p<.0001).

Fig. 20

Note that 62.8% of Blacks as compared to 37.5% of the White did not receive instruction.

There is also greater inclination for Blacks to address with the deferential terms a female or male who is not boss or superior when the female or male is older than the age considered proper by Whites. Seventy-four percent of the Blacks as compared to 88% of the Whites deemed it proper to address by age 20 a female who is not a boss or superior; and thus, about 26% of the Blacks and only 12% of the Whites deemed the appropriate age for the addressee to be later--at 25 or 30. Moreover, the number of Blacks who considered the earliest age to be appropriate--namely, 10 years older for the addressee--was greatly less in proportion to the number of White informants: 24.7% Blacks to 40.8% Whites:

Age for Addressing Female When Not a Boss/Superior

Answer in Number of Years Older	Black	White
By 10:	24.7% (38)	40.8% (167)
By 15:	24.0% (37)	21.8% (89)
By 20:	25.3% (39)	25.4% (104)
By 25:	12.3% (19)	5.6% (23)
By 30:	13.6% (21)	6.4% (26)

Missing cases = 77

Statistical analysis resulted in a significant X^2 value of 22.139 ($p<.0002$).

Fig. 21

A similar pattern holds for Black versus White responses for the proper age of addressing a male who is not a boss or superior:

Age to Address Male When Not a Boss/Superior

Answer in Number of Years Older	Black	White
By 10:	20.0% (31)	36.2% (148)
By 15:	19.4% (30)	23.2% (95)
By 20:	27.1% (42)	26.4% (108)
By 25:	11.6% (18)	7.6% (31)
By 30:	21.9% (34)	6.6% (27)

Missing cases = 76

Statistical analysis resulted in a significant X^2 value of 36.6 ($p<.0001$).

Fig. 22

Although, as discussed earlier, Blacks often followed White trends in giving a positive response to use of the terms, they exceeded Whites in addressing Ministers and Clergy. Even the 40-year-old Blacks tended to do so, although this age bracket droppped drastically in their address to Doctors and Dentists, Nurses, Employers and Supervisors. Compare these charts of address to Ministers and Clergy:

Blacks' Address to Minister/Clergy by Age Bracket

Answer	18-29	30s	40s	50s	60s
Yes:	90.8% (118)	68.2% (15)	83.3% (5)		100.0% (1)
No:	9.2% (12)	31.8% (7)	16.7% (1)		

Missing cases = 1

Statistical analysis resulted in a significant X^2 value of 8.966 ($p<.03$).

Fig. 23

On the other hand, for 40-year-old Whites, the percentage of those addressing Ministers/Clergy diminished to 46.9%:

Whites' Address to Minister/Clergy by Age Bracket

Answer	18-29	30s	40s	50s	60s
Yes:	88.9%	69.7%	46.9%	62.5%	100.0%
	(313)	(23)	(15)	(10)	(1)
No:	11.1%	30.3%	53.1%	37.5%	
	(39)	(10)	(17)	(6)	

Missing cases = 2

Statistical analysis resulted in a significant X^2 value of 44.331 ($p<.0001$).

Fig. 24

Perhaps the reason for this difference in 40-year-old Blacks greatly exceeding Whites in addressing Ministers and Clergy is the great role the Black Church has played among its members not only in spiritual, but also in economic and political matters, and perhaps the inclination to use the deferential terms shows a greater reverence toward its religous leaders. In contrast, 40-year-old Blacks when addressing other persons often decline below the level of Whites. Note, for example, the difference between 40-year-old Blacks and 40-year-old Whites in their address to Nurses, where 40-year-old Blacks' low positive responses--16.7%--is even lower than their White counterparts' responses--31.3%:

Blacks' Address to Nurses by Age Bracket

Answer	18-29	30s	40s	50s	60s
Yes:	70.0%	31.8%	16.7%	100.0%	
	(91)	(7)	(1)	(1)	
No:	30.0%	68.2%	83.3%		100.0%
	(39)	(15)	(5)		(1)

Missing cases = 0

Statistical analysis resulted in a significant X^2 value of 19.6 ($p<.0006$).

Fig. 25

Whites' Address to Nurses by Age Bracket

Answer	18-29	30s	40s	50s	60s
Yes:	70.2%	42.4%	31.3%	50.0%	100.0%
	(247)	(14)	(10)	(8)	(1)
No:	29.8%	57.6%	68.8%	50.0%	
	(105)	(19)	(22)	(8)	

Missing cases = 2

Statistical analysis resulted in a significant X^2 value of 29.443 (p<.0001).

Fig. 26

When educational status as a variable is examined, the Faculty seems to be nonconventional in not using the terms of deference. When the other categories responded mostly with a positive response to using the deferential terms with Ministers and Clergy and with the Police, the faculty clearly showed an independence of mind by not responding with as great an inclination:

Address to Ministers/Clergy by Educational Status

Answer	Freshman/ Sophomore	Junior/ Senior	Graduate Student	Faculty
Yes:	89.0%	81.8%	72.5%	56.3%
	(373)	(108)	(37)	(18)
No:	11.0%	18.2%	27.5%	43.8%
	(46)	(24)	(14)	(14)

Missing cases = 6

Statistical analysis resulted in a significant X^2 value of 32.397 (p<.0001).

Fig. 27

Don't Use Terms with Police Officer When Informant Is Confronted for a Possible Violation

Answer	Freshman/ Sophomore	Junior/ Senior	Graduate Student	Faculty
True:	11.4% (47)	18.3% (24)	21.3% (10)	40.6% (13)
False:	88.6% (364)	81.7% (107)	78.7% (37)	59.4% (19)

Missing cases = 19

Statistical analysis resulted in a significant x^2 value of 22.98 ($p<.0001$).

Fig. 28

Their responses to Doctors/Dentists and especially to Nurses also seemed low:

Address to Doctors/Dentists

Answer	Freshman/ Sophomore	Junior/ Senior	Graduate Student	Faculty
Yes:	74.2% (311)	66.7% (88)	50.0% (26)	46.9% (15)
No:	25.8% (108)	33.3% (44)	50.0% (26)	53.1% (17)

Missing cases = 5

Statistical analysis resulted in a signficant x^2 value of 21.87 ($p<.0001$).

Fig. 29

Address to Nurses

Answer	Freshman/ Sophomore	Junior/ Senior	Graduate Student	Faculty
Yes:	68.5% (287)	62.9% (83)	46.2% (24)	37.5% (12)
No:	31.5% (132)	37.1% (49)	53.8% (28)	62.5% (20)

Missing cases = 5

Statistical analysis resulted in a significant X^2 value of 20.673 ($p<.0001$).

Fig. 30

Although their percentages remained below other groups for address to Employers/Supervisors and Older Persons, Faculty responses at least reached figures above 60% for these two categories. Probably the Faculty response was higher for Employers/Supervisors because of the necessity of being accommodating or ingratiating enough, although Faculty in oral interviews and written comments indicated that they differed on the rank of the official when the the deferential terms should be used: on whether, for example, the terms should begin with the Department Chair, the Dean, or the Vice-President, or be restricted only to the President of the university. Note the results for Employers/Supervisors by educational status:

Address to Employers/Supervisors

Answer	Freshman/ Sophomore	Junior/ Senior	Graduate Student	Faculty
Yes:	84.5% (354)	75.8% (100)	65.4% (34)	69.7% (23)
No:	15.5% (65)	24.2% (32)	34.6% (18)	30.3% (10)

Missing cases = 4

Statistical analysis resulted in a significant X^2 value of 16.05 ($p<.001$).

Fig. 31

The Faculty showed an unusually high response in address to Older Persons of both races, if one considers its even lower positive responses on other items of the questionnaire. The Faculty also showed the most percentage of those who chose other options: address only to those of the same race and also nonuse of the terms:

Address to Older Persons

Answer	Freshman/ Sophomore	Junior/ Senior	Graduate Student	Faculty
Older persons of only the same race:	4.0% (17)	4.7% (6)	2.4% (1)	15.2% (5)
Older persons of both races:	89.5% (376)	88.3% (113)	88.1% (37)	69.7% (23)
Do not use at all:	6.4% (27)	7.0% (9)	9.5% (4)	15.2% (5)

Missing cases = 17

Statistical analysis resulted in a significant X^2 value of 13.529 ($p<.04$).

Fig. 32

Probably the result for this mixed pattern is that the Faculty varied greatly in age and thus voted individually the way their age bracket tended to vote, producing mixed results. Here is the breakdown of the Faculty by age:

Faculty by Age

Age	Percentage	Frequency
18-29	11.1%	4
30s	22.2%	8
40s	36.1%	13
50s	27.8%	10
60s	2.8%	1

Missing cases = 0

Fig. 33

Whenever the variable of sex proved to be statistically significant, it was males who used the deferential terms more in these areas: address to Police Officers, Doctors/Dentists, and Ministers/Clergy:

Methods in Dialectology

Address to Police Officers upon a Possible Violation: Race, Sex, and Age Do Not Matter

Answer	Female	Male
True:	80.1%	88.4%
	(286)	(243)
False:	19.9%	11.6%
	(71)	(32)

Missing cases = 8

Statistical analysis resulted in a significant X^2 value of 7.16 ($p<.008$).

Fig. 34

Address to Doctors/Dentists

Answer	Female	Male
Yes:	65.7%	74.3%
	(236)	(205)
No:	34.3%	25.7%
	(123)	(71)

Missing cases = 5

Statistical analysis resulted in a significant X^2 value of 4.97 ($p<.03$).

Fig. 35

Address to Ministers/Clergy

Answer	Female	Male
Yes:	81.6%	88.8%
	(292)	(245)
No:	18.4%	11.2%
	(66)	(31)

Missing cases = 6

Statistical analysis resulted in a significant X^2 value of 5.7 ($p<.02$).

Fig. 36

This pattern is also statistically significant when the data are broken down by race and sex for Address to Police Officers and Address to Ministers/Clergy: Black males are always ahead of Black females; White males always surpass White females:

Address to Police Officers upon a Possible Violation: Race, Sex, and Age Do Not Matter
Answer by Race and Sex

Answer	Black Females	White Females	Black Males	White Males
True:	69.4%	80.9%	73.3%	90.9%
	(84)	(228)	(44)	(241)
False:	30.6%	19.1%	26.7%	9.1%
	(37)	(54)	(16)	(24)

Missing cases = 71

Statistical analysis resulted in a significant x^2 value of 30.644 (p<.0001).

Fig. 37

Address to Ministers/Clergy
Answer by Race and Sex

Answer	Black Females	White Females	Black Males	White Males
True:	83.6%	72.4%	88.1%	80.5%
	(102)	(205)	(52)	(214)
False:	16.4%	27.6%	11.9%	19.5%
	(20)	(78)	(7)	(52)

Missing cases = 69

Statistical analysis resulted in a significant x^2 value of 11.89 (p<.008).

Fig. 38

But the questionnaire not only tested how various segments of the population answered various questions, but also whether oral in-depth interviewees' comments could be confirmed concerning how the terms can be interpreted in specific contexts. For example, the use of Ma'am/Sir, according to interviewees can be a hard, bottom-line negative, but socially acceptable answer. Negative feelings and intentions can thus be stated, in the language of assertiveness training, assertive rather than aggressive (Galassi and Galassi, 1977, 14-16). That is, these expressions allow a Southerner to indicate negative feelings in a socially acceptable way, still maintaining the speaker's composure and self-respect and still giving due respect to the listener, without recourse to vile words or unacceptable emotional outbursts, because against these negative meanings and feelings are the basic meanings of politeness and deference.

To test this hypothesis of the function of Ma'am/Sir, five questions were placed on the questionnaire. They are reproduced, as follows, with the results: the frequencies of responses placed in parentheses after the percentage figures:

Suppose a telephone operator, upon the request of a male caller, has looked up a person's telephone number 3 times by using the computer, but the operator cannot find any listing of the person. Then this conversation takes place:

    Operator: I am sorry. There's no listing.
    Caller: It's got to be there!
    Operator: Sir. I'm sorry. I've checked the list three times. If you want to, you can talk to my supervisor.

Which one or which ones of these statements give a correct interpretation:

1. The operator's answer shows the operator feels true respect for the caller because the operator addresses the caller with Sir.
    A. True   27.1% (171)
    B. False   72.9% (460)
              Missing cases = 9

2. Although the operator gives this answer, using Sir, the operator probably does not have true respect for the caller:
    A. True   71.2% (449)
    B. False   28.8% (182)
              Missing cases = 9

3. The caller would interpret the operator's remark as an unfriendly act.
    A. True   24.8% (156)
    B. False   75.2% (473)
               Missing cases = 11

4. The caller knows that there is a good possibility that the caller can still change the operator's mind because the operator used <u>Sir</u>.
      A. True   13.2% (83)
      B. False   86.8% (546)
                       Missing cases = 11

   5. The operator has used proper business etiquette.
      A. True   94.5% (601)
      B. False   5.5%   (35)
                       Missing cases = 4

Note that respondents overwhelmingly indicated that the operator has used proper business etiquette, but all the time accomplishing the following:

1. The operator has been able to be assertive without being aggressive when giving the caller the hard-line or bottom-line <u>Sir</u>, from which the operator refuses to budge.
2. The caller does not interpret the operator's strong assertion as an unfriendly act, probably because proper business etiquette has been followed.
3. The operator has gone through all of the forms of etiquette without necessarily feeling or possessing true respect for the caller.

These accomplishments show that <u>Sir</u> in this context definitely is an acceptable mode of mitigation and politeness, achieving understanding and peace in a difficult situation when the caller seems to be insistent and unreasonable.

Another item tested in the questionnaire came from some oral in-depth interviewees' comments that three respectful, quick-sounding <u>Yes, Sirs</u>--<u>Yes, Sir, Yes, Sir, Yes, Sir</u>--or <u>Yes, Ma'ams</u>--<u>Yes, Ma'am, Yes, Ma'am, Yes, Ma'am</u>--may indicate impatience in a respectful way with what is being said because the addressee already understands or already has heard what the speaker is saying. The addressee wishes the speaker to cut short his/her remarks. Respondents indicated this interpretation to be correct with the highest responses given out of the three options on the questionnaire. The questionnnaire tested this use of 3 <u>Yes, Sirs</u>, by asking the questions below (the results are placed adjacent to the options given):

Suppose an employer reminds an employee how <u>one</u> task--<u>not several</u> tasks--is done. In the midst of the explanation, the employee says <u>respectfully, but rather quickly, 3 Yes, Sirs</u> in a row: "Yes, Sir, Yes, Sir, Yes, Sir." By saying these <u>3 respectful and quick Yes, Sirs,</u> the employee indicates that:

   1. The employee is extremely respectful toward his/her employer, is appreciative of the employers' reminder, and wants the employer to go through with the full explanation of the task to be done.
      A. True   36.2% (226)
      B. False   63.8% (399)
                       Missing cases = 15

2. The employee already knows what the employer wants and that the employer should cut short the explanation.
   A. True   62.8% (394)
   B. False   37.2% (233)
   Missing cases = 13

3. The employee wants to show he or she understands all of the explanation thus far and will proably say, "No, Sir," when the explanation is not clear.
   A. True   56.8% (358)
   B. False   43.2% (272)
   Missing cases = 10

Another comment tested on the questionnaire was the remark by some interviewees that Yes, Sir, and Yes, Ma'am, can be used in some instances among speakers to show close bonding and cordiality, even if the age of the addressee is younger or is the same age as the speaker. A Black female instructor explains the feeling of camaraderie created by using these terms among peers by stating that saying Ma'am to a fellow female friend of the same age is like saying, "Oh, girl, do you know that such and such a thing happened?" Perhaps this explanation may liken the use of Ma'am and Sir among peers to the use of brother and sister in evangelical churches to create bonding.

Respondents on the questionnaire recognized the deferential terms being addressed to younger speakers or to peers, but rejected the notion that they were for camaraderie. Instead, the interpretation was that of hearty affirmation, another function of Yes, Sir, and Yes, Ma'am, which interviewees usually cited as one of the uses of these terms. However, I have personally observed these terms used for camaraderie among peers and among persons younger than the speaker. I have even noted a long-time senior professor in our department, for example, who upon three occasions greeted me with "Yes, Sir," upon first seeing me in the morning, instead of using the salutation "Good morning." Moreover, I observed a basketball guard dribbling the ball down court with "Yes, Sir," to his teammates to indicate a good feeling of camaraderie with his team players because the team had the situation in hand, under control--an interpretation he gave when he was personally interviewed after the game. I also observed two young Black men who greeted each other from their cars with a "Yes, Sir," before they conversed.

Thus, the questionnaire may not confirm some interviewees' comments which are borne out by personal observation, demonstrating the need for personal observation as a necessary ingredient in the determination of the meaning of the deferential terms.

Moreover, the objective portion of the questionnaire is like a skeleton without the flesh and blood of the organism. Only the personal interviews and the free-response portion of the questionnaire can produce the personal anecdotes giving insight into the colorful interactions and social dynamics by the use of these terms. For example, interviewees recounted painful experiences of a teacher chiding them or hitting them upon the hand with a ruler in elementary and secondary school if they forgot to use these terms when addressing the teacher. A Black maid, 57, remembers how angered she was in the '50s and '60s at Blacks' being made to use the deferential terms when addressing Whites, when Whites did not use these terms with Blacks. At a downtown restaraurant, she was particularly angered by a sign on the wall, which stated: "All Black help are to say, 'Yes, Sir, and Yes, Ma'am,' to all White employees." In contrast, today, a White public school instructor said that a Black mother inquired whether children in school were taught to use the terms, because the mother was disturbed that her children were not using them. In reply, the White instructor stated that all the children needed to say were a plain "Yes" or a plain "No."

But in some places, the deferential terms are still required. One person said that in juvenile court in Memphis a sign on the wall states that all persons are to answer or address adults with Ma'am or Sir. Moreover, two individuals said that some karate instructors require their pupils to address their instructors with these terms, one of whom said that she has seen karate instructors requiring their students to use these terms while carrying out punishment during each push-up. Thus, if a student is required to do push-ups, he will say, "1, Sir! 2, Sir! 3, Sir! 4, Sir!" etc. as he exercises.

Interviewees, free-response comments, and personal observations also indicate the versatile function of M'am and Sir. Sometimes they are used by White instructors with students much younger than their instructors to create closeness by indicating racial and age equality. At times, they are used, instead, to create distance, seriousness, and formality, as in the case of a Mother who says to her three-year-old girl requesting sweets early in the morning, "No, Ma'am. You may not have candy before breakfast." Moreover, a child who usually does not say "Yes, Ma'am," to her mother, will do so, when reprimanded to show her seriousness of intent, her respect of her mother, and her contrition.

The questionnaire also does not measure frequency of using the terms. Interviewees, free-response comments, and personal observations indicate that there is a type of person who punctuates his/her statements with "Yes/No, Sir," and "Yes/No, Ma'am," at the drop of a hat, creating the image of a clean-cut, extremely well-mannered indvidual, while others will use the terms sporadically in their conversation. Sometimes, individuals who frequently use the terms say that they do so deliberately to create a good image: in the words of one college male, "a good-boy image." In the words of a Northerner, such use is like saying, "Yes, thank you," or "No, thank you," in the North, instead of a plain "Yes" or "No," which does not convey a well-mannered speaker.

Thus, all three methods--the objective questions on the questionnaire, the subjective methods of oral interviews and of free-response comments on the questionnaire, and personal observation--are needed to indicate the function and uses of Ma'am and Sir as modes of mitigation and politeness in the South and the variables which influence those who use these terms.

References

Galassi, Merna Dee, and John P. Galassi. (1977) <u>Assert Yourself!: How to Be Your Own Person</u>. New York: Human Sciences Press

Some Innovative Linguistic and Procedural Solutions, Relative to Sea Island Creole, in General; Some Aspects of the Sea Island Creole Verbal Auxiliary, in Particular

IRMA ALOYCE EWING CUNNINGHAM
North Carolina A & T State University

Here, my primary linguistic focus, relative to Sea Island Creole, will be that of some aspects of the verbal auxiliary. As these are considered, some of the varied techniques employed and challenges met in eliciting, analyzing and presenting the data for the grammar --- from which they have been taken --- will be pointed out, either directly or indirectly. Before beginning this discussion, however, I will provide you with some background information, regarding Sea Island Creole --- sometimes called "Gullah" or "Geechee."[1]

This tongue is significant for a number of reasons -- one being -- unlike other varieties of English spoken in the United States, which are mutually intelligible from one region to another, this is <u>one</u> which is most often unintelligible to people, outside the area in which it is spoken.

Sea Island Creole is an English-based Creole language spoken by Black slave descendants on the islands and coastal mainland from southern North Carolina to northern Florida.

In addition to the English element which constitutes the basic vocabulary of Sea Island Creole, it has many linguistic characteristics which are ascribable to a West African substratum, resulting from the languages spoken by the slaves who were brought to this area during the 18th and 19th centuries. Here, we see a second reason for the significance of the tongue; it <u>clearly</u> reflects the African linguistic heritage of the Black American. (Note -- If we were ever going to call <u>anything</u> "Black English," this would be it.)

I have chosen the name, Sea Island Creole [hereafter, generally, referred to as SIC], because the names, "Gullah" and "Geechee," have a derogatory connotation and denotation for the speakers of this tongue.

The attitude of authors writing about SIC has been negative until very recently. These authors did not recognize SIC as a creole language at all -- but as a degenerate form of the 17th and 18th century English employed by masters and overseers in communicating with the slave ancestors. (In other words, they saw SIC as simply <u>bad English</u>.) Some even called it "the worst English in the world."[2] Their attitudes, coupled with the adverse attitudes of lay observers and _even_ commercial recordings, utilizing the tongue for comical purposes --[3] convinced the islanders that their language really was _and_ is inferior. This, combined with many other factors, has made any effort by linguists to investigate the tongue, extremely difficult, for every attempt possible has been made by islanders to conceal its _very_ existence from outsiders. "Standard" English, then, which is spoken along side the Creole, has become a winning competitor.

It was not until 1949, when Lorenzo D. Turner published his <u>Africanisms in the Gullah Dialect</u> (resulting from fieldwork, which he began in the early thirties), that SIC was seen for what it really is -- a genuine creole tongue.[4] Linguistically, Turner's focus was phonology and vocabulary. Then, it was not until 1969 that any additional definitive work was done on the tongue. That work was my <u>Syntactic Analysis of Sea Island Creole</u>, based on my own field work in the area. The approximate 40 year hiatus between Turner's fieldwork and my own should serve as some indication of the difficulty of fieldwork in that territory.

Most of the information I will share with you, in reference to the SIC Verbal Auxiliary, is a result of the research I began in 1969.

SETTING THE STAGE

As I share with you certain linguistic specifics, please be mindful of the following challenges, which had to be met, before I could have anything <u>to</u> share:

(1) To my surprise ..... the language was unintelligible to me. Having conducted two pilot studies, employing the limited printed resources available (i.e., the textual data employed in Turner's work), I thought myself fairly well equipped to handle the fieldwork, in terms of basic audio understanding of the tongue. I sincerely expected another dialect -- not another language.[5] Countless hours had to be devoted to just learning to understand the tongue, and I am not talking semantic maneuvers either.

(2) In addition to the lack of textual information regarding the tongue -- at that time, there was a lack of procedural information for eliciting <u>syntactic constructions</u>.

(3) These challenges, combined with unwilling informants (some reasons for this unwillingness already given), might give you some notion of what the research entailed, from which I have drawn the following aspects of the SIC verbal auxiliary, that I will now share with you.

THE VERBAL AUXILIARY

Members of the verbal auxiliary are: (1) the tense indicator, been/bɪn/, (2) the progressive, habituative and perfective aspect markers, (3) do/du/, and the (4) modal.[6] Here, I will concentrate on the tense indicator, been, the progressive and perfective aspect markers, and the very intricate relationship among them. Each considered member of the auxiliary will be discussed as it functions with the transitives, non-transitives and verbal adjectives. The SIC Creole parallels to the English verb "to be" in its function as a copula preceding nouns and adverbs are not included in this discussion.

The adjective is being treated as a predicator, along with all other non-copulative verbs, because it has the capacity to occur as the sole predicating element and because of its direct co-occurrence possibilities with various members of the auxiliary. The verbal adjective is common in many West African languages (Ewe, Fante, Yoruba, Kongo).

Tense (in general)

In S.I. Creole, the verbal categories are marked for _aspect_ rather than _time_. A single verb form may do service for the past, present or future. The preference for aspectual marking over tense marking might be evidenced by the fact that the sole tense indicator, been, which marks past tense, rarely occurs alone as a simple past tense indicator, although it occurs frequently in combination with the progressive aspect markers. The tendency toward a strongly marked aspectual system with little or no formal indication of tense is found in many West African languages, (e.g., Ewe, Mandinka, Yoruba). (In other words, the manner of action—and not the time — is the most important consideration to the Creole speaker.)

The Tense Indicator - Been

Been always precedes the verb or predicating adjective that it marks. With the transitives and non-transitives, the simple past is seldom marked but is either represented by the unmarked form of the verb (in which case tense must be determined from context) or the past progressive. The following illustrate the marked past tense, as well as the unmarked tense used with reference to past time:

(Note)   "C" preceding an example = Sea Island Creole sentence
         "E" preceding an example = "Standard" English translation

Marked: (Preceding a Verbal Adjective)
                       C: I been mad.

                       E: I was angry.

                       (Preceding a Verb)
                       C: We been see that man thief that man car.

                       E: We saw that man steal that man's car.

Unmarked: with Verb (V)
                       C: The rest of them -- I meet them here.

                       E: I met the rest of them here.

The Aspect Markers

Now, to consider the progressive and perfective aspects--this should give some indication of the purpose, form and behavior of these aspectual types, as well as the importance of aspect marking over tense marking.

1.   The present progressive aspect markers

These are /də/ and /ɪŋ/.   ɪŋ = ing

də always precedes the verb; ɪŋ always follows, thus resulting in the forms /də/+V or V+ɪŋ. The two progressive markers do not co-occur. Neither co-occurs with the verbal adjective. Examples of the present progressive as rendered by both forms follow:

C: I still də look.   C: My head də hurt me.

E: I am still looking.   E: My head is hurting me.

C: I still looking.

(də is paralleled in the W.A. languages, Ewe and Ibo.)

As in other cases, the present form sometimes does service for the past, as well as the present.

2.   The past progressive

The present progressive forms combine freely with the tense indicator (which must always precede). As a result, just as there are two present progressive forms, there are also two past progressive forms:

Past	Present
bɪn+ə + V (Note - bɪn+ də-→ bɪn+ə)	də + V
bɪn+ V + ɪŋ	V + ɪŋ

The past progressive is versatile. It may do service for the English simple past (I cooked), past progressive (was cooking), present perfect progressive (have been cooking) and the future perfect progressive (shall have been cooking). It may <u>sometimes</u> do service for the past perfect progressive (had been cooking), if the speaker focuses on the action <u>before</u> it terminated, rather than the fact that it has terminated. Usually, the Creole speaker focuses on the latter; therefore, he employs the perfective aspect marker, <u>done</u> /dʌn/ . (<u>been</u>- ə /bɪn-ə/ and <u>done</u>/dʌn/ do not co-occur.)

<u>Examples of the past progressive form</u>
past progressive
C: When you call me, I been-ə cook my dinner. (bɪn +ə + V)

E: When you called me, I was cooking my dinner.
(or, in rare cases)
E: When you called me, I had been cooking my dinner.

present perfect progressive
C: I been-ə see that boy a long time. (bɪn + ə + V)

E: I have been seeing that boy for a long time.

future perfect progressive
C: I been-ə cook for five years next month. (bɪn +ə + V)

E: I shall have been cooking for five years next month.

simple past
C: I been doing that till July gone. (bɪn + V +ɪŋ)

E: I did that until last July.

The Roving Perfective, Done

The perfective, <u>done</u>, may render any <u>action</u> or <u>state</u> as being complete. It has a wide range of occurrence within the Creole sentence. (This form is paralleled in Jamaican Creole.) Here, we will consider it only in its function as an auxiliary.

Done may occur with some other members of Aux., but, in so doing, it is always the last in the series. It occurs preceding the predicating adjective and transitive and non-transitive verbs as in:

with Verbal Adjective
C: Your blood done normal.

E: Your blood pressure is completely normal now.

with Linking Verb
C: I done got fainty.

E: I had become faint.

with Transitive Verb
C: You see, you done do it.

E: You see, you have done it.

with Modal
C: I must to done sell about two hundred fish sandwich.

E: I must have sold about two hundred fish sandwiches.

In some instances I have mentioned co-occurrence restrictions among the members of Aux themselves and their restrictions preceding the verbal adjective, transitive and non-transitive verbs. The following should serve to clarify the co-occurrence restrictions of the aspect markers. (These are unfactored rules, for illustrative purposes only.)

Aux is optional in its entirety
$$\text{Aux} \longrightarrow (\text{Aux}_1) \quad (\text{Aux}_2)$$
$$\text{Aux}_2 \longrightarrow \left\{ \begin{array}{l} \text{(Habituative)} \quad \text{(Progressive/-V)} \\ \text{Perfective} \end{array} \right\}$$

The habituative and progressive do not co-occur with the perfective.

You may choose either the habituative or the progressive or both, but if the progressive is chosen, the predicator following must be a verb and not a verbal adjective.

The following is a *general* unfactored rule, illustrating the immutable co-occurrence restrictions, among the members of Aux_1. It shows schematically the incompatibility of modal (M) and (do), of do and be, and of be and tense (T). Be, in this case, is the base form of the verb, to be, which is required by (M), in some contexts, and *not* the be which marks the habituative aspect.

$$\text{Aux}_1 \longrightarrow \left\{ \begin{array}{ll} (M) & \left(\begin{Bmatrix} \text{be} \\ T \end{Bmatrix} \right) \\ (do) & (T) \end{array} \right\}$$

ON THE PRESENTATION AND COLLECTION OF DATA

In order to best address the varied focal strengths of my audience, the textual type explanation of constructions, such as the preceding, is presented -- along with specific data illustrating it (as shown on the accompanying handout). Transformational rules summarizing the preceding are also given (see handout and the last portion of the discussion of the "Verbal Auxiliary"). Whenever possible, I give my audience an opportunity to hear the tongue, as rendered by native speakers, for only, in this way, can the true distinctiveness of SIC be fully appreciated.

(PLAYING OF TAPES)
FIRST -- I will play a short passage from my chief textual informant, Henrietta -- Yonges Island, S.C.[7]

The linguistic focus, here, is the present progressive, in both of its forms. I, particularly, would like to alert you to the /də/ form, since it is peculiar to SIC. As she moves along, you will hear other members of the auxiliary, as well.

Conversational Context -- Care of ill husband.

Technique -- Continuous discourse, since my target was syntax.

SECOND -- Part of a Direct Questioning Session with Eloise, my chief technical informant -- Edisto Island, S.C.[8]

The linguistic focus here is the differentiation between bɪnə and done. This session ended one of my greatest analytical challenges. (Remember the overlap between the past progressive and the perfective, mentioned earlier in this paper?)

Additional Techniques -- The frame and translation

THIRD -- Focus -- Contrast between Creole to Outsider vs. Creole to Creole.
Conversational Context - A general three-way discussion, among two creole speakers and me. Note the contrast, when another creole speaker enters abruptly, causing the existing creole linguistic shield to be dropped.

Now, (what I suspect to be) a very necessary translation of the interruptive creole statement, you have just heard --

Technique -- Continuous discourse and keeping the recorder rolling at all times that were appropriate.

NOTES

[1] Most of the information contained throughout this paper and on all accompanying material has either been taken from my work, *A Syntactic Analysis of Sea Island Creole*, 1970 or was acquired during the course of my research for that work. In a few instances, materials, from later work in the area, have been included.

[2] Some authors, mirroring this belief, were John Bennett, George Krapp, Ambrose Gonzales and Reed Smith.

[3] The recordings done by Dick Reeves of Charleston, for example.

[4] Lorenzo Dow Turner, *Africanisms in the Gullah Dialect* (Chicago: University of Chicago Press), 1949.

[5] Despite my *theoretical* knowledge that this was a creole language in its own right, *true* knowledge of this fact did not occur until my first direct encounter with it.

[6] All linguistic representations, after this point, will be given in regular English orthography, unless clarity dictates otherwise.

[7] Because of the delicate and sensitive nature of this fieldwork, it was necessary that I create, on the spot, a different kind of informant format from the type(s) that preceded me. Informants were, systematically, divided into two categories-- textual and technical.

The textual informants were those who retained the strongest creole influence in their tongues. These informants talked without any interruption or subsequent interrogation from me, relative to the language, itself. The technical informants knew the creole as well as anyone but considered their link to the tongue indirect. These informants responded freely to my questions (from any format) about the structure of the tongue and *even* volunteered information.

[8] The basic existing Kurathian direct questioning and frame techniques contributed greatly to two of my eliciting devices. With constant modification of these, I was able to create workable tools, first for syntax, in general -- then, for Sea Island Creole, in particular.

REFERENCES

Cunningham, Irma A.E. (1970) <u>A Syntactic Analysis of Sea Island Creole ("Gullah")</u>. Ph.D. diss., The University of Michigan.

_____. (1984) "Problems Confronting the Investigator of Sea Island Creole ('Gullah') 30+ Years after Turner". Paper. Greensboro, North Carolina.

Kurath, Hans. (1939) <u>Handbook of the Linguistic Geography of New England</u>. Washington, D.C.: American Council of Learned Societies.

Labov, William. (1966) <u>The Social Stratification of English in New York City</u>. Washington, D.C.: Center for Applied Linguistics. This work was extremely helpful, in terms of pointing out conversational topics which would carry emotional charges strong enough to elicit unguarded responses.

Turner, Lorenzo D. (1949) <u>Africanisms in the Gullah Dialect</u>. Chicago: University of Chicago Press.

Canadian Urban Survey Methodology: A Summary of Research Techniques and Results

GAELAN DODDS DE WOLF AND ERIKA HASEBE-LUDT
University of Victoria and Freie Universitaet Berlin

I INTRODUCTION

A result of nearly ten years of collaboration and research under the direction of Dr. Robert J. Gregg, from the University of British Columbia in Canada, the Survey of Vancouver English represents the world's largest urban socio-dialectology survey to date (UBC Reports, April 29, 1981). Officially titled An Urban Dialect Survey of the English Spoken in Vancouver and for short referred to as SVEN,[1] the plans for this survey were based on Dr. Gregg's long-term involvement in Canadian English dialectology, particularly in the study of British Columbian and Urban West Coast dialect features.[2]

SVEN was preceded by a two-year pilot project that lasted from 1976 to 1978 and prepared the groundwork for the more comprehensive and complex main survey which began in 1979 and was formally completed in 1984.

Three years after the official Final Report to the Social Sciences and Humanities Research Council of Canada was submitted by Dr. Gregg, research on various aspects of the collected data is still continuing with forthcoming publications and theses that show the wide range and depth of the material and its potential for further investigation.[3]

The following presentation endeavours to give a comprehensive account of this unique survey with respect to the methods that were used during the various procedures and steps of the research, from the early stages of designing the questionnaire and collecting the data on to the statistical analyses and evaluation of results and the final archiving of the data. Not only within the framework of Canadian urban dialectology and sociolinguistics, but also on a worldwide scale, the SVEN survey is a pioneering effort in survey methodology. It is the intention of this summary of research techniques and results to provide a useful tool for linguistic investigation and to evaluate the theoretical and empirical findings from the perspective of application to future survey methodology.

II INNOVATIVE METHODS OF DATA COLLECTION

During the process of data collection which lasted roughly from 1979 to early 1981, an enormous number of approximately 150 phonological, syntactic and lexical variables were gathered to constitute the body of data that describes, or even circumscribes, the dialect of Vancouver, one of Canada's major urban centres. In order to cope with the massive amount of material, innovative methods of data collection, transcription, coding and statistical orientation had to be employed.

Informant selection

With respect to the number of informants interviewed and the amount of data amassed, the SVEN survey can claim to be the largest sociolinguistic or dialect survey to date.

A total of 300 interviews comprising 240 in the main survey and 60 in the pilot study were conducted,[4] with each interview an average of one-and-a-half hours in length.

The informants were rigorously chosen according to stratified random sampling procedures which were performed following guidelines from sociological survey techniques involving computer scrambling of both census tract and enumeration area division (v. de Wolf 1985b; forthcoming).[5] These divisions were later matched with the Vancouver Criss Cross Directory which supplied the informants' names, addresses and telephone numbers. This entire procedure, necessary for reasons of statistical reliability, proved to be rather problematic for a city with a demographic structure like Vancouver that consists of a large number of non-native English speakers (up to 84% in the East End area) and non-Vancouverites.[6] The acceptance rate in the initial informant selection by telephone was only 7%. This means that out of the 3700 telephone calls that were originally made, 3460 had to be rejected mainly because of the large number of non-native speakers and non-Vancouverites. Furthermore, for the stratified sample (v. Clarke, forthcoming), that fit these two criteria, equal numbers of male and female speakers as well as of the three age groups and four socio-economic groups had to be selected in order to fill the 24 cells of 10 informants (i.e., 10 young female upper-middle class informants etc.) from the SVEN population of 240.

Geographical area selection

The territory that is covered by the Greater Vancouver Area posed another challenge to sociolinguistic survey methodology in that in a population of over 1 million, with areas as far as 50 kilometers apart, the interviewing often involved extensive travelling on the part of the field worker. The benefits of extending the original boundaries from the pilot study to the whole urban area known as Greater Vancouver lay in reaching older speakers who had been born in Vancouver and had moved out of the urban core to one of the outlying municipalities on retirement (Gregg 1981).

Apart from the lengthy and meticulous process of informant selection, based on statistical methods derived from accepted social science practices and adapted to the specific linguistic criteria involved, the procedure of revising and extending the existing questionnaire for this large-sclae survey was a major innovative task and challenge in survey methodology.

Interview and Questionnaire Design.

One of the unique features of the SVEN questionnaire and of the interview structure was the high success rate in creating an informal setting in which the informant was able to relax and come as close as possible to an every day speech situation within the formal constraints of a structured interview.[7] This was particularly evident in three of the twelve sections of the questionnaire, namely the ones entitled Background Information, Questions About Vancouver and the Spontaneous Narrative proper. Despite the position of the Background Information as the first section of the interview, it elicited a large amount of spontaneous, informal speech owing to the expansive questions on informants' family history, cultural interests and opinions regarding radio, TV and so on, to which most informants responded with enthusiasm and eloquence, providing us with a large number of continuous spontaneous speech sequences. As Woods (1979: 67), in his Ottawa survey, and as the majority of other dialect surveys have shown, the background section at the beginning would normally elicit formal speech. Since this has not been found valid for the SVEN survey, it can be claimed that, with respect to spontaneous speech, the interferences and restrictions that result from an interview situation were greatly reduced in favour of a speech environment that closely resembles every day language and communication.[8]

The questionnaire, with over a thousand questions in the twelve sections, was designed to elicit various degrees of formality in the speech styles and produced, apart from the traditional formal styles in the Word List (Section III) and Minimal Pairs (Section X), various degrees of informal registers in at least six of the sectints, with the surprising result of an often very casual style of speech in the Reading Passage (Section VI) which, according to Gregg (1984: A4), demonstrates that reading as such does not necessarily involve a formal speech style. Also, as Murdoch (1981: 51) pointed out, the expended Visual-Aural Prompting Section with its 22 charts of mainly pictures proved to be the most informal of the non-continuous speech styles and was highly successful in eliciting a less formal style for specific variables than the word list (Murdoch 1981).

The fundamental principle underlying the structural composition of the questionnaire was to ensure statistical validity for the analysis of the data. Therefore it was decided, in collaboration with experts in education and sociology and after the evaluation of Woods' Ottawa survey, to test the same variable at least three times -- wherever possible -- in each section.

Transcription

During the three-year long transcription process, which proved to be very highly labour-intensive and time-consuming owing to the vast number of phonological, syntactic and lexical variables elicited, the two principal research assistants had to maintain a strictly regulated time schedule in order to complete the extremely detailed and narrow transcription process on time. Heavy-duty office tape recorders with a backspacing device, reverse time control and speed control were used not only to ensure smooth operation but also to verify sounds in case of doubt or interference from background or surface noise on the tapes. The reviewing of early transcriptions was a necessary ongoing part of the work in order to warrant continuity and consistency for coding and computer programming.

Also, collaboration between the transcribers who were each responsible for different sections of the questionnaire, in the form of constant revision and discussion$_9$of the new material was a vital part of the transcription process.

III COMPUTER PROGRAMMING AND STATISTICAL ANALYSIS

Coding

While the transcription process was still ongoing, coding and computerizing for all 300 interviews began in early 1981 in conjunction with the University of British Columbia's Arts Computing Department and the University's Computing Centre. This complex task, which lasted well over two years, involved choosing the most suitable computer programmes for the multitude of linguistic information generated from the interviewing and transcription, and designing basic model codes for the 39 rule-governed phonological variables together with the large variety of grammatical and lexical forms.

After the first initial coding stage, it became necessary to devise a merged version since it was not possible to fit in the quantity of different pronunciations that occurred for individual variables — sometimes up to 15 values per variable. In the second stage of coding, similar values were combined in phonetic mergers. Finally, this coding system was standardized to allow survey-internal comparison and frequency counts throughout all sections of the questionnaire, giving the same code number to one particular variant in all the different occurrences of the same or similar word (Gregg 1984: A8).

Coding for each informant included the variables for age, sex, socio-economic status, generation, ethnic background and linguistic speech style, level of education, as well as the ares(s) of Greater Vancouver where the informant lived and the length of time lived in each area (de Wolf 1981: 63-64).[10] This resulted in a detailed documentation of the correlation between linguistic variables and sociological parameters with regard to sound change and social mobility as perceived by the Labovian model (Labov 1980).

Eventually, with respect to external correlation of variables across survey boundaries, the data from Woods' survey of Ottawa English, for example, had to be converted to the SVEN system because of the difference in coding and the statistical package used.

Statistical analysis

Whereas the compatible Woods' survey used the MIDAS package,[11] the main computer programme recommended for SVEN was SPSS and later SPSS:X, i.e. Statistical Package for the Social Sciences, which, as the name suggests, was specifically designed for social science research. With the help of programmers from U.B.C.'s Arts Computing Department, the members of the SVEN research team received the necessary basic training in computer use in order to be able to carry out the variable tasks involved in the statistical analysis.

With regard to the spontaneous speech textual sequences that were analysed, the Oxford Concordance Programme was used in combination with SPSS: (Hasebe-Ludt 1981). Eventually, after 3 years of intense collaboration, the intricate and tedious process of computerization and statistical analysis resulted in a valuable compilation of print-outs of frequency counts and cross-tabulations that correlate linguistic speech styles with sociological parameters based on methodological principles that allow conclusions on the the nature not only of the particular speech variety under investigation, but also on general trends in language behaviour within a larger sociolinguistic framework.

IV EVALUATION OF RESEARCH TECHNIQUES

When the Survey of Vancouver English was officially completed with a <u>Final Report to the Social Sciences and Humanities Research Council of Canada</u> in April 1984, the data had been stored along with the Ottawa Survey data and those from the earlier Gregg/Polson Linguistic Survey of British Columbia in the UBC Computing Centre. The vast amount of data generated from this large-scale linguistic investigation, with its carefully designed questionnaire, has made it possible for the first time to make use of a combination of innovative methods in survey research based on quantification techniques used in the field of social science, thus strongly linking linguistics more than ever with this scientific discipline. The particular socio-dialectology orientation of the survey has proven to be a highly effective tool in dealing with linguistic speech variables, balancing the dialectology component of more traditional geographically oriented survey research with the innovative sociological parameters of statistical analysis, random sampling and socio-economic group identification.

In this framework, SVEN confirms the validity of regional sociolinguistic urban area studies such as Labov's (1966) landmark New York City study, Trudgill's (1974) Norwich study in Great Britain and Woods' (1979) Canadian urban socio-dialect survey of Ottawa by carrying those methodological approaches further on a larger and more intricate scale of a geographical and statistical nature. At the same time, the recurring question concerning the definition of a so-called 'Canadian Standard' is addressed through SVEN's grounding on the previous surveys in B.C. (Polson 1969) and the nationwide survey of Canadian English (Scargill/Warkentyne 1972) in that it supplies the sorely needed data for an eventual comparison of various regional sociolinguistic probes. Although it is unlikely that the vernacular of Vancouver and other Canadian urban centres would differ so markedly from the standard as in Welsh (Thomas 1985), Gregg (1985) points out, in his recent discussion concerning the search for a Canadian standard, that the creation of authentic Canadian computer data bases for specific reference on Canadian usage has to rely on accurate and detailed linguistic research, computer programming and coding in order to assess these differences. In this sense, the SVEN survey presents a workable model for a possible series of Canadian urban surveys (Gregg 1985: 23), which could eventually lead to the establishment of guidelines for Canadian usage.

On a more pragmatic basis, the effectiveness of the SVEN model was generally confirmed despite a series of adjustments in coding and experimental programming owing to the unavailability of existing models (v. Murdoch 1985). The questionnaire itself, in its highly labour-intensive nature, posed a true challenge to both informants and researchers, but the success and benefits of this large-scale approach are confirmed by the results from the elicited data and by far outweighed the problems in coding that were caused by the larger than expected variety in response to the posed questions.

V IMPLICATIONS AND GUIDELINES FOR FUTURE RESEARCH

The SVEN survey's methodological procedures, as described above, can be of particular help to researchers in the field of linguistic survey investigation and analysis through its data collection principles, such as random sampling, the use of identical code numbers, and cross-tabulations for each individual variable. The standardization of the coding system (Murdoch 1984) represents a vast step towards a universally accepted system of computer coding for survey research, in particular in the area of phonology, for both survey-internal and -external research in North America and possibly elsewhere. In this sense, the SVEN coding system can be seen as a possible working model.

Furthermore, based on the statistical methodology of representative random sampling and controlled by the rigorous criteria of informant acceptability, the data allowed for the study of various topics of particular relevance in current sociolinguistic and dialect research, such as the differences between male and female speech, the impact of the level of education on so-called linguistically 'prestigious' or 'stigmatized' variables, the role of age combined with any one of the other sociological parameters and the impact of a sound change in progress. Only the scientific, statistically-oriented basis could ensure the reliability of the results.

In summary, it can be said that on all levels of linguistic parameters -- the phonological, syntactic as well as the lexical level, the innovative methodology of the SVEN survey presents a working model for future survey research, providing practical tools as well as theoretical guidelines to Canadian linguists and researchers involved in sociolinguistic research in general.

The SVEN research team members thoroughly believe in the need for similar Canadian urban surveys; by comparing and correlating data bases from various regional varieties, we will eventually obtain the information necessary for setting up guidelines for Canadian usage (Gregg 1985: 21). Already, a forthcoming study comparing the two surveys of Ottawa and Vancouver will be a most valuable contribution towards this goal.[12] Numerous papers and publications by the SVEN research team have documented the continuing progress and development of the project, pointing towards different aspects and angles of the present and future research involved (de Wolf 1986a and 1986b and Hasebe-Ludt 1986a and 1986b). It would be desirable if eventually this collection of data across urban centres could lead to the publicatin of a textbook on Canadian English that is based on statistically representative empirical linguistic probes (Gregg 1984). For the present time, this third and conclusive contribution on the SVEN survey to the Methods conferences constitutes for us a means of documenting the life-long commitment to the investigation of regional as well as national variability in Canadian English by the founder and initiator of the SVEN project, Dr. Robert J. Gregg, and his immense contribution to the study of Canadian English.

Notes

1. 'SVEN' was also the identification code for the print-outs of the computer programming of the data.
2. 'See Gregg (1957a), (1957b), (1971), (1973) on aspects of Vancouver and British Columbia speech characteristics.
3. Cf. de Wolf's forthcoming thesis on A Comparison of Speech Variables in the Sociolinguistic Surveys of Ottawa and Vancouver as well as Hasebe-Ludt's (1986b) article on Stereotypes of Language in Vancouver English.
4. For an in-depth account of the general background of the survey, see Gregg (1981).
5. Dr. Martin Meissner and Dr. George Gray of the Anthropology and Sociology Department, UBC, were among the experts consulted by the SVEN research team.
6. The term "Vancouverite" in the SVEN definition applied to individuals "who were born and educated within the limits of Greater Vancouver and had never left the area for any considerable stretch of time." (Gregg 1984, A6).
7. Cf. Labov's (1981) keynote address to Methods IV: "Can Dialectology Deal With Spontaneous Speech: The Technical and Scientific Challenge."
8. See Hasebe-Ludt (1981) and (1983) for further discussion of spontaneous speech methodology and analysis.
9. See de Wolf, G. (1981) for a detailed account fo the transcription process and technical equipment used.
10. This particular methods uses the boundaries established by the Gray Report (Gray and Boreham 1979).
11. Woods' survey was later transferred from MIDAS into SPSS by de Wolf with the help of Jean Wu from the Arts Computing Department (v. de Wolf 1985a).
12. Cf. de Wolf's forthcoming Ph.D thesis on "A Comparison of Speech Variables in the Sociolinguistic Surveys of Ottawa and Vancouver" forthcoming Ph.D thesis, University of Victoria.

References

Clarke, S. (forthcoming) "Linguistic Variation in the Non-stratified Social Context". *Papers from the Sixth International Conference on Methods in Dialectology*, ed. A. Thomas. Bangor: University College of North Wales

de Wolf, G. Dodds (1981) "Transcription, Coding, and Data Analysis of the SVEN Survey". *Papers From the Fourth International Conference on Methods in Dialectology*, ed. H.J. Warkentyne, University of Victoria: Department of Linguistics, 62-65

—————(1985a) "Methods in Statistical Analysis of Compatible Data From Two Major Canadian Urban Sociolinguistic Surveys". *Papers From the Fifth International Conference on Methods in Dialectology*, ed. H.J. Warkentyne, University of Victoria: Department of Linguistics, 191-196

—————(1985b) *A Comparison of Speech Variables in the Sociolinguistic Surveys of Ottawa and Vancouver*. A dissertation proposal for the Department of Linguistics, University of Victoria

—————(1986a) *The Pronunciation of Lexical Items in Canadian English*. University of California, Riverside: Eighty-Fourth Annual Meeting of the Philological Association of the Pacific Coast

—————(1986b) *Regional Differences in Syntactic Choice* New York: Annual Meeting of the American Dialect Society

Gray, G.A. and Boreham, M. (1979) *Vancouver and Political Communities: A Social Ecological Analysis*. Report to the Commission on Governmental Reorganization, City of Vancouver

Gregg, R.J. (1957a) "Neutralisation and Fusion of Volcalic Phonemes in Canadian English as Spoken in the Vancouver Area". *Journal of the Canadian Linguistic Association*, 3, 78-83

Gregg, R.J. (1957b) "Notes on the Pronunciation of Canadian English as Spoken in Vancouver, B.C." *Journal of the Canadian Linguistic Association*, 3, 20-26

————— (1971) "The Phonology of Canadian English as Spoken in the Area of Vancouver, British Columbia." *Readings on Language in Canada*, ed. R.H. Southerland, Calgary: University of Calgary, 34-54

---------- (1973) "The Linguistic Survey of British Columbia: The Kootenay Region". *Canadian Languages in their Social Context*, ed. R. Darnell. Edmonton: Linguistic Research, 105-116.

---------- (1981) "General Background to the Survey of Vancouver English (SVEN)" *Papers from the Fourth International Conference on Methods in Dialectology*, ed. H.J. Warkentyne, University of Victoria: Department of Linguistics, 41-47

---------- (1984) *Final Report to the Social Sciences and Humanities Research Council of Canada on an Urban Dialect Survey of the English Spoken in Vancouver*. Linguistics Department: University of British Columbia

---------- (1985) "The Standard and Where We Stand Now." *In Search of the Standard in Canadian English*, ed. W.C. Lougheed, Occasional Papers No. 1, Strathy Language Unit, Kingston: Queen's University, 157-168

Hasebe-Ludt, E. (1981) "Aspects of Spontaneous Speech in the Urban Dialect Study of Vancouver English". *Papers from the Fourth International Conference on Methods in Dialectology*, ed. H.J. Warkentyne, University of Victoria: Department of Linguistics, 57-61

---------- (1983) *Elicitation and Analysis of Spontaneous Speech in the Survey of Vancouver English (SVEN)*, University of British Columbia: Annual Meeting of the Canadian Linguistic Association

---------- (1985) "Methodology of Spontaneous Speech Analysis", *Papers from the Fifth International Conference on Methods in Dialectology*, ed. H.J. Warkentyne, Department of Linguistics: University of Victoria, 197-200

---------- (1986a) *Male-Female Differences in Lexical Variable Choice in Canadian English*. University of California, Riverside: Eighty-Fourth Annual Meeting of the Philological Association of the Pacific Coast

---------- (1986b) *Stereotypes of Language in Vancouver English*. New York: Annual Meeting of the American Dialect Society

Labov, W. (1966) *The Social Stratification of English in New York City*. Washington, D.C.: Center for Applied Linguistics

---------- (1980) *Locating Language in Space and Time*. New York: Academic Press

Labov, W. (1981) "Can Dialectology Deal with Spontaneous Speech: The Technical and Scientific Challenge." *Papers from the Fourth International Conference on Methods in Dialectology*, ed. H.J. Warkentyne. University of Victoria: Department of Linguistics, 7-28

Murdoch, M.M. (1981) "Visual-Aural Prompting in the Vancouver Survey Questionnaire". *Papers from the Fourth International Conference on Methods in Dialectology*, ed. H.J. Warkentyne. University of Victoria: Department of Linguistics, 48-56

———— (1985) "A Proposal for Standardization of Computer Coding Systems in Linguistic Surveys," *Papers from the Fifth International Conference on Methods in Dialectology*, ed. H.J. Warkentyne. University of Victoria: Department of Linguistics, 185-190.

Polson, J. (1969) *A Linguistic Questionnaire for British Columbia*. Unpublished M.A. thesis. Vancouver, B.C.: University of British Columbia

Scargill, M.H. and Warkentyne, H.J. (1972) "The Survey of Canadian English: A Report". *The English Quarterly* 5, 47-104

Thomas, A. (1985) "Sociolinguistic Variation in a Minority Language". *Papers from the Fifth International Conference on Methods in Dialectology*, ed. H.J. Warkentyne, University of Victoria: Department of Linguistics, 457-464

Trudgill, P. (1974) *The Social Differentiation of English in Norwich*. Cambridge: University Press

UBC Reports, "Urban English Survey Most Extensive Ever". April 29, 1981, V. 27, No. 3, 3

Woods, H.B. (1979) *A Socio-Dialectology Survey of the English Spoken in Ottawa: A Study of Sociological and Stylistic Variation in Canadian English*. Unpublished Ph.D dissertation. Vancouver, B.C.: University of British Columbia

Linguistic Variation and Welsh Mutations in Children

WYNFORD BELLIN
University of Reading

WELSH MUTATIONS AND LINGUISTIC VARIATION

One of the hallmarks of a Celtic language is the system whereby the initial segments of citation forms of words may change in a wide variety of environments. The interest of the mutation system for sociolinguistics is that in adults there is considerable variation (see, for example, Thomas, 1984) and a classic set of issues is raised as to how children come to acquire rules where variation abounds. These issues are more acute in the case of Welsh since most speakers live in areas of considerable language shift.

This contribution compares two methodologies as alternatives to analyzing any corpus of conversational material or informal story telling, since any corpus analysis is bedevilled by the all-pervasive nature of the environments which condition the phonological changes. Some are purely lexical, some phonological, and in Welsh, as distinct from other Celtic languages, some involve major syntactic categories (see Bellin, 1984, pp. 168-174).

Owing to developments in Welsh bilingual education (see further in Bellin, 1986), it is of considerable interest to compare children undergoing a home-school language switch with children from homes where Welsh is spoken.

To keep investigation within practical bounds it was necessary to choose some particular environments for testing purposes. The ones chosen were connected with possessive pronouns. Thus the word for "house" which begins with /t/ may appear as:

    dy dŷ 'your (familiar) house' with initial /d/

    ei thŷ 'her house' with initial /θ/

    fy nhŷ 'my house' with initial /nh/

In most linguistic descriptions of the mutation system,

the citation form is treated as the base form, and the other forms are derived by mutation rules. These rules fall into three sets known as

soft

aspirate

and nasal mutations.

The changes in initial segments are summarized in Table 1a.

TABLE 1: Welsh Consonants and the Mutations Shown

a) Consonants transcribed

Initial segment of citation form	Soft mut.	Aspirate mut.	Nasal mut.
p	b	f	mh
t	d	θ	nh
k	g	x	ngh
b	v		m
d	ð		n
g	zero		
m	v		
ɫ	l		
r	r		

b) Consonants in conventional spelling

Initial segment of citation form	Soft mut.	Aspirate mut.	Nasal mut
p	b	ph	mh
t	d	th	nh
c	g	ch	ngh
b	f		m
d	dd		n
g			ng
m	f		
ll	l		
rh	r		

The testing procedures used were oral, but since all the children involved were of school age, and teachers might ask what was going on, conventional spelling was used in the test materials handled by the investigators. Table 1b can be compared with Table 1a for a summary of conventional spelling. The reason for picking the particular environments used for the investigation was that possessive pronouns can be regarded as having communicative relevance, whereas other environments conditioning mutation such as those involving gender distinctions would not provide such an obvious relevance for testing purposes.

CHILDREN IN THE INVESTIGATION

The children in the investigation attended a Welsh medium primary school in the Ystalyfera area of Swansea in West Glamorgan. The age range was between five and nine years. There were twelve children from each age group with roughly equal proportions of boys and girls. They were selected at random from enrolment lists. Only a third of the children had parents who both spoke Welsh. However, the basis for categorizing the children was whether they were addressed in Welsh at home, and whether they used the language in reply. The school policy was to teach all children entirely through the medium of Welsh until the age of seven, after which part of the curriculum was taught in English.

AN ELICITATION PROCEDURE

An elicitation test with twelve items was devised, using vocabulary judged to be straightforward for the age groups. Each item was a text two or three sentences long. The final sentence in each text stopped with a possessive pronoun, and the child was meant to complete the sentence. The nouns which were targets for completion are given in Table 2.

TABLE 2: Nouns used in the elicitation test

	Mutation		
	Soft	Aspirate	Nasal
'head'	pen -> ben	pwrs -> phwrs 'purse'	pwrs -> mhwrs 'purse'
'tea'	te -> de	...	tegannau -> nhegannau 'toys'
'cap'	cap -> gap	...	cap -> nghap
'brother'	brawd -> frawd	***	...
'clothes'	dillad -> ddillad	***	drôr -> nrôr 'drawer'
'gloves'	menig -> fenig	menig (no mutation)	***

Key to symbols
...   no examples were used
***   the consonant never shows this mutation

Notes

In one case, with the word for "gloves", the citation form was elicited, since no mutation would be shown in the context.

Brightly coloured cartoons were prepared - portrayal of the central characters (Dafydd and Siân) for a warm-up item, and then a cartoon for each elicitation item. So, for example, when showing a picture of the central characters with Siân holding a broken doll, the elicitation context was:

Mae Dafydd a Siân yn cweryla. Mae Dafydd wedi torri tegannau Siân Mae Siân yn gwaeddu: "Paid a chwarae gyda fy ___ "	Dafydd and Siân are quarelling. Dafydd has broken Siân's toys. Siân shouts: "Don't play with my ___ "

where the target form was <u>nhegannau</u> mutated from the citation form <u>tegannau</u> 'toys'. (Although translations are given here, the whole investigation was conducted exclusively in Welsh.)

In conducting the test, all sessions were recorded, and transcription relied on agreement between two judges.

Results of the elicitation test

Figure 1 plots the average number of items where children in an age group in Wales produced the target mutated form, showing the average for Welsh speaking homes with the symbol "W" and the average for English only homes with "E".

```
                plot of means*age    symbol is value of home
  MEANS |
        |
     9  +
        |
        |
        |                                                            W
     8  +                                        W
        |
        |
        |
     7  +
        |
        |
        |                                                       E
     6  +
        |
        |                 W                 E
     5  +
        |                      E
        |
        |
     4  +
        |                           W
        |                                E
     3  +
        |
        |
        |
     2  +E
        |
        |
     1  +
        |
        |
     0  +
        +------------+------------+------------+------------+
        5            6            7            8            9
                                 AGE
```

There were no children from Welsh speaking homes in the youngest group. The results were analysed by comparing the fit of a number of possible regressions. First a simple regression on age was tried, and then extra terms were added in and improvement in fit was tested for significance. As would be expected from the impression given by Figure 1, there was a significant regression on age. But the R squared was only .33. Adding the effect of home language increased the R squared significantly to .83. So parallel slopes can be regarded as the best fitting regression, instead of a joint regression on age. Both subgroups improve with age but children from Welsh speaking homes can be expected to keep a little ahead of the others on this particular set of items. However, only one or two items were implicated in the separation.

A careful item analysis was conducted using methods described in Bellin (1985) to find whether any particular items from the test were responsible for the slight separation of the Swansea subgroups.

There were two items which distinguished between the language backgrounds. About two was the number to be expected from looking at the separation between the trends in Figure 1.

On items requiring te 'tea' to mutate to de and cap 'cap' to mutate to nghap there were different age trends in children from homes where Welsh was spoken and the "immersion" children. (Parallel lines, both improving, in the case of te/de, and separate lines with English speaking homes getting slightly less likely to produce the target for cap/nghap). So it was possible to detect which items had caused the slight separation between the trends in Figure 1.

Conclusions from the elicitation test

The elicitation test established that the children undergoing a home-school language switch were becoming more likely to produce mutated forms with age, in spite of the fact that formal teaching of such rules is neither practical nor part of the curriculum in bilingual schools. (Formal teaching of Welsh as a foreign language occurs only in schools where the medium of instruction is English, although reading, spelling and writing in Welsh obviously have a role in the bilingual school curriculum.)

Careful item analysis of the elicitation test isolated two items where the children who did not speak Welsh at home behaved differently from those who did. It would be surprising if no such items could be discovered. A suggestion as to why those items in particular distinguished tbe language backgrounds has been made by Dressler (personal communication). In research on Breton, evidence was found that speakers who make use of the language only in specific situations are less likely to produce mutated forms of loan words than other speakers (cf. Dressler & Wodak-Leodolter, 1977). Since the two items distinguishing the language backgrounds in this investigation involve loan words, there may be a reluctance on the part of children from monolingual English homes to submit them to the full mutation system. It is as if they were treated as particularly blatant borrowings. If such a difference in behaviour underlies the results, then these children nevertheless are behaving like speakers whose Welsh was acquired under home or community influence. Lexical imports which have not yet been established as loan words fail to show mutation even in literary registers. The main finding is that all the children improve in control of the phonological changes as they grow older.

CONTRIVING TO RECORD SPONTANEOUS USAGE

A common criticism of the kind of elicitation test reported here is that it will underestimate children's likelihood of following a rule, since the adult has a definite target form in mind, and will create some test anxiety by the formality of the procedure. Because of such assumptions, the children in Swansea were revisited to try a procedure devised by Mair Rees, a Reading psychology student. The aim of the procedure was to involve children in a game which would require the use of possessives in child-to-child communication, rather than at the insistence of an adult.

The game involved three pairs of identical objects:

- two ping-pong balls (involving the mutations pêl -> bêl/mhêl 'ball')

- two small cars (involving the mutations car -> gar/nghar 'car')

- two bus tickets (involving the mutations tocyn -> docyn/nhocyn 'ticket'

The members of each pair were marked with either a blue or red sticker. Otherwise they were indistinguishable. The game was played between two children seated either side of a small table on which all the objects were positioned. Each child was allocated a colour (red or blue) and told that objects bearing that colour were his/her property for the duration of the game. In the game, a child was asked to turn away from the table, while the partner removed an object. Then the one who had turned away was to look and say which object was missing and whose it was. Taking turns at removing objects and saying what was missing created opportunities for the phonological contrasts with the voiceless stops to be produced.

Children who played the game

The Swansea school was revisited several weeks after the elicitation test, and four subjects from each of the six to nine-year-old age groups took part in the game. These children were selected for being close to the median score for their age groups on the elicitation test. Their partners in the game were selected at random from the same class. All sessions were recorded and decisions about whether or not target forms had been produced depended on two judges. The whole procedure was conducted in Welsh.

Results from the procedure with the game

Since the same children from each age group had taken part in the game and the elicitation test, it was possible to compare the likelihood of producing a target form in either situation. The number of children was small, and only the voiced/voiceless distinction on stops was involved. But the main result was clear and surprising.

Comparing the procedures

Every child provided six contexts in both the elicitation test and the game where forms showing mutation could have been produced. That meant that the likelihood of producing such forms in the one situation or the other could be compared. Details of the statistics are given in Bellin (1985).

What actually happened was the opposite of what was anticipated. All the six year olds were better in the formal procedure. Only the oldest children had a higher proportion of target forms in the game procedure - all being more likely to produce mutated forms in that situation assumed to be nearer to spontaneous usage. This was very surprising for two reasons:

- different procedures often give different results, but their relative difficulty stays stable over age ranges as a rule

- there was so much more adult pressure to produce target forms in the elicitation test

Since it was never expected that any of the children would be better in the formal test, the results of the youngest children need to be explained.

REGISTERING VARIATION AND RULE ACQUISITION

The obvious factors for explaining the children's behaviour would be

- citation form awareness

- literary influence.

However growth of citation form awareness cannot explain why the younger children should behave so differently from the older ones. Literary influence could be expected to have a uniform influence with older children producing more mutations in either procedure.
An admittedly speculative account of how bilingual children deal with the mutation system might account for the surprising superiority of the six year old children in the formal test rather than the game.

Suppose that bilingual competence has different levels. That is to say, besides practical pronunciation procedures, another level occurs when faced with a linguistic system that pervades phonology, lexicon and syntax, like the Welsh mutation system. There may be a kind of tacit strategic knowledge developing before following the mutation rules in production is tried out.

First of all, an appreciation of what is happening develops at the strategic level. So adult-like pronunciation might be more variable than later on. But the child is sizing up the acquisition task for this aspect of the language. What happened with the formal test was an uncovering of the extent of this strategic level knowledge. Because the adult elicitation method was so pressing, the strategic level knowledge alerted children to what was wanted without self-consciousness. Providing the lexical items in the eliciting context, meant that the phonological change was the sole requirement for practical knowledge. Hence, the tacit growing awareness of the system could inform performance on the formal test.

The situation of the youngest group, then, is that they register that there is a rule without following it in spite of adult variation. With older children, who are producing the mutated forms in ordinary contexts, there is now reliance on practical production procedures, and any meta-level knowledge comes from awareness of what they are doing in ordinary speech. When a formal elicitation test is administered, it is not tapping a tacit unselfconscious strategic knowledge, but a more conscious awareness of what is going on. The element of self-consciousness may cause unease. Hence, only the oldest children behaved as anticipated, showing superior performance in the less formal game.

So after registering the rules without following them, children begin to follow them tacitly in some situations, and later with growing literacy, they follow rules with awareness and are perturbed by too blatant a probe of what they know they do with adult-like variation.

Such a speculative account of what happens goes beyond the evidence. Some cross-checking in pairs of lexical items might help out. The pattern shown by individual children was only clear in one of the pairs of lexical items used in both procedures - the pair consisting of cap which was to mutate to nghap in the formal procedure, while car was to mutate to nghar in the game, if adult categorical rules were applied. So the finding for individual children clearly depends on the lexical items selected. But it may be the case that some stage of registering the presence of a rule and being aware of it as if it were a categorical rule precedes variable production in other languages where linguistic variation is studied.

REFERENCES

Bellin, W. (1984) Welsh phonology in acquisition. In Ball, M. J. & Jones, G. E. (eds.) Welsh Phonology: Selected Readings. Cardiff: University of Wales Press.

Bellin, W. (1985) The linguistic competence of bilingual children in Welsh medium schools. Child Language Seminar Papers: 1985, pp. 131-147

Bellin, W. (1986) Welsh and English in Wales. In Mayor, B. & Pugh, A.K. (eds.) Language, Communication and Education London: Croom Helm, pp. 99-123

Dressler, W. & Wodak-Leodolter, R. (1977) Language preservation and language death in Britanny. International Journal of the Sociology of Language, 12, 33-44.

Thomas, P W (1984) Variation in South Glamorgan Consonant Mutation. In Ball, M. J. & Jones, G. E. (eds.) Welsh Phonology: Selected Readings. Cardiff: University of Wales Press

Stylistic Variation in Nova Scotia Acadian French

KARIN FLIKEID
Saint Mary's University

The French-speaking population in Nova Scotia is in the unusual situation of being located in a number of distinct geographical areas, spread out from one end of the province to the other. This is not without historical reason: after the treaty of Paris in 1763, Acadians who had been deported from Nova Scotia in 1755 and in following years were allowed to return and resettle, on the express condition that they would not form large groups anywhere (this requirement stemmed of course from the fear that they might again achieve power if they were to regroup.) The linguistic consequence of this situation is that while before the Deportation the Acadian population was in all likelihood well on its way to forming a fairly homogenous speech community after 150 years of settlement in a concentrated area, the isolation which has prevailed since the Deportation between the various geographical areas resettled by the Acadians has led to noticable dialect differences affecting pronunciation, grammar and vocabulary.

Research funding was granted by the Social Sciences and Humanities Research Council of Canada in 1984 for a comprehensive study which has as its general objective the linguistic description of the French spoken in Nova Scotia, encompassing its geographical and social variation. Because the five main areas where French is spoken are geographically distinct, the situation lends itself ideally to a comparative approach, both on the level of linguistic description of the present-day varieties and in a sociolinguistic perspective. The project thus involves the systematic collection of spoken language data from the five areas, using identical techniques in each, in view of a comparative study designed as such from the start.

In determining the composition of the corpus, consideration was given to the various purposes it was intended to serve. It encompasses a stratified sociolinguistic sample as well as interviews to be used primarily for the comparative linguistic description. There is considerable geographical variation within several of the major areas, and to include this dimension within the sociolinguistic sample would have meant increasing the sample size considerably and would also have made the identification of sociolinguistic patterns more complex. It was therefore decided to focus on one particular community in each area for the central comparative sociolinguistic study, and to do an additional exploration of the geographic variation within each area. The community

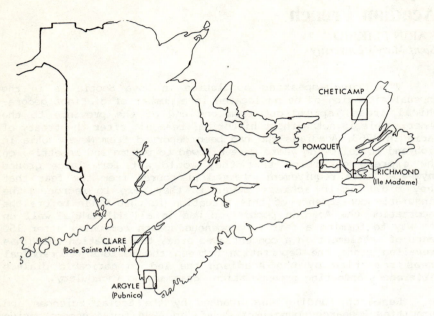

FIGURE 1: MAP OF THE FIVE MAIN ACADIAN AREAS IN NOVA SCOTIA

chosen was in each case the one which had the largest and most homogenous Francophone population. These communities are indicated on the map given in Figure 1.

Each of the Acadian communities in Nova Scotia has its distinct historical evolution and present-day socio-economic situation. The sociolinguistic component of the study addresses the question of how these different situations are reflected in the language use in each community. Before describing the actual features studied, let me give a brief outline of some of the social and historical factors involved, and the types of contrasts found between the major areas. A basic tenet of life in Nova Scotia Acadian communities has been the coexistence with the English-speaking population. Settlement patterns vary from area to area. Whereas in Clare and Cheticamp the French formed a homogenous group geographically, although bordered by English-speaking areas, in Argyle and Richmond, English and French settlers were interspersed from the beginning. This in its turn has entailed a difference in the degree of control over the language of services, particularly that of the schools. Where services had to be shared by the two language groups, purely French-language services were far less likely to evolve. The socio-economic development of each community has also been different, determining to what extent people have had to leave the community to work in nearby English-speaking areas. The degree of contact with Francophones from outside the area varies widely, linked partly to the development of tourism. I have found language attitudes to be to a large extent shared by the members of each community, often being expressed in the same words. These attitudes differ from community to community, ranging from being generally apologetic to expressing pride in the Acadian heritage.

The gradual encroaching of the English language can be measured through various indices of assimilation. One such measure, based on census figures, shows the proportion of respondents of French descent who learned French as their mother tongue but at the time of the census no longer spoke French in the home. This figure is 7% in the Baie Sainte-Marie area, as compared to 42% in the Pomquet area. The provincial school system has since the beginning been reluctant to allow French in the schools. French language schools only became legal a few years ago. To varying degrees, French has been in use, according to the local situation in each area. Very few textbooks were ever available. The presence of written French was thus minimal until fairly recently.

METHODOLOGY: INSIDER AND OUTSIDER INTERVIEWS

The choice of interviewers being crucial to the speech style elicited, an approach was devised which would ensure that spontaneous speech was obtained, as well as giving some indication of the speakers' stylistic range. Each informant was interviewed on two occasions, once with an interviewer from the same community, once with an interviewer from outside the community. A number of the local interviewers were initially recommended by the Fédération Acadienne de la Nouvelle-Ecosse, which has been very helpful both in the planning stages and in the course of the field work, through their regional offices. Two interviewers were chosen for each of the five areas. I myself travelled to each area in turn, choosing the most suitable candidates and providing the necessary training in interview techniques and use of the technical material. The interviewers proved to be extremely dedicated and enthusiastic, and the quality of the interviews surprisingly good. In addition, the intimate knowledge they displayed of their communities was extremely valuable.

The local interviewers were seldom unknown to the informants. If they did not know them personally in some capacity, the informants knew their parents or the interviewers knew the informants' children or grandchildren, or some other connection was present. (The interviewers were encouraged to establish the connection at the beginning of the interview, and also to write it down on the interview schedule.) The speech variety used by the interviewers was very informal, local speech. They did not use a written questionnaire when interviewing, but had read one beforehand, prepared in order to give them an idea of the areas they could explore. Questions were of course rephrased by the interviewers, to fit the local context. In the recorded interviews, the language of the interviewers is often as interesting as that of the informants. Conversation flows freely and both express opinions.

This first series of interviews was intended to elicit informal speaking style among members of the community, modified only by the interview situation and the presence of the tape recorder. As a contrast, the idea of having a separate interview with someone from outside the community, speaking standard French, was implemented, in order to see to what extent the speakers would accomodate to this speech style. It was hypothesized that both the capacity to modify towards a more standard style of speech and the inclination to do so would vary from individual to individual, but also from community to community. In this second interview, explicit questions on language use were asked, and an attempt was made to probe as far as possible informants' feelings about their way of speaking. It was felt that this double approach would prove to be valuable for quantitative contrasts between the stylistic contexts represented by the two types of interview, both among individuals and among geographical areas. Although it meant a considerable investment of time and effort, it seemed best to conduct these interviews myself, because it was crucial that the interviewer be familiar with the various Acadian dialects, in order to understand and respond to what was being said during the interview.

To date, 230 interviews have been gathered by the local interviewers. Of these, 120 constitute the core sociolinguistic sample, which is stratified by age, sex and geographic area. I myself have conducted second interviews with 145 of the informants.

For a major study of this type, involving large quantities of transcribed data, the use of computer analysis makes possible a far more comprehensive examination of the data than could be envisaged otherwise. Transcribed texts from all areas have been entered onto the Saint Mary's computer (VAX 11/780) in the course of the past two years, in modified orthographic transcription.

The interviews presently transcribed now constitute a total of over 800,000 words of text. Using the Oxford Concordance Program, specially designed for this type of analysis, printouts of all occurrences of each feature to be studied can be obtained within minutes. Certain categories have been marked in the text and can be systematically retrieved. The program is proving useful both for linguistic description and for sociolinguistic analysis. Statistical programs for variation analysis, Varbrul 2S and 3, have been implemented on our computer. The S.P.S.S.-X statistical package is being used as well for complementary analyses.

STYLISTIC VARIATION

The results that follow are based on 120 double interviews which have been conducted and transcribed in the manner described above. The sociolinguistic variables involved are currently being analysed in their multiple dimensions and will be presented in detail elsewhere; I am here focusing on the stylistic shifts and the interaction between these and some of the other dimensions considered. Three variables are discussed, two of a morphological nature, showing the extent to which Acadian features continue to be used, and one lexical, examining the presence of words of English origin in the informants' speech.

Variable 1: Presence of English Elements: Code-switching and Borrowing

A detailed study of code-switching and loan-words from English is presently underway. However, an initial indicator of the overall presence of words of English origin was obtained by use of the concordance programs, extracting all words (tokens) which had been marked as English in the course of the transcription and calculating for each individual informant the proportion that these represented of the total number of tokens. A breakdown of the results by age group, stylistic context and geographical area is given in figure 2. Although the overall tendency reflects the encroaching role of the dominant culture, with increasing use of English elements by the younger speakers in all areas, strong regional contrasts emerge. The highest proportions were found, as could be expected, in those areas which have the weakest concentration of Francophones and the highest degree of assimilation.

The most interesting aspect emerged from the examination of the differences between the two speech styles elicited, the one used with the local interviewers and one used with an outsider to the community. The proportion of English forms proves to be markedly reduced, for all informants in all areas, in the second type of interview. The degree of reduction varies both individually and between communities. Examination of explicit language attitudes expressed in the interviews throws light on this tendency. There appears to be strong pressure within Acadian communities not to deviate from customary speech style, which involves considerable code-switching and borrowing from English. To use the

French equivalents of established loan-words, even when these have become familiar through school and the media, is not usual when speaking to peers. Such a usage would expose one to being ridiculed or thought pretentious. On the other hand, when speaking to a Francophone from outside the community, one of the ways of accomodating is in fact to choose just these French equivalents, if known to the speaker.

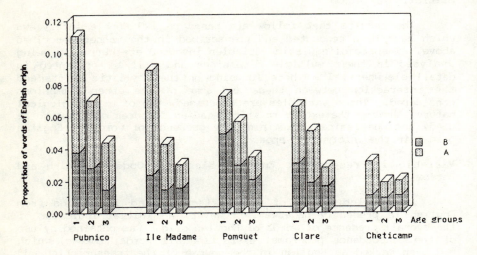

Figure 2: Presence of elements of English origin (code-switching and borrowing) Distribution by geographical area, age group and contextual style.
(A: Informal Style; B: Formal Style; 1: Age 15-34, 2: Age 35-54, 3: Age 55+)

The use of English words is one of the features which seems to be stigmatized among Acadian speakers. It is in fact almost a stereotype, and, as such, is generally greatly exaggerated by outsiders and by Acadians themselves, who regularly claim that their language is "half English, half French". One of the interesting results of this study is that the true proportion of English penetration can be evaluated, and proves to be far lower than popular perception would have it. The data collected reveals that even in the most informal circumstances, the total proportion of English words is generally below 10%, and examination of the language used in a situation where individuals exercise strong control over their language production shows that most Acadians can without difficulty reduce their code-switching and use of loan-words to a great extent if they so desire. In informal speech style, code-switching and borrowing are thus maintained as much through the pressure to conform to local speech norms as because of any inability to modify speech behavior.

Variable 2: Third Person Plural Verb Endings in "-ont"

A variable which shows a very different type of patterning is the use of the third person plural ending, where the traditional Acadian forms "-ont" and "-iont" alternate with the standard forms (e.g. "ils parlont" - "ils parlent"; "ils parlont" - "ils parlaient"). One important finding is simply the very high overall use of these forms in the interviews with the local interviewers. This is a very strong indication that the speech style recorded in these interviews is close to the style which would be natural between the speakers. Individual differences are more marked in the case of this feature, which appears to reflect with greater sensitivity the educational and social background of the speakers, whereas the preceding variable tends to be more indicative of group norms.

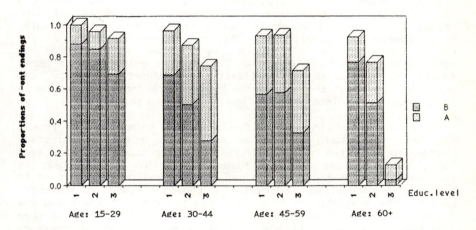

Figure 3: Presence of third person plural verb endings in -ont, present and imperfect tenses. Distribution by age group, educational level and contextual style (A: Informal Style, B: Formal Style; 1: 0-7 yrs of schooling, 2: 8-11 yrs, 3: 12+ yrs)

In the more formal style, there is a reduction in the use of the Acadian forms for the majority of the speakers and many switch styles markedly. However, in all geographical areas, there are speakers who maintain a high level of Acadian forms even when speaking with an outsider. Figure 3 shows the distribution of individual scores on this variable (proportion of "-ont" endings) in regard to age group, educational level and stylistic context. The proportion of Acadian forms used decreases as the level of education increases, as might be expected, but it also decreases with age. There is a compounding or interaction effect as well in that older speakers with higher levels of education use fewer Acadian forms than any other group. (These tendencies, illustrated graphically here, have been analyzed statistically through multiple regression analysis and found to be significant.) A significant reduction in the proportion of "-ont" endings in the more formal interview situation is found for all the groups considered. It is however interesting that this reduction is least marked in the youngest age group, regardless of educational level.

Variable 3: Plural "je"

As can be seen in figure 4, a similar pattern, even more sharply marked, emerges for the third feature examined, the use of the pronoun "je" in the first person plural. This plural use of "je" was known to be common to a number of Acadian areas, though its exact present-day distribution had not been examined. Analysis of the data shows this form to be strongly present in all five areas. The form with which "je" alternates proves, interestingly, to be almost exclusively "on". All occurrences of "nous" in the corpus were examined, and only a very few cases were found of its being used as a subject pronoun. "Nous" is of course used in other functions, e.g. as object, reflexive or disjunctive pronoun, and both "je" and "on" are reinforced by the form "nous autres" as in "nous autres, je disons..." or "nous autres, on pense...".

Analysis of the individual use of this variable proves extremely interesting in that an even stronger age-related trend emerges than for the preceding variable, where older speakers favor "on", while younger speakers favor "je". This is obviously in contrast to any decline in the use of the Acadian form that could have been hypothesized, and calls for thorough study and interpretation. The stylistic shift between the two types of interview was found to be highly significant overall, and more pronounced than for the preceding variable, though a good number of speakers maintained a high or intermediate level in both interviews. Regression analyses showed the patterns of variation to be similar in both speech situations; of particular interest is that the stratification by age is as marked in both styles.

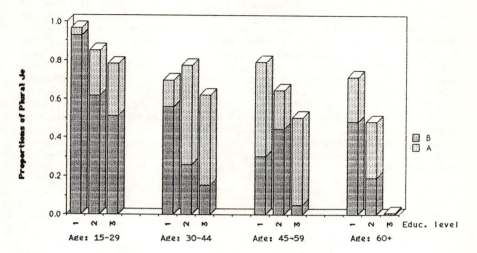

Figure 4: Presence of Je as third person plural pronoun. Distribution by age group, educational level and contextual style (A: Informal style, B: Formal Style; 1: 0-7 yrs of schooling, 2: 8-11 yrs, 3: 12+ yrs)

These results are quite different from those I found in an earlier study of New Brunswick Acadian French, where the use of Acadian forms was found to be declining overall among younger speakers. There, French is in a much stronger position in the schools and used extensively outside of home and village, whereas in Nova Scotia French is on the whole still inadequate in the schools. Many young people have a stylistic repertoire where the shift into a more formal style generally coincides with switching into English because they are then dealing with members of the English-speaking community. It would seem, from the analysis of the two morphological variables, that the capacity for stylistic shift in the communities examined is not so much a function of level of education as it is of the experience gained through exposure to other varieties of French and contact with Francophones from outside the community.

CONCLUSION

The results of this initial series of analyses seem to indicate that the systematic use of both insider and outsider interviews to investigate stylistic shift is highly appropriate to the situation in the speech communities studied. It is of value to find that close to authentic speech style can be obtained, despite the presence of the tape recorder, by having the interviews conducted by members of the same community as each informant. The extremely high use of Acadian grammatical forms reported on here are a clear indication of this. The major stylistic shifts observed when these interviews are compared with those I conducted myself show the necessity of this approach. Informal Acadian speech cannot be elicited by an outside observer, and descriptions of the basic linguistic systems of Acadian should not be based on such interviews. The dual approach adopted has thus proved extremely useful in obtaining material for studying a wide range of aspects of the linguistic situation in the Acadian communities of Nova Scotia.

Commercial Television as a Source of Language Data

TIMOTHY C. FRAZER
Western Illinois University

This paper is about language and television. But I want to begin with an apology to this international audience, because I am well aware that the use of television varies considerably from one nation to the next, and that what follows is based on my own experience with television in the United States; the exact kind of data provided by U.S. television may not be available elsewhere. Still, television remains as a massive source of language data, and given its powerful impact as a tool for political and economic control, we can expect to see its use expand and diversify everywhere. In recent years, moreover, television has received increasing attention from scholars in the humanities and social sciences alike, due in part to increasing concern over the power of television as a social force, but also to changing technology, especially the advent of the moderately priced videocassette recorder. The VCR makes it possible to record television content on the spot and allows for analysis at leisure. The VCR is particularly valuable for the linguist, for, unlike audio tapes of spoken language, the video tape allows the observation not only of spoken language, but of all the communicative codes -- dress, gesture, facial expression, even physical surroundings -- employed by the linguist's "informant" or "consultant." All of this of course suggests that investigators need their own video cameras and equipment, but I believe that an excellent source of data for linguistic studies can be found on commercial television.

In this paper I would like to examine two particular areas of commercial television content which should be useful to the dialectologist or sociolinguist. First, I will examine the use of local television news as a supplement or substitute for the traditional elicitation of actual language use. Second, I will discuss the use of television drama as an important source of information for studies in language attitudes and perceptual dialectology.

Television news in the United States traditionally occupies an hour in the evening, with a half hour given to events of national interest and a half hour given to news of local interest; most of the content of local news programs is repeated later in the evening. The content of local news programs is dominated by stories covering the activities of local government -- city councils, county boards, school boards -- and to events of particular dramatic interest, ranging from elections to crimes to natural disasters. Since some of these events do not provide much to photograph, and since others happen unpredictably, preventing the local camera crews from arriving in time to film the event itself, television news people often supplement their accounts with interviews of ordinary citizens. Sometimes these people are stopped at random on the street to get their reactions to the event; sometimes they are witnesses to the event itself. In either case, the interviewees speak in a state of excitement -- their favorite candidate may have just won the election, the grain elevator may have just exploded and burned to the ground -- providing an excellent sample of speech in a casual, unmonitored register.

Unmonitored speech from video, I believe, should be accepted at the very least as supplemental to the kinds of linguistic evidence traditionally elicited by fieldworkers. Unlike most television speech, which comes from actors or newspersons who have been to dialect coaches, we hear the authentic speech of members of the community we want to investigate. Interviews like these also provide a wealth of information about the interviewees. Visual cues often provide correlative social data about the interviewee: sex, social class, sometimes ethnicity. At other times, interviewers often ask enough personal questions about the interviewee, especially name, occupation, place of residence, that what information remains to be gathered can easily be filled in. In particular, interviewees who give their names can be checked in documents like city or county directories, which provide information about occupation and neighborhood of residence.

Given the difficulties of obtaining field interviews -- especially those of time, help, funding -- television local news can supply valuable linguistic data about the communities where the news originates. These data should be at least as reliable as supplemental data used in other studies (Labov's 1966 department store survey is the most famous example). I have begun to use such data in a study which tests Craig Carver's (1986) assertion that the Mississippi River functions as a dialect fault line in the middle western United States. Television stations in Quincy, Illinois, cover news on both the Illinois and Missouri sides of the Mississippi River. I have begun to record local news interviews from both sides of the Mississippi, and while I have not yet collected enough tokens to present any conclusive results, it appears from my preliminary data that fronting of /au/ and flattening of /ai/ occur with significantly higher frequency on the Missouri side of the river than they do on the Illinois side. If this apparent trend continues, it will show Carver's claim to be correct.

I would like to move now to another way in which television content can provide useful data for linguists, this time in the areas of perceptual dialectology and language attitudes. Since Labov's early work in New York City, sociolinguists have sought to monitor society's negative or positive attitudes toward sociolinguistic variables; as Dennis Preston (1986) has shown, moreover, people have definite perceptions about the kinds of regional and social variation that exist around them, whether these perceptions are accurate or not. These perceptions are obviously worthy of study. In examining the use of television as a source of information about language attitudes and perceptions, I want first to examine two domestic situation comedies which depicted working-class figures. These programs flourished in the United States during the 1970s: "Happy Days" and "Laverne and Shirley."

As Robert Sklar observes in "The Fonz, Laverne, Shirley, and the Great American Class Struggle," the American Broacasting Company's "Happy Days" began something of a revolution on

American television. The program was originally conceived as a domestic comedy which featured a middle-class family in the comic tradition of "Ozzie and Harriet," "Father Knows Best," and others which flourished in the 1950s and early 60s. For a note of originality, the program also featured Arthur Fonzarelli, a working-class young man who drove a motorcycle. The "Fonz," as he came to be called, featured, in Sklar's words, a "black leather jacket, [a] ducktail haircut, [and] tight blue jeans, those fifties´ stigmata of a badass hood" (1980:78). So much did Fonzie´s appearance contribute to "Happy Days"´ rise to the top of the Nielsen ratings that ABC soon spun off another comedy series, "Laverne and Shirley," about two working-class girls who share an apartment.

What interested me about both of these programs is that they are set in Milwaukee, Wisconsin, although the only exteriors we see of Milwaukee appear during the credits at the opening of each episode -- the shows themselves were shot in ABC´s studio in California. Now I have never conducted a systematic study of Milwaukee speech, but I lived there during the summer of 1985, and am familiar with the speech of white Milwaukeeans. I observed no major difference between white Milwaukee speech and the American English dialect which Linguistic Atlas scholars have characterized as "Inland Northern." White Milwaukee speech and Inland Northern both differ from many dialects of the Eastern United States in that postvocalic /r/ is always pronounced with some degree of constriction; if we were to describe this pattern according to the "(r) index" William Labov constructed for his New York City study (1972:114) we would say that white Milwaukeans have an (r) index of 100.

What is remarkable about Fonzie´s pronunciation is his frequent use of unconstricted /r/. From a single episode of "Happy Days," I counted exactly 100 /r/ tokens in Fonzie´s speech. 81 of these tokens were unconstricted and 19 were constricted. According to Labov´s index, Fonzie´s /r/ score is 19. On "Laverne and Shirley," Shirley Feeney´s /r/s are always constricted, but Laverne De Fazio´s /r/s frequently lack constriction. From a single episode of "Laverne and Shirley," I counted 55 /r/ tokens for Laverne. Only 26 of these were constricted, giving Laverne an (r) score of 47. The most obvious things these figures tell us is that Laverne and Fonzie do not talk like the native white Milwaukeeans they are intended to portray. What is more difficult is to figure out just what this working-class "television dialect" implies.

First, let´s state the obvious: although neither of their /r/ scores are as low as those of Labov´s New York city sample in casual style (where /r/ values for the lower-middle, working and lower classes are below 10), Fonzie and Lavernes´s speech is modeled on that of lower-class white New Yorkers. Other features from their speech which I did not try to quantify also are frequent in New York speech: frequent rendering of interdental fricatives as stops, extreme raising of low-front and low-back vowel phonemes. But why use New York City speech to depict the Milwaukee working class? There may be answers in the tradition of popular culture itself, but I think this is also a sociolinguistic question. The attitudes Labov uncovered about New York City speech, on the part of New Yorkers and non-New Yorkers alike, were mixed: on the one hand, people thought New York City speech was "tough," cool and macho, and therefore just right for a working-class hero like the Fonz. On the other hand, New Yorkers also give negative value to their own speech, and abandon its marked features as they move up the stylistic or social scale; Labov called New York a "great sink" of linguistic insecurity. So it is that on "Laverne and Shirley," it is Laverne De Fazio who is the "bad girl" of the pair and who also uses much unconstricted /r/. Those who have seen the program know that Shirley Feeney, whose /r/ score is 100, is the "good girl" who (unlike Laverne) aspires to adopt middle-class values and obeys authority figures. What is suggested here is that some powerful stereotypes about language exist in society at large, stereotypes which are reflected -- and perhaps perpetuated -- by the electronic media.

Our examination of working-class figures on TV suggests, then, that television, as Raymond Williams (1986) has suggested, relies on the conventions and stereotypes of everyday discourse to make sense to its audience. My next example shows this to be true even when the producers and directors seem be to trying to do something else.

A few years ago, June Frazer and I began to examine the relationship between real-world interactive discourse and the dramatized discourse that took place on television (Frazer & Frazer, 1985). The model of real-world discourse we wanted to apply was Pamela Fishman's study of cross-sex conversation (Fishman, 1977, 1978). Fishman found that male-female conversation was dominated by an unequal power relationship: more than twice as often as women, men initiated topics, interrupted their female partners, asserted truths in statements, and, by a variety of additional means, controlled the interactive process. Women, on the other hand, performed what Fishman calls the "interactional shitwork" of conversation maintenance; their job is to keep the male-controlled conversation going by such devices as maintenance questions or other utterances ("Oh, really?" "Uh-huh") which signal interest and encourage the partner to continue. We examined the television drama "Policewoman" to see if the male-female discourse on that program was similar to such real discourse as reported by Fishman.

"Policewoman," a police procedural drama from the 1970s starring Angie Dickenson, interested us for several reasons. First of all, it was the first police drama to feature a team consisting of a male and female partner. Secondly, it attempted to respond to the growing feminist movement of the seventies by symbolically promising that its heroine will perform the same violent tasks traditionally reserved for males; this is promised both by the title and by the program's logo, a still of Ms. Dickinson aiming a pistol in the two-handed grip favored by TV producers. But instead of delivering on these promises, the show reverts to visual stereotypes in its treatment of Sgt. Pepper Martin, Dickinson's character. We are often treated to shots of Pepper in costumes that reveal as much flesh as allowed in prime time, reducing her to the traditional sex object. In her role as a policewoman, Pepper is usually confined to traditional feminine roles, posing as a prostitute, caring for child crime victims. Often she herself becomes victim, captured, tied up, threatened by criminals, needing rescue, finally, by Bill, her macho partner.

Given the mixed bag of signals "Policewoman" sends out to its audience, we began our analysis of dialogue between Pepper and her male partner. Would Sgt. Martin at least get to be a verbal equal, or would the program offer more realism than its director intended by reducing Pepper to the traditional role of conversation maintenance?

During our analysis, we did have to take into account a number of differences between the televised discourse of "Policewoman" and real discourse. One important difference, of course, is that TV discourse, like all dramatized discourse, has a third participant, the audience -- much of the discourse in drama is expository. Also, the discourse depicted on police shows is most of the time consultative, not interactive. Still, taking into account the illocutionary force of the utterances we recorded in a single segment of "Policewoman," we found the following differences between male and female utterances:

Statements (We counted only statements which introduce new propositional content or which alter the propositional content of a previous turn): We found a total of 56 statements, 32 of which were Bill's, 24 Pepper's. Of the staments in this segment, 57% are male, 43% are female.

Maintenance utterances ("Of course," "Uh-Huh," etc.): We found only six of these, a lower number than we might expect to find in a chunk of real interactive discourse, but only one was Bill's; five were Pepper's.

Imperatives (Includes both grammatical imperatives and utterances with imperative illocutionary force like "will you get me out of here?"): We found a total of ten imperatives; eight were Bill's, two Pepper's.

Despite the difficulties of comparing real and dramatized discourse -- which I have have not gone into detail about because of the nature of this conference -- we see that this segment of television discourse illustrates the important differences in male and female talk discovered by Pamela Fishman, and which have been observed anecdotally by Robin Lakoff (1975) and others: male speech is empowered, female is not; males control discourse, females support them. All of this happens on a program which has sought feminist credentials, which suggests that people who create television scripts know something about real-world discourse, and that knowledge is deeply engrained enough not to be conscious to its observers. Once again, television tells us what people THINK about language, even if, as "Policewoman" suggests, they don't know that they think it.

Present in this paper, I realize, are some incomplete and limted data. But my point here has been to emphasize their source, to suggest some ways in which it can be used. Television is a powerful communicative tool, and a great potential source of data about language and about human communication.

REFERENCES

Carver, Craig. 1986. The influence of the Mississippi River on Northern dialect boundaries. *American Speech*, 61, 245-61.
Fishman, Pamela M. 1977. Interactional shitwork. *Heresies: A Feminist Publication on Arts and Politics*, 2, 99-101.
_____. 1978. The work women do. *Social Problems*, 23, 397-406.
Frazer, June M., and Timothy C. Frazer. 1985. Cross-sex conversation. Paper presented to Language and Society Division, Modern Language Association of America.
Labov, William. 1966. *The Social Stratification of English in New York City*. Washington, D.C.: Center for Applied Linguistics.
_____. 1972. *Sociolinguistic Patterns*. Philadelphia: University of Pennsylvania Press.
Lakoff, Robin. 1975. *Language and Woman's Place*. New York: Harper and Row.
Preston, Dennis. 1986. Five visions of America. *Language in Society*, 15, 221-240.
Sklar, Robert. 1980. The Fonz, Laverne, Shirley, and the great American class struggle. In Horace Newcomb, ed., *Television: The Critical View*, 3rd edition. New York and Oxford: Oxford University Press.
Williams, Raymond. 1986. In Stephen Heath and Gillian Skirrow, An interview with Raymond Williams. In Tania Modleski, ed., *Studies in Entertainment*. Bloomington and Indianapolis: Indiana University Press.

The Construction of Rural Sociolinguistic Corpus: The Prince Edward Island Study[1]

RUTH KING and ROBERT RYAN
York University, Canada

INTRODUCTION

In this paper we will report on a new variabilitiy study, begun in the spring of 1987, of the Acadian French spoken in Prince Edward Island, Canada. In his recent bibliography of Acadian linguistics, Edward Gesner (1986) comments upon the healthy state of linguistic research on Acadian, noting more than sixty-five conference presentations and/or publications between 1980 and 1985. Sociolinguistic research on Atlantic Canada Acadian dates from the late 1970's and includes studies of Acadian varieties of northeastern New Brunswick and of five dialect areas in Nova Scotia, all conducted by Karin Flikeid, and four varieties of western Newfoundland, conducted by Ruth King. Surprisingly, however, Gesner's exhaustive bibliography contains no references at all, either early or recent, to the variety of Acadian French which is the mother tongue for some 6000 people in Prince Edward Island.[2]

It is this lacuna which we seek to fill in our present study, in which we have undertaken the systematic investigation of the speech of a relatively large, representative sample of the francophone population of Prince Edward Island, stratified according to age and sex, drawn from both major Acadian areas of the province. Our objectives are (a) to describe phonological, morphological, and syntactic features of Prince Edward Island Acadian French; (b) to identify, interpret, and explain variation in the light of both linguistic and social constraints operating within the speech community; and (c) to compare the sociolinguistic patterning we find within the francophone regions of the island and to compare the Prince Edward Island results with those for the other Acadian varieties of the Atlantic Provinces already investigated or currently under investigation. Our work is done in collaboration with Gary Butler who is ethnographic consultant for this project and who will, in a separate project reported on in this volume, extend the analysis of Prince Edward Island Acadian to some aspects of discourse. We will first present some background into the history and present-day status of Acadian French in Prince Edward Island, followed in turn by results of our pilot study and the methodological techniques which we have implemented in our large-scale study.

HISTORICAL BACKGROUND

The first important influx of French-speaking settlers to Prince Edward Island, composed largely of natives of the centre-west region, arrived directly from France, from the port of La Rochelle in 1720 with secondary settlement from Acadian areas of Nova Scotia largely between 1749 and 1755. Following the *grand dérangement* (or "big expulsion") in 1755, several thousand Acadians arrived from Nova Scotia to avoid deportation to the United States. On the island they farmed the land of anglophone absentee landlords. The subsequent history of Prince Edward Island's Acadian inhabitants has been no less troubled than that of their counterparts in Nova Scotia: lack of economic and educational opportunity and steadily increasing linguistic and cultural assimilation have been their lot over the centuries. The decline of French, both as a mother tongue and as home language, is particularly dramatic, as is shown in the following table from Statistics Canada:

PRINCE EDWARD ISLAND ACADIAN POPULATION EVOLUTION: 1931 - 1981

	1931	1941	1951	1961	1971	1981
Total pop P.E.I.	88,038	95,047	98,429	104,629	111,640	122,506
French origin	12,962	14,799	15,477	17,418	15,325	14,770
	(14.7%)	(15.6%)	(15.7%)	(16.6%)	(13.7%)	(12.1%)
Fr. mother tongue	10,137	10,678	8,477	7,958	7,365	5,915
	(11.5%)	(11.2%)	(8.6%)	(7.6%)	(6.6%)	(4.8%)
French spoken at home						3,420
						(2.8%)

We see that, of the 12.1% of the total population of the island listed as being of French origin in 1981, less than half had actually learnt French has their mother tongue. Only half of this latter group reported their home language as being French (this last question was not asked for previous censuses).

The present-day geographic distribution of Prince Edward Island francophones is given in the table below, along with the rate of assimilation to the anglophone majority. This latter figure was determined by comparing census data for French as a mother tongue to those for French as a home language.

FRANCOPHONE POPULATION OF PRINCE EDWARD ISLAND ACCORDING TO COUNTY, 1981

	Total pop.	French origin	French mother tongue	French home language	Rate of assim.
Total pop.	122,506 (100%)	14,770 (12.1%)	5,915[3] (4.8%)	3,420 (2.8%)	42.2%
Prince Co.	42,821 (100%)	9,255 (21.6%)	4,895 (11.4%)	3,290 (7.7%)	32.8%
Queen's Co.	60,470 (100%)	4,520 (7.5%)	900 (1.5%)	120 (0.2%)	86.7%
King's Co.	19,215 (100%)	995 (5.2%)	115 (0.6%)	10 (0.05%)	91.3%

We see that the francophone population is concentrated in Prince County in the north-west of the island, in its Tignish region (which includes the communities of Tignish, Palmer Road, Saint-Edouard and Saint-Louis) and Evangéline region (which includes the communities of Baie-Egmont, Wellington, Mont-Carmel and Abram's Village). These communities are shown on the map on the following page. With the exception of the town of Bloomfield, there has been almost total assimilation in the geographical area between Evangéline and Tignish. While there is also a substantial francophone population in the two urban centres on the island, Charlottetown and Summerside, it is heterogeneous in character. Charlottetown, the provincial capital, is the site of the federal Ministry of Veterans' Affairs and Summerside is the site of a large airforce base, both of which have attracted francophones from other provinces.

Today's Acadian population, then, is situated principally in the Evangéline region (with a total population of 2900 of whom 46.8% are of French origin) and the Tignish region (with a total population of 2306 of whom 45.2% are of French origin), with Evangéline in particular displaying active interest in the preservation of French culture and language. The Evangéline region is the site of an Acadian museum, Acadian cultural associations and an annual Acadian festival. Unlike the Tignish region, where only a French "immersion" educational system is in place, there are French elementary and high schools in the Evangéline region. The variety of French taught and sanctioned by the educational system is, however, a standard Québécois, which appears to separate the home variety from that of institutionalized settings.

THE PILOT STUDY

A preliminary investigation of PEI Acadian was undertaken in 1985 and 1986, for which we gathered historical, demographic, and sociocultural information and arranged the recording (principally by local contact people) of a limited corpus of some twenty hours of speech samples representative of both major Acadian regions, both sexes, and various age groups. We subsequently transcribed the corpus and undertook a preliminary analysis of the phonology.

Not surprisingly, we found evidence of traditional Acadian features such as *ouisme* (i.e. the realization of [u] where standard French has [o] or [ɔ], as in *connaître* [kunɛ:t] "to know") and palatalization of /k/ and /g/ before non-low front vowels (as in *calculer* [kaltʃyle] "to calculate"). We have found nasal vowel patterning, as in Nova Scotia and New Brunswick varieties, to be conditioned by stress and syllable structure: phonological processes such as diphthongization operate in stressed, open syllables, e.g. *garçon* [garsõʷ] "boy".

Of particular interest in the data analysed thus far (and confirmed by more recent fieldwork) is the existence of variants which to our knowledge are not found in other Acadian varieties and which are typically associated with Québécois, i.e., affrication of /t/

and /d/ before high, front vowels (as in *tirer* [t^{s}ire] "to pull" and *dur* [d^{z}yr]) "hard"), and raising of oral mid vowels (as in *manger* [mãẓeˆ]) and of the nasal vowel /ɛ̃/ (as in *y en avait un* [j ãn avɛ jẽ] "there was one"). Further, we have evidence of regional variation in that speakers in the Evangéline region display much more vowel raising than do Tignish speakers. It must be emphasized that all of our informants for the pilot study were born in Prince Edward Island and had spent all of their lives there: they range in age from adolescents to octogenarians. There is no evidence in Prince Edward Island settlement history of extended contact with Québec nor is their reason to believe that our older speakers, late in life, are accommodating to a Québécois prestige model. Thus far the evidence suggests that these features have developed independently in Prince Edward Island Acadian; clearly, though, the question needs further research.

THE PRESENT STUDY

Our large-scale study is an examination of the synchronic social patterning of Prince Edward Island Acadian, i.e., the correlations which exist between linguistic usage and social phenomena (e.g., gender, education, and social identity) both within and between communities. Through the systematic investigation of the speech of different age groups, it is potentially a study of linguistic change in apparent time. The linguistic phenomena we will investigate include those suggested by the pilot study, e.g. nasal vowel variation, affrication of /t/ and /d/, palatalization of /k/ and /g/, *ouisme*, and mid vowel raising. Other variables have been chosen because a variant is typical, conservative Acadian and/or because they have been investigated in studies of other Acadian varieties. These include choice of subject pronoun in the first person plural (*je* is the typical Acadian first person subject clitic, regardless of number), presence or absence of the complementizer *que*, agreement marking on the verb in the third person plural, usage or nonusage of the *passé simple*, and patterns of cliticization of object pronouns.

The major theoretical questions addressed by this study may be classified as follows:

A. QUESTIONS ARISING FROM THE RURAL CONTEXT:

How does linguistic variation in nonurban Prince Edward Island compare with that found in speech communities which exhibit strong social stratification (e.g., Are sex and/or some measure of socio-economic class related to linguistic variation?)?

What finer social variables (e.g. vernacular loyalty, social network) might be correlated with linguistic variation?

B. QUESTIONS ARISING FROM THE LANGUAGE CONTACT SITUATION:

What is the relative status of French and English? In what domains do each tend to be spoken? Are younger speakers in particular abandonning the minority language and if so, why? Do certain social characteristics promote language shift?

How prevalent are codeswitching and codemixing? How are they constrained? What are the effects of grammar contact?

C. QUESTIONS ARISING FROM THE DIALECT CONTACT SITUATION:

Has Acadian dialect mixture played a role in the development of Prince Edward Island Acadian? How have the linguistic effects of dialect contact been integrated?

Has Québécois had any effect on Prince Edward Island Acadian?

What is the status of standard and nonstandard varieties of French? What is (are) the prestige model(s)?

How does phonological and grammatical change in Prince Edward Island Acadian compare with change in other Acadian varieties (and indeed with change in French in general)?

Methodology

The methodology implemented in this study has been strongly influenced by previous work done in non-urban contexts, i.e. by Clarke for Montagnais in Sheshatshui, Labrador (reported on in this volume), by King for Acadian French in western Newfoundland, and especially by Flikeid for several Nova Scotia Acadian varieties (also reported on in this volume). The rigourous methodology employed by Poplack in her Ottawa-Hull French study (see Poplack, in press), particularly in terms of data computerization and manipulation, has also set for us an excellent example. In this section we will outline the sampling procedure, research instruments, and role of local research assistants in our project, pointing out in particular adaptations made to the local context.

Sampling Procedures

Our first goal has been to collect a corpus of natural speech from both Acadian regions of the province for a relatively large sample stratified according to age and sex, consisting of people who were raised in their community, are of Acadian origin, are fluent French speakers, and are of the same socio-economic class. The communities we have chosen are Saint-Louis in the Tignish region and Abram's Village in the Evangéline region. fairly homogeneous francophone populations and because they display an active interest in the preservation of French culture and language. Census data for these particular communities were difficult to obtain due to their small populations: each was included in an enumeration area with other communities and it was impossible to obtain individual figures for such questions as the number of people who report speaking French as their home language. The official data therefore had to be supplemented with information obtained by local contact people. In the case of Saint-Louis we also found disparity between the community's view of its geographical boundaries and that of the federal government, in which case we adopted the community's cognitive map.

We have hired as field research asssistants natives of each area who are Acadians fluent in the local variety and well-known in the community. For each community they compiled a list of residents who met the above-mentioned criteria and further subdivided this list according to sex and age group, drawing on their personal knowledge. From each sublist, potential informants were randomly chosen until a quota for each community was reached. In the event that a potential informant did not wish to or was unable to participate in the project, another name was randomly selected from the sublist. The final sample of 48 speakers is as follows:

Age	Tignish Region: Saint-Louis		Evangéline Region: Abram's Village	
	Male	Female	Male	Female
15-24	2	2	2	2
25-34	2	2	2	2
35-44	2	2	2	2
45-54	2	2	2	2
55-64	2	2	2	2
65+	2	2	2	2

As Poplack (in press) points out, such a stratified sample is more useful in sociolinguistic research than a purely random sample since the relatively small number (from a mathematical point of view) of speakers would cause serious skewing if a purely random procedure were employed. For example, such a sample would probably have unequal representation of males and females. The rural, bilingual context also makes sampling techniques such as knocking on every tenth door exceedingly time-consuming. Since in Atlantic Canada a French surname is no guarantee of fluency in French, use of the telephone directory as a list of potential informants would also have been difficult.

It will be noted that there are fine divisions in the sample according to age but that it is not stratified according to any social measure. We believe that greater familiarity with each community must first be obtained by working closely with our research assistants and by examining the ethnographic information and survey data which the interviews provide. Such information will allow us to rearrange and refine our groupings and should be accomplished fairly easily, given the sample size.

We also plan in the second year of the project to interview, for geographical-comparative purposes, a smaller sample of speakers from Rustico where only a small (12%) minority of the population are of Acadian backgound, as well as a smaller sample of speakers from the community of Bloomfield, which borders both the Evangéline and Tignish regions. Here we will interview five males and five females from our oldest age group in each of the communities. The sampling procedure will be as for our primary sample.

The Interview Schedule

Since our goal is the collection of a large volume of natural speech from a relatively large number of individuals, we have made every effort to lessen the Observer Effect. Before beginning data collection, our Acadian research assistants (two for each community, along with a part-time worker) underwent an intensive week-long training period in field techniques since we had found in the pilot study that ingenue interviewers, however well-intentioned, did not possess the necessary technical skills nor the interviewing skills to conduct high quality, sociolinguistic interviews. Trained local interviewers have also contributed to the success of Flikeid's Nova Scotia project and Poplack's Ottawa project.

During the training period, the assistants were familiarized with the manipulation of the equipment, with interviewing techniques and with the questionnaires themselves through demonstration and through a set of three practice interviews conducted with members of the community. All interviews for the study were recorded on Sony TCM-5000 cassette tape recorders equipped with two lavalière microphones, the combination of which results in near-broadcast sound quality. The subsequent transcription of the interviews will begin fifteen minutes into each tape in order to allow time for the informants to become more comfortable with the interview situation.

Our interview format is modelled on those techniques developed by William Labov and his associates (cf. Labov 1984), focussing on the particular interests of the local population, with a general conversational module as a guide. We developed a total of four questionnaires, of which three are designed for use during the interview itself. A short questionnaire presented at the beginning of the interview session elicits demographic information about the informants and their families (e.g. educational and employment background, place of birth, names and ages of children, parents, grandparents, etc.) and forms part of what we call the Individual Profile. The interviewer, to the extent that is necessary, makes use of the general conversation module to obtain the speech which makes up the bulk of the interview. The second part of the Individual Profile consists of a set of questions, asked near the end of the interviews, about past and present linguistic usage (e.g. which language, French or English, is spoken to which people and in what contexts). The Individual Profile is modelled on previous questionnaires used by King (1983) and Dorian (1981).

Each informant was interviewed for a total of at least two hours in order that we might accumulate enough data for morphological and syntactic analysis, with the corpus as a whole consisting of some 100 hours. In some cases the interview was completed in more than one session with the informant. The interviews were finished within a one-month period.

A fourth research instrument is a set of questions designed to establish what we call a Community Profile, based on one by Arensberg and Kimball (1965) and adapted to the local context by Butler. It serves as an aid to the collection, organization and analysis of data concerning the spatiotemporal and sociocultural aspects of the community and of the behaviour of its members, which may directly or indirectly be related to language use. It is organized so that the local research assistants can record information, based on their own experiences and those of other members of the community, in a readily accessible way. For example, specific sections cover genealogical information, others oral history of settlement, others the structure of work and leisure activities. These data, initially recorded on large file cards by the research assistants, will be stored on computer diskette and will serve to complement ethnographic information contained in the actual interviews.

Stages to Follow

The next phase of the project will be computerization of the corpus collected during the summer of 1987 and of the data from the Individual and Community Profiles. For maximum efficiency in data transcription, we will follow the example of Poplack and Flikeid: the entire corpus will be transcribed in modified orthography by a research assistant, equipped with a transcribing machine with headphones and a footpedal, who will type directly into a computer and store the data on diskette. A correction phase, involving a computer-assisted spelling check, relistening to each interview and correcting all errors on the printout and then in the data file will follow. Approximately ten minutes per informant, or eight hours overall, of the corpus will be transcribed phonetically and computerized.

For data storage, manipulation and analysis we will use an IBM-compatible Zenith microcomputer equipped with a twenty-megabyte hard disk. The microcomputer version of the Oxford Concordance Program will be used to manipulate the corrected corpus (e.g. produce word-frequency lists, lists of borrowings, etc.). Statistical analysis will be effected through the use of SPSSX-PC, the microcomputer version of the Statistical Package for the Social Sciences, and of the VARBRUL-2S computer program developed by David Sankoff).

Allowing time for the evaluation what sorts of information -- e.g. linguistic, ethnographic, etc. -- are missing from the large corpus, supplementary interviews will be conducted during the summer of 1988. In order to be able to compare contextual styles, we also plan to re-interview approximately twenty of the original informants of our primary sample at this time. In these interviews we hope to elicit a formal speech style since the interviewer will be an outsider and a speaker of European standard French. This method of comparing insider and outsider interviews has been successfully employed by Flikeid in the Nova Scotia study reported on in this volume.

Our goals for the second year of the project include the transcription and computer storage of the data from the supplementary interviews. Computer-assisted linguistic analysis of the entire corpus will continue during this period.

SUMMARY

Our primary objective, then, is the collection, computerization, and analysis of a large corpus of natural speech, geographically and socially representative of Prince Edward Island's Acadian population, which should allow a description of this previously-undescribed variety of Acadian, including the sociolinguistic patterning of major phonological, morphological and syntactic variables and the identification of linguistic change in progress. The data studied thus far indicate interesting patterns of variation which analysis of a large sociolinguistic corpus should elucidate and which should advance our knowledge of the structure of linguistic variation in the rural context.

FOOTNOTES

[1] We would like to acknowledge the support provided by a two-year research grant from the Social Sciences and Humanities Research Council of Canada.

[2] In her major lexical study Les parlers français de l'Acadie (1962), Massignon did have one Prince Edward Island informant, a female resident born in 1889, of Mont-Carmel in the Evangéline region, who not only gave information for her home community but also for three geographically disparate villages, Rustico, Miscouche and Tignish! Fortunately, given this dubious methodology, the Prince Edward Island villages figured only as secondary localities for Massignon's study. Dulong and Bergeron's Atlas linguistique de l'est du Canada (1980) which concentrated for the most part on the province of Québec, has one Prince Edward Island locality, Baie Egmont, also in the Evangéline region. For this locality there were several informants, both males and females, who were born around the turn of the century in nearby villages. Surprisingly, Massignon's phonetic transcriptions do not reveal what we believe to be distinctive traits of Prince Edward Island Acadian French, namely vowel raising and affrication of /t/ and /d/, whereas Dulong and Bergeron's contain the expected affrication. The latter do not appear to have recorded vowel raising in their phonetic transcription for any of the varieties they investigated, although its occurrence in Québécois is well-documented (cf. Gendron (1966).

[3] Data for five individuals are also missing in the original document.

References

Arensberg, C. and Kimball, S. (1965) *Culture and Community.* New York: Harcourt, Brace & World, Inc.
Arsenault, B. (1978) *Histoire des Acadiens* Editions Lemeac.
Arsenault, G. (1980) *Histoire de l'émigration chez les Acadiens de l'Ile-du-Prince-Edouard* Summerside, Prince Edward Island: La societé Saint-Thomas d'Aquin.
Arsenault, S. et al. (1976) *Atlas de l'Acadie: Petit atlas des francophones des Maritimes* Editions d'Acadie.
Blanchard, J.H. (1927; New edition 1964) *Histoire des Acadiens de l'Ile-du-Prince-Edouard* Imprimerie de l'Evangéline.
Dorian, N. (1981) *Language Death* Philadelphia: University of Pennsylvania Press.
Flikeid, K. (1979) *La variation phonétique dans le parler acadien du nord-est du Nouveau-Brunswick: Etude sociolinguistique* Peter Lang.
_____. (1984) A comparative study of Acadian French: Report on the first phase. Paper presented at NWAVE-XIII, University of Pennsylvania, Philadelphia, PA; October 27, 1984.
Gendron, J.D. (1966) *Tendances phonétiques du français parlé au Canada* Paris: Klinksieck and Québec: Les Presses de l'Université Laval.
Gesner, B.E. (1986) *Bibliographie annotée de linguistique acadienne* Québec: Center for International Research on Bilingualism.
King, R. (1985) Linguistic variation and language contact: A study of the French spoken in four Newfoundland communities. In H.J. Warkentyne (ed) *Methods V: Papers from the Fifth International Conference on Methods in Dialectology.* Victoria, B.C.: University of Victoria, 211-237.
King, R. and R. Ryan. (1987) La phonologie des parlers acadiens de l'Ile-du-Prince-Edouard. In M. Kinloch et al (eds) *Papers from the Tenth Annual Meeting of the Atlantic Provinces Linguistic Association* Fredericton, N.B.: University of New Brunswick, 95-108.
Labov, W. (1972) *Sociolinguistic Patterns* University of Pennsylvania Press.
_____. (1984) Field techniques of the project on linguistic change and variation. In John Baugh and Joel Sherzer (eds)

Language in Use: Readings in Sociolinguistics. Englewood Cliffs, New Jersey: Prentice-Hall.

Massignon, G. (1962) *Les parlers français d'Acadie: Enquête linguistique.* 2 vol. Paris: Klincksieck.

Poplack, S. (In press) The care and handling of a mega-corpus: The Ottawa-Hull French project. In R. Fasold and D. Shiffrin (eds) *Proceedings of NWAVE-XII.* Georgetown University Press.

Statistics Canada. (1981) *Canadian Census,* Doc. E-572.

Written Records of Spoken Language: How Reliable Are They?

NATALIE MAYNOR
Mississippi State University

One of the biggest obstacles facing linguists researching changes in spoken language is that of finding data that accurately represent the speech of earlier periods--periods before the advent of the tape recorder. Reliable sources for such research do, of course, exist. In spite of some questions that have been raised about their methodology, people like Edmond Edmont, who bicycled through France gathering data for Jules Gilliéron, Alexander Ellis in Britain, the fieldworkers employed by Jaberg and Jud in Italy and Switzerland, and those under the direction of Hans Kurath in the United States were well trained in listening carefully and transcribing the spoken words as accurately as possible. Problems arise, however, when linguists, in their enthusiastic quest for data from earlier periods, rely on written sources that are not so accurate.

The problem is perhaps especially serious in the United States, where only one carefully prepared linguistic atlas, the Linguistic Atlas of New England (Kurath et al., 1939-43), was completed before World War II and where questions about the historical relationship between the speech of blacks and whites continue to be debated but have yet to be answered satisfactorily. Because the Linguistic Atlas of New England includes only a few black informants and because clear answers to historical questions require even earlier examples than those in LANE, linguists researching the history of Black English Vernacular have been forced to turn to other sources of early data.

One source for diachronic study of language is writing samples from people whose dialects are being examined. Works like Norman Eliason's <u>Tarheel Talk</u>, an analysis of language in North Carolina before 1860, have been based on personal writings of a wide variety of people, including the barely literate, whose "naive records," to quote Eliason, "are particularly illuminating" (1956, p. 28). Even though, as Eliason points out, "writing almost inevitably induces some restraint" (1956, p. 49), diaries or letters to family and friends are sometimes revealing in their vocabulary, usage, and phonetic spellings. An obvious limitation, however, when trying to examine diachronically a dialect like Black English Vernacular is the scarcity of such early writings. Although Eliason's book does include excerpts from a few letters from ex-slaves to their former masters and mistresses, the fact is that very few slaves were able to write at all.

Another source that has been used fairly often, possible too often, is literary dialect. The use of literary sources for linguistic research has, of course, a long and respectable history. Evidence such as that drawn from rhyme in the poetry of early writers has been accepted by language historians for years. Reconstructing phonetic values from rhyme, however, is not exactly the same thing as making pronouncements about dialects based on dialogue in fiction, especially fiction written by someone who does not speak the particular dialect being depicted. Linguists who have carefully examined literary dialect, Constance Weaver (1970) for example, have concluded that writers, including those who are bidialectal themselves, tend to exaggerate certain features. My own very cursory examination of the dialect in Alice Walker's novel <u>The Color Purple</u> (1982) in comparison with taped samples of rural Southern black speech supports this conclusion. As Walt Wolfram has said in discussing Dillard's use of literary sources in his book <u>Black English</u>, "the tendency to represent those things that are most different may focus on those considered 'exotic' by the writer (or linguist), resulting in a representation which is linguistically overdone" (1973, p. 674). Ralph

Fasold's review of Dillard's book makes basically the same point, concluding that "it is valid for Dillard to use literary sources to support the broad outlines of his historical hypothesis, but not to rely on them too heavily for detail" (1975, p. 201). This is not to say that the writers who exaggerate their literary dialect are in error. After all, fiction is not real life, and literary dialect is not real speech.

Ruling out fiction because it is fictional, linguistic researchers sometimes turn to seemingly more reliable sources of data, for example the WPA slave narratives, a collection of interviews with former slaves conducted in the United States during the 1930's as part of the Federal Writers' Project of the Works Progress Administration (WPA).[1] The WPA slave narratives, sometimes claimed to be verbatim records of the ex-slaves' words (Yetman 1967, p. 534), would seem at first glance to be a goldmine of linguistic data. A closer examination, however, reveals that the records of these interviews are of questionable reliability for linguistic purposes and that they are certainly not verbatim.

In 1972 Greenwood Press published George P. Rawick's compilation of over two thousand of the WPA narratives, some of which had already been published in part or whole, for example the excerpts by B.A. Botkin in _Lay My Burden Down_ (1945) and whole interviews by Norman Yetman in _Life Under the "Peculiar Institution"_ (1970). At the time, Rawick believed that the manuscripts which he found in the Rare Book Room of the Library of Congress in Washington probably represented the entire WPA collection. Subsequently he found thousands of additional pages of WPA interviews in various parts of the country. These additional interviews, published in 1977 and 1979 as supplements to Rawick's earlier collection, include entirely new material as well as different versions of some of the interviews in Rawick's 1972 collection. The noticeable differences between the two or more versions of the same interviews raise serious questions about the reliability of these interviews as linguistic data.

In many cases the versions of the interviews poublished in Rawick 1972 (the versions at the Library of Congress) indicate historically and sociologically interesting editing of content, editing which Rawick believes was done before the narratives were sent to Washington. For example, references to cruelty by overseers or masters were sometimes deleted and the happy life of the slaves emphasized (or fabricated). Of more interest to linguists are the language differences that appear in the different versions of the same interview. In his introduction to the supplemental Mississippi narratives, Ken Lawrence, who along with Jan Hillegas helped edit the Mississippi supplements, says "<u>None</u> [emphasis Lawrence's] of the dialect in these narratives can be considered authentic. The interviewers had been instructed in the 'proper' renderings, and most strove to comply" (Rawick 1977, vol. 6, p. xciv). In reference to the seemingly routine editing of "we" to "us," Lawrence says: "In his book <u>Black English</u>, J.L. Dillard refers to this usage as an 'undifferentiated pronoun.' However, all of his examples showing 'us' used in this fashion are taken from Botkin's slave narrative selections in <u>Lay My Burden Down</u> and therefore are suspect" (Rawick 1977, vol. 6, p. xciv). The narratives in Rawick 1972 indicate frequent use of "us for "we." The presumably earlier versions of the same interviews, which appear in Rawick 1977/79, occasionally use "us" for the subject of a sentence but far more often use "we."

The evidence of linguistic tampering is strengthened by some of the correspondence found in state archives. For example, a letter from Marjorie Woods Austin, one of the interviewers in Mississippi, protests some of the instructions from Washington on the handling of dialect in the narratives (Rawick 1977, vol. 6, p. xciv-xcv). Among other things, Austin says "Never in my life have I ever heard a negro say de for the . . . . However, since "de" seems to be part of Washington's idea, fine, I am using it--under protest." Austin goes on to say, "I have not used 'mammy' as of your correction because none of these negroes have used the word."

A memorandum to the workers in South Carolina from Miss Mabel Montgomery, State Director, reads as follows:

> Please follow carefully the instructions, originating in Washington, which have been sent you from time to time, particularly those relating to modified dialect. Some of you have transgressed in this regard. Consult the list of tabooed words and <u>do not use them</u>. Our desire is for easy reading and a complicated dialect does not produce that result. We who live in the south are so accustomed to Negro speech that we forget how difficult it is to be understood by people from other sections. (Rawick 1977, vol. ii, pp. 323-24)

My own suspicions about the reliability of the narratives as linguistic data were aroused when I was first looking at some of the interviews in Rawick 1972 and Rawick 1977/79, having not yet read the introductory material and having very little knowledge of the overall project. My initial feeling was that the versions in Rawick 1972, those found in Washington, showed more deviation from so-called Standard English than did the versions in Rawick 1977/79. Table 1 lists a few random examples of the kinds of discrepancies I first noticed.

As a test of my initial reaction I examined three interviews for verb use in clauses which appear in both Rawick 1972 and the supplements. With present-tense forms of all verbs and past-tense forms of the verb <u>be</u> I found a discrepancy rate of approximately thirty percent, with the majority of the discrepancies resulting from use of the "standard" forms in Rawick 1977/79 and "non-standard" forms in Rawick 1972. For example, one of the ex-slaves in Mississippi in quoting a question asked him by his master, says "Prince, do you know who you were named for?" in Rawick 1977 (vol. 8, p. 1168) and "Prince does you know who you is named for?" in Rawick 1972 (vol. 7, p.77). The questions of exactly how, when, where, and why these changes were made is interesting. Even without answering these questions, however, such discrepancies are one indication that the narratives may be of limited usefulness for linguistic research.

In his general introduction to the supplemental collection Rawick also questions the reliability of these narratives as linguistic data:

> There are three fundamental ways that the slave narratives should not be used in my opinion, although they have already been used for these purposes in the published work of some scholars.

Table 1
Random Discrepancies Between Versions of WPA Narratives in Rawick 1972 and Rawick 1977/79

Alabama Narratives

R 72   : Joe and Jerry, dey was de table boys.
R 77/79: Jo and Jerry were de table boys.

R 72   : Dey did'n' have a thing to do.
R 77/79: They didn't have to do a thing.

R 72   : I ain't seen none planted 'tell after I was free.
R 77/79: I neber seed no cotton planted til' a'ter I was free.

R 72   : . . . but I 'spec's hit won't be long twell I is ober de ribber wid de bles'.
R 77/79: . . . but it wont be long now 'til I jines dem 'ober de riber.'

Mississippi Narratives

R 72   : Dey names was Dennis when dey come.
R 77/79: There [sic] names were Dennis when they came.

R 72   : Us all lived in de quarters an' de beds was home made.
R 77/79: We all lived in the quarters and our beds were home made.

R 72   : Candy an' presents was put in piles for ever'one.
R 77/79: Candy was put in piles for each person.

Texas Narratives

R 72   : De women am off Friday afternoon . . . .
R 77/79: The wimmen was off Friday afternoon . . . .

R 72   : . . . us all have plenty meat.
R 77/79: . . . we all have plenty of meat.

R 72   : I 'magines I seed ghosties two, three times.
R 77/79: I 'magine I see ghos'es two or three time.

Methods in Dialectology 115

> First, the slave narratives do not generally provide a reliable source for those seeking to study black speech patterns and black English. However, for certain subjects, particularly the study of Gullah and related black linguistic patterns in coastal South Carolina and Georgia, the narratives may prove of use. A few interviewers seem to have been particularly concerned about and competent in the rendering of speech patterns. However, although some efforts were made to record faithfully what was heard by other interviewers, both the very way in which the narratives were recorded and developed and the way the matter of dialect was handled should preclude much confidence in the use of the narratives in this respect. (Rawick 1977, p. xxix)

There was, of course, a great deal of variation from state to state in how much editing was done to the narratives before sending them to Washington. The Georgia and Indiana narratives, for example, do not seem to have been heavily edited, although many of the Georgia narratives were not originally sent to Washington. But the fact that some interviews are almost identical in the version appearing in Rawick 1972 and that in Rawick 1977/79 does not necessarily prove that these narratives are "pure." The question is not simply a matter of discrepancies between the versions of the interviews sent to Washington and those found later in state archives. Assuming that the versions in Rawick 1977/79 are earlier or purer versions than those in Rawick 1972, there is still the question of how close to verbatim the earlier or purer versions are. Pointing out that "the narratives were taken down in pencil or pen, most often after the interview, from memory or from scattered field notes supplemented by memory," Rawick states simply in his introduction to the supplements: "these are not verbatim recordings of conversations" (Rawick 1977, p. xxxi). Such an observation is really not much more than common sense. How many highly trained linguistic fieldworkers would be able to write down every word of a conversation? The interviewers for the WPA project were for the most part neither linguists nor stenographers.

Are the WPA narratives, then, useless as linguistic data? Probably not entirely. Some of Jeutonne Brewer's findings (1979) on the present-tense of *be* in the WPA narratives, the relatively rare use of invariant *be* for example, are quite similar to what Guy Bailey and I have found in our analysis of taped interviews with thirteen former slaves, most of whom were interviewed in the 1940's (Bailey and Maynor 1987).[2] These tapes, which we bought from the Library of Congress, include those recordings mentioned in Rawick's introduction to the supplements as having "some direct reference to the slave narrative collection" (Rawick 1977, p. xxx).

Because we had already analyzed all instances of the present tense of be in these tapes, I chose that feature to analyze in some of the WPA narratives for comparative purposes. Table 2 indicates my findings. In choosing the thirteen WPA narratives to examine, I first tried to match the informants geographically with our taped informants. However, complications like the matter of where the interviews took place as opposed to where the informants had actually lived as slaves, length and style of the interviews (some of the WPA interviews are recorded in third person), and an attempt to avoid using too many interviews from the same state or conducted by the same fieldworker resulted in my use of what may be considered a more or less random sample of the narratives. Table 3 lists the thirteen taped interviews and the thirteen interviews recorded in Rawick 1972 and 1977/79.

The results given in Table 2 suggest that the WPA narratives are in some respects parallel with our taped interviews. For example are is never used in the first person singular and almost never in the third person singular, and invariant be is not a common variant in any environment. In other respects, however, the representation of the present tense of be in the WPA narratives appears questionable. The seemingly capricious use of am, for example, does not correspond at all with what we have found in our tapes of the former slaves or with tapes we have analyzed of the speech of other older black folk speakers (Bailey and Maynor 1985). The distribution of is and zero in the plural and second person singular also raises questions.

The versions of the narratives published by Rawick in 1977/79 are

PERSON/NUMBER DISTRIBUTION OF THE PRESENT TENSE OF BE IN THIRTEEN WPA NARRATIVES FROM RAWICK 1972 AND 1977/79 AND THIRTEEN TAPED NARRATIVES OF FORMER SLAVES

	1st Singular				3rd Singular					Plural & 2nd Singular			
	am	is	∅	are	be	am	is	∅	are	be	am	is	∅	are	be
Taped Narratives*	85 (94%)	0	3 (3%)	0	2 (2%)	0	159 (88%)	22 (12%)	0	0	0	18 (19%)	55 (59%)	17 (18%)	4 (4%)
Rawick 1972	1 (4%)	18 (75%)	5 (21%)	0	0	18 (20%)	42 (48%)	28 (32%)	0	0	2 (4%)	33 (66%)	11 (22%)	2 (4%)	2 (4%)
Rawick 1977/79	11 (28%)	19 (49%)	8 (21%)	0	1 (3%)	1 (1%)	54 (61%)	32 (36%)	1 (1%)	1 (1%)	0	33 (62%)	11 (21%)	8 (15%)	1 (2%)

*Audited and analyzed in collaboration with Guy Bailey

Table 3

Taped Interviews

Wallace Quarterman. Recorded at Frederica, Georgia, 1935.
Uncle Billy McCrea. Recorded at Jasper, Texas, 1940.
Uncle Bob Ledbetter. Recorded at Oil City, Louisiana, 1940.
Irene Williams. Recorded at Rome, Mississippi, 1940.
Joe McDonald. Recorded at Livingston, Alabama, 1940.
Isom Moseley. Recorded at Gee's Bend, Alabama, 1941.
Alice Gaston. Recorded at Gee's Bend, Alabama, 1941.
Laura Smalley. Recorded at Hempstead, Texas, 1941.
Aunt Harriet Smith. Recorded at Hempstead, Texas, 1941.
Mr. Johnson. Recorded at Mound Bayou, Mississippi, 1942.
Fountain Hughes. Recorded at Baltimore, Maryland, 1949.
Celia Black. Recorded at Tyler, Texas, 1974.
Charlie Smith. Recorded at Bartow, Florida, 1975.

Interviews in Rawick 1972 and 1977/79

Rev. W. B. Allen, Georgia.
Charity Anderson, Alabama.
Henry Barnes, Alabama.
Harriet Barret, Texas.
Harrison Beckett, Texas.
James Bolton, Oklahoma.
Lewis Bonner, Oklahoma.
Rachel Bradley, Arkansas.
Fannie Brown, Texas.
Tom Chisolm, South Carolina.
Charlie Davenport, Mississippi.
Lizzie Davis, South Carolina.
Prince Johnson, Mississippi.

probably more reliable than the versions published in 1972. However, neither of these collections should be considered anything approaching verbatim records of speech. As Jeutonne Brewer has said, while calling the slave narratives "an important source of information about the form of BE grammar in the 1930s," they should not be considered the "fifth avenue" that Marion Starling claimed them to be. As Brewer goes on to say, "if they are a fifth avenue, they are a cobblestone fifth avenue, without street lights or traffic police during a five o'clock rush hour" (1980, p. 52). Returning to my earlier quotation from Fasold's review of Dillard, "it is valid for Dillard to use literary sources to support the broad outlines of his historical hypothesis, but not to rely on them too heavily for detail" (1975, p. 201), I suggest that the same can be said for the use of the WPA narratives. Just as with spoken language reflected in fiction, records of this kind may provide some general insights into the language of the informants. However, the limitations of such sources must be taken into consideration. Even in the best of circumstances it is difficult for dialectal research to be completely accurate. In order for dialectologists to maintain credibility, it is necessary that more attention be given to the reliability of their data.

Notes

[1] The name Works Progress Administration was changed on July 1, 1939, to Work Projects Administration.

[2] Typescripts of these tapes are currently being edited by Bailey, Maynor, and Patricia Cukor-Avila for publication by John Benjamins as part of the Creole Language Library Series.

References

Bailey, Guy, and Maynor, Natalie. (1985) The present tense of be in Southern black folk speech. American Speech, 60, 195-213.
‾‾‾‾‾‾. (1987) The divergence controversy. Paper presented to the Southeastern Conference on Linguistics, Washington, D.C. Botkin, B.A., ed. (1945) Lay My Burden Down: A Folk History of Slavery. Chicago: University of Chicago Press.
Brewer, Jeutonne P. (1979) Nonagreeing am and invariant be in early black English. The SECOL Bulletin, 3, 81-100.
‾‾‾‾‾‾. (1980) The WPA slave narratives as linguistic data. Orbis, 29, 30-54.
Eliason, Norman E. (1956) Tarheel Talk. Chapel Hill: University of North Carolina.
Fasold, Ralph. (1975) Review of J. L. Dillards's Black English. Language in Society, 4, 198-221.
Kurath, Hans, et al., eds. (1939-43) The Linguistic Atlas of New England. 3 vols. Providence, R.I.: Brown University Press.
Rawick, George, ed. (1972) The American Slave: A Composite Autobiography. 19 vols. (1977) Supplemental Series 1. 12 vols. (1979) Supplemental Series 2. 10 vols. Westport, CT: Greenwood Press.
Walker, Alice. (1982) The Color Purple. New York: Harcourt Brace Jovanovich.
Weaver, Constance. (1970) Analyzing literary representations of recent northern urban Negro speech: a technique with application to three books. East Lansing: Michigan State University dissertation.
Wolfram, Walt. (1973) Review of J.L. Dillard's Black English. Language, 49, 670-79.
Yetman, Norman R. (1967) The background of the slave narrative collection. American Quarterly, 19, 534-53.
‾‾‾‾‾‾, ed. (1970) Life Under the "Peculiar Institution": Selections from the Slave Narrative Collection. New York: Holt, Rinehart and Winston.

Diachronic Interlinguistic Contact as Reflected in the Typological Structure of Today's Acadian Fishermen's Terminology

ROSE MARY BABITCH
Université de Moncton

ABSTRACT

The lobster-fishing terminology of Acadian fishermen on Miscou and Lamèque Islands in northeast New Brunswick is of French, English, Dutch and Acadian typologies. It was analysed quantitatively by the Séguyian dialectometric method, adapted by incorporating a proximity evaluation as well as cluster analysis and correspondence procedures.

INTRODUCTION

The data analysed in this paper is the lobster-fishing terminology of Acadian fishermen living on Miscou and Lamèque Islands situated in northeastern New Brunswick (map Annex 1). The terminology consists of a cumulation of terms which the fishermen obtained by incorporating:
- metropolitan French fishing terms;
- English fishing terms, including terms used by New England fishermen in the 19th century;
- two Dutch nautical terms which were not retained in the dialectometric analysis of the terminology because of insufficient occurrences and;
- Acadian terms which are word formations based on derivations, compounding and phonetic change of both French and English terms for example, the Acadian equivalent for the English compound standing buoy is stand "bouille".

Of the two islands, Lamèque is the larger. It is 22 miles long and 10 miles wide with one coastline bordering the Bay of Chaleur and the other the Gulf of St. Lawrence. Thirteen communities with a population of 9000 people entirely French speaking except for a few English families, are situated along each coast. In contrast to Lamèque Island, Miscou is 8.5 miles long and 4.5 miles wide. The Island is also bounded by the Bay of Chaleur and the Gulf of St. Lawrence, and is separated from Lamèque Island by Miscou Harbour. Francophones and anglophones constitute the population of 810 people living on the island. The table in annex 3 shows in percent, the distribution of French and English presently spoken in each community. Most of the fishermen, both Acadian and English, have their fishing boats docked at the main wharf which is Miscou Harbour.

Permanent settlement of both islands occurred during the late 18th and the beginning of the 19th centuries according to Hughes (1978, p. 4). A number of Acadians who were refugees of the 1755 expulsion from ancient Acadia which is known today as the province of Nova Scotia, some French Canadians from Quebec and Norman French from Gaspé, settled on Miscou Island and along the Bay of Chaleur coast of Lamèque Island. Immigrants from the British Isles, some from Scotland, also settled on Miscou and Lamèque Islands in communities apart from the French settlements. The Gulf of St. Lawrence coast of Lamèque Island was settled totally by French-speaking fishermen in the latter half of the 19th century.

English terms to be found in today's Acadian fishermen's terminology therefore, do not come from an interlinguistic contact of the first British and Acadian settlers. It is hypothesized that the presence of some English terms come from an interlinguistic contact of Acadians with New England fishermen. An attempt to verify this hypothesis will be made firstly, by obtaining the typological structure of the terminology by means of correspondence procedures and then correlating the structure with plausible interlinguistic contacts with New England as well as metropolitan French commercial fishermen and secondly, by using individual isoglosses to show the geographic spread of two New England terms throughout both islands.

METHOD

Thirteen fishing wharfs used by the lobster fishermen of Lamèque Island, and the main wharf used by the fishermen of the five communities of Miscou Island, constitute the geo-linguistic space studied in this paper (map Annex 2). The number of fishermen interviewed on both islands, 132 in the 1981-82 surveys, constitutes about 60% of the population of lobster fishermen in the age group 20 to 60 years and over owning their fishing boat and gear. The questionnaire, the same for both islands was designed and interviews conducted, to elicit the term which a fisherman used to name the parts of a lobster-fishing rig. The informants' responses on Miscou Island were noted phonetically during the interviews, while those on Lamèque were recorded and then transcribed after the survey. A research team comprising of an analyst, a computer programmer and myself then undertook to adapt Séguy's dialectometry in the analysis of the terminology.

After the raw data had been filtered, 26 significant terms and their variables were retained for a study of the lexical, typological and morpho-syntactic parameters. The data was then coded for computer processing. The Hamming method was used to measure the linguistic distance between informants on one hand and between fishing localities on the other. To analyze the typological parameter, twelve terms and their variables were retained. These were coded according to their typologies as shown in the table annex 4A. The informants' responses were then compared according to the Hamming method which evaluates a certain degree of ressemblance between two objects in a grill structure as shown in annex 4B.

The grill structure shows that a fisherman may ennunciate more than one term while another might not even have a term to designate the same object. Therefore, the comparison obtained in the grill structure is an approximate and not a precise evaluation. The similarities and differences obtained, were then coded 0 or 1, thus dissociating the concept of distanciation from that of differentiation. A computer program permitted the linguistic comparisons to be cumulated in matrix form. The next step was to synthesize the linguistic comparisons so that they become an evaluation of a typological degree of similarity and difference obtained from the linguistic comparisons. It is at this point that Eric Lebrun, the analyst, chose to work with an evaluation of proximity instead of the CHI-2 distributional distance used by Dennis Philps in his doctorat d'état thesis (1985).

A proximity degree for each two fishermen was obtained by subtracting their total number of differences from their total number of similarities. After a computer program had operated the calculation, it was possible to know the percentage of proximity of fishermen fishing from the same wharf as well as the difference for example between fisherman R21 of Pigeon Hill, and fisherman F3 from Petite Lamèque.

To get the typological structure of the terminology for both islands, it was necessary first, to get the amalgamated proximity degree for each locality. This was obtained by calculating the mean proximity degree of the fishermen in a locality, and then constructing a histogram (Annex 5). The histogram contains information about the distributional occurrences of inter-locality proximity degrees. The pointed line represents the mean deviation and the unbroken line represents the mean. Those localities where the proximity level is greater than the mean deviation for example, in the case of locality M where the proximity level MM is situated to the right of the pointed line, are considered as homogeneous groups with regards to our typological study. Those localities whose proximity level is situated between the mean and the mean deviation, are considered as having a sufficiently significant proximity level but are not very homogeneous. No locality, in the study, has an insufficient proximity level. The structure defined by the inter-locality proximity tables resulting from the computerized calculation is represented by two diagrams, a tree diagram and a cluster diagram (Annex 6, 7). The tree diagram permits a quantitative study of inter-locality relationships, whereas the cluster diagram has the advantage of permitting the visualization of the same relationships in geographic space. To obtain a more meaningful interpretation of the structure, information represented in the tree diagram was converted into a table giving the profile of the typological responses, that is to say, the distribution of a variable and its occurrences in each locality (Annex 8).

INTERPRETATION OF THE STRUCTURE

The tree diagram (Annex 6) shows that the typological structure divides Miscou and Lamèque Islands into two major opposing groups. Localities G, H,

L, M, N, P, and R, form a homogeneous group of 90% and over similarity. To it are attached at a rather low degree (65-70%), the group E, F on one hand and K on the other. Localities A, B, C, D, form an opposing group: A, B on one hand, and C, D on the other. Each sub group being more than 60%, is therefore rather homogeneous.

The areal structure represented by the cluster groupings (Annex 7), suggests that localities C and D constitute the boundary separating the two major groups. Correlation of the typological profile (Annex 8) with the groupings either in annex 6 or annex 7, shows that localities B, C, D, constitute a transitional zone. The profile table (Annex 8), indicates that there is a gradient from a significant to a less significant use of English terminology: A 44%, B; C; D 35-40%, while for the rest of Lamèque Island, use of English terms is about 25% except for localities K (33%) and E (17%). The gradient for the use of French terms on the other hand is from less significant to significant: A 40%, B; C; D 53%, and about 67% for the rest of Lamèque Island. The use of Acadian terms for both islands averages 17-18%. The variation of this percentage is not significant enough to influence the locality group formations.

CORRELATION OF THE TYPOLOGICAL STRUCTURE WITH DIACHRONIC ACADIAN INTERLINGUISTIC CONTACTS

Two metropolitan French fishing terms, hallope; tangon, and two English terms jig; snood which were traced as being part of New England 19th century fishing terminology, led to postulate an Acadian interlinguistic contact with metropolitan French and New England commercial fishermen. The two French terms which are part of the Lamèque fishermen's terminology, are not included in the terminology of the Miscou Island fishermen. As equivalents for the two French terms, the fishermen of Miscou Island use the English terms jig and snood.

Individual isoglosses indicating the transitional zone of the terms jig; snood (Annex 9), corroborate the cluster groupings (Annex 7) in showing that the linguistic boundary is not Miscou Island where an English-French population still exists, but that it includes localities Pte. Rivière-de-l'île and Ste. Cécile on Lamèque Island (Annex 9 localities 3, 4). The isogloss for the term snood is fragmented (Annex 9 T2) in that it cuts off at locality 4, is replaced by the term hallope as shown in the table annex 10A, and then reappears at locality 9 (Annex 9 T3) after which, it is again replaced for the most part by the term hallope (Annex 10A). The isogloss for the term jig on the other hand cuts off at locality 3 (Annex 9 T1), and is replaced by the term tangon throughout the rest of Lamèque Island as shown in the table annex 10B. The fact that there is a 100% usage of the terms jig and snood on Miscou Island (Annex 10 A, B), makes plausible the hypothesis of an interlinguistic contact of Miscou fishermen with New England commercial fishermen in the 19th century.

English terms to be found in the Acadian fishermen's terminology of both islands form two sets. The terms in Set 1 are used to name the different parts of a lobster trap, while those in Set 2 designate the different parts of the lobster gear used in submerging the traps into the sea. Chronological classification showed that the terms forming Set 1 date back to the latter half of the 19th century whereas two terms in Set 2 date back to the first part of the 19th century. The terms in Set 2 for the most part influence the formation of the locality groupings represented both in the tree and the cluster diagrams (Annex 6, 7). The English terms jig; snood and the French terms tangon; hallope, belong to this set.

SET 1 - ENGLISH CORE TERMS

English terms designating the parts of a lobster trap form a core terminology which is used today by the fishermen of both islands. The terms date to the last quarter of the 19th century which marks the establishment of lobster fishing as a complementary industry to cod fishing in Atlantic Canada. It was during this period that anglophone companies set up fish shops on both islands. Material was supplied by the companies and traps were built by the fishermen at the shops before the fishing season began. This is where the Acadian fishermen learned English terms such as palings, crosspiece and bow which designate the different parts of a lobster trap. The construction of a lobster trap has not changed significantly since the time it was introduced. This explains why this set of terms forms a core terminology.

SET 2 - ENGLISH TERMS JIG - SNOOD

As documented by Innis (1954, p. 223), New Englanders traded and fished for cod and mackerel in the Gulf of St. Lawrence in the first part of the 19th century. Acadians at this time in history consisted of refugees who had migrated from Nova Scotia and had changed their occupation from farming to fishing, but had not as yet stabilized into forming permanent settlements. The fishermen, some of whom lived on Miscou Island, sold their cod to the Anglo-Norman Jersey firm Charles Robin and Company which used either French or English as needed in all business transactions. The company which specialized in cod, had a fishing station at Paspébiac in Quebec. Boats were sent to collect cod at Miscou Island.

New England fishermen fished for mackerel as well as for cod in the same waters as the Acadians who fished mainly for cod. The Acadians must have observed and were curious about the lure the New Englanders called jig. The jig was used to fish mackerel as stated in McFarland (1911, p. 315). The cod was caught by using a hand-line to which were attached a smaller line called snood and a hook. The Acadians traded the mackerel they caught with the New Englanders. During the barter and plausible linguistic exchange, the Acadians could have picked up the terms jig and snood. This is supported by the fact that the terms have been retained for the most part on Miscou Island (Annex 10 A, B). Jig today is used to designate the gear used to submerge traps into the sea, while snood designates the rope used to attach a trap to the mainline.

SET 2 - FRENCH TERMS   TANGON - HALLOPE

According to the dictionary Paul Robert (1964), tangon has its origin either in an Old-French nautical term, or in a Middle Dutch term tange which referred to a long mobile pole extending horizontally from the exterior part of a sailing vessel. In today's lobster-fishing terminology, tangon refers to a long wooden pole to which a mainline with traps is attached. It is the equivalent of the English term jig. According to Morandière (1962, vol. 1, p. 183), the term hallope appeared in French cod-fishing terminology about 1753. It referred to a net used to fish cod. In today's lobster-fishing terminology, hallope is the equivalent of the English snood, and so does not refer to a net as in the 18th century, but rather to a rope.

That the terms hallope and tangon were borrowed from the metropolitan French fishermen is supported by the fact that the two terms are mentioned by Charles de la Morandière (1962, vol. 3, p. 1111) in his history of the French cod-fishing in Atlantic Canada. Miscou Island was a French fishing station at various intervals throughout the 17th century; furthurmore, there was a continued presence of metropolitan French fishermen in Nova Scotia in the first part of the 18th century and yet, contact of colonial Acadians with the French fishermen is sparsely documented. Clark (1968, p. 248), mentions that Acadians worked as extra hands both for French and New England fishermen.

At the beginning of the 18th century, some metropolitan French fishermen preferred to fish in the Bay of Chaleur and the Gulf of St. Lawrence where they fished until Canada was conquered by England in 1763. Although it is not supported by documents, Acadian refugees who had migrated from Nova Scotia to the area where the French fished, undoubtedly worked as extra hands for them and also traded their dry cod. Contact with the French fishermen safeguarded the Acadians' knowledge of French fishing terms. This knowledge was then transmitted into the 20th century by a continued use of Acadian speech in connection with their trade. This was made possible through contact with first, the Jersey firm Charles Robin and Company in the 18th century, and then by the establishment of other Jersey fish companies on Miscou and Lamèque Islands in the 19th century which employed the Acadians with whom the companies' staff communicated in French.

CONCLUSION

A synchronic analysis effected by an adaptation of the Séguy-Philps dialectometric method revealed a typological structure which localized geographically, and determined the English-French usage boundary of Acadian fishermen's lobster-fishing terminology. Diachronic analysis permitted to define the boundary in relation to hypothesized Acadian interlinguistic contacts with both metropolitan French and New England commercial fishermen.

Individual isoglosses showing the geographic spread of two English terms and the transition zones to the use of French terms, furnished supportive evidence of Acadian fishermen's borrowings of both New England and metropolitan French fishing terms.

REFERENCES

Babitch, R. M. (1984). "The Georgraphic Spread and Transition Areas of Lexical Variations in the Lobster-fishing Terminology on Miscou and Lamèque Islands," Paper presented at the seventh annual meeting of the Atlantic Provinces Linguistic Association. Moncton, N. B.: Université de Moncton.

Clark, Andrew Hill. (1968). Acadia the Geography of Early Nova Scotia. Madison, Wisconsin: The University of Wisconsin Press.

Innis, Harold, A. (1954). The Cod Fisheries. Toronto: University of Toronto Press.

Haines, Cederic, L. (1979). "The Acadian Settlement of Northeastern New Brunswick: 1755-1826," M. A. Thesis. Fredericton: University of New Brunswick, microfilm.

Hughes, Gary. (1978). Two Islands, Miscou and Lamèque and Their State of Bondage 1849-1861. A New Brunswick Museum Publication.

McFarland, Raymond. (1911). A History of New England Fisheries. N. Y.: D. Appleton and Company.

Morandière, Charles. (1962). Histoire de la Pêche Française de la Morue Dans l'Amérique Septentrionale. Tomes I, III. Paris: Maisonneuve et La Rose.

Oxford Dictionary on Historical Principles. (1933). Oxford: Clarendon Press.

Philps, D. (1985). "Atlas Dialectométrique des Pyrénées Centrales," thèse pour le doctorat d'état ès lettres et sciences humaines. Toulouse: Université de Toulouse - Le Mirail, 2 tomes.

Robert, Paul. (1964). Dictionnaire de la langue française. Paris: Société du Nouveau Littré.

Seguy, J. (1973). "La dialectométrie dans l'Atlas Linguistique de la Gascogne," in Revue de Linguistique Romane. Strasbourg:37.1-24

Van Wijvan, Franck. (1912). <u>Etymologisch Woordenbock der Nederlandshe</u>. La Haye: Martinus Nijhoff.

Annex 1

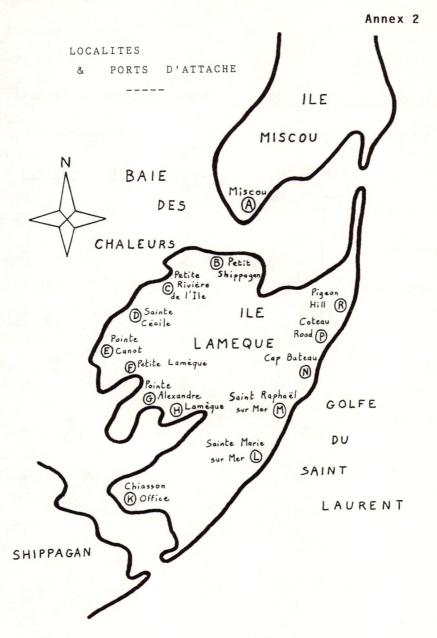

Annex 3

Languages in % spoken in each community of Miscou Island

Community	Population	French	English
Miscou Harbour		50%	50%
Miscou Centre	760	99%	1%
Miscou Plains		98%	2%
Miscou Light		1%	99%
Wilson's Point	50	10%	90%

Typological Coding

Annexe 4A

Term	Typology	Code
taquet	French	Z
tire d'char	Acadian	Y
clip	English	X
no term	—	L

Annex 4B

Grill Structure

Occurrences of Terms
Coded Typologically

	1	2	3	4
Informant A	Z	X	ZY	L
Informant B	Z	ZX	Y	Z
Similarity	Yes	Yes	Yes	No
Difference	No	Yes	Yes	Yes

Annex 6

STRUCTURE TYPOLOGIQUE

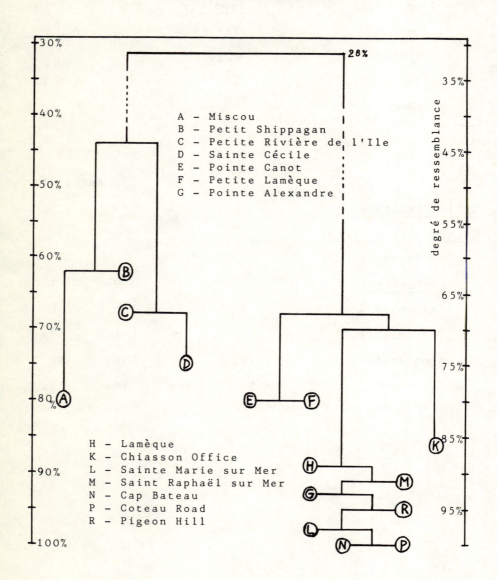

Methods in Dialectology

Annex 5

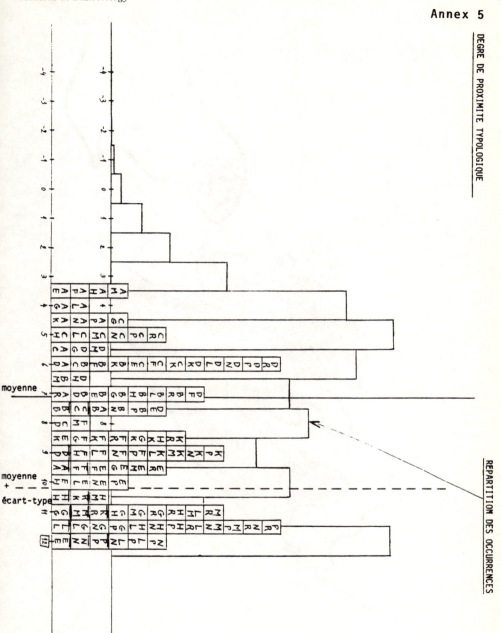

REGROUPEMENTS TYPOLOGIQUES

Annex 7

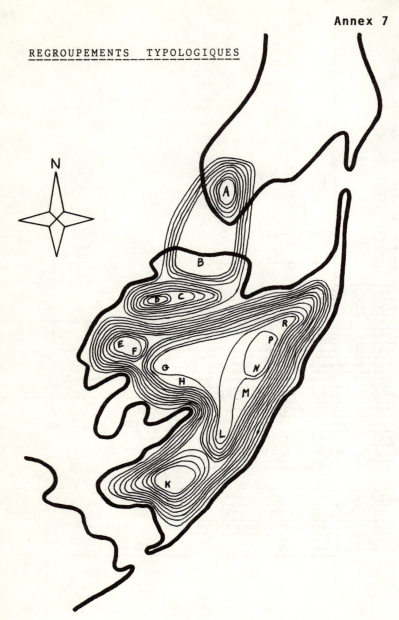

Annex 8

PROFIL MOYEN

TYPOLOGIQUE (%)

	AN. (X)	AC. (Y)	FR. (Z)
A	44	20	40
B	40	18	52
C	40	16	54
D	36	21	54
E	17	17	58
F	27	17	72
G	29	17	67
H	22	17	69
K	33	11	67
L	24	17	68
M	24	18	68
N	25	17	67
P	25	17	67
R	26	17	65

Annex 9

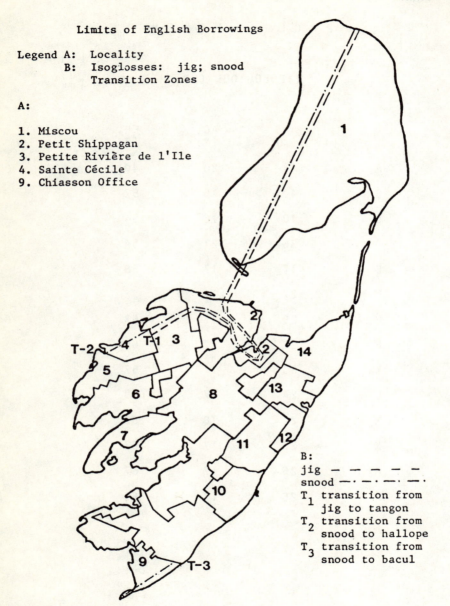

Limits of English Borrowings

Legend A: Locality
B: Isoglosses: jig; snood
   Transition Zones

A:

1. Miscou
2. Petit Shippagan
3. Petite Rivière de l'Ile
4. Sainte Cécile
9. Chiasson Office

B:
jig — — — — —
snood —·—·—·—
T_1 transition from jig to tangon
T_2 transition from snood to hallope
T_3 transition from snood to bacul

Annex 10A

Term:	Locality	% using Term & V.	% Interviewed
snood	1	100	80
	2	100	66.66
	3	100	62.50
	4	66.66	60
	9	58.33	66.66
Variants:			
snood or hallope	4	33.33	60
snood or cable	9	16.66	60
snood or bacul	9	8.33	60
bride	9	8.33	60
snood or bride	9	8.33	60
hallope	5	100	100
	6	100	60
	7	100	66.66
	3	100	60
	9	100	66.66
	10	100	64.28
	11	100	61.53
	12	87.50	61.53
	13	100	100
	14	100	59.63
towline	12	12.50	61.53

Annex 10B

Term:	Locality	% Using Term & V.	% Interviewed
jig	1	100	80
	2	33.33	66.66
Variants:			
jig or tangon	2	33.33	66.66
	3	10	62.50
tangon	2	33.33	66.66
	3	90	62.50
	4	100	60
	5	100	100
	6	100	60
	7	100	66.66
	8	100	60
	9	100	60
	10	100	64.28
	11	100	61.53
	12	100	61.53
	13	100	100
	14	100	59.09

Verb Analysis of the Linguistic Atlas of the North Central States: A Case Study in Preliminary Analysis of a Large Data Set

MICHAEL D. LINN and RONALD R. REGAL
University of Minnesota, Duluth, USA

This paper reports work in progress on the statistical methods for the volume on the verb analysis of the Linguistics Atlas of the North Central States (LANCS). Of the regional linguistic surveys in the United States, LANCS has had a particularly complicated history. Field work began with a preliminary survey of Michigan and Indiana under the direction of Albert H. Marckwardt in the summer of 1938. Work in Ohio, Illinois, Kentucky, and Wisconsin followed. Only in Wisconsin was the field work completed before the United States entered World War II. Field work was resumed in 1948 and completed in 1977. The North Central archives are comprised of 564 field records. Because of incomplete records, 543 records are being used for this analysis. Only the 128 questions on grammatical forms are used here. The work reported here covers the preliminary stages in the analysis. These stages include coding the data, checking the data, producing summary tables, screening for the more interesting questions and looking for patterns which further analysis will refine.

DATA CODING

The data had already been collected by twenty-six field workers from 1938 to 1977. However to be machine read, the data needed to be coded. This coding presented problems. First of all, it was expensive, and second, the records at that time were housed at the University of Chicago. Fortunately, Virginia McDavid graciously came to our aid. She agreed to cover the cost of key punching and coding the forms, if we would work out the format. However, before she could begin transcribing the material, some decisions had to be made. First what should be done with multiple answers to the same question? Since there were very few questions that had more than two responses, we decided to limit the coded responses to two. Thus every question was assigned two columns in the coding format, one for each response. If a question had only one response, the first column was left blank, but if a question had two responses, the appropriate number was entered respectively in each column. The education, age, sex, race, year of birth, date of recording, and the longitude and the latitude of the community were coded for each informant. The data coding stage needs to be coordinated with the keypunching. The keypunching personnel need to be contacted early to agree on a coding form which can be keypunched from easily and accurately. The keypunching should be verified, that is keypunched twice.

DATA CHECKING

Once the data have been coded into a computer, it is tempting to charge into the analysis, especially since the coding probably took longer than expected for one reason or another. However, the data need to be checked and cleaned up before any analyses are done. With large data bases, it becomes particularly important to check the accuracy of entering the data into the computer. Even with verification there can be errors in either coding or keypunching. A good first step is to read the data into the computer and print the data in an easy to read format. Hard copy listings of the data should be made and saved for the project's archives. Original records for several people should be compared to the printed output. Any changes that are made to the data base need to be documented. Editing should be done on a copy of the original files in order to protect against accidental file obliteration and to keep the documentation intact. For documentation one should keep notes of what steps are taken and what changes are made to the data files. These notes are invaluable in redoing the steps if necessary and in documenting. Without proper notes, it is hard enough to remember what one did the day before, let alone a year ago. For the project the initial reading of the coded files and the creation of more convenient files were done with a simple FORTRAN program. Several coding errors were caught, documented and fixed at this stage.

The first computer runs after initial listings of the files were checks for consistencies of the data with known constraints. Each question has an allowable range of coded answers. Each answer by each person should be checked to assure that the answer is a legal code for that question. This can be handled by writing special purpose programs, i.e. FORTRAN programs, or by utilizing software packages, SAS or S. This part of the project and the analysis described later were handled conveniently with the Bell Laboratories statistical package S (Becker and Chambers, 1984). The files created by the FORTRAN programs were read by S to create S data structures. The answers were read into data sets FIRST and SECOND. FIRST is a 128 × 543 matrix with the answers for the 128 questions and 543 informants. FIRST contains the unique response if the response is unique and one of the dual responses if two responses were elicited. SECOND contains the other answer if two answers were recorded. When two responses were elicited, there is no precedence implied between FIRST and SECOND. A zero is recorded in FIRST if no responses were coded for that question. A zero is coded for SECOND if no second response was recorded. Unfortunately, we do not know if a question is unanswered because (1) the informant had no vocabulary item to match the question or (2) the field worker failed to try to elicit a response to the question. In future interviews this distinction should be coded explicitly.

Other S data sets were created as 543 long vectors for the informants' state, community, informant ID within the community (A, B, etc.), age, sex, race, latitude and longitude. Vector INFCODE was created by encoding together the informants' state, community and ID codes. A vector CODELIMIT 128 long was created for the maximum possible allowable code for each question. To record which FIRST answers out of bounds was accomplished by the S command

for (ques in 1: 128){
print (encode ("question", ques))
Print (infcode [first [ques,] > codelimit[ques]])

First [ques,] is the ques-th row of the matrix FIRST. The square brackets [] indicate subsets of the data sets. There are other methods that can be used, but it is important to develop a system where coding errors can be investigated. Another inconsistency check was to look for answers where FIRST = 0 and SECOND > 0. Latitudes and longitudes were checked by plotting the points coded by state number. The plotting was handled with S also. Visual inspection of the map indicated informants with incorrectly coded locations, leading to a point falling outside the state boundary. The identity function in S allowed us to plot the points on a graphics terminal and then use the cursor hairs or mouse to display the informant codes for problem points. Obvious problems with latitudes could be spotted by looking at a stem-and-leaf diagram of the latitudes and noticing that latitudes below 36 were obviously out of place. The corresponding informant codes could be identified with the S command infcode [lat < 36].

There are still possibly latitudes or longitudes coded incorrectly but still falling within the correct state boudaries. Verified keypunching would help keep these errors down but will not catch errors from original coding mistakes. At least catching the gross mistakes will eliminate the problems which have a drastic effect on the analysis to be run later. For example, later we use the determinant of the variance–covariance matrix of latitudes and longitudes as a measure for clustering. Since we used standard non-robust estimators for variance and covariance, a single extremely aberrant latitude could sabotage the estimate. At least assuming that the locations are within the correct state boundaries protects the analysis from such gross coding errors.

SUMMARY TABLES AND STATISTICS

After cleaning up the data, we produced summary tables and statistics for future reference and benchmarks. Useful statistics included the fact that about 10% of the questions answered had dual responses. Hence multiple responses should not be ignored in the analysis. Overall, 24% of the possible responses are missing and every question had some missing responses. Hence missing data is a major concern for the analysis.

INFORMANT CLASSIFICATION

Classification by Sex

As the Table 1, Informants Classified by Sex, demonstrates, there are considerably more male than female informants in LANCS in every state.

Table 1
Informants Classified By Sex

State	Number			Percent	
	Males	Females		Males	Females
Wisconsin	35	14		71	29
Michigan	52	19		73	27
Illinois	84	49		63	37
Indiana	53	28		65	35
Ohio	82	20		80	20
Kentucky	<u>73</u>	<u>19</u>		<u>79</u>	<u>21</u>
Total	379	149	Average	72	28

The largest variation by sex is in Ohio with 80% being male and the smallest in Illinois with only 63% being male. Because in the Linguistic

Atlas of the Upper Midwest, "grammatical features are more significant as social indicators than as regional determiners and that the Upper Midwest is fairly homogenous as to grammatical features" the grammatical features will be examined for gender differences (Linn and Regal, p. 260).

As Table 2 (Informants Classified by Type) illustrates, there are considerable differences in the number and percentages of Type I, II, and III informants in the North Central States. As in the other Atlas studies, Type I informants have the least amount of schooling, usually eighth grade or less; Type II the next least amount, generally less than high school; and Type III has the most schooling, usually a high school diploma and often college, some even being graduated from college. In addition, Type I informants are the oldest and Type III the youngest.

Table 2
Informants Classified By Type

	Number			Percent		
	Type I	Type II	Type III	Type I	Type II	Type III
Wisconsin	31	19	02	60	37	04
Michigan	31	32	09	43	44	13
Illinois	72	45	17	54	34	13
Indiana	36	37	08	44	46	10
Ohio	48	44	10	46	43	10
Kentucky	<u>55</u>	<u>29</u>	<u>12</u>	<u>57</u>	<u>30</u>	<u>12</u>
Total	273	206	58	51	38	11

Multivariate statistics will be used to check for the influence of social type. With over half (fifty-one percent) of all the informants being Type I informants, some bias is likely. Some variation between the states might be due to distribution of informant type with Michigan and Indiana having more Type II informants than Type I informants while the other states have more Type I informants. Map 1 plots the informants by type with 1 representing Type I, 2 representing Type II, and 3 representing Type III.

Methods in Dialectology

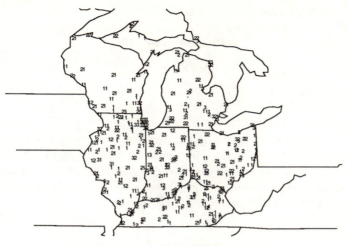

Map 1. Informant Type

Response Counts for Each Question

A very useful set of tables was the counts of how many responses were given for each possible answer. Chart 1 shows the results for the first five questions.

Chart 1
Summary of Responses
for Questions 1-5

Question 1: At Once
Answer   1   2
                 406   17

Question 2: Rise
Answer   1   2   3   4   5   6   7   8
                 293   17   37   18   16   99   68   3

Question 3: Half Past
Answer   1   2   3
                 427   37   163

Question 4:   Quarter Of
Answer   1   2   3   4   5
              113   219   164   52   2

Question 5:   Blow
Answer   1   2   3   4
              331   155   6   1

Thus for Question 1 ([all] at once), there were 406 responses for answer 1 ([all] at once), and 17 responses for answer 2 ([all] to once). By listing the responses in this manner, one can also determine if further investigation of an answer is worth pursuing. The investigator can set the lower limits for what he feels is a useable number of responses.

FINDING SIGNIFICANT RESPONSES

In the verb analysis of the North Central States, there were 128 questions and 581 different answers. With such a large number of different answers, it was necessary to find a method of identifying the interesting answers. We did this by screening for answers where informants with the same answer to a given question fall within a small area as compared to the total area. We chose to do this by finding answers where the informants had a small generalized variance of their positions, as defined by latitude and longitude. The variance of the bivariate latitudes and longitudes of particular informants is measured by their variance–covariance matrix. The generalized variance is the determinant of the variance–covariance matrix, $|S|$. The measure of similarity in the locations was defined to be

$$-\frac{\sqrt{N}}{2}\left\{\ln[|S_1|/|S|] - \ln\left[\frac{(N-2)(N-3)}{(N-1)(N-1)}\right]\right\}$$

where

S_1 = Variance–covariance matrix for the subset of informants with given response.

S = Variance–covariance matrix for all the positions which answered the question.

N = the number of people giving the answer.

In essence what this formula does is looks at

$$\frac{\ln(|S_1|/|S|) - \text{"expected value"}}{\text{"standard deviation"}}$$

The "expected value" and the "standard deviation" are actually approximations to the asymmetric distribution when the data are multivariant normal (Anderson, 1958). This statistic will be large if the informants giving a particular response are distributed around a point such as a city or along a line such as a linear migration path or a river. Initially we tried looking just at $\ln(|S_1|/|S|)$, but some responses given by a small number of informants were considered to be more clustered than we thought appropriate. The formula given above adjusts for the number of informants in the proposed cluster. The adjustment is not technically exact since the clustered informants' location are part of the finite population of informants in the study, but the formulas from asymmetric normal theory at least give a reasonable adjustment.

Because some informants responded with two answers and some responded with only one answer, it was felt that a single answer should be given more weight than one when an informant gave two responses. To do this in S_1, a point was counted twice if a unique answer were given and once if a nonunique answer were given. For $\underline{S}$ each point was counted once. The result of these calculations are shown in Chart 2 where the larger the number, the greater the similarity.

Chart 2
Listing of Informants' Similarity for Questions 1-4

Question No.	Answer No.	Similarity Value
1	1	0.269
1	2	-0.651
2	1	0.622
2	2	-0.213
2	3	<u>4.485</u>
2	4	0.237
2	5	<u>6.966</u>
2	6	-0.363
2	7	-1.459
3	1	-0.175
3	2	0.828
3	3	1.684
4	1	2.483
4	2	-0.492
4	3	<u>6.832</u>
4	4	<u>3.073</u>

In this chart, only answers 3 and 5 for question 2 (<u>raised</u> and <u>riz</u>) for the preterite of <u>rise</u> and answers 3 and 4 for question 4 (<u>till</u> and <u>forty-five</u>) for (<u>quarter of</u>) have similarities large enough to be considered further in the analysis. Thus in these four questions, ten answers can be eliminated as being not interesting. In the corpus for verb analysis, the greatest geographical similarity is shown in Question 68 (the preterite of <u>sit</u>), answer number 4 (<u>sot</u>). To mark the response, a "*" is used if it is a unique response for that informant, and a "+" is used if it is not a unique response. As the Map 2 shows, only eight informants gave this response, but they are clustered around Southeastern Kentucky and three of these informants gave no other response. Thus the small number is overridden by the tightness of the cluster. On these maps, informants that gave a response to this question other than the one being analyzed are marked on the map by a dot. This was done to show the area where this question was asked and the number of informants responding to it with some response. Because of the time taken to collect the material, all questions were not elicited in all areas.

Methods in Dialectology 147

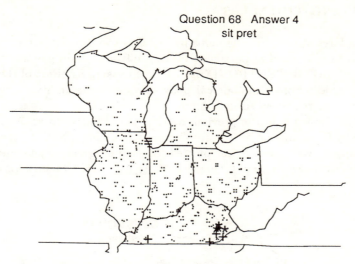

Map 2. Sot As Preterite of Sit

Map 3, Question 18 (<u>Shafts</u>), Answer 4 (<u>fills</u>) shows a wider geographical pattern with a fairly tight cluster. The value was 5.19 as compared to 9.72 for Question 68, Answer 4.

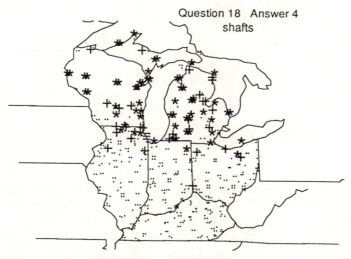

Map 3. Fills for Shafts

PLOTTING THE MAPS

In a large study, drawing maps by hands is too time consuming to allow extensive exploration of patterns. Writing software to do plotting using for example PLOT10 TEKTRONIX is also time consuming. Part of the success of this project from a methodical point of view is the ability to draw high quality maps relatively easily with S.

All of the maps in the previous section were plotted on an Apple Laser Writer by S running on an Encore Computer running UNIX. In these maps each (up to two) response was plotted for each informant by longitude and latitude, as shown in Map 4, Question 18, shafts. When two responses come

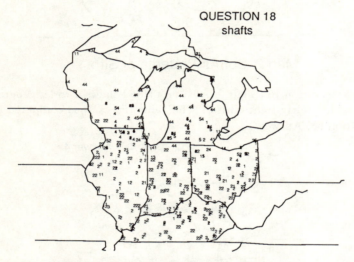

Map 4. Responses for Shafts

from the same informant, one is printed over the other, which can make it hard to read. In addition to being hard to read, the sheer amount of information on the page can obscure the patterns. For this reason, it was decided to print maps with only one answer as shown in Map 3, Question 18, shafts Answer 4 (fills). The stars (*) record fills as a unique answer, a cross (+) records fills as a nonunique answer, and a dot (·) marks where an informant answered with a response that was not fills. This was done with

Program New Map which plots the responses by longitude and latitude.

Program New Map

(1) postscript
(2) for (resp in 1:49) {
(3) par (cex=1.0)
(4) usa (xlim=c(80,93), ylim=c(26,48)
(5) target ← keep [resp,2]
(6) ques ← keep [resp,1]
(6) text (-83,48.5, encode ("Question", ques, "Answer", target)
(8) text (-83,48,question [ques])
(9) pick ← (first [ques,]==tar) & (second [ques,]==0)
(10) par (cex=1.6)
(11) if (sum (pick) > 0) {
(12)   text (-map [pick,2],map [pick,1], "*")}
(13) pick ← ((first [ques,]==target & (second [ques,]>0)) | (second [ques,]==target)
(14) par (cex=1.2)
(15) if (sum (pick) >0) {
(16)   text (-map [pick,2],map [pick,1],"+")}
(17) pick ← (first [ques,]>0) & (first [ques,] !=target) & (second [ques,] !=target)
(18) par (cex=0.75)
(19) if (sum (pick)>0) {
(20)   text (-map [pick,2],map [pick,1],".")}
(21) }

The numbers in parentheses at the beginning of each line are not part of the program, but were put there for ease of explication here. A line by line explication of the program follows.

(1) Postscript tells the computer that the graphics output of the program will be sent to a postscript driver which creates files printable on the Apple Laser Writer.
(2) Establish looping and create maps 1 through 49.
(3) Set the relative expansion of the characters at 1.0.
(4) The latitudes on the map to be drawn will be between 36 and 48 degrees and the longitudes will be between 80 and 93 degrees.
(5) Establishes the target answer to the $resp^{th}$ clustered response for the first answer given by each informant (see line 2).

(6) Ques is the question number for the $resp^{th}$ clustered response.
(7) and (8) Write the question and the answer numbers in the upper right hand corner of the map.
(9) First [Ques,] is the 543 long vector of first answers to the question and second [Ques,] is the 543 long vector of second answers to the same question. Pick is the logical vector 543 long which is true if and only if the answer is target. In other words, pick is true only if the informant has a unique response matching the targeted response.
(10) Enlarges the relative print size to 1.6.
(11) Tests whether there are points to be plotted.
(12) Plot all unique responses as "*".
(13) Pick the informants with nonunique responses. The symbol "&" is the logical "and"; the symbol "|" is the logical "or".
(14) Changes the relative print size to 1.2.
(15) Checks to see if there are points to be plotted.
(16) Plots all nonunique responses as "+".
(17) Picks the informants with nonunique responses.
(18) Changes the relative print size to 0.75.
(19) Checks whether there are points to be plotted (see line 9).
(20) Plots all responses other than the targeted answer as ".".
(21) Closes loop for lines (3) through (20).

Correlation Between Answer and Informant Type

To measure the strength of the association between answers to a given question and informant type, we decided to use correspondence analysis to measure the maximal correlation achieveable between scaled responses and informant type. We considered X^2 significance levels but many of the tables are sparse and have widely varying numbers of possible answers. The scales from the correspondence analysis may also be useful for later analyses. In correspondence analysis, the maximal correlation comes from the square root of the first nontrivial eigenvalue from the correspondence analysis. This singular value decomposition and subsequent matrix manipulations were again handled conveniently with S. Thus it is a singular value decomposition of particular matrices (Greenacre, 1985). What it does in essence is to show how closely the answers correspond between the various groups being compared. The higher the value, the greater the likelihood that the differences in the data can be attributed to the classification. A correlation of 1.0 would mean that the different answers were absolutely correlated with the classification. Correlation Analysis was done for informant type. The first four are shown in Table 3.

Table 3
Correlation Between Answer and Informant Type

Question 1, At Once

Percent Answer	1	2
Type I	95	5
Type II	93	2
Type III	100	0

Maximum Correlation 0.11

Question 2, Rise

Percent Answer	1	2	3	4	5	6	7	8
Type I	52	3	9	5	5	11	16	1
Type II	57	5	5	1	0	24	8	0
Type III	77	1	1	1	0	18	2	0

Maximum Correlation 0.29

Question 3, Half Past

Percent Answer	1	2	3
Type I	75	6	18
Type II	75	4	21
Type III	67	6	27

Maximum Correlation 0.07

Question 4, Quarter of

Percent Answer	1	2	3	4	5
Type I	16	43	36	5	0
Type II	23	42	29	6	1
Type III	35	36	17	12	0

Maximum Correlation 0.20

Question 21, I am not

Percent Answer	1	2	3
Type I	29	64	7
Type II	69	29	2
Type III	85	15	0

Maximum Correlation 0.46

The variation in answers for questions 1 and 3 do not seem ascribable to classification by informant type. The largest correlation is for Question 21, "I am not" which has a maximal correlation of .46. Several other questions have maximal correlations of over .40 so further analysis is needed to determine if the informant type has had a confounding effect on the geographical distribution of grammatical forms.

MULTIVARIATE ANALYSIS

For the multivariate analysis only answers that show a potential for being interesting and are answered by a sufficient number of informants will be used. For this study only questions with an answer clustered at +3.00 or higher and had 10 or more responses will be used. This limited the questions to 32. The number of informants is limited to 378 if we choose those informants answering 24 or more of these questions, or 75% of them. The questions being used in this analysis are shown in Chart 3.

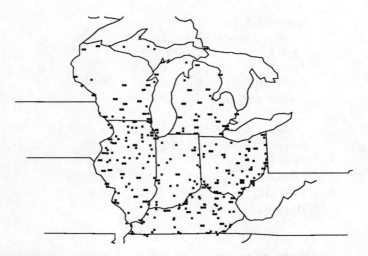

Map 5. At Least 24 Responses on 32 Questions

As Map 5 demonstrates, the informants to be used in the final analysis are fairly evenly distributed over the North Central States. Only nothern Wisconsin has a noticeable gap, but this area was sparcely populated at the time of the interviews and is still not heavily populated. All-in-all those informants left in the analysis cover the area of the North Central States.

Since all of the informants to be used in the multivariate analysis did not answer all 32 questions, the problem of what to do about missing data remains. This problem is complicated by having no way to determine if an informant did not have a term for the question or if the field worker did not ask that particular question. For this subset of the data 14% of the responses are missing, and at the present time a decision is being made as to how to treat this missing data.

Chart 3
Questions To Be Used In Multivariate Analysis

2,	pret. rise	33,	toward	55,	who-all	88,	didn't used to
4,	quarter of	36,	bite	56,	who all's	90,	take
8,	pret. drive	49,	yours	65,	pret. drink	98,	want to get off
9,	ppl drive	50,	hers	70,	an apple	102,	costs
10,	roughs	51,	his	72,	over yonder	104,	dive
18,	shafts	52,	theirs	79,	hadn't ought	107,	ppl. climb
19,	am/are	53,	you	80,	I won't	114,	wait for
21,	I am not	54,	you'll	85,	look here	121,	see

CONCLUSIONS

LANCS has had a long and complicated history. The large amount of data collected has presented several problems common to large data bases. What we have presented here describes the preliminary stages that we will be using for the investigation of the verb analysis of LANCS. Among the important stages that are needed for the analysis of such large data bases are the coding of the data so that it is as useful as possible. For the LANCS project this entailed coding for two answers per question and classifying informant by education, age, sex, race, year of birth, date of recording, and the longitude and latitude of community. Data checking is also important, even with verification. Summary table and preliminary statistics help plan future analyses. Since it is impossible to examine every possible answer, it is necessary to find interesting questions and to find patterns which look promising for further analysis. Computer drawn maps can greatly reduce the time formerly needed to search for isoglosses. Variance-covariance analysis can be used to discover which responses are interesting geographically and worth further analysis. Correspondence analysis is helpful to determine if responses are influenced by informants' gender or type. While we are just beginning our analysis and will be doing other statistics, these suggestions should aid in the analysis of other large data bases where the computer can be an essential tool.

References

Anderson, (1958) *An Introduction to Multivariate Statistical Analysis*. New York: John Wiley & Sons.

Becker, R. A. and Chambers, J. M. *S: An Interactive Environment for Data Analysis and Graphics*. Belmont, California: Wadsworth.

Greenacre, M. J. (1984) *Theory and Applications of Correspondence Analysis*. Orlando, Florida: Academic Press.

Linn, M. D. and Regal, R. R. (1985) Numerical Taxonomy as a Tool in Dialect Research. *Papers from the Fifth International Conference on Methods in Dialectology.* ed by H. J. Warkentyne. Victoria, British Columbia: University of Victoria.

Terminology vs Jargon: Canadian hockey talk

JAMES ARTHURS
University of Victoria, Victoria, B.C.

In this presentation, I approach my topic as a lexicographer, i.e. as one whose work is always only more or less correct. By that I mean that I am typically concerned about portraying a particular lexicon in an adequate way, rather than completely (since I find I have no satisfactory definition of "complete"). In order to do that, I take a particular lexicon to be a relatively closed system -- a kind of English for a Special Purpose, in fact. Next, I try and define for it a characteristic function (or Special Purpose) against which I can then evaluate what constitutes adequacy. In this instance, the particular lexicon is Canadian hockey talk and I have defined the function that an adequate lexicographical portrayal of it should serve as that of enabling a novice, e.g. an immigrant knowing English, to achieve an adequate-to-full understanding of the ice hockey commentaries available on CBC-TV. I shall talk about certain aspects of the task that this characteristically Canadian E.S.P. presents for the lexicographer, aspects rooted for the most part in the need to reconcile the data from both written and oral sources.[1]

The T.V. commentaries themselves are not only a significant source of data for my purpose but, given the size of the audience that the broadcasts reach every week for several months of the year, they are also an especially powerful means of both disseminating and fixing the lexicon of which they are constituted and with which one must be or become very familiar in order to participate fully as a viewer/listener. With this in mind, I have made transcriptions of the English and French commentaries of 7 games (amounting to some 14-15 hours) but I shall restrict myself here to the English text of a single game.

In practical terms, the usual first source of hockey talk, as with any game, might very well be the Book of Rules of the game, where one expects to find the terms and descriptions that define the game and its conduct. Upon inspection, however, it soon became clear that by itself a close study of the Rules would not equip me to "participate fully as a viewer/listener", to use my expression of a moment ago. Indeed, the question of how big is the gap between the lexicon of the Rules and that of the commentaries and, along with that, the further question of the nature of these respective lexicons together form the theme of this paper.

I shall look first at the Rules.[2] Within their general context, the Rules present a series of subcontexts, each with its theme. These are: Rink, Teams, Equipment, Penalties, Officials and Playing Rules and within each of the subcontexts, further context specification occurs. We can see this fairly readily in even the partial list of items presented in Fig. 1, dealing with the shape and dimensions of the Rink, its parts both internal and external, the various special persons, markings, devices and practices, down to the more mundane things like dressing-rooms and lighting in the arena.

fence	posts	light
boards	nets	red
blue line	spots	green
"Blue Lines"	circles	toilet
goal lines	bench	shower
"Goal Line"	gong	Referees
zone	clock	spectators
		acrimonious discussion

Figure 1. The Rink.

The list contained in Fig. 1 is a curious one: all of its items are common enough words and yet they are more than that, of course. Because of their context, they are also terms. Each is in context a technical expression designating a notion or concept intrinsic to that context. It is not to be identified with other instances of the same form in other contexts, no matter how similar. Goal, line, goal-line, zone, post, net are all different in hockey talk from what they may be not only in general parlance but also in the parlance of football, basketball and the like.

Extracting terms from a textual data-base presents certain problems of recognition and/or definition but in the case of the hockey Rules they were alleviated somewhat by the fact that in many cases the writers had employed upper-case spellings, boldface and quotation marks, singly or in combination, to highlight certain words or phrases. Thus in **Fig. 2**, we see in Rule 1 that "Ice", "Hockey" and "Rink" are all given special status and, in Rule 3(d), that "DEFENDING ZONE", "NEUTRAL ZONE" and "ATTACKING ZONE" are to be regarded as imbued with a particular, localised meaning. Instances of similar usage may be seen in **Fig. 1** also.

Rule 1:
    Ice Hockey shall be played on an area of ice called a "Rink".

Rule 3(d):
    That portion of the ice surface in which the goal is situated shall be called the "DEFENDING ZONE" of the team defending that goal; the central portion shall be known as the "NEUTRAL ZONE" and that portion furthest from the defended goal as the "ATTACKING ZONE".

    Figure 2. Orthographic definition.

Using these forms of orthographic designation as a basic guide, as well as noting all cases of words or strings introduced in sentences containing such forms as *shall be* ..., *must be* ..., *is to be* ..., *should be* ..., etc., I drew up a list of terms and regular expressions amounting to some 498 forms. The list contains a number of repetitions of items differentiated only typographically (in the sense already mentioned): these were included merely because they were there to be seen in the Rules and were retained even in cases where the importance of the distinction was not clear. Many items in the list show collocational information for the use of certain forms. A number of these are shown in **Fig. 3**. In each case, the item expresses some notion or concept that is held -- either by the writers of the Rules or in my judgement -- to be of intrinsic importance to the lexicon of hockey.

The list allows for occasional synonymy -- we have an example in _Fig. 3_ in the case of _completed_ or _conducted_ in collocation with _face-off_ -- but only for cases within the text of the Rules. This leads to the question of which may be the term and which the variant but the statistics of frequency of occurrence were not considered for this list and so no answer is offered at

                10-minute misconduct (penalty)
                (make contact) above shoulder height
                approved (regulation equipment)
                approved (whistles)
                "icing the puck" (is called)
                bat (the puck, in the air)
                bat (the puck, with the hand)
                carry (the puck)
                clean (interception)
                complete (a pass)
                complete (a face-off)
                conduct (a face-off)
                control (of the puck)
                displacing (a goal post)
                possession (of the puck)

                    Figure 3. Collocations.

present. The same question arises with regard to certain practices of the writers of the Rules, who from time to time will define a term only to subsequently refer to the concept it embodies by use of a paraphrase. Thus, having defined "_Rink_" (cf. Rule 1), they then refer to _the ice surface_ (cf. Rule 3d), meaning the same as "_Rink_" or _rink_. In other cases, they will use a phrase that seems to have terminological force even though it has never been actually defined as a term. Thus _Centre Ice_ is used to refer to a part of the rink already defined as "_Neutral Zone_". The relationship in each of these cases is represented in _Fig. 4_: the arrows indicate items of the commentary usage

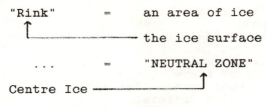

Figure 4. Synonymy.

that have come to be almost the standard or preferred paraphrase for the previously defined term, identified here by its relation to the = sign. The ellipsis (...) signifies the definition that exists for "NEUTRAL ZONE" but which is omitted here.

Finally, considering the list from the point of view of an English for Special Purposes, one recognises even intuitively that certain of the terms and/or regular expressions are more useful and appropriate for the specific activity of writing Rules rather than for watching or talking about actual games. For instance, the phrase approved whistles is not likely to be of much help to the immigrant watching hockey on the CBC. A number of other such cases are shown in Fig. 5, along with collocational information as appropriate.

Let us turn now from the Rules to the commentary. Comparing it with the list of items extracted from the Rules, one finds that slightly more than half of the Rules list -- some 260 items -- do not appear anywhere in the text of the commentary. This is a large proportion but perhaps not too surprising all the same, since most of the missing items are of the type exemplified in Fig. 5 and reveal a preoccupation with themes that do not generally engage the attention of spectators. Nonetheless, the situation presents to the lexicographer a problem of selection, perhaps distinguishing him thereby from the terminologist or terminographer in the delicate matter of adequacy.

```
abandoned stick
(the team) at fault
deliberate illegal substitution
eligible (to play the puck)
(the "slow whistle" is) exhausted
```

```
"fair game"
fence
fisticuffs
Illegal Puck
illegal stick
Kicking Player
line-ups (are collected)
Molesting Officials
Official Report of Match
premature entry (into face-off circle)
washed out
```

Figure 5. Items of limited distribution.

Even that is only the beginning of the problem. A close lexical analysis of the commentary brings out the fact that it contains some 325 words and recurring expressions that are nowhere to be found in the Rules list.[3]

In a number of cases, these items are related to items in the Rules list. There appear to be three main types, as shown in Fig. 6:[4]

    1 - strings containing new collocational information pertaining to the same sense of the original item
    2 - strings providing a new sense for the original form
    3 - new forms, found only in the commentary.

Thus we see in Fig. 6 that of the two senses of goal, only one receives an extended range of collocations in the commentary. I should point out too that the table I have shown does oversimplify a little in the case of ahead, for which one might well claim that there are indeed three more or less distinct senses at work in

---

Rules list	Commentary
==========	==========
1. goal (line/post)	goal (line/post) (career/open/overtime /tying) goal
possession (of the puck)	(with)/(get/gain/struggle for) possession

2. ahead (of the puck) (get) ahead (of the puck)
 (dump/get/pass/play/nudge
 /tip) (it/the puck)
 ahead (to X)
 (put Montreal) ahead (2-1)
    change (of possession of (make) changes (while the
     the puck)   play goes on)

3.   good penalty
 head man (the puck)
 line up (with a shot)
 loose (puck)
 open ice
 overskate (the puck)
 (a good) takeout

Figure 6. **Lexical extension**.

---

the examples shown: *in front of* (the puck), *in front of* (oneself) and *in front of* (the other team). So also with *change*, meaning -- in the usage of the commentary -- a change of players on the ice, rather than of possession of the puck.[5]

From a stylistic point of view, all three types are recognisably jargonesque and accordingly provoke quite a range of reactions from those who encounter them. However, the fact is that they recur with high frequency and so it may already be true to say that hockey talk without them becomes undeniably long-winded and rather less than authentic.

Although many of the items seem to be the result of ordinary association of syntactic categories, many others -- especially of types 2 and 3 -- are genuine innovations that are not commonly susceptible to paraphrase. So, for instance, while the form *away* is used infrequently in the Rules and the expression *away from the play* never, the same expression in the commentary is of very high frequency and invariable. Likewise, although the phrase *Centre Ice* occurs infrequently and undefined in the Rules, it turns out to have in the commentary a very high frequency -- namely, in the string *centre ice area*, a form with the same meaning as the original but which doesn't appear in the Rules. Conversely, the form *Rink* or *rink*, though common in the Rules, is scarcely heard in commentary and then mostly as a synonym for *ice* (-*surface*) and in the phrase *rink*-*wide* *pass*.

The type of innovation is sometimes quite surprising, as in the case of the verb *to* *clear*. This form doesn't appear in the Rules but in sports talk generally it is known to refer to a move intended to foil or weaken an attack by the opponents and collocates most often with *out* or *away*. In the commentary, however, its distribution is as shown in *Fig*. *7*.

---

clear the puck (back) (in/out) (to) (X/the corner/line)

Figure 7. Innovation.

SUMMARY

The commentary I have discussed has better than 300 items (words or strings) that do not appear in the Rules. These items for the most part are formed with quite ordinary words but occur with high frequency in their particular context and are found to require definition for the viewer/listener, who without them is unable to follow the commentary correctly.

I submit that the description I have just given makes these items sound remarkably like terms. This leads me to postulate two complementary series of terms in this context -- an official (written) one and an unofficial (oral) one. I propose that both of them must find a place in any adequate lexicographical or dialectological account of Canadian English.

NOTES

[1] I wish to acknowledge the help I have received from the Canadian Amateur Hockey Association. Their kindness in furnishing the text of the Rules in computerised form has greatly facilitated the analysis. My gratitude goes also to Bob Croteau, of the Wang Corporation in Victoria, for his invaluable services in converting the CAHA files to a form compatible with the system I use for my work.

[2] C.A.H.A.'s <u>Official Hockey Rules 1985-86, 1986-87</u>, adopted at the December meeting, 1984.

[3] It should be noted that some of these items have been extracted on the basis of their appearance in hockey talk generally rather than on the basis of this one commentary alone. It is expected of course that the selection will be confirmed by the results of the analysis of the remaining texts.

[4] In <u>Fig. 6</u> and <u>Fig. 7</u>, as throughout this paper, the parentheses mark collocational (sometimes optional) information: the slashes mark items in complementary distribution within the given context.

[5] A brief explanation of the new senses shown may be in order at this point:
-- a <u>good penalty</u> is one incurred in preference to the risk of a probable goal
-- to <u>head man</u> the puck is to pass it quickly to your man closest to the opponents' goal
-- to <u>line up</u> with a shot is to take dead aim at the goal
-- a <u>loose</u> puck is simply there on the ice, under no one's control
-- <u>open ice</u> is an area of the ice surface temporarily uncontrolled by anyone
-- to <u>overskate</u> the puck is to skate past the puck in the process of trying to gain or maintain possession of it, usually while advancing down the ice
-- a good <u>takeout</u> is checking an opponent or otherwise nullifying his efforts to carry out an attack in the defending zone, by taking him out of/on the play.

Slander and Defamation as a Source for Historical Dialectology

G.M. AWBERY
Welsh Folk Museum

Ready access to large amounts of raw data is now taken for granted by both dialectologists and sociolinguists. Since the early 1950s it has been possible to taperecord natural speech in a wide variety of situations and to store it for later analysis. There is therefore a wealth of material available for synchronic descriptive work on the linguistic usage of this recent period, and it is a comparatively simple matter to fill gaps with further programmes of recording.

For those wishing to look at the spoken language as it was in earlier periods however, the situation is rather more frustrating. We can achieve an element of apparent time-depth by recording speakers of different ages and assuming that the speech of older members of the community represents an earlier stage, that of younger members a later development. It is possible in fact, where a sound archive has been in existence for some time, to extend the time depth quite considerably. The earliest speakers recorded for the Welsh Folk Museum sound archive were born in the 1860s, and one or two as early as the late 1850s. The number of tapes which allow one to go back as far as this are comparatively few however, even in a large and long-established archive of this kind.

Very occasionally one may come across much earlier recordings of natural speech. In 1907 and 1909, for instance, an Austrian professor, Dr. Rudolf Trebitsch, visited Wales and recorded a total of fourteen speakers on phonographic roles. These recordings have been preserved in the Phonogrammarchiv of the Austrian Academy of Sciences in Vienna, and tape copies have now been deposited in the Welsh Folk Museum sound archive (1). The oldest of these informants was born in 1840, and several others in the 1850s and 1860s. I have never come across live recordings in Welsh of anyone born earlier than 1840 though; somewhere around this date must come a cut-off so far as direct evidence of linguistic usage is concerned.

Relying on the work of early dialectologists, we can reach back a little further. Fynes-Clinton's study of Bangor Welsh, published in 1913, quotes informants born as early as 1835 and 1839. And Henry Sweet's description of the dialect of Nant Gwynant, published in 1883, must surely take us back further again, though sadly he does not give details of who his informants were and when they were born.

Beyond this point evidence inevitably becomes anecdotal, and it is more difficult to gather reliable information about the spoken language. We turn, for instance, in Wales to the comments of antiquaries, in particular to the <u>Parochialia</u> of Edward Lhwyd who in 1696 drew up a questionnaire which he distributed throughout Wales. This questionnaire concentrated largely on farming methods, historical remains and local traditions, but one question did concern local dialect, "What Words, Phrases, or Variation of dialect in the Welsh seems peculiar to any Part of the Country?" A potentially fruitful source of information for an early period. Unfortunately very few of the clergymen who replied to Edward Lhwyd bothered with this particular question, and those who did try to answer it provided only scanty and unsystematic information.

Other sources are equally frustrating. Something can be made of the way in which place names are written in various kinds of legal documents. Though, of course, these were not drawn up with dialectal forms as a primary consideration, and other factors may well determine the exact spelling used in any one case. The actual legal documents involved - wills, inventories and accounts - were often written in English, and so of themselves cast no light on the spoken Welsh of the area. And where we do have access to letters, folk poetry and so on, written in Welsh and from a specific locality, there is always the problem of interference between the dialect and standard Welsh. Anyone literate in Welsh, from the end of the Sixteenth Century onwards, would have been familiar with the Welsh Bible, and its forms would inevitably influence their written usage. Such texts cannot be treated as straightforward examples of local dialect, even when clear traces of it appear.

It is heartening therefore to discover an abundant and hitherto unexplored source for the spoken language in the legal records of early modern Wales. From the Sixteenth Century to the Nineteenth Century actions for slander and defamation were brought before the civil and ecclesiastical courts, and the records of such cases have survived in considerable numbers. A large proportion of this material has now been transcribed and edited in calendar form by a historian, Richard Suggett, and it is therefore for the first time easily accessible to linguists who might find dealing with the original documents an onerous and daunting task. I am greatly indebted to him for his ready co-operation in making available these calendar summaries, not all of which have as yet been published (2).

The most important of the secular courts which heard actions for slander was the Court of Great Sessions, which held sessions twice a year in each Welsh county between 1542 and 1830. Defamation cases, on the other hand, were brought before the Consistory Courts of the four Welsh dioceses, and survive in considerable quantities from the Eighteenth Century onwards.

The complainant's case was set out in a writ and declaration in the case of the secular courts, or a 'libel' in the case of the ecclesiastical courts. These set out the main facts of each case: the names of the parties in dispute, the residence and style or occupation of the defendant, and in the case of ecclesiastical courts of the plaintiff too, the date and place of the offence, and – most importantly for the linguist – the exact wording of the slander or defamation. This was given in Welsh or English, according to the language of the original insult, and where the abuse was in Welsh, an English translation generally follows.

Examples of cases from both the secular and ecclesiastical courts are given below in calendar form, that is a type of summary which omits the repetitive common form of the legal documents, but preserves the unique detail of each case. The first is a case from the Court of Great Sessions for Anglesey:

1660   Sessions held at Beaumaris on 1 Oct. 12 Charles II
(reference: Wales 16/9)
David Griffith v. David ap Moris of Llangristiolis,
yoeman (damages claimed: 100)
<u>Declaration</u> (Membrane 8b): the def. on 16 Sept.
12 Chas II at Erriannell spoke of the plt. these
scandalous Welsh words:
"Lleidir wyt ti a ladrottaist ddau oyn o ddar
John Owen David."
In English:
"Thou art a theefe and thou hast stolen two lambs
from John Owen David."
Plea: Not guilty: issue [not tried]

The second example is taken from the records of the Consistory Court of Llandaff, and illustrates the form of cases brought before the ecclesiastical courts.

1738   Jennett John of Baislegg, spinster c. Samuel David of
Michaelston y Vedw.
<u>Libel</u> (reference: LL/CC/G 850): Exhibited 12 May.
The def. in Nov. – April last at Coed Kernew defamed
the plt. by speaking these Welsh words:
"Whore iw hi a myfi gesim hi gant waith."
In English:
"She is a whore and I have had her a hundred times."

Some entries are considerably longer, involving a series of pleas and the depositions of witnesses, but the two shown here are in the main typical, as the majority of cases did not proceed to trial or judgement. They are also typical as to content, in that the secular courts dealt largely with accusations of theft and other felonies, while the ecclesiastical courts heard allegations of sexual misdemeanours.

We find then in these records numerous examples of reported speech dating from the period 1542 to 1830, and we have reasonably full information as to when and where they were spoken, and some detail about the social status of the people involved. Since the crux of the legal case was the actual slander or defamation, the words complained of had to be accurately reported, with no temptation for the clerks of the court to modify natural, informal language in the direction of the literary norm.

So far, so good. There are however, inevitably, problems. The records have not survived evenly. Some periods and localities are more fully represented than others, and there are frustrating gaps in the available data. The content of these cases is rather monotonous, being limited to actionable verbal abuse. And there are also some difficulties with the varying spelling conventions used by the clerks of the courts.

Overall, however, this is a potentially fruitful source of information on the spoken language of periods for which such data is otherwise rare and at best anecdotal.

Information on a wide range of dialectal features can be gleaned from these documents then, and the distribution of lexical items, morphological markers and phonological variants at different periods can be mapped. It is possible in many cases to compare the resulting picture with what is known of the distribution of the corresponding forms in contemporary Welsh. And for areas on the English border where the language has now been lost this material provides priceless evidence as to the nature of the spoken Welsh once current there.

First, then, an example of morphological variation. There are in modern Welsh two alternative realisations of the 3sg past inflection on the verb, <u>odd</u> and <u>ws</u>, giving for instance <u>gwelodd</u> and <u>gwelws</u> for 'he/she saw'. Of the two, <u>odd</u> is found in the standard language, and in the dialects of north Wales and the south-west. <u>Ws</u> is limited to the the dialects of the south-east.

It is a comparatively straightforward matter to map the distribution of these variants in the slander data for different periods. 3sg past forms of the verb are common and the two realisations quite distinct. Examples of such forms are given below.

1731   Trefdraeth (Anglesey)
       "..fe a ddygodd oen o'r morfa.."
       "..he stole a lamb out of the marsh.."

1726   Gladestry (Radnor)
       "Di girn di dorrws y twlle sydd in di hatt di."
       "Thy horns did break the holes that is in thy hatt."

Map 1 shows the distribution of these variants in the Eighteenth Century data, and although there are inevitably gaps in the available information, the picture is very similar to that of the present day. The ws variant is characteristic of the south-east, with odd found in the north and west. Mapping the data for the Sixteenth and Seventeenth Centuries gives very similar results, allowing us to extrapolate back that much further again.

I should perhaps add that this map, and indeed all the maps on this handout, have been prepared using the location of the quarrel as a basis, as this information is given in almost every case. The home village of the speaker is given less regularly and is therefore less useful for this purpose. It seems unlikely that any serious bias results from this decision since home villages usually turn out, when they are mentioned, to be identical with the location of the quarrel or at least close by.

A third variant realisation of the 3sg past form of the verb exists in contemporary spoken Welsh, a periphrastic form involving the auxiliary ddaru. This is in modern Welsh confined to north Wales. And here again, mapping the forms which arise in the slander cases, as in the example below, reveals that this distribution was already in force in earlier times.

1760   Llansannan (Denbigh)
       "..fe ddarfu hi ddwyn y blawd."
       "..she stole the meal."

Map 2 shows the position in the Eighteenth Century, and here again, mapping the equivalent material for the Sixteenth and Seventeenth Centuries gives very similar results.

It is worth perhaps making the point that the southern border counties, which have long since been completely anglicised, are shown here to be part of the south-eastern area characterised by the ws inflection. Material of this kind, which allows us to draw reliable conclusions as to the dialectal affiliations of such areas, is of considerable value.

Lexical variants characteristic of the modern dialects can also be found in this material, and mapped appropriately. Though here the examples for any one item tend to be rather thinner on the ground. Whereas the 3sg past inflection will show up on any number of different verbs, any one specific lexical item will inevitably turn up less frequently.

Here are some typical examples: first, the distribution of varying terms for 'heifer'. In north Wales we find <u>heffer</u>, a loan from English; in mid Wales <u>anner</u>; and in the south-east <u>treisiad</u>. Examples of each are shown below, and their geographical distribution is summed up in Map 3.

1773   <u>Pwllheli</u> (Caernarfon)
        "Ti a ddygaist <u>heffer</u>."
        "Thou hast stolen an heifer."

1577   <u>Defynnog</u> (Brecon)
        "Thomas ap Madock aeth am <u>hanneyr</u> i yn lledraddaidd."
        "Thomas ap Madock toke away my heyfor theveshlye or feloniously."

1758   <u>Llantrisant</u> (Glamorgan)
        "Beth am y <u>trisedy</u>."
        "What of the heyfers."

Map 4 shows the equivalent map for 'barley', with the loan form <u>barlish</u> in the south-west and the native <u>haidd</u> elsewhere. Examples of both lexical items are shown below.

1634   <u>Denbigh</u> (Denbighshire)
        "..lleidr fy <u>haidd</u> i.."
        "..theefe to my barly.."

1706   <u>Roch</u> (Pembrokeshire)
        "Llydyr y <u>marlish</u> y.."
        "Theefe of my barly.."

In neither case is there enough data to justify drawing up separate maps for different periods. The picture is clear, and compatible with the maps of lexical distribution drawn up by Alan Thomas in his dialect atlas <u>The Linguistic Geography of Wales</u>. Here again then the earlier picture as gleaned from the slander data is similar to that which still exists in the modern dialects.

The third type of variation which can be mapped from this material is phonological variation. This is rather more problematic than either morphological or lexical variation, where all that was required of the clerk of the court was that he should note the lexical items and inflections used by the speaker correctly. When we come to the question of the speaker's accent we are asking rather more of him, namely that he should manipulate the spelling conventions in such a way as to reveal the characteristic accent of the speaker, departing if necessary from the normal literary convention of the day.

Surprisingly, this does actually happen, though not with complete regularity. In the south-east, for instance, we find that the south-eastern realisation of word-initial <u>chw</u> as <u>hw</u> is often noted, with <u>chwaer</u>, 'sister' being written as <u>whar</u>, and <u>chwech</u>, 'six', as <u>hwech</u>, as in the example shown below.

1725 <u>Neath</u> (Glamorgan)
".. y mae iti <u>whech</u> o blant heb yr un o'r un tad ai gilidd.."
".. thou hast six children & not any one hath ye same man to his father as the other.."

Map 5 shows the distribution of such forms as found in material dating from the Eighteenth Century. It is difficult to know what weight to place on the standard language forms here. Do they reflect actual usage, with initial <u>chw</u> appearing side by side with dialectal <u>hw</u> ? Or do they merely reveal uncertainty over spelling conventions among the clerks noting down the details of each case?

In this same area the diphthong <u>au</u> in monosyllables is often realised as <u>ou</u>, with <u>aur</u>, 'gold', being pronounced <u>our</u>, and <u>dau</u>, 'two', being pronounced <u>dou</u>, as in the example below.

1707 <u>Trallwng</u> (Brecon)
"..fe fi iddo <u>ddoi</u> o blant o ordderch.."
"He had two bastards."

This also shows up in the data, as we see from Map 6, which again draws on Eighteenth Century material. And here again there is some variation, with the local form appearing in some cases and not in others. The precise status of this variation is again uncertain.

These maps again allow us to draw conclusions as to the dialectal affiliation of the southern border counties. As with the morphological example discussed earlier, we find these areas linking in neatly with the south-east as a whole.

In this paper it has been possible only to present a brief sample of the kind of material one can derive from these early slander and defamation cases. Work now in progress should allow a fuller picture to emerge of the range of dialectal charcteristics which can be extracted from this promising source.

NOTES

1. W.F.M. sound archive tape no. 6832. Transcripts of these recordings, some made by Dr. Trebitsch himself, and others by his informants, are also held in the museum, together with full details of the name, age and background of each informant. (W.F.M. Accessions Correspondance F83.150) For an account of this early programme of recording, see Trebitsch (1908 and 1909).

2. Suggett (1983) and Suggett (unpub.). Suggett (1983) contains a calendar of the following cases: Court of Great Sessions for Denbighshire, Montgomeryshire and Glamorgan; Llandaff Consistory Court (Part 1), and the Consistory Court of the Archdeaconry of Carmarthen. Suggett (unpub.) contains a calendar of the following cases: Court of Great Sessions for Anglesey, Caernarfonshire, Flintshire, Breconshire, Radnorshire, Cardiganshire, Pembrokeshire, Carmarthenshire and Glamorgan (additional cases). Llandaff Consistory Court (Parts 2 and 3), Bangor Consistory Court, and the Consistory Court of the Archdeaconry of Brecon.

REFERENCES

Fynes-Clinton, O.H. (1913) The Welsh Vocabulary of the Bangor District. Oxford: Oxford University Press.
Lhwyd, E. (1909-1911) Parochialia. Addendum to Archaeologia Cambrensis.
Suggett, R.F. (1983) An Analysis and Calendar of Early-modern Welsh Defamation Suits. SSRC Final Report (HR 6979).
Suggett, R.F. (unpub.) Supplementary Parts of the Calendar.
Sweet, H. (1882-4) Spoken north Welsh. Transactions of the Philological Society, 409-484.
Thomas, A.R. (1973) The Linguistic Geography of Wales, a Contribution to Welsh Dialectology. Cardiff: University of Wales Press.
Trebitsch, R. (1908) Phonographische Aufnahmen der irischen Sprache in Irland und einiger Musikinstrumente in Irland und Wales, ausgefuhrt von Dr. Rudolf Trebitsch im Sommer 1907. Berich xii, Phonogramm-Archivs-Kommission, Vienna.
Trebitsch, R. (1909) Phonographische Aufnahmen der welschen Sprache in Wales, der manxschen Sprache auf der Insel Man, der gaelischen Sprache in Schottland und eines Musikinstrumentes in Schottland ausgefuhrt im Sommer 1909. Berich xviii, Phonogramm-Archivs-Kommission, Vienna.

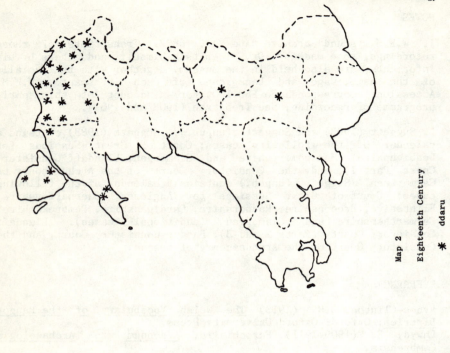

Map 2
Eighteenth Century
✱ ddaru

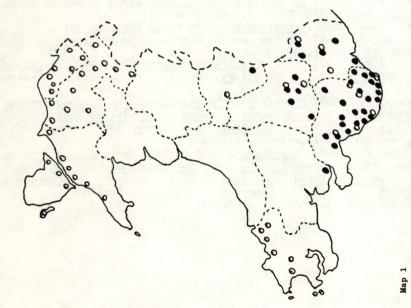

Map 1
Eighteenth Century
○ odd ● ws

Methods in Dialectology

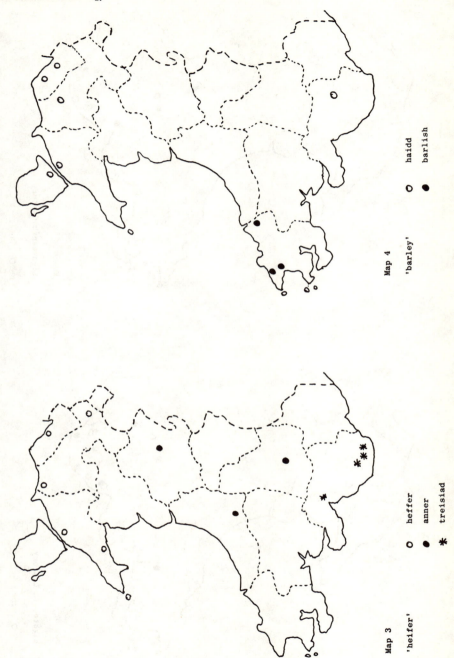

Map 4
'barley'   ○ haidd
           ● barlish

Map 3
'heifer'   ○ heffer
           ● anner
           * treisiad

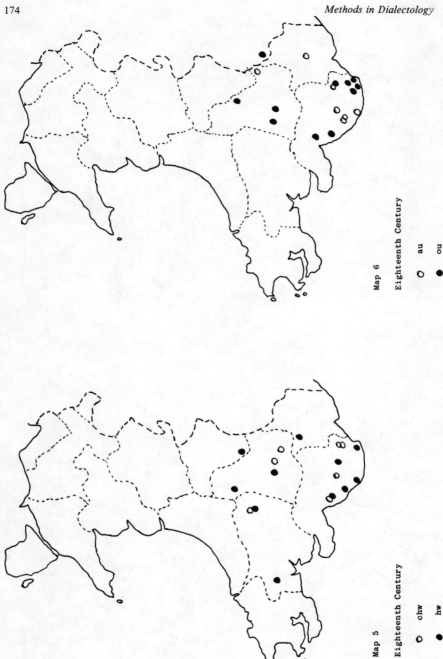

Beyond Linguistic Divergence in Black American English: Competing Norms of Linguistic Prestige and Variation

JOHN BAUGH
Department of Linguistics. The University of Texas at Austin

INTRODUCTION

The most recent issue of <u>American Speech</u> (Spring, 1987) is devoted to the following question, "Are Black and White Vernaculars Diverging?" Scholars diverge in their response to this question. The present discussion, based on long-term studies of adult black English, reflects a more complex picture of relevant linguistic variation. Labov (1987:6) speaks for the proponents of the view that the dialects are drifting apart; "we suspected that divergence was taking place because all of the social and economic conditions for divergence were there." Vaughn-Cooke (1987:32) captures the sentiment of those who are skeptical of this linguistic abyss; "the divergence hypothesis [sic] is uninformed and simplistic, and [sic] it cannot provide a coherent account of language change in black English."

Claims of linguistic divergence are primarily based on the speech of younger blacks. These young speakers have begun to use nonstandard forms in ways that were previously unattested. However, there are two ways to view this lack of attestation: first, the recent claims may reflect linguistic innovations, or, prior research may not have revealed the usage that is now viewed as novel. Fasold (1987:4-5) offers complementary observations regarding contrasting grammatical interpretations; "A linguist who assumes that grammatical structure is to be discovered in language use is more likely to find a change in grammar, say between present-day and earlier records of vernacular black English (VBE) speech, if a difference in use of a particular feature can be demonstrated. Other linguists, assuming that grammatical structure often stays constant while community conventions for its use change, will probably assert that the grammar is still the same, even if they agree with the first linguist that the feature is now used in somewhat different ways than it formerly was."

It comes as no surprise to learn that younger members of the black English speech community maintain, and perpetuate, nonstandard norms. Indeed it was for this very reason that Dillard (1972) focused his study of black English on the speech of children; they tend to be less formal than adults, and therefore provide the most convenient linguistic picture of the vernacular in use. Much like Cunningham's research, presented at this conference, I too needed considerable cooperation from the adult informants that were the object of my analysis, because they are justifiably suspicious of any investigation. They also resent the personal invation of privacy that is the keystone of our profession. As a black man I was accutely aware of the special nature of the "observer's paradox" in our community, which is why I devoted several years of my fieldwork to interviews with the same informants. This effort was essential to earning their trust, which in turn allowed me to record their uninhibited speech.

Despite modest social and educational advances for some black Americans, the vast majority still suffer from poverty and cannot share the full advantages of the mainstream culture. Much like the youth that Cheshire (1982) studied in Reading, black youth tend to be proud, and preservation of the street vernacular is a reflection of that pride. The adults that I interviewed, who were quite active members of their community, were linguistic pragmatists; they are clearly proud of their black heritage, but they also know that racism prevails in the larger society, and their linguistic behavior reflects these competing norms, which have not yet influenced their children.

These opposing norms are the primary object of my remarks. Although the evidence that has been presented in support of linguistic divergence is important, these linguistic innovations among black youth reflect a well established trend, where younger members of the community employ the most extreme form of the vernacular. Depending upon opportunity and social circumstance, these youth are likely to respond to the linguistic demands of their adult environments. Those who have opportunities to enter the professions will attempt to learn the dialect of wider communication (i.e. standard English), whereas those who remain in the vernacular community will, in all likelihood, maintain the street vernacular throughout much of their ordinary discourse.

The remainder of this paper examines the methods, analyses, and some established results that confirm the linguistic osmosis of black America. Black speech is socially stratified, and the prevalence of racism, segregation, and a lack of linguistic understanding among members of the majority culture will continue to perpetuate the diversification of black American speech patterns. Some of this diversity will consist of linguistic changes toward the standard, while other changes will serve to reinforce the independent vitality of the street vernacular.

METHODS

The data for this research were collected during the 1970's and the 1980's by the author. The early research was conducted as part of an extensive participant observer survey when I served as a lifeguard at the local public pool in Pacoima, California. This area is a long established black ghetto in Los Angeles, and reflects all of the problems that are typical of many impoverished ghettos. There are, nevertheless, pockets of modest affluence, and many middle class families reside in some of the

"Joe Lewis" housing tracts that were built during the late 1950's and early 1960's. Other residents have witnessed the transition from agriculture to industry. Throughout the process the citizens of Pacoima have remained among the lowest paid workers in the city, and unemployment rates are well above average. A large hispanic population lives, quite literally, on the other side of the tracks. There have been some long-standing conflicts between the black and brown communities which occassionally flare up or subside depending upon a variety of capricious social circumstances. Public recreational facilities were divided along these racial boundaries as a pragmatic response to the history of these conflicts. I was employed to work on the black side of town for over ten years, and I collected most of the data reported herein during the last six of those years.

Two years ago I was able to return to the community and re-interview some of my key informants. Others had moved or were serving time in jail. During these follow-up interviews I was able to solicit opinions regarding the divergence hypothesis. Most of my informants agreed with Labov's observation that social conditions for blacks have not truly improved. They also felt that younger members of the speech community were constantly engaged in the processes of linguistic innovation. Most of the examples that they cited referred to slang, such as "They don't say 'Right on' like we used to, now they say 'Word'." Also, "It ain't hip to say 'cool' no more; that's out. Now these brothers 'chill out' and it's just us 'old folks' that be saying 'cool'." When general comparisons with adults were discussed linguistic accommodation, or style shifting, was reaffirmed; "These kids don't be going through no changes when they talk to they friends or they teacher cause it ain't hip to talk white, but we [adults] have to deal with the man, and you just gotta be able to rap to him in the language that he understands."

Elsewhere (Baugh, 1983) I describe the gradual familiarization process that allowed me to interview adult informants in the four following situations:

1) Intimate speech events among fimiliars, all of whom are natives of the black vernacular culture.

2) Speech among newly acquainted members of the black vernacular culture.

3) Speech events among familiars, including outsiders to the black vernacular culture.

4) Speech between strangers, including individuals who are foreign to black vernacular culture.

A major methodological difference between my research and that conducted by Labov and Harris (1986) in Philadelphia stems from my decision to develop new social networks for the purpose of this research. Harris conducted interviews within his existing social networks, consisting primarily of type 1 and 2 situations. I had very limited success with this procedure, because my close friends were not used to being interviewd by me. After several attempts to interview members of my existing social networks I determined that they changed their manner and mode of speaking during these interviews; I therefore found that I was unable to record my closest friends or family without distorting the data. In the case of my Pacoima interviews, however, I always had my tape recorder in hand, and whenever I made new friends these individuals were aware of my research goals at the outset. In other words, these new friendships grew out of my research, and did not tax my rapport with established friends. Rickford's (1987) discussion of sociolinguistic surveys and assessing speaker competence reinforce the value of such long-term procedures.

Wolfson (1976) challenged fieldworkers to demonstrate that our interviews could reflect "natural speech." That is, she argued that interviews, by their nature, were not comparable to ordinary conversations where people were not being recorded. The typical interview takes place between individuals who do not already share extensive common knowledge. When a television reporter conducts an interview they presumably do not already know the answers to the questions they are asking. By contrast, I usually knew the answers to many of the questions I would ask of my friends or family, and they knew that I knew those answers. Once I realized that my interviews with friends did not produce their colloquial vernacular, I was compelled to engage in the gradual familiarization process that provided me with access to new informants.

The full details of my field procedures are available in other manuscripts (see Baugh 1983). Briefly, I would inform prospective informants of my desire to study the oral history of black America. This topic holds considerable interest for the vast majority of black Americans, regardless of background, and I was able to overcome the initial reservations of most informants because my questions were organized in ways that demonstrated my support of black culture, and the importance of black Americans to the history, development, and evolution of American culture as a whole. The trust that I earned allowed me to conduct interviews under several circumstances, and these data in turn provided a valuable profile of linguistic accommodation in social context.

PHONOLOGICAL ANALYSES

Linguistic variability can be observed at several levels within the grammar, particularly in the adult black English speech community. This discussion concentrates on phonology because these data occur with sufficient frenquency within the corpus that patterns of linguistic accommodation can be confirmed quantitatively.

A) Suffix /-s/ variability

Three suffix /-s/ functions have been analyzed in comparison to the four situational contexts identfied previously, including: plural /-s/, possessive /-s/ and third person singular /-s/. Figure 1 illustrates the overall variability of these forms, as well as their respective response to social circumstances. The final analysis demonstrates a combination of linguistic and social influences.

The linguistic variability is ranked; plurals are perserved with greatest frequency, followed respectively by possessive /-s/ and third person singular /-s/. There are semantic explanations for this pattern. In ordinary discourse plural /-s/ often carries the full semantic burden, whereas the possessive and third person singular morphophonemes tend to correspond to redundant semantic functions. For example, "My brother('s) car" or "He like('s) hot cars" convey all of the essential semantic information irrespective of the presence or absence of the suffix /-s/ forms. Where as "The kid(s) ran" requires the plural /-s/ to disambiguate two different meanings.

In addition to this functional linguistic explanation we also find that adult black English speakers produce situational variation. They tend to preserve the vernacular with familiars, regardless of their social background, and more standardized forms tend to be used with those who are newly acquainted. Figure 2 illustrates this variability for each suffix /-s/ form individually.

B) /-t/ and /-d/ variability

The case of consonant cluster reduction reflects some similarities to suffix /-s/ variability, but significant differnces also exist. Three types of /-t/ and /-d/ final consonant clusters were observed, including:

monomorphemic   (e.g. past, lift)

ambiguous   (e.g. kept, told)

past tense   (e.g. passed, walked)

As with the suffix /-s/ variability, there are linguistic explanations for the distribution of these three functions within the corpus, as illustrated in figure 3. The monomorphemic forms are absent most frequently, followed respectively by the ambiguous and past tense forms. This trend is similar to other studies of these morphophonemes (see Guy, 1980). In monomorphemic contexts both /-t/ and /-d/ are vulnerable because they do not convey distinct semantic information. In ambiguous consonant clusters they perform a redudant function. Only the past tense forms represent instances where the semantic function can rest soley on these variables, and often the discourse context conveys

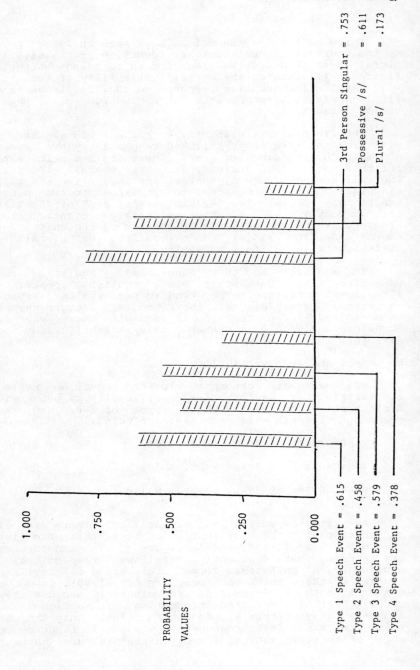

FIGURE 1
Suffix /s/ Absence

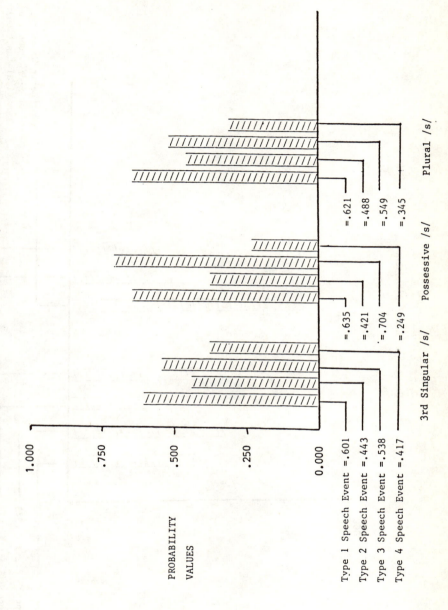

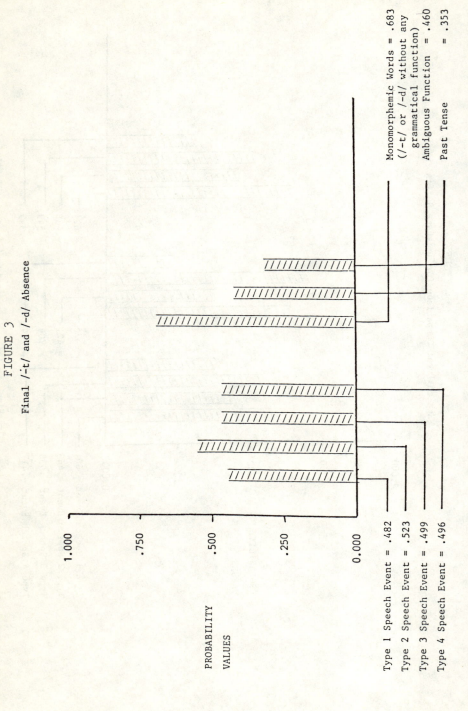

FIGURE 3

Final /-t/ and /-d/ Absence

the nature of past events, hence providing another basis of the observed variability.

Unlike suffix /-s/, the /-t/ and /-d/ variability is dominated by linguistic constraints; situational factors do not convey any appreciable impact on this variation. This would also suggest that /-t/ and /-d/ variability is not highly stigmatized within the speech community. Stigmatized features tend to exhibit greater situational variaiblity, as speakers accommodate to alternative speech events.

C) Copula variability

Wolfram (1974) observed significant differences between the 'is' and 'are' forms of the copula with respect to the relationship between black and white vernaculars in the southern United States. The present results correspond to the 'is' form, which exhibits unique variability in the black English speech community. Figure 4 demonstrates a shift in emphasis with respect to the primary influence on the relevant variability.

Copula variaiblity reflects slight situational variaiblity, which conforms to the same pattern as does suffix /-s/ accommodation. This trend is illustrated in figure 4. The relevant grammatical findings have been discussed in more thorough detail in my earlier examinations of this variability (see Baugh 1980, 1983). In those earlier analyses I was able to confirm the historical association of this variability to prior creolized forms, based on the pioneering works of Beryl Bailey (1965, 1966) and Labov (1969).

Despite the fact that this linguistic variation corresponds closely to Bailey's (1965, 1966) early comparative observations for standard English, black English, and Jamaican Creole, the present findings also show slight situational variability where the vernacular is used most among familiar individuals, regardless of their racial background. Speech events among the newly acquainted tend to be more formal, just as they are with suffix /-s/ variability.

D)   CONCLUSION

Adults within the black English community exhibit bidirectional linguistic accommodation depending upon social circumstances. Since adults have had greater linguistic exposure to other dialects and norms outside of their community, these data confirm that they have both the experience and ability to alter their speech to meet the demands of alternative discourse contexts. Other aspects of linguistic variation can be attributed to internal linguistic processes.

The vast majority of research on black American English focuses on youth, and this trend grows out of two well intended goals: first, these younger members of the speech community are the most active users of the vernacular; it is an important part

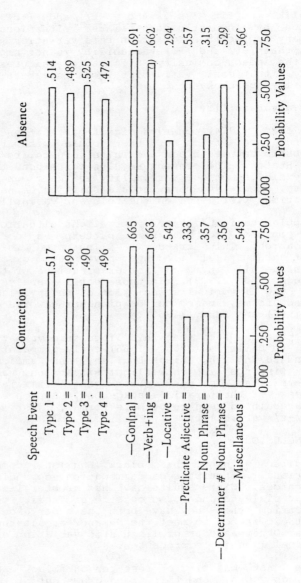

FIGURE 4
PROBABILITY VALUES FOR COPULA VARIABILITY

of their local culture, and fluency in the vernacular (i.e. a slick rap) is highly prized; second, given the educational thrust of many pioneering studies within the black community, scholars were most concenred with the language of youth because they were the target of educational objectives. In spite of these worthy intentions, the inherent bias toward younger speakers has resulted in distorted interpretations of the black English speech community as a whole.

The black Speech community is highly stratified, both socially and linguistically, and scholars who have been critical of the recent divergence hypothesis are reacting, at least in part, to the implication that this diversity is diminished by claims that black and white speech patterns are merely drifting apart. Our best evidence suggests that there are considerable forces operating at both ends of the linguistic continuum. Many urban youth continue the process of linguistic innovation that has been a hallmark of "hip" black speech. Those blacks who seek acceptance within the majority culture attempt to embarce the standard, which is often determined by social circumstances.

These competing linguistic trends are attributable to a common, perhaps universal, linguistic principle. Once a child becomes socialized they begin to make value judgments regarding language, among other apsects of culture. They then attempt to adopt linguistic behavior that is designed to gain repsect from those individuals from whom they seek respect. Those who strive to maintain strong ties within the vernacular community tend to preserve the vernacular through active use, whereas those who wish to "escape" the ghetto often view linguistic accommodation as a first step on the path out of the community.

While I believe the findings that have been presented in support of linguistic divergence, which I would characterize as evidence of linguistic innovation, are important and provacative, they are by no means comprehensive, and they do not reflect a comprehensive view of the black speech community. The competing linguistic norms that are evident among adult blacks reflect the growing complexity of the speech community, which defies any theory of unidirectional linguistic change. As long as racism and poverty persist we will find a broad range of personal linguistic strategies employed by various black Americans. The present discussion is offered in support of clarifying this fact.

REFERENCES

Bailey, B. (1965) Toward a new perspective in Negro English dialectology. American Speech, 40, 171-77.

―――― (1966) Jamaican Creole Syntax: A transformational approach. Cambridge: Cambridge University Press.

Baugh, J. (1980) A reexamination of the Black English Copula. In W. Labov, ed. Locating Language in Time and Space. New York: Academic Press.

―――― (1983) Black Street Speech: Its History, Structure, and Survival. Austin: University of Texas Press.

Cheshire, J. (1982) Variation in an English dialect: A sociolinguistic study. Cambridge: Cambridge University Press.

Dillard, J.L. (1972) Black English. New York: Random House.

Fasold, R.W. (1987) Introduction. Are black and white vernaculars diverging? American Speech, 62, 3-5.

Guy, G. (1980) Variation in the group and the individual: The case of final stop deletion. In W. Labov, ed. Locating Language in Time and Space. New York: Academic Press.

Labov, W. (1969) Contraction, Deletion, and Inherent Variability of the English Copula. Language, 45, 715-62.

―――― (1987) II. Are black and white vernaculars diverging? American Speech, 62, 5-12.

Rickford, J.R. (1987) The haves and have nots: Sociolinguistic surveys and the assessment of speaker competence. Language in Society, 16, 149-78.

Vaughn-Cooke, F.B. (1987) III. Are black and white vernaculars diverging? American Speech, 62, 12-31.

Wolfram, W. (1974) The relationship of white Southern speech to vernacular black English. Language, 50, 498-527.

Wolfson, N. (1976) Speech events and natural speech. Language in Society, 5, 81-96.

Uses of Dual Scaling in Social Dialectology: Multidimensional Analysis of Vowel Variation

WLADYSLAW CICHOCKI
University of New Brunswick

This paper presents an approach to the problem of how to quantify sociolinguistic variables which have more than two variants. A solution is presented in terms of Dual Scaling, a multivariate statistical technique related to Correspondence Analysis, which is especially suited to the study of the categorical type of data found in sociolinguistic research. Applications to Glasgow English (i) and Toronto English (aw) illustrate the advantages of a unitary and multidimensional approach to this problem, and also show how a graphical representation of variation enhances its analysis.

The Problem

The basic approach to the quantification of linguistic variation has been to calculate subject scores using the weighted-index method (Labov 1966). An often cited example is the (eh) vowel in New York English: the five phonetic realisations are ordered along a continuum of phonetic height, which also corresponds to the social continuum of standard/non-standard.

(eh − 1) [ɪˤ:ə]
(eh − 2) [eˤ:ə] [ɛˤ:ə]
(eh − 3) [æ^:]
(eh − 4) [æ:]
(eh − 5) [a:]

To arrive at a subject's score the index assigned to a variant is multiplied by the proportion of tokens of that variant used by the subject, and these products are added together. The higher the score the closer a subject's pronunciation is to the lower vowel and, in this case, to the standard. The subject scores are used subsequently to establish correlations with linguistic and social constraints.

The method appears to be straightforward, but underlying it are statistical assumptions that need to be stated explicitly. The main assumption is that the variants are considered to be interval-type data: i.e. they can be arranged in a linear order with an equal distance or weight between the successive points of this order. In many cases there is a linguistic or social factor which is inherently gradient and thus provides a basis for linearly ordering the variants. There are cases, however, for which there is no continuum on which to establish an order. Scottish English (r), for example, has three phonetic variants – [r, ɹ] and ∅ – among which there is no phonetic gradient and no unequivocal social gradient (Romaine 1978). In Belfast English (a) there is a curvilinear correspondence between social and phonetic facts: the local prestige form associated with the middle class is [a] but working class speakers use [ɛ] as well as [ɑ, ä, ɔ] (Milroy 1982). Headless relatives in Montréal French have three variants – ce que, qu'est-ce que and qu'osque – which cannot be ordered (Kemp 1979). Similarly, Ontario French has a discourse conjunct with four variants – donc, alors, ça fait que and so – which resist ordering (Mougeon et al 1985).

It is fair to say that users of the weighted-index method have generally avoided pitfalls associated with these difficulties. Nevertheless, it is clear that we are still in need of a generalised procedure which is flexible enough to accomodate all the data types found in sociolinguistic inquiry.

Various solutions have been proposed. One approach is to analyse variants separately (see Hudson 1980, Romaine 1980). Such analyses are, however, subject to experimentwise error (known as type 1 error). Statistical practice suggests a unitary approach which studies the variants together. This is the approach used in cluster analysis (Jones-Sargent 1983), in principal component analysis (Berdan 1978) and in the dual scaling analyses we present below.

Dual Scaling

Dual Scaling (DS) is a member of the growing family of multivariate statistical techniques. It is closely related to correspondence analysis, Hayashi's quantification, homogeneity analysis and optimal scaling (see Nishisato 1980). The technique makes no assumptions about data distributions (such as normality), and is adapted to quantify categorical type data (i.e. categories which cannot be ordered along a continuum). These features make it attractive for exploring the data structures found in sociolinguistic and dialectological research, and a few applications are found in the literature (for example Cichocki 1986, Inoue 1986, Philps 1984). In this paper we focus on two applications in the study of vowel variation.

Glasgow English (i)

This variable is found in words such as hit, thing and children, and has five variants which Macaulay (1978) arranges along a linear scale as follows:

(i - 1) [ɪ]
(i - 2) [ɪ̌] [ɛ^]
(i - 3) [ï̌] [ɛˀ]
(i - 4) [ə^]
(i - 5) [ʌ^]

In phonetic terms the variants fall into two dimensions – height and front-backness. Using the weighted-index approach Macaulay finds a linear relation between social group and vocalic variant: speakers from the higher end of the social scale tend to use the higher, more front variants; those from the lower end the mid central variants. His sample includes 16 subjects, four from each socioeconomic class (professional, white collar, blue collar, semi-skilled); both genders are equally represented across the social groups.

The DS formulation for this analysis is in terms of a table of frequencies (as in Table 1). The rows are the 16 individual subjects; columns are the 5 variants of (i); the entries are the frequencies with which each subject uses each variant. The procedure treats the rows and columns as two separate spaces – subject space and phonetic space – and objectively determines the optimal association or correlation between them. This association is displayed in the form of a graph which summarizes both indices assigned to variants and scores attributed to subjects. These indices and scores depend strictly on the data structure itself as no preset order is input (1), and they indicate the extent to which subjects' linguistic performance are similar or different.

The application of DS to the Glasgow English (i) data produces a two-dimensional plane (see Figure 1) which accounts for over 90% of the variance in the data. The first (vertical) dimension is the more important (77.2%), the second (horizontal) is less important (16.2%). Locating the phonetic space, we note that the configuration of the vocalic variants corresponds to the familiar pattern of the vowel triangle: the high vowels are at one end of the graph; the mid vowels are spread out along

| | Phonetic Variants | | | | |
Subject	[ɪ]	[ε^],[ɪᵛ]	[ε`],[ɪ̈ᵥ]	[ə^]	[ʌ^]
1	24	40	13	3	0
2	22	48	10	0	0
3	28	45	7	0	0
4	47	30	2	0	0
5	0	16	24	2	0
6	0	32	37	11	0
7	10	36	2	0	0
8	1	38	9	2	0
9	0	12	36	19	7
10	1	28	37	13	1
11	0	22	32	8	0
12	2	33	38	7	0
13	0	15	38	22	5
14	0	34	30	13	3
15	1	19	21	2	1
16	1	18	15	5	1

Table 1   Frequency-table data matrix for Glasgow English (i). The
           table lists frequencies of occurrence of each variant for
           each subject.
           (Source - Macaulay 1978: 140)

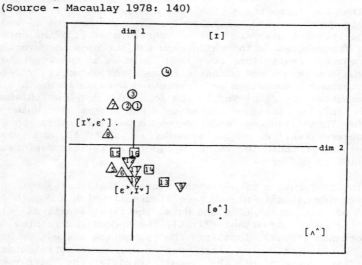

Figure 1   Graph of the dimension 1 - dimension 2 plane for Glasgow
            English (i). Five vocalic variants constitute phonetic
            space. Each number locates a subject in phonetic space;
            social group membership is marked as: ◯ professional,
            △ white collar, ▽ skilled, ☐ semi-skilled.

the opposite end. The positions of individual subjects within the phonetic space also present a fairly clear pattern. Members of the highest social group and two females of the second highest group use the high variants; other subjects use the mid variants, showing variation on the front-back phonetic plane.

The most obvious feature of this analysis is the close correspondence it has with Macaulay's (weighted-index) analysis. The order of variants along dimension 1 is exactly the same as their order in his approach. Also, the subject scores calculated by the two approaches are strongly related ($r=-0.988$). This similarity, however, is apparent if one considers the status of the assumption of order among the variants. DS makes no assumptions and arrives at an analysis which is identical to the weighted-index analysis, which requires the ordering assumption.

A second feature is the possibility of examining information represented on the higher dimensions. In particular, it is interesting to examine usage by those subjects who have (near)identical scores on dimension 1 and different scores on dimension 2. Comparing subjects 1 and 7 (in Table 1) we observe that subject 1 (professional and male) has a broader range of variants - 30% (i-1), 50% (i-2), 17% (i-3), 3% (i-4) - than subject 7 (white collar and female) - 21% (i-1), 75% (i-2), 4% (i-3). A similar comparison holds for subjects 5 and 14 as well as for subjects 6 and 16. Thus dimension 2 isolates subjects who have a greater (to the right) or lesser (to the left) spread of variants. While this difference is statistically significant, its sociolinguistic relevance and interpretation must be determined by the researcher. Is the spread due to the particular lexical items elicited? Are there attitudinal reasons why certain subjects have greater dispersion of variants than others? Answers to these and similar questions will determine whether or not to retain this higher dimension in the analysis.

A third feature of the DS analysis is the graphic display of the results. Not only does the graph show the data by simultaneously representing subject and phonetic spaces, it also induces the researcher to think further about certain details which may have substantive value for the analysis. Such a visual approach to exploring data is receiving increasing attention among statisticians (Tufte 1983).

This Glasgow English (i) application is an example of the elegant quantification of sociolinguistic variation that DS offers, and provides some justification for using DS in quantifying variables with multiple variants (2). We turn now to the analysis of a more complex vocalic variable.

Toronto English (aw)

Toronto English (aw) has six vocalic variants – three low [æw, aw, ɑw] and three mid [ɛw, ɐw, ʌw] – which fit the phonetic dimensions of height and front-backness. The diphthong is found in words such as <u>mouse</u>, <u>trout</u> and <u>couch</u> (in what is called the voiceless environment) as well as in <u>cow</u>, <u>down</u> and <u>aloud</u> (the elsewhere environment). Using data from 18 subjects of three ages groups (children, young adults, adults) and both genders, Chambers (1980) shows that there is a (putative) change of (aw)-fronting taking place. The change is occurring regularly across the age groups and is faster in the elsewhere environment. He also discusses a second process, (aw)-non-raising which involves the voiceless environment but which has less well-defined social correlates.

Chambers' analysis is based on a grouping of variants according to the dimensions of vowel space: variant onsets are front [æ, ɛ], central [a, ɐ] or back [ɑ, ʌ] in the case of (aw)-fronting; they are mid [ɛ, ɐ, ʌ] or low [æ, a, ɑ] for (aw)-non-raising. In terms of the problem of quantification, the researcher must be careful here to verify the pattern of the social-linguistic correlation for each of the variants that have been grouped together. This is also possible in a unitary approach which handles all six variants simultaneously. The DS formulation is to combine the two (18 x 6) tables which summarize the usage by the 18 subjects of the 6 variants for the two phonological environments (or word classes). This (36 x 6) table (see Table 2) is a super-matrix which we can represent formally as Z = [Zv, Ze], where Zv is the table summarizing data in the voiceless environment and Ze is the table for the elsewhere environment.

The DS analysis of this super-matrix reveals three interpretable dimensions which account for 82.4% of the variance in the array. These are displayed as pairs of planes in Figures 2a, 2b and 3. Figures 2a and 2b (the dimension 1 - dimension 2 plane) show the vowel triangle with the low vowels spread out at the lower end and the mid vowels grouped together at the upper end. The cluster of mid vowels is broken up in the dimension 1 - dimension 3 plane (Figure 3).

The graph in Figure 2b locates subjects' usage in the elsewhere environment along the [æ] - [a] - [ɑ] continuum. This

Subject	Phonetic Variants						
	[ɑ]	[ʌ]	[a]	[ɐ]	[æ]	[ɛ]	
1	0	7	0	8	0	0	
2	0	3	0	12	0	0	
3	1	6	0	8	0	0	
4	0	9	0	6	0	0	
5	0	9	0	5	0	1	
6	1	10	0	3	0	0	
7	0	15	0	0	0	0	
8	0	11	1	0	1	2	*voiceless environment*
9	0	0	8	7	0	0	
10	0	15	0	0	0	0	
11	0	2	7	0	6	0	
12	1	13	1	0	0	0	
13	0	14	0	1	0	0	
14	0	14	0	1	0	0	
15	7	8	0	0	0	0	
16	0	15	0	0	0	0	
17	0	12	0	3	0	0	
18	0	14	0	1	0	0	
1	4	0	11	0	0	0	
2	1	0	14	0	0	0	
3	5	0	7	1	2	0	
4	5	0	4	0	6	0	
5	0	0	4	0	11	0	
6	0	0	3	0	12	0	
7	7	0	8	0	0	0	
8	6	0	6	0	3	0	*elsewhere environment*
9	0	0	14	0	1	0	
10	9	0	6	0	0	0	
11	1	0	8	0	6	0	
12	5	0	9	0	1	0	
13	10	0	5	0	0	0	
14	13	0	2	0	0	0	
15	13	0	1	0	0	0	
16	15	0	0	0	0	0	
17	5	0	10	0	0	0	
18	15	0	0	0	0	0	

Table 2   Frequency- table data matrix for Toronto English (aw). The super-matrix lists frequencies of occurrence of each variant for each subject in both voiceless and elsewhere environments.
(Source - Chambers p.c.)

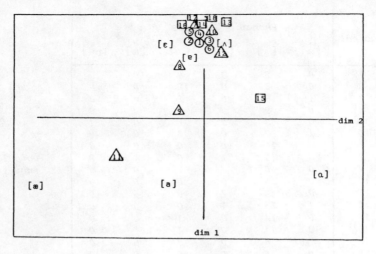

(a) voiceless environment

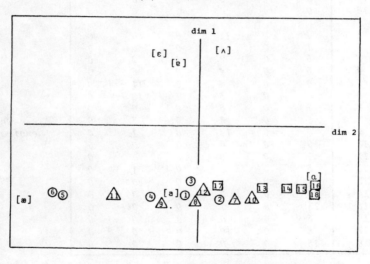

(b) elsewhere environment

Figure 2 Graphs of the dimension 1 - dimension 2 plane for Toronto English (aw), based on DS analysis of data super-matrix. Subjects are located in phonetic space according to their production in (a) voiceless and (b) elsewhere environments. Age group membership is marked as: ○ children, △ young adults, □ adults.

is the (aw)-fronting sound change, with children leading, followed by young adults and adults. The subject scores calculated by DS correlate very strongly with those of the weighted-index approach (r=-1.00). The same plane (Figure 2a) also represents subjects' production in the voiceless environment. The graph points to four subjects (8,9,11 and 15) who do not always raise the (aw) onset - this is (aw)-non-raising which also involves some fronting as shown in the graph. The correlation between the subject scores from the two approaches is strong (r=0.994).

The dimension 1 - dimension 3 plane (Figure 3) further analyses the voiceless environment, focusing primarily on the continuum between [ɐ] and [ʌ]. (We note that the production of [ɛ] is considered to be a separate process and appears on dimension 4.) The process of (aw)-fronting with raising in this plane is characteristic of children, especially boys who are ahead of girls, and a few male adults. There is a fairly strong correlation with weighted-index scores (r= 0.687). This dimension points to a small discrepancy between DS and Chambers' treatments.
DS insists that (aw)-fronting is two separate processes depending on the environment, and not one process as in Chambers' analysis. The DS position appears to be due to a gender x environment x process interaction. Females in general lead in the elsewhere environment, which involves (aw)-fronting; males (particularly boys) lead in the voiceless environment, which involves (aw)-fronting with raising. While this difference in linguistic interpretation is not great, neither position overtly distorts the data found in the matrix in Table 2.

The quantification of Toronto English (aw) illustrates that whereas the classical method assumes that variants can be grouped and deals with these groups separately, DS takes a unitary approach. The DS results correspond closely to the classical treatment as shown by the strong subject score correlations. They also show a multidimensional structure which isolates several processes and their interactions. These are: (aw)-non-raising with fronting in the voiceless environment (dimension 1), (aw)-fronting in the elsewhere environment (dimension 2), (aw)-fronting with raising in the voiceless environment (dimension 3), and the production of [ɛ] (dimension 4). For the most part these receive a reasonable linguistic interpretation.

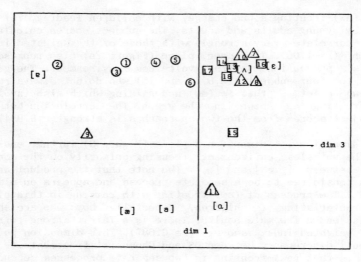

Figure 3   Graph of the dimension 1 - dimension 3 plane for Toronto English (aw). Each number indicates the position of a subject in phonetic space, given his/her production in the voiceless environment. Age group membership is marked as: ◯ children, △ young adults, ☐ adults.

Conclusion

This paper shows how DS provides an objective and generalised approach to the quantification of variables with more than two variants. DS makes no assumptions about the distribution of sociolinguistic data such as the order of variants, and it uses a mathematically-based approach to produce results which correspond closely with those proposed in studies using the weighted-index method.

Among the advantages of the technique are its unitary approach (which coincides with statistical practice and which avoids experimentwise error), its use of multidimensionality (so that significant and interesting patterns are isolated beyond those one finds in a linear or unidimensional perspective), and its graphical representation (which both clarifies the description of variation and enhances our understanding of it).

The paper also suggests a direction for further research. The analyses presented here make use of two types of frequency tables: a simple (16 x 5) matrix in the case of Glasgow English (i) and a two-part super-matrix (i.e. two simple (18 x 6) matrices) for Toronto English (aw). From these we can generalise to a super-matrix with n parts; that is, $Z = [Z_1, Z_2, ..., Z_n]$, where each Z_i represents the simple matrix with information about the i-th of n word classes. Such a super-matrix could in fact include many variables, and its analysis awaits further empirical testing.

Notes

(1) It is possible to input a set of constraints on, for example, the order of the phonetic variants by formulating a design matrix (see Nishisato 1980, chapter 8).

(2) Berdan (1978) proposes a similar approach to the Glasgow data using principal component analysis. DS is a variant of principal component analysis devised to analyse qualitative data such as the frequency tables which represent this and other variables, while the version used by Berdan is intended for interval and ratio data types. This suggests that data structures derived by the two techniques are not always identical (Lebart, Morineau & Warwick 1984, chapter 2).

References

Berdan, R. (1978) Multidimensional analysis of vowel variation. In D. Sankoff (ed) 149-60.

Chambers, J.K. (1980) Linguistic variation and Chomsky's 'homogenous speech community'. In A.M. Kinloch' & A.B. House (eds) **Papers from the fourth meeting of the Atlantic Provinces Linguistic Association**, 1-32.

Cichocki, W. (1986) **Linguistic Applications of Dual Scaling in Variation Studies**. Unpublished Ph.D. dissertation, University of Toronto.

Hudson, R. (1980) Sociolinguistics. Cambridge, UK: Cambridge University Press.

Inoue, F. (1986) Sociolinguistic aspects of new dialect forms: language change in progress in Tokyo. International Journal of the Sociology of Language, 58, 73-89.

Jones-Sargent, V. (1983) **Tyne Bytes: A Computerized Sociolinguistic Study of Tyneside**. New York: Verlag Peter Lang.

Kemp, W. (1979) L'histoire récente de ce que, qu'est-ce que et qu'osque à Montréal: Trois variantes en interaction. In P. Thibault (ed) 53-74.

Labov, W. (1966) **The social stratification of English in New York City**. Washington, DC : Center for Applied Linguistics.

Lebart, L., Morineau, A. & Warwick, K.M. (1984) **Multivariate descriptive statistical analysis**. New York: John Wiley & Sons.

Macaulay, R. (1978) Variation and consistency in Glasgow English. In P. Trudgill (ed) 132-43.

Milroy, J. (1982) Probing under the tip of the iceberg: phonological 'normalization' and the shape of speech communities. In S. Romaine (ed) 35-48.

Mougeon, R., Beniak E. & Valois, D. (1985) Issues in the study of language contact: evidence from Ontarian French. Unpublished MS, Ontario Institute for Studies in Education.

Nishisato, S. (1980) **Analysis of categorical data: Dual Scaling and its applications**. Toronto: University of Toronto Press.

Philps, D. (1984) La structure de l'espace dialectal: essai

méthodologique. In H. Warkentyne (ed) (1985) **Papers from the fifth international conference on methods in dialectology**, 351-62.

Romaine, S. (1978) Postvocalic /r/ in Scottish English: sound change in progress? In P. Trudgill (ed) 144-58.

Romaine, S. (1980) A critical overview of the methodology of urban British sociolinguistics. **English World Wide**, 1/2, 163-98.

Romaine, S. (ed) (1982) **Sociolinguistic variation in speech communities.** London : Edward Arnold.

Sankoff, D. (ed) (1978) **Linguistic variation: models and methods.** New York: Academic Press.

Thibault, P. (ed) (1979) **Le français parlé: Études sociolinguistiques.** Edmonton: Linguistic Research.

Trudgill, P. (ed) (1978) **Sociolinguistic patterns in British English.** London: Edward Arnold.

Tufte, E.R. (1983) **The Visual Display of Quantitative Information.** Cheshire, CT: Graphics Press.

Computers and the American Linguistic Atlas

WILLIAM A. KRETZSCHMAR
University of Georgia

I am here today as a representative for computer work on large-scale projects in American dialect geography. I can describe for you something of the history, present status, and future of the Middle and South Atlantic and Gulf States Atlases; in this I will be a realist. Yet I hope you will indulge me if I depart at times from the actual to talk about a dream -- about a combined American Linguistic Atlas. It has now been 62 years since Kurath made his first field trip to investigate variation in American English, 62 years since the conception of the dream. 62 years ago I was not even a gleam in my grandmother's eye, but now I find myself taken up with it as was Kurath, and quite likely with a better chance of doing something about it. For the last decade I have participated in work on two projects and watched the others; I could not have thought seriously of a combined American Atlas at any time during that period, and nobody else had thought seriously of it since the 1960s. Today the situation has changed. As a realist (if my claim to that label has not already worn thin), I will talk about our situation, especially computer developments, and you can see just how far the vision might be justified by our current status.

As most of you are aware, our American regional projects can be traced back to 1929, when Hans Kurath proposed a plan for a Linguistic Atlas of the United States and Canada. This rather ambitious title -- all of the US and Canada? -- represented a dream rather than an expectation even from the beginning; Kurath's sponsoring agency, the American Council of Learned Societies, rejected the proposal for a national survey and recommended instead an exploratory survey of a limited area (Kurath et al. 1939, pp. ix-xii; O'Cain 1979, pp. 244-54). Kurath subsequently completed the pilot survey of New England in good time (Kurath et al. 1939-43), despite the Depression and approaching War, but other regions had to await time and resources. Kurath himself directed work in the Middle Atlantic States and the South Atlantic States, later combining these two areas into a single project, our current LAMSAS. Perhaps in recognition of the difficulty of completing entire regional surveys in timely fashion, much less completing a Linguistic Atlas of the United States and Canada, between 1949 and 1961 Kurath (1949), Atwood (1953), and Kurath and McDavid (1961) published three summary volumes on the vocabulary, grammar, and pronunciation of the Eastern US, still the basic resources for American dialect patterns. At any rate, Raven McDavid has written that "by 1963 the original concept of a unified Linguistic Atlas of the United States and Canada, under a single director, had been abandoned" (1984, p. 7). The effort did go forward in other areas of the country. Albert Marckwardt continued the survey of the North-Central region. Harold Allen directed work in the Upper Midwest, bringing his *Atlas* to publication in the 1970s (1973-76). David Reed managed efforts on the Pacific Coast, in California and Nevada. The latest major project has been directed by Lee Pederson in the Gulf States, and he has published a good deal of his material already (Pederson *et al*. 1981, 1986a, 1986b). Other linguistic geographers worked in other places on a smaller scale, such as William R. Van Riper in Oklahoma (see McDavid [1984] for the best recent overview). There were also cognate ventures in dialect lexicography, culminating in the recent publication of the first volume of *DARE*, but I must leave those aside for present purposes. In the course of fifty years there have been occasional changes in the leadership of different projects and the inevitable accession of a younger generation of scholars. Raven McDavid succeeded Kurath on LAMSAS, for instance, and I in turn have followed him. Nonetheless, after more than fifty years and despite the fragmentation of the proposed American Atlas into separate and unequal regions, that original ambitious dream still has life for a good part of the land area of the US, including all of it east of the Mississippi -- though Canada will have to be treated separately -- since all of these investigators used basically the same methodology and conducted interviews at roughly the same time, call it "mid-century". It may still be possible to prepare a Linguistic Atlas of the United States based on these records.

The most important factors for realizing an American Atlas are now coming together. First of all, many of the separate regional projects are coming physically together. In the Fall of 1986, I moved to the University of Georgia with the collections that Raven

McDavid had assembled in Chicago and South Carolina, which include either the original records or paper copies of LAMSAS, the North-Central project, the New England project, and numerous smaller surveys, such as Miller's records from Augusta, Georgia. To augment that already fine collection, we are now preparing a complete copy of the Gulf States tapes, and have a commitment to receive the Pacific Coast records. It may well be possible to acquire other important surveys as time goes on, though at the moment we are buried in the hundreds of thousands of pages we already have, preparing for archiving them in the Special Collections Department of the Georgia Library. The University has been most generous in providing working space, facilities, equipment, assistants, and administrative cooperation -- all those things that have been lacking for the past 62 years. Major funding to complement this excellent groundwork will probably have to come from our National Endowment for the Humanities; NEH has provided well over a million dollars for linguistic atlas work during the past decade or so, for which we are all most grateful, and we hope that NEH will continue to lend us support. The table is set for a feast of work.

A second major factor is the security of the projects under the sponsorship of the American Dialect Society. While the original Linguistic Atlas of the US and Canada project began under the auspices of the American Council of Learned Societies, the break-up into smaller projects meant the abandonment of any central responsibility. When all of the separate projects were independently the business of their directors, there was no assurance about whether research materials would be, or would continue to be, available to others. For example, I cannot discover that anybody knows for sure what has happened to Kimmerle's Colorado records. Our Georgia agreement is actually between the Dialect Society and the University, with ultimate title to the collections residing with the Society. In this way the resident editor can trust that the work will continue, and that scholars will always be able to use the materials. Any research materials that we receive for archiving and future processing will fall under the agreement, and so will benefit from its protection. Nobody doubts the time it will take to complete editing of all of the materials, much less their assembly into a larger unit; we cannot, and now need not, afford the impermanence of merely personal responsibility.

The last major factor in realizing the dream of an American Atlas is the main subject of my talk, the development of computer methods. The advantages of using computers for our work must be obvious to all; for LAMSAS alone, we have something like one and a quarter million responses to questions; since each response might also be analyzed by its phonetic constituents, we might settle on an estimate of 10-15 million individually sortable pieces of information in the LAMSAS corpus. Computer assistance is not just a convenience for us; it is absolutely necessary if we are to do anything more than scratch the surface of our data in analysis. In addition, we must have computer assistance in the publication process. Our former method of producing the fascicles of LAMSAS (McDavid *et al*. 1980-; see McDavid *et al*. [1986] for a more detailed description of the process) involved the typing of camera-ready columns of fine phonetics at a Selectric II typewriter, which required enormous amounts of time and detailed work by a skilled compositor, who spent additional hours stripping manual corrections into the inevitably imperfect typescript. With a computer not only can the keyboarding be vastly expedited, but editing is easier and the result is a database, not just a typescript, and from that we can conduct our automated analyses as well as publish in print form.

The history of the use of computers in American linguistic geography is longer than one might think; there is an excellent article on that subject by Viereck and Schneider (1984). Let us go back, though, only as far as 1982, when I began investigating computerization for LAMSAS and when Lee Pederson had already spent two years entering Gulf States data on the Emory University mainframe. For LAMSAS, Raven McDavid had considered using computers as early as the 1960s but rejected the means then available as too cumbersome and ill-suited to the work. He asked me to take up the subject again when I left Chicago for a teaching post in Wisconsin and so would be unavailable for first-hand work with the records. My primary brief at that time was to find out how computers could help us publish LAMSAS in fascicles, with fine phonetic detail, and I quickly learned that there was no good way to do it. For one thing, there was no good means to represent phonetic characters on the computer screen. There was also no good way to print them out. Of course there were things that IBM and DEC and other companies recommended, but they were either vastly too expensive if they could actually display or print phonetics, or they would have to rely on complicated coding schemes for data entry, which would not make our keyboarding and editing any easier. Pederson's goal was different. When he began work on the concordance in 1980 (with the help of John Nitti of the University of Wisconsin, a key figure in LAGS computerization), he was concerned only to enter data in standard spelling, so he could use available equipment. Pederson found the Emory mainframe more than suitable for his purpose.

The only thing left for me to do, however, was to start from scratch. From the beginning I intended that our LAMSAS methods should be portable to any dialectologist, not limited to one-of-a-kind equipment, so development should rely on software, to be designed for available hardware of at most moderate price. I knew what our specific needs were for LAMSAS, and I also advertised for advice among dialectologists and other linguists so that our development work might have as wide an application as possible. The result of my inquiries indicated strongly that the software should be written for increasingly popular microcomputers rather than for mainframes -- because of downtime and competition for mainframe processing time on many campuses (though these problems were only marginal for Pederson) -- but that was as far as the consensus went. In 1983 and 1984 I wrote three separate grant proposals for the development of software which would enable us to computerize LAMSAS, and which would also have provided a basic integrated software package for anyone who needed phonetics, but all three proposals went unfunded. Reviewers generally thought the idea a good one, but most had their own ideas about what microcomputer or printer or computer language or set of phonetic symbols should be included, and most worried about the broad, speculative nature of the proposal and about development costs; no expensive proposal was ever funded when so many disagreed about so many of the details.

In the meantime, during 1983, McDavid and I prepared a proposal to create a word index for LAMSAS on computer, following an NEH recommendation. That task could be accomplished with available commercial products because it required no phonetics; NEH funded it. We began with a planning meeting in the summer of 1984, with Pederson -- fresh from completing data entry for his LAGS Concordance (Pederson et al. 1984, 1986a) -- and a software consultant, Jeffrey Huntsman, who himself taught linguistics at Indiana and had wide experience in the kind of development work we envisaged. At that meeting we confirmed our general goal of devising methods of general utility, not just for LAMSAS alone. We provided for entering the complete set of LAMSAS responses in standard spelling into a database instead of only the unique responses, and we explicitly allowed for the eventual addition of phonetic data when the means became available. It was a heady two days, to be followed by two years of frustration. Even the best of plans is subject to the humanity of its agents: McDavid died suddenly in October of 1984, and the software consultant was never in two years able to deliver a fully satisfactory version of the software we had outlined. Our NEH grant money bought hardware and paid for student assistants, and we did manage to encode about 30Mb of data (perhaps 30% of our corpus), but we ended up with no indices and an unreliable (in computer terms, "flaky") database. In a moment I will discuss the details of our plan and the reasons it failed; for now, it is enough to say we learned that computers and software are not the essential problem, a role reserved for the people manipulating them.

During our two years of headaches on LAMSAS, Pederson went forward with work on LAGS. He shifted over to microcomputers from the mainframe and began reentering data. It was not possible to convert data from the Concordance for reasons I will discuss below, but the reentry of data in these databases was made easier, indeed made possible, by the existence of the Concordance, worth every moment of the two years for data entry and three years of editing that it took to make. He completed entry of a database in systematic phonetic coding, which replaces each sound with a string of up to nine letters representing distinctive features (Pederson 1985, 1986b), and now has completed entry of another database in what he calls Automatic Book Code, a separate system which respells words in the Roman alphabet in order to represent pronunciation while still retaining a recognizable word shape (Pederson 1987). Pederson has also worked with programmers to create several mapping programs to be used with these databases. Pederson is now ready to proceed rapidly with publication of different volumes of LAGS featuring these databases and related maps; he also has plans to distribute the LAGS databases on floppy disks.

At this point, then, to bring these historical remarks to a close, LAGS is the only major American Atlas project to be fully entered into computer databases (though still without using phonetic symbols per se), LAMSAS is partially entered but in a dubious form, and none of the several other major Atlas surveys has been entered at all. LAGS is the only project at a point where analytical and mapping programs could be applied to a complete database, and in fact Pederson is in process of using such programs. LAGS and LAMSAS, at least, are committed to using microcomputers as basic tools, though none of us is averse to using mainframe processing when we have a real need for it. The crucial issues facing us now are the use of phonetics and methods of data entry. The first, actually, is now possible: in 1986 Hercules Computer Technology released an inexpensive graphics card which allows the user to define and display any characters he wants to on IBM and compatible microcomputers, in a manner which will work with applications software not designed for the card and which will allow for printout without excessive coding in the data file itself. The marketplace has caught up to the needs we identified five years ago. For phonetics on printout, the pages of Journal of English Linguistics (if I may insert a brief plug) will continue to show the state-of-the-art in cost-effective, desk-top representations. The second issue, methods for data entry, must be our main concern because we have to have compatible databases for our separate surveys if we are later to make combined analyses, and we must have a rapid, labor-saving way to enter our enormous quantities of data. It will not do to enter and reenter data as Pederson has had to do, but we would be silly not to construct new databases which did not conform to the pattern set by LAGS. Let us now turn to the technical matters of the structure of a database and means for rapid entry of text into that structure. The remarks to follow will be more technical than many people are used to; I hope attention to the Figures will help explain.

"Structure" in a database refers to the arrangement of information: what different kinds of files will be included within the overall database; then, what data will be listed within each file; and then, with what coding will the data be entered. LAGS offers us two separate models for database structure (see Figure 1). The LAGS concordance was structured on the mainframe as a series of files, all of the same type, one file for each informant in the survey; later these files were all appended together to create one huge file. Each line in the file constituted a "record" (one unit of data) and thus was devoted to a single response by an informant; each "record", in this case each line, contained six "fields" (places to put individual pieces of data): a code number to identify the informant, the page of the questionnaire, the question on the page, a symbol characterizing the response (to mark scribal error or other anomalies), a grammatical tag, and the response itself. Comments by the fieldworker or informant were actually entered in the same field as the response, but were set off with angle brackets and so amount to a separate field. All data was entered in standard spelling, but there was some added coding: an asterisk marked a "phantom space" in phrases and compounds to tell the concording program to count each word as well as the phrase or compound as a whole; and there was information in square brackets about grammatical elements deleted from phrases. The LAGS microcomputer databases for lexical, pronunciation, and grammatical items are even simpler. Each of these databases has two types of files: a response file and a code-list file. There is a pair of these files for each relevant item in the questionnaire. Within each response file separate lines again constitute a record, and within each record there are just two fields: one for the code number of the informant, and one for the response. Multiple responses by the same informant are listed in the same field, but are separated by "+" signs. In order to save keyboarding and processing time, the responses are entered as single symbols, and the legends to the single-symbol codes are contained in the code-list file. The only difference between the lexical, pronunciation, and grammatical databases is that the files with keys to the symbols have the responses listed in standard spelling for the lexical database, and in the Automatic Book Code for the pronunciation and grammatical databases. In order to analyze the information in these databases, LAGS keeps a single master file for information about each informant (sex, age, race, social class, and so on) and the terms of the interview (date, place, and interviewer). There is one other LAGS database, for systematic phonetics, but since that database was created from LAGS idiolect synopses we will leave it out of account here.

Data entry for LAGS has been only minimally automated, and the microcomputer databases were reentered using paper copies of the concordance or the transcriptions of interviews. It is important here to recognize the path-finding nature of LAGS data entry -- until the job had been done, nobody could predict ways to save time. For the concordance database, the keyboarder would enter the code number of the informant whose responses would be keyed at that session, and then the program would bring up screens with the page numbers of the questionnaire and the item numbers in order, and the keyboarder would type in coding and responses for each record. For the microcomputer databases, the keyboarder would call up a text editor (typically the WordStar wordprocessing program), then name a file for the item to be entered, and then copy into it a serial listing of the 914 primary informants, each on a separate line. Then the keyboarder would enter the appropriate code letters, from a code-list of the possible responses, on the line for each informant. LAGS microcomputer methods represented an advance in entry speed and accuracy because only a single letter had to be typed for each response; the improvement was possible because the concordance had already been constructed and so the keyboarder knew what responses were possible.

We designed our ambitious LAMSAS data structure when only the LAGS concordance database had been entered, but we planned for something quite similar to what LAGS ended up with (see Figure 2). Instead of a mainframe program and later WordStar on microcomputers, we intended an integrated database to be made from dBase III, a powerful commercial database program. The whole idea was to enter our data only once in a file structure which, later, would allow us to create a concordance and also allow the use of the analytical tools provided within dBase III; moreover, we wanted a customized look for the program (in computer terms, a "user-interface") which would be (again in computer terms) "bulletproof", that is, one that would not require the keyboarder to know anything about the program itself but would lead him through the steps of data entry via menus. Still further, we wanted the customized version to be adaptable to any survey, not just usable for LAMSAS. Accordingly, our database had many files. First, there was a master file which contained a list of all of our informants with their characteristics, like the LAGS master file. Next, we had a second master file with a list of all of the headwords from the separate items in the questionnaire. The data files consisted of a main file of responses to be created for each item in the questionnaire, with each of these response files linked to separate files for a list of common responses, for comments on individual responses, and for responses which were too long to fit into the standard length allowed in the main response file. Instead of one huge data file, as with LAGS on mainframe, or two file types for each questionnaire item as with LAGS on microcomputer, for LAMSAS we had no fewer than four files for each questionnaire item.

The larger number of linked files was the beauty, in principle, of the ultra-rapid and "bulletproof" data-entry system for LAMSAS. When the keyboarder called up our customized version of dBase III he had only to enter the number corresponding to the headword, and the program would create a file containing entry screens for each of our 1216 informants, and each of the screens would already have most of the data filled into the fields: the headword, other item and informant coding information, and flags to indicate that that response had no special characteristics and no comment attached (the usual status of our responses). The program then opened the linked files for comments, for responses too long to fit into the standard field of the entry screen, and the common-response file. If this was a new headword file, the program then asked the keyboarder to fill in the fields of the common-response file, and when that was done it jumped immediately to the first record so the keyboarder could begin filling in responses. The program automatically checked to see whether it could find a set of files already created for a given headword, and if so, did not recreate them but skipped ahead to the first blank record, the precise spot that the keyboarder had gotten to in the previous session, in the main response file. The keyboarder usually pressed just two keys for each record, the appropriate letter from the common-response file (the codes were displayed at the top of the screen for reference), and the "Enter" code to save that record and bring up the next screen. If the response was not contained in the common-response file, the keyboarder could enter it manually; if there was some special characteristic for the response, he just changed the flag to the appropriate code for "suggested", "forced", or the like; if there was a comment he simply pressed one key to make the program bring up a field from the comment file for it to be entered; if the response was too long to fit into the standard response field, the program automatically copied that field as a record in the long-response file. If an informant had given multiple responses, the keyboarder just pressed a key and the program automatically created a new entry screen for the second or third or whatever response. If the keyboarder ever pressed the wrong key, either the program would not accept the keystroke or he could go back later to edit an erroneous response. When the keyboarder was finished with an entry session, the program automatically converted the single-key responses into the full response listed in the common-response list before saving all of the files. All the time it was running it was lovely, it was wonderful when all went well: the LAMSAS program allowed the entry of the 1200-plus responses for one questionnaire item in as little as three hours, and typically in four, compared to about eight hours for the 800-plus responses for one informant in the LAGS concordance.

But all did not go well. We devised our linked file structure for speed and "bulletproofing", and also to save space; every character saved in one of our entry screens meant over a megabyte of storage space would be saved for the final database, since each entry screen for a record corresponded to a just one of our million-plus responses. The design, however, put a great burden on the software consultant who did the programming. All of those files and the linkages between them had to be kept straight, and he just could not do it. His first few attempts were outright failures. I remember clearly the day he brought the first version to Chicago -- six months late, and both of us driving for hours through a snowstorm just to get there. We sat before the computer until late at night and, for all that, the program would not even allow us to get past the opening menu -- at which point we both drove more hours through the same snowstorm to get home. After fifteen months of more and more corrections, talk of firing the consultant, even talk of suspending work on the grant, the program would finally allow us to enter data without absolutely fatal errors. Even then, however, the program was "flaky": it occasionally and unpredictably refused to save responses or comments, it could not keep multiple responses in order, it even failed to find responses for editing that actually were in the data file. Having gone so far already, however, we kept our commitments to our students and forged ahead to enter as much data as we could before the grant period ended and the project moved to Georgia. Now, every data file in the 30Mb we managed to enter will have to be collated with our original paper records to locate and correct these "flaky" errors. This is less than wonderful.

Pederson's progress on LAGS and our failure with the custom LAMSAS program result from a fundamental difference in viewpoint. Pederson places great confidence in and reliance on the keyboarder, especially since he and one or two staff members of long tenure on the project have done all of that work. On LAMSAS, we had been used to employing graduate student assistants for repetitive, clerical tasks and to reserving senior staff time for highly skilled jobs like transcription and editing. Evidently we shall have to change our minds. If a "bulletproof" program is too unwieldy, we will just have to remove the armor and try to protect ourselves by controlling who sits at the keyboard -- and that is our new plan. The LAMSAS database may be flawed, but it is far from unusable. Its data structure can be converted from a linked system of files to the less automated, simpler LAGS system. The linkages existed only in the program, not as a part of the files themselves; therefore, we can adapt our basic data structure to one which combines elements of the LAGS mainframe and microcomputer structures. In so doing we can still use edited versions of the files from our initial keyboarding. Our redesigned database will serve both to create an index and also, once converted to compatible files, to make use of LAGS analytical programs. We will retain the dBase III software with which the LAMSAS database was originally created (a few LAGS files were made with it, too), but instead of an overall customized version for data entry we will have to rely on skilled keyboarders to manipulate the files.

Our new data structure will have two files per questionnaire item, like the LAGS microcomputer databases, one for responses in which each record will contain one response, the other for a key to single-letter codes for the possible responses (see Figure 2). Unlike the LAGS microcomputer databases, the records in our response files will contain information encoded only in the LAGS mainframe concordance file, that is, a comment field, fields for page and item number from the questionnaire, and flags for special characteristics and grammatical function in addition to informant number and response. We will add one additional field not found in LAGS, a project identifier for LAMSAS, looking forward to the day when we will want to make cross-survey analyses. In dBase III it is possible to modify the structure of each record after the fact, so we have the means to add a field for the phonetic transcription of the response once we finish the first run with responses in standard spelling. We will no longer keep separate files for comments and for extra-long responses; we will just have to accept inflation of the total final size of the database in order to dispense with the linked files. We will still have a code-list file, but now it will contain all possible responses and not just common responses; we can make the code-list file ahead of time for many items, because of previous work on LAMSAS list manuscripts. The code-list file will not be linked to the main response file during data entry; that linkage will only be necessary during later file conversions. We will also have to construct a master informant file just like the LAGS master.

Data entry for this system can be more automated than data entry for the LAGS concordance, about the same as entry for the LAGS microcomputer databases, but will include more data per record. LAGS has given us clues for time-saving. For new files the keyboarder will use dBase III to copy a model file onto the new filename, with the response field already filled in with the most common response if that is desirable; these steps will require the keyboarder to know how to use dBase III, and will no longer be performed automatically. Then the keyboarder would call up the new file and proceed through it record by record, filling in fields with special information as needed. If the most common response is copied along with the model and there are no comments or flags to be written, in many cases the keyboarder would have to type only one keystroke to go on to the next record; two keystrokes if a single-letter code for a response was all that was needed; and more keystrokes as necessary to add comments or change flags. It will take half a dozen keystrokes and more knowledge of the dBase III program to insert a record in the event an informant gave multiple responses, another case where the process is no longer automatic. The procedure will be reasonably speedy, but quite dangerous; every time the keyboarder has to use commands in dBase III there is a chance of fouling up the database, and there is even some danger without special commands -- accidentally pressing the wrong key in dBase III can cause the loss of the file one is working on. There will be mistakes, but at least with this method it will be the keyboarder and not the program at fault.

I have mentioned file conversions at several points. There is nothing mysterious about them, but some are more difficult than others. It would have been next to impossible to convert the LAGS concordance file into the files for different microcomputer databases; going from complete responses to single-letter codes would have required a complicated conversion program for each questionnaire item, not to mention changing representation systems for the grammatical and pronunciation databases. Another problem was the inclusion of more than one kind of information in a single field, particularly comments and "phantom space" coding and grammatical deletion codes all in the response field. For LAMSAS we will be starting with dBase III and can use the commands of that commercial program to make most conversions. File conversions in such a case are quite easy if all one wants to do is to add or delete fields from the records in a file. For example, when we want to delete the headword field from the old LAMSAS structure to get to the new one, or later to add a phonetics field to the new LAMSAS structure, that will be quite simple. To achieve versions of the new LAMSAS files compatible with the LAGS microcomputer files, we will delete the unwanted fields useful only for the index, but we will have to adjust files manually to meet the LAGS practice in such files of putting more than one response into a record; this is another case where a field has more than one piece of information. To make an index, we will have to convert our responses coded as single letters into the complete, spelled-out response. That will require a small conversion program to relink each response file with its code-list file; the conversion will be time-consuming but not impossible, and will certainly take less time than rekeyboarding everything. The conversion is possible because we will have started with single-letter entries, the reverse of the LAGS procedure. It will be easiest to use one of the mainframes at Georgia for the index: it will not be a problem to append all of our response files together (that function is supported in dBase III), but the resulting combined file will be a monster and could only be stored and processed on a mainframe. dBase III creates its data files according to a standard configuration (comma delimited ASCII), so using the capacity of the mainframe will be possible.

It will all, I think, be worth the trouble. We will have keyboarded the LAMSAS database only once, and then can automate most of the conversions. The system is portable to other surveys once we finish LAMSAS; it will not be as easy for other dialectologists to use our new method as it would have been for them to use the one we originally designed -- other users will have to learn dBase III, whereas before they would not have -- but the methods are simple enough to work well. When we get to the point of crossing survey boundaries to make meta-analytical studies, the LAGS databases will have to have a field added for a project identifier, but the groundwork will have been laid to make that quantum leap to truly large-scale analysis. As it happens Georgia has an underutilized supercomputer, and we might be one of the few projects to make use of it for humanities research.

Let me conclude today by illustrating some of the analytical programs already developed for LAGS. The programs were written for the microcomputer databases by Susan Leas McDaniel, one of Pederson's long-standing assistants on the project, along with William McDaniel. All are written in compiled BASIC, and are able to produce screen displays, disk files, or printouts for output. There are five programs. The first and simplest program, called "lexsort", sorts a given data file, either for a single variant or for a combination of variants. The program then lists all of the informants for the target response or combination, with all of their characteristics. I have not illustrated this simple listing. The other four programs produce maps of different kinds, as illustrated on Figures 4 through 6.

The mapping programs all depend on the principle of the graphic plotter grid (Pederson 1986a), for which Thomas's 1980 book on areal analysis served as inspiration. Rather than plot symbols upon a base map, which would require fairly sophisticated graphics software for either screen displays or printout, Pederson prefers to define a grid for the LAGS region using the regular character locations on the screen or print positions on the printout page (Figure 3 shows the LAGS region; Figures 4-5 the maps). His 70 by 34 grid provides 2380 possible points. In the map, each displayed or printed dot or letter corresponds to one of the 914 primary LAGS informants, and spaces are used to show places where there is no informant -- such as the ocean, or gaps in the less-dense pattern of interviewing in Florida and Texas. The completely filled eastern area of the region represents the dense interviewing there, but also results from the need to spread out slightly the multiple informants from urban places into adjoining rural areas. The abstraction renders quite a good likeness of the boundaries of the Gulf States region. When a map is displayed on the computer monitor, the heading plus the grid require two consecutive screens; on printout, the entire heading and map fit nicely onto a single page. The arrangement is an elegant solution, I think, in not requiring special equipment to produce a picture for computer maps.

Two LAGS programs generate maps of this kind. The first, called "lagsmap", prompts the user for one, two, or three variables, single variant responses from a data file. The program then plots each occurrence of the specified variables and their combinations on the grid, using a separate symbol for each variable or combination of variables; for informants who gave none of the variables as responses, the program plots a full stop. Figure 4 shows an example of this kind of map: for the question about kindling, the responses _fatwood_ and _rich-pine_ are plotted, and have a distinct pattern. The second program, called "codemap", is illustrated in Figure 5. For this program, the user selects a variant response from a data file, and can then specify any of nine codes referring to the age, social status, and education of informants, for both Black and white informants. The program will then plot a separate symbol for each code specified for the variant response. Figure 5 shows the plot for _fatwood_, which shows that that variant occurs most frequently among older informants. These two graphic-plotter mapping programs can satisfy most common mapping needs.

The last two LAGS programs produce a more abstract and compact representation of the data (see Figure 6). In the original design for interviewing, the LAGS region was divided into 16 different sectors (see Figure 3). The program called "sectotal" counts the occurrences of a specified variable in each sector, and represents the totals in a 4 x 4 matrix. As in the graphic-plotter grids, each sector is in the relative position it occupies within the actual LAGS area, but here the sectors simply compose a square matrix rather than a picture. In Figure 6, the "sectotal" matrices for _fatwood_ and _rich-pine_ give a good indication of the complementary distribution of the variants. The last and newest program, called "soctotal", compiled only in recent weeks, uses a similar matrix, but does not represent a geographic area. The 4 x 6 matrix instead compactly shows the total number of informants who gave the target response in 24 different social categories, as labeled on Figure 6. The greater number of older informants using <u>fatwood</u> and <u>rich-pine</u> shows up here, and for <u>rich-pine</u> there is also an apparent difference by degree of insularity (Kurath's Type A rather than his Type B) and educational level. With a little practice in looking at them, the matrices give a fast indication of the potential patterning of a variant on an actual map.

All of these programs run in about 15 seconds on a standard IBM PC, in as little as five seconds on a fast machine like an AT. That is a result of good programming, but also of a good data structure in the databases. The segmentation of the data into files according to the separate items on the pages of the questionnaire limits the quantity of data the computer must search in order to produce results. These programs link the separate files for responses and the code lists (which the user refers to outside of the programs) with the master file of informant information; linkage <u>after</u> data entry is much easier to maintain than our LAMSAS idea of linkage from the beginning. The analytical system defined by the separate programs can be added to and might be improved. For instance, there might be a shell for the programs which could help the user select data files, variables, and codes, when now the user must look up all of that information separately. Wishful but not implausible thinking might suggest a system using Artificial Intelligence which could "decide" which files and criteria were relevant to a question -- but to return from airy castles, any additions and improvements would only make this already good system better.

All in all, LAGS sets a fine model for our further work on the separate regions of the American Atlas, and suggests how possible a combined Atlas has actually become. Nobody will underestimate the time and work it will require to encode the data for all the separate regions, or even for <u>one</u> of the regions, but we have hope today which we could not have had as little as five yeas ago, hope brought by the computer and recent developments for it, of realizing Kurath's original dream for an American Atlas.

References

Allen, H. B. (1973-76) *Linguistic Atlas of the Upper Midwest*. 3 vols. Minneapolis: University of Minnesota Press.
Atwood, E. B. (1953) *A Survey of Verb Forms in the Eastern United States*. Ann Arbor: University of Michigan Press.
Kurath, H. (1949) *A Word Geography of the Eastern United States*. Ann Arbor: University of Michigan Press.
-----, and McDavid, R. I., Jr. (1961) *The Pronunciation of English in the Atlantic States*. Ann Arbor: University of Michigan Press. Rpt., 1982 (University, AL: University of Alabama Press).
Kurath, H., et al. (1939) *Handbook of the Linguistic Geography of New England*. Providence: Brown University, for the American Council of Learned Societies. 2nd ed., 1973, with additions by A. R. Duckert and R. I. McDavid, Jr. (New York: AMS Press).
----- (1939-43) *Linguistic Atlas of New England*. 3 vols. in 6. Providence: Brown University, for the American Council of Learned Societies. Rpt., 3 vols., 1973 (New York: AMS Press).
McDavid, R. I., Jr. (1984) Linguistic geography. *PADS*, 71 [*Needed Research in American English (1983)*], 4-31.
----- et al. (1980-) *Linguistic Atlas of the Middle and South Atlantic States*. Chicago: University of Chicago Press.
----- (1986) Inside a linguistic atlas. *Proceedings of the American Philosophical Society*, 130, 390-405.
O'Cain, R. K. (1979) Linguistic Atlas of New England. *American Speech*, 54, 243-78. [review article after rpt.]
Pederson, L. (1985) Systematic phonetics. *Journal of English Linguistics*, 18, 14-24.
----- (1986a) A graphic plotter grid. *Journal of English Linguistics*, 19, 25-41.
----- (1986b) A survey in deductive phonetics. *Zeitschrift für Dialektologie und Linguistic*, 53, 289-309.
----- (1987) An automatic book code (*ABC*). *Journal of English Linguistics*, 20, 48-71.
----- et al. (1981) *The Linguistic Atlas of the Gulf States: The Basic Materials*. Microform. Ann Arbor: University Microfilms.
----- (1984) The LAGS concordance. *American Speech*, 59, 332-39.

----- (1986a) <u>The Linguistic Atlas of the Gulf States: The Concordance of Basic Materials</u>. Microform. Ann Arbor: University Microfilms.
----- (1986b) <u>The Linguistic Atlas of the Gulf States: Volume 1, Handbook</u>. Athens: University of Georgia Press.
Schneider, E., and Viereck, W. (1984) The use of the computer in American, Canadian, and British English dialectology and sociolinguistics. <u>Dialectology</u>, ed. by H. Goebl (Bochum: Brockmeyer), 15-60.
Thomas, A. R. (1980) <u>Areal Analysis of Dialect Data by Computer: A Welsh Example</u>. Cardiff: University of Wales Press.

Figure 1   LAGS Data Structure

Concordance structure: one file per informant, later one large file.

Example of LAGS mainframe concordance file:

```
BOOK   PAGE   LINE   SG   GG   ENTRY
-----------------------------------------------------------------
0387   038    6      f    s    harnessing him <to attach to a wagon>
...
0007   020    4      b         harp <=harmonica>
0015   020    4                harp
0029   020    4                harp
0030   020    4                harp
```

Microcomputer databases: master file of informants, with one response file and one code-list file per questionnaire item, unlinked.

Example of structure in LAGS microcomputer lexical file {008.6}:

```
"001","bh+ec"
"002","A+bh+cx"
"003","B+ec+eh"
"004","bh"
"005","bh+ff"
"006","bh"
"007","bh"
"008","bh+cx+eh"
"009","fg"
```

Example of structure in LAGS microcomputer code-list file:

                    CODE LIST FOR {008.6} (KINDLING)

A = black pine knots (1)   ba = firewood (22)
B = burrs (1)   bb = heart of pine (3)
C = cedar (3)   bc = heart of the pine (2)
D = cedar kindling (1)   bd = hearts (2)
E = cedar shavings (1)   be = huisache wood (1)
F = cedar shingles (1)   bf = kindle (n.) (1)
G = cedar splinters (1)   bg = kindle wood (2)
H = chip kindling (1)   bh = kindling (578)
I = chips (38)   bi = kindling-like, a (2)

Figure 2   LAMSAS Data Structure

Original automated program: 4 files per item, linked to each other and to master files by automated program.

master informant file   master headword file

                response file

common-response file   comment file   extra-long response file

Example entry screen:

                        Procedure for adding item data

List MS No: 137   HOG PEN

1--pig pen
2--hog pen
3--pig sty
4--hog house
5--hog lot
6--xxxx
7--xxxx
8--sty
9--hog pasture
0--NO RESPONSE

List MS No.: 137   Headword: HOG PEN
Informant: NC49   [421]   Worksheet No.: 15.3
Item: _____
Doubtful Record? N   Another reply? N   Comment (Y/N/Q[uit] N

            Press ^W when you are finished with the record.

New LAMSAS structure: master file of informants, with one response file and code-list file for each item, unlinked. Page and question numbers to serve as filename.

Fields per record, response file: project id, informant no., response, special characteristics, grammatical tag, comment, [response in phonetics].

Fields per record, code-list file: code letter (e.g., aa,ab), unique response.

Figure 3   Map of LAGS Region by Sector

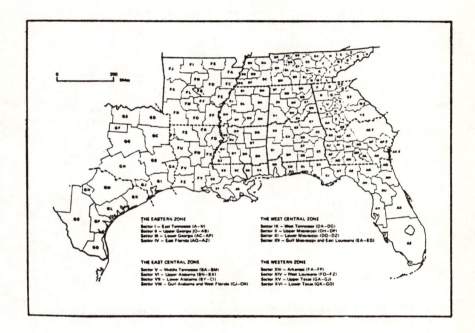

Figure 4   Kindling

A = fatwood (total: 34)
B = rich-pine (total: 43)
+ = fatwood + rich-pine
. = another response or no response

```
                    1         2         3         4         5         6         7
           1234567890123456789012345678901234567890123456789012345678901234567890
       A                                              .........B........BBB..B          A
       B                                                        ........B..........     B
       C                                    ...............              B..B.........B C
       D                                    ...............                     B.BBB   D
       E                                    ...............              B........      E
       F                                    ..B............B................B...        F
       G                                    ..B............B........B......B..B.B..     G
       H               ..          .        .B.............B........B...B....A....      H
       I                                    .BB..................................B..    I
       J               .           .        ..........A......B..........B............B..J
       K            ....         ..         .......................A........A.......    K
       L            ...         ..          ..............................A.......      L
       M            ..          .           ..........A.........B...........           M
       N                         .          ...B......B....A...........A.......A....    N
       O               .                    .....B............A..................A...A. O
       P                       .BB          .....B.......B......A...........A....A.     P
       Q               ..         ..        BB.........A..A....A..A..A........           Q
       R                .         ..        B..............A........A..A        A       R
       S                                    ..............AA....    .AA..         ..    S
       T              ..         ...        .........                        ..A        T
       U             ..          .          ............                      .  ..     U
       V              ..          .         ...........                      ...        V
       W             ...         ...                                         ...        W
       X              ..                                                    ..          X
       Y              .          ....                                   A .. A          Y
       Z                         .                                         ..           Z
       AA              .          ..                                        ....  .     AA
       AB             ..          ..                                     A...           AB
       AC             ..           .                                         .. A A     AC
       AD             ..                                                      . ..      AD
       AE             ..                                                       ....     AE
       AF              ...                                                     ...      AF
       AG                                                                       .       AG
       AH                                                                               AH
                    1         2         3         4         5         6         7
           1234567890123456789012345678901234567890123456789012345678901234567890
```

Figure 5   Kindling (008.6)   Variant: fatwood   34

```
                   Code 1: Race/Class/Age
            1 = W/L/13-30    0/5      A = B/L/13-30    0/13
            2 = W/M/13-30    0/67     B = B/M/13-30    0/13
            3 = W/U/13-30    0/10     C = B/U/13-30    0/0
            4 = W/L/31-60    1/25     D = B/L/31-60    1/19
            5 = W/M/31-60    4/117    E = B/M/31-60    1/25
            6 = W/U/31-60    1/33     F = B/U/31-60    0/5
            7 = W/L/61-99    4/149    G = B/L/61-99    5/84
            8 = W/M/61-99    13/257   H = B/M/61-99    1/35
            9 = W/U/61-99    3/54     J = B/U/61-99    0/3


              1         2         3         4         5         6         7
     12345678901234567890123456789012345678901234567890123456789012345678901234567890
A                                                ........................           A
B                   .........          .........................................   B
C                   .........          .........................................   C
D                   .........          .........................................   D
E                   .........          ........................................    E
F                   .........          ........................................    F
G                   .........          .......................................     G
H        .       ..  .........          .........................8....            H
I            .        .........          .........................                 I
J           .   .   .  .........9          ...................                     J
K   . ...           ..    ...........8.........D.........                          K
L   ...         ..        ..............................9..                        L
M    .           .         ...................H..........                          M
N                          ..............5......8...7....                           N
O    .           .            ...............8..........7..8.                       O
P           .       ...        ...................8.........8....6..                P
Q   ..       ..                .........G..9...8..7..5.............                 Q
R    .        ..                .........8.......G..5         ..  8                 R
S                                .............5G....   .   8G..   ..                S
T         .              ...        .............            ..  ..E               T
U   ..        ..   .         ..........                        .   .                U
V   ...      .   ..           ..........                     ... .   .              V
W   ...        .                                              ..  .  .              W
X   . ...        ...                                       G  ..    4              X
Y             ....                                            ..  .                 Y
Z   .             ...                                        ....  .  .             Z
AA                 ..                                        8.. .                  AA
AB  ..               .                                         ...  .8 7            AB
AC  ..    .                                                      .   .              AC
AD         ..    .                                                 .  .             AD
AE        ..                                                       ....             AE
AF          ...                                                     ...             AF
AG                                                              .                   AG
AH                                                                                  AH

              1         2         3         4         5         6         7
     12345678901234567890123456789012345678901234567890123456789012345678901234567890
```

Figure 6   LAGS Matrix Programs

SECTOTAL

all infs. (000.0) 914	fatwood (008.6) 34	rich-pine (008.6) 43
82 34 47 60	1 0 0 0	4 0 2 12
62 49 53 87	0 0 0 2	3 3 4 8
54 47 62 78	0 0 5 9	2 5 0 0
40 61 34 64	0 3 6 8	0 0 0 0

SECTOTAL matrix key: AR WT MT ET
                       WL UM UA UG
                       UT LM LA LG
                       LT WG EG EF

SOCTOTAL

all infs. (000.0) 914	fatwood (008.6) 34	rich-pine (008.6) 43
197 108 224 582	8 0 8 26	4 0 5 38
717 197 317 400	26 1 13 20	39 2 15 26
422 350 333 231	15 20 8 6	15 22 14 7
492 295 513 106	19 11 19 4	28 23 18 2
529 344 352 218	18 17 11 6	34 23 16 4
385 349 348 217	16 17 11 6	9 25 14 4

SOCTOTAL matrix key:

Col. 1	Col. 2	Col. 3	Col. 4
Black	age <30	age 45-60	age 60+
White	age 30-45	age 60-70	age 70+
Female	elem. ed.	high-schl. ed	college ed.
Male	lower soc. cl.	middle soc. cl.	upper soc. cl.
Insular	Type I	Type II	Type III
Worldly	folk spkr.	common spkr.	cultivated spkr.

The Limits of Chi Square
LAWRENCE M. DAVIS
Ball State University

Perhaps the best known of all statistical tests is the nonparametric test,[1] chi square (X^2). Generally speaking, it can be used to test the relationship of several percentages; that is, we can test the null hypothesis (H_o) that there is no relationship in Table 1, between educational level and the responses to Received Pronunciation (RP).

TABLE 1

EDUCATIONAL LEVEL

Response	Primary	Secondary	College	Total
Positive	72	400	201	673
Neutral	20	123	56	199
Negative	8	77	43	128
Total	100	600	300	1000

Of the total 1,000 subjects, then, 673 (67.3%) responded positively to RP, 128 (12.8%) responded negatively and 199 (19.9%) were neutral. If these scores were not a function of education, we would expect that, for example, 67.3% of the 100 subjects with a primary school education would respond positively, 67.3% of those with a secondary school education would respond positively and so on. These calculations are in Table 2.

TABLE 2

	Primary	Secondary	College
Positive	100 x .673 = 67.3	600 x .673 = 403.8	300 x .673 = 201.9
Neutral	100 x .199 = 19.9	600 x .199 = 119.4	300 x .199 = 59.7
Negative	100 x .128 = 12.8	600 x .128 = 76.8	300 x .128 = 38.4

We can list the actual scores and the expected scores, as we have done in Table 3. The expected scores are in parentheses.

TABLE 3

	Primary	Secondary	College
Positive	72 (67.3)	400 (403.8)	201 (201.9)
Neutral	20 (19.9)	123 (119.4)	56 (59.7)
Negative	8 (12.8)	77 (76.8)	43 (38.4)

Now we calculate x^2, which involves subtracting the expected score from the actual score, squaring that difference, dividing by the expected score and adding all those results. These calculations are in Table 4.

TABLE 4

$$x^2 = \frac{(72 - 67.3)^2}{67.3} + \frac{(400 - 403.8)^2}{403.8} + \frac{(201 - 201.9)^2}{201.9}$$

$$+ \frac{(20 - 19.9)^2}{19.9} + \frac{(123 - 119.4)^2}{119.4} + \frac{(56 - 59.7)^2}{59.7}$$

$$+ \frac{(8 - 12.8)^2}{12.8} + \frac{(77 - 76.8)^2}{76.8} + \frac{(43 - 38.4)^2}{38.4}$$

$$= .33 + .04 + 0.00 + 0.00 + .11 + .23$$

TABLE 4 (CON'D)

+ 1.80 + 0.00 + .55

= 3.06

Our calculated x^2 = 3.06. To find the level of significance, we turn to the x^2 *Distribution Table*, presented here as Table 5.

TABLE 5:

THE x^2 DISTRIBUTION

Degrees of Freedom	.30	.20	.10	.05	.02	.01	.001
1	1.074	1.642	2.706	3.841	5.412	6.635	10.827
2	2.408	3.219	4.605	5.991	7.824	9.210	13.815
3	3.665	4.642	6.251	7.815	9.837	11.345	16.268
4	4.878	5.989	7.779	9.488	11.668	13.277	18.465
5	6.064	7.289	9.236	11.070	13.388	15.086	20.517
6	7.231	8.558	10.645	12.592	15.033	16.812	22.457
7	8.383	9.803	12.017	14.067	16.622	18.475	24.322
8	9.524	11.030	13.362	15.507	18.168	20.090	26.125
9	10.656	12.242	14.684	16.919	19.679	21.666	27.877
10	11.781	13.442	15.987	18.307	21.161	23.209	29.588
11	12.899	14.631	17.275	19.675	22.618	24.725	31.264
12	14.011	15.812	18.549	21.026	24.054	26.217	32.909
13	15.119	16.985	19.812	22.362	25.472	27.688	34.528
14	16.222	18.151	21.064	23.685	26.873	29.141	36.123
15	17.322	19.311	22.307	24.996	28.259	30.578	37.697
16	18.418	20.465	23.542	26.296	29.633	32.000	39.252
17	19.511	21.615	24.769	27.587	30.995	33.409	40.790
18	20.601	22.760	25.989	28.869	32.346	34.805	42.312
19	21.689	23.900	27.204	30.144	33.687	36.191	43.820
20	22.775	25.038	28.412	31.410	35.020	37.566	45.315
21	23.858	26.171	29.615	32.671	36.343	38.932	46.797
22	24.939	27.301	30.813	33.924	37.659	40.289	48.268
23	26.018	28.429	32.007	35.172	38.968	41.638	49.728
24	27.096	29.553	33.196	36.415	40.270	42.980	51.179
25	28.172	30.675	34.382	37.652	41.566	44.314	52.620
26	29.246	31.795	35.563	38.885	42.856	45.642	54.052
27	30.319	32.912	36.741	40.113	44.140	46.963	55.476
28	31.391	34.027	37.916	41.337	45.419	48.278	56.893
29	32.461	35.139	39.087	42.557	46.693	49.588	58.302
30	33.530	36.250	40.256	43.773	47.962	50.892	59.703

Along the left margin of the table, we find degrees of freedom. For x^2 degrees of freedom are calculated in Table 6.

TABLE 6

$$df = (r - 1)(c - 1)$$

The "r" stands for horizontal *rows* and the "c" stands for vertical *columns*. Since we have 3 rows and 3 columns in our problem, df = (3 - 1)(3 - 1) = 4.

Table 5 tells us that, at df = 4, X^2 must equal at least 9.488 for the results to be significant at p < .05, meaning, as you probably know, that there is a 5% probability that results are a function of chance alone, and are valid only for the sample involved. Clearly, p < .01 is still better, since there would be only a 1% probability that the results happened by chance. It should be noted that p < .05 is the generally the lowest level of significance accepted in the social sciences. Since our results (3.06) are well below the number for a p < .05 level of significance, we cannot say that there is a relationship between level of education and the response to RP; in fact, the table indicates that the results are valid at less than p < .30, so we cannot reject the null hypothesis for the data in Table 1.

We can take a further example from Labov's (1966, p. 81) work in New York City--the department store survey--to illustrate further the use of X^2. The numbers in Table 7 refer to subjects who had all, some or no postvocalic /r/ constriction in their responses to Labov's questionnaire. All the subjects were from Saks Fifth Avenue, and are divided in terms of whether they worked on the lower floors or on the (more prestigious) upper ones. The null hypothesis, of course, is that there is no relationship between postvocalic /r/ constriction and the prestige of the floor on which the employees worked.

Using the percentages for the rows, we first calculate the expected scores for each column. After we apply the formula, we find that, at 2 degrees of freedom, our result of 5.231, calculated here in Table 8, is significant only at p < .10. It is larger than 4.605, but smaller than 5.991, the critical value for x^2 at p < .05 when df = 2.

TABLE 7

	Ground Floor	Upper Floors	Total	%
all /r/	7	13	20	29.4
some /r/	7	15	22	32.4
no /r/	16	10	26	38.2
Total	30	38	68	100.0

Table 8

$$x^2 = \frac{(7 - 8.82)^2}{8.82} + \frac{(7 - 9.72)^2}{9.72} + \frac{(16 - 11.46)^2}{11.46}$$

$$+ \frac{(13 - 11.17)^2}{11.17} + \frac{(15 - 12.31)^2}{12.31} + \frac{(10 - 14.52)^2}{14.52}$$

$$= .376 + .761 + 1.79 + .300 + .588 + 1.407$$

$$= 5.222$$

Therefore: p < .10

Labov (1966, p. 81) says that, given the more prestigious

status of the upper floors at Saks, "we should find a differential of [postvocalic /r/ constriction]." Perhaps we *should* have, but there is still a 10% probability that his results are a function of chance alone, and are valid only for his limited sample. Put simply, given the level of significance generally accepted in the social sciences, we should not posit a relationship between the prestige of the floor on which the employees worked and their levels of postvocalic /r/ constriction.

Several linguists, notably Fasold (1972), Wolfram (1974), Biondi (1975), and Feagin (1979) use x^2 in what are called 2 by 2 tables. That is, there are 2 rows and 2 columns, so df = (2 - 1)(2 - 1) = 1. The table looks like Table 9 here.

TABLE 9

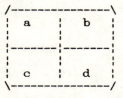

The x^2 calculation is much simpler for such tables, and is presented here as Table 10. The "n" is the total number of observations, and we put in the numbers for each cell.

TABLE 10

$$x^2 = \frac{n(ad - bc)^2}{(a + c)(a + b)(b + d)(c + d)}$$

TABLE 11

$$\chi^2 = \frac{n\,([ad - bc] - \frac{n}{2})^2}{(a + c)(a + b)(b + d)(c + d)}$$

Some statisticians recommend using the *Yates Correction for Continuity*, which involves adding 1 additional element to the above formula: subtracting 1/2 of the total n from the difference between ad and bc in the table, as in Table 11.[2] Although statisticians such as Connover (1974) have objected to the Yates Correction for Continuity, it seems wise to use it, mainly because it helps prevent the rejecting of the null hypothesis with insufficient evidence (a Type I error, as it is known).

Note the data in Table 12: the results of Labov's (1966, p. 446) subjective reaction test to postvocalic /r/ constriction.

TABLE 12

	From /r/-pronouncing region	From /r/-less region	Total
/r/ positive	10	5	15
/r/ negative	7	10	17
Total	17	15	32

TABLE 13

$$\chi^2 = \frac{32\,([\langle10 \times 10\rangle - \langle7 \times 5\rangle] - \frac{32}{2})^2}{17 \times 15 \times 15 \times 17}$$

$$= \frac{32\,(49)^2}{65{,}025} = \frac{76{,}832}{65{,}025} = 1.18$$

Using the Yates Correction, we calculate x^2 as in Table 13. We noted earlier that df = (2 - 1) (2 - 1) = 1, and Table 5 indicates that the results are valid only at p < .30. The calculated x^2 (1.18) is larger than 1.074 (x^2 at p < .30, where df = 1). We cannot, therefore, reject the null hypothesis. Given the p < .05 level of confidence, we must admit that there is not a statistically significant relationship between the subjects' responses to postvocalic /r/ constriction and the dialect area from which the subjects came.

Here, a few words of caution are in order insofar as the use of x^2 is concerned. Cochran (1954) has demonstrated that, for the test to be valid, no expected frequency can be less than 1, and no more than 20% of all the expected frequencies can be less than 5. For 2 x 2 tables, all of the expected frequencies must be 5 or more.

Moreover, I would argue that there are alternatives to x^2, especially when 2 x 2 tables are concerned. Note the example in Table 14: Labov's data for the pronunciation of *floor* at Saks Fifth Avenue and at Macy's.

TABLE 14

Saks (n_1 = 49) p_1 = .63

Macy's (n_2 = 110) p_2 = .40

Using the Yates Correction, x^2 = 6.454, and, as Table 5 indicates, p < .05. However, an alternative test, the proportion test, can also be used to evaluate the data. This test involves, first, calculating *pi*, or the actual number of subjects who exhibit the form under consideration. The formula for *pi* is presented here as Table 15, and the calculation for Macy's and Saks is in Table 16.

TABLE 15

$$\pi = \frac{n_1 p_1 + n_2 p_2}{n_1 + n_2}$$

TABLE 16

$$= \frac{(49 \times .63) + (110 \times .40)}{49 + 110} = .680$$

$$z = \frac{p_1 - p_2}{\sqrt{\pi(1-\pi)(1/n_1 + 1/n_2)}}$$

$$= \frac{.63 - .44}{\sqrt{(.680 \times .321)(1/49 + 1/110)}}$$

$$= 2.375$$

Since, z is more than 1.96, we can say that our results are significant at $p < .05$. In fact, they are significant at $p < .02$, since the z is more than 2.326. Had z been 2.576, we could have rejected the null hypothesis at $p < .01$.

Up to this point, we have been using x^2 and the proportion test to test percentages of *subjects*. When we are concerned with percentages of *responses*, however, we should set up a frequency distribution, if at all possible. The reason for this is that the x^2 test, and the proportion test as well, are really quite limited, in that they require grouping all the subjects into categories, and this, in itself, may suggest more homogeneity in the data than the data themselves warrant.

To illustrate this point, we can turn to Feagin's (1979) study of the speech of Anniston, Alabama. Her results for multiple negation for the older men and women of the rural working class (p. 232), presented here as Table 17, show that the women, as a whole, used multiple negation 75.73% of the time and the men used it 88.97% of the time. x^2, she says, is 9.00, so the results are valid at $p < .01$ (p. 284).

TABLE 17

Multiple Negation	Women	Men	Total
+	128	129	257
-	41	16	57
Total	169	145	314

Table 18 presents the calculation of x^2, with the Yates Correction, for the data in Table 17.

TABLE 18

$$x^2 = \frac{314 \left([\langle 129 \times 41 \rangle - \langle 128 \times 16 \rangle] - \frac{314}{2} \right)^2}{145 \times 257 \times 169 \times 57}$$

$$= 8.32$$

If we had not used the Yates Correction, our results would have been 9.19--slightly higher than the 9.0 suggested by Feagin. At df = 1, Table 5 indicates that, in any case, $p < .01$ for the difference between the men and the women insofar as multiple negation is concerned. It seems, then, that we surely can reject the null hypothesis, and say that the men of the rural working class in Anniston, Alabama, definitely do exhibit more multiple negation than do the women. And the proportion test gives similar results.

However, as I have already suggested, the data should have been presented in a frequency distribution, and only then tested. Feagin (1979, p. 359) does present the subject by subject responses in an appendix, and we would do well to examine these results, listed here in Table 19.

TABLE 19

RURAL WORKING CLASS

Women		%	Men		%
1	59/66	89.39	9	55/65	84.62
2	24/31	77.42	10	30/33	90.91
3	14/16	87.50	11	12/12	100.00
4	7/13	53.85	12	5/5	100.00
5	4/4	100.00	13	11/12	91.67
6	2/6	12.50	14	11/12	91.67
7	10/11	90.91	15	5/6	83.33
8	8/12	66.67			
Total	128/169	(75.73)	Total	129/145	(88.97)

Note that Feagin's means, are a function of the *total* cases of multiple negation for the women and the men. If we calculate the means for the frequency distributions, however, we obtain different results. The means are 72.28 ($s = 28.31$) for the women and 91.74 ($s = 6.56$) for the men--a difference of nearly 20%.

It should also be noted that subjects 1 and 2 produced well over half of the potential and actual multiple negations of the women, and likewise for subjects 9 and 10 for the men. The data are hardly homogeneous. Because the F-test shows wide differences between the variances of the two samples, and since the number of subjects in each group is not equal, we probably should not perform the t-test. In this case, however, the Mann-Whitney test (1947), a nonparametric test which is less well-known than X^2, is indeed appropriate. First, we rank the men and the women, as in Table 20.

TABLE 20

Women	Men	Rank of Women	Rank of Men
1. 89.39	9. 84.62	8	6
2. 77.42	10. 90.91	4	9.5
3. 87.50	11. 100.00	7	14
4. 53.85	12. 100.00	2	14
5. 100.00	13. 91.67	14	11.5
6. 12.50	14. 91.67	1	11.5
7. 90.91	15. 83.33	9.5	5
8. 66.67		3	
$n_1 = 8$	$n_2 = 7$	$R_1 = 48.5$	$R_2 = 71.5$

The calculation and results of the Mann-Whitney test, presented here in Table 21,[3] reveal that Feagin's results do not justify rejecting H_o at $p < .05$, even though the x^2 test was valid at an even higher level of confidence ($p < .01$).[4] Such is the problem which can result when one groups frequencies together.

TABLE 21

$$u = n_1 n_2 + \frac{n_1(n_2 + 1)}{2} - R_1$$

$$= 8 \times 7 + \frac{8(7 + 1)}{2} - 48.5$$

$$= 56 + \frac{64}{2} - 48.5$$

$$= 39.5$$

$$z = \frac{u - \frac{n_1 n_2}{2}}{\sqrt{\frac{n_1 n_2 (n^1 + n^2 + 1)}{12}}}$$

$$= \frac{39.5 - 28}{\sqrt{\frac{56(7 + 8 + 1)}{12}}} = \frac{11.50}{8.64}$$

$$= 1.331$$

Therefore: $p > .05$

It might be argued, and with some justification in fact, that the Mann-Whitney test here might not be appropriate, because, as I pointed out earlier, 2 female and 2 male subjects contributed disproportionately to the totals of their respective groups. This is surely true, but true all the more so insofar as Feagin's use of X^2. The Mann-Whitney test at least does not force us to group the responses of all the men and all the women together; indeed, we have more control over the data when we use Mann-Whitney than we do with X^2.

As noted earlier, X^2 is a very useful test when comparison of mean levels of responses are *not* involved. When they are so, we should set up frequency distributions. When parametric tests (the *t*-test, for example) are possible, we should use them to test for the difference between means. If not, then the nonparametric Mann-Whitney (1947) test is an adequate substitute. Moreover, the proportion test is a helpful check to X^2 analysis in 2 x 2 tables. In any case, there are alternatives to X^2, in spite of its popularity today.

NOTES

[1] Nonparametric tests make fewer assumptions about samples and the populations from which samples are drawn. For example, the *t*-test assumes that the two samples come from populations with equal variances, and most statisticians argue that one should demonstrate this, using the F-test, before applying the *t*-test. Parametric tests also generally assume that the variable(s) under consideration are normally distributed throughout the population. Nonparametric tests make no such assumptions, but, on the other hand, they are also somewhat less robust than their parametric counterparts.

[2](ad-bc) must be set up so that it is a positive number.

[3]Zar (1974, p. 112) points out that the approximation of z here is for levels of significance of $p < .01$ or lower ($p < .02$, $p < .05$, etc.). Strictly speaking, the formula for z is also different when ties are involved. Zar (1974, p.113) notes that the main denominator in the equation for z should, in fact, be as follows:

$$\sqrt{\frac{n_1 \, n_2}{(n_1 + n_2)^2 - (n_1 + n_2)} \times \frac{(n_1 + n_2)^3 - (n_1 + n_2) - T}{12}}$$

Where $T = \sum(t_i^3 - t_i)$, and where t_i is "the number of ties in a group of tied values, and the summation is performed over all groups of ties."

If we calculate z using this formula, the result is 1.339--still far from the required 1.960 for a $p < .05$ level of significance.

[4]The section on Feagin's (1979) use of x^2 is a revision of an earlier approach to the problem, which appeared in Davis (1982)

REFERENCES

Biondi, L. (1975) *The Italian-American Child: His Sociolinguistic Acculturation.* Washington, D. C.: Georgetown Univ. Press.

Cochran, W. G. (1954) Some Methods for Strengthening the Common x^2 Tests, *Biometrics* 10, 417-51.

Connover, W. J. (1974) Some Reasons for Not Using the Yates Continuity Correction on 2 X 2 Contingency Tables, *Journal of the American Statistical Association,* 69, 374-82.

Davis, L. M. (1982) American Social Dialectology: A Statistical Appraisal, *American Speech*, 57, 83-94.

Fasold, R. W. (1974) *Tense Marking in Black English: A Linguistic and Social Analysis*. Washington, D. C.: Center for Applied Linguistics.

Feagin, C. (1979) *Variation and Change in Alabama English: A Sociolinguistic Study of the White Community*. Washington, D.C.: Georgetown Univ. Press.

Labov, W. (1966) *The Social Stratification of English in New York City*. Washington, D. C.: Center for Applied Linguistics.

Mann, H. B. and Whitney, D. R. (1947) On a Test of Whether One of Two Random Variables is Stochastically Larger than the Other, *Ann. Math. Statist.*, 18, 50-60.

Trudgill, P. J. (1974) *The Social Differentiation of English in Norwich*. Cambridge: Cambridge Univ. Press.

Wolfram, W. A. (1974) *Sociolinguistic Aspects of Assimilation: Puerto Rican English in New York City*. Washington, D. C.: Center for Applied Linguistics.

Zar, J. H. (1974) *Biostatistical Analysis*. Englewood Cliffs, N. J.. Prentice-Hall.

The Quantitative Paradigm and the Study of Literacy: A New Initiative in Variation Studies

RICK EVANS
Texas A & M University

INTRODUCTION

In recent years, literacy has become one of the most discussed and, perhaps as a consequence, one of the most confounding subjects in the academic world.[1] Social historians, psychologists, sociologists, political scientists (as well as politicians), educators, rhetoricians, literary critics, and even linguists have all tried their hand at definition. And, while the different representatives of these various disciplines might at least agree that literacy involves the ability to read and the ability to write, each would more than likely disagree about what those abilities themselves involve. For some, reading and writing offer a new mode of consciousness. For others, they represent a collection of conventions to be mastered. And for still others, reading and writing are cultural or social or educational survival skills. However, even though these various understandings appear quite different, they do indicate a steady progression of important discoveries concerning literacy. In fact, it is this very progression that encourages the application of William Labor's quantitative paradigm as an appropriate methodology for literacy research.

PROGRESSION OF LITERACY RESEARCH

The first of these discoveries is essentially a reaction against Ferdinand de Saussure's (1962, p. 23) belief that "language and writing are two distinct systems of signs; [and] the second exists for the sole purpose of representing the first." Interestingly, the one to initiate this contrary reaction, Eric Havelock (1976, pp. 12-19), seems in some of his statements at least to agree with Saussure. He says, for example, that "the habit of using written symbols to represent . . . speech is just a useful trick," or that a "successful writing system is . . . the purely passive instrument of the spoken word." However, Havelock (1976, p. 9) also says that as more and more people began to read and write, that useful trick for representing language gradually evolved into something new, a system of signs "that provided a fresh release, a freedom for language and its resources to expand beyond previous oral standards." Accordingly, this written language not only began to develop in ways different from oral language, but even "changed somewhat our habits of thought" (Havelock 1976, p. 51). Jack Goody affirms and extends Havelock's claims with his own. Writing, he (Goody 1968, p. 1) says, constitutes a "new medium of communication." He goes on to assert that this "literate communication" has had profound effects on the evolution of our western culture (Goody 1968, p. 4). Our understanding of democracy, our concept of a past as distinct from the present (history vs. myth), and our emphasis on the individual all are the consequences of literacy (Goody 1968). Finally Walter Ong (1977, p. 256) exceeds both Havelock and Goody with his claim that the historical movement from primary orality to literacy represents a significant "evolution of consciousness." For Ong (1982, p. 7), writing is not the passive instrument of the spoken word at all; instead writing, and reading, enlarge "the potentiality of language almost beyond measure." He (Ong 1982, pp. 14-15) even maintains that "without writing human consciousness cannot achieve its fuller potentials, cannot produce other and powerful creations." "In a sense," he (Ong 1982, p. 15) says, "orality needs to produce and is destined to produce writing." This assertion, along with those made by Havelock and Goody, clearly express a kind of textual elitism. How, after all, can one claim that literacy makes possible new habits of thought, momentously important cultural innovations, and indeed an evolution of human consciousness without implying the original "primitiveness" of orality? Havelock, Goody, and Ong reject such an implication. Still, simply rejecting the implication does not make it disappear. Others, like David Olson, do attempt to avoid, if not quite remove, this implication in the next of our discoveries concerning literacy.[2]

In his often cited article, "From Utterance to Text: The Bias of Language in Speech and Writing," Olson (1977) adopts a slightly different perspective on literacy. While still viewing it as an historical phenomenon rooted in the gradual invention of the alphabetic writing system, he also looks at literacy as a phenomenon of language development. Olson (1977, p. 262) contends that there is a developmental "transition from utterance to text," and that this transition can be described by carefully looking at the different ways that utterance, oral language, and text, written language, realize meaning. Clearly, he (Olson 1977, p. 275) implies that becoming literate is essentially a matter of learning to "conventionalize" meaning in written language.

Before exploring Olson's different perspective and its significance any further, notice how he avoids the above expression of elitism. Olson assumes that the first of our discoveries concerning literacy is true. Written language is not simply a representation of oral language. He also assumes that oral language is equal to written language. And, without subjugating either one to the other, he claims, for instance, that each exhibits ways of representing meaning unique to itself. He (Olson 1977, p. 258) even avoids the primitivist suggestion inherent in his own developmental transition from utterance to text by explaining that his concerns are the consequences associated with the "schooled language of written texts." This distinction of a certain <u>variety</u> of written language will become important later. For now, it is enough to understand that Olson considers this developmental transition to be a social rather than a natural one.

If utterance and text realize meaning in different ways, then the obvious question becomes -- what are these different ways? According to Olson (1977, p. 259), textual meaning, or "meaning in the text," has a few, very significant characteristics. It is, first of all, autonomous. This suggests that a text must be fully adequate, indeed "formally adequate" for the purposes of communicating meaning (Olson 1977, p. 277). Second, the meaning communicated in a text must be explicit. There can be little, if any, ambiguity, and the text must always be able "to stand up to analysis of its [own] implications" (Olson 1977, p. 268). (Olson often refers to the sentence as a kind of idealized text and, at one point, claims that a sentence should be written to have only one meaning.) Third, the meaning in a text must be "logically connected" (Olson 1977, p. 269). And according to Olson, textual meaning is logically connected if we appropriately use the "conventionalized rules" of written language necessary to legitimize the implications arising from such use (Olson 1977, p. 273). Whether or not we consider the meaning plausible or congruent with our ideas or experience of the world is irrelevant. That these characteristics of textual meaning are related to one another is obvious. That they appear to be related generally to the claims of Havelock, Goody, and Ong, even though less obvious, lends them perhaps too much credibility. Yet, Olson, with his particularization of meaning in the text, has suggested the second of our discoveries concerning literacy: written language is not simply a representation of oral language, but instead "is best seen as a distinct subsystem within the larger grammar" of the language generally (Labov 1972a, pp. 63-64).

However, Olson, like Havelock, Goody, and Ong before him, also fosters an implication that I suspect he would rather avoid. Remember my earlier reference to Olson's claim that he was concerned only with the schooled language of written texts. Well, either this "schooled language" and the language that exhibits "meaning in the text" are the same (this implication seems inescapable given Olson's reference to the tradition of the British essayists and the evolution of the "essayist technique") or they are not the same. If they are the same, then there is but a single written language. If, on the other hand, they are not the same, or if we might posit an "unschooled" language of written texts that is also different from oral language, then we might have more than a single written language. We might have several written languages, various grapholects, even the possibility of different codes each distinctive in its own unique ways. This possibility leads to the last of our important discoveries.

To my mind, some of the most interesting and provocative research done on literacy has explored its various inter- and intracultural, social and educational contexts. For example, Ron and Suzanne Scollon (1981) argue that Athabaskan and English language users act out of very different "reality sets" and that these differing reality sets affect each culture's understanding of literacy. They (Scollon and Scollon 1981, p. 53) claim that learning to write in the "essay-text" manner, a kind of literacy closely related to Olson's schooled language of written texts, would involve not only learning new patterns of discourse, but would constitute for the Athabaskan writer a socially inappropriate display of dominance. They further suggest that if we encourage the Athabaskans to master such a variety of literacy, then we are also encouraging them to "experience a change in their ethnicity as well as a change in reality set" (Scollon and Scollon 1981, p. 42). The Scollons clearly demonstrate that the variety of literacy adopted by a particular culture depends in large measure on that culture's sense of its own identity.

That different cultures exhibit different varieties of literacy, or literacies, at least suggests the possibility that different literacies may exist within a single culture. Sylvia Scribner and Michael Cole (1981) explore this possibility in their Vai Project in Liberia. In fact, they find three kinds of literacy, each tied to a particular intracultural context. There is an English literacy associated with the government and the schools; a Vai literacy used primarily for commerce, record keeping, and personal letters; and an Arabic literacy used for reading, writing, and memorizing the Quarian (Gee 1986, p. 729). When comparing the discourse practices of those capable in one or more of these literacies, Scribner and Cole find no evidence for the grandiose claims (similar to those made by Ong) of the globally positive effects of literacy. They did however find evidence to suggest that each type of literacy does enhance the specific skills practiced in carrying out that literacy (Gee 1986, p. 730). In other words, they were able to link literacy as a skill or collection of skills with certain very specific social tasks. In effect, Scribner and Cole (1981, p. 236) suggest that literacy is "a set of socially organized practices."

Shirley Brice Heath (1983) further explores this contextually based understanding of literacy in her research of three communities in the Piedmont Carolina area of the United States.

James Paul Gee (1986, p. 737) summarizes her research quite well. He states:

> Heath analyzes the way . . . [three] different social groups "take" knowledge from the environment, with particular concern for how "types of literacy events" are involved in this taking. Literacy events are any event involving print, such as group negotiation of meaning in written texts (e.g., an ad), individuals "looking things up" in reference books or writing family records in the bible, and the dozens of other types of occasions when books or written materials are integral to interpretation in an interaction. Heath interprets these literacy events [then] in relation to the larger sociocultural patterns which they may reflect or exemplify . . . .

In fact, Heath is able to describe the different kinds of literacy events that occur in each of these three communities. As a result, she (Heath 1983, pp. 367-369) claims that because certain social subgroups encourage different, and sometimes exclusive ways of using written language, our society's educational system must either attempt to integrate those ways with its own, or suffer those students who are not mainstream literates to be excluded.

APPROPRIATENESS OF THE PARADIGM

In his introduction to <u>Sociolinguistic Patterns</u>, William Labov (1972a) describes the academic environment for the study of speech during the 1960's. He (Labov 1972a, p. xiii) says that, "[in] spite of a considerable amount of sociolinguistic activity, a socially realistic linguistics seemed a remote prospect." He goes on then to list some of the "ideological barriers" that had to be overcome. Currently, in spite of the work of the Scollons (1981), Scribner and Cole (1981), Heath (1983), Cook-Gumperz (1986), Street (1984), and many others, a socially realistic understanding of literacy too seems a remote prospect. However, there is a growing realization of the complexity of literacy. And in the above progression of important discoveries concerning literacy, a few, certainly not all, of the ideological barriers have been overcome. We know, for example, that writing is language and "not merely a way of recording language by means of visible marks" (Bloomfield 1983, p. 21). We know too that writing or written language is best understood as a distinct subsystem with many of its own "rules for comprehension and production. And finally, we know that there are several of these distinct subsystems, various grapholects, each intimately joined to and capable of changing with different cultural, social, and educational contexts. The recognition that literacy may actually involve the use of a number of different grapholects within a variety of social and cultural contexts makes it crucial to understand both how those grapholects operate -- that is, their various linguistic realizations -- and how they are embedded within their socio-cultural contexts. To do that, students of literacy must employ a research methodology which can account for variation in a way that specifies both its linguistic and its extralinguistic constraints. In other words, we need a methodology which can account for the languages of literacy. The methodology that seems most appropriate is the Labovian quantitative paradigm.

APPLICATION OF THE PARADIGM

Perhaps the most accessible description of Labov's quantitative paradigm is not given by Labov himself, but instead by Richard Hudson (1980). Hudson (1980, p. 144) states that there are five stages in the application of the quantitative paradigm: 1) selecting informants, circumstances and linguistic variables; 2) collecting texts; 3) identifying the linguistic variables and their variants in the texts; 4) determining the number, distribution, and the constraints of those variants; and 5) exploring the operations of these variables within different linguistic and extra-linguistic contexts. Hudson (1980, p. 144) also suggests that even though the stages generally follow this linear order, there is "usually some cyclicity" involving small-scale pilot studies and the not-so-strict sequential application of the stages themselves. Such pre-study preparation and in-study cross-checking is important for avoiding possible methodological pitfalls -- the most frightening of which is unrevealing results.

Just like Labov (1972a, p. 208) and his "need to obtain large volumes of well-recorded natural speech," so too our initial approach is governed by the need to obtain large volumes of the different varieties of written language in various contexts and responses to those different varieties. The importance of selecting our informants, carefully attending to the circumstances of their lives, and judiciously choosing, or being sensitive enough to choose only the most appropriate linguistic variables for observation has been clearly demonstrated by the Scollons, Scribner and Cole and Heath. The textual elitism of Havelock, Goody and Ong forewarns us of some of the difficulties involved in collecting written texts and responses to those texts. And finally, the considerable degree of subjectivity apparent in Olson's analysis of the distinctive features of textual meaning suggests how "scientific" we must try to be when we attempt to identify those linguistic variables, their variants and determine their number, distribution and constraints. However, if we are cognizant of the social situation, the cultural context, in which the languages of literacy are used; if we can collect representative samples of those languages and reliable responses to them; and if we can generate further discoveries about those languages and responses; then we will have begun to answer at least a few of the fundamental questions about literacy. Interestingly, I believe that those fundamental questions are similar to the ones that Labov (1972a) suggest are key to the study of language in its social context. Those questions, rephrased slightly for their new application, are:

1) In written languages, what are the distinctive forms and rules and how they do operate? Also, what constraints may be placed on them?

2) How are the rules combined into systems in written languages? How are they conventionalized and even deconventionalized within those systems? And, what is it that is distinctive about those conventions?

3) How are these systems related to each other across all their various linguistic and extra-linguistic contents?

4) How do these forms, rules, and rule systems change?

It should be clear from the above discussion that my own understanding (or definition) of literacy is closely related to the user's understanding of written language -- its forms, the rules that govern those forms, the systems of conventions generated by those rules, how those forms, rules, and systems vary within different contexts, and lastly, how they all change. It should also be clear that I believe the best way to get at that user's understanding is through a careful study of the varieties of written languages in their different sociocultural contexts. And finally, it should be clear that I believe that the Labovian quantitative paradigm provides us with a particularly effective methodology for such study. My contention is simply that the more we know about written language in use, the more we will know about literate communication, specifically, and literacy, generally.

FINAL COMMENT

In my title to this paper, I suggest that the use of the quantitative paradigm represents a new initiative in the study of the languages of literacy. While this is true in the main, attentive research into the varieties of written language is as old as the discipline of philosophy. Further, we know that more recently David Crystal and Derek Davey (1969) have suggested a very similar methodology for the study of the "many different varieties" of English. They call their approach "stylistics."[3]

And, even more recently, Charles Ferguson (1983) has been attempting to "locate" some of the different registers in English. He calls his approach "register analysis."[4] Perhaps, however, the research tradition with which I most identify is represented by Labov's (1972b) well-known article "The Logic of Non-Standard English." In that article, Labov was extremely successful demolishing the myth of language deficit and in promoting the reality of language difference. I would like to argue that there is another myth that needs our attention -- the myth of invariance in written language. And, I would like to replace that myth with a reality -- the reality of the many different varieties of written language.

Notes

1) I would like to thank Guy Bailey for his helpful responses and supportive encouragement so crucial to the completion of this paper.

2) Olson, far from rejecting those elitist sounding statements in Havelock, Goody and Ong, begins his article with the sentence: "The faculty of language stands at the center of our conception of mankind: speech makes us human and literacy makes us civilized" (p. 257).

3) In their introduction, Crystal and Davey propose a threefold methodology that bears a striking resemblance to the last three steps of Labov's quantitative paradigm. An interesting study would be to trace the historical development of Labov's paradigm.

4) Even though Ferguson, in his 1982 article, "Simplified registers and linguistic theory" argues against the application of the variable rule model for the analysis of register variation, the Labovian quantitative paradigm remains for him a useful methodology.

References

Bloomfield, L. (1933) *Language*. New York: Holt, Rinehart and Winston Inc.

Crystal, David, and Davey, Derek. (1969) *Investigating English Style*. Bloomington: Indiana University Press.

Cook-Gumperz, J. (ed.) *The social construction of literacy*. Cambridge: Cambridge University Press.

Ferguson, C. (1983) "Sports announcer talk: Syntactic aspects of register variation." *Language in Society*, 12, 152-172.

Gee, J. P. (1986) "Orality and Literacy: From the Savage Mind to Ways with Words." *TESOL Quarterly*, 719-746.

Goody, J. (ed.) (1968) *Literacy in traditional societies*. Cambridge: Cambridge University Press.

Havelock, E. A. (1976) *Origins of Western Literacy*. Toronto: Ontario Institute in Education.

Heath, S. B. (1982) "What no bedtime story means: Narrative skills at home and school." *Language and Society*, 11 (2), 49-75.

Heath, S. B. (1983) *Ways with words: Language, life and work in the communities and classrooms*. Cambridge: Cambridge University Press.

Hudson, R. A. (1980) *Sociolinguistics*. Cambridge: Cambridge University Press.

Labov, W. (1972a) *Sociolinguistic Patterns*. Philadelphia: Pennsylvania University Press.

Labov, W. (1972b) *Language in the Inner City*. Philadelphia, Pennsylvania University Press.

Olson, D. R. (1977) "From utterance to treat: The bias of language in speech and writing." *Harvard Educational Review*, 47 (3), 257-281.

Ong, W. J., S. J. (1977) *Interfaces of the word: Studies in the evolution of consciousness and culture*. Ithaca: Cornell University Press.

Ong, W. J., S. J. (1982) *Orality and literacy: The technologizing of the word*. London: Methuen.

Saussure, Ferdinand de. (1959) <u>Course in General Linguistics</u>. trans. by Wade Baskin, ed. by Charles Bally and Albert Sechehaye, in collaboration with Albert Reidlinger. New York: Philosophical Library.

Scollon, R., and Scollon, S. B. K. (1981) <u>Narrative, literacy and face in interethnic communication</u>. Norwood, NJ: Ablex.

Scribner, C., and Cole, M. (1981) <u>The psychology of literacy</u>. Cambridge: Cambridge University Press.

Street, B. V. (1984) <u>Literacy in theory and practice</u>. Cambridge: Cambridge University Press.

Log-Linear Statistical Models: Explaining the Dynamics of Dialect Diffusion

DENNIS GIRARD and DONALD LARMOUTH
University of Wisconsin-Green Bay

INTRODUCTION

Dialectologists have generally recognized that a number of social variables can influence the diffusion of features from one dialect to another or account for the inherent variability of performance demonstrated by different groups of speakers. Accordingly, it is now virtually standard practice to group informants according to age, sex, and socioeconomic status in trying to account for dialect variation, although there are still problems associated with such groupings (see Davis 1985, Trudgill 1984, and Linn 1983). Beyond these more or less "standard" social variables, studies such as Trudgill (1974) and Larmouth (1981) have shown that diffusion can be influenced by the relative sizes of the populations of the communities in the region, and work by Milroy (1980) shows that the social network(s) in which a speaker participates can also be significant.

Naturally, all of these social variables occur simultaneously in real life; indeed, they may act in concert, such that they could have a greater effect in tandem than they might have individually. A model which relates such composite or multivariate effects to observed linguistic variation in different stylistic registers would be intuitively more satisfying than one which simply demonstrates a two-way relationship between separate social variables and linguistic variation--the kind most readily shown through conventional chi-square statistical methods.

In this discussion, we will outline a strategy for statistical analysis which enables the discovery of multivariate effects of different social variables that seem to account for the variation observed in a 63-informant sample from east central Wisconsin and explain the ways in which these social variables interact in diffusing linguistic innovations from one population to another. This strategy involves the use of log-linear statistical models.

LOG-LINEAR MODELS AND CONVENTIONAL CHI-SQUARE ANALYSIS

It will be important at the outset to explain the differences between log-linear statistical models and conventional chi-square statistics. We are all familiar with the conventional chi-square test of count data arranged in a two-way table and its applications in dialectology (see Davis 1982 for several good examples). The typical procedure is to calculate expected values by the formula

$$\frac{\text{Row Total} \times \text{Column Total}}{\text{Table Total}}$$

These are then compared with the observed values using Pearson's statistic

$$\sum \frac{(\text{Observed Value} - \text{Expected Value})^2}{\text{Expected Value}}$$

which is a measure of the discrepancy between observed and expected values. It is important to note that these expected values are calculated with a particular assumption in mind; namely, that the row classification in the table is not associated with the column classification. That is, the reason an observation falls into a particular row has nothing to do with the reason that it falls into a particular column in a two-way table. This is called a "model of independence." If the model of independence is correct, then the expected values are close to the observed values and Pearson's statistic is a small number providing no evidence of association between row classification and column classification. However, if the value of Pearson's statistic is large, indicating a significant discrepancy between observed and expected values, this provides evidence of a lack of independence between row and column classifications and we conclude that there is an association between the two variables used for classifying the observations. In such a case, the assumption of independence is a poor model to explain the data.

The notion of a "model" is extremely important in the analysis of multi-way (two-way, three-way, four-way, n-way) classifications of categorical data. The calculation of expected values in a two-way table, as mentioned earlier, depends upon the assumption of independence; but there are only two possible models for a two-way classification—independence or no independence. Thus, if we reject independence as a model, we are left with only one alternative model. This is not the case with multi-way tables. There are eight models which could explain a relationship among the variables in a three-way table (using all the variables) and 113 models that involve all the variables in a four-way table—many more if one or more of the classifying variables is not used—and each model its own different set of expected values. Thus, the strategy of looking for a large discrepancy between observed and expected values will not work. Instead, we must invert our perspective and look for a model in which, in some sense, the discrepancy between observed and expected values is as small as possible.

This process is akin to fitting a regression function to a set of data. We are looking for the best explanation of the data, given a set of underlying categorical variables. In a fashion analogous to regression analysis, we try to write the logarithms of the expected values as a function of the categorical variables:

$$\log e = \theta + \lambda^A + \lambda^B + \lambda^C + \lambda^{AB} + \lambda^{AC} + \lambda^{BC} + \lambda^{ABC}$$

where

    e = expected value

    θ = a constant (the mean of the logs of all expected values)

    λ^Z is the component of the (log of) the expected value due to factor Z

The letters A, B, C . . . indicate that the model contains the main effects due to the categorical variables themselves. The letter pairs AB, AC, BC . . . indicate that interactions between the main variables are in the model. The term ABC represents the presence of a three-way interaction among the variables A, B, and C in the model, and so on.

A model is "good" if a measure of the differences between observed values and expected values (which are calculated relative to the model) is small. The measure commonly used is G-square, which is approximately the same as Pearson's chi-square statistic. If G-square is small, the model fits the data well; if G-square is large, indicating significant discrepancies between observed and expected values, the model is a poor fit to the data. To paraphrase in terms of chi-square, we would say: large chi-square, poor fit; small chi-square, good fit. To amplify this a bit, consider the case of a simple two-way table. Here is a table relating informant age and use of the plural form of <hoof> (Miller 1984):

	Plural Form	
Age	-fs	-ves
40+	10	4
18-39	4	15

If age and plural form are independent, then the model which will fit the data is

$$\log e = \theta + \lambda^A + \lambda^B$$

but if age and plural form are not independent, the model will be

$$\log e = \theta + \lambda^A + \lambda^B + \lambda^{AB}$$

where the λ^{AB} term represents the interaction between age and plural form.

In constructing a model of this type it is usual to follow what is known as the hierarchy principle:

> If a model uses interaction terms [such as AB or ABC above], it must, <u>a priori</u>, involve any simpler interactions and main effect terms involving these same variables.

Thus, if a model contains the interaction term ABC, then it must also involve the terms AB, AC, BC as well as the main effects A, B, and C. As another example, the model AB,ACD would involve the terms ACD, AC, AD, CD, AB, A, B, C, and D (but not BC and BD). The notation <u>AB,ACD</u> is customary shorthand for the model

$$\log e = \theta + \lambda^A + \lambda^B + \lambda^C + \lambda^D + \lambda^{AB} + \lambda^{AC} + \lambda^{AD} + \lambda^{CD} + \lambda^{ACD}$$

It can be seen, then, that the basic objective of the log-linear method, as we are applying it in dialectology, is to discover which among many possibilities represents the "best-fit" model to represent the interactions between social and linguistic variables, including the possibility of multivariate interactions. As we will show later, the method can also be used to infer the relative importance of each social variable in these multivariate interactions. [An introductory treatment of log-linear methods is presented in Fienberg (1980) and Upton (1978); more detailed discussion is available in Goodman (1978) and Bishop <u>et al</u>. (1975).]

BACKGROUND COMMENTS ON THE DATA SET

The data set explored in this discussion was collected in east central Wisconsin as part of a project to test the applicability of gravity models in regional dialectology. The region is populated by several different ethnic groups. Residue from previous bilingual generations remains in the speech of quite a few informants. There was a total of 63 informants in the sample, including speakers from Green Bay (the regional center or focal area), Manitowoc (a competing city of moderate size), the towns of Denmark and Mishicot, and several smaller villages such as Maribel, Kellnersville, Whitelaw, Francis Creek, and some unincorporated communities which don't appear separately in census records because they are too small. The fieldwork was conducted using Alva Davis' questionnaire, Standard English in the United States and Canada, to elicit responses in three styles or registers: a word-list (responses to circumlocution questions), a reading sample (the story of "Arthur the Rat"), and an open-ended conversational section for casual discourse. [Note: there is also a specific word-list in the Davis questionnaire which is intended to be read aloud by the informant, but this part was omitted from the sample because it produced unnatural results.]

The informants were classified according to sex, age (younger/older), socioeconomic status (middle class/working class), size of the community population (big city/smaller city/town/village), and social network ("local"/"outside" orientation). The latter variable takes account of the fact that some people who reside in small outlying communities may nevertheless be socially oriented to a larger city instead of their actual residence, while others living in the same small community are socially oriented to the immediate locality and not "outside" to a city in the region. In this sample there were no instances where an informant living in a city was socially oriented to an outlying rural community; hence, all city informants were classified as having an "outside" (that is, "city") orientation. Their linguistic performance was classified according to the degree to which archaic forms such as an apico-dental [t] or [d] vs. a "modern" interdental [θ] or [ð] are evident in their speech. For our purposes here, this was made into a two-way classification ("archaic" vs. "modern") based on the percentage of occurrence of the modern forms, using Bailey's notion of categorical and variable linguistic rules (Bailey 1973). Tables 1, 2, and 3 summarize the data set in terms of the three registers obtained in the questionnaire and the significant social variables (community population, socioeconomic status or class, and social network).

The data set is problematic: each of the registers along with the social variables produces a multi-way table with 128 cells. Since there are only 63 informants in the sample, the result is a table with many zero cells. Such tables are difficult to handle. Many log-linear models do not have exact formulas for the computation of expected values, and iteration algorithms are used. These algorithms often will not converge if the table is too sparse. Accordingly, Goodman (1970) recommends adding 0.5 to each cell frequency before undertaking an analysis of the data, and this was done in the present instance to compensate for the sparseness of the table.

DATA ANALYSIS

To demonstrate how to apply log-linear models to the analysis of our data, we will walk through a detailed example. We used the P4F program in the BMDP statistical analysis system (University of California); other systems such as SAS and ECTA can also be used. The first step in any analysis of a data set of this dimension is to consider the possibility of reducing the dimensions of the problem. Are all of the variables really necessary or significant? If a variable is statistically independent of <u>each</u> variable in a set of other variables, the interaction among these other variables may be measured from a table of sums constructed by collapsing over the independent variable (Fienberg 1980, Bishop <u>et al</u>. 1975). Demonstrating independence can be done using chi-square tests, and in the present instance, both age and sex are independent of the other variables, permitting a collapse of the initial table to one of four dimensions.

This effort to reduce the complexity of the data structure would be standard in any event, whether or not log-linear models were employed. For example, in order to treat three-dimensional tables, this initial chi-square analysis would be done to see if they could be reduced to two-dimensional tables. It is worth noting that, had age and sex turned out to be significant in this data set, we would have been obliged to keep them in, and then we would have been confronted with an enormously complicated problem, especially given the sparseness of the table. As it was, we were lucky.

The search for an appropriate model to explain a table with several dimensions can be a time-consuming process. It is common to use a stepwise procedure, either adding or removing variables from a chosen model to arrive at a better model. Once the variables of age and sex have been shown not to interact significantly with any of the other variables, we are left (after collapsing) with a four-dimensional table. These data can be completely explained using the so-called "saturated model"—the model having a four-way interaction term, and where the expected values must exactly equal the observed values. For example, looking at the word-list data, the four-way interaction among word-list register (W), community population (P), social network (N), and social class (C) is designated as WPNC. Similar four-way interactions would appear in saturated models for reading register and casual speech register and would perfectly fit the data. However, a four-way interaction is very complex, so such models are difficult to interpret and hence not necessarily useful.

The next step, and the real entry into log-linear analysis, is motivated by the general principle of parsimony—an attempt to discover a simpler model which will still explain the data with a minimal discrepancy between observed and expected values. The table will still be four-dimensional, but the number of log-linear parameters that we will be using as components of the logarithmic expected values will be reduced as we look to eliminate interactions which are not significant.

In a stepwise procedure analogous to a forward or backward regression analysis, we begin with a model with a four-way interaction among word-list register, community population, social network, and social class (WPNC). This model has a perfect equality between observed and expected values (chi-square value 0.000) and zero degrees of freedom. Recalling the hierarchy principle, within this four-way interaction are contained all possible three-way interactions (PNC, WNC, WPN, and WPC) as well as all other interactions. The BMDP program searches among these possibilities to see which one can be eliminated with the least increase in the discrepancy between observed and expected values. In this instance, as the tree diagram in Figure 1 shows, elimination of the WPC interaction creates the least discrepancy. This yields the next simplest model containing three three-way interactions PNC,WNC,WPN with a chi-square value of 1.37 and six degrees of freedom.

With PNC,WNC,WPN as the next simplest model, we again note, invoking the hierarchy principle, that all possible two-way interactions are contained within this model, and the BMDP program can search for the next simplest model by eliminating another three-way interaction. In this instance, again referring to the tree-diagram in Figure 1, the model which creates the least discrepancy between observed and expected values is PNC,WC,WPN. It maintains an insignificant chi-square value of 1.37 and adds one degree of freedom. This step has thus eliminated one three-way interaction WNC (which essentially contributed nothing to the explanation) and preserves a two-way interaction (WC), which was present within WNC because of the hierarchy principle: WN, NC, and WC are present within WNC, and WN and NC are present within the other multivariate factors PNC and WPN.

In the same fashion, the program searches all the possibilities implicit in the PNC,WC,WPN model for the next simplest model which creates the smallest additional discrepancy between observed and expected values and comes up with the model PNC,WC,WN,WP where the three-way interaction WPN is eliminated in favor of three two-way interactions (WC, WN, WP), while retaining the three-way interaction PNC as a component of the model. This model has a chi-square value of 2.84 (1.47 was added) and ten degrees of freedom (three have been added), showing that WPN did not contribute significantly to the explanation.

It should be noted here that what we have up to now called a chi-square value is really the G-square value which, though analogous to chi-square, has an additive property. G-square statistics are totally additive from model to model, while chi-square produces approximate additivity. Since the procedure we are following is totally additive, we will call these G-square values by their right name henceforth. This also means that the net effect of going down the tree several levels step by step is exactly equivalent to going down several steps in one fell swoop.

Again, reiterating the same procedure, any of the four terms in the model PNC,WC,WN,WP can be eliminated, and the BMDP program searches all the possibilities to find that the model PNC,WN,WP creates the least increase in the discrepancy between observed and expected values, adding a G-square value of 0.55 and adding one degree of freedom, from 10 to 11. Now, with the PNC,WN,WP model, we can go further and eliminate one of these components and see what the program will discover. As shown in Figure 1, the next simplest model is PNC,WN, which eliminates WP as a component but retains the three-way interaction PNC. This step adds a G-square value of 6.55 and three degrees of freedom, but the total G-square value of 9.94 is still not significant, so explanatory power has not been damaged seriously by this step in reducing the complexity of the model.

However, as Figure 1 indicates, if we go beyond this point and attempt to eliminate PNC or WN from the PNC,WN model, the situation changes fundamentally. If the two-way interaction WN is eliminated, the G-square value is increased by 16.68 to 26.62, and if PNC is eliminated, the G-square value is increased by 8.48 to 18.43. Both of these resulting G-square values are significant; thus, if either of these components is eliminated from the model, there are major losses in explanatory power. This means that PNC,WN is a promising model to account for the word-list register data.

The BMDP program will produce a variety of output associated with the PNC,WN model: observed values, expected values, standardized deviates, components of chi-square, the log-linear parameters, etc. A careful examination of this output is necessary in order to evaluate the proposed model in terms of realistic interpretations. No judgment about a "best model" can be made without such an examination. Table 4 displays expected values and Table 5 the standardized deviates for the PNC,WN model. (The standardized deviate is the difference between observed and expected values divided by the square root of the expected value.) The standardized deviates for the PNC,WN model are approximately normally distributed; thus, a value of a standardized deviate exceeding 2.0 in magnitude reflects a significant difference between observed and expected values. In the present instance, all of the standardized deviates associated with the PNC,WN model are very small, which indicates a "good fit" of expected values to observed values. (In an instance where more than one promising model emerges, a comparison of the tables of standardized deviates is very useful in deciding which has a better fit, as we will see later.) A more detailed analysis would also examine the log-linear parameters to assess the contribution of each of the factors to the the model, but we will show later that a similar assessment can emerge from continuing the stepwise process of eliminating factors from the model.

As a result of examining the PNC,WN model and judging it to fit the word-list register data well, we see that a three-way interaction among community population, social network, and social class and a two-way interaction between word-list register and social network are both necessary to explain the data. We will return to a more detailed interpretation of this after we have examined models for reading register and casual speech register.

Moving on to an analysis of the reading register data, we will not walk through every step, because the process is represented in the tree-diagram in Figure 2. However, it is worth noting that a three-way interaction among community interaction, social network, and social class emerges as part of the most promising model PNC,RN (where R = reading register). There is also a two-way interaction between social network and reading register (RN) analogous to WN in the word-list model. Table 6 displays the expected values for the PNC,RN model, and as shown in Table 7, the standardized deviates for this model are also very small, indicating a good fit of observed values to expected values.

Concerning the casual register data, Figure 3 summarizes the stepwise analysis, and again a three-way interaction among community population, social network, and social class emerges as a factor in the most promising model. Likewise, as in the models for word-list register and reading register, there is a two-way interaction between register and social network. However, the interaction between casual register (K) and social class (C) is also significant, and that factor is retained in the most promising model. If any of the factors PNC, KC, or KN is removed from the PNC,KC,KN model (which has a G-square value of 5.66 and 13 degrees of freedom), there is a significant increase in the discrepancy between observed and expected values, as seen at the bottom of the tree-diagram in Figure 3. This is not a surprising result, because the initial chi-square analysis of interactions among all the variables showed that the interaction between social class and casual speech register was very significant (Pearson's chi-square value was 9.39 with one degree of freedom, and $p = <.002$). Table 8 displays the expected values for the PNC,KC,KN model.

Given the previous success of the PNC,WN and PNC,RN models, it is tempting to consider what the difference between the simpler model PNC,KN and the more complex model PNC,KC,KN model might be. If the standardized deviates of the two models are compared (the measure of "goodness of fit" of observed values to expected values), we find that they are small in both models (see Tables 9 and 10), even though there was a significant increase in the discrepancy between observed and expected values as the KC interaction is eliminated from the model. This indicates that the contribution of the KC factor (interaction between casual register and social class) may not be as important as its initial chi-square value might have suggested. The significance of the KC interaction is reduced because of the three-way PNC interaction in the model of the casual speech register data. It is a subtle point, but we do obtain a more accurate sense of the dynamics of the data as a result of this analysis than we would from a straightforward chi-square analysis of two-way tables. The two-way interaction between social class and casual register is important—just not as important as a traditional chi-square analysis would have led us to believe.

Returning now to the issue of the relative importance of the main effects in the model, we go back to the stepwise procedure which initially produced the most promising models (beyond which the G-square values go up significantly). If we take the process beyond this point anyway, we can begin to discover how important the factors are. In the instance of the word-list register model in Figure 4, our most promising model was PNC,WN (which now appears at the top of the tree-diagram), and if we go beyond this to the next simplest model, ignoring the significant increase in G-square, we discover that the interaction between community population, social network and social class is dropped out, so the next simplest model is NC,PN,WN. The three-way interaction PNC is eliminated, and the two-way interactions present within it now become the targets of further elimination. The contribution of PN, PC, and NC are each examined, and PC contributes the least to the adequacy of the model. In other words, elimination of either PN or NC would result in a greater increase in the G-square value than PC would, so PC is eliminated.

Continuing in the same fashion (recognizing that we are no longer looking for a best-fit model), the program reveals that NC is the next factor to be eliminated, leaving a model C,PN,WN as the next simplest model, and when this in turn is subjected to further analysis, the main effect or singlet factor C (social class) can be dropped with the least increase in G-square value, yielding a model PN,WN. If any further simplification is attempted (either PNW or P,WN), the G-square values go up so high (39.16 and 39.88) that there is no point in continuing. However, the process to this point suggests that social class contributes less to the explanation of the observed variation in word-list register than the two-way factors PN and WN (community population/social network and word-list register/social network). Thus, in seeking a sense of the relative importance of the main effects in the PNC,WN model (the singlets P, N, C, and W), social class is the least important—less important than the remaining doublets PN and WN.

In some ways, this procedure is more revealing that the log-linear parameters which are also part of the output of the BMDP program. The log-linear parameters are estimates of the the magnitude of each parameter and how a large a component each one was relative to the log of the expected values. But a significance level was not attached to those parameters. The stepwise procedure has the benefit of attaching a significance level (G-square) to each of the interaction terms and each of the main effect terms, which provides some basis for deciding which terms could be eliminated and what effect that elimination would have.

INTERPRETATION OF "BEST FIT" MODELS

Although the primary focus here has been upon the implementation of log-linear statistical analysis in discovering parsimonious "best-fit" models, it seems appropriate to attempt a brief interpretation of the results of this process, so that the significance of the procedure will perhaps be more apparent.

As was noted in the introduction, conventional data gathering in sociolinguistics regularly includes the specification of age, sex, and social class as social variables, while community population and social network have not been so well established as useful social variables. Yet, in this data set (with all the limitations noted earlier), age and sex were eliminated from the model early on, because there were no significant interactions between these and any other variables, while community population and social network (local vs. outside orientation) are consistently shown to be the most salient social variables in accounting for the variability to be found in each of the three registers sampled. Social class seems also to be significant in accounting for the variability ob-observed in the casual register, though less powerful than population or social network.

Even more interesting than the discovery of the most important social variables in this data set is the discovery that a three-way interaction among community population, social network, and social class is necessary to explain the variation between observed and expected values in each of the registers sampled (word-list, reading, and casual speech). The models which best fit the data sets must involve a multivariate interaction among these three social variables—they act together to generate the observed effect (the inherent variability between archaic and modern forms across the three registers sampled), above and beyond what is explained by the two-way interaction between register and social network.

On the face of it, this is an intuitively satisfying conclusion. Community population size is not a static measure, but in fact a determinant in the patterns of interaction among communities in region and has been utilized in gravity models of regional dynamics for many years. The regional center or focal area's features diffuse outward, not in oil-spot fashion, but through a hierarchy of larger to smaller communities in the region, following general patterns of social and economic activity (Larmouth 1981). Likewise, specification of an informant's social network is a description of the pattern of most frequent and significant contact and interaction, which can either operate to diffuse a new feature or to retain and reinforce a familiar one. With vastly improved roads and transportation systems, social networks can more easily transcend spatial limitations which would have sharply constrained a rural person's social contacts a half-century ago. Similarly, while social class is perhaps a more indirect factor in a person's patterns of social interaction, it is not surprising to see it emerge as an important factor in casual discourse. And since all of these factors occur simultaneously, it seems entirely appropriate that they act together to account for the movement of linguistic features from one group to another; indeed, the best-fit models for all three registers consistently show that such simultaneous interactions are necessary to account for the dynamics of the data set.

Thus, the multivariate interactions among the social variables seem to offer a more plausible and direct specification of the dynamics of social contact and interaction, and these multivariate interactions, as revealed through log-linear methods, appear to be useful in explaining the mechanisms by which dialect features diffuse from one population to another. It would be interesting to see whether the same or similar inferences could be drawn from other (and richer) data sets if log-linear statistical models were employed, but this is a task which awaits further effort if, as we hope, this approach has been of some interest here.

Table 1: Observed Frequency for Word-List Register

Social Class	Social Network	Community Population	Word-List Register Archaic	Modern	Total
Working	Local	Village	7	2	9
		Town	1	4	5
		City	0	0	0
		BigCity	0	0	0
		Total	8	6	14
	Outside	Village	0	0	0
		Town	0	5	5
		City	0	6	6
		BigCity	0	9	9
		Total	0	20	20
Middle	Local	Village	1	0	1
		Town	0	4	4
		City	0	0	0
		BigCity	0	0	0
		Total	1	4	5
	Outside	Village	0	7	7
		Town	0	4	4
		City	0	4	4
		BigCity	0	9	9
		Total	0	24	24

Table 2: Observed Frequency for Reading Register

Social Class	Social Network	Community Population	Word-List Register Archaic	Modern	Total
Working	Local	Village	6	3	9
		Town	4	1	5
		City	0	0	0
		BigCity	0	0	0
		Total	10	4	14
	Outside	Village	0	0	0
		Town	0	5	5
		City	0	6	6
		BigCity	0	9	9
		Total	0	20	20
Middle	Local	Village	0	1	1
		Town	3	1	4
		City	0	0	0
		BigCity	0	0	0
		Total	3	2	5
	Outside	Village	2	5	7
		Town	0	4	4
		City	0	4	4
		BigCity	0	9	9
		Total	2	22	24

Table 3: Observed Frequency for Casual Speech Register

Social Class	Social Network	Community Population	Word-List Register		
			Archaic	Modern	Total
Working	Local	Village	9	0	9
		Town	5	0	5
		City	0	0	0
		BigCity	0	0	0
		Total	14	0	14
	Outside	Village	0	0	0
		Town	1	4	5
		City	2	4	6
		BigCity	3	6	9
		Total	6	14	20
Middle	Local	Village	1	0	1
		Town	3	1	4
		City	0	0	0
		BigCity	0	0	0
		Total	4	1	5
	Outside	Village	2	5	7
		Town	0	4	4
		City	0	4	4
		BigCity	0	9	9
		Total	2	22	24

Table 4: Expected Values for PNC,WN Model

Social Class	Social Network	Community Population	Word-List Register Archaic	Modern	Total
Working	Local	Village	4.8	5.2	10.0
		Town	2.9	3.1	6.0
		City	.5	.5	1.0
		BigCity	.5	.5	1.0
		Total	8.7	9.3	18.0
	Outside	Village	.1	.9	1.0
		Town	.5	5.5	6.0
		City	.5	6.5	7.0
		BigCity	.8	9.2	10.0
		Total	1.8	22.2	24.0
Middle	Local	Village	1.0	1.0	2.0
		Town	2.4	2.6	5.0
		City	.5	.5	1.0
		BigCity	.5	.5	1.0
		Total	4.3	4.7	9.0
	Outside	Village	.6	7.4	8.0
		Town	.4	4.6	5.0
		City	.4	4.6	5.0
		BigCity	.8	9.2	10.0
		Total	2.2	25.8	28.0

Table 5: Standardized Deviates for PNC,WN Model

Social Class	Social Network	Community Population	Word-List Register Archaic	Modern
Working	Local	Village	1.2	-1.2
		Town	-.8	.8
		City	.0	-.0
		BigCity	.0	-.0
	Outside	Village	1.5	-.4
		Town	.1	-.0
		City	-.1	.0
		BigCity	-.3	.1
Middle	Local	Village	.5	-.5
		Town	-1.2	1.2
		City	.0	-.0
		BigCity	.0	-.0
	Outside	Village	-.1	.0
		Town	.2	-.1
		City	.2	-.1
		BigCity	-.3	.1

Table 6: Expected Values for PNC,RN Model

Social Class	Social Network	Community Population	Word-List Register Archaic	Modern	Total
Working	Local	Village	6.3	3.7	10.0
		Town	3.8	2.2	6.0
		City	.6	.4	1.0
		BigCity	.6	.4	1.0
		Total	11.3	6.7	18.0
	Outside	Village	.1	.9	1.0
		Town	.7	5.3	6.0
		City	.8	6.2	7.0
		BigCity	1.2	8.8	10.0
		Total	2.8	21.2	24.0
Middle	Local	Village	1.3	.7	2.0
		Town	3.1	1.9	5.0
		City	.6	.4	1.0
		BigCity	.6	.4	1.0
		Total	5.7	3.3	9.0
	Outside	Village	.9	7.1	8.0
		Town	.6	4.4	5.0
		City	.6	4.4	5.0
		BigCity	1.2	8.8	10.0
		Total	3.2	24.8	28.0

Table 7: Standardized Deviates for PNC,RN Model

Social Class	Social Network	Community Population	Word-List Register Archaic	Modern
Working	Local	Village	.1	-.1
		Town	.4	-.5
		City	-.2	.2
		BigCity	-.2	.2
	Outside	Village	1.1	-.4
		Town	-.2	.1
		City	-.3	.1
		BigCity	-.6	.2
Middle	Local	Village	-.7	.9
		Town	.2	-.3
		City	-.2	.2
		BigCity	-.2	.2
	Outside	Village	1.6	-.6
		Town	-.1	.0
		City	-.1	.0
		BigCity	-.6	.2

Table 8: Expected Values for PNC,KC,KN Model

Social Class	Social Network	Community Population	Word-List Register Archaic	Modern	Total
Working	Local	Village	6.9	.9	7.8
		Town	6.3	.8	7.1
		City	1.2	.1	1.3
		BigCity	1.2	.1	1.3
		Total	15.5	2.0	17.5
	Outside	Village	1.5	2.8	4.2
		Town	1.8	3.4	5.2
		City	2.0	3.7	5.6
		BigCity	3.3	6.2	9.4
		Total	8.5	16.0	24.5
Middle	Local	Village	2.9	1.3	4.2
		Town	2.6	1.2	3.9
		City	.5	.2	.7
		BigCity	.5	.2	.7
		Total	6.5	3.0	9.5
	Outside	Village	.6	4.2	4.8
		Town	.7	5.1	5.8
		City	.8	5.5	6.4
		BigCity	1.4	9.2	10.6
		Total	3.5	24.0	27.5

Table 9: Standardized Deviates for PNC,KC,KN Model

Social Class	Social Network	Community Population	Word-List Register Archaic	Modern
Working	Local	Village	1.0	-.4
		Town	-.3	-.3
		City	-.6	.9
		BigCity	-.6	.9
	Outside	Village	-.8	-1.4
		Town	-.2	.6
		City	.4	.4
		BigCity	.1	.1
Middle	Local	Village	-.8	-.7
		Town	.5	.3
		City	.0	.6
		BigCity	.0	.6
	Outside	Village	2.4	.7
		Town	-.3	-.3
		City	-.3	-.4
		BigCity	-.7	.1

Table 10: Standardized Deviates for PNC,KN Model

Social Class	Social Network	Community Population	Word-List Register Archaic	Modern
Working	Local	Village	.5	-1.0
		Town	.3	-.6
		City	-.3	.7
		BigCity	-.3	.7
	Outside	Village	.6	-.3
		Town	.1	-.1
		City	.7	-.4
		BigCity	.8	.4
Middle	Local	Village	-.1	-.2
		Town	-.3	.6
		City	-.3	.7
		BigCity	-.3	.7
	Outside	Village	-.1	.2
		Town	-.6	.3
		City	-.6	.3
		BigCity	-1.2	.7

Figure 1: Diagram of BMDP Evaluation of Word-List Register Models

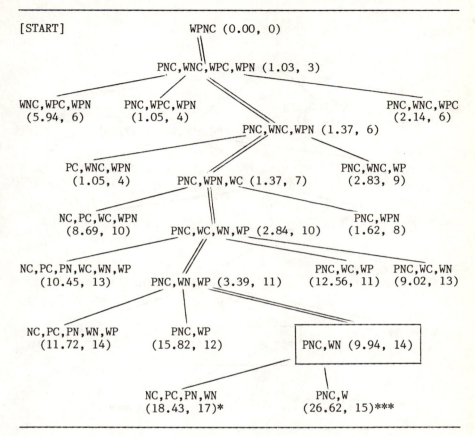

KEY: First number in parentheses is the added G-square value

Second number in parentheses specifies degrees of freedom

"Most Promising Model" appears in a box

Bold line marks pathway through best-fit models

W - word-list register   N - social network

P - community population size   C - social class

* - significant discrepancy created between observed and expected values (*** - <u>really</u> significant)

Figure 2: Diagram of BMDP Evaluation of Reading Register Models

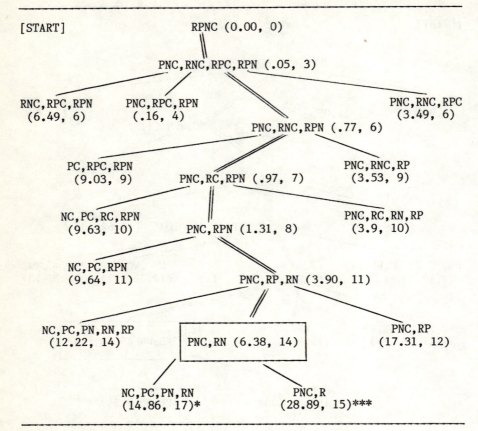

KEY: First number in parentheses is the added G-square value

Second number in parentheses specifies degrees of freedom

"Most Promising Model" appears in a box

Bold line marks pathway through best-fit models

R - reading register   N - social network

P - community population size   C - social class

* - significant discrepancy created between observed and expected values (*** - <u>really</u> significant)

Figure 3: BMDP Evaluation of Casual Speech Register Models

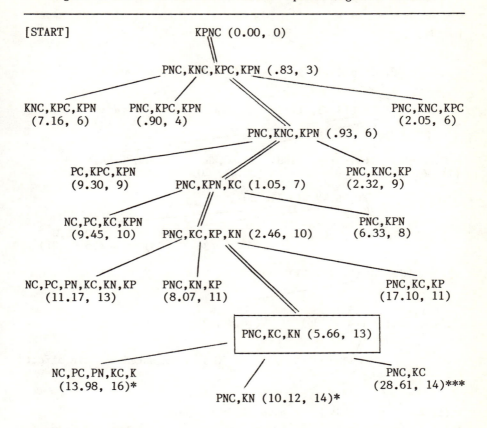

KEY: First number in parentheses is the added G-square value

Second number in parentheses specifies degrees of freedom

"Most Promising Model" appears in a box

Bold line marks pathway through best-fit models

K – casual speech register   N – social network

P – community population size C – social class

* – significant discrepancy created between observed and
   expected values (*** – really significant)

Figure 4: Diagram of BMDP Evaluation of Main Effect Variables

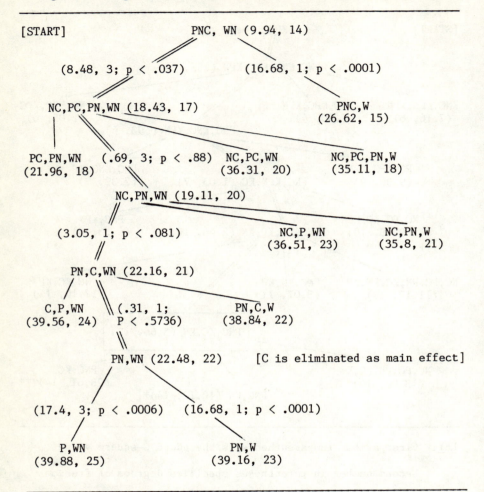

KEY: First number in parentheses is the added G-square value

Second number in parentheses specifies degrees of freedom

p-values are included within parentheses

W - word-list register   N - social network

P - community population size   C - social class

REFERENCES

Bailey, C.-J. (1973). *Variation and Linguistic Theory*. Washington D. C.: Center for Applied Linguistics.

Bishop, Y., Fienberg, S. & Holland, P. (1975). *Discrete Multivariate Analysis*. Boston: MIT Press.

Davis, L. (1982). American social dialectology: a statistical appraisal. *American Speech*, 57, 83-94.

--------- (1985). The problem of social class grouping in sociolinguistic research. *American Speech*, 60, 214-221.

Fienberg, S. (1980). *The Analysis of Cross-Classified Categorical Data*. 2nd ed. Boston: MIT Press.

Goodman, L. (1978). *Analyzing Qualitative/Categorical Data*. Cambridge: Abt Books.

--------- (1970). The multivariate analysis of qualitative data: interactions among multiple classifications. *Journal of the American Statistical Association*, 65, 226-256.

Larmouth, D. (1981). Gravity models, wave theory, and low-structure regions. In H. Warkentyne (ed.), *Methods IV: Papers from the 4th International Conference on Methods in Dialectology*, 199-219. Victoria, British Columbia: University of Victoria.

Linn, M. (1983). Informant selection in dialectology. *American Speech*, 58, 225-243.

Miller, M. (1984). The city as a cause of morphophonemic change. *The SECOL Review*, 8, 28-59.

Milroy, L. (1980). *Language and Social Networks*. Oxford: Blackwell.

Trudgill, P. (1974). Linguistic change and diffusion: description and explanation in sociolinguistic dialect geography. *Language in Society* 4, 215-246.

--------- (1984). Sex and covert prestige: linguistic change in the urban dialect of Norwich. In J. Baugh & J. Sherter (eds.), *Language Use: Readings in Sociolinguistics*, 54-58. Englewood Cliffs, N. J.: Prentice-Hall.

Upton, G. (1978). *The Analysis of Cross-Classified Data*. New York: John Wiley & Sons.

Research on Mural Sprayscripts (Graffiti)

URS DÜRMÜLLER
University of Berne

Research on mural sprayscripts from a sociolinguistic point of view is still in its intial phase -in spite of the many publications on graffiti. As socio-political, psycho-social, and generally cultural signs, graffiti have been studied by anthropologists, folklorists, social psychologists and ethnographers, among others (see Dürmüller 1987). The data contained in these articles, however, have been recorded in such a way that many of the questions to be asked in sociolinguistic research cannot be answered.

There can be no doubt that sociolinguists and dialectologists must take a keen interest in the collection of graffiti data and their analysis as examples of language in society and forms of particular language varieties. Interesting aspects of graffiti may be revealed if graffiti defined according to social groups and/or locality are checked for specific linguistic features, such as use of diverse writing symbols and spelling conventions in general; use of keywords and lexical items in general; use of syntactical patterns, of speech acts; as well as for the interplay between linguistic and contextual features. On the other hand, the social response to graffiti, i.e. the decoding of sprayscripts by readers from various social groups deserves the attention of researchers as well. Here it should be particularly rewarding to focus on the difficulties people have in interpreting some graffiti correctly, due to such factors as ignorance of the special writing conventions, ignorance of the special meanings of cultural keywords, inability to contextualize appropriately the verbal part of a graffito with the other features of its total semiotic make-up.

Such graffiti have become a part of everyday life in most urban societie In recent times most of them have been spraypainted on walls with public access - hence their name. As mural sprayscripts they contain conventionally defined text in one or several languages; they contain alphabetic signs as well as pictograms, ideograms or logograms, or any combination of these. They can vary letter and picture size, they may appear in one or many colours, and they may include the surface on which they appear as an essential part of their semantic structure. Mural sprayscripts offer possibilities to study written language of a particular kind, of language that is not spoken although it shares many characteristics of spoken language, of language that is written only. Mural sprayscripts are intended for reading, they aim for visual effects, they want to be seen. Thus letter shape, color, general appearance become important, often more so than the semantic contents of the words used.

Sprayscripts fall between the categories of written and spoken language. Murals are part of written language, and they do not occur in face-to-face situations where temporal commonality is of importance. Nevertheless, most of them seem to be spontaneous rather than edited, informal rather than formal, non-standard rather than standard.
This peculiar kind of language variety should in addition be analyzed for: genre or text type, textual structure, authorship, motivation for production, socio-cultural domains of reference, communicative function, language variation and standardization, lingua franca function, multilingualism and code-switching, attitudes and reactions of readers.

Data elicitaion, which so often appears as one of the main problems in sociolinguistic research, does not present the familiar problems if the researcher turns to graffiti. Mural sprayscripts and the verbal messages they contain are simply there, available as data in exactly the way they were produced or read when no researcher was secretly or openly observing the process. The graffiti speak to the researcher in exactly the same way as to anyone else. He finds himself in exactly the same situation as any of his fellow citizens when reading the writing on the wall. However, when deciphering the walls, the researcher cannot rely on his own intuition alone. He must have it counterchecked by asking for the opinion of representatives of various population groups to whom the data may be shown in slide form. This seems especially important with regard to assigning graffiti texts to socio-cultural domains, and to the reading of these texts as speech acts. People should be asked for a paraphrase of the graffiti text in their own words, and they should be encouraged to identify and describe the speaker, the addressee, and the topic of the speech event.
Data collection must be contextual, and it must be either complete in a certain well-defined area, or at random in a larger area. Since locality is also part of the information, the language medium is not the only one to consider. Graffiti integrate language into the larger medium of painted or sprayed art in an architectonically defined area. Which means that graffiti are fully understanable only within their wider context. Taking slides when procuring the data will ensure that there is information on the form and color of the graffito, on the text contained by it, on the interplay of text and non-text, and on the background against which the script is to be read -the surface on which it is painted, scribbled, or sprayed; whether this is concrete, wood, or brick, etc.; whether this material is architectonically perceived to be part of a church, a supermarket, a railway station (and which part of it), or whatever.

The use of such additional non-linguistic means is the reason why there are no identical sprayscripts. Variation appears as an essential characteristic of mural scripts. It is true that messages re-appear in different places, and often they are identical on the word level and on the syntactic level. Often, however, they are varied in accordance with the particular locality they appear in. Variation is also found if the text as such remains the same, because in these cases some other parts of the total semiotic build-up of the graffito has changed: letter size, letter form, coloring, embedding among other sprayed items, ornamentation, placement on surface, surface type, wider locality. It can be claimed that if all the aspects of mural sprayscripts are taken into consideration, there are no identical graffiti.

Determining the communicative genre to which graffiti might belong, one cannot fail to notice certain parallels of mural sprayscripts with advertising. But while advertising in the public media manifests some of the most deliberately controlled and highly purposeful use of language in society, murals are also open towards spontaneous and unreflected creation. As in advertising, again, the "speaker-sprayer" of mural scripts cannot rely on getting a response from his addressees since graffiti constitute "one-way" communication (dialogue exceptions have been recorded in restrooms and elevators). The sprayer has no way of picking up immediate cues about what effect his message is having on the addressee as he is reading it, and for that reason the sprayer cannot make any immediate adjustments to what he is saying or how he is saying it, as it is possible in face-to-face communication. Also there is no social obligation on the reader/addressee of a graffito to appear agreeable to the communicative act; he is free to disregard anything or everything expressed in the graffito.

Graffiti are essentially public, theoretically open to all and everyone to read and - with some social and psychological restrictions - also to produce. Though, while everybody can (or already has) read one or several graffiti and thus functions as a receiver of messages coded in mural sprayscript form, in practice only a few people produce or actually have produced murals in order to express themselves or to address others graffiti-wise.
Sociologists suggest that not persons, but social conditions should be addressed as authors of graffiti. And anthropologists maintain that graffiti mirror hidden cultures. Sociolinguists, however, would like to detect the people behind the words on the wall, seeing the study of graffiti in relation to the individuals or the social groups that are responsible for their production as of central importance. In graffiti people use language (and other semiotic means) to share their thoughts and feelings with others, to mark their social and cultural identity, and to define their social relationship with people belonging to the

same group or people outside that group. Language easily acquires a
symbolic function both for individuals (with regard to personal self-
presentation) and within smaller groups (where it functions as an
emblem of ethnicity).
Only rarely has it been possible to identify the authors of mural sprayscripts. In the case of American cities like New York or Philadelphia
authorship was attributed not only to definite social groups but even to
individuals. Most of the authors, however, remain anonymous, except
where script turns into art. Indeed, the urge for artistic expression
may be just as important a motivation as any ideological one. Becoming
a graffito king among the young sprayers means to be highly original,
to be playful, to be a master of the technique, and to produce
something esthetically pleasing. These cases show that the written
language may get fresh calligraphic impetus from mural sprayscripts.
Many of the attractive scripts seem to be inspired by or even copied
from commercially available letter shapes. Often, not only picture
graffiti, but also some of the sprayscripts can rank as art. Comparing
these more sophisticated graffiti with the many drab ones, one might
conclude that the former are a later development. While on a first
stage, graffiti texts tend to be not signed, primarily verbal, aiming
for clarity in order to get across the political or sexual message,
and often making a gesture of offence, on a secondary stage they tend
to be signed pseudonymically, they are primarily graphic, aiming for
ambiguity in order to increase the poetic status of the text and in
order to make movement within fashion possible, making a gesture of
art.

Since, to some extent, mural sprayscripts are also pictographic and
ideographic, a part of their texts should be internationally understandable. When ideas are represented literally, directly, often
even non-symbolically, mural sprayscripts may be said to use primitive
language, i.e. a kind of language that does not have any direct
relationship to the spoken language since the signs used represent
objects in the real world rather than their linguistic names. Because
such texts do not depend on the sounds of any particular language, they
can be understood by anyone. Indeed, mural sprayscripts exhibit
universal hieroglyphs belonging to a world language. There are international symbols for sex and love, there are political symbols (like
the Swastika) and symbols for anarchy, there are signs for longing
(like palms, flowers, sharks and butterflies), and there are signs
for terror (like the skull and the nuclear cloud). To some extent, then,
mural sprayscripts have helped to develop a world-wide lingua franca
restricted, however, to the written public medium. Research here
should begin to list these symbols and work out the way they are being
used in different places, and the ways they are combined with alphabetic signs. Although, on the one hand, the style of writing may be
locality and group specific, thus highly idiosyncratic, there may,

on the other hand, exist certain international conventions that will
make it possible to discuss standardization processes in graffiti texts.
Generally, however, although they are examples of written language,
graffiti texts are not cast in standardized language. The forms of
language used are highly diverse precisely because social identity
is marked by language - by one of several languages in multilingual
settings, by one of several language varieties in monolingual settings.
In mutlilingual Switzerland, e.g., the various national languages are
used in varying varieties. In addition there appear foreign languages,
above all world English and the languages of migrant workers. Graffiti
texts thus contain fascinating material for the study of the various
aspects of bi- and multilingualism, of language choice, including
code switching, and the study of language attitudes.

Researchers will find it rewarding to examine the languages or
language varieties used in graffiti texts in terms of what is
being expressed in them. In a city whose inhabitants use language
A predominantly, what does it mean if a sprayscript is written in
language B? or C? And what might it mean if a graffito text also
uses additional languages, thus switching between A, B, and C? In
order to find answers to such questions, establishing correlations
between language(s) and domains of reference (such as music, politics,
drugs, sex, law and order) might prove helpful.

Since many items seem to defy classification along these terms, the
data should also be handled in terms of communicative function(s).
The functions identified most often so far are (1) naming of self
and other, self-identification, self-assertion, self-advertising;
(2) territorial marking and occupation; (3) venting tensions and pro-
testing; (4) in-group communication, sending messages to others;
(5) intimate communication as between lovers; (6) political activism,
calling others to act; (7) and showing off originality and playful-
nessin nonsense and concrete poetry texts.
In order to establish the communicative function of spraytext, the
visual information of the whole graffito must be taken into consideration again. Correlations must be established between colors
and linguistic characteristics, between relative size of the
graffito and the linguistic characteristics and between ornamentation
and linguistic characteristics.
It would appear that the affective component of spraytext may be enhanced by the use of colors. A certain relationship between kind
of message andcolor can be suggested following the work of Berlin &
Kay, 1969. Statistics show that basic color terms (black, red and white)
are used most often in graffiti. On the other hand, the so-called
younger colors, i.e. those known in highly technological civilizations,
are used more rarely in the graffiti. Such sophisticated color terms

are blue, brown, and, especially, purple, pink, orange, and grey.
Here, correlations should be established between color type and and
simplicity or elaboration of message structure, lexicon and syntax of
the texts.

Certain words in the graffiti texts appear as clearly emblematic of
particular social stances; members of particular groups will be expected to use them in their mural writing in specialized meanings
not necessarily available to the general public. Since it is supposed
that many graffiti have their origins in subcultural domains, we may
expect the murals to exhibit a heightened awareness of language, to
use words intentionally, letting them play a vital part in the
exercise and consolidation of power. Such outwardly directed words
will be more easy to recognize than those that are inwardly directed,
the so-called keywords. As the term hints, keywords act as keys to
whole systems of belief; they open up worlds that are often foreign
to the ordinary citizen, they give away the secrets of what in Western
industrialized nations is now called "the scene". Research here should
try to establish which words belong to which group and to which domain,
and to describe the semantic shifts that make them meaningful for
insiders, but leave them quite uninteresting for outsiders.

The syntax of mural sprayscripts can also be analyzed. It offers
many good examples for ambiguous sentences; their pragmatic status
becomes clear only if one succeeds in contextualizing them appropriately. The data from mutlilingual Switzerland (Dürmüller, 1986)
suggest that phrasal and clausal examples occur with similar frequency and allow for great variation. Complex sentences, however,
could be attested only in the native local languages. Again the
types of syntactic patterns found ought to be correlated with the
message type of the mural in question, with the locality in which
it is found, and, if possible, with the social groups or the individuals with whom it can be linked up.

It is the interplay between the linguistic and the contextual features
one should constantly bear in mind. Dealing with decontextualized
linguistic data collected from graffiti may produce nice results;
but once the researcher goes back to check on the whole graffiti,
he will unfailingly notice that he may have interpreted much of the
data wrongly. It is this constant interplay of diverse public signs
that makes the sociolinguistic study of graffiti so difficult and
often quite frustrating. Students of mural sprayscripts should therefore recognize the elusiveness of mural scripts as one of their
essential characteristics. This, however, should not intimidate
prospective researchers; quite on the contrary: they should face the
challenge and begin to work all those walls filled with culturally
and socially relevant linguistic signs.

References

Berlin, B. and P. Kay. 1969. Basic Color Terms. Berkeley and Los Angeles: University of California Press.
Dürmüller, Urs. 1986. Sociolingvisticki aspecti zidnih natpisa sprejom (graffiti). Polja (novi Sad), 327, 253-354.
Dürmüller, Urs, 1987. Sociolinguistic Aspects of Mural Sprayscripts. Sociolinguistics, XVI, 1.

Linguistics and Dialectology: Controlling Strange Data

ROBERT B. HAUSMANN
University of Montana

INTRODUCTION

During my first course in linguistics, my professor told me something that seemed on the surface patently false; he said that you could say the same word 100 times in a row and never say it the same way twice. At the time, I was certain that I--at least--said a given word the same way every time I said it, even though I was vaguely aware that others might say it differently on occasion (and therefore, of course, wrong). And while my professor may have been exaggerating slightly, careful listening over the years (and a few days' work with a sound spectrograph) have led me to accept his statement as more true than false.

I know now, after 20 some years of studying language, that a lot more language variety comes out of our mouths than exists in our heads; I have come, that is, to accept the notion that our psychological awareness of language is more or less <u>emic</u> even though what comes out of our mouths is decidedly <u>etic</u>. Put another way, I have come to accept the fact that we are a reductionist creature. We seem to simplify the world we are confronted with.

Since we have this tendency as speakers of language to reduce the phonetic variety we hear to a single phonemic or morpho-phonemic set, dialect geographers are on more secure ground when they do word geography rather than anything else. To lift a classic question from the various linguistic atlases of the United States, that someone would decide to chart the distribution of <u>SKILLET</u> versus <u>FRYING PAN</u> versus <u>SPIDER</u> for the 'utensil you use to cook eggs in the morning' should surprise no one. First of all, different words for the same thing is something that anyone who has ever travelled 20 miles from home will almost certainly have run into. Second, different words for the same thing is exactly how languages seem to differ. And, third, our reductionist instincts are hardly powerful enough to reduce the sound sequence in <u>SKILLET</u> to the sound sequence in <u>FRYING PAN</u>.

But coming up with different words for the same thing only whets our dialect geographer appetites. In fact, from the very beginning of dialectology in 1876 when Georg Wenker (Wrede, et al. 1926) was seeking phonetic variation to check on the sound law theories of the Young Grammarians, dialectologists have been interested in charting other kinds of differences. To draw examples from the history of American dialectology, they started charting underlying phonological differences (ROOF pronounced [ruf] or [rʊf]). They started charting narrow phonetic differences in the syllable nucleus of the first vowel in words like MOUNTAIN or in the onset of the syllable nucleus in words like TUBE or NEW (Kurath 1939:26,35). And in morphology, they started charting the differences in the preterit and past participle in irregular verbs, the principal parts of LIE, for example, and LAY (Atwood 1953, V. McDavid 1957).

All of this time, the dialect geographers were very aware that they were sampling the population, and that there were some risks involved in making too much of what was found. Because they knew that speakers might have different forms for different occasions (and even different forms for the same occasion), fieldworkers were cautioned by their trainers to probe and probe again to make certain that a given response was as accurate a representation of how people actually spoke as possible (Kurath 1939:39-53; V. McDavid 1957:5ff). And we were cautioned to choose people who truly represented the speech community (no self-appointed guardians of the language, for example, and no people with no teeth). We were careful, even before discussions of the Observer's Paradox or discussion of linguistic styles, about how we asked what we asked. And even before dialectologists started to learn about statistics and sampling techniques, we were careful who it was we selected to ask what we wanted to ask.

Curiously enough, we have spent relatively little time talking about what it is that we ask. To be sure, the creators of questionnaires have spent hour upon hour deciding what questions to ask and what questions not to ask. I have never been charged with designing such a questionnaire. Almost certainly those who have been so charged have been guided by the principle that an appropriate question is one that can be reasonably expected to elicit the most variation across the population. But we have not talked among ourselves as much as we might about what language variation we do not or should not study, at least in the broad-stroke formats designed to cover large geographical areas and large populations in the shortest time possible. And it is this question of what we study that I want to address here, for I feel that we can profit much by considering directly the relationship of a particular linguistic form to the linguistic system from which it arises.

I want to begin this discussion of the relationship between form and system by reporting on a comparative study I have done (under the direction of the late Raven I. McDavid, Jr.) of the field records of the <u>Dictionary of American Regional English</u> and <u>The Linguistic Atlas of the North Central States</u> for the principal parts of some irregular verbs. From there, I will report on some variation in pronunciation I have collected from university faculty members for various 'learned' or 'big' words. I will conclude from both instances that a direct examination of these kinds of linguistic variation in the context of what we know about speaker grammars can predict that these forms may be a mistake to collect, at least for the typical purposes of dialect geography. I make this suggestion not to criticize any dialect questionnaire but to open to more discussion what we should ask when we design dialect questionnaires.

THE THESIS

My thesis is that the dialect geographer must use particular care with just those linguistic forms that have a dynamic relationship to a speaker's linguistic system. Put another way, we must know whether the surface linguistic form is vulnerable to change or adjustment from its participation in the phonological, morphological, or syntactic components of the speaker's grammar.

Systematic Phonetic Variables

Take, as an example, the pronunciation [bɛ̃], meaning "bend." While this surface form almost certainly does not ever occur in isolation, it commonly occurs when the word following begins with a consonant, as in the construction, "[bɛ̃] back his finger." If, in fact, we could successfully elicit the word in every field interview, we could expect great variety in the forms we would get. Depending on the "fast speech" rules of the speaker (Stampe 1969, 1972), we might get the "citation" (the most formal) form [bɛnd], or we could get a less formal form [bɛ̃n], or we could get the fully reduced form [bɛ̃]. Because there is almost certainly a "variable" rule (Fasold and Shuy 1975) that has the effect of deleting the final consonant in a nasal cluster when the following word begins with a consonant, and because there is another rule of English that reduces a final nazal consonant after it has nazalized the preceding vowel (again, only before a following word that begins with a consonant), we get variation in the form. In this case, matters are complicated because consonant cluster simplification (in American English, at least) is a mark of informality.

In our field interviews, therefore, we will get a get a variety of forms for this word. Subsequent analysis of these forms may imply a geographical distribution for this word when what may be the case is that we have been incapable of replicating the degree of formality of the interview situation. Instead of a geographical distribution of forms, we may be getting a geographical distribution of our interviewing formality. What complicates matters further for any form vulnerable to fast speech rules is the fact that various speakers choose, no matter what the social environment, to use more or fewer of their "fast speech" options; some people simply speak more formally than others. But here is a clear case where a particular linguistic surface form participates directly in a linguistic system that can affect the form--and therefore our analysis of the significance of the variation.

But few of us, the psychological reality of the citation form firmly in our brains, would collect such phonological variation. Intuitively, it seems, we would steer away from it. But there are other forms where our intuitions might not serve us as well, and such forms simply emphasize the need to consider carefully what it is we are seeking. What I have in mind is the status of post-vocalic /r/ in American and British English. In the Handbook of the Linguistic Geography of New England, Kurath (1939:34) charts the distribution of post-vocalic /r/. We know now, from intense studies of the form in the same speakers (Labov 1966), that post-vocalic /r/ varies in some American English dialects. Not only do some speakers have post-vocalic /r/ and others not, but some speakers have post-vocalic /r/ only some of the time. Furthermore, Labov (1972) has shown that the percentage of the time a speaker has post-vocalic /r/ can determine social status and formality. The point here is that the field records collected on this form almost certainly are a simplification of the facts of post-vocalic /r/ in New England. Again, because the form is part of a linguistic system, and because this form is affected by linguistic rules in that system, we as dialect geographers have learned that we must be particularly cautious about how we collect post-vocalic /r/ and what we conclude we have when we look at our field records.

DARE Versus LANCS

A good way to show the danger in collecting some kinds of geographical data would be to replicate a study, to go through a community asking the same question of the same kinds of people. If we get strong correlation between the two studies, we would be certain that our questions were revealing a genuine dialect distribution. If, however, we get great conflict between our two studies, we would have reason to believe that something is wrong--either with our questions or our interviewing techniques (or both). Fortunately, with the publication of The Dictionary of American Regional English we have opportunity to check on some of our data, for DARE fieldworkers asked many of the same questions in exactly the same geographical areas as did the fieldworkers working on The Linguistic Atlas of the United States.[1]

While participating in an NEH sponsored seminar directed by Raven I. McDavid, Jr., I was in a position to compare the field records of The Linguistic Atlas of the Northern Midwestern States (which were housed with McDavid at the University of Chicago) with the field records of Dictionary of American Regional English (housed with Professor Frederic G. Cassidy at the University of Wisconsin). I chose to examine the responses to questions designed to elicit the principal parts of irregular verbs. I limited my comparative investigation to the State of Illinois, partly because the fieldworkers who collected that data were experienced (Professor McDavid and Professor Harold B. Allen collected almost all of them (V. McDavid 1957:16)), partly because there was a large number of communities studied in each case, and partly because Virginia McDavid's 1957 doctoral dissertation seemed to suggest that one could draw isoglosses based on the data (V. McDavid 1957). As everyone familiar with the State of Illinois knows, there is a rather dramatic difference in the settlement history (and consequently, the dialect) between the northern and the southern regions of the State. My hypothesis was that I would find little correlation between the verb paradigms for irregular verbs as revealed in the field records of the two studies.

The background of the two studies is pretty unremarkable. The LANCS field records were collected between 1948 and 1956. 72 field records were collected in communities well distributed throughout the State. From 1 to 17 informants were interviewed in each of the towns, although the verb forms were not collected from each of the informants interviewed.

The DARE field records were collected between 1967 and 1970. Field records were collected in 55 communities well distributed throughout the State. From 1 to 5 informants were interviewed in each community, although, as with the LANCS study, not all informants gave responses to all verb form questions.

My attempt at a comparative analysis was slightly frustrated by the fact that not all irregular verbs were sought in both studies. Furthermore, not all forms for all the regular verbs were sought, for reasons that are not at all clear to me. For example, while forms of LIE (as in 'to lie down') were sought in both DARE and LANCS, DARE sought both the preterit and the past participle while LANCS sought only the preterit. Similarly, while both sought RUN as in 'to run ashore', DARE, again, sought both the preterit and the past participle while LANCS sought only the past participle.

But there was enough overlap to give a notion of the correlation between the two studies, at least as that correlation is represented in the data on five verbs: dive, DRINK, RUN, COME, and LIE. The comparative data are displayed in Figure 1.

DARE Versus LANCS

Irregular Verbs: Taught vs. Taught-against Forms²

		PRETERIT			PAST PARTICIPLE		PRET=PT PAR	
1.	dive	dived	dove	dive				
		# (%)	# (%)	# (%)				
	A. DARE	21 (45)	26 (55)	0				
	B. LANCS	71 (56)	53 (42)	2 (2)				
2.	drink	drank	drunk		drank	drunk	drank	drunk
		# (%)	# (%)		# (%)	# (%)	#	# (%)
	A. DARE	48 (96)	2 (4)		25 (49)	26 (51)	25	1 (52)
	B. LANCS	114 (95)	6 (5)		75 (61)	47 (39)	74	4 (65)
3.	run	ran	run					
		# (%)	# (%)					
	A. DARE	40 (78)	11 (22)					
	B. LANCS	80 (57)	61 (43)					
4.	come	came	come					
		# (%)	# (%)					
	A. DARE	46 (90)	11 (22)					
	B. LANCS	80 (57)	61 (43)					
5.	lie	lay	laid	lied				
		# (%)	# (%)	# (%)				
	A. DARE	20 (43)	25 (53)	2 (4)				
	B. LANCS	38 (32)	76 (65)	3 (3)				

Figure 1   DARE versus LANCS for Five Irregular Verbs

As with most such charts, there is much to be drawn from it. I want, for the purposes of this paper, to concentrate only on the correlations between the two studies. For the preterit of DIVE, for example, DARE informants used DIVED 45% of the time; LANCS informants used DIVED 56% of the time. For DRINK, the correlation between LANCS and DARE was much better; 96% of the DARE informants used DRANK while 95% of the LANCS informants used that form. For RUN, the data are less correlate. DARE informants used RAN 78% of the time, while LANCS informants used RAN only 57% of the time. For COME, the data are even more skewed. DARE informants used CAME 90% of the time, while LANCS informants used CAME only 57% of the time. For the preterit of LIE, the correlation is a little better, with DARE informants using LAY 43% of the time and LANCS informants using LAY 32% of the time.

Methods in Dialectology

I do not find these correlations to be particularly satisfying. If we were checking on FRYING PAN versus SKILLET, I would expect that we would find higher correlations.[3] It might, however, be argued that the data show little correlation because there is a higher percentage of Type III informants in the DARE studies than in the LANCS studies.[4] In order to control for that possibility, I have broken the responses down by informant type (as determined by the fieldworkers). These data are displayed in Figures 2–4.

ANALYSIS OF DARE VERSUS LANCS
BY TYPE I INFORMANT

	PRETERIT			PAST PARTICIPLE		PRET=PT PAR	
A. TYPE I							
1. dive	dived	dove	dive				
	# (%)	# (%)	# (%)				
a. DARE	5 (50)	5 (50)					
b. LANCS	35 (51)	31 (46)	2 (3)				
2. drink	drank	drunk		drank	drunk	drank	drunk
	# (%)	# (%)		# (%)	# (%)	#	# (%)
a. DARE	8 (89)	1 (11)		6 (75)	2 (25)	6	1 (77)
b. LANCS	58 (92)	5 (8)		49 (76)	15 (34)	74	4 (74)
3. run	ran	run					
	# (%)	# (%)					
a. DARE	8 (73)	3 (27)					
b. LANCS	35 (47)	40 (53)					
4. come	came	come					
	# (%)	# (%)					
a. DARE	7 (78)	2 (22)					
b. LANCS	46 (46)	49 (54)					
5. lie	lay	laid	lied				
	# (%)	# (%)	# (%)				
a. DARE	2 (25)	6 (75)	0				
b. LANCS	18 (26)	49 (72)	1 (2)				

AVERAGES (4 verbs; dive excluded)[5]

	PRETERIT		PAST PARTICIPLE		PRET=PT PAR
	Taught	Taught Against	Taught	Taught Against	
a. DARE	66.25	33.75	51	49	52
b. LANCS	52.75	47.25	39	61	65

Figure 2 Numbers and Percentages of Verb Forms for TYPE I Informants

You will notice in Figure 2 that the averages for TYPE I informants for the irregular verbs that we have collected are in each of the principal parts no closer than 13%. We are getting, I hope it is safe to say, little correlation for TYPE I informants. For the TYPE II informants, the data are displayed in Figure 3.

While the averages for the past participle look pretty good--50% versus 57%, we still have little correlation between the two studies in the preterit, where the differences are 15 percentage points apart. Again, I think we can conclude that there is little correlation between the two studies, at least for TYPE II informants.

And, finally, we have the correlation statistics on TYPE III informants. They are displayed in Figure 4 below. In the data for TYPE III informants, we have the best correlation imaginable, no more than 4 percentage points off and often better. Unfortunately, there is reason to suspect these data. First off, the number of TYPE III informants in the State of Illinois is unreliably small. LANCS only asked verb morphology questions (for these verbs) of 17 informants of TYPE III; and DARE interviewed a smaller number of TYPE III informants. For these questions, DARE only shows records from 7 TYPE III informants. Furthermore, that there is strong correlation between the studies may reflect less on the mutual confirmation of the two studies than it does on the relative success of the public schools to weed out the non-standard (in our terms, the "taught-against") forms from the speech of TYPE III speakers.[8]

If the case has not been made strong enough already, consider the following displays of the LANCS and DARE statistics. In Figure 5 below, are displayed the preterit of DIVE for the two studies for the State of Illinois. There is no isogloss one can draw for such data. The forms DOVE and DIVED for the preterit are generously distributed throughout the State.

The lack of correlation so far suggests strongly, I think, that verb morphology should not be sought for the purposes of showing dialect areas in any broad based questionnaire. The reasons why this can be predicted come from our current understanding of how people learn verb morphology. We know that children learning English verb morphology go through the following stages. First, they learn the infinitive form: I GO; He GO, Mommy. Second, curiously enough, they learn the irregular forms of frequently occurring irregular verbs: John IS nice, John ATE dinner. Third, somewhere between three and four, they start changing their already correct irregular verbs to forms like: EATED, SLEEPED. Fourth--over a period of some years, they correct their EATED and SLEEPED forms back again to standard English ATE and SLEPT (McNeill 1970:84-5).

If Chomsky has done nothing else, he has forced us to recognize the degree to which an individual child is forced to devise, to construct, his

ANALYSIS OF DARE VERSUS LANCS
BY TYPE II INFORMANT

	PRETERIT			PAST PARTICIPLE		PRET=PT PAR	
B. TYPE II							
1. <u>dive</u>	dived	dove	dive				
	# (%)	# (%)	# (%)				
a. DARE	15 (48)	16 (52)					
b. LANCS	28 (67)	14 (33)					
2. <u>drink</u>	drank	drunk		drank	drunk	drank	drunk
	# (%)	# (%)		# (%)	# (%)	#	# (%)
a. DARE	35 (97)	1 (3)		18 (47)	20 (53)	18	0 (50)
b. LANCS	44 (98)	1 (2)		23 (55)	19 (45)	23	1 (57)
3. <u>run</u>	ran	run					
	# (%)	# (%)					
a. DARE	27 (82)	6 (18)					
b. LANCS	28 (57)	21 (43)					
4. <u>come</u>	came	come					
	# (%)	# (%)					
a. DARE	33 (92)	3 (8)					
b. LANCS	35 (64)	20 (36)					
5. <u>lie</u>	lay	laid	lied				
	# (%)	# (%)	# (%)				
a. DARE	16 (44)	18 (50)	2 (6)				
b. LANCS	13 (36)	21 (58)	2 (6)				

AVERAGES (4 verbs; <u>dive</u> excluded)[6]

TYPE II

	PRETERIT		PAST PARTICIPLE		PRET=PT PAR
	Taught	Taught Against	Taught	Taught Against	
a. DARE	78.75	21.25	53	57	50
b. LANCS	63.75	36.25	45	55	57

Figure 3 Numbers and Percentages of Verb Forms for TYPE II Informants

ANALYSIS OF DARE VERSUS LANCS
BY TYPE III INFORMANT

	PRETERIT			PAST PARTICIPLE		PRET=PT PAR		

C. TYPE III
1. <u>dive</u>

	dived		dove		dive				
	# (%)		# (%)		# (%)				
a. DARE	1 (17)		5 (83)						
b. LANCS	8 (50)		8 (50)						

2. <u>drink</u>

	drank	drunk	drank	drunk	drank		drunk
	# (%)	# (%)	# (%)	# (%)	#	#	(%)
a. DARE	5 (100)	0 (0)	1 (20)	4 (80)	1	0	(20)
b. LANCS	15 (100)	0 (0)	3 (19)	13 (81)	2	0	(13)

3. <u>run</u>

	ran	run
	# (%)	# (%)
a. DARE	5 (71)	2 (29)
b. LANCS	17 (100)	0 (0)

4. <u>come</u>

	came	come
	# (%)	# (%)
a. DARE	6 (100)	0 (0)
b. LANCS	16 (100)	0 (0)

5. <u>lie</u>

	lay	laid	lied
	# (%)	# (%)	# (%)
a. DARE	2 (67)	1 (33)	
b. LANCS	7 (54)	6 (46)	

AVERAGES (4 verbs; <u>dive</u> excluded)[7]
TYPE III

	PRETERIT		PAST PARTICIPLE		PRET=PT PAR
	Taught	Taught Against	Taught	Taught Against	
a. DARE	84.5	15.5	80	20	20
b. LANCS	88.55	11.5	81	19	19

Figure 4 Numbers and Percentages of Verb Forms for TYPE III Informants

language out of the language data to which he is exposed (Chomsky 1957, 1965). That explains why the child "unlearns" so many "correct" verb morphology forms. As the child is exposed to more and more regular verbs, verbs that have the same morpheme for both the preterit and the past participle ("kick<u>ED</u>" and "stabb<u>ED</u>", for example), the child trusts his own abilities to generalize over the data he is receiving from the adult speakers around him. That is why, of course, the child often comes up with forms that are uniquely "child" forms, that is, forms that <u>no</u> adult ever uses, no matter what his social background (the double preterit <u>WENTED</u>, for example).

Methods in Dialectology

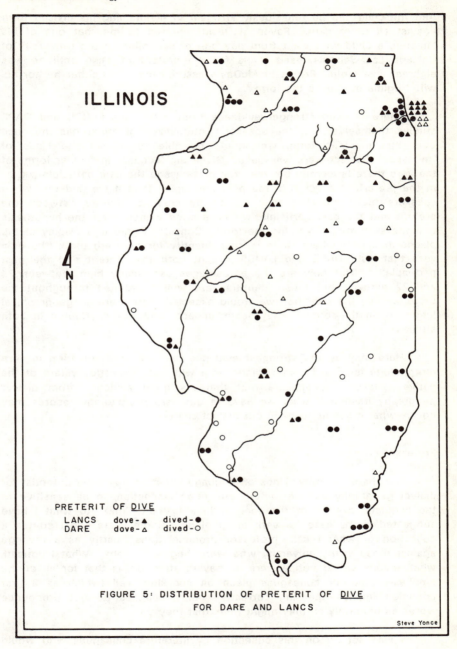

FIGURE 5: DISTRIBUTION OF PRETERIT OF DIVE FOR DARE AND LANCS

And the child can be tenaciously arrogant in maintaining his divised form against all other data. Raven McDavid reported to me that one of his children, a child who went from day one of schooling to the University of Chicago Lab Schools, used BRANG for the preterit of BRING until he was eighteen years old. Professor McDavid assured me that neither he nor his wife Virginia ever used the form.[9].

There is even stronger evidence from within the LANCS and DARE studies themselves. If the speaker's internalized grammar has influence over the linguistic form, we should be able to predict the kinds of "mistakes" that speakers will make. Given the fact that in regular forms of the verb there is identity between the preterit and the past participle (KICKED in the preterit and KICKED in the past participle), then if we find that when speakers make mistakes they do so by creating identity between the preterit and the past participle, we have good evidence for the hypothesis that the system is governing the form. Consider Figure 6, a display of the places in Illinois where there is such identity for the verb DRINK (the only verb that both DARE and LANCS sought both the preterit and the past participle):[10] Not only are the percentages particularly high (between 74 and 77 percent) but these identities are well distributed throughout the State, exactly the condition we would expect if there were no geographical influence on the forms. They seem, in fact, randomly distributed in both studies.

Here may be the strongest evidence that the linguistic form in verb morphology is in a dynamic relationship with the linguistic system of the native speaker. It appears that there is good evidence from dialect geography itself that what we have in our verb morphology records may not be what it seems to be in our dialect charts.

Professor Errors

But there are other kinds of language variation that have potential for dialect geography but which turn out, upon inspection, to be sensitive to the linguistic system of the speaker in a fashion similar to what I have suggested is the case for verb morphology. Some years ago I started a collection of what I call "professor pronunciations," partly as a revenge against those in my university who were language snobs. What I noticed, what anyone would notice were he paying attention, is that for all of the emphasis that our colleagues place on speaking well (which as a first condition implies speaking correctly), our colleagues do not pronounce words as uniformly as they might think that they do.

I was set off on this collection by literature colleagues who would stop me in the halls to tell me of the latest student howler. Whether it was

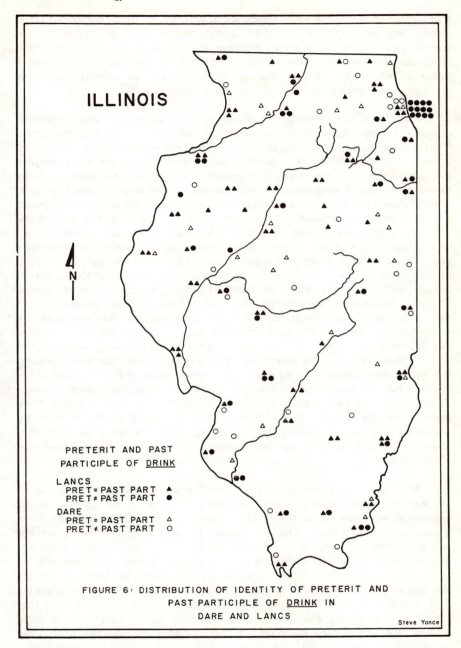

FIGURE 6: DISTRIBUTION OF IDENTITY OF PRETERIT AND PAST PARTICIPLE OF DRINK IN DARE AND LANCS

a professor showing me an exam paper in which a student remarked that it was a "Dog eat dog world" spelled "Doggy dog world"[11] or reporting on a student use of the word SUAVE pronounced [swev], I was struck by how mean-spirited my colleagues were. I started my own collection when I heard a colleague[12] remark that so-and-so "can not change his mind through sheer CAPRICE" pronouncing the last word ['kæprɪs].

And from this collection I began to think about my own linguistic history and how I have changed some of my pronunciations over the years. It takes an embarrassing moment (or a potentially embarrassing moment as in the case that follows) in order for you to remember them, but I imagine that each of you--if put to the task--could come up with something similar to my own. Some time before I was nineteen, I ran into the word EPITOME. From the context, from the sentence in which I heard it, I must have figured out what the word meant. I am sure, since the word is not particularly difficult to spell, that I even used it in the papers and essay examinations I wrote, and I used it correctly--if not impressively; EPITOME (for a nineteen-year-old, at least) is a hotshot word. I don't know if I ever said it out loud or not; I may have. One day I was sitting in a modern drama class in college, and one of my fellow students was giving an oral report on Synge. To prove some point or another, she read a passage from some critic. I don't remember what the point was, but I do remember that she used the word EPITOME and that she pronounced it with stress on the first syllable, not [ɛpɪtəmi] but [ɛpɪˌtom]. A very smart, beautiful young woman with whom I was madly in love and on whom I was (alas, unsuccessfully) putting the move was sitting next to me. She leaned over and whispered softly into my ear, "Imagine. She doesn't even now how to pronounce EPITOME." Terror froze my heart, for [' pɪˌtom] was exactly the way I would have pronounced the word. But I leaned over to Joy (Joy Dixon was my enchantress' name) and whispered, "Amazing. And she probably thinks that she's well educated." As you can imagine, I've never mispronounced the word since.

Now curious as this is, what is really interesting is not that a fellow student mispronounced a word. When you think of all of the sound sequences we have stored in our little brains, it is no wonder that we mess a word up now and then. I have a brother, for example, who simply can not say the word SPECIFIC. It comes out for him, for some reason I do not understand, invariably [p 'sɪfɪk]. He hears it as wrong when it comes out; he tries to correct it, but unless someone says the word for him, he can not say [spə'sɪfɪk]. My brother's kind of mistake is not what I find interesting. And further, I am not interested in malipropisms, either of the "Doggy Dog World" kind or of the kind where a speaker has simply substituted a word that is close phonologically--but off semantically--for another word. For example, I am not interested in, as one of my most brilliant undergraduates once wrote, "His was a most heart RENDERING experience" (or as another student put it, "He needed to WRETCH nourishment from the earth"). These are nonce forms; they are amusing perhaps, but they are not systematic, and therefore they are not linguistically significant. What is interesting--what should interest us as linguists--is that I wanted to pronounce the word EPITOME with the same stress and vowel qualities as did my hapless fellow student. And it was this replication of error that made me begin to take these mistakes seriously.

But before I give my interpretation of what all of this means--both for child language acquisition and for dialect research--let me share a small part of my "professor pronunciations" list. I will give my explanation, as best as I can, of where the mistakes come from as we go along. I will try, that is, to articulate the principle that makes this an analysis of linguistic competence rather than an analysis of linguistic performance.

One of my colleagues (MA, PhD Columbia, if that matters) was going off to read a paper and was reading his paper aloud to himself. In that it was one of the first papers he had ever read, he checked the pronunciation of every word "bigger"[13] than a preposition. In the course of this process, he looked up CHAOS to find--to his absolute amazement--that the word is pronounced ['ke ,as] rather than, as he would have said it, ['če ,as]. He was so certain of his [mis]pronunciation, in fact, that he came to my office to enlist my aid in a challenge of the dictionary. He swore that he had never heard anyone pronounce the word with a [k] in the place of his [č].[14]

An art professor--again, someone who might be expected to know better--pronounces[15] the word CHARISMA [čar'Izm]. In both cases, I suspect the explanation is straightforward. These people are using their reading attack skills to predict that the orthographic <ch> value is the equivalent of the early spelling convention <ch> in CHURCH, CHOOSE or CHIMNEY for the alveolar-palatal affricate [č] rather than the late-borrowed [k] from Greek.

As you can imagine, many other of the "mispronunciations" were of this ilk, readers assuming that the orthography was English orthography rather than an orthography representing a foreign pronunciation, a situation arising when English speakers borrow a foreign pronunciation complete with a foreign spelling. And so I got a professor who says [poygnənt] for POIGNANT, one who says [ri'ku] for RECOUP as in "recoup their losses," one who says the word CONCUPICENT [kan'kʌpəsənt] instead of [kan'kyupəsənt], one who says the word BAS-RELIEF [,bæsri'lif] instead of [,bari'lif] and the like.

In another kind of "mistake," a history professor pronounces the word PERSEPHONE [pər'sɛfən,i] ['pʌrsə,fon]. Like my own EPITOME ['ɛpItom], I suspect this is also a reading pronunciation. Here the speaker is attacking from the end of the word to the front and assigning a silent value to the final <e> (as in HOME and ROME). Such an attack has the effect of tensing the preceding vowel. But combined with this end-to-beginning attack is an underlying assumption that the word is stressed on the first syllable. Under these assumptions, ['pʌrsɪˌfon] and ['ɛpɪˌtom] are perfectly reasonable pronunciations.

The assumption that the word was (or was not) stressed on the first syllable was a common one among the mistakes. For example, I found among my collection:

1. RESPITE pronounced [rə'spayt] instead of ['rɛspɪt],
2. CHAMELEON pronounced ['šæmələn] instead of [kə'milyən],
3. COMPROMISE pronounced [kam'pramɪs] instead of ['kamprəˌmayz],
4. NONCHALANT pronounced [nan'čælənt] instead of [nanšə'lant],
5. DEBRIS pronounced ['dɛbrɪs] instead of [də'bri],
6. BLASE pronounced [blez] instead of [bla'ze],
7. REVERE pronounced ['revər] instead of [rə'vir],
8. LABORIOUS pronounced ['lebərəs] instead of [lə'boriəs].[16]

These are, in my opinion, even more interesting than the reading pronunciations, if a little less straight-forward to explain. As is well known, the words of English, a Germanic language, are mainly stressed on the first syllable (assuming that the first syllable is not a prefix). But we also have thousands of words that are not stressed on the first syllable, and most of them--although not all, of course--are stressed on some non-initial syllable, the syllable chosen dependent on all kinds of factors (the language from which the word was borrowed, the century during which the word was borrowed, the degree to which the word has been assimilated into the language). I could call this the non-Germanic stress rule, although it serves truth well enough to call it the Romance stress rule, since Romance words make up the bulk of the lexical stock that exhibit non-initial word stress.

In order to find out which of the two rules is the more powerful, one only has to note the direction in which the stress tends to move. The evidence, fortunately, is in. It is well documented that words that historically had stress on the non-initial syllable are changing to stress the first syllable. We have POLICE, therefore, not stressed on the final syllable but on the first, not [pə'lis] but ['poˌlis]. While this pronunciation for POLICE is more commonly reported in the southern United States, the word INSURANCE pronounced ['ɪnšurəns] instead of [ɪn'šurəns] is common through the US. Even in my own university, in the past sixteen years the word INCOMPLETE[17] has gone from being pronounced universally as [ɪnkəm'plit] to being pronounced almost universally as ['ɪnkəmˌplit] by student and faculty alike.

We have now an explanation, or a start of an explanation, for why all of these professors mispronounced the stress on the words I collected. Words in English are classifiable--at least on the basis of sound/spelling correspondence and stress rules--as either native or non-native. When coming to terms with a new word, it appears that speakers first must determine if the word is native or non-native in nature. If you analyze, for example, EPITOME as Romance, you get something close to the proper pronunciation. If, however, you decide it is Germanic, then you pronounce it as I did as a teenager, [ˈɛpɪtom]. And so up and down the list. For every mis-stressing of the word, we can propose that the word has been incorrectly assigned to a lexical class. A language situation like this is very rare, of course, for most borrowed words conform to the native phonological rules and constraints. But the history of the English lexicon is--while not unique--very unusual. During the Norman domination of England (and English), native speakers of English borrowed a very large number of words in a short period of time. In fact, we borrowed so many--and they had such high social status--that we also borrowed the stress system associated with those words. Unfortunately, that stress system was in direct conflict with the native stress system. And that is why it can be claimed that we are still fighting the Battle of 1066, The Battle of Hasting. And while the military battle with the Norman French may have ended in 1066, the linguistic battle continues on. Each of our children is doomed to fight that battle whenever he or she tries to come to terms with the English lexicon. The only consolation is that the Germanic stress rule is almost certain to prevail over the Romance stress rule. While we may have lost the military battle, we are almost certain to win the linguistic battle--even though that final victory may be centuries down the road.

The conclusion we can draw from all of these professor errors is that they are clear evidence that language is not transferred between speakers by word of mouth alone. Sometimes it is learned from the orthographic system first, and even when it is not, the orthographic system can favor what we have read over what we have heard. And even when we learn words by word of mouth, these professor errors reveal one more area where the linguistic system of the language user has impact on the linguistic form.

CONCLUSION

We can argue, therefore, that all of our efforts to collect language tokens must be done in full awareness that individual speakers can have forms which were not derived from what I will call for lack of a better term "contact transmission." They can come--as the verb forms from Illinois illustrate--from morphology, or they can come--as the professor pronunciations illustrate--from phonology. In both cases, there is dynamic interaction between the surface form of the language and the underlying linguistic system. While speakers are certainly not free to make up just any form, speakers do have some influence--will they or will they not--over the lexicon of their language.

I do not want to single out the verb morphology and the professor error data as the only kinds of data that are vulnerable to influence from the grammars of speakers of the language. In syntax, we can predict that "multiple negatives" are a mistake[18] to collect, since they are almost certainly a linguistic variable dependent on linguistic style. The same case probably obtains--at least for some speakers--for "double modals."[19] And, as a final example, "positive ANYMORE"[20] is so elusive that many speakers who use it have little knowledge that they do so, and--as such--would be particularly difficult and risky to collect through systematic sampling. I would like the argument behind these examples to begin a discussion of what we should ask when we design dialect questionnaires. With more perfectly designed questionnaires we will save ourselves valuable research time. But perhaps more important, if we do not attend to such matters as the relationship between linguistic form and linguistic system, we dialect geographers may risk collecting data that suggest a kind of regional variation that may not actually exist in the language.

Notes

[1]Before I begin, I want to start with a caution. I intend these remarks as no criticism of any dialect project or of any dialect study. The plight of the dialect geographer is a real one. It is hard to design questionnaires that elicit data when one does not know for certain what is out there to be found. And if one does know what is out there, looking for it again seems almost a redundancy. And, furthermore, almost every questionnaire I have seen has included questions that hindsight would reveal as in no way 'interesting.' The designer of the questionnaire should not be criticized for this, for it is always better to collect that which is not significant rather than wish one had looked for something after all of the fieldwork has been done.

[2]Because these verbs are taught directly in the public schools--and taught again and again and again, the schools help determine which verb forms are seen as standard and, consequently, which verb forms win in a competition between any two. Some may want to make something of this

in the interpretation of these data, and so I have chosen to indicate the "taught" and "taught against" forms overtly in the figure.

[3]Sadly, I did not draw such data when I had access to the field records. I think, however, that even without such data, we can speculate that if we do not get better correlations for such lexical distributions than we seem to be getting for verb forms, our methods of research are seriously to be questioned.

[4]Type III informants are the most "cultured," often informants with college educations.

[5]I have excluded _dive_ from the averages table for all verbs because the status of the preterit _dived_ versus _dove_ is unclear. Some teachers teach the one; others teach the other.

[6]See note 5.

[7]See note 5.

[8]While it is beyond the scope of this paper, these data suggest that the Illinois public schools succeed in teaching standard English verb morphology only to TYPE III speakers. If one were to filter out of those TYPE III speakers those whose parents are also TYPE III speakers (to find those whom the school and not the parents have taught the standard forms), my guess is that the public schools do even worse at teaching verb morphology than we might otherwise think.

[9]Personal communication, 1978

[10]And consider the right-most column in figures 1-4, headed Pret=PtPar, where percentages are given for the number of such identities out of the possibilities for such identities.

[11]Or even more unbelievable (if I hadn't seen the student paper with my own eyes), a student remark about HITLER'S YOUTH IN ASIA PROGRAM for HITLER'S EUTHANASIA PROGRAM.

[12]PhD Princeton, if that matters, and a man who has even gone so far as to publish part of his personal collection of these errors (Bier 1985).

[13]The child's notion of "big" words or "long" words or "hard" words is interesting. It is the nature of learned words that they are learned later in a child's life--well after the child starts to school. Because many of these words are Romance, they have more unanalyzable morphemes than their

comparable Germanic words. They are in a sense "bigger" because they are "longer"; because they are unanalyzabled, they are more "difficult". (See Hausmann ms.)

[14] He was almost certainly both correct and incorrect in his assessment; he could not have lived for 40 years as an academic and not have heard it, but the conventional pronunciation simply never registered.

[15] When I used the term pronounces, I mean to imply habitual use. For all of my collected pronunciations, the term was not registered unless the speaker used the term more than one time

[16] I have dozens more.

[17] A grade for a student who has not completed all of the work in a class by the end of the term.

[18] HE DOESN'T KNOW NOTHING.

[19] HE MIGHT COULD GO.

[20] HE SMOKES A LOT ANYMORE.

Works Cited

Atwood, E.B. (1953) *A Survey of Verb Forms in the Eastern United States.* Ann Arbor, Mich.: University of Michigan Press.

Bier, J. (1985) Faculty evaluations and higher English usage or zyrcons and piglets, *Journal of Higher Education*, Vol. 56, Sept., 564-72.

Chomsky, N. (1957) *Syntactic Structures.* The Hague: Mouton.

____ (1965) *Aspects of a Theory of Syntax.* Cambridge: MIT Press.

Fasold, R.W. and Shuy, R.W.,eds. (1975) *Analyzing Variation in Language.* Washington, D.C.: Georgetown University Press.

Hausmann, R. (1986) "Big" words in English. Unpublished Manuscript.

Kurath, H. (1939) *Handbook of the Linguistic Geography of New England.* Providence, Rhode Island: Brown University.

Labov, W. (1966) *The Social Stratification of English in New York City.* Washington, D.C.: Center for Applied Linguistics.

____ (1972) *Language in the Inner City.* Philadelphia: University of Pennsylvania Press.

McDavid, V.G. (1957) *Verb Forms of the North Central States and Upper Midwest.* Unpub. Doctoral Dissertation: University of Minnesota.

McNeill,D. (1970) *The Acquisition of Language.* New York: Harper and Row.

Stampe, D. (1969) The acquisition of phonetic representation. In R.I. Binnick et al, eds. *Papers from the Eighth Regional Meeting of the Chicago Linguistic Society*, 443-54.

____ (1972) *How I Spent My Summer Vacation.* Unpub. Doctoral Dissertation: University of Chicago.

Wrede, F. et al. (1926) *Deutscher Sprachatlas.* Marburg.

Acoustic Comparative Study of Contradictory /a:/ and /æ/ between Maine Dialect and General American

TSUNEKO IKEMIYA
Tezukayama University in Nara City, Japan

1.0 INTRODUCTION

This comparative study is the test and the analysis of /a:/ and /æ/ in two word groups between Maine dialect and General American and tries to show by sound spectrographic data their contradictory phenomenon. The two word groups are the following:

	Maine Dialect	General American
Group 1	ask [ɑ:sk] aunt [ɑ:nt] half [hɑ:f] bath [bɑ:θ] answer [ɑ:nsə]	[æsk] [ænt] [hæf] [bæθ] [ænsɚ]
Group 2	garden [gædn] guard [gæd] park [pæk] car [kæ] farm [fæm]	[gɑɚdn] [gɑɚd] [pɑɚk] [kɑɚ] [fɑɚm]

Note: In Maine dialect [ɑ:] in Group 1 might be written as [a] because it is rather fronted as compared with RP [ɑ:], while [æ] in Group 2 might be written as [aᴱ] since it is not completely fronted.

(For reference the dialect map of the U.S. and maps of New England and Maine are shown on following pages).

1.1 MOTIVATION

This study is based upon the author's auditory impressions during her Master's study in linguistics at Kansas State University from 1961 - 1963 under the guidance of Dr. Ernest Haden and Dr. Leo Engler (4), and then during the five-month research work done at the University of Maine at Orono 1983 with the suggestions and help in collecting data of Prof. Jacob Bennett (5). The author's impression about the above mentioned two group words in both areas tempted her to do the acoustic study as to whether or not this contradictory phenomena can be confirmed by sound spectrography.

2.0 PRELIMINARY INFORMATION

The recorded data were taken both in General American and Maine areas, and in the case of Maine, especially around Hancock County, Maine with a little data of Washington county. Sound spectro-graphic work was done in Japan since the instrument was available in Tezukayama University, Nara City. The informants of both Maine and General American were at least second generation natives in both dialectal areas with the age range of 50-85.

2.1 METHOD

Five informants were selected for each and male and female group from Maine native and General American speakers, totalling 20 informants, and the voice was recorded for the words by the Sony TCM-111 Cassette Corder (6) with FCM-16 electric condenser microphone attached for clear recording. As for the sound spectrographic data, the Japanese-made Lyon Spectrograph was used.

The recorded data was put into the spectograph, the frequencies of cycle per second (Hz) of formant 1 and 2 of each vowel of the words of each informant were measured, and average Hz's of difference of formant 1 and 2 were calculated. Finally, the average Hz figures were transcribed into histograms in order to compare the contradictory nature of the vowels in Maine dialect and General American.

This measurement is based upon the application of the principle that the difference between formant 1 and 2 becomes smaller in the case of back low vowel /ɑː/, and becomes larger in /æ/ (Ladefoged, 1975: 176-7; Potter, 1966: 46).

2.4 OBSERVATION AND DISCUSSION

1. The word "ask" does not conform to the rest of the data.

2. In group 1 in General American /æ/ before the nasal /n/ has larger length or difference between formant 1 and 2, showing the General Americal characteristic more clearly than the rest of the group 1 words.

3. Group 2, in contrast to group 1, Maine data shows the low

308   *Methods in Dialectology*

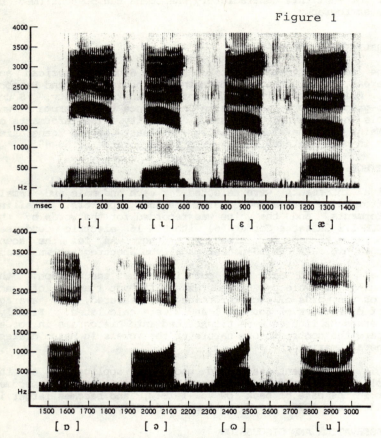

Figure 8.6 *A spectrogram of the words "heed, hid, head, had, hod, hawed, hood, who'd" as spoken in a British accent.*

by Peter Ladefoged

Figure 2

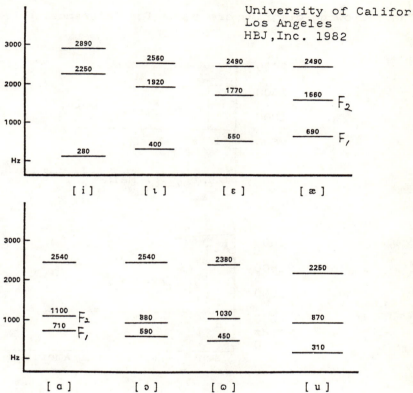

Figure 8.5 *The frequencies of the first three formants in eight American English vowels.*

Figure 3

The following diagrams are shown for reference:

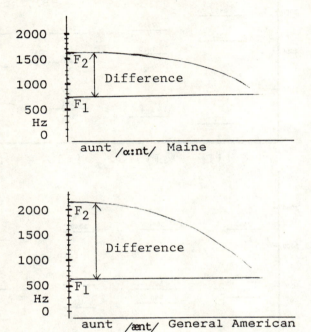

Total and average figures of Hz of each informant, and histograms are shown in the following figures.

Figure 4 General American

		ask		aunt		half		bath		answer	
MAN		Hz	(mm)	Hz	(mm)	Hz	(mm)	Hz	(mm)	Hz	(mm)
P. Lapointe	F2	1804.8		2105.6		1804.8		1729.6		2105.6	
	F1	676.8		526.4		752.0		676.8		601.6	
	F2-F1	1128.0	15.0	1579.2	21.0	1052.8	14.0	1052.8	14.0	1504.0	20.0
D. Carson	F2	1579.2		1955.2		1654.4		1391.2		1761.2	
	F1	752.0		451.2		601.6		601.6		564.0	
	F2-F1	827.2	11.0	1504.0	20.0	1052.8	14.0	789.6	10.5	1197.2	16.0
R. Carson	F2	1763.4		1955.2		1541.6		1466.4		1955.2	
	F1	676.8		564.0		714.4		714.4		601.6	
	F2-F1	1086.6	14.4	1391.2	18.5	827.2	11.0	752.0	10.0	1353.6	18.0
M.Carson	F2	1767.2		2256.0		1692.0		1579.2		1955.2	
	F1	789.6		564.0		827.2		670.8		827.2	
	F2-F1	977.6	13.0	1692.0	22.5	864.8	11.5	908.4	12.1	1128.0	15.0
C. Rogers	F2	1837.7		1504.0		1504.0		1466.4		1616.8	
	F1	601.6		601.6		601.6		714.4		564.0	
	F2-F1	1236.1	16.4	902.4	12.0	902.4	12.0	752.0	10.0	1052.8	14.0
WOMAN											
J. H. Lapointe	F2	1804.8		2180.8		1729.6		2180.8		2256.0	
	F1	902.4		601.6		977.6		977.6		601.6	
	F2-F1	902.4	12.0	1579.2	21.0	752.0	10.0	1203.2	16.0	1654.4	22.0
H. J. Carson	F2	2105.6		2444.0		2180.8		2030.4		2481.6	
	F1	1052.8		827.2		977.6		864.8		752.0	
	F2-F1	1052.8	14.0	1616.8	21.5	1203.2	16.0	1165.6	15.5	1729.6	23.0
J. Hopkins	F2	1880.0		2444.0		1767.2		1880.0		2331.2	
	F1	827.2		639.2		827.2		902.4		676.8	
	F2-F1	1052.8	14.0	1804.8	24.0	940.0	12.5	977.6	13.0	1654.4	22.0
J. Carson	F2	1992.8		2895.2		1729.6		1804.8		2744.8	
	F1	827.2		601.6		940.0		977.6		676.8	
	F2-F1	1165.6	15.5	2293.6	30.5	789.6	10.5	827.2	11.0	2068.0	27.5
L. Johnson	F2	2030.4		2744.8		2250.6		1616.8		2444.0	
	F1	940.0		676.8		902.4		864.8		752.0	
	F2-F1	1090.4	14.5	2068.0	27.5	1348.2	18.0	752.0	10.0	1692.0	22.5

Figure 5 General American

		garden		guard		park		car		farm	
MAN		Hz	(mm)	Hz	(mm)	Hz	(mm)	Hz	(mm)	Hz	(mm)
P. Lapointe	F2	1128.0		977.6		977.6		977.6		827.2	
	F1	601.6		676.8		601.6		676.8		676.8	
	F2-F1	526.4	7.0	300.8	4.0	376.0	5.0	300.8	4.0	150.4	2.0
D. Carson	F2	1090.4		977.6		1052.8		1015.2		902.4	
	F1	564.0		526.4		601.6		601.6		526.4	
	F2-F1	526.4	7.0	451.2	6.0	451.2	6.0	413.6	5.5	376.0	5.0
R. Carson	F2	1090.4		1015.2		977.6		940.0		940.0	
	F1	676.8		601.6		601.6		601.6		601.6	
	F2-F1	413.6	5.5	413.6	5.5	376.0	5.0	338.4	4.5	338.4	4.5
M. Carson	F2	1165.6		1128.0		1090.4		1128.0		977.6	
	F1	639.2		639.2		676.8		714.4		601.6	
	F2-F1	526.4	7.0	488.8	6.5	413.6	5.5	413.6	5.5	376.0	5.0
C. Rogers	F2	1353.6		1278.4		1240.8		1165.6		1052.8	
	F1	676.8		714.4		676.8		676.8		752.0	
	F2-F1	676.8	9.0	564.0	7.5	564.0	7.5	488.8	6.5	300.8	4.0
WOMAN											
J. H. Lapointe	F2	1353.6		1278.4		1278.4		1278.4		1203.2	
	F1	827.2		827.2		752.0		827.2		752.0	
	F2-F1	526.4	7.0	451.2	6.0	526.4	7.0	451.2	6.0	451.2	6.0
M. J. Carson	F2	1391.2		1353.6		1353.6		1165.6		1052.8	
	F1	752.0		676.8		676.8		639.2		676.8	
	F2-F1	639.2	8.5	676.8	9.0	676.8	9.0	526.4	7.0	376.0	5.0
J. Hopkins	F2	1278.4		1240.8		1165.6		1203.2		1015.2	
	F1	676.8		752.0		752.0		827.2		789.6	
	F2-F1	601.6	8.0	488.8	6.5	413.6	5.5	376.0	5.0	225.6	3.0
J. Carson	F2	1203.2		1240.8		1165.6		1090.4		1052.8	
	F1	752.0		789.6		789.6		864.8		714.4	
	F2-F1	451.2	6.0	451.2	6.0	376.0	5.0	225.6	3.0	338.4	4.5
L. Johnson	F2	1278.4		1165.6		1090.4		1015.2		977.6	
	F1	752.0		752.0		789.6		789.6		864.8	
	F2-F1	526.4	7.0	413.6	5.5	300.8	4.0	225.6	3.0	112.8	1.5

Methods in Dialectology 313

Figure 6 Maine American

		ask		aunt		half		bath		answer	
		Hz	(mm)	Hz	(mm)	Hz	(mm)	Hz	(mm)	Hz	(mm)
MAN											
H. Ingalls	F2	1692.0		1428.8		1466.4		1466.4		1955.2	
	F1	601.6		639.2		864.8		752.0		639.2	
	F2-F1	1090.4	14.5	789.6	10.5	601.6	8.0	714.4	9.5	1316.0	17.5
R. Randall	F2	1729.6		1504.0		1579.2		1428.8		1880.0	
	F1	676.8		864.8		676.8		676.8		526.4	
	F2-F1	1052.8	14.0	639.2	8.5	902.4	12.0	752.0	10.0	1353.6	18.0
D. A. Brown	F2	1692.0		1504.0		1353.6		789.6		1804.8	
	F1	601.6		789.6		752.0		639.2		601.6	
	F2-F1	1090.4	14.5	714.4	9.5	601.6	8.0	150.4	2.0	1203.2	16.0
M. Jordan	F2	1654.4		1804.8		1504.0		1391.2		1804.8	
	F1	714.4		752.0		902.4		752.0		714.4	
	F2-F1	940.0	12.5	1052.8	14.0	601.6	8.0	639.2	8.5	1090.4	14.5
H. Jordan	F2	1603.1		1616.8		1616.8		1541.6		1717.6	
	F1	714.4		902.4		902.4		902.4		752.0	
	F2-F1	888.7	11.8	714.4	9.5	714.4	9.5	639.2	8.5	965.6	12.84
WOMAN											
H. Bowden	F2	1992.8		1504.0		1353.6		1917.6		2218.4	
	F1	789.6		752.0		864.8		714.4		676.8	
	F2-F1	1203.2	16.0	752.0	10.0	488.8	6.5	1203.2	16.0	1541.6	20.5
D. Smith	F2	2068.0		1616.8		1654.4		1504.0		1917.6	
	F1	827.2		864.8		902.4		752.0		752.0	
	F2-F1	1240.8	16.5	752.0	10.0	752.0	10.0	752.0	10.0	1165.6	15.5
J. Ingalls	F2	1992.8		1992.8		1917.6		1804.8		2556.8	
	F1	864.8		977.6		940.0		714.4		714.4	
	F2-F1	1128.0	15.0	1015.2	13.5	977.6	13.0	1090.4	14.5	1842.4	24.5
P. Jordan	F2	1616.8		1616.8		1616.8		1541.6		2368.8	
	F1	902.4		526.4		902.4		789.6		526.4	
	F2-F1	714.4	9.5	1090.4	14.5	714.4	9.5	752.0	10.0	1842.4	24.5
A. Wilbur	F2	1616.8		1616.8		1504.0		1428.8		1917.6	
	F1	789.6		752.0		752.0		676.0		714.4	
	F2-F1	827.2	11.0	864.8	11.5	752.0	10.0	752.0	10.0	1203.2	16.0

Figure 7 American

		garden		guard		park		car		farm	
MAN		Hz	(mm)	Hz	(mm)	Hz	(mm)	Hz	(mm)	Hz	(mm)
H. Ingalls	F2	1504.0		1466.4		1504.0		1504.0		1353.6	
	F1	714.4		714.4		676.8		639.2		601.6	
	F2-F1	789.6	10.5	752.0	10.0	827.2	11.0	864.8	11.5	752.0	10.0
R. Randall	F2	1541.6		1466.4		1391.2		1504.0		1278.4	
	F1	639.2		564.0		752.0		676.8		601.6	
	F2-F1	902.4	12.0	902.4	12.0	639.2	8.5	827.2	11.0	676.8	9.0
D. A. Brown	F2	1466.4		1541.6		1428.8		1504.0		1391.2	
	F1	676.8		676.8		752.0		714.4		752.0	
	F2-F1	789.6	10.5	864.8	11.5	676.8	9.0	789.6	10.5	639.2	8.5
M. Jordan	F2	1654.4		1504.0		1466.4		1504.0		1391.2	
	F1	676.8		714.4		827.2		827.2		714.4	
	F2-F1	977.6	13.0	789.6	10.5	639.2	8.5	676.8	9.0	676.8	9.0
H. Jordan	F2	1654.4		1767.2		1616.8		1729.6		1541.6	
	F1	752.0		827.2		827.2		752.0		940.0	
	F2-F1	902.4	12.0	940.0	12.5	789.6	10.5	977.6	13.0	601.6	8.0
WOMAN											
M. Bowden	F2	1729.6		1541.6		1428.8		1428.8		1428.8	
	F1	864.8		789.6		864.8		827.2		789.6	
	F2-F1	864.8	11.5	752.0	10.0	564.0	7.5	601.6	8.0	639.2	8.5
D. Smith	F2	1692.0		1804.8		1541.6		1729.6		1541.6	
	F1	827.2		827.2		827.2		864.8		864.8	
	F2-F1	864.8	11.5	977.6	13.0	714.4	9.5	864.8	4.5	676.8	9.0
J. Ingalls	F2	1729.6		1880.0		1804.8		1880.0		1804.8	
	F1	827.2		827.2		864.8		864.8		902.4	
	F2-F1	902.4	12.0	1052.8	14.0	940.0	12.5	1015.2	13.5	902.4	12.0
P. Jordan	F2	1767.2		1729.6		1729.6		1729.6		1616.8	
	F1	752.0		789.6		601.6		902.4		488.8	
	F2-F1	1015.2	13.5	940.0	12.5	940.0	15.0	827.2	11.0	1128.0	15.0
A. Wilbur	F2	1729.6		1729.6		1428.8		1579.2		1504.0	
	F1	714.4		789.6		827.2		789.6		714.4	
	F2-F1	1015.2	13.5	940.0	12.5	601.6	8.0	789.6	10.5	789.6	10.5

Figure 8 General American

		ask		aunt		half		bath		answer	
		Hz	(mm)	Hz	(mm)	Hz	(mm)	Hz	(mm)	Hz	(mm)
Total Amount (10)	F2	18565.9		22484.8		17854.6		17145.6		21651.6	
	F1	8046.4		6053.6		8121.6		7965.2		6617.6	
Average	F2	1856.59		2248.48		1785.46		1714.56		2165.16	
	F1	804.64		605.36		812.16		796.52		661.76	
Δ difference F2-F1		1051.95	14.0	1643.12	21.85	973.8	12.94	918.04	12.21	1503.4	20.1
Men's Total (5)	F2	8752.3		9776.0		8196.8		7632.8		9394.0	
	F1	3496.8		2707.2		3496.8		3378.0		3158.4	
Average	F2	1750.46		1955.2		1639.36		1526.56		1870.8	
	F1	699.36		541.44		699.36		675.6		631.68	
F2-F1		1051.1	14.0	1413.76	10.0	940.0	12.5	850.96	11.32	1247.12	16.58
Women's Total (5)	F2	9813.6		12708.8		9657.8		9512.8		12257.6	
	F1	4549.6		3346.4		4624.8		4587.2		3459.2	
Average	F2	1962.72		2541.76		2931.56		1902.56		2451.52	
	F1	909.92		669.20		924.96		917.44		691.84	
difference F2-F1		1052.8	14.0	1872.48	24.9	1006.6	13.39	985.12	13.1	1759.68	23.4

Figure 9 General American

		garden		guard		park		car		farm	
		Hz	(mm)	Hz	(mm)	Hz	(mm)	Hz	(mm)	Hz	(mm)
Total Amount	F2	12332.8		11656.0		11317.6		10979.2		10001.6	
(10)	F1	6918.4		6956.0		6918.4		7219.2		6956.0	
Average	F2	1233.28		1165.6		1131.76		1097.92		1000.16	
	F1	691.84		695.6		691.84		721.92		695.6	
Δ difference	F2-F1	541.44	7.2	470.0	6.25	439.92	5.85	376.0	5.0	304.56	4.05
Men's Total	F2	5828.8		5376.8		5339.2		5226.4		4700.0	
(5)	F1	3158.4		3158.4		3158.4		3271.2		3158.4	
Average	F2	1165.6		1075.36		1067.84		1045.28		940.0	
	F1	631.68		631.68		631.60		654.24		631.68	
	F2-F1	533.92	7.1	443.68	5.9	436.16	5.8	391.04	5.2	380.32	4.1
Women's Total	F2	6504.8		5978.4		5978.4		5752.8		5301.6	
(5)	F1	3760.0		3760.0		3760.0		3948.0		3797.6	
Average	F2	1300.96		1195.68		1195.68		1150.56		1060.32	
	F1	752.0		752.0		752.0		769.6		759.52	
difference	F2-F1	548.96	7.3	443.68	5.9	443.68	5.9	360.96	4.8	300.8	4.0

Methods in Dialectology 317

Figure 10 Maine American

		ask		aunt		half		bath		answer	
		Hz	(mm)	Hz	(mm)	Hz	(mm)	Hz	(mm)	Hz	(mm)
Total Amount (10)	F2	17658.3		16205.6		15566.4		14814.4		20141.6	
	F1	7482.4		7820.8		8460.0		7369.6		6617.6	
Average	F2	1765.83		1620.56		1556.64		1481.44		2014.16	
	F1	748.24		782.08		846.0		736.96		661.76	
Δ difference	F2-F1	1017.59	13.5	838.48	11.15	710.64	9.45	744.48	9.9	1352.4	17.98
Men's Total (5)	F2	8371.1		7858.4		7520.0		6617.6		9162.4	
	F1	3308.8		3948.0		4098.4		3722.4		3233.6	
Average	F2	1674.22		1571.68		1504.0		1323.52		1832.48	
	F1	661.76		789.6		819.68		744.48		646.72	
difference	F2-F1	1012.46	13.5	782.08	10.4	684.32	9.1	579.04	7.7	1185.76	15.77
Women's Total (5)	F2	9287.2		8347.2		8046.4		8196.8		10979.2	
	F1	4173.6		3872.8		4361.6		3647.2		3384.0	
Average	F2	1857.44		1669.44		1609.28		1639.36		2195.84	
	F1	834.72		774.56		872.32		729.44		676.8	
difference	F2-F1	1022.72	13.6	894.88	11.9	736.96	9.8	909.92	12.1	1519.04	20.2

Figure 11 Maine American

		garden		guard		park		car		farm	
		Hz	(mm)	Hz	(mm)	Hz	(mm)	Hz	(mm)	Hz	(mm)
Total Amount	F2	16468.8		16431.2		15340.8		16092.8		14852.0	
(10)	F1	7444.8		7520.0		7820.8		7858.4		7369.6	
Average	F2	1646.88		1643.12		1534.08		1609.28		1485.2	
	F1	744.48		752.0		782.08		785.84		736.96	
Δ difference	F2-F1	902.4	12.0	891.12	11.85	752.0	10.0	823.44	10.95	748.24	9.95
Men's Total	F2	7820.8		7745.6		7407.2		7745.6		6956.0	
(5)	F1	3459.2		3496.8		3835.2		3609.6		3609.6	
Average	F2	1564.16		1549.12		1481.44		1549.12		1391.2	
	F1	691.84		699.36		767.04		721.92		721.92	
	F2-F1	872.32	11.6	849.76	11.3	714.4	9.5	827.2	11.0	669.28	8.9
Women's Total	F2	8648.0		8685.6		7933.6		8347.2		7896.0	
(5)	F1	3985.6		4023.2		3985.6		4248.8		3760.0	
Average	F2	1729.6		1737.12		1586.72		1669.44		1579.2	
	F1	797.12		804.64		797.12		849.76		752.0	
difference	F2-F1	932.48	12.4	932.48	12.4	789.62	10.5	819.68	10.9	827.2	11.0

Methods in Dialectology

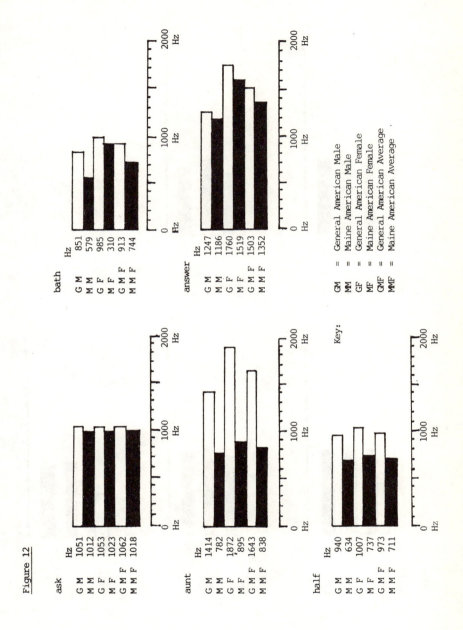

Figure 12

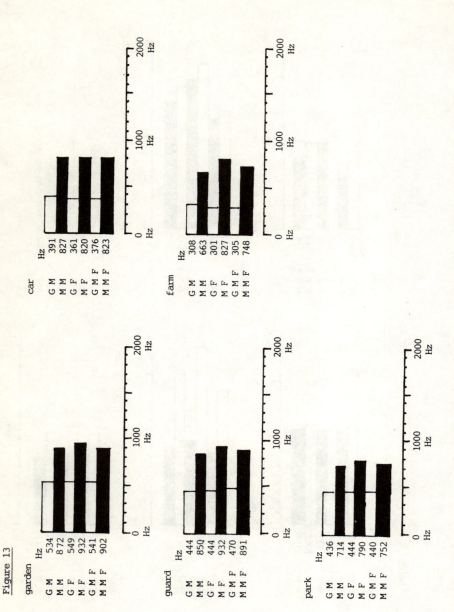

Figure 13

fronted tendency of /æ/.

4. In group 1, in General Americn, the female data shows the characteristic of /æ/ more than the male ones.

2.5 CONCLUSION AND THE CUE FOR FURTHER STUDIES

Acoustic data as a whole, shows the interesting phenomena of contradiction between Maine dialect and General American.

The stabilization of /ɑ:/ from /æ/ in "ask", "half", "answer" and "bath" in the 17th century, is mentioned by McDavid, (7) Samuel, Kenyon (8) and by others. However, the retention of /æ/ in "garden", "guard", "park" and "car" is seldom discussed in the United States except being taken up by comedians such as in Bert and I (9).

Though some work has been done from the point of view of articulatory phonetics by Margaret Thurston (10), Tsuneko Ikemiya (11) and by Professor Jacob Bennett (12), future studies are needed in connection with origin of colonial English, some of which Professor Jacob Bennett will refer to in the session on the 5th of August.

NOTES

1. McDavid, Raven I., "The Dialects of American English", by Francis, W. Nelson (N.Y.: Ronald Press Co., 1954), p. 496.

2. Ikemiya, Tsuneko. "Language in New England – vocabulary around Ellsworth, Maine. Tezukayama Univ. Reviews. No. 20 (1978) p. 174.

3. Ibid. p. 174.

4. Haden, Ernest and Leo Engler. "Status of Utterance, "Acta Linguistica IX, No. 1 (1965) 25-36.

5. Bennet, Jacob. "Maine's Dialect – Signposts to History" Univ of Maine Alumni Journal (1977) p. 14.

6. As for the instruments, the Sony TCM-111 Cassette Corder was used with FCM-16 electric condenser microphone attached for recording, and Lyon spectrograph made in Japan was used for the data.

7. McDavid (1954: 496).

8. Kenyon, Samuel, J. American Pronunciation. George Wahr Publishing Co., Ann Arbor, U.S.A., 1949. p. 13.

9. Bryan, Robert and M. Dodge. Bert & I. (Ipswich, Mass: 35 Mill Road, 01938, 1985).

10. Thurston, Margaret. The Eastern Coastal Maine Dialect. The Master's Thesis for The Ohio State University, U.S.A. (Columbia, Ohio: Ohio State University, 1983).

11. Ikemiya, Tsuneko. "On the Archaic Nature Seen in Maine Dialects I", Tezukayama Univ. Reviews, No. 51 (1986) 27-53.

12. Bennett, Jacob. "The Folk Speech of Maine: Clue to Colonial English," The Dublin Seminar for New England Folklife (1983) 27-34.

REFERENCES

Algeo, John. The Origins and Development of the English Language. N.Y.: HBJ Co., 1982.

Ballew, Stephen & E. Ives. "Suthin". Orono, Maine: UMO Press, 1978.

Baugh, Albert C. History of the English Language. N.Y.: D. Appleton-Century Co., 1935.

Bennett, Jacob. "George Savary Wasson and the Dialect of Kittery Point, Maine," American Speech 49 (1974), 54-66.
------. "Maine Speech . . . not a laughing matter," Maine Alumnus UMO 57, No. 4. (Summer 1976) 14 & 45.
------. "Approach to Dialect Writing",AS, 54. No. 2 (1979) 90-101.
------. "The Folk Speech of Maine: Clue to Colonial English",The Dublin Seminar for New England Folklife (1983) 27-34.

Cercignani, Fausto. Shakespeare's Works and Elizabethan Pronunciation. Oxford: Clarendon Press, 1981.

Cutler, Evelyn Starr. "Representation of Maine Coast Dialect in the Work of Sarah Orne Jewett," New York Univ., Ph.D., Ann Arbor: xerox Univ. Microfilms (1976) 1-162.

Dodge, Marshall & R. Bryan. Bert & I. Books and Records. Ipswich, Mass.: 1981.

Haden, Ernest & L. Engler. "Status of Utterance," Acta Linguistica IX, No. 1. (1965) 25-36.

Engler, Leo. "Studies Shore Dialects," The Daily Times, Salisbury, Maryland, (Sunday, June 26, 1983), p.a. 8.

Francis, W. Nelson. The Structure of American English. N.Y. Ronald Press Co., 1958.

Gould, John. Maine Lingo. Camden, Maine: Down East Magazine, 1975.

Ikemiya, Tsuneko. "Language in New England," Tezukayam Univ. Review (No. 20, 1978), 1-31.
------. "Sound Spectographic Study of /a/ in half, and the final /r/ in door, fire, air, and steer in General American, New England American, and British English", Tezukayama Univ. Review (No.. 39, 1982), 46-69.
------. "On the Archaic Nature Seen in Maine Dialects I," Tezukayama Univ. Review (No. 51, 1986), 27-53.

------. "On the Archaic Nature Seen in Maine Dialects II," *Tezukayama Univ. Review* (No. 52, 1986), 25-43.

Jewett, Sarah Orne. *The Country of the Pointed Firs*. Boston: Houghton, Mifflin, 1896.

Kenyon, John S. and Thomas A. Knott. *A Pronouncing Dictionary of American English*. Springfield, Mass.: G. and C. Merrian, 1944.

Ladefoged, Peter. *A Course in Phonetics*. N.Y.: HBJ. Co., 1982.

Lehiste, Ilse. "An Acoustic-Phonetics. Study of Internal Open Juncture", *Phonetica* 5 (Supplement) (1960), 20-21.

Kokeritz, Helge. *Shakespeare's Pronunciation*. New Haven: Yale University Press, 1953.

Kurath, Hans. *The Linguistic Atlas of New England*. 3 vols. in 6 parts. Providence: Brown University, 1939-1943.
------. *A Word Geography of the Eastern United States*. Ann Arbor: University of Michigan Press, 1949.
------. "The Origin of the Dialectal Perspectives in Spoken American English," in *A Various Language: Perspectives on American Dialects*. Ed. by J. Williamson & V.M. Burke. N.Y.: Holt, Rinehart & Winston, Inc., 1971. p. 12-21.
------. "Some Aspects of Atlantic Seaboard English, Considered in Their Connection with British English," in *A Various Language*, 101-107.

McDavid, Raven I. "The Dialect of American English," Chapter 9 in *The Structure of American English*. by Francis W. Nelson, New York: Ronald Press Co., 1954, 480-543.

Marckwardt, Albert. H. *American English*. N.Y.: Oxford Univ. Press, 1958, 147.

Oxford English Dictionary. vol. 1-vol. 12. Oxford: Clarendon Press, 1970.

Pierce, Joe E. "A Spectrographic Study of English Vowel Phonemes Under Primary Stress", *Linguistics* LXXXIV (1972), 65.

Potter K.R. et al., *Visible Speech*, N.Y.: Dover Publications Inc., 1966.

Reed, Carroll. E. *Dialects of American English*. The World Publishing Co., 1967.

Shakespeare - Complete Works. Ed. Craig, W.J. London: Oxford University Press, 1894.

Trudgill, Peter. *Sociolinguistics*. Penguin Books, 1974.

Thurston, Margaret. "The Eastern Coastal Maine Dialect," The Master's Thesis for The Ohio State University. Columbia, Ohio: Ohio State Univ., 1983.

Webster's Third New International Dictionary, Merriam, 1971.

Wentworth, Harold. *American Dialect Dictionary*. N.Y.: Thomas Y. Crowell Co., 1944.

Focus of Change in American Folk Speech

FREDERIC G. CASSIDY
Dictionary of American Regional English

The title of this Conference has been troubling me. I am always worried by the word <u>dialect</u> or the term <u>dialectology</u>. This is the disease of lexicographers: they are forever trying to <u>define</u> things. Defining means drawing boundaries or setting up synonyms or descriptions when we know perfectly well that words, whatever they are, or phrases, whatever <u>they</u> are, are pieces arbitrarily pulled out of a web of language, pulled out of contexts on which they depend for such <u>ad hoc</u> precision as they can have. To pull the word or phrase out of its contextual web is to tear and deactivate its vital connections, to leave the threads hanging.

Or, to change the figure and think of those admirable models that chemists make to show the composition of matter -- with atoms of one shape or color joined in various complexes and clusters to atoms of other kinds: Language is somewhat like those models, except that the components of a language "unit" are less definite and less rule-governed than atoms of matter. Our phonemes are generalizations, our "parts of speech" and "syntactic units" are simplifications made for practical reasons. In the new physics, even atoms are no longer irreducible units (as etymologically they once were): they too can be decomposed. In order to deal with matter and assign names one has to set up arbitrary boundaries and to some extent ignore known differences, sweeping them for a time under the semantic rug.

So -- back to <u>dialectogy</u>. I tried some years ago to improve on the common dictionary definitions of <u>dialect</u>. Dictionaries agree in a general way, of course, in recognizing the subordination of a dialect as a variant form of a language; they note its primary connection with geography, and they recognize the extension of the term to other varieties of language--social, occupational, and so on. But the concept remains fuzzy. The lexicographer would like to see something more clearly definable. Alas, it is not to be. My attempt (see handout) is the best I have been able to do, using a grid with plus and minus features. Apply this to a map and one can talk of "dialect areas" with a fair degree of comfort. Yet I confess that I have often found the isogloss a discomforting device, only broadly acceptable. Especially when based on old historical sources, it reflects a paucity of evidence; there is always some correlation with geography -- a very broad or general one that does not fully represent the realities of human settlement and intercommunication. No doubt there really are or have been some Southern vulture <u>Cathartes aura</u> is known in various parts of its range as <u>buzzard</u>, <u>carrion crow</u> (usuallly pronounced <u>caren crow)</u>, <u>turkey buzzard</u>, <u>john crow</u>, etc. This range is geographically limited, but there is language variance within it. As just noted, where the range is small or the life-form rare, with only one name, <u>DARE</u> does not usually enter it. But some difficult decisions have to be made. We have had two editors doing only the scientific terms, identifying the plants, animals, and some minerals with folk names as exactly as they can. But scientific names, the familiar "binomials", make much exacter distinctions than folk names do. The <u>turkey buzzard</u> just mentioned has a bald red head. There is a very similar counterpart with a bald black head, also called <u>turkey buzzard</u> though it is not even of the same genus -- not <u>Cathartes</u> but <u>Coragyps</u>. People are annoyingly casual about the application of names. This is especially true of city people talking about country things. <u>DARE</u> lists in Volume I names for the three distinct plants called <u>bittersweet</u> in various parts of the country. First, <u>Solanum dulcamara</u> commonly <u>nightshade</u>, also called <u>dwale</u>, <u>fever-twig</u>, <u>felonwort</u>, <u>matrimony vine</u>, <u>morel</u>, <u>poison berry</u>, <u>poison flower</u>, <u>pushionberry</u>, <u>scarlet berry</u>, <u>skawcoo</u>, <u>snakeberry</u>, <u>terididdle</u>, <u>tetherdevil</u>, <u>violet bloom</u>, and <u>wolf grape</u> (fifteen regional names). The second plant called bittersweet, <u>Celastrus scandens</u>, has at least nine other names: <u>climbing bittersweet</u>, <u>climbing orangeroot</u>, <u>false bittersweet</u>, <u>fever twig</u>, <u>fever twitch</u>, <u>gnome's gold</u>, <u>jacob's ladder</u>, <u>Roxbury waxwork</u>, and <u>yellowroot</u>. The third kind of "bittersweet", <u>Chimaphila umbellata</u> and other species, best known by its Indian name <u>pipsissewa</u>, goes by at least fifteen other names. It has been a special task of <u>DARE</u> to document and clarify this confusing situation and to work out the regionality of these folk names. One of our difficulties has been to validate the evidence. Some names, reported by early botanists, have been repeated by later ones apparently just because they had found them listed. The lexicographer can neither check the first record for accuracy nor know whether the later recorder actually knew the plant and its name, or merely copied his predecessor, giving the name a kind of factitious-- sometimes, we suspect, a fictitious -- existence. Here the direct evidence from our Questionnaire is often the decisive factor. At least we can be sure the term is alive if an informant, innocent of botanical books, furnishes it spontaneously.

Another point: localized informants who know the things of their own area and can vouch for them may never have heard names used in other areas. For our purposes, this gives a real value to ignorance. <u>DARE</u> informants were chosen always as people living at or near their birthplaces who had not traveled or stayed away long enough for their local speech to have been affected. We repeatedly heard elderly informants boast that they had never been more than twenty or thirty miles from home, or that they were still living in the house they were born in. With the advent of automobiles, of course, that condition is becoming rare. Radio and television, once again, stir restlessness-- especially in the young people. For the best field collecting one has to catch the speaker at ease in his normal environment, speaking on a thoroughly familiar topic. <u>DARE</u> fieldworkers made 1843 tape recordings averaging half an hour each on dozens of such topics. We have used them for phonology, morphology, and the lexicon, but hardly for syntax. Covering all fifty states, that is a rich, not fully exploited archive.

The <u>Times Literary Supplement</u> review of <u>DARE</u> (May 9, 1986) by Hugh Kenner, speaks out for the importance of <u>written</u> sources as against oral ones and makes the valid points that the oral is limited to an informant's brief lifetime, and that in a full treatment of a word in <u>DARE</u> is likely to take far more from printed sources than from oral ones. He praises the <u>OED</u> for having limited itself to printed sources -- almost implying that oral ones would not have added much. This requires some corrective comment. Since Joseph Wright's <u>English Dialect Dictionary</u> was in preparation concurrently with the first fascicles of the <u>OED</u> and was fully in print by 1905, Murray was able to use Wright's great work for the recorded dialect element. Wright's chief sources had been printed by the English Dialect Society but the data had been mainly collected from local speakers all over England. Thus the oral element was by no means neglected, and in many instances it was the only evidence.

One is glad to have the reassurance of print, which outlives the speaker but preserves his speech. On the other hand, print itself confers no authority. <u>DARE</u> has excerpted several hundred volumes of "regional" literature, also travel accounts, diaries, local newspapers, and many more. This is all valuable material but must be treated with caution. When an author really knows the dialects he or she purports to be presenting -- such writers as William Faulkner, Mary McCarthy, Eudora Welty -- excellent! Also some older authors: Lowell, Eggleston, Simms. But others try to write "Yankee dialect" or "Southern dialect" without direct knowledge, with predictably disastrous results. Since Volume I of <u>DARE</u> appeared I have had wistful enquiries from would-be authors who find the variety of forms we record quite disheartening. Such people should do comic strips, not novels.

Another danger is that the author should patronize his dialect speaker, deliberately distorting or exaggerating the speech for comic effect or to show social disdain. This was far more common in the eighteenth and nineteenth centuries than it is today, and I believe democracy has something to do with it. Social lines still exist, and language still has its shibboleths, but there seems to be more tolerance of differences and certainly among dialectologists a more scientific approach. Some early records in <u>Dialect Notes</u> show that the collector's interest was too often in the queer, laughable <u>mistakes</u> that uneducated folk speech. Conversely, the cultivated speech of a region reshapes the speech of the middle class, the common speech; and features of the common speech encroach upon folk speech. The unmistakable trend from local to regional usage and from regional to national usage that characterizes the National Period of our linguistic history is essentially a process of the dissemination of upper-class speech forms to lower social levels and across earlier local or regional boundaries.

In planning <u>DARE</u> we were fully aware of Kurath's great work, the <u>Linguistic Atlas of New England</u>. He saw clearly the triple division of the American language scene: the national, regional, and local features coexisting within the language. <u>DARE</u> chose not to limit itself to folk speech or to separate that from the broader colloquial speech with which it often merges. To separate folk and regional on one side from national on the other could be made more meaningfully: the national equates with the language of education and upper-level discourse -- what we consider the "standard" language (even though <u>that</u> is not strictly uniform). So, for the sake of brevity, <u>DARE</u> uses the term "regional" to subsume both regional and local. To quote from the Introduction, "Regionality, as defined in DARE, bears no relation to the size of the area of use, so long as it is less than total", the whole country. General dictionaries take care of standard words and phrases: DARE enters regionalisms (including localisms) and folk usages whether regionally, restricted or not.

Our use of the word folk has also been questioned. The definition given in the Introduction (p.xvi) is mine. I quote:

> For DARE, folk usage is that which is learned in the home and in the community, from relatives and friends, not from schooling, books, or other outside forms of communication. It is traditional and largely oral; it includes anything that can be called "dialect" in the United States.

Having written this, I came upon the statement of purpose set out by the United States Library of Congress' Folk Life department and was gratified to find that their definition of "folk" agreed comfortably with mine. The fact is that the conditions which produced dialects in old countries are found less and less in the United States today. Universal education even with regional differences, easy communication and movement over great distances, mechanized farming, the powerful influence of cities, and most recently the overwhelming success of radio and television all tend toward uniformity, raising the fear that the language may suddenly become homogenized. This is somewhat exaggerated, though true, for counter forces are at work. Nevertheless, DARE has come along just in time to catch the bulk of the more local usages. Our field collecting, done in all fifty states some twenty-plus years ago, has saved a very great deal of local usage from oblivion.

There was another check on what might be considered folk speech, or regional non-standard usage. DARE devised for field collecting a questionnaire to be used uniformly in every part of the country, with every question phrased exactly and not to be altered by the fieldworker, to ensure that responses would be comparable. The same method was adopted independently by Professor Harold Orton for his Survey of English Dialects. We met cordially in Chicago in about 1966 and compared notes, but our systems were already fully worked out and did not need to be changed.

All questionnaires have to face the matter of limitations. Obviously, one cannot ask about everything under the sun for which a sought response might be made -- in our case, a regional word. Further, and especially when a huge area is to be covered in a short enough time so that the data may be synchronic, one cannot prolong the questioning of informants to the uttermost point. So, how to set limits? In the case of DARE, our task was to survey all fifty states in five years -- the farthest that our funds would stretch. Allowing one week for each community, fifty weeks to the year, and a thousand communities, we had to complete four questionnaires per week for five years. This imposed a strict limit -- we could not afford, in money or time, to ask all the possible questions. How to find those likely to yield the maximum number of regionally varying responses?

To this end we analyzed the approximately 40,000 examples already printed in Dialect Notes -- six volumes of material collected over a fifty-year period -- and sorted them by semantic categories. Reasoning that any item or subject which proved to have many variant names probably had others as yet unrecorded, we made sure to include a question for each. It has been truly observed that certain subjects stimulate the naming process, while others do not. Adapting the sense of Wordsworth's lines about Peter Bell,

> A primrose by a river's brim
> A yellow primrose was to him
> And it was nothing more.

So -- "primrose" -- what else?

On the other hand, the dragonfly, from its distinctive shape and actions, stirs the naming interest in us. DARE has collected more than seventy different names, including <u>darning needle</u>, <u>snake doctor</u>, <u>mosquito hawk</u>, <u>water dipper</u>, <u>skimmer</u>, <u>spindle</u>, <u>stitcher</u>, <u>ear cutter</u>, <u>gauze hawk</u>, and of more recent origin and application, <u>airplane fly</u> and <u>helicopter</u>.

Our reasoning in preparing the Questionnaire was correct, to judge by the huge number of variant responses our field workers collected. All will be printed as the Data Summary in the final volume. The DARE Questionnaire, then, was derived from what members of the American Dialect Society had collected over a sixty-year period: it represents what they found to be nonstandard, regional, examples of folk usage. One may correctly call this a definition by consensus. Almost everything so collected, once edited in the light of other evidence, will find its way into the five projected volumes of DARE.

The borderlines of what is called regional in DARE are further drawn by excluding other types of discourse. Let me quote again from the Introduction (pp.xvi-xvii):

> DARE does not cover artificial forms of speech such as Boontling (the private language used by the inhabitants of Boonville, California, and its environs) or any whose purpose or effect is to exclude the general listener. Criminal argot is of this kind, an in-group code intentionally separated from the general idiom. DARE includes such terms only if they have escaped into wider use. The same policy is followed with occupational language, sometimes called trade jargon, which only its users understand. For example, the hobo word <u>gump</u>, a chicken, is not known otherwise, but the jazz musician's <u>cool</u> has long since come into wider use. DARE does not attempt to cover restricted occupational vocabularies--especially when the occupation is highly specialized or esoteric, such as the sexing of chicks or the wrapping of cigars. On the other hand, the vocabularies of widespread occupations such as farming, housekeeping, mining, lumbering, cattle-raising, which involve entire communities and even entire regions, are necessarily included.

One more consideration must be mentioned, the effect of natural factors on the concept of regionalism as applied to language. Any large area is bound to have natural variations of topography, climate, fauna, flora, and so on. In the parts of the United States where there is plenty of snow, children go out to convenient slopes and fling themselves down on sleds, taking what they call a <u>belly-flop</u>, <u>belly-flapper</u>, <u>belly-flouncer</u>, <u>belly-flumps</u>, <u>belly-gutter</u>, <u>belly-jumper</u>, <u>belly-plumper</u>, <u>belly-slider</u>, <u>belly-smacker</u> and a dozen more. The distribution of these terms is clearly regional, as DARE maps demonstrate (pp.214

forward). But of course they can only be Northern or North Midland terms. On the other hand, water in lakes, ponds, swimming pools is found over the entire area, so that when inexpert divers land flat on the surface, they may also take a belly-flop, belly-whopper, belly-whacker, or a belly-splasher (compare the maps on p.217).

Many other terms are necessarily limited by nature, the occurrence of special winds (the Chinook, Santa Ana, blue norther), of mineral and land forms (alkali, needles, salt-licks), the range within which birds, animals, and plants are found. In such cases, regionality is natural and may or may not be linguistic. If the range is limited, there may be a single name for the object, and that is necessarily standard, DARE does not generally include these. If the range is large, though less than the entire country, there is room for name-variants. The lost valleys where everybody spoke exactly the same dialect which differed from the dialect on the other side of the mountain. Except, of course, for a few odd folk who spoke idiolectally. The question is, how many differing features must a variant have to deserve properly to be called a dialect? I take it the question is unanswerable except by fiat.

The problem came up, necessarily, in planning and setting the boundaries for the Dictionary of American Regional English (DARE). Volume I, published in September 1985, has received many notices, in a number of which reviewers seem to question the term "regional". In the most recent review (the London Review of Books, 5th March 1987) Walter Nash writes, "Even after reading Professor Cassidy's explanation of the term, I am not sure what 'regional' includes or excludes." The difficulty is the same as with the term 'dialect': one cannot be precise, beyond a point, about so complex a concept. Nevertheless, one must make the attempt. So I do in the Introduciton to DARE (pp.xvi-xviii), under the heading Inclusions and Exclusions, which I shall summarize in a moment. But first I should note that the title which the founders of the American Dialect Society (1899) expected to use for their projected Dictionary was simply parallel to Joseph Wright's English Dialect Dictionary: it was to have been American Dialect Dictionary. Over the years this expectation prevailed, and Harold Wentworth did indeed bring out a small book under this title in 1944, though the Society did not accept it as fulfilling their plan.

Meantime, and considering what dialect meant in Europe and other long-settled countries where local varieties of language had had time to become established, and how inexactly that term applied to the American scene, where expansion of miscellaneous peoples into a vast territory had taken place rapidly and was still proceeding, the term dialect took on a generally derogatory sense. The notion of there being limited areas with distinctive varieties of speech simply did not suit the American scene. It was evident that there were three broad types: Northern, Southern, and Western, but the country was too new and the movement of population too fluid to make the European sense of the term applicable.

My understanding is that regional and regionalism, which had been used chiefly about political matters (check your OED and the Supplement volume 3), was first applied to language a little before the middle of this century. I quote from Hans Kurath's A

Word Geography of the Eastern United States (1949) page 7:
> What has been clearly visualized hitherto is the supreme importance of knowing all the levels of speech in their local, regional, and national variations if we would understand the history of our language in all its complexity. Our regional types of cultivated speech rest upon the regional types of common speech as much as upon literary English, and common speech in turn has its roots in

speakers make. Their usage labels are often quite sharp. The later volumes are far more objective. DARE's labels try to reflect this objectivity -- see the Introduction, p.xx. Even at its best, literary dialect is two removes from the "real thing". The first remove is what the writer may do in creating a specific character; the second remove is the editing that he or the publisher may require to make the book "acceptable". The real thing is language unselfconsciously spoken in a normal environment by someone who is not on guard and is not trying to impress an outsider. He is "warbling his native woodnotes wild." This is no condemnation of literary dialect -- that has a life of its own. Some created literary characters are, as they say, "larger than life". But that is something different: that is art, not dialectology.

Despite our editors' best efforts to define, to make clear to ourselves and others the sense of the words "regional" and "folk speech", it must be confessed that we ourselves meet occasional uncertainties, borderline cases. Fieldworkers were told to err on the side of inclusiveness -- to leave final decisions to the editors. With such forms, when the evidence is slight but, in the light of editorial experience, seems genuine, we precede it with a double dagger. This is better than to exclude it. We recall that when Wright printed in the English Dialect Dictionary certain forms still alive in dialect but unrecorded in Middle English, they were later shown to have descended from Old English. Better to include a warningly marked uncertainty than to reject it outright. Further evidence may turn up later. DARE has probably saved a number of terms, finding them still in oral use, unrecorded otherwise. A small thing, perhaps, but not without value. And the work as a whole should excuse some small shortcomings.

Sex-Linked Differences Among Atlas Informants: Irregular Verbs

VIRGINIA G. McDAVID
Chicago State University

It is often said that women adhere more closely than men to what we call the standard in language. That is, they tend to use the forms preferred by usage guides, textbooks, and editors. It is also often said that among speakers of English, social class and educational background are more clearly revealed by choice of verb form -- particularly preterit or past participle form -- than by any other variant.

One source of data for testing whether this impression is supported by fact lies in the collections of the various linguistic atlases of the United States. Here I shall be dealing specifically with materials from New England, the Middle and South Atlantic States (New York, New Jersey, Pennsylvania, Delaware, Maryland, West Virginia, Virginia, and North Carolina, but here excluding South Carolina, Georgia, and Florida), and the North-Central States (Wisconsin, Michigan, Illinois, Indiana, Ohio, and Kentucky). The data in the Linguistic Atlas of the Upper Midwest has already been studied for this purpose by Harold B. Allen in a series of articles (Allen 1986).

The informants, or subjects, in these Atlas investigations are classified into three groups on the basis of education, reading, and social contacts. Most important is education. Those with college education are Type III, those with high-school education are Type II, and those with grammar school education or less are Type I. Typically the Type I informant is elderly and very likely a farmer, and representative of folk speech. The Type II informant is likely to be somewhat younger and representative of common speech, what might be called blue-collar English. Type III informants all have a college education. All are natives of their communities and have spent little time elsewhere. The mean age of the Type I informants in the areas studied is 73; that of the Type II informants is 66; and that of the Type III informants is 63. Seventy percent are men and about thirty percent women. The atlases provide a body of stable folk evidence -- not a representative and complete picture of American speech in all its complexities.

The New England interviews were made from 1931 to 1933. Those for the Middle and South Atlantic States were made in the 1930s and late 1940s. Those for the North-Central Atlas were made largely in the 1950s with the exception of Wisconsin, where the interviewing was done in 1939 and 1940 by Professor Cassidy. Many of these records are now more than fifty years old, and some of the informants were in their 80s at the time of the interviews. Several of the New England informants had sailed to China on clipper ships.

One study based on grammatical items in the atlas work sheets is E. Bagby Atwood's *A Survey of Verb Forms in the Eastern United States* (1953), which deals with more than one hundred verb constructions. Atwood is concerned principally with regional differences, between occurrences of *dived* and *dove* for example and with differences between the three types of informants. Nowhere does he sort out responses by the sex of the informant, nor did I sort them by sex in my 1956 dissertation dealing with verb forms in the North-Central States and Upper Midwest.

The first person to use atlas data for the study of differences that might be sex-related was Robert Van Riper in "Usage Preferences of Men and Women: DID, CAME, and SAW" (1976). After examining the responses of men and women in different age groups and in the three educational levels, Van Riper concludes:

"It is meaningful that in the Upper Midwest more women than men on the lower and middle levels show a preference the 'standard' forms of the past tense of these verbs, and that on the upper level the preference is fairly even. It must be more than coincidental that the same pattern of preference also appears in the North-Central States, and it seems likely that it will be the pattern in the other regions as well.... This can be summarized in the form of a theory, subject to further testing, which is this: If a verb form ... is strongly supported by school handbooks of usage and by editors of widely read publications, and if the competing forms are censured by usage handbooks, more women than men in any age group or on any level except the highest will favor the supported form; and sometimes this is the case even on the highest level."

Van Riper's hypothesis was tested by Allen (1986), who concludes that it does indeed hold for his data from the Upper Midwest, and that the standard forms have a higher frequency in the speech of women. My own conclusions from the data that follow seem to be in general agreement with Allen's, though comparison is not possible because he does not report numbers of informants, only percentages.

Let us turn to the data on six verb forms: *blow, come, drown, give, run,* and *tear*. There are some 60 preterit and participle verb forms in the atlas questionnaires. I selected these six because they are common verbs, because the choice of the correct form is a matter of textbook concern, because they have (mostly) only one nonstandard alternative (unlike *SEE* for example), and because -- frankly -- I have worked with some of these for many years. They are old and familiar friends, and I wanted to see what they were up to.

I report data from six geographical areas in the United States. (1) New England; (2) New York (including a few records from adjoining Ontario); (3) New Jersey and Pennsylvania; (4) Wisconsin, Michigan, Illinois, Indiana, and Ohio; (5) Delaware, Maryland (including the two informants from the District of Columbia), and West Virginia; and (6) Virginia, North Carolina, and Kentucky. A list of these areas is printed at the bottom of each odd-numbered table. From time to time I shall refer to these areas by number.

The basis for this division was Atwood's analysis in *Verb Forms* and my own experience working with these and other atlas materials. The number of speakers offering a response is indicated in parentheses on the tables. No responses suggested by the field worker have been included, nor any marked as old-fashioned, 'heard', or in any way not the informant's natural use. In addition, a chi-square test has been used to determine the significance of variation in the use of the standard as opposed to nonstandard forms. Differences significant at the .05 level or beyond (the 95 percent level of confidence; there is a 5 percent probability that the difference is the result of chance alone) are marked on the tables and charts. A separate table for each verb form indicates which of various comparisons are significant according to this test.

----

blow, preterit   Tables 1, 2; Charts 1, 2

The standard form *blew* is least common among the Type I informants and most common among the college-educated. This pattern is one that prevails among all six verbs. The differences between Types I and II and Types I and III are significant. Those between Types II and III often are not.

Among the Type I informants in areas 1 through 4, more than half of both sexes use the standard form. In the two southernmost areas, less than half do. Only in the North-Central area are the differences between male and female significant. Among the Type II informants, the differences between male and female are significant in two areas: New England and the southernmost one of Virginia, North Carolina, and Kentucky.

The differences between the males of the three types are everywhere significant. The differences between the Type I females and the Type II males are not significant except in the two southernmost areas. Differences between Type III males and females are nowhere significant; those between Type I males and female are significant only once, in area 4; and between Type II males and females significant only twice, in areas 1 and 6.

----

come, preterit   Tables 3, 4; Charts 2, 3

The standard form *came* is least common among the Type I informants and most common among the college-educated. Differences among all types of informants are significant. Women have a higher proportion of the standard form in almost all areas and in all three types of informants, but only once, between Type II male and female informants in the North-Central area, is this difference significant. Differences between males of the three types are almost everywhere significant, but not differences between females. There is no significant difference between Type I females and Type II males in three areas.

----

drown, past participle   Tables 5, 6; Charts 4, 5

Again the standard form is least common among the uneducated and most common among the college-educated. Differences between Types I and II informants are significant as are those between Types I and III. Differences between Types II and III are not. Type I and II females generally have a higher proportion of the standard forms than do males. Nowhere are differences between Type III males and females significant. Such differences are significant between Type I males and females in Delaware, Maryland, and West Virginia, and they are significant between Type II males and females in areas 1. 3. and 6. Differences between Type I and II males are significant in all six areas; between Type II and III males in none. There are no significant differences between Type I females and Type II males except in Virginia, North Carolina, and Kentucky.

----

give, preterit   Tables 7, 8; Charts 5, 6

The standard form *gave* is least common among the Type I informants and most common among the Type III informants. Type I and II women generally have a higher proportion of the standard form than do men. There is little difference between Type III men and women. There are significant differences between Type I men and women in areas 1 and 4 and between Type II men and women in the same two areas -- New England and the North-Central states -- as well as in Virginia, North Carolina, and Kentucky. Everywhere there is a significant difference between Type I and II males, but almost never between Type I and II females. There is no significant difference between Type I females and Type II males except in the two southernmost areas.

----

run, preterit   Tables 9, 10; Charts 7, 8

The standard form *ran* is most common among the college-educated. Differences between all three types of informants are significant. Type I and II women almost always use a higher proportion of the standard form than do men, and often Type III women as well. The differences between Type I males and females are significant in areas 1, 2, and 4; and between Type II males and females in areas 1 and 4.

Differences between Type I and II males are significant in all areas; those between Type II and III males only in areas 1 and 4. Differences between Type I females and Type II males are nonsignificant except in area 5.

----

tear, past participle   Tables II, 12; Charts 8, 9

Again the standard form is least common among the uneducated, and commonest among the college-educated. Differences between the three types of informants are significant except in one area. And again, women of all three types quite consistently use a higher proportion of standard forms than do men. Among the Type I men and women the difference is significant only in the North-Central area. Between the Type II men and women it is significant in areas 1, 3, and 4.. Differences between Type I and II males are everywhere significant. Differences between Type I females and Type II males are nonsignificant except in the southernmost area.

Do the data from these six verbs support Van Riper's hypothesis that except among the most highly educated, more women than men use the standard forms? The answer is a qualified one.

First, the data support the hypothesis more strongly for some verbs than for others. The verbs that show significant variation in the largest number of cells are *give* and *run*. No verbs show significant variation between Type III males and females, and these are omitted here.

	I	II	
blow	1 (area 4)	2 (areas 1, 6)	3
come	0	1 (area 4)	1
drown	1 (area 5)	3 (areas 1, 3, 6)	4
give	2 (areas 1, 4)	3 (areas 1, 4, 6)	5
run	3 (1, 2, 4)	2 (areas 1, 4)	5
tear	1 (area 4)	3 (areas 1, 3, 4)	4
	--	--	--
	8	14	22

Second, the data support the hypothesis more strongly for some geographical areas than for others.

	I	II	
Area 1	2	5	7
2	1	0	1
3	0	2	2
4	4	4	8
5	1	0	1
6	0	3	3
	--	--	--
	8	14	22

Area 4, the North-Central one, has the most cells with significant differences; right behind it is New England.

Finally, the data support the hypothesis more strongly for Type II informants than for Type I informants, as Table 13 shows. With six verbs in each of six areas, there are thirty-six possibilities for significant male-female differences among Type I informants, and such differences do appear eight times, or twenty-two percent of the time. For the Type II informants, again there are thirty-six possibilities for male-female differences. Here significant differences appear fourteen times, or thirty-nine percent of the time. For both groups of informants, even where there are no significant differences, the women almost always have a higher percentage of the standard forms. There are no examples of significant differences between male and female Type III informants, the most highly educated.

Differences between Type I and Type II males are significant for all six verbs in all areas with no exceptions. Differences between Type I and Type II females are significant less than half the time. For the verb *run* they are never significant, and for the verb *give* they are significant only in area 6. Differences between Type II and Type III males are significant less than half the time, and for Type II and III females, even less than that. The clearest and most consistent difference for all verbs is between Type I and Type II males. There are no significant differences between Type I females and Type II males in the four northernmost areas, and not always in the two southernmost areas. In other words, the least educated women use about as many standard forms as the men with high-school education.

Many verb forms remain to be studied in the atlas data. Further study should reveal much more about language differences between men and women.

References

Allen, Harold B. (1986) Sex-Linked Variation in the Responses of Dialect Informants. Part 3: Grammar. *Journal of English Linguistics*, 19.2, 149-76.
Atwood, E. Bagby. (1953) *A Survey of Verb Forms in the Eastern United States*. Ann Arbor, Michigan: University of Michigan Press.
Linguistic Atlas of New England (1941) Ed. Hans Kurath. Providence, Rhode Island: Brown University.
Linguistic Atlas of the Middle and South Atlantic States. Editor-in-Chief William A. Kretzschmar, Jr. University of Georgia. Unpublished.
Linguistic Atlas of the North-Central States. Editor-in-Chief William A. Kretzschmar, Jr. University of Georgia. Unpublished.
McDavid, Virginia. (1956) Verb Forms of the North-Central States and Upper Midwest. University of Minnesota dissertation. Unpublished.
Van Riper, William R. (1979) Usage Preferences of Men and Women: *Did, Came,* and *Saw*. *American Speech* 54.279-84.

Table 1   b<u>low</u>, preterit   LWS 6.3   SWS 5.5   LANE 637   VF 6, 38, 42.

		I		II		III			I M		I F		II M		II F		III M		III F		
1	blew	59%	67	84%	155	95%	40	262	56%	50	74%	17	78%	104	100%	51	91%	20	100%	20	262
	blowed	41%	46	16%	29	5%	2	77	44%	40	26% ◆	6	22%	29	0% ●	0	9%	2	0%	0	77
		113		184		42		339	90		23		133		51		22		20		339
2	blew	69%	45	93%	65	100%	21	131	66%	37	89%	8	94%	45	91%	20	100%	8	100%	13	131
	blowed	31%	20	7%	5	0%	0	25	34%	19	11%	1	6%	3	9%	2	0%	0	0%	0	25
		65		70		21		156	56		9		48		22		8		13		156
3	blew	77%	81	97%	74	100%	19	174	75%	71	100%	10	97%	64	100%	10	100%	12	100%	7	174
	blowed	23%	24	3%	2	0%	0	26	25%	24	0%	0	3%	2	0%	0	0%	0	0%	0	26
		105		76		19		200	95		10		66		10		12		7		200
4	blew	67%	114	86%	123	98%	40	277	62%	89	93%	25	82%	68	92%	55	100%	22	95%	18	277
	blowed	33%	56	14%	20	2%	1	77	38%	54	7%	2	18%	15	8%	5	0%	0	5%	1	77
		170		143		41		354	143 ●		27		83		60		22		19		354
5	blew	41%	39	76%	54	100%	13	106	44%	35	25%	4	76%	51	75%	3	100%	4	100%	9	106
	blowed	59%	56	24%	17	0%	0	73	56%	44	75%	12	24%	16	25%	1	0%	0	0%	0	73
		95		71		13		179	79		16		67		4		4		9		179
6	blew	3%	6	44%	62	97%	31	99	4%	5	2%	1	33%	20	75%	42	80%	4	100%	27	99
	blowed	97%	192	56%	80	3%	1	273	96%	134	98%	58	67%	41	48%	39	20%	1	0%	0	273
		198		142		32		372	139		59		61 ●		81 ●		5		27		372

1: NEng. 2: NY. 3: NJ, PA. 4: WI, MI, IL, IN, OH. 5: DE, MD, WV. 6: VA, NC, KY.   p .05 ●   p .10 ◆

Table 2
blow, preterit

✓ significant at $p < .05$

	1y	1n	2y	2n	3y	3n	4y	4n	5y	5n	6y	6n
I & II	✓			✓	✓		✓		✓		✓	
I & III	✓			✓	✓		✓		✓		✓	
II & III			✓		✓		✓		✓		✓	✓
I M & I F			✓		✓		✓	✓			✓		✓
I M & II M	✓			✓	✓		✓		✓		✓	
I M & II F	✓		✓				✓	✓			✓	✓
I M & III M	✓				✓		✓	✓			✓	✓
I M & III F	✓		✓		✓		✓				✓	✓
I F & II M			✓		✓		✓		✓	✓		✓	
I F & II F	✓				✓		✓		✓		✓	✓
I F & III M	✓				✓				✓	✓		✓	
I F & III F	✓								✓		✓	✓
II M & II F	✓			✓					✓		✓		✓
II M & III M			✓		✓		✓		✓		✓	✓
II M & III F									✓		✓		✓
II F & III M			✓		✓				✓		✓	✓
II F & III F				✓	✓				✓		✓		✓
III M & III F			✓						✓				

Table 3

ċome, preterit   LWS 102.4   SWS 74.1   LANE 640   VF 9.

		I		II		III			I		E		M		F		M		F	
1	came	20%	30	35%	81	66%	39	150	19%	22	25%	8	31%	50	42%	31	61%	20	73%	19	150
	come	80%	120	65%	153	34%	20	293	81%	96	75%	24	69%	111	58%	42	39%	13	27%	7	293
			150		234		59	443		118		32		161		73		33		26	443
2	came	36%	22	68%	39	96%	25	86	30%	16	75%	6	65%	24	75%	15	100%	10	94%	15	86
	come	24%	39	32%	18	4%	1	58	70%	37	25%	2	35%	13	25%	5	0%	0	6%	1	58
			61		57		26	144		53		8		37		20		10		16	144
3	came	35%	36	70%	52	100%	19	107	34%	31	50%	5	66%	42	100%	10	100%	11	100%	8	107
	come	65%	66	30%	22	0%	0	88	66%	61	50%	5	34%	22	0%	0	0%	0	0%	0	88
			102		74		19	195		92		10		64		10		11		8	195
4	came	36%	46	67%	71	89%	34	151	32%	34	55%	12	56%	34	82%	37	90%	19	88%	15	151
	come	64%	82	33%	35	11%	4	121	68%	72	45%	10	44%	27	18%	8	10%	2	12%	2	121
			128		106		38	272		106		22 ◆		61		45 ●		21		17	272
5	came	9%	8	47%	32	94%	17	57	10%	8	0%	0	48%	31	25%	1	100%	4	93%	13	57
	come	91%	86	53%	36	6%	1	123	90%	70	100%	16	52%	33	75%	3	0%	0	7%	1	123
			94		68		18	180		78		16		64		4		4		14	180
6	came	1%	2	23%	34	97%	31	67	1%	2	0%	0	16%	10	29%	24	100%	4	96%	27	67
	come	99%	200	77%	111	3%	1	312	99%	141	100%	59	84%	52	71%	59	0%	0	4%	1	312
			202		145		32	379		143		59		62		83 ◆		4		28	379

1: NEng.   2: NY.   3: NJ, PA.   4: WI, MI, IL, IN, OH.   5: DE, MD, WV.   6: VA, NC, KY.

Table 4
come, 'preterit

	1		2		3		4		5		6	
	y	n	y	n	y	n	y	n	y	n	y	n
I & II	✓		✓		✓		✓		✓		✓	
I & III	✓		✓		✓		✓		✓		✓	
II & III	✓		✓		✓		✓		✓		✓	
I M & I F		✓	✓			✓		✓		✓		✓
I M & II M	✓		✓		✓		✓		✓		✓	
I M & II F	✓		✓		✓		✓			✓	✓	
I M & III M	✓		✓		✓		✓		✓		✓	
I M & III F	✓		✓		✓		✓		✓		✓	
I F & II M		✓		✓		✓	✓	✓			✓	
I F & II F		✓	✓	✓		✓				✓	✓	
I F & III M	✓			✓	✓		✓		✓		✓	
I F & III F	✓			✓	✓		✓	✓			✓	
II M & II F		✓	✓		✓	✓			✓			✓
II M & III M	✓			✓	✓		✓				✓	
II M & III F	✓			✓		✓	✓		✓		✓	
II F & III M		✓	✓					✓	✓	✓		
II F & III F	✓				✓			✓	✓		✓	
III M & III F		✓			✓			✓		✓		✓

Table 5
drown, past participle   LWS 96.1   SMS 69.6   LANE 522   VF 12.

		I			II			III			M	E	M	F	M	F
1	drowned	67%	78	89%	166	98%	49	293	63%	59	86%	19	86%	113	98%	53	96%	25	100%	24	293
	drownded	33%	38	11%	20	2%	1	59	37%	35	14%	3	14%	19	2%	1	4%	11	0%	0	59
		116		186		50		352	94		22		132		54		26		24		352
2	drowned	57%	38	92%	54	100%	22	114	56%	32	60%	6	90%	38	94%	16	100%	7	100%	15	114
	drownded	43%	29	8%	5	0%	0	34	44%	25	40%	4	10%	4	6%	1	0%	0	0%	0	34
		67		59		22		148	57		10		42		17		7		15		148
3	drowned	38%	40	64%	47	94%	17	104	38%	36	40%	4	59%	37	100%	10	91%	10	100%	7	104
	drownded	62%	65	36%	26	6%	1	92	62%	59	60%	6	41%	26	0%	0	0%	0	0%	0	92
		105		73		18		196	95		10		63		10		10		7		196
4	drowned	57%	106	81%	113	97%	36	255	54%	84	71%	22	81%	66	80%	47	100%	22	93%	14	255
	drownded	43%	80	19%	27	3%	1	108	46%	71	29%	9	19%	15	20%	12	0%	0	7%	1	108
		186		140		37		363	155		31		81		59		22		15		363
5	drowned	12%	10	61%	43	100%	13	66	7%	5	31%	5	61%	41	50%	2	100%	4	100%	9	66
	drownded	88%	76	39%	28	0%	0	104	93%	65	69%	11	39%	26	50%	2	0%	0	0%	0	104
		86		71		13		170	70		16		67		4		4		9		170
6	drowned	19%	37	73%	92	91%	31	160	18%	24	22%	13	55%	27	84%	65	100%	5	90%	26	160
	drownded	81%	159	27%	34	9%	3	196	82%	112	78%	47	45%	22	16%	12	0%	0	10%	3	196
		196		126		34		356	136		60		49		77		5		29		356

1: NEng. 2: NY. 3: NJ, PA. 4: WI, MI, IL, IN, OH. 5: DE, MD, WV. 6: VA, NC, KY.

Table 6
drown, past participle

	1 y	1 n	2 y	2 n	3 y	3 n	4 y	4 n	5 y	5 n	6 y	6 n
I & II	✓		✓		✓		✓		✓		✓	
I & III	✓		✓		✓		✓		✓		✓	
II & III		✓		✓	✓		✓		✓		✓	
I M & I F	✓			✓	✓		✓		✓			✓
I M & II M	✓		✓		✓		✓		✓		✓	
I M & II F	✓		✓		✓		✓		✓		✓	
I M & III M	✓			✓	✓		✓		✓		✓	
I M & III F		✓	✓		✓		✓		✓		✓	
I F & II M		✓		✓	✓		✓		✓		✓	
I F & II F		✓		✓	✓			✓	✓		✓	
I F & III M		✓		✓	✓		✓			✓	✓	
I F & III F	✓			✓	✓			✓	✓		✓	
II M & II F		✓		✓	✓			✓	✓			✓
II M & III M		✓		✓		✓		✓		✓		✓
II M & III F		✓		✓		✓		✓		✓	✓	
II F & III M		✓		✓		✓		✓		✓		✓
II F & III F		✓		✓				✓		✓		✓
III M & III F		✓			✓			✓				✓

Table 7   give, preterit   LWS 102.1   SWS 73.5   LANE 649   VF 15.

	I		II		III			M	E	M	F	M	F	
										II		III		
1	gave	46% 46	68% 95	95% 42	183	38% 30	80% 16	86% 43	92% 23	100% 19	183
	give	54% 53	32% 45	5% 2	100	62% 49	20% 4 ●	14% 7	8% 2	0% 0	100
		99	140	44	283	79	20	50	25	19	283
2	gave	40% 27	83% 55	100% 22	104	36% 22	83% 5	87% 20	100% 9	100% 13	104
	give	60% 40	17% 11	0% 0	51	64% 39	17% 1 ♦	13% 3	0% 0	0% 0	51
		67	66	22	155	61	6	23	9	13	155
3	gave	35% 36	79% 59	100% 19	114	33% 31	50% 5	91% 10	100% 11	100% 8	114
	give	65% 68	21% 16	0% 0	84	67% 63	50% 5	9% 1	0% 0	0% 0	84
		104	75	19	198	95	10	11	11	8	198
4	gave	48% 78	69% 83	91% 32	193	43% 59	70% 19	80% 40	91% 20	92% 12	193
	give	52% 85	31% 37	9% 3	125	57% 77	30% 8	20% 10 ●	9% 2	8% 1	125
		163	120	35	318	136	27	50	22	13	318
5	gave	23% 22	63% 45	100% 11	78	22% 17	29% 5	75% 3	100% 4	100% 7	78
	give	77% 72	37% 27	0% 0	99	78% 60	71% 12 ●	25% 1	0% 0	0% 0	99
		94	72	11	177	77	17	4	4	7	177
6	gave	4% 8	69% 97	100% 34	139	3% 4	7% 4	81% 64	100% 5	100% 29	139
	give	96% 190	31% 43	0% 0	233	97% 138	93% 52	19% 15	0% 0	0% 0	233
		198	140	34	372	142	56	79 ●	5	29	372

1: NEng. 2: NY. 3: NJ, PA. 4: WI, MI, IL, IN, OH. 5: DE, MD, WV. 6: VA, NC, KY.

Table 8
give, preterit

	1		2		3		4		5		6	
	y	n	y	n	y	n	y	n	y	n	y	n
I & II	✓		✓		✓		✓		✓		✓	
I & III	✓		✓		✓		✓		✓		✓	
II & III	✓			✓	✓	✓		✓			✓	
I M & I F	✓			✓	✓	✓			✓			✓
I M & II M	✓		✓		✓		✓		✓		✓	
I M & II F	✓		✓		✓		✓			✓	✓	
I M & III M	✓		✓		✓		✓		✓		✓	
I M & III F	✓		✓		✓		✓		✓		✓	
I F & II M		✓		✓		✓	✓	✓			✓	
I F & II F		✓		✓		✓	✓		✓	✓		
I F & III M		✓		✓	✓			✓	✓		✓	
I F & III F		✓		✓	✓		✓	✓		✓		
II M & II F	✓			✓	✓	✓			✓	✓		
II M & III M	✓			✓	✓	✓			✓			✓
II M & III F	✓			✓	✓		✓		✓	✓		
II F & III M		✓		✓		✓	✓		✓			✓
II F & III F		✓		✓		✓	✓		✓	✓		
III M & III F		✓					✓					

Table 9   run, preterit   LWS 102.3   SWS 73.7   LANE 658   VF 20.

Left portion (age groups I, II, III):

		I	II	III	Total
1	ran	11% 13	30% 48	68% 30	91
1	run	89% 106	70% 112	32% 14	232
		119	160	44	323
2	ran	37% 27	64% 44	100% 23	94
2	run	63% 46	36% 25	0% 0	71
		73	69	23	165
3	ran	33% 35	64% 36	95% 18	89
3	run	67% 70	36% 20	5% 1	91
		105	56	19	180
4	ran	30% 53	48% 58	92% 34	145
4	run	70% 123	52% 63	8% 3	189
		176	121	37	334
5	ran	12% 12	47% 33	100% 13	58
5	run	88% 85	53% 37	0% 0	122
		97	70	13	180
6	ran	2% 3	16% 23	90% 28	54
6	run	98% 157	84% 117	10% 3	277
		160	140	31	331

Right portion (sex × age: I, II, III with M, F):

		I-M	I-F	II-M	II-F	III-M	III-F	Total
1	ran	6% 6	39% 7	25% 28	44% 20	50% 11	86% 19	91
1	run	94% 95	61% 11●	75% 86	56% 26	50% 11	14% 3	232
		101	18	114	46	22		323
2	ran	31% 20	78% 7	60% 28	73% 16	100% 8	100% 15	94
2	run	69% 44	22% 2	40% 19	27% 6	0% 0	0% 0	71
		64	9	47	22	8	15	165
3	ran	31% 29	60% 6	59% 27	90% 9	91% 10	100% 8	89
3	run	69% 66	40% 4	41% 19	10% 1	9% 1	0% 0	91
		95	10	46	10	11	8	180
4	ran	26% 39	50% 14	42% 31	57% 27	90% 19	94% 15	145
4	run	74% 109	50% 14	58% 43	43% 20●	10% 2	6% 1	189
		148	28	74	47	21	16	334
5	ran	12% 10	12% 2	47% 31	50% 2	100% 4	100% 9	58
5	run	88% 71	88% 14	53% 35	50% 2	0% 0	0% 0	122
		81	16	66	4	4	9	180
6	ran	1% 2	14% 1	14% 8	18% 15	50% 1	93% 27	54
6	run	99% 151	86% 6	86% 50	82% 67	50% 1	7% 2	277
		153	7	58	82	2	29	331

1: NEng.   2: NY.   3: NJ, PA.   4: WI, MI, IL, IN, OH.   5: DE, MD, WV.   6: VA, NC, KY.

Table 10
run, preterit

	1 y	1 n	2 y	2 n	3 y	3 n	4 y	4 n	5 y	5 n	6 y	6 n
I & II	✓		✓		✓		✓		✓		✓	
I & III	✓		✓		✓		✓		✓		✓	
II & III	✓		✓		✓		✓		✓		✓	
I M & I F	✓		✓			✓	✓		✓			✓
I M & II M	✓		✓		✓		✓		✓		✓	
I M & II F	✓		✓		✓		✓			✓	✓	
I M & III M	✓		✓		✓		✓		✓		✓	
I M & III F	✓		✓		✓		✓		✓		✓	
I F & II M		✓		✓	✓		✓	✓				✓
I F & II F		✓		✓	✓			✓	✓			✓
I F & III M		✓		✓	✓	✓	✓					✓
I F & III F	✓			✓	✓	✓		✓	✓			
II M & II F	✓			✓	✓	✓			✓			✓
II M & III M	✓			✓	✓	✓			✓			✓
II M & III F	✓		✓		✓	✓		✓			✓	
II F & III M		✓		✓	✓	✓			✓			✓
II F & III F	✓			✓	✓	✓			✓	✓		
III M & III F	✓					✓	✓					✓

Table 11 tear, past participle LWS 102.6 SWS 74.3 LANE 665 VF 64

		I		II		III			I		II		III		
									M	E	M	F	M	F	
1	torn	31%	37	53%	97	88%	42	176	28% 27	48% 10	47% 61	65% 36	83% 20	92% 22	176
	tore	69%	81	47%	87	12%	6	174	72% 70	52% 11	53% 68	35% 19	17% 4	8% 2	174
		118		184		48		350	97	21	129	55 ●	24	24	350
2	torn	44%	30	83%	59	100%	23	112	40% 23	70% 7	76% 34	96% 25	100% 9	100% 14	112
	tore	56%	38	17%	12	0%	0	50	60% 35	30% 3	24% 11	4% 1	0% 0	0% 0	50
		68		71		23		162	58	10	45	26 ◆	9	14	162
3	torn	37%	38	64%	49	91%	18	105	35% 33	50% 5	59% 39	100% 10	91% 10	100% 8	105
	tore	63%	66	36%	27	8%	1	94	65% 61	50% 5	41% 27	0% 0	8% 1	0% 0	94
		104		76		19		199	94	10 ◆	66	10 ●	11	8	199
4	torn	42%	73	70%	98	89%	34	205	37% 52	64% 21	60% 48	83% 50	88% 21	93% 13	205
	tore	58%	102	30%	42	11%	4	148	63% 90	36% 12	40% 32	17% 10	12% 3	7% 1	148
		175		140		38		353	142	33 ●	80	60	24	14	353
5	torn	11%	10	45%	32	92%	12	54	10% 8	14% 2	46% 31	25% 1	100% 4	89% 8	54
	tore	89%	85	55%	39	8%	1	125	90% 73	86% 12	54% 36	75% 3	0% 0	11% 1	125
		95		71		13		179	81	14	67	4	4	9	179
6	torn	6%	11	49%	71	94%	33	115	5% 7	7% 4	46% 28	51% 43	83% 5	97% 28	115
	tore	94%	187	51%	74	6%	2	263	95% 135	93% 52	54% 33	49% 41	17% 1	3% 1	263
		198		145		35		378	142	56	61	84	6	29	378

1: NEng. 2: NY. 3: NJ, PA. 4: WI, MI, IL, IN, OH. 5: DE, MD, WV. 6: VA, NC, KY.

Table 12
tear, preterit

	1 y	1 n	2 y	2 n	3 y	3 n	4 y	4 n	5 y	5 n	6 y	6 n
I & II	✓		✓		✓		✓		✓		✓	
I & III	✓		✓		✓		✓		✓		✓	
II & III	✓			✓	✓		✓		✓		✓	
I M & I F		✓		✓		✓	✓			✓		✓
I M & II M	✓			✓	✓		✓		✓		✓	
I M & II F	✓		✓		✓		✓			✓	✓	
I M & III M	✓		✓		✓		✓		✓		✓	
I M & III F	✓		✓		✓		✓		✓		✓	
I F & II M		✓		✓		✓	✓			✓	✓	
I F & II F		✓		✓	✓		✓			✓	✓	
I F & III M	✓				✓	✓			✓	✓		✓
I F & III F	✓			✓		✓		✓	✓		✓	
II M & II F	✓				✓	✓		✓			✓		✓
II M & III M	✓				✓		✓	✓			✓		✓
II M & III F	✓				✓		✓	✓			✓	✓	
II F & III M		✓	✓		✓		✓		✓			✓
II F & III F	✓			✓				✓	✓	✓		
III M & III F		✓			✓		✓		✓			✓

Table 13

Number of Significant Occurrences

	I	II	
blow	1 (area 4)	2 (areas 1, 6)	3
come	0	1 (area 4)	1
drown	1 (area 5)	3 (areas 1, 3, 6)	4
give	2 (areas 1, 4)	3 (areas 1, 4, 6)	5
run	3 (areas 1, 2, 4)	2 (areas 1, 4)	5
tear	1 (area 4)	3 (areas 1, 3, 4)	4
	8	14	22

Table 14

Significant Occurrences and Geographical Areas

	I	II	
Area 1	2	5	7
2	1	0	1
3	0	2	2
4	4	4	8
5	1	0	1
6	0	3	3
	8	14	22

Methods in Dialectology

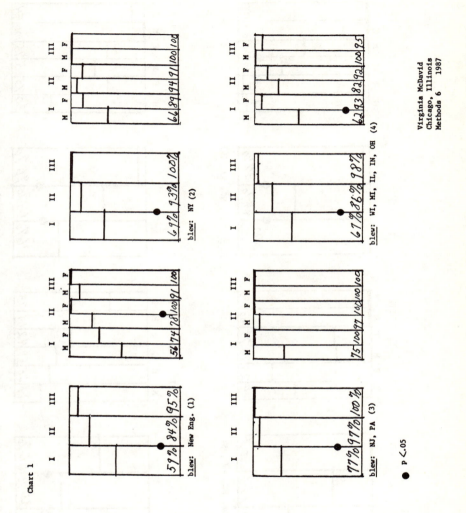

Chart 1

Virginia McDavid
Chicago, Illinois
Methods 6   1987

Chart 2

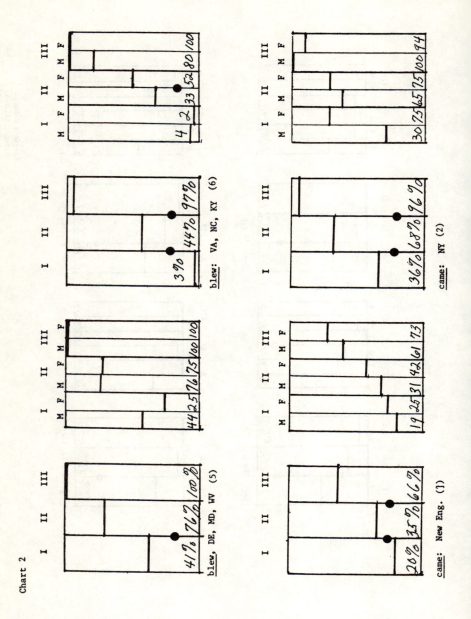

Methods in Dialectology

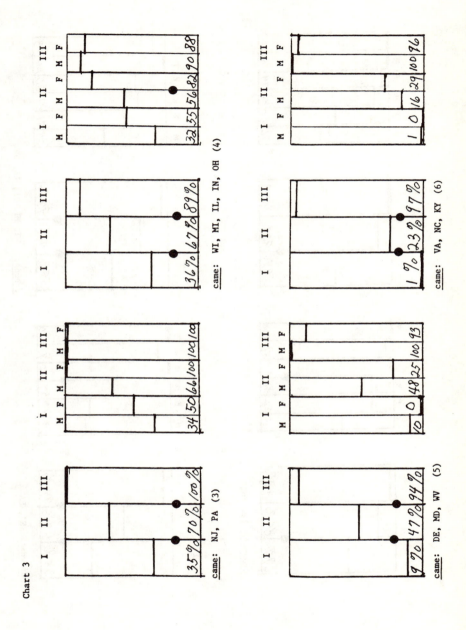

Chart 3

356   *Methods in Dialectology*

Chart 4

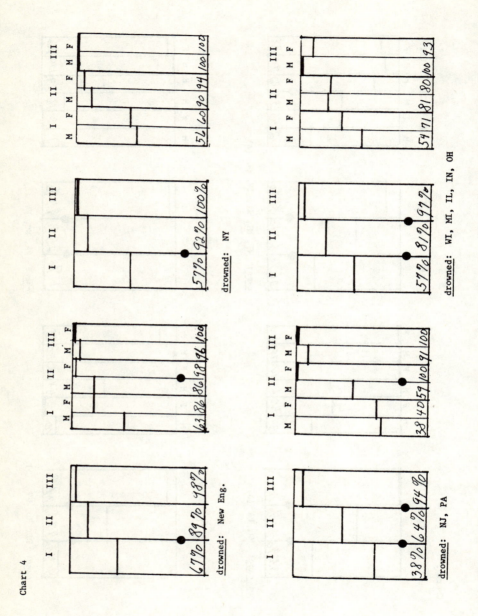

Methods in Dialectology

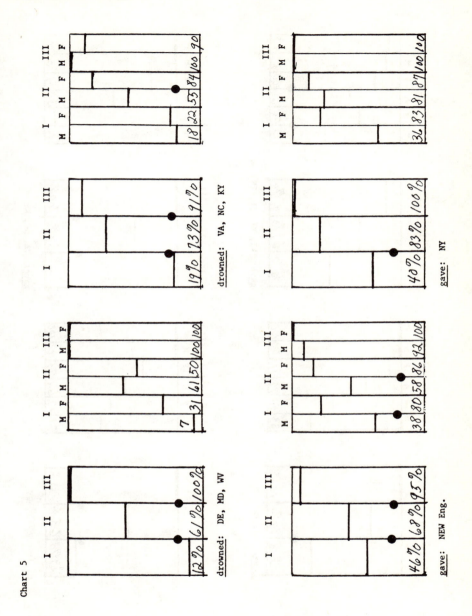

Chart 5

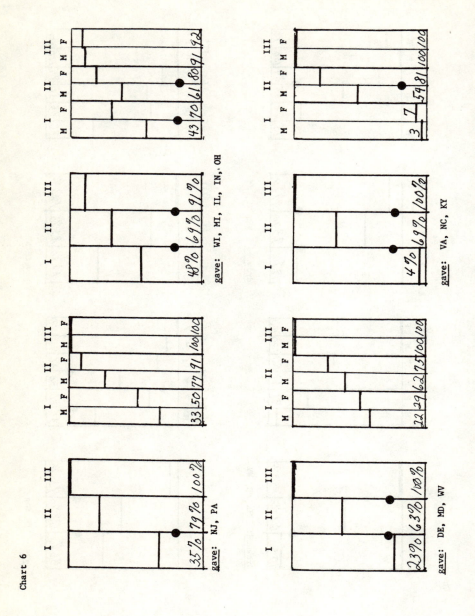

Chart 6

Methods in Dialectology

Chart 7

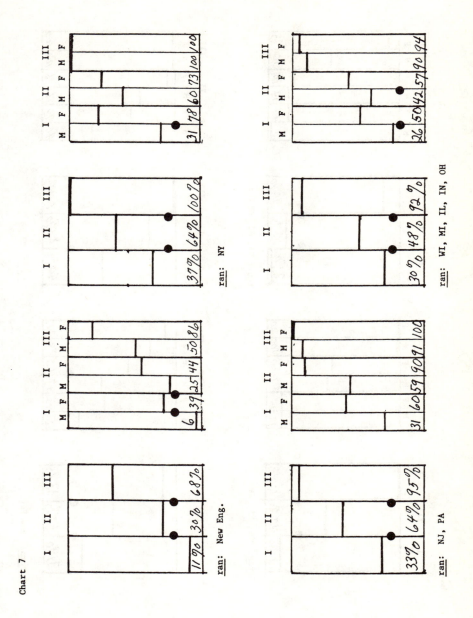

360 Methods in Dialectology

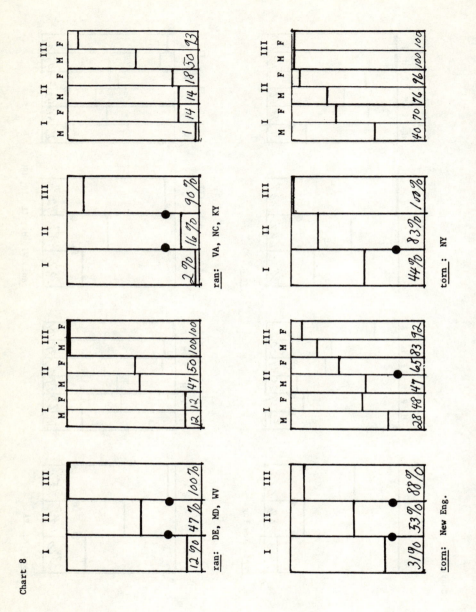

Chart 8

Methods in Dialectology

Chart 9

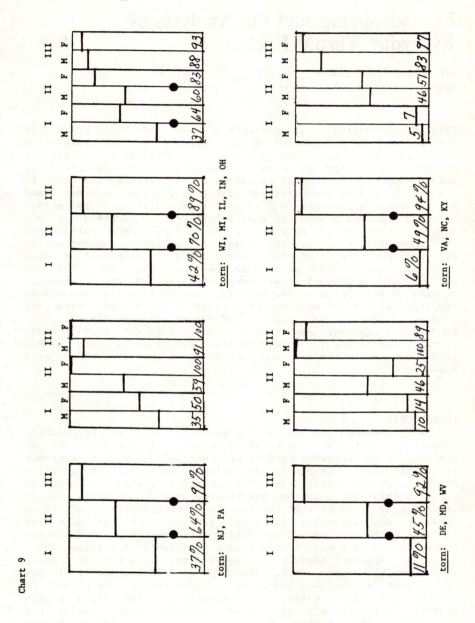

Eavesdropping and the Analysis of Everyday Verbal Exchange

GRAHAM McGREGOR
University of Newcastle upon Tyne

This paper outlines a programme of research whose principle concern is the development of an interpretive sociolinguistic framework for analysing everyday communicative activity. Following the lead of Gumperz's recent work on conversational inferencing, the method of investigation is based on the need to provide a closer understanding of how linguistic knowledge and social factors interact in discourse interpretation. The method involves various studies of what I have called "eavesdropping", that is, the process by means of which third-person participant and non-participant listener judges are invited to comment on the tape-recorded talk of others. The results of three such studies are considered with particular reference to the types of descriptive statement that were elicited in the research. Discussion will focus on the nature, distribution and theoretical implications of the most commonly cited of these types which are termed "observations" and "inferences" respectively. In conclusion, further empirical work is suggested to examine what, if any, sociolinguistic pattern there may be across and within individual eavesdroppers and the kinds of inference that were made.

INTRODUCTION

The research of which this paper is part is principally concerned with the study of interpersonal communication as manifest in the language used by speakers and hearers in everyday verbal exchange. In particular, it seeks to explore the question of what is communicated and what communicates when language is used in this way. But how can this question be broached when it is generally accepted that the face-to-face activities, of which speaking and listening are part, involve real-time processes subject to the ongoing and coordinated efforts of the individuals concerned and as a consequence cannot be directly investigated?

This apparent impasse for analytic method is not of course insurmountable since one can always proceed in a theoretical way by presenting idealised models of the kind recently developed by Sperber and Wilson (1986), for example, who identify a single property ("relevance") as the key to human communication and cognition. The problem about such models, as Lesley Milroy (1987) suggests is that whatever methods are concerned, the theoretical goals and assumptions that underlie them *always* bear an indirect relationship to data. This problem is particularly salient for the would be analyst of talk in naturally occuring social contexts because if the real-time processes of everyday verbal exchange are not amenable to direct investigation, one wonders what *evidence* an investigator might use in support of his/her analytic claims? Presumably, the more evidence we provide, the stronger our claims will be, but the question remains, what sort of evidence can we bring?

STUDIES IN INTERACTIONAL SOCIOLINGUISTICS

The beginnings of an answer to this question are inherent in Survey sociolinguistic analyses of the kind pioneered by William Labov in the United States of America and later by Peter Trudgill (1974) in Britain. As is well known, Labov's (1966) work was devoted to eliciting natural speech in a variety of different settings. The work is a landmark of its kind and far too well known to need detailed exposition here. Suffice to say, he then used this speech as a data base for examining the distribution of segmentable features of linguistic form in order to develop a model of sociolinguistic structure. What interests me particularly is what Labov did next, for a third of the work is devoted to supplementing his linguistic analysis through measures of social evaluation. These either draw on idependently collected ethnographic data, or on attitude measurements patterned on the match guise technique developed by Wallace Lambert. This technique makes use of panels of judges who are asked to evaluate samples of natural speech passages reflecting particular combinations of variables and then to rate the prestige and other characteristics of their speakers. Investigations of this kind have subsequently been taken up by social psychologists (see Giles and St. Clair, 1979; Ryan and Giles, 1982, for examples of studies in this tradition) but their work is centred on the study of attitudes to language, or patterns of language use, in controlled and experimental contexts.

Whilst data from subjective evaluation or matched guise tests demonstrate speakers' awareness of appropriate language behaviour in different situations, such data tells us relatively little about what is being communicated in the situation in hand as Gumperz (1982a) points out. This is not to criticise either Labov or the social psychologists because their work on social evaluation has provided a useful and perfectly valid means of making statements about behavioural trends. The crucial question is whether the trends the analyst has observed as part of the speech communication process are *the same* as those experienced by the actual participants during whatever exchange has taken place?

AN INTERPRETIVE SOCIOLINGUISTIC APPROACH

I want to suggest that this question is in fact researchable and more than that needs to be researched in a systematic way. But research of the kind I have in mind requires a rather different perspective from the Labovian paradigm we have considered thus far since the methods and goals of the latter are relatively abstract in nature. Gumperz (1982a) indicates how so very clearly as Lesley Milroy (1987, p.2) points out;

> "... although Labov rejects Saussurian and Chomskyan assumptions of uniformity in grammatical systems, he shares with other linguists an interest in understanding the general character of grammars, believing these to be affected by the social charactersitics of human groups. Gumperz then goes on to argue that the relatively abstract approach associated with this theoretical goal entails a neglect of the speaker as participant in interaction, and that quite different methods are needed to investigate issues arising from the ability of speakers to interact".

By proposing a speaker-oriented approach to the study of everyday verbal exchange, Gumperz work is significantly different from other linguistic and sociolinguistic traditions since it "...focuses on the strategies that govern the actor's use of lexical, grammatical, sociolinguistic and other knowledge in the production and interpretation of messages in context" (1982a, p.35). This interpretive sociolinguistic approach as he calls it aims to document and test the claim that interpretive analysis of talk in key naturally occuring situations "...can yield significant insights into the communicative processes that underlie categorization, intergroup stereotyping, evaluation of verbal performance and access to public resources in modern societies" (1982b, p.vii).

The substance of this claim is investigated in Gumperz (1982a; 1982b) through a series of case studies exploring situations of intergroup communication and the role of particular communicative phenomena therein. In order to find out what is going on in such situations from the participants' point of view, Gumperz develops a general theory of 'conversational inferencing', that is, "the situated or context bound process...by means of which participants in an exchange assess each others' intentions, and on which they base their responses" (1982a, p.153).

A typical method which is used to find out what kind of inferences are made is to play a recording of a particular exchange, or at least some episode from it, to a panel of listeners, including some of the individuals who were involved as participants. Individuals are then asked "to explain what they thought the speaker intended to convey in speaking as he did and to evaluate the effectiveness of his verbal strategies". This method enables Gumperz to develop hypotheses about the kind of social assumptions that judges must have made in order to interpret and evaluate the exchange in a particular way. However, the method does not offer any systematic framework for dealing with these judgements, nor for making use of particular judges, nor for explaining any variations that might have occured within different judgers and the judgements they made.

I would suggest that the development of such a framework could serve a number of important functions, not least in providing analysts of talk with a potential source of evidence in support of their own intuitive claims. It would also provide a means of circumventing the difficulty of direct observation. Afterall as Kibrik (1977, p.2) notes, "the concrete utterances which represent the realisation of linguistic competence of speakers who know the language can be observed". Since presumably participants in verbal exchange may be supposed to know what is going on in them, we might reasonably expect individuals from the same speech community to possess the ability to describe such exchanges, if only from their own point of view, and this ability is researchable as Gumperz has shown. The question that remains is to determine what it is members might have to say about what goes in talk, albeit from outside the participation event, since I take it that if a linguistic phenomenon is spoken about by native language users it must be worth investigating (cf. Hoenigswald, 1966).

This is not to argue that what participant and non-participant observers have to say about episodes of verbal exchange will necessarily match their experience as speaker-hearers (what they have to say may reveal only peripheral aspects of various underlying complex processes as Dore and McDermott, 1982 suggest) but rather to aver that an examination of what ordinary language users have to say about what is going on in their own and other peoples' talk promises to be at least as interesting as theoretical introspection about what such an activity might constitute. At least this is what I hope to demonstrate in the second half of this paper by presenting the results of studies based on the interpretive capacity of such users.

EAVESDROPPING

The research programme I have initiated towards this end focusses on what members have to say about what goes on in talk from outside the participation event, that is by providing them with opportunities to act as participant and non-participant observers, or "eavesdropper" judges as I prefer to call them, of previously recorded speech activities. The method of investigation is thus "listener" - rather than speaker-oriented, though the listeners concerned undertake their work in the third rather than the first person as the following diagram shows.

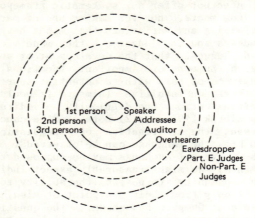

In contexts where we are ratified participants, we presumably listen to talk because we expect to make use of it in some way; let's say for purposes of comprehension and recall. Where we are overhearers, or eavesdroppers, our motivation for listening must be different. Compare the roles of Othello and Iago as addressees and overhearers respectively or the politically motivated eavesdropping of Richard Nixon. In circumstances where individuals have been asked to make subjective evaluations or do so as a matter of professional course, I suggest that their listening behaviour might best be thought in a critical sense; they are listening in order to make judgements about others. But what kinds of judgements might individuals make if their listening behavior was not directed in any specific way?

The studies which I have undertaken to date have attempted to investigate the interpretive capacity of participant and non-participant eavesdropper judges without attempting to pre-empt or pre-judge what they might listen for. Three pilot projects using different judges (singly and in pairs) were undertaken with the aim of eliciting as wide a range of judgements as possible.[1] The use of pairings was an attempt to minimise the effect of audience design (Bell, 1984), and hence analyst influence, by encouraging spontaneity of interaction between judges. In these studies, the instructions eavesdroppers were given were made as general as possible in order to try to avoid directing their listening behaviour. Thus judges were simply invited to listen to and comment on various different extracts of talk on the basis that one could not predict the signficance of particular kinds of information, for particular individuals, in advance. All comments which judges gave were noted and form the basic corpus of data for the analysis which follows. On this occasion, I will deal with the comments of non-participant judges only.

In all 30 non-participant judges, fifteen men and fifteen woman of varying ages from the University community at Newcastle participated in the research. They included undergraduate and postgraduate students, as well as academic and ancillary staff. None of the judges had any linguistic training. Each judge listened to segments of talk ranging from 40 seconds duration to five minutes selected from tape-recordings I had made. The selection of segments was problematic because I did not want to provide either too much, or too little material for individuals to listen to. Thus on the one hand, I wanted to avoid overtaxing eavesdroppers' short-term memory, and on the other, I wanted to be certain there would be enough material to prompt some comment rather than none at all. All the recordings were of dialogues to help facilitate speaker recognition for purposes of eavesdropper and analyst reference.

Inspection of the comments revealed that whilst eavesdroppers provided extremely variable responses to the conversational extracts, a great many of them consisted of very similar kinds of declarative statement. Excluding comments about what they could actually hear due to the quality of the recordings, and comments addressed to me directly, two major types of statement were identified. These typically involved a predicator and argument describing some state of affairs about either perceived surface characteristics of the exchanges, or providing information about who the participants were and what they were involved in doing. Some 1,277 descriptive statements of these types were identified and provide the basic data for the discussion which follows.

I have labelled these statement types "observations" and "inferences" respectively, on the model of Hayakawa's (1952, Chapter 3) categorisation of the language of reports, where Hayakawa suggests that the report of what we have seen, heard or felt constitutes the basic symbolic act for purposes of the interchange of information.

On further inspection, "observations" were found to refer to four distinguishable characteristics of the exchanges. These include in ascending order of frequency:
(1) Observations about lexis (e.g. "They use words like bona fide and relationship"; "Words such as junk and rip-offs are used"). There were 14 descriptive statements of this type referring to the participants use of particular words and phrases.
(2) Observations about subject matter. 32 descriptive statements were of this type and these referred to what the participants talked about (e.g. "They talk about a range of topics, black

holes, how to teach, how to get money"; "They talk about student-teacher relations";
(3) Observations about sequential organization. These included descriptions of within-turn verbal phenomena (e.g. "There is lots of hesitancy, uhm, uh and so on"; "There are plenty I means, uhms and you knows") as well as descriptions of dialogic phenomena (e.g "There is some overspeaking"; "It's interspersed with them talking over each other"; "There are gaps when they didn't know what to say"). 93 examples were of this kind.
(4) Observations about prosody. In this category, eavesdroppers offered descriptive statements about a variety of prosodic and paralinguistic phenomena. (e.g. "He was a bit low and mumbly at times"; "She spoke very quickly"; "Her voice went up when she said 'however'"; "The word 'mud' was stressed"). 146 statements of this type were identified.

The frequency and distribution of "observations" in the three studies is given in the following table.

OBSERVATIONS

	LEX.	SUB.	SEQ.	PRO.	TOTAL
Study 1	7	12	23	8	50
Study 2	1	7	37	71	116
Study 3	6	13	33	67	119
TOTAL	14	32	93	146	285

LEX. = Lexis; SUB. = Subject Matter; SEQ. = Sequential Organization; PRO. = Prosody.

The nature of comments such as these are indicative of the ability of particular eavesdroppers to act as naive discourse analysts. Indeed, the descriptions they offered about such textual phenomena could be inspected for pattern in much the same way as ethnomethodological studies try to establish how participants act within their own social worlds. In this sense "observations" could always be verified by checking them against a transcribed record of the exchanges. 285 or 22.3% of the total number of statements were of this kind. Now what about "inferences"?

As far as possible, "observations" exclude "inferences" since "inferences" cannot be verified in the same way, that is, they consist of descriptive statements about matters which non-participant eavesdroppers could not have directly known, nor which participant eavesdroppers could have predicted prior to listening to the exchanges. 992 descriptive statements, or 77.6% of the total number were of this kind. That gives us a ratio of about 3 inferences to every 1 observation. This ratio may be simply be a function of the role in which eavesdroppers are cast, or the way different individuals attended to different extracts. On the other hand, it may reflect the attentional strategies that one might employ in face-to-face encounters since I presume that ordinary languge users are more likely to be concerned with inferencing of the kind Gumperz (1982a; 1982b) suggests than with the particular structure and content of exchanges, or the kinds of pattern recurrently displayed therein.

Three major categories of "inference" were identified. These include, again in ascending order of frequency:
(1) Inferences about setting, in which eavesdroppers not only prescribed the spatial and temporal parameters of the exchanges but also their presumed purpose (e.g. "It's a casual encounter"; "It's a discussion between colleagues, not intimate but relaxed"; "They're just filling in time because they happened to be there. It wasn't for a purpose"). Only 38 statements of this kind were offered.
(2) Inferences about the participants. These provided indexical details about individuals as well as describing the nature of interpersonal and discourse relations (e.g. "The first guy was a Geordie"; "One was older than the other"; "They didn't know each other very well"; "One man is entertaining another to coffee. He plays the role of host and asks all the questions"). A total of 345 statements of this type occured in the corpus.
(3) Inferences about the text. 609 statements of this type were offered giving descriptions of different activity types, or speech events, (e.g. "It's easy chatty conversation"; "It's a discussion between colleagues"; "It's a coffee interim conversation") and also particular communicative strategies and effects within those types or events (e.g. "He wants to do something but isn't sure about it. He was sounding out"; "One of the speakers was probing for advice"; "'Really' is ambiguous. It's not convincing. It had shades in it"; "'Yes' marks understanding rather than agreement"). The frequency and distribution of each type are summarised in the table which follows.

INFERENCES

	SET.	PAR.	TEX.	TOTAL
Study 1	21	75	122	218
Study 2	9	108	288	405
Study 3	8	162	199	369
TOTAL	38	345	609	992

SET. = Setting; PAR. = Participants; TEX. = Text.

We come then to the question of what might have prompted such judgemental and evaluative remarks? "Inferences" could have been and sometimes were based on what had been "observed". Occasionally, the two would be directly linked by eavesdroppers in statements such as, "One of the speakers sounded eager but hesitant. It came from the way he said things, may be his tone"; "They were obviously educated, they used words such as bona fide and relationship". However, whether or not this link was made in any overt sense, we presume that eavesdropper inferences could only have been deduced or based on guesses from necessary forms of social and linguistic knowledge, whether this knowledge was based on real or imagined, interactional experience. In order to begin to determine more precisely what this knowledge might be, we can work backwards as it were from each type of inferential statement. This procedure obviously entails a higher level of inferencing based on the kinds of professional knowledge that analysts necessarily bring to bear in handling their data (cf. the ethnographic approach of Agar, 1980).

In offering comments about setting, eavesdroppers presumably provided answers to the questions of where, when and why the exchanges took place. These answers could only be based on knowledge about the temporal and spatial parameters of speech events. To identify and describe the individuals concerned in these events, eavesdroppers would have to ask who the participants were and what they were like. This would require knowledge not only of individual person prototypes but also social group and relational stereotypes. To then answer the question of what these participants were doing in communicative terms, knowledge of communicative norms and processes would be pre-requisite. A detailed exposition of these sources of knowledge and eavesdropper inferencing in general is presented in McGregor (forthcoming).

CONCLUDING REMARKS

By proceeding in this way with different kinds of talk and different eavesdroppers, we ought to be able to generate and test hypotheses about possible co-ocurrence relationships between eavesdropper judgers and the judgements they make. The following questions could be usefully investigated within controlled experimental work, for example: Is there a relationship between structurally specifiable styles of speech and eavesdropper inferencing? By what criteria are different individuals judged to be communicatively successful and by what kind of judge? What, if any, is the relationship between perceived communicative strategies and effects and the social network ties of different individuals? But to what end might such questions be broached?

The end surely has to do with the original question that we posed. What communicates and what is communicated when language is used in naturally occuring social contexts? Sperber and Wilson

(1986, p.1) list some of the possible answers that have been mooted in response to this question *vis a vis*, "meanings, information, propositions, thoughts, ideas, beliefs, attitudes, emotions" and so on. Because these answers have been put forward by professional analysts does not necessarily make them right. Indeed, as far as ordinary talk is concerned, I would argue that without the kind of supporting evidence we have suggested here, analysts judgements may be both simplified and distorting since they must to an extent be artifactual and influenced by their strong theories.

By using eavesdropper judges, who presumably do not have such strong theories, we can begin to elicit and identify forms of social and communicative knowledge that are not normally verbalized by participants in everyday verbal exchange from the ordinary language users point of view. Morevover, we will have done so in manner that effectively neutralises the observer's paradox, since eavesdropper judges cannot and do not affect speaker style.

NOTE

[1]These studies are variously reported in McGregor (1983; 1984; 1985; 1986a; 1986b; forthcoming).

REFERENCES

Agar, M. (1980) Stories, Background Knowledge and Themes: Problems in the Life History of Narrative. *American Ethnologist*, 7, 223-39.
Bell, A. (1984) Language Style as Audience Design. *Language in Society*, 13, 145-204.
Dore, J. and McDermott, R.P. (1982) Linguistic Indeterminacy and Social Context in Utterance Interpretation. *Language*, 58, 347-398.
Giles, H. and St. Clair, R. (1979) (eds.) *Language and Social Psychology*. Oxford: Blackwell.
Gumperz, J.J. (1982a) *Discourse Strategies*. Cambridge: Cambridge University Press.
Gumperz, J.J. (1982b) *Language and Social Identity*. Cambridge: Cambridge University Press.
Hayakawa, S.I. (1952) *Language in Thought and Action*. London: Allen and Unwin.
Hoenigswald, H.M. (1966) A Proposal for the Study of Folk-Linguistics. In W. Bright (ed.) *Sociolinguistics*, 16-26. The Hague: Mouton.
Kibrik, A.E. (1977) *The Methodology of Field Investigations*. The Hague: Mouton.
Labov, W. (1966) *The Social Stratification of English in New York City*. Washington, D.C.: Center for Applied Linguistics.

McGregor, G. (1983) Listeners' Comments on Conversation. *Language and Communication*, 3, 271-304.
McGregor, G. (1984) Conversation and Communication. *Language and Communication*, 4, 71-83.
McGregor, G. (1985) Lissnty Mi Toknty Yi: A Look at Linguistic Variation from the Listener's Point of View. In H.J. Warkentyne (ed.) *Papers from the Fifth International Conference on Methods in Dialectology*, 285-299. B.C., Canada: University of Victoria.
McGregor, G. (1986a) The Hearer as 'Listener Judge': An Interpretive Sociolinguistic Approach to Utterance Interpretation. In McGregor, G. (ed.) *Language for Hearers*, 153-184. Oxford: Pergamon.
McGregor, G. (1986b) Listening Outside the Participation Framework. In McGregor, G. and White, R.S. (eds.) *The Art of Listening*, 55-72. London: Croom Helm.
McGregor, G. (forthcoming) *Eavesdropping: Studies in Sociolinguistic Inferencing*. University of Newcastle upon Tyne.
Milroy, L. (1987) *Observing and Analysing Natural Language*. Oxford: Blackwell.
Ryan, E.B. and Giles, H. (1982) (eds.) *Attitudes Towards Language Variation*. London: Arnold.
Sperber, D. and Wilson, D. (1986) *Relevance*. Blackwell, Oxford.
Trudgill, P. (1974) *The Social Differentiation of English in Norwich*. Cambridge: Cambridge University Press.

Methods in the Study of Dialect Perceptions

DENNIS R. PRESTON
Eastern Michigan University

The study of folk dialect boundaries has been of limited interest to traditional dialectologists, but more recent concentration on ethnographic and attitudinal language facts makes such studies an important part of determining the boundaries and composition of speech communities.

The earliest studies of folk accounts of dialect differences were based on respondent rankings of surrounding communities.

Figure 1: A perceptual dialect map of Dutch-speaking areas (Rensink 1955, 22)

The little arrow method ('Pfeilchenmethode'), introduced by Weijnen (1968), was used in preparing an elaborate folk map of Dutch-speaking areas (Figure 1). To see how this map was derived, consider actual responses on this map of the Netherlands--West German border (Figure 2).

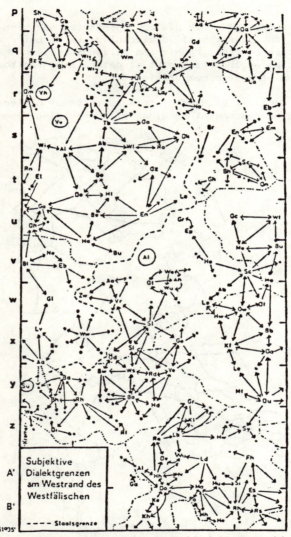

Figure 2: The 'little arrow' method applied to a section of the Netherlands-German border (Kremer 1984, 79)

Each arrow indicates that a respondent from the site at its base has named the site at its head as dialectally the same; two-headed arrows indicate reciprocal judgments. Figure 3 shows how perceptual areas are derived -- a boundary line is drawn through the blank spaces left among the bundles of connecting arrows.

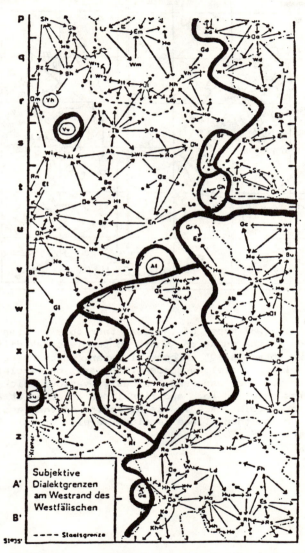

Figure 3: Figure 2 with perceptual speech area borders drawn in

Grootaers (1959) derives folk dialect maps by grouping together sites which share opinions about where significantly different speech is located (Figure 4).[1]

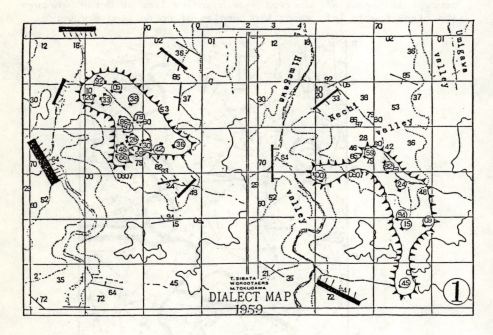

Figure 4: Two maps of the same territory showing patterns of responses to the question 'Where do people speak differently than in your own village?' in coastal Japan. Each number represents a single (older, male) respondent. Squares on circles point in the direction of the responses. Lines of various thicknesses are at the sites referred to, and fine lines attached at angles to the thicker ones point back in the direction of the respondent's home site. The toothed lines enclose areas of similar responses (Grootaers 1959, 359).

Oliveira (1980, summarized in Preston 1985a, Forthcoming.) uses perceived differences and similarities to study the perception of dialects in Rio Grande do Sul (the southernmost state in Brazil) from the point of view of Santa Maria (a city near the geographical center of the state).

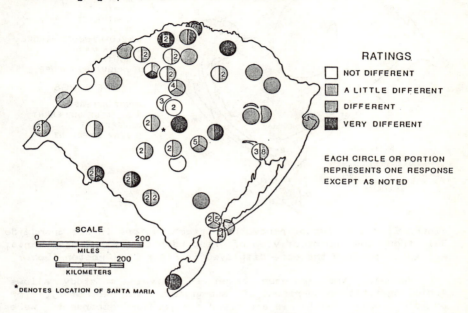

Figure 5: Frequency and type of response to speech difference ratings of sites around Santa Maria, Rio Grande do Sul (Brazil) (data from Oliveira 1982; map from Preston 1985a)

The tally of responses to different sites is represented in Figure 5; Figure 6 shows boundaries extrapolated from those site-referenced data. Oliveira's work is a definite improvement over earlier work in Japan and Europe for several reasons. First, and most importantly, she charts the perception of dialect differences from one site only, gathering the opinions of several respondents from that site. Separate studies from other sites would be necessary before a composite of the entire region from the point of view of a number of representative sites in the region could be prepared. In fact, there is no reason to assume that a composite might evolve from such separate studies. That is, the perception of dialect differences from one site to another might be so radically different that a composite of what representative speakers from an entire area thought about its dialect composition would be too complex to represent in a single map.

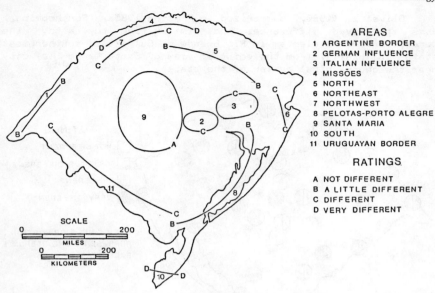

Figure 6: Boundaries of perceptual speech regions in Rio Grande do Sul from the point of view of respondents from Santa Maria; extrapolated from the data displayed in Figure 5 (Preston 1985a)

Second, the approach taken in Oliveira's study allows sociolinguistic comparison of sub-groups. In her study, for example, male and female and older and younger respondents were treated separately, and it was found that both sex and age were important variables in variety perception.[8]

Preston (In Progress) has used this technique, among others, in studying the perception of dialect differences in the United States from the point of view of southernmost Indiana (the area directly across the Ohio River from Louisville, Kentucky -- hereafter SI) and southeastern lower Michigan (the area around Ann Arbor, Michigan -- hereafter SM). That study classifies respondents on the basis of sex, age, and social status and includes smaller substudies of Blacks and Appalachians (in SM only). Since the vast majority of respondents referred to entire states in their rankings, statistical analyses were possible. Figure 7 shows the areas created by a four-way difference ranking by all SI respondents.

The ranking of area differences does not, however, directly provide the outlines of folk dialect regions. In all these approaches, boundaries are extrapolated from clusters of areas of perceived similarity or difference from the point of view of the

Methods in Dialectology

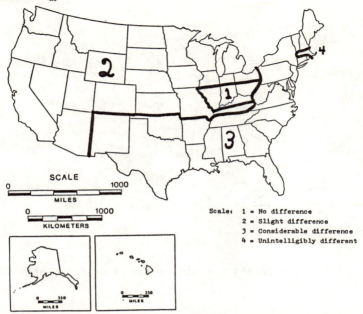

Figure 7: Degrees of speech difference in the United States from the point of view of southern Indiana respondents (Preston In Progress)

respondent's home site (or sites). It is obvious that an area which is different from the respondent's home site might also be different from another site, but these methods would group the two together on the basis of their similar degree of difference from the respondent's home site (as, in fact, the East Coast and South are grouped together in Figure 7). Preston (1982, 1985a, Forthcoming a,b,) introduced a technique for deriving composites of folk dialect boundaries from respondent hand-drawn maps.[3]

Figure 8 is an example of such a respondent map. Given a blank map and unlimited reference to a detailed road map of the area being studied, a respondent is asked to outline and label all the areas where there are 'different ways of speaking' or where 'people talk differently.'[4]

The difficulty with hand drawn maps arises in the preparation of a composite. Since the respondents are permitted to draw lines wherever they see fit, the task of showing where a majority of respondents believe a speech area exists is a difficult one. Figure 9 shows how the speech region 'Northern' was determined from a number of hand-drawn maps procured from young, white, college-enrolled SI respondents.

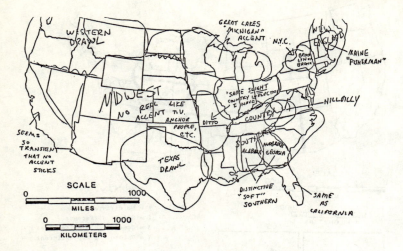

Figure 8: A respondent's hand-drawn map of United States dialect areas

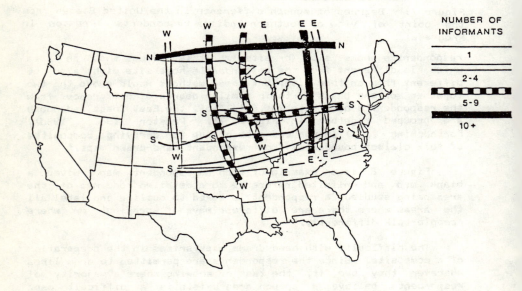

Figure 9: The determination of the 'Northern' speech area for a group of southern Indiana respondents (Preston 1986, 227)

Methods in Dialectology

The rough limits of each map's outline of the region were copied onto a separate map. A tally was kept of where the lines overlapped (or very nearly overlapped). Such overlapping was taken to be similar to the familiar 'bundling of isoglosses' in traditional dialectology, and the bundle representing the greatest number of respondent-drawn boundaries was taken to be a speech area boundary. In Figure 9, for example, it is clear that most respondents believe that the northern limits of 'Northern' are at the US-Canadian border and that the eastern limits bisect Ohio; though the southern limits are a little more complex, the majority agree on the southern boundaries of Michigan and Wisconsin. The only substantial split decision is the western boundary -- about the same number include Minnesota as leave it out. In this case, the final boundary (see Figure 10) was placed through the middle of the state.

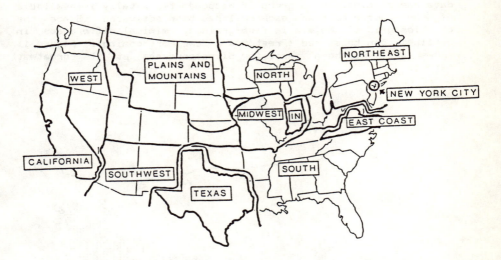

Figure 10: A generalized map of southern Indiana respondents' perceptions of the dialect aras of the United States (Preston 1986, 230)

Though this technique is crude, it is justified, at least in part, by the fact that the original drawings are inexact representations of the respondents' impressions. When each region is derived (as in Figure 9), a general map may be prepared (Figure 10).

The biggest problem in deriving composite maps in this way is not, however, its inexactness. All the sociolinguistic gains reported above for the work by Oliveira are made nearly impossible by such a time-consuming method of map preparation. What is needed is a way to derive best-agreed on boundaries from large numbers of respondent maps and to be able to return to the same data for similar derivations from different subgroups of the population. It is clear that only a quantified approach to these data would allow such sociolinguistically sophisticated treatment. To allow for this, the outline of each respondents' areas were traced onto a digitizing pad. A microcomputer record of the areas outlined was kept along with the complete demographic information about each respondent. These data may be combined according to the demographic profile required by the investigator.

The digitizing process activates each cell which falls within the boundaries of the respondent's hand-drawn area. When these data are combined for a group of respondents, a tally is available of the number of times each cell has been activated. Since the graphics grid of the map is fine-grained, minimal differences in outlines can be stored (Preston and Howe Forthcoming). Figure 11 shows the 'Southern' area for SI respondents at its greatest extent.

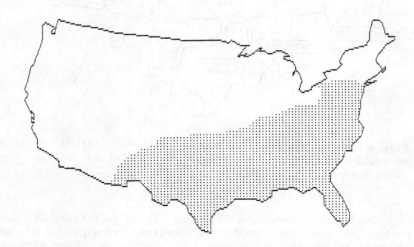

Figure 11: SI respondents' (N = 202) perception of the 'Southern' speech area at its greatest extent (.5%)

Methods in Dialectology

If a cell of the grid were activated even once -- if only one respondent included that cell in his or her representation of 'Southern' -- it is marked in Figure 11. Of course, such a map is not a generalization at all, but an indication of the greatest possible extent of the area 'Southern' for SI respondents. Figure 12 shows the area outlined by cells activated by eighty percent of the respondents. In this case, the opposite effect is produced. A very large number of respondents must agree that the territory represented here is 'Southern,' and one might regard Figure 12 as a 'core' map of the SI perception of 'Southern.'

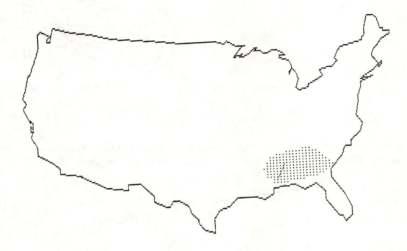

Figure 12: SI respondents' perception of the 'Southern' speech area at an 80% cell activation level; a 'core' area definition

Once the researcher has the ability to look at any group or sub-group at any level of cell activation, the preparation of many different sorts of maps is possible. Figure 13, for example, is a map which displays the twenty, forty, sixty, and eighty percent cell activations of 'Southern' for the entire SI population. Like a geographical contour map, it shows the onset and increasing density of agreement. Additionally, it allows for a careful inspection of agreements of percentage levels. If the contours are widely separated (as they are in Figure 13), one may assume that the folk definition of the region is gradient, reflecting either an indecisiveness about the boundaries of the region or a sensitivity to the gradual onset of features which define it. If,

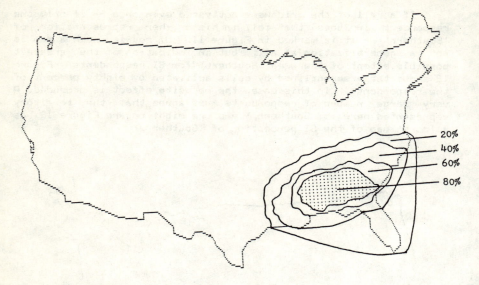

Figure 13: SI respondents' perceptions of the 'Southern' speech area at 20%, 40%, 60%, and 80% cell activation levels

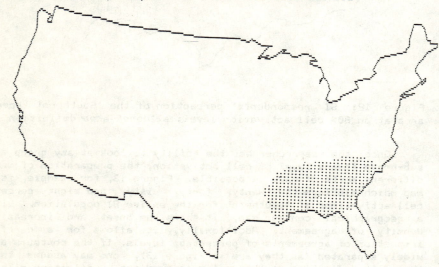

Figure 14: SI respondents' perception of the 'Southern' speech area at a 50% cell activation level

on the other hand, the contours derived from the various percentage levels fall close together, one might assume that the definition of the region is sharp.

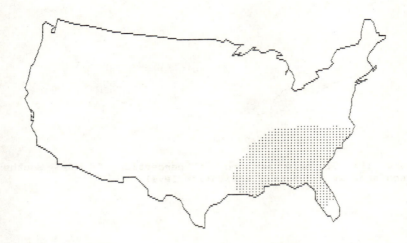

Figure 15: SM respondents' perception of the 'Southern' speech area at a 50% cell activation level

For the construction of general maps, however, it may be satisfactory to take fifty percent cell activation as most representative of the group. Figure 14, for example, shows that level of cell activation for the entire SI group. It contrasts rather strikingly, however, with Figure 15, the most general SM map. Michigan respondents include the 'Inner' and 'Outer' South (or 'South Midlands' and 'South') in their perceptual 'Southern.' Indiana respondents, however, have a more limited view of 'Southern,' due, most likely, to their greater proximity to the area and their own South Midland variety.[6]

Fifty percent activation maps are used as well in the contrast between SI male (Figure 16) and female (Figure 17) perceptions of 'Southern.' The 'Southern' area reaches a little farther north for men than for women, but the western extension for women is considerably greater than that for men. Such contrasts may be sought among classes and ages as well or even for smaller subgroups.

Figure 16: SI male respondents' perception of the 'Southern' speech area at a 50% cell activation level

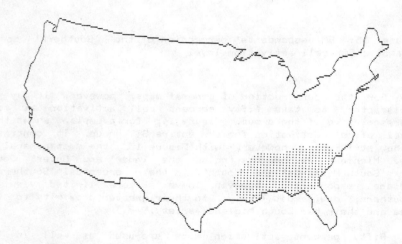

Figure 17: SI female respondents' perception of the 'Southern' speech area at a 50% cell activation level

Methods in Dialectology 387

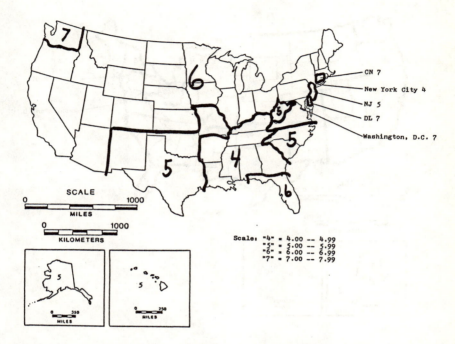

Figure 18: A mean scores 'correct speech' map of the United States from the point of view of SI respondents (1 = least correct, 10 = most correct)

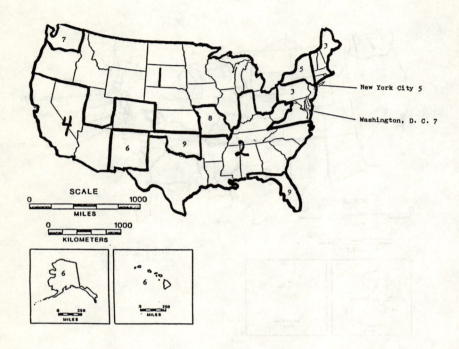

Figure 19: Regional groupings which emerge from a factor analysis of the 'correct speech' ratings of the United States by SI respondents (Figure 18); region #1 is the strongest factor group, #2 the second strongest, and so on

Methods in Dialectology

In addition, these generalizations from hand-drawn maps may be compared to ones derived from other techniques in perceptual dialectology, to ones representing production rather than perception dialect facts, or to ones which represent such nonlinguistic geographically distributed phenomena as perception of regions, residential preference, and so on. For example, the 'Southern' area determined in this generalization of hand-drawn maps (Figure 14) is rather different from the 'Southern' area which emerges from the similarity and difference technique (Figure 7). Of course, many more such contrasts, involving subgroups as well as entire populations, might be made.

In the progress of research on hand-drawn maps, it was noticed, not unexpectedly, that respondents' concerns in outlining areas were often prescriptive rather than descriptive. A method used to determine such facts as desirability of residence or political climate in cultural geography was borrowed and modified to elicit these responses more directly (Preston 1985a, b, In Press, Forthcoming$_{a,b}$, Maciel 1982, Faggion 1982 -- the last two summarized in Preston 1985a and Forthcoming$_a$.). Generally speaking, such research is simple; a respondent is asked to rank a predetermined area along some dimension (e.g., correctness of speech). Experience with earlier studies led to the following practices in the current research (Preston In Progress):

Respondents are asked to rank the areas on a scale or scales (here one to ten for 'correct' and 'pleasant' speech) rather than to rank order all the areas. In Preston 1985a and In Press, respondents reacted negatively to the task of having to rank the fifty states, Washington, D.C., and New York City on a continuous scale of one to fifty-two. They objected not only to the tediousness of the task but to the fact that they could not give the same ranking to several areas. Figure 18 shows the mean ratings for SI respondents to the 'correct' task.

The patterns which emerge from these ratings may be compared to earlier findings, and, of course, more careful internal studies of subgroups might be done on these data alone. Since the data are quantitative, other sorts of statistical tests may be conducted on them. A factor analysis, for example, groups together those states with the greatest similarity of ratings. Figure 19 shows the nine factor groups which emerge from the SI 'correct' data. It is interesting to note that Indiana, kept so distinct from its southern neighbors when a simple comparison of means is used, is here grouped together with the area the same respondents regard as 'Southern' in the other tasks.

Finally, in a research technique carried out for the first time in Preston In Progress (though suggested in Preston 1982, Forthcoming..), respondents are asked to identify what site a regional speaker is from. In this first attempt, it was decided to explore the North-South dimension of United States dialects along a line from Saginaw, Michigan to Dothan, Alabama. First, that line included the home sites of the SI and SM speakers; second, after the complexities of the East Coast are sorted out, the most interesting middle United States dialect boundaries appear to be those which separate the country into northern and southern areas.

Figure 20 is the map which was shown to the respondents while tape recorded voices from the sites marked on it were played in scrambled order. The respondents were instructed to assign each voice to a site. The voices were all male, well-educated speakers between the ages of twenty-seven and fifty-eight, and all were discussing a dialect-related topic in a reasonably casual manner.

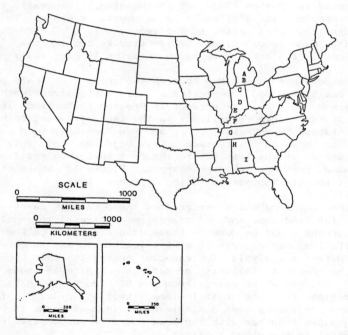

Figure 20: Actual home sites of voices played for respondents

Methods in Dialectology

Mean scores for the association of voices with sites were derived from an arbitrary assignment of numbers one through nine (from south to north) to the sites. The lower the mean score for the voice, the more 'Southern' the respondents thought it was; the higher the mean, the more 'Northern.' Obviously each voice could achieve a 'correct' score by having its mean match its position. The nine areas (from north to south) and the mean scores assigned them by the total SI population were as follows:

9	Saginaw, Michigan	6.59
8	Coldwater, Michigan	6.31
7	South Bend, Indiana	6.38
6	Muncie, Indiana	6.06
5	New Albany, Indiana	5.83
4	Bowling Green, Kentucky	5.09
3	Nashville, Tennessee	3.75
2	Florence, Alabama	2.63
1	Dothan, Alabama	2.45

In a first attempt to analyze these data, it was decided to use a difference of 1.00 or more between means as an indication of a perceived major dialect boundary; a difference of .50 to .99 was taken to be a minor boundary. When this rationale is applied to the above data, Figure 21a emerges. Figure 21b compares a similar treatment of data for the SM population.

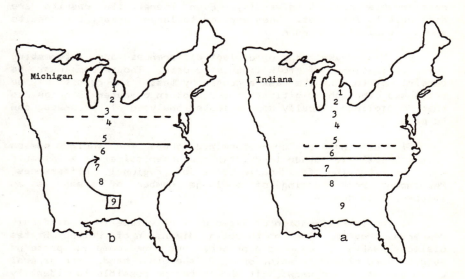

Figure 21: SI (a) and SM (b) north-south speech boundaries based on the distance between the mean scores of the respondents' identification of taped regional voice samples

The box and arrow accompanying area nine in Figure 21b indicates that SM respondents misplaced that voice drastically, assigning it a value which placed it between sites six and seven. On the one hand, that is not so dramatic, since areas six through nine did not contain a major boundary for SM raters. On the other hand, it is precisely between areas six and seven (and seven and eight) where SI raters find major boundaries.

These results clearly invite comparison with different production dialect studies as well as internal evaluation and comparison with other perceptual linguistic data. The SI line between sites seven and eight supports an interpretation of a limited 'Southern' area for these respondents (see Figure 14), and the SM line between sites five and six supports the more extensive 'Southern' region seen by this group (see Figure 15).

In general, then, the following specific techniques have developed in the study of the folk perception of dialect differences:

1) The rating of differences or similarities between the respondent's home area and other sites is perhaps a most limited and confusing way of approaching this question. It may be of most utility in small, densely populated areas which support considerable dialect diversity. Even there, its results are difficult to interpret. When applied to larger areas, the results are disappointing (Figure 7).

2) Hand-drawn maps of dialect differences are interesting characterizations of folk linguistic data. Though one must be careful not to make the task a geography test, the results may be processed through digitization and kept in computer storage so that sociolinguistically sophisticated analyses of responses can be made.

3) Rankings of pre-determined areas for their speech 'correctness' (or other linguistic characteristics) is a valuable way of studying folk caricatures of regional differences. Respondent rank-ordering of a large number of areas is an inappropriate design.

4) The identification of taped dialect voices is a difficult research program. The north-south dimension of United States dialects makes it easy to approach, but more complex patterns suggest more elaborate solutions. On the other hand, once general characteristics are knows, it should become possible to identify the precise signals which respondents base their judgments on. Eventually, research which focuses on the identification of only a few regions may prove more worthwhile.

These studies of the folk perception of dialects are only a small part of the investigation of folk linguistics, or, more elaborately put, the metalinguistics of nonlinguists. It is clear that such findings have value to those who want to understand the composition and boundaries of a speech community. It could be argued, however, that such findings have practical value for educational linguistics and contrastive value for production studies or other linguistic studies which focus on variation (e.g., attitude studies).

In a fuller ethnographic account, the methods described here are best supplemented with extensive respondent interviews (both before and after the tasks) and other participant observer strategies. By themselves, however, they provide a valuable supplement to the study of a speech community's use of and regard for language.

Notes

1   Preston (Forthcoming.,.) provide fuller historical accounts of methods in perceptual or folk dialectology.

2   Oliveira (1982) is a small, pilot study, concentrating on the methods of data collection and map preparation. The resulting composite map should, therefore, be treated with some suspicion.

3   Respondent hand-drawn maps have been used in cultural geography, e.g. Ladd (1967).

4   Naturally, such words as 'dialect' are specifically avoided.

5   And, of course, irregularities in the shapes of the contours may lead to interesting interpretations, particularly those which occur at some percentage levels and not others. Some such irregularities may lead to a suspicion that the subgroups which make up the population are interestingly different.

6   Little interpretation is given here since the focus is on methodology.

References

Grootaers, W. A. (1959) Origin and nature of the subjective boundaries of dialects. *Orbis* 8, 355-84.

Kremer, L. (1984) Die Niederländisch-Deutsch Staatsgrenze als subjective Dialektgrenze. *Grenzen en grensproblemen* (Een bundel studies nitgegeren door het Nedersaksich Instituut van der R. U. Groningen ter gelegenheid van zijn 30-jarig bestaan = *Nedersaksiche Studies* 7, zugleich: Driemaandelijkse Bladen 36), pp. 76-83.

Ladd, F. (1967) A note on 'The world across the street.' *Harvard Graduate School of Education Association Bulletin* 12, 47-8.

Maciel, M. I. P. (1982) O Portoalegrense e os falares do Rio Grande do Sul. Seminar paper. Porto Alegre: Universidade Federal do Rio Grande do Sul. (Summarized in Preston 1985a, Forthcoming.

Oliveira do Canto, M. L. (1982) Atitude de pessoas que moram em Santa Maria com relacão a fala de outras regiõs de estado. Seminar paper. Porto Alegre: Universidade Federal do Rio Grande do Sul. (Summarized in Preston 1985a, Forthcoming.).

Preston, D. R. 1982. Perceptual dialectology: mental maps of United States dialects from a Hawaiian perspective. *Working Papers in Linguistics* (University of Hawaii), 14, 5-49.

---- (1985a) Mental maps of language distribution in Rio Grande do Sul (Brazil). *The Geographical Bulletin* 27, 46-64.

---- (1985b) Southern Indiana perceptions of 'Correct' and 'Pleasant' speech. In H. J. Warkentyne (ed.) *Methods/Méthodes V* (Papers from the Fifth International Conference on Methods in Dialectology), Victoria, British Columbia: Department of Linguistics, University of Victoria, pp. 387-411.

---- (1986) Five visions of America. *Language in Society*, 15, 221-40.

---- (In Press) The nicest English is in Indiana. Festschrift for W. Bzdęga. Poznań, Poland: Adam Mickiewicz University Press.

---- (Forthcoming.) *The Perception of Language Differences.* Dordrecht: Foris.

Preston, D. R. (Forthcoming.) The methods of perceptual dialectology. Proceedings of the fourteenth NWAV (New Ways of Analyzing Variation) Meeting, ed. by R. Fasold, Georgetown University.

---- (In Progress) *Perceptual Dialectology: Folk Views of Dialects in the United States.* A study of the folk perceptions of United States dialects from southern Indiana and southeastern Michigan; supported by the National Science Foundation.

---- and Howe, G. (Forthcoming) Computerized generalizations of mental maps. Proceedings of the fifteenth NWAV (New Ways of Analyzing Variation) conference, ed. by J. Rickford, Stanford University.

Rensink, W. G. (1955) Dialectindeling naar opgaven van medewerkers. *Mededelingen der centrale commissie voor onderzoek van het nederlande volkseigen*, 7, 20-3.

Weijnen, A. (1968) Zum wert subjektiver Dialektgrenzen. *Lingua*, 21, 594-96.

Informants' Response Ratings in the
Survey of English Dialects

EDGAR W. SCHNEIDER
University of Bamberg

INTRODUCTION

Dialect atlas projects have always been carried out with specific aims in mind - commonly to determine the regional distribution of speech forms and the dialectal division of an area, or - explicitly in the case of the <u>Survey of English Dialects</u> (SED) - to establish regional reflexes of historical processes or stages in the development of a language. Yet in addition to the systematically collected "core data" (responses to the questionnaire items at selected localities), they have normally yielded all sorts of further and more or less incidental material not directly sought for or elicited. In the editing process, such information is made publicly accessible to varying extents, but much of it frequently seems to be eliminated and ignored. I would like to call for a more conscious consideration of such data, for it may permit the posing of additional and different kinds of questions which may be of general linguistic interest and relevance. Let me offer you a brief personal credo. I think dialectology should not be content with finding localisms or archaisms, and not even with establishing linguistic boundaries (which is problematic enough anyway, both theoretically and methodologically). What fascinates me about dialects is the fact that this is where language exists in its purest form - where it operates most naturally, without the interference of prescriptive or logical considerations. Therefore, the study of dialects should contribute to our overall understanding of how human language is organized, and the collection and interpretation of dialect data should take that position into account whenever possible.

For this paper, I have chosen to analyse a sub-set of such rather marginal information in the SED from this perspective, namely informants' ratings and qualifications of their own responses. Quite frequently, the SED informants not only responded to the question posed to them but also added that this response or one of the responses given was "older", "better", "less frequently used", "more refined", and the like. These ratings may indirectly offer us some insights into the structure of the dialectal lexicon, into the nature of the dialect speakers' pragmatic and linguistic competence, also into their awareness of ongoing lexical change.

To my knowledge, these ratings, which in the "Basic Materials" are added to the responses in square brackets, have not received any attention in interpretive studies hitherto. In the conception of the SED project, they seem to have been envisaged and regarded as an intrinsic part of the responses, but allowed for only marginally. In the project's <u>Introduction</u>, Harold Orton acknowledges their existence twice, but only in passing. First, when describing the special sheets for the field recordings, he explains: "The left side was reserved for the informant's responses and for any remarks or explanations about them." (17). Second, the locality entries are said to comprise "lastly, enclosed within square brackets, any relevant <u>explanatory information</u> or <u>illustrative material</u>". (24) In the <u>Linguistic Atlas of England</u>, the existence of "critical observations by informants on the currency or obsolescence of the response" as part of the "incidental material" is mentioned (Orton, Sanderson and Widdowson, 1978; Introduction, unpaged). Otherwise, these utterances have remained unnoticed and have not been taken into consideration. My paper is based upon an exhaustive listing of the ratings added to the responses in Book I "The Farm", i.e. - quantitatively - about one-ninth of the whole "Basic Materials". This soon turned out to yield more than sufficient material for the present purpose and scope, and I assume - without any indications to the contrary - that it is basically representative of the whole data set. I am not considering semantic distinctions, which are also quite frequently indicated in the same fashion and concern the size, shape, material or purpose of some devices. For regional reference, I use the county structure and designations plus the respective locality numbers as given in the Basic Materials of the SED. I will describe and comment on - first - the quantitative and qualitative incidence of the ratings given, and - second - some linguistic patterns and observations concerning the distributions of the ratings found in this corpus.

INCIDENCE

Even after having worked with the SED for years, I was surprised by the extraordinary frequency and variety of these qualifications once I actually worked out their incidence. I counted a total of 969 tokens, which, related to the corpus size of 313 localities and 107 questions in Book I (I.6.4.a and b were treated separately) means that 2.89 per cent of all responses, on the average, receive an additional rating. This strikes me as quite high considering that the information is fully volunteered and apparently not sought for. These tokens are distributed unevenly over 79 different types of ratings, even with full synonyms (such as "commoner" and "more common") taken together. Some of these are idiosyncratic, a few may be haphazard, and many are near (though not full) synonyms, but the number and variety of expressions is still impressive and indicates the fine grading and complexity of speakers' lexical knowledge. Slightly more than half of these qualifications (42, to be exact) occur only once. On the other hand, some are exceptionally frequent. This applies above all to "older", which was recorded 425 times, i.e. 43.9 % of all tokens. Also, "preferred" accounts for another 21.5 %, with 208 instances in the corpus. At some distance, a few more adjectives and adverbs are quite frequent, namely "modern" (62 occurrences, i.e. 6.4 %), "usual(ly)" (50; 5.2 %), "old" (34; 3.5 %), and "rare" (26; 2.7 %). The frequency of the others ranges up to 11.

As far as their regional distribution is concerned, the analysis reveals that the ratings are generally scattered over the whole area, without any significant concentrations in particular counties or localities. Thus, they are not due to the eagerness or the carefulness of some particular informants, but obviously reflect the intrinsic subtlety of dialect speakers' lexical competence. Also, the ratings are not restricted to only a sub-set of the questions. Naturally, this distribution varies, i.e. some attract more and others fewer such specifications, but there is only a single question out of the 107 in Book I which has no such qualification whatsoever (viz. I.9.5. 'WHEEL*'). Alternatively, some questions have an extraordinary number of dialectal variants which are marked as "older" as opposed to the standard key-word, which is obviously gaining ground. Examples are I.1.10 'PADDOCK', I.2.3 'COWMAN', I.9.4 'SHAFTS' and I.9.10 'TIRE'. As to the distribution over linguistic forms, too many are affected to permit a listing of reasonable length, and again, many are idiosyncratic. Nonetheless, some consistent patterns and concentrations which are more or less limited will be mentioned below in the interpretive discussions.

According to the kind of meaning conveyed, the types of response ratings can be categorized into a few major semantic classes. These concern the presumed age of words or forms, their frequency of usage, stylistic evaluation, regional or technical restrictedness, and finally their semantic status in comparison with other items.

Qualifications concerning the "age" comprise 20 different types, amongst them some of the most frequent ones, namely "older", "modern", and "old". Their interpretation demands a brief comment but is basically unproblematic. It seems clear that a dialect speaker's reference to the age of an item cannot be understood in the literal sense, i.e. concerning the etymological age or period of integration of a word in the English vocabulary. Rather, these ratings indicate the fact that speakers consciously notice lexical change in the course of time, presumably over generation distances. Thus, qualifications such as "used by the very old"[1], "used by older farmers", "formerly used" (3) and "in old days"

(2) indicate more precisely what is meant than somewhat general terms such as "older" (425), "old" (34), etc. Obviously, the dimension of age permits a binary subclassification into "older" or, presumably, obsolescent forms and "more recent", innovative ones, with the possibility of further internal gradings. The first group comprises at its extreme end the rating of a form as "obsolete" (6; 2 of these were "suggested") or "older; almost extinct". The other qualifications in this group, in addition to the above-mentioned, are "oldest" (2), "very old" (7), and, more reluctantly, "probably older" (6) or even "possibly older". In the alternative group, we have "modern" (62), "more modern" (8), "more recent" (4), "later", "used today", "used nowadays", "new word", and "very modern". On the whole, this reflects a subtle awareness of ongoing lexical change.

The second class, which concerns indications of a form's frequency of usage, again permits a rough arrangement along a continuum between two extreme ends. These forms, which are self-explanatory, are: "always" (2), "most usual", "most common / commonest" (5), "used more often", "more usual" (7), "commoner / more common" (9), "usual(ly)" (50), "sometimes", "rarer", "less common" (3), "less frequent" (2), "less usual" (2), "less often", "less used", "little used", "occasional", "seldom", "not normally used", "not usually used", "rarely used" (3), "rare" (26), "infrequent", "unusual", "not usual", "very rare" (5) and "not used" (11).

Class 3 consists of stylistic evaluations and indicates that the informants are fully aware of the fact that some of their words are explicitly "dialectal" while others are "more refined", and the like; in addition to this dichotomic distinction, further, fairly subtle qualifications are introduced. Relative proximity to the linguistic standard is indicated by "polite" (3), "the proper name" (3), "proper" (2), "used in 'careful speech'", "refined", "more polite" (2), "more refined", and, with an additional overtone, "'posh' word". "Familiarly" (2, both in 32W) expresses a positive attitude towards a dialectal term. "More genuine" (2, both at 6Y-9) evaluates dialect words positively, while "dialectal" and "more dialectal" remain neutral in that respect. The other ratings seem to indicate consciousness of the stigma of dialect forms - less clearly so with "broader" (4) and "broadest", very obviously in the case of "least acceptable", and, with an obvious awareness of the word's vulgarity in the standard, "rougher" (for cow-piss, I.3.10., 3Du-6). Somewhat outside this scale, a word may be rated as a "nickname" (4; 3 of these, in different regions, concern (old) shep, I.2.1.), as "facetious", or, in contrast, as "not jocular".

A few other ratings are related to the latter group but pose serious problems because their interpretation is unclear. These are "better" (2), "best" (2), also "more natural" and "most natural" and, primarily, the form second in the frequency ranking, "preferred" (208). Preference is a highly subjective attitude unless the underlying value system is uniform or generally known. This, however, is not the case here, for we know that in linguistic matters, and especially with respect to dialectal usage, two norm systems, which are positively evaluated in certain contexts and negatively in others, are in conflict: the dialectal speech norm to express group solidarity, and the standard norm that is associated with education and an upper class orientation. Which value system underlies an individual response in a particular case cannot be determined with certainty. Closer scrutiny of the evidence reveals that for the majority of informants the "preferred" form is the more strongly dialectal one, as not infrequently this rating co-occurs with "older" (e.g. at I.2.3, 33Brk-3; I.5.4, 31So-10; I.10.2, 9Nt-2; and others), or, in one case, it contrasts with an alternative form at the same locality which is labelled "proper" (I.7.4, 4We-1). On the other hand, the reverse may also be the case, i.e. the form which is "preferred" competes with an alternative one which is marked as "older" (I.3.6, 4OSx-6).

The items in the remaining two clases are few but interesting because they introduce new facets of lexical knowledge. First, there are two regional references to areas other than the informant's familiar surroundings. The informant at 4OSx-2 believes that the pronunciation /æmiz/ rather than the local /$\varepsilon_l$mz/ for 'HAMES*' (I.5.4) is typical of Surrey (incidentally, he is wrong – Surrey also has the diphthong), and the form close for 'FIELD' (I.1.1) is "regarded as Scots" (which it is, but not exclusively) by the informant at 1Nb-1. In a similar vein, the word mallet (I.7.5) is recognized as a technical term ("used by joiner/carpenter") independently by five speakers in the eastern region (as opposed to beetle, which is always given as an alternative response). Second, a few expressions relate to the lexico-semantic status of a given word. "No special name" suggests that the form offered is a semantically general hypernym. Similarly, "special term" and, in contrast, "general term" (both used at the same locality – I.1.10, 21Nf-3) also express a hyponymic relationship between the two items marked in this way. The information "both mean the same" characterizes two lexemes as synonyms, and "another name" also identifies a word as a synonym of the second response, while "no other word" indicates the lack of such a form and the semantically unchallenged functional range of the response, in terms of the lexical field concept.

DISTRIBUTION: SOME PATTERNS AND OBSERVATIONS

Before interpreting specifically linguistic patterns in the response ratings, a word of caution is necessary concerning the distinction between the reference to a linguistic item and to the extralinguistic subject matter. In some cases, it is very obvious and in others it seems reasonable to assume that the qualification given relates not to the word but to the thing denoted by it. In particular, this concerns the word "modern" with respect to newly-introduced techniques and devices in farming, such as the cow-through (I.3.6, 6Y-30), which replaced an earlier wooden cow-kit; the gangway (I.3.7,1Nb-7), also called alley-way (1Nb-4), passage (19Hu-2) or hay-hole (26Bk-2), as there were "none in older buildings" (cf. 26Bk-2); or the 'CESS-POOL' (I.3.11), labelled tank (5La-3, 250-2, 250-6), sock-tank (7Ch-6), sock-pits (7Ch-6), cistern (17Wa-1), or cess-pit-tank (24Gl-6), which was only recently introduced (e.g. "formerly ran out into strawyard", 250-2). Similarly, the object rather than the word is probably meant when the suggested item straw-yard (I.1.9) is qualified as "very rare" at 5La-7; when side-ladders (I.10.6) are said to be "not used" at 29Ess-11; when a bar for "TETHERING-STAKE' (I.3.3) is called "modern", with the additional comment "formerly chained to ring on trough" (17Wa-6), and in other cases as well (although their number constitutes a very small minority).

As to the purely linguistic evaluations, two less important categories must be mentioned before dealing with the really interesting systematic qualifications. First, many of the ratings are idiosyncratic. For example, when bullock-yard is called "most common" (I.1.3, 29Ess-13), when grip for 'DRAIN' (I.3.8) is "preferred" by the speaker at 35K-3, and when garthy for the 'COW-MAN' (I.2.3) is offered as a "nickname" (9Nt-1), and we have no comparable statements nearby in any of these cases, little of general relevance is to be gained from these ratings - although they may of course be invaluable for a detailed study of the items concerned. Such individual qualifications may even come as a surprise, e.g. when hen-house (I.1.6), which is otherwise used generally in the area, is regarded as "rare" at 29Ess-2.

Second, there are even some cases when ratings of related responses found in neighbouring localities appear to be conflicting. The same form may receive different qualifications in an area. For example, pig-cree (I.1.5 'PIGSTY') is considered "older" at 3Du-2 but "more modern" at 3Du-4; stand (I.3.1 'STALL') is "older" at 18Nth-1 but "more recent" at 26Bk-2; dray (I.9.2 'WAGON') is rated "older" at 7Ch-6 but "modern" at 8Db-2. In other cases, alternative items are rated identically or similarly, e.g. both shepherd and herd (I.2.1 'SHEPHERD') as "(probably) older" in 1Nb; twine and string (I.7.3 'STRING', contrasted with the other form) as "older" at 1Nb-4 and 2Cu-6, respectively; swingletree and tawtree (I.8.3 'SWINGLETREE') as "older", opposed to each other, at 7Ch-6 and 11Sa-8; dig and delve (I.7.8 'DIG') as "more modern" in 2Cu, 3Du and 5La; rods and shafts (I.9.4 'SHAFTS') as "preferred" in 35K; etc. Even at the same locality, ratings may remain unclear, as at 6Y-14, where two variant pronunciations of cow-man (I.2.3) are offered, one being "preferred" and the other one "more usual". In all these cases, it is impossible to determine whether these patterns reflect very subtle local distributions or are due to erroneous opinions on the part of one of the informants.

In the majority of cases, however, the ratings given appear to be adequate, as can be deduced mainly from their internal consistency and systematicity, or from other considerations. Although the stylistic value and the frequency of words as well as other parameters may be affected, most of these distributions concern the progressive obsolescence of dialect words and the intrusion or modern expressions, often standard words. Again, this category can be divided into three sub-groups according to their distributional patterns: alternative qualifications at single localities, unique ratings supported by other considerations, and similar ratings at several localities within an area.

In cases belonging to the first of these groups, several responses are offered at the same locality, each is qualified in some way, and the relationship of these qualifications is consistent insofar as they normally represent opposite ends of the same scale. For example, at 6Y-10 we find two pronunciations of fold-yard (I.1.3 'FARMYARD'), one (/faɒldjaːd/) considered "older", the other one (/fɔɒldjaːd/) "modern". At 5La-8, the word hen-house (I.1.6 'HEN-HOUSE') is rated as "older", while hen-cote is "more refined", i.e. in this case the parameters of age and style coincide. For the same question, the frequency of two pronunciations of hen-house ("very rare" vs. "more common") is compared at 29Ess-8. A threefold distinction is offered with reference to question I.1.5 'PIGSTY' at 39Ha-4: hoghouse is "old", pigsty is unmarked, and piggery is "modern". Similarly, concerning the stylistic value of variants of 'HEN-HOUSE' (I.1.6) at 6Y-30, hen-hut is not qualified, while hen-cote is said to be "broader" and hen-hole "broadest".

The second group comprises primarily local dialect words which have a limited distribution and are obviously on the point of becoming extinct, being both restricted to generally no more than a single occurrence in the area and marked as "older" (or the like) by the respective informant. Examples of this pattern are: farm-garth (I.1.3 'FARMYARD', 1Nb-7); court-yard (I.1.3, 25O-3); barton (I.1.3, 38Do-5; three more occurrences in the South); pigeon-pen (I.1.7 'DOVE-COTE, 12St-11); hoppet (I.1.10, 29Ess-12; twice more in 29Ess); butt (I.1.10, 39Ha-7); sheep-man (I.2.1, 31So-3); clod-hopper (I.2.2 'CARTMAN', 15He-7); baiseler (I.2.3, 1Nb-5); cow-banger (I.2.3, 6Y-26), bungey (I.2.3, 8Db-7; also twice in 12St); dummock-man (I.2.3, 40Sx-3); stall-tree (I.3.3

'TETHERING-STAKE', 31So-8); hop-spud (I.3.13 'MUCK-FORK', 40Sx-4); haft (I.3.16 'HANDLE', 10L-10); lease (I.6.1 'TEAM', 29Ess-7); scale it (I.7.1 'WEIGH IT', 33Brk-3); thills (I.9.4 'SHAFTS', 21Nf -11). In addition, parallel reactions by a single informant to parallel questions can be mentioned here. The speaker at 35K-2 "prefers" both near-horse (I.6.4a) and off-horse (I.6.4b) to his alternatives left-hand-horse and right-hand-horse; the one at 33 Brk-2 has near and off for both concepts but qualifies both as "rare".

Finally, the most comprehensive group consists of fairly unanimous judgements of certain words or distributions of a few items at several localities within a larger area. Thus, we can safely assume that these are cases where the respective qualifications are appropriate and inherent elements of the speech community's lexical knowledge, being widely shared by many dialect speakers. Presumably obsolescent forms which are more or less frequently and consistently marked as "older" or "old" (etc.) are close (I.1.1. 'FIELD'), as opposed to field, in 6Y, 9Nt and 10L; rick-yard, (I.1.4), gradually replaced by the key-word 'STACK-YARD' in 8Db and 11Sa; close in the North, West, and East and plat in the South (I.1.10), mostly in contrast with the key-word 'PADDOCK'; wagoner (I.2.2 'CARTMAN') in the West; fogger (I.2.3) in 25O and 33Brk; the pronunciations /jamz/ rather than /ɛəmz/ in 6Y, /oɷmz/ rather than /eɪmz/ in the West, and /e·əmz/ rather than /eɪmz/ in the East (I.5.4 'HAMES'); beetle (I.7.5 'MALLET') primarily in the South; spittle in contrast with the key-word (I.7.6 'SPADE') in the West; tine and (only in the South) spean (I.7.10 'PRONG'); steal (I.7.12 'SHAFT) in the North, West, and East; stee (I.7.14) vs. standard 'LADDER' (which is also rated as "not used", "rare", or "the proper name") primarily in the North; round (I.7.15 'RUNG') in the West and South; and shut-knife rather than pocket-knife in 21Nf (I.7.18 'KNIFE'). Sometimes the standard words which are becoming more common are explicitly rated "modern" or similarly, such as farm-labourer (I.2.4) in the North, partition (I.3.2) in the West, bin (I.7.4), and share (I.8.7) in 6Y. Furthermore, not only the age of words is rated so unanimously. Informants in the South, in particular in 32W, agree that prongs (I.7.9 'FORKS'), not the key-word, is used "usually" or even "always", and those in the East regard mallet (I.7.5) as a technical term and beetle as the normal expression. Speakers also know that cow-piss (I.3.10) is "rougher" and cow's water "more polite" but disagree on which is "(more) usual"; one speaker even claims that he has "no other word" than water.

Etymological considerations have yielded little of interest. Words of various etymologies occur, of course; e.g., from those found to be disappearing, stee is probably from Scandinavian, wagoner is from Dutch, and close 'field' is from French (Orton and

Wright, 1974). However, most of the words affected are of native origin, and this factor does not play a significant role in this context.

CONCLUSION

The analysis of informants' response ratings has revealed the existence of fairly subtle qualifications and detailed opinions on lexical items in the minds of the English dialect speakers interviewed for the SED; it has shown that the English dialectal vocabulary is far from being a homogeneous set of independent lexical items of equal standing. In particular, the ongoing process of lexical change, which is primarily the replacement of dialect words by standard lexemes, and the fact that dialect speakers are highly aware of this process could be demonstrated very clearly. Thus, I conclude that this material is certainly relevant and useful for dialectological and linguistic research, though with some natural limitations. For example, a more systematic procedure in the elicitation and definition of the response ratings would have been desirable from this point of view. Generally, my conclusion is that in large-scale dialectological projects as much of the original data as possible should be made accessible to the potential user to permit not only the traditional types of analyses but also innovative approaches and the posing of questions that could otherwise not be asked.

NOTE

1) Following a form, its frequency in the corpus is indicated, unless it occurs only once.

REFERENCES

Orton, H. (1962) Survey of English Dialects (A). Introduction. Leeds: E.J. Arnold.
Orton, H. and W. J. Halliday (eds) (1962) Survey of English Dialects (B). The Basic Material. Vol. I: The Six Northern Counties and the Isle of Man. Part I. Leeds: E.J. Arnold.
Orton, H. and M. V. Barry (eds) (1969) Survey of English Dialects (B). The Basic Material. Vol. II: The West Midland Counties. Part I. Leeds: E.J. Arnold.
Orton, H. and Ph. M. Tilling (eds) (1969) Survey of English Dialects (B). The Basic Material. Vol. III: The East Midland Counties and East Anglia. Part I. Leeds: E.J. Arnold.
Orton, H. and M. F. Wakelin (eds) (1967) Survey of English Dialects (B). The Basic Material. Vol. IV: The Southern Counties. Part I. Leeds: E.J. Arnold.

Orton, H. and N. Wright (1974) _A Word Geography of England._ London, New York, San Francisco: Seminar Press.
Orton, H., S. Sanderson and J. Widdowson (1978) _The Linguistic Atlas of England._ London: Croom Helm.

Accent and Identity

GARY NEAL UNDERWOOD
The University of Texas at Austin

Through the years, many linguists have made incidental reference to the concepts of identity and identification to explain socially patterned language variation. For example, in a discussion of the significance of conflicting value systems with respect to the status of variants in a language, Labov (1964, p. 94) commented, 'Identification with the class of people that includes one's friends and family is a powerful factor in explaining linguistic behavior.' Others have speculated about the importance of one's identification in learning a second language. Reflecting on the success of Americans in their attempts to learn second languages in order to conduct business in Latin America, Whyte and Homberg (1965, p. 13) suspected that identification might be more important than aptitude:

> A strong psychological identification with other people and culture may more than make up for below average learning ability whereas a man of superior language ability may fail to make the necessary psychological identification and make poor progress.

Casual statements such as these about speakers' identification with groups have been paralleled by equally glib remarks about the use of language to identify groups. Typical is this declaration by Hertzler (1965, p. 40):

> The function of language as a means of *group* [his emphasis] identification is important from the sociological point of view. He who speaks a language can be located socially as to the group or groups to which he belongs. By means of it, others can tell some of his characteristics, whether he is a friend or foe, whether he is an 'in-group' or 'out-group' person.

Despite an awareness of identity as an important factor in sociolinguistics, it has tended to be peripheral to the interests of linguists.

It was left, therefore, to the British creolist, Robert Le Page, to propose a theory of language acquisition based upon the concept of identity. Le Page developed his Theory of Acts of Identity while studying the language of children in multilingual communities in a 'state of flux' in which children make clear choices from among competing language systems. In his attempt to explain how these children go about acquiring their language rather than another one spoken in their community, Le Page (1974, p. 2) reasoned that individuals search for and create for themselves their own senses of identity. The linguistic consequences are, according to Le Page, that

> each individual creates the systems for his verbal behaviour so that they shall resemble those of the group or groups with which from time to time he may wish to be identified....

Further, Le Page has added four riders to his theory, for he reckons that one's linguistic achievement is constrained by whether

(a) he can identify the groups
(b) he has the opportunity and ability to observe and analyse their behavioural systems
(c) his motivation is sufficiently strong to impel him to choose, and to adapt his behaviour accordingly
(d) he is still able to adapt his behaviour.

Although Le Page developed his Theory of Acts of Identity in Belize, where children may acquire English, Spanish, an indigenous Indian language, or Belize Creole English as their dominant or only language, he has also tested that theory in St. Lucia, Singapore, and West Indian communities in England. While his own research has not been concerned with either monolingual communities or intralanguage choices, Le Page states that he intends for his theory to be 'universally applicable' (Le Page and Tabouret-Keller, 1985, p. 181; see also Le Page, 1968, 1975, 1978, 1986; and Le Page et al., 1974). Indeed, he interprets the evidence of social dialect research by Labov, Peter Trudgill, and Lesley Milroy as support for his theory (Le Page and Tabouret-Keller, 1985, p. 84), even though the studies by these three people have not been designed to test Le Page's hypothesis.

Trudgill appears to have been the first sociolinguist to apply Le Page's Theory of Acts of Identity to the study of accent variation within a single language. In his chapter, 'Acts of conflicting identity: The sociolinguistics of British pop-song pronunciation', Trudgill (1984) utilized Le Page's theory to provide a post hoc explanation of why British rock singers modified their pronunciation while singing to sound more like Americans. While Le Page's theory provided insightful explanations for the behavior of the Beatles, the Rolling Stones, Dire Straits, and other British rock vocalists, Trudgill's work still did not provide the desired test of the Le Page hypothesis.

In contrast to Trudgill's study, on-going research begun at The University of Texas at Austin in 1984 is designed expressly to test the Theory of Acts of Identity with phonological variation within a single language.[1] Of general interest is a better understanding of why people--especially those who are socially and geographically mobile--develop particular accents instead of others that are also available to them in their linguistic milieu. Specifically, Le Page's theory is proposed to explain why some native Texans talk with a 'Texas accent' and others do not, and why some some accents of Texans are deemed to be 'stronger' than others. Within the context of the Le Page theory, it is hypothesized that a speaker's Texas accent bears a direct relationship to that person's sense of identity as a Texan. This claim is significantly different, it should be stressed, from asserting that the accent is an indicator, marker, or stereotype (see, e.g. Labov 1964, p. 102) of speakers who are assigned by objective criteria to a particular social category.

Using Le Page's theory to account for variation in the pronunciation of English by Texans presents two immediate problems, one inherent in the notion of identity and the other created by the subtle differences between accents in contrast to differences between two clearly distinct languages.

Le Page and the other linguists who have noted the significance of identity on one's language have not specified exactly what the concept of identity entails. When used by linguists, identity is at best a vague concept which is closely related to, if not synonymous with, 'membership' or 'association'. This would explain how Le Page interprets the findings of Labov, Trudgill, and Milroy as support for his theory when Milroy's research would appear to others to be quite different from that of Labov or Trudgill, and, furthermore, the hypotheses of all three would seem to be in clear conflict with Le Page's. Labov and Trudgill have typically analyzed linguistic variants in terms of social grouping. Labov (1966, p. 210), for example, has argued that studying variation in language with respect to membership in social groups 'seems more fundamental and more closely tied to the genesis of linguistic differentiation.' Continuing, Labov specifically argues that 'the social group of peers in which a speaker spends his preadolescent years is the main force in establishing his linguistic pattern.' Labov (1966, p. 272) attributes, therefore, one's basic linguistic patterns to one's 'sex, ethnic group, and parental background' with the recognition that later in life one's speech is influenced by membership in groups based upon education, occupation, and income. In contrast to Labov's stress of the importance of group membership, Milroy's analysis of patterned variation in Belfast English (Milroy, 1980), for example, is not in terms of membership in groups but in terms of networks of social interaction (i.e., association or affiliation). At one point Le Page (1978, p. 17) comes close to equating identity with membership in a group, for he proposes that, as one matures, a person evaluates various groups according to

a) his wish to be identified with them
b) his assessment, in light of the cues they give him, of his chance of being accepted by them
c) his wish to retain a separate identity for himself.

Thus, it would appear that Le Page, like Labov and others, is simply reaffirming a point of view expressed over a half-century ago by Edward Sapir. Sapir (1933, p. 64) argued that certain linguistic features were shared by select individuals to symbolize their belonging to an 'unorganized but psychologically real' group and that members of the group intuitively perceived each other's membership by those liguistic features. In simple terms, according to Sapir, '"He talks like us" is equivalent to saying "He is one of us."'

If identity is simply another term for group membership and affiliation, then Le Page's theory would be not merely unoriginal but incapable of providing new, insightful accounts for language behavior. However, it should be noted that in the statement by Whyte and Homberg which was quoted in the opening paragraph *identification with a group* is clearly different from *membership in a group*. Although Whyte and Homberg failed to explain precisely what they meant by 'identification', their use of the word suggests the existence of a clear and meaningful concept of identity which can give Le Page's theory special significance.

Fortunately, this desired concept of identity is provided by field theory in social psychology, as formulated by Kurt Lewin (1951) and elaborated by John Shelton Reed (1983). As explained by Reed (1983, p. 9),

> to say that people *identify* [his emphasis] with a group....means simply that the group has a strong positive valence [i.e., sum of forces of attraction or repulsion] for them. This implies that the group exists cognitively for them, and it usually means that they will belong to it, although the possibility exists that someone can identify with a group that he does not belong to--for instance, because he lacks the prerequisites or sees the group as closed to him--just as someone can fail to identify with a group that he does belong to but believes he cannot leave.

In addition to making a clear distinction between identification with a group and membership in it, Reed (1983, p. 64) is careful to point out that identification is an emotional construct. Unlike consciousness, which is cognitive, one's identification with a group is in simple terms a feeling of closeness to members of that group. Consequently, it is possible to determine not only one's identification with a group apart from one's membership or non-membership in that group but also to measure the strength of that identification on a linear scale.[2]

With the incorporation of this concept of identification from field theory, Le Page's hypothesis becomes for the first time genuinely testable and, more significantly, distinctly different from Labov's theory of group membership. Drawing upon Reed's research into the regional identification of Southerners, it has been possible to construct an Index of Texan Identification. The identification index is based upon scored responses to three questions closely patterned after those used in Reed's study of Southern identification. The questions with scores for answers indicated in parentheses are as follows:

Some people in Texas feel they have a lot in common with other Texans, but others don't feel this way. How about you? Would you say you feel pretty close to other Texans in general, or that you don't feel much closer to them than you would to people from somewhere else?

    a. Feel closer to Texans (2)
    b. No closer than to others (0)
    c. Don't know, can't say (0)

Suppose that you are the manager of a company that must hire a scientist. Two persons apply--one born and educated in another state, the other born and educated in Texas. If they were equally qualified, which would you prefer, the person from Texas or the person from somewhere else?

    a. Person from Texas (2)
    b. Person from some other state (0)
    c. It depends, don't know, etc. (1)

Suppose that two good persons are running for Congress in your district. One was born and raised in Texas, and the other was born and raised in another state. If both people had moved to the district five years ago, which one would you favor, the person born and raised in Texas or the person born and raised in some other state?

    a. Person from Texas (2)
    b. Person from some other state (0)
    c. It depends, don't know, etc. (1)

Whereas the first question directly asks subjects to say whether they feel close to other Texans, the other two measure what Reed (1983, p. 57) calls 'in-group preference' in a situation that forces the subject to make a choice. By the tabulation of scores appropriate to a subject's responses to these questions, an individual's level of Texan identification can be scored on a scale from 0 to 6, from low identification to high.

There still remains, however, the problem of selecting an appropriate variable from the 'Texas accent' in order to test the hypothesis. Although several linguistic variables were considered, the pronunciation of /ai/ was selected since the monophthongal pronunciation, typically [a], appears to be the most persistently stereotyped feature of the 'Texas accent'.[3] Almost every popular commentator from the humorist H. Allen Smith (1974) to Robert Reinhold (1984), the Houston Bureau Chief for the *New York Times*, suggests that Texans lack the /ai/ diphthong, substituting a low central or low back unrounded vowel--the vowel of *palm* or *father*--in its place. Similarly, Herman and Herman (1959, p. 112) and Machlin (1975, p. 34) instruct actors who are portraying Texans to substitute the low monophthong for the diphthong /ai/. During the height of the Texas chic phenomenon, both Hicks (1981, n.p.) and Kemp (1981, p. 222) informed those who wanted to become Texans to substitute a retracted low vowel for the diphthong. Kemp's advice is to 'use short *a* sounds when a long *i*, might ("maht") seem to be in order.' Even Jim Everhart's *The Illustrated Texas Dictionary of the English Language* (1967-85), the purpose of which is primarily to entertain tourists, informs its readers that *kite* and *cot*, *pride* and *prod*, *eyes* and *ahs*, *blind* and *blond*, *dial* and *doll*, *tire* and *tar*, *bye* and *bah* are all homophonous pairs in Texas English. Although these and other laywriters are not accurate in their impressions of the monophthongized /ai/, clearly an unglided variant is a sterotyped pronunciation feature of Texans.

In addition, over the years a number of serious linguistic investigators have attested that the monophthongal /ai/ is a pervasive and salient pronunciation feature in the Lone Star State. Researchers have established the monophthongal variant-- which for convenience, and certainly not accuracy, I shall hitherto call the 'Texas /ai/'--in the speech of Texans from East Texas (Smith, 1973; Stanley, 1936, 1937, 1941; Tarpley, 1970; Wheatley & Stanley, 1959), North East Texas (Tarpley, 1970), Central Texas (DeCamp, 1978; Heard, 1969; Nail, 1948), the Gulf Coast (Norman, 1955, 1956), West Texas (Stanley, 1971) the Panhandle (SoRelle, 1966a, 1966b), the German Hill Country (Klipple, 1944, 1945), and Southwest Texas (Labov et al., 1972.[4] It has also been reported from such metropolitan centers as Beaumont and Port Arthur (Norman, 1955, 1956), San Antonio (Sawyer, 1957, 1959, 1964, 1970), Austin (Baird, 1971), Dallas (Hinton et al., 1977), Fort Worth (Lawrence, 1963, 1970), Lubbock (Stanley, 1971), and Amarillo (SoRelle, 1966a, 1966b). (See Map 1.)

Therefore, the Texas /ai/ seems to be a logical variant to use in the testing of the identity hypothesis. Accordingly, a one-page biography of a fictional Texan was contrived, containing a total of 62 occurrences of /ai/ which can be scored. An audiotape recording is made of each subject's reading of the biography, and each tape is analyzed by the author, the variant for each instance of /ai/ being identified as either a diphthong or a monophthong. An /ai/ score, representing the frequency of the monophthongal variant, is then calculated.[5]

To date recordings of 134 subjects have been analyzed. The geographical distribution of these subjects according to cultural area or metropolitan city is indicated on Table 1. Because of the small numbers of subjects from many of these locales, no analysis of /ai/ scores by geographical grouping is offered at this time. However, Table 2 offers a conventional analysis of mean /ai/ scores by social grouping according to age, background,[6] educational attainment, sex, and socioeconomic class.[7] Although cross-tabulations would yield a more refined correlation of the Texas /ai/ to social grouping, this table is sufficient, however, to suggest that some factor other than group membership is at work here. First of all, the differences between the mean /ai/ scores of any set of subcategories and the percent of difference between /ai/ scores for subcategories in

Table 1. *Geographical Distribution of Subjects*

LOCALE	NUMBER (134)
CULTURAL AREA	
Panhandle	0
West	11
North East	4
Southwest	2
German Hill Country	6
Central	26
East	9
South	5
Gulf Coast	14
CITIES	
Austin	15
Beaumont	3
Corpus Christi	4
Dallas	6
El Paso	2
Fort Worth	2
Galveston	3
Houston	9
Laredo	6
Lubbock	2
San Antonio	4
Tyler	1

Methods in Dialectology

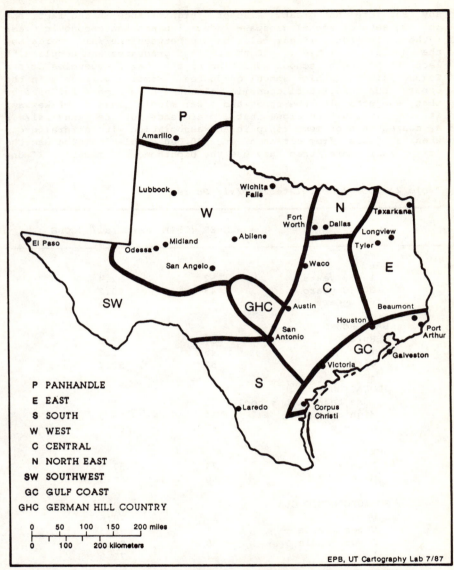

Source: D.W. Meinig, Imperial Texas: An Interpretive Essay in Cultural Geography Austin, UT 1969

Map 1. Cultural areas and major cities of Texas

any set are not great. Also of significance is the fact that in two sets of social groups-- education and socioeconomic class --there is not a linear relationship between the /ai/ scores and the social variables. Both college graduates and people with less than a high school education have higher frequencies of the Texas /ai/ than high school graduates. Similarly, people in the upper and lower socioeconomic classes have higher /ai/ scores than subjects in the upper and lower middle classes. Likewise, it is difficult to argue that a preference for the Texas /ai/ is a consequence of membership in and association with a rural group when subjects from cities of over 50,000 population also use the Texas /ai/ more than they use the diphthong. Similarly, if one

Table 2. *Social Correlates of /ai/ Scores*

GROUP	NUMBER (134)	MEAN /ai/ SCORE
AGE		
10-30 years	52	52.4
30-60 years	43	60.2
60+ years	39	68.4
BACKGROUND		
Rural	35	67.2
Town	45	61.6
City	53	52.7
EDUCATION		
Less than high school	23	61.9
High school	54	58.3
College	47	62.6
SEX		
Female	74	57.1
Male	60	62.5
SOCIOECONOMIC CLASS		
Upper	13	70.6
Upper middle	71	58.5
Lower middle	38	53.3
Lower	12	71.9
ETHNICITY		
Afro-American	10	67.4
Anglo	113	62.7
Hispanic	11	29.2

claims that the use of the monophthongal /ai/ is identifies one as a Texan born before 1927, there is no young group which does not tend to use it, either. The point is that there is not one group listed on Table 2 which prefers to use the diphthong instead of the Texas /ai/; there is no negative correlation between any of these social groups and a tendency to use the distinctive feature of the Texas accent. In every social group the Texas /ai/ is dominant.

It is at this point that the Index of Texan Identity becomes important. Table 3 reveals that not all of these 134 native Texans feel close to other Texans, and some of those who do identify with other Texans have feelings of closeness that are stronger than others'. While the majority of these subjects have very strong identification with other Texans, as revealed by their high scores on the Index of Texan Identity, some have weak identification as Texans. Six subjects appear to have no identification at all as Texans.

Table 3. *Index of Texan Identity*

	SCORE	NUMBER (134)
High	6	69
	5	19
	4	24
	3	4
	2	10
	1	2
Low	0	6

Given the subjects' /ai/ scores and their scores on the Index of Texan Identity, an important decision with regard to analyzing the data concerns whether to base that analysis on social or linguistic grouping. As explained by Barbara Horvath (1985, p. 63),

> The first approach, which we will call social grouping, involves sorting speakers into social groups and then averaging the values of the linguistic variables across these speakers; in the second approach, which we will call linguistic grouping, the overall distribution of the linguistic variables is determined and then the people who speak that way are identified.

Most sociolinguistic analysis has been based upon social grouping. Labov argued (1966, p. 210), for example, that social grouping 'seems more fundamental and more closely tied to the genesis of linguistic differentiation' and, further, it 'avoid[s] any error which would arise from assuming that a group of people who speak alike is a fundamental unit of social behavior' (Labov 1966, p. 211). In response, Horvath (1985, p. 63) remarks, 'There does seem to be the makings of a Labovian Paradox here: members of a social group speak alike but people who speak alike may not be members of a social group.' Indeed, the rejection of linguistic grouping would also appear to be a rejection of the assertions of Sapir and Hertzler (quoted above) and others who insist that shared linguistic features are crucial to signaling group membership or recognition. More importantly, social grouping is rejected in this analysis for theoretical reasons. Since identity theory holds that one's identification with a group does not require membership in that group, then it follows that people with shared identity do not necessarily constitute a social group. On the other hand, being a member of a group does not mean that one will identify with that group. In fact, all 134 subjects in this study do belong to a single group: they are all Texans. Clearly though, they do not all identify with that group. Thus the relationship between scores on the Index of Texan Identity and /ai/ scores is based on linguistic grouping.

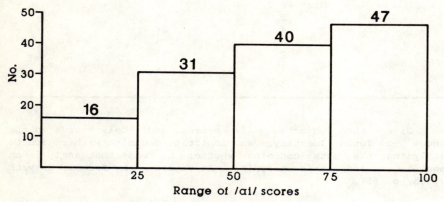

Figure 1. Distribution of /ɑi/ scores

Figure 1 is a histogram which represents the distribution of /ai/ scores where the bases of the rectangles correspond to four ranges of /ai/ scores and the heights correspond to the number of /ai/ scores within those ranges. For convenience, /ai/ scores in

Methods in Dialectology

the 0 to 25 range are called 'rare', those in the 25 to 50 range 'occasional', scores in the 50 to 75 range 'common', and those in the 75 to 100 range 'usual'. Significantly, for over 35% of the subjects the use of the Texas /ai/ is either occasional or rare: 16 (11.9%) rarely use the Texas /ai/ and another 31 (23.1%) use it only occasionally. Of the remaining 65%, the Texas /ai/ is the common form for 40 subjects (29.9%) and the usual variant for 47 others (35.1%).

The crucial test of the identity hypothesis requires the computation of the mean scores on the Index of Texan Identity for the group of subjects in each range of /ai/ scores. The results of this correlation are presented in Figure 2. There is a clear linear relationship of scores on the Index of Texan Identity to the range of /ai/ scores. Those subjects who use the Texas /ai/ rarely have a mean identity score of only 3.38. The mean identity score increases to 4.00 for subjects who use the Texas /ai/ occasionally. Common users of the Texas /ai/ have an even higher mean identity score of 5.05, and those subjects who usually pronounce /ai/ as a monophthong have the highest mean

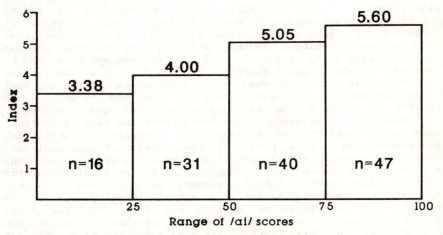

Figure 2. Mean Index of Texan Identitiy by /ɑi/ scores

identity score of all, 5.60. In addition to the linear relationship between the linguistic and identity variables, it will be noticed that the largest separation between the linguistic groups distinguishes those speakers who tend to use the Texas /ai/ from those speakers who tend to use the diphthongal variant. Thus, the evidence displayed on Figure 2 answers the crucial question of this study, for it confirms that a speaker's Texas accent, as revealed by the use of the Texas /ai/, is directly related to that person's sense of identity as a

Texan. 'Strongest' accents (i.e., those marked by highest frequency of the Texas /ai/) are characteristic of those subjects with strongest senses of identity as Texans. Texas accents progressively 'weaken' with progressively lower senses of identity as Texans by the subjects.[8] Thus, the Le Page hypothesis, as refined by this study, is accepted.

This research validates the Theory of Acts of Identity. In the study of sociolinguistic variation, language variation must be understood in terms of speakers' identification rather than their assignment to or membership in social groups. As these Texas subjects have demonstrated, people may very well be members of a group with which they do not want to identity or be identified by others. Consequently, they may choose to be linguistically different from their group. On the other hand, people may desire to identify and be identified with a group to which they may not belong. They will attempt to pattern their language after that of the members of the group with which they seek identification. Their success, of course, depends upon the four riders to LePage's theory.

This study has at least two additional implications that are significant. First, it affirms the desirability of basing quantitative analysis of sociolinguistic data in terms of linguistic grouping--a technique pioneered by Horvath--rather than social grouping. Second, in addition to providing clearer insights into idiolect formation--i.e., into why speakers tend to acquire certain characteristics of pronunciation at the expense of others at their disposal--, it promises to explain why some sound changes succeed and others do not and to improve our ability to predict the efficacy of sound changes in progress. For instance, many regionalists worry about the fate of regional accents or dialects as a result of increased urbanization, geographic and social mobility, the impact of mass media and improved national and international networks of communication, and increased education. Such worries may be misdirected, for instead the fretters should perhaps be concerned with the strength of people's sense of regional identity. It would appear, for example, that despite the fact that the Texas population has become not merely overwhelmingly urban but metropolitan in this century (in addition to being over 80% urban, in 1982 over 78% of the population of Texas was estimated to be located in in twenty-eight Primary Metropolitan Statistical Areas and Metropolitan Statistical Areas[9] of Texas [Kingston, 1985, pp. 441-2]), the regional Texas /ai/ has retained its popularity because many Texans, regardless of their social transformations, have not abandoned their identity as Texans.

Despite the encouraging results of this analysis, the on-going study of the relationship between accent and identity is moving into other areas of concern. First is a refinement of the measurement of identification. In addition to measuring identity with the type of questions used by Reed, a Likert-type scale is being used to measure one's degree of closeness to a group, and a comparison of the two methods will be undertaken. Second is the expansion of the study of identity into dimensions other than one's sense of being Texan. People's identities are complex because they belong or aspire to belong to numbers of groups simultaneously. Since identities are multi-dimensional, a linguistic variant may relate positively to more than one identity, thus enhancing one's motivation to acquire it. On the other hand, a variant may be positively associated with identification with one group and negatively with that of another. If a speaker aspires to identify with both groups, a conflict results, and one's linguistic behavior will consequently be affected by which of the identities is the stronger one. To date 129 subjects have been tested for their strength of identity with respect to 20 separate social groups, but those data have not yet been analyzed. Also of interest is the relationship of accent to consciousness--as opposed to identity--and traditional value orientation. Whereas identification is emotional, consciousness is a cognitive construct. Consciousness, as explained by Reed (1983, p. 33), is a contrastive concept; people's awareness and anaysis of their distinctiveness from others is heightened through increased education, contact with outsiders, urbanization, upward social and occupational mobility, and attention to the mass media (see Reed, 1983, pp. 27-54). Traditionalism, consciousness, and identity are interrelated. Reed (1983, p. 65) points out that

> modernizing, consciousness-raising backgrounds and experiences...operate both to increase identification, by increasing consciousness, and to decrease it, by decreasing the traditional value orientation.

The effects, therefore, of changes in Texan consciousness and traditional value orientation upon Texan identification are of considerable interest. To date 243 subjects have been tested with respect to an Index of Texan Consciousness as well as the Index of Identity, but at present those data are also unanalyzed. It remains to be seen, therefore if increased 'modernization' of Texas is enhancing Texan identity and thus reenforcing the Texas accent or if it is diminishing Texan identity and consequently eroding the Texas accent.

Notes

1. This research has been supported in part by funds from the University Research Institute of The University of Texas at Austin.

2. In 'The social motivation of a sound change' Labov (1963) comes close to attributing the popularity of centralized /ai/ and /au/ diphthongs in the speech of Martha's Vineyard to identity, but he neglects to to do so. At one point he (Labov 1963, p. 304) asserts:

> It is apparent that the immediate meaning of this phonetic feature [i.e., centralization of the diphthongs] is 'Vineyarder.' When a man says [rɐɪt] or [hɐʊs], he is unconsciously establishing the fact that he belongs to the island: that he is one of the natives to whom the island really belongs.

Significantly, Labov never uses either the term 'identity' or 'identification' with reference to these speakers and their motivations. Also of interest is the fact that instead of associating the raised diphthongs with speakers' feelings of closeness to each other, he ties it to their feelings of closeness to place. Labov (1963, p. 306) writes:

> In summary, we can then say that the meaning of centralization, judging from the context in which it occurs, is *positive orientation towards Martha's Vineyard* [his emphasis].

Labov even devises an index of orientation towards Martha's Vineyard with three categories:

> *positive*--expresses definitely positive feelings towards Martha's Vineyard; *neutral*--expresses neither positive nor negative feelings towards Martha's Vineyard; *negative*--indicates a desire to live elsewhere.

It is noteworthy that Labov's interview format lacks any provision for a suitable means of measuring his subjects' orientation to the island. Instead Labov explains his assignment of speakers to categories in this fashion: 'An examination of the total interview for each informant allows us to place him in one of three categories....' Of course, there is a final problem with Labov's orientation scale--it is not linear. It is entirely possible that subjects may have a positive orientation towards a place yet prefer to live elsewhere, or one may (perversely, perhaps) prefer to live somewhere despite negative feelings about that place. For example, I know several colleagues at The University of Texas at Austin who rarely, if ever, have anything positive to say about Austin or Texas. They complain about the heat, the isolation, the lack of desired cultural amenities, their allergic reactions to the abundant junipers of the Hill Country area, the university administration, the attitudes and behavior of Texans, Texas music and food, state and local politics, and everything else--yet they will not consider moving to accept a position in another university. Likewise, there are any number of expatriate Texans with very positive feelings for their state who choose not to live there, preferring New York, Boston, or perhaps even Denver.

In a fashion similar to Labov's, Hinton et al. (1977, p. 3) sought to relate the pronunciation of /ai/ by native-born Anglo residents of Dallas County to their 'orientation toward Texas'. In addition to repeating Labov's error in failing to devise a means of quantifying their subjects' orientation (they merely asked, 'Would you like to live here all your life, or do you think you'd rather settle down somewhere else?' and judged their responses to be either 'positive' or 'non-positive' [Hinton et al., 1977, p. 7]), Hinton et al. compound their problems by proceeding to confuse their subjects' preferences of places to live with their 'attitude toward being a Texan' (1977, p. 7)--which was not elicited and which is definitely not the same as their attitude toward desirable places to live.

3. The monophthongal /ai/, of course, is not unique to Texas. In the South it is so pervasive, in certain phonological environments, that James Sledd (1955) nicknamed it the 'confederate vowel'. Indeed, evidence of its widespread use in the South may be found in a variety of sources (e.g., Kurath & McDavid, 1961; Sledd, 1966; Underwood, 1971; Wolfram and Christian, 1976; Crane, 1977). Actually, the monophthongal /ai/ has currency outside Southern states, being reported, for example in western Pennsylavnia and eastern Ohio (Hankey, 1965, 1972) and Indiana (Carmony, 1970). Monophthong pronunciations of /ai/ have also been attributed to varieties of Black English in the United States without regard to locale (e.g., Dillard, 1972; Burling, 1973; Labov, 1973). In fact, monophthongal /ai/ is not confined to accents of American English, for Wells (1982, Vol. 1, p. 238) reports that in RP and various English regional accents monophthongal /ai/ occurs in certain syllable types as a result of a phonological process he calls 'smoothing'. Lanham (1982) also reports that a monophthonged /ai/ is also characteristic of Natal English in South Africa.

4. The regional labels are those for the cultural areas of Texas established by Meinig (1969).

5. Reported frequencies for monophthongal pronunciations of /ai/ must be viewed with caution. It is possible to manipulate such scores through the selection of syllable types, level of stress, or degree of formality in which the /ai/ occurs. Previous reports of the use of monophthongal variants of /ai/ (see note 3), for example, have shown that monophthongization occurs as a rule only in some syllable types or in weakly-stressed syllables. In the southeastern United States it has traditionally been de rigueur for educated speakers to use diphthongal variants before voiceless consonants, even though they may have monophthongal variants elsewhere. Thus, a researcher in that area could presumably inflate /ai/ scores by excluding from consideration words such as *night* or deflate them by concentrating upon words in which /ai/ precedes a voiceless consonant. Even though this shibboleth does not appear to operate in Texas English, the test passage has been designed to include at least five instances of /ai/ preceding a syllable boundary and each of the following types of sounds in closed syllables-- voiceless stops, voiceless fricatives, voiced stops, voiced fricatives, nasals, /l/, and /r/. Each /ai/ which is scored occurs in a stressed syllable. In this study each syllable type has an equal weight in the determination of the /ai/ score. The /ai/ scores reported in this study, therefore, have a relative value for allowing the comparison of speakers in this study to each other; they should not be used to compare these speakers with those included in any other study.

6. Subjects are group according to the types of communities in which they spent their primary language-learning years. 'Rural' identifies residence on farms or ranches or in incorporated and unincorporated communities of less than 2,500 people. 'Town' means residence in incorporated and unincorporated places with populations between 2,500 and 50,000. Though considered urban by the U. S. Bureau of the Census, these communities, which Hodges (1964) calls 'Anytowns', are separated from larger communities because of differences in social stratification and language variation. Galvan and Troike (1969, p. 31), for example, noted linguistic complexity in Tyler (population 70,508 in 1980) that was not present in four smaller East Texas towns. 'City' refers to residence in metropolitan communities with populations in excess of 50,000

7. Socioeconomic class is assigned on the basis of a weighted three-component (education, occupation, and primary source of income) scale expressly designed for use in Texas by McGuire and White (1955). The scale has been up-dated for the present study.

8. For those who insist upon analyzing /ai/ scores in terms of scores on the Index of Texan Identity, the relationships are as follows:

IDENTITY SCORE	MEAN /ai/ SCORE
0-1	30.8
2-3	42.4
4	51.5
5	56.9
6	69.7

Subjects with scores of 0 and 1 and those with scores of 2 and 3 on the Index of Texan Identity are grouped together because of the small number of subjects with each of these scores. (See Table 3.) Regardless of whether subjects are clustered in terms of their /ai/ scores or their scores on the Index of Texan Identity, the relationship between identity and accent is the same.

9. According to the U. S. Bureau of the Census a metropolitan area consists of a city with a population of 50,000 or more or 'twin cities' with a combined population in excess of 50,000, the county or counties in which such cities are located, and surrounding counties that are economically and socially integrated with the central city or cities. A Metropolitan Statistical Area is a free-standing metropolitan area or cluster of such areas with a total population between 50,000 and one million. A Primary Metropolitan Statistical Area is a sub-unit of a Consolidated Metropolitan Statistical Area, which has a population in excess of one million people.

References

Baird, S.J. (1971) *Employment Interview Speech: A Social Dialect Study in Austin, Texas*. PhD Dissertation, The University of Texas at Austin.

Burling, R. (1973) *English in Black and White*. New York: Holt, Rinehart, and Winston.

Carmony, M. (1970) Some phonological rules of an Indiana Dialect. In J. Griffith and L.E. Miner (eds.), *The First Lincolnland Conference on Dialectology*. University: University of Alabama Press.

Crane, L.B. (1977) The social stratification of /ai/ in Tuscaloosa, Alabama. In D.L. Shores and C.P. Hines (eds.), *Papers in Language Variation: SAMLA-ADS Collection*. University: University of Alabama Press.
DeCamp, S. (1978) American speech from Central Texas. *Journal of the International Phonetic Association* 8, 81-82.
Dillard, J.L. (1972) *Black English: Its History and Usage in the United States*. New York: Random House.
Everhart, J. (1967-85) *The Illustrated Texas Dictionary of the English Language*. 6 vols. Omaha: Cliffs Notes.
Galvan, M.M. and Troike, R.C. (1969) The East Texas Dialect Project: a pattern for education. *Florida FL Reporter* 7(1), 29-31, 152-53.
Hankey, C.T. (1965) Tiger, tagger and [ai] in western Pennsylvania. *American Speech* 40, 226-28.
--(1972) Notes on West Penn-Ohio phonology. In L.M. Davis (ed), *Studies in Linguistics in Honor of Raven I. McDavid, Jr.* University: University of Alabama Press.
Heard, B.R. (1969) *A Phonological Analysis of the Speech of Hays County, Texas*. PhD Dissertation, Louisiana State University.
Herman, L. and Herman, M.S. (1959) *American Dialects*. New York: Theatre Arts Books.
Hertzler, J.O. (1965) *A Sociology of Language*. New York: Random House.
Hicks, M. (1981) *How to Be Texan*. Austin: Texas Monthly Press.
Hinton, L. et al. (1977) The sociology of dialect variation in Dallas. Unpublished manuscript.
Hodges, H.M., Jr. (1964) *Social Stratification: Class in America*. Cambridge, MA: Schenkman.
Horvath, B.M. (1985) *Variation in Australian English: The Sociolects of Sydney*. Cambridge: Cambridge University Press.
Kemp, R. (1981) *The Genuine Texas Handbook*. New York: Workman.
Kingston, M. (ed.) (1985) *Texas Almanac and State Industrial Guide*. 53rd ed. Dallas: Dallas Morning News.
Klipple, F.C. (1944) *A Study of the Speech of Spicewood, Texas*. MA Thesis, The University of Texas.
--(1945) The speech of Spicewood, Texas. *American Speech* 20, 187-91.
Kurath, H. and McDavid, R.I., Jr. (1961) *The Pronunciation of English in the Atlantic States*. Ann Arbor: University of Michigan Press.
Labov, W. (1963) The social motivation of a sound change. *Word* 19, 273-309.
--(1964) Stages in the acquisition of standard English. In R.W. Shuy (ed.), *Social Dialects and Language Learning*. Champaign: National Council of Teachers of English.
--(1966) *The Social Stratification of English in New York City*. Washington: Center for Applied Linguistics.

--(1973) Some features of the English of Black Americans. In R.W. Bailey and J.L. Robinson (eds.), *Varieties of Present-Day English*. New York: Macmillan.
-- et al. (1972) *A Quantitative Study of Sound Change in Progress*. 2 vols. Philadelphia: The U.S. Regional Survey.
Lanham, L.W. (1982) English in South Africa. In R.W. Bailey and M. Gorlach (eds.), *English as a World Language*. Ann Arbor: University of Michigan Press.
Lawrence, T.Z. (1963) *An Analysis of the Speech of Twenty Students at Texas Christian University*. MA Thesis, Texas Christian University.
--(1970) Certain phonetic tendencies perceived in the dialects of selected Texans. In B. Hala et al. (eds.), *Proceedings of the Sixth International Congress of Phonetic Sciences*. Prague: Academic Publishing House of the Czechoslovakian Academy of Sciences.
Le Page, R.P. (1968) Problems of description in multilingual communities. *Transactions of the Philological Society*, 189-212.
--(1975) Polarizing factors: political, social, economic, operating on the individual's choice of identity through language use in British Honduras. In J.G. Savard and R. Vigneault (eds.), *Les Etats Multilingues*. Quebec: Laval University Press.
--(1978) Projection, focussing, diffusion. *Society for Caribbean Linguistics Occasional Paper 9*.
--(1986) Acts of identity. *English Today* 8, 22-24.
-- and A. Tabouret-Keller (1985) *Acts of Identity: Creole-Based Approaches to Language and Ethnicity*. Cambridge: Cambridge University Press.
-- et al. (1974) Further report on the sociolinguistic survey of multilingual communities: survey of Cayo District, British Honduras. *Language in Society* 3, 1-32.
Lewin, K. 1951. *Field Theory in Social Science: Selected Theoretical Papers*, ed. D. Cartwright. New York: Harper and Brothers.
Machlin, E. (1975) *Dialects for the Stage*. New York: Theatre Arts Books.
McGuire, C. and White, G.D. (1955) *The Estimation of Social Status*. Austin: The University of Texas, Department of Educational Psychology Laboratory of Human Behavior.
Meinig, D.W. (1969) *Imperial Texas: An Interpretive Essay in Cultural Geography*. Austin: University of Texas Press.
Milroy, L. (1980) *Language and Social Networks*. Baltimore: University Park Press.
Nail, W.A. (1948) *The Phonology of the Speech of Crawford, Texas*. MA Thesis, The University of Texas.
Norman, A.M.Z. (1955) *A Southeast Texas Dialect Study*. PhD Dissertation, The University of Texas.
--(1956) A southeast Texas dialect study. *Orbis* 5, 61-79.

Reed, J.S. (1972) *The Enduring South: Subcultural Persistence in Mass Society*. Chapel Hill: The University of North Carolina Press.
--(1983) *Southerners: The Social Psychology of Sectionalism*. Chapel Hill: The University of North Carolina Press.
Reinhold, R. (1984) How to talk 'Texian'. *New York Times Magazine* (July 22) 8, 10.
Sapir, E. (1933) Language. In *Encyclopaedia of Social Sciences*. 9 vols. New York: Macmillan.
Sawyer, J.B. (1957) *A Dialect Study of San Antonio, Texas: A Bilingual Community*. PhD Dissertation, The University of Texas.
--(1959) Aloofness from Spanish influence in Texas English. *Word* 15, 220-31.
--(1964) Social aspects of bilingualism in San Antonio. *Publication of the American Dialect Society* 41, 7-15.
--(1970) Spanish-English Bilingualism. In G.G. Gilbert (ed), *Texas Studies in Bilingualism*. Austin: University of Texas Press.
Sledd, J.H. (1955) Review of *Outline of English Structure*, by G. Trager and H.L. Smith. *Language* 31, 312-45.
--(1966) Breaking, umlaut, and the Southern drawl. *Language* 42, 18-41.
Smith, H.A. (1974) How to talk Texian in tin easy lessons. *Smithsonian* 5(2), 108.
Smith, R.B. (1973) *Some Phonological Rules in Negro Speech of East Texas*. PhD Dissertation, The University of Texas at Austin.
SoRelle, Z.R. (1966a) *Segmental Phonology of Texas Panhandle Speech*. PhD Dissertation, University of Denver.
--(1966b) Segmental phonology of Texas Panhandle speech. *Study of Sounds. Vol. 12: Papers Delivered at the Second World Congress of Phoneticians, Tokyo, 26-31 August 1965*. Tokyo: Phonetic Society of Japan.
Stanley, G. (1971) Phoneaesthetics and West Texas dialect. *Linguistics* 71, 95-101.
Stanley, O. (1936) The speech of East Texas. *American Speech* 11, 3-36, 145-66, 232-52, 327-55.
--(1937) *The Speech of East Texas*. New York: Columbia University Press.
--(1941) Negro Speech of East Texas. *American Speech* 16.3-16.
Tarpley, F. (1970) *From Blinkey to Blue-John: A Word Atlas of Northeast Texas*. Wolf City: The University Press.
Trudgill, P. (1984) *On Dialect: Social and Geographical Perspectives*. New York: New York University Press.
Underwood, G.N. (1971) *Some Rules for the Pronunciation of English in Northwest Arkansas*. ERIC ED 957 652.
Wells, J.C. (1982) *Accents of English*. 3 vols. Cambridge: Cambridge University Press.

Wheatley, K.E. and Stanley, O. (1959) Three generations of East Texas speech. *American Speech* 34, 83-94.
Whyte, W.F. and Homberg, A.R. (1965) Human problems of U.S. enterprise in Latin America. *Human Organization* 15, 11-15.
Wolfram, W. and Christian, D. (1976) *Appalachian Speech*. Arlington: Center for Applied Linguistics.

A Method for Discovering Historical Language Variation

JACOB BENNETT
University of Maine

There is a period in the past history of the English language which, in the estimation of this writer, should be examined more closely and analyzed more vigorously than it has been, at least for the past two or three generations. It is difficult to pin the chronology down exactly, but roughly it spans the years from the beginning of the Fifteenth Century until the establishment of the printing press about seventy-five years later. There is no dearth of material for study. True, as is well known, the Fifteenth Century did not produce a large quantity of memorable English literature--to put it tritely, it was that fallow time before the flowering of the Renaissance--but the era did bequeath an amazingly large body of writings in manuscript form, much of it regional, much of it autograph, and much of it localized. There are, for example, the dramatic works; there is the corpus of ordinances of the English gilds, brought together by Toulmin Smith for the Early English Text Society, a compendium, in various localized and dated hands; the Promptorium Parvulorum, an English-Latin dictionary containing a mine of folk language in contemporary English, set down, as the compiler explains in his preface, in his own native dialect; the voluminous works of such authors as John Capgrave; the colloquial Book of Margery Kempe; and a multitude of others.

It is not valid, however, to imply that this period has always been neglected by language scholars. A good deal of work, in fact, was done at one time, but that was in a distant past, when workers in the field were called philologists; one need only recall such names as Lorenz Morsbah, Karl Luick, Wilhelm Dibelius, Richard Jordan. However, somehow their labors, as well as the language they worked on, has since been largely slighted, even, it is fair to add, by modern dialectologists. The results of what Sever Pop once called the bahnbrechenden Arbeiten of these pioneers still remain powerful and valuable, although the discrete works remain unorganized and far from assembled into any sort of cohesive pattern.

There is much more that supplementation, further analysis, and ultimately consolidation could accomplish. First of all, it could possibly lead the way to a more comprehensive description of Early Modern English than we have. Furthermore, the results of such study could even throw new light on the nature of Middle English dialects. And finally, pertinent to one of the main theses of this paper, the effort could possibly lead to new information about the origins of later varieties of English, such as that which was originally transported to North America.

Methods in Dialectology

There have been a few attempts in more recent times to describe and sort out the earlier stages and varieties of English, such as Middle English, Elizabethan English, the English of even later times, but the results, in the opinion of this writer, have been thin and, at the best, moot. This failure is possibly the result of a couple of misconceptions which seem almost universally to have beset the latter-day workers in the diachronic vineyards, misconceptions brought about by a too ready and facile acceptance of two works which came to be pronounced seminal after their respective publications, and which have proven to be dominant influences. The first is the monograph by Samuel Moore, Sanford B. Meech, and Harold Whitehall, "Middle English Dialect Characteristics and Dialect Boundaries," and the other is Helge Kökeritz' Shakespeare's Pronunciation. The former, mostly because it is too simplistic, has affected (negatively, it seems) our outlook on Middle English dialectology, and the latter, in spite of occasional mild disagreement, has become accepted too readily as the point of departure for consideration of the origin of Early Modern varieties of English, such as the variety which was transported to Colonial America and about which we actually know so little.

The main purpose of this paper is not merely to present an analysis and critique of what has gone on before, but rather to suggest a new approach (one might even use the word 'method') for examining the English language of the past and particularly that of the late Middle Ages. It will probably be helpful, however, first to summarize briefly the objections to what was referred to above as the two misconceptions which have influenced the approaches of recent workers.

It is no doubt true that the work of Kökeritz and others in what might aptly be termed the Shakespeare approach has been a valuable contribution, but it is wrong to assume that it is anything more than what Kökeritz himself called it, i.e. an attempted reconstruction, worked out from such things as rhymes, homonymic puns, and the writings of orthoepists, of Shakespeare's Pronunciation. Furthermore, even within the narrow parameters set by Kökeritz, there has been and still is considerable disagreement as to the conclusions that the approach has encouraged. One fact should have seemed apparent from the start: the reconstructed Shakespearean literary language is a far cry from the speech of the Englishmen who came to Plymouth and Massachusetts Bay, most of whom, incidentally, emigrated from places far from London and most of whom were illiterate.

It is equally fallacious to accept the boundaries of Moore, Meech, and Whitehall as representing a depiction of the English language of the Middle Ages. The study has been useful, perhaps, as a general guide to a few wide geographical linguistic regions which might be called dialect areas. Again, this is no help in determining what the language was really like. In most cases the period under examination for Middle English dialectology has been, basically, the Fourteenth Century (chosen, perhaps, because the few selected criteria are more obvious and more easily extrapolated). That period is too early to be by itself effective; the criteria used are too broad and too few; and the sources used for evidence are at least in part questionable.

Since the characteristics which have been culled from the heart of the Middle Ages are too broad, too general, and too few, and since the rhymes and homonymic puns of Shakespeare are of questionable validity for effective reconstruction of the true language (spelling of course is of negligible value in the Renaissance because with the advent of the printing press orthography rapidly became standardized), it seems logical that the place to search is somewhere in between, and that place would be the pre-Caxton period of the Fifteenth Century. As a result of a number of decades of labor with a considerable body of manuscript material from this period it is the conclusion of this writer that this is indeed the case.

This writer's work with this body of fifteenth century material has consisted for the most part of linguistic analysis, but paradoxically the objective has not been until now to study the language itself or to throw light on the nature of historical English dialects. The purpose rather was to localize certain problematical works of literature, particularly in the field of medieval drama. It is relevant to assert that the analyses yielded considerable success since the specific provenances of a number of the works under study were established primarily on grounds of linguistic evidence. It is quite safe to state, for example, that the morality play The Castle of Perseverance was composed in or near the cathedral city of Lincoln; that the early fragment The Pride of Life is in the language not of some locale in western England, as has been claimed, but rather in a form of Anglo-Irish (the manuscript was discovered in Dublin); that the Hegge plays, the so-called Ludus Coventriae, were a product of Norwich in East Anglia; and that the morality The Mary Magdalene can be accurately pinned down to a single community, Bishop's Lynn in Norfolk. Now, these works are all products of the pre-Caxton fifteenth century, and since it is possible to localize these works on the basis of their language characteristics, the indication is that this period should be a fruitful one for further linguistic analysis and consideration.

There has been the inclination by some to assume that the dialects, especially in the East Midlands, had largely levelled into a kind of regularized Schriftsprache by now so that differences are no longer recognizable in the written language. This is probably true of the broad features established by Moore, Meech, and Whitehall and which have been suitable for designating the few large and general dialect regions of the earlier Middle Ages. The standard, especially in the East Midlands and the South, was indeed rapidly developing. But a goodly number of features, fine ones, more subtle ones, other than the general broad ones, continued to exist in the manuscripts (most of which have largely been ignored by students of dialect). These features are numerous, and they are distinctive to specific regional areas, a fact which is it hoped can be demonstrated.

As for a methodical approach to the problem, it is necessary, first of all, to conduct close and complete analyses of individual localized manuscripts of this period under consideration. This does not mean merely the exercise of placing a given work into a dialect area on the basis of any given number of traditionally accepted characteristics and isoglosses, but rather an exacting examination of all its lexical, morphological, and phonological features. It is the contention of this writer that in the works of the later Middle Ages, especially in those of the Fifteenth Century, a texture of distinctive features, dialectal and otherwise, is indeed present. From the point of view of establishing dialect areas, this kind of exacting consideration could lead ultimately to new isoglosses for Middle English based on entirely different features; one can envision, for this period, at least, maps which are more complex than the existing ones for the Middle Ages and which have more exact, though much more involved, lines of demarcation.

For a number of reasons fifteenth century East Anglia is an appropriate provenance to use to demonstrate how the process can apply. In the first place, the intensive analysis by this writer over many years in an attempt to localize a number of late medieval works has led to considerable familiarity with the language of the region. Secondly, since the standard had been and still was rapidly developing in the East Midlands, so that the Schriftsprache had levelled more radically there than in most other locales, results of analyses from that area can present more suitable grounds for strengthening the thesis that fine features can be extrapolated even from apparently linguistically levelled manuscripts. Besides, as has been pointed out, there is a surprisingly large corpus of material from East Anglia available to work with, much of it, it bears repeating, autograph and dated, and a considerable body of it (including some of the drama) reflecting the important informal language of the folk.

Demonstration of the method will consist of taking two communities from one shire and separating them linguistically on the basis of differences isolated in contemporaneous manuscripts of that time and place. The shire is Norfolk. The cities are Norwich and Bishop's Lynn. They are about forty miles apart.

In all general respects the language of Norwich conforms morphologically and phonologically to that of the rest of the shire; that cathedral city perhaps could possibly be termed an important focal point for the East Anglian region. These features are the following: $\bar{e}$ for OE i in open syllables and also for i in words of French origin; occasional $\bar{e}$ for OE $\bar{i}$; e frequently for OE y (at times long before lengthening groups); $\bar{e}$ occasionally for OE $\bar{y}$; loss of the sound [x] in OE-<u>ht</u>; both <u>be</u> and <u>are</u> for the third person plural of 'to be'; both <u>hem</u> and <u>them</u> for the objective case of the third person plural pronoun; the spellings <u>ei</u> (<u>ey</u>) for ME $\bar{e}$; <u>x</u>- to represent the initial sound in 'shall' and 'should'; and <u>qw</u>-, <u>qwh</u>- for ME <u>w(h)</u>-.

Bishop's Lynn, forty miles away on the shore of the Wash, was linguistically similar, and its language was typified to a large extent by these same characteristics. However, it is possible to isolate a cluster of distinctive features from its language, a subsidiary group, which effectively sets the town linguistically apart. These secondary features are -<u>ar</u> as the usual ending for both the noun agent and the comparative of adjectives; -<u>n</u> for the ending of the past participle of strong verbs; <u>i</u> (<u>y</u>) as the vowel in inflectional endings; the form <u>systyr</u> (as contrasted to <u>sustyr</u> elsewhere in Norfolk); <u>be</u> in weak or unstressed position and <u>by</u> in strong position for the preposition 'by'; and the frequent use of -<u>t</u> for -<u>th</u> in the third person singular present tense of verbs.

It is safe to say that, as far as could be determined, this combination of features from Bishop's Lynn, the bundle of general Norfolk characteristics combined with the cluster of subsidiary features, can be found in no other place in Norfolk, or, for that matter in East Anglia. Moreover, this technique, it may be noted, has successfully been applied to other specific provenances, such as Lincolnshire (Lincoln) and Ireland (Anglo-Irish, probably Dublin).

Not only does it seem apparent that this approach could throw new light on the English language of the late Middle Ages and the Early Modern Period, but the possibility exists that the method has no small relevance to the study of the origins of later varieties of the language, and in particular to the nature of the language which was first transported to America. To discover anything about Colonial English it seems logical that one must first learn something about the language of its source. It remains doubtful, at any rate, that the source was in any way Shakespearean.

There is some evidence (reported on elsewhere) that there could be, in fact, a demonstrable linguistic connection between East Anglia and the early colonies. Some of the lexical items, chiefly on the level of folk speech, which have been uncovered from fifteenth century Bishop's Lynn, for example, have to have a familiar ring to all who are acquainted with the <u>Linguistic Atlas of New England</u> and Kurath's <u>Word Geography</u>. There are words such as <u>botery</u> (Kurath's <u>buttry</u>), <u>sek</u> ('paper sack'), <u>totyr</u> (cf <u>teeter-totter</u>), <u>tonowre</u> (<u>tunnel</u> for <u>funnel</u>), <u>ese</u> (<u>eace worm</u>), <u>grawcyr</u> (<u>grand-sir</u>). Moreover, further research, with literary dialects in the Northeastern United States, and with field work with aged informants in Maine, a prime relic area, has uncovered still more lexical items which seem to point back to the eastern regions of fifteenth century England. Since these words, so far as this writer can determine, can be found nowhere else in England, past or present, and since the only other place they do exist is in the folk speech of certain areas of the northeastern United States, the implication is tantalizing.

It is estimated that about eighty-five percent of the original colonists in America came from East Anglia. East Anglia, it has been pointed out, was the hotbed in England of Puritanism.

WORKS CITED

Bennett, J. (1962) The "Castle of Perseverance": redactions, place, and date. Mediaeval Studies, 24, 141-152.
_____ (1985) The folk speech of Maine: clues to Colonial English. American Speech: 1600 to the Present, Annual Proceedings of the Dublin Seminar for New England Folklife, 8, 27-34.
_____ (1974) George Savary Wasson and the dialect of Kittery Point, Maine. American Speech, 49, 54-66.
_____ (1973) The language and the home of the Ludus Coventriae. Orbis, Bulletin International de Documentation Linguistique, 22, 43-63.
_____ (1978) The "Mary Magdalene" of Bishop's Lynn. Studies in Philology, 75, 1-9.
Dudley, D. (1972) An Edition with Linguistic Analysis of the Morality Play "The Pride of Life". M.A. Thesis, University of Maine.
Kökeritz, H. (1953) Shakespeare's Pronunciation. New Haven: Yale University Press.
Kurath, H. (1949) Word Geography of the Eastern United States. Ann Arbor: University of Michigan Press.
Moore, S., Meech, S., and Whitehall, H. (1935) Middle English dialect characteristics and dialect boundaries. Essays and Studies in English and Comparative Literature, 13, 1-60.

The Study of Linguistic Change in the Survey of Vancouver English

ROBERT J. GREGG
University of British Columbia

The topic of linguistic change has fascinated many linguists - and the philologists before them -- over a long period of time. It was actually the Indo-European specialists who paved the way for the study of language change during the eighteen hundreds and well into our own century with their quest for Ursprachen or Proto-languages, and the ultimate Ursprache: the original ancestral Proto-Indo-European (PIE) mother tongue itself.

Their research hinged on the notion that, throughout pre-history, sets of speech sounds had undergone regular changes in certain branches of the Proto-language which led ultimately to regular correspondences of sounds in all of the related languages. These languages were eventually recorded in written form from the beginnings of documented history onwards.

Once it was established that they were dealing not with arbitrary letters or symbols but with speech sounds that could be analysed into component features, they were able to form workable theories of what physiological changes had taken place in order to produce a given modification of the original PIE sounds.

The only problem was that some philologists became so impressed by their ability to reconstruct ancestral phonological forms that they got carried away, and a small fanatical group among the Junggrammatiker (the so-called Neo-Grammarians) declared dogmatically that there were no exceptions to their phonological rules which they rather arrogantly called 'laws'.

These extremist views, however, have not marred the value of the monumental pioneer work done by the Indo-Europeanists on linguistic change since the early 19th century.

Nowadays, of course, especially since the advent of urban social dialectology, we are becoming increasingly interested in the possibility of a totally different kind of approach to the study of language change.

In current projects such as our sociolinguistic Survey of Vancouver English (SVEN for short) we are able to examine the responses of three age groups - old (O), middle (M), and young (Y) - noting the values chosen for any particular variable by the members of each group. The quantification of these values for each group then allows us to make a realistic estimate of the direction, the social locus, and the rate of any change that is observed to be in progress.

Using the SVEN data we can study the phenomenon of change under the headings of lexicon, grammar, and phonology.

LEXICON (Gregg, 1981 & 1983)

Some of the typically Canadian and, more narrowly, local lexical items provide interesting evidence of change. Because of its long-standing reputation as a Canadianism, for example, we made a very thorough investigation of the present status of the word <u>chesterfield</u> which is currently in competition with <u>couch</u> and <u>sofa</u>.

Before proceeding with the analysis of the responses relating to this word, however, brief explanation of our method of presenting data is necessary. It is effectively summarized in a compact table:

AGE/SEX/SE STATUS:CROSS-TABULATION

	Y		M		O	
	M	F	M	F	M	F
I						
II						
III						
IV						

Across the top: <u>Y</u>, <u>M</u>, <u>O</u>, stand for the young, middle, and old age groups.
Next line down: M, F, stand for Male and Female.
Down the side: <u>I</u>, <u>II</u>, <u>III</u>, <u>IV</u>, stand for the socio-economic status groups, ranging from lowest to highest.

The four speech styles covered here are:

<u>MC</u>: Minimal Contrast
<u>WL</u>: Word List
<u>VA</u>: Visual-Aural
<u>RP</u>: Reading Passage

To return to 'chesterfield', we find that 69 percent of the old males of socio-economic status group II (OM-II) used this word exclusively as against only 8 percent of the young males of SE group I (YM-I). There is a similar polarization between the 46 percent for the old females of SE group III (OF-III) and the zero percent of YM-I who have 'chesterfield' as their first choice and 'sofa' as their second. The YM-I fare a little better (23 percent) with 'chesterfield' as first choice and 'couch' as second. On the whole, however, the future of this acknowledged Canadianism does not seem too bright with this obvious decline in its use among the young speakers, for the young females score only marginally better than the males.

A local lexical item, the Vancouver place name Kitsilano (ultimately derived from the name of a Squamish Salishan chief) refers to a trendy district on the south shore of English Bay. The main reason for its inclusion in SVEN was to check on the variant pronunciations of the vowel in the third syllable which bears the primary stress and to assess their sociolinguistic significance. In defiance of all orthoepic rules this stressed syllable for almost half (48 percent) of our total population of 300 had - exclusively - the diphthong /aɪ/. The second largest group (35 percent) had /ɑ/, and in third place came the much smaller group (6 percent) with /æ/. The remainder fluctuated between /aɪ/ and one of the simple vowels. In this way a further 9 percent used /aɪ/ at least some of the time.

Our statistics show, incidentally, that the /aɪ/ variant belongs essentially in the district itself but it has spread to other parts of the city as a result of the internal "migration" of Kitsilano dwellers. The /ɑ/ variant seems to be favoured by the top SE status groups, while /æ/ crops up sporadically all over the urban area.

When we check the three age groups we find that /aɪ/ is used increasingly by the young of both sexes. The actual overall range of increase from O to Y for males is from 33 percent to 49 percent. For females it goes from 45 percent to 51 percent.

Other local words such as saltcheck (=sea), skookum (=sturdy, etc.), Siwash (=Indian, derog.), etc., are rapidly losing ground with young speakers, especially females. One local word we discovered by a kind of linguistic archeology, namely saskie (< Squamish Salishan/tsaʔtsqi/: edible shoots of the salmonberry), was known nowadays to only 9 out of our 300 informants. Only one of the nine was in the young category and he had acquired it directly from a Squamish Indian friend.

GRAMMAR (Gregg, 1985)

We decided to analyse our grammatical data on a special basis with the intention of ascertaining the impact of education on current usage. Accordingly, we arranged for printouts to give the results – regardless of age – for those informants who had had post-secondary education and those who had not, as well as a third sizable category – the teachers.

We do, however, have the age-group percentages for two of our grammatical sections, the first dealing with the choice between past participle got vs. gotten, the latter archaic or regional/dialectal form being highly stigmatized by those who use got exclusively. In spite of this opprobrium, we found that the young groups scored 54 percent in favour of gotten, the middle groups, 39 percent, and the old only 19 percent, so clearly, regardless of its supposed stigma, gotten is on the increase.

The breakdown by age and sex shows the following percentage scores for the use of gotten, with the young females well in the lead:

YM: 43   MM: 42   OM: 21
YF: 63   MF: 36   OF: 17

It is obvious, of course, that among our informants as a whole, the overall score was 63 percent against gotten and only 37 percent for.

The second controversial question of usage was the famous – or infamous – multi-purpose particle, the so-called Canadian eh? The scores show a very slight percentage increase in the acceptance of eh? in the middle and young groups taken together as against the old:

Y: 26   M: 29   O: 25

Further in contrast to the situation with gotten, it is the males in general (with 32 percent) who show a sizable lead over the females (with only 22 percent). SE status seems to have no correlation with the incidence of this usage.

PHONOLOGY (Gregg, 1984)

In SVEN we investigated a total of 39 phonological variables involving systematic sound changes. Nine of these dealt with variants of medial /t/ in different environments, the first five directly, the last four indirectly.

We can observe, for example, from our SVEN data that a well-known change – the voicing of medial intervocalic /t/ – is progressing rapidly. This shift is maximal with the youngest speakers in general who have a score of 48 percent for voicing in Minimal Contrast (MC) style (the most formal) as against 25 percent for the middle age groups and 17 percent for the old. Further important information about this change is that male speakers are ahead of female, and the lowest status groups show more than double the percentage of the highest.

These polarizations become even more pronounced when we look at the cross-tabulations, especially those involving the three social factors: age, sex and socio-economic status. For MC style, for example, where the overall mean for voicing is 30 percent, this three-factor tabulation shows that the young males of the lowest SE group (YM-I) scored 77 percent over against the oldest women of the top SE group with a mere 4 percent. From this evidence there would seem to be no doubt which social class is leading in this change and which is resisting it.

The four speech styles considered here, however, also show that there is a clearly graded percentage increase in voicing from the most formal to the most informal register:

Minimal Contrast (MC)	Word List (WL)	Visual-Aural (VA)	Reading Passage (RP)
30	49	61	76

which demonstrates the obvious correlation of voicing with speech style.

The same polarizations also appear in all of the three-factor cross-tabulations:

	YM-I	OF-IV
MC	77	4
WL	90	12
VA	94	33
RP	87	54

What is really noteworthy here is that the oldest women in class IV (OF-IV) actually scored 54 percent for voicing in the most casual style covered here, namely the RP. This marks a 50 percent increase over their score in the most formal speech register (MC) which was only 4 percent.

It seems quite likely that in the truly casual speech style elicited by SVEN (the Spontaneous Narrative which is not yet completely analysed) this voicing process will have reached even higher percentage scores in all age, sex, and SE groups.

For words like city, butter, etc. the most famous American dictionary - Webster's Third New International Dictionary (1961) - puts the pronunciation with /d/ in first place, but does list /t/ in second. We have not yet reached this point in dictionaries of Canadian English, but figures such as those quoted will henceforth call for careful consideration.

The change just dealt with is thus a wide-spread phenomenon in the U.S. as well as Canada and it involves a shift which our three-generation study shows to be conspicuously on the increase, especially with the young.

Intersecting with this shift of medial /t/ —> /d/, however, there is a special Canadian phenomenon affecting the diphthongs /aɪ/ and /aʊ/ when they occur immediately before the set of voiceless obstruents which, of course, includes /t/. In this environment the two diphthongs are regularly represented by high-onset variants, [əi] and [ʌu], respectively. If the /t/ is final or if it remains voiceless medially there is no problem: write [rəit], and writer [rəitər], etc. If, however, as is more likely, the medial /t/ —> /d/, then some linguists have felt that a dilemma may arise: will the Canadian speaker retain the high-onset variant [əi] that he would have selected in the environment of the underlying /t/, or will he adjust to the "new" /d/ and pronounce writer not as [rəidər] but as [raɪdər]-- identical with rider?

Our SVEN data show that there is no evidence of any serious dilemma. The special Canadian variants remain, scoring up to the 100 percent mark before medial intervocalic /t/ whether it has been shifted to /d/ or not. In the case of the /a / diphthong, the overall mean before medial /t/ (or its frequent replacement /d/) is 90 percent for the retention of the Canadian variant [əi] as compared with 94 percent before final C^{-vc}. For the /aʊ/ diphthong, the incidence of the Canadian variant [ʌu] is actually higher by one point before medial /t/ (94 percent) than before final C^{-vc} (93 percent)!

As for any change indicating a general loss of the special Canadian diphthong variants [əi] and [ʌu], which some pessimists have predicted, the SVEN data show for the most part no serious weakening in their position as the following composite percentage scores for young and old groups indicate:

Variable 6--$əiC^{-voice}$
Y: 95
O: 96

Variable 7--$əitV$
Y: 90
O: 91

Variable 8 $-ʌuC^{-voice}$
Y: 92
O: 99

Variable 9 $-ʌutV$
Y: 88
O: 99

Other phonological changes of current interest include the deletion of yod after the alveolars /t/, /d/ and /n/ and before /u:/, i.e., /ju:/ —> /u:/, as in tune /tju:n/ or /tu:n/, dew, due /dju:/ or /du:/, new /nju:/ or /nu:/.

For this change the SVEN statistics show a stratification very similar to tht for the medial /t/, Variables, 1 to 5. The YM-1 have the highest score for yod deletion, while the OF-IV have the highest score for its retention.

The overall percentage figures for the whole SVEN population of 300 show the two variants to be relatively close to each other, with yod retention a little ahead:

	Value 1 /ju:/	Value 2 /u:/
MC	54	46
WL	58	42
VA	57	43
RP	54	46

In the three-factor cross-tabulation, however, the old and young are polarized as before:

SE/AGE/SEX		Variable 14		Value 2 --/u:/
MC		73		23
WL	Y	49	O	22
VA		57		17
RP		57		35

One final phonological variable where the new "changed" form is well in the lead is the replacement of voiceless /hw/ by voiced /w/, i.e., there is a merger of /hw/ and /w/. This means that the traditional distinction between words like whet and wet, which and witch, whales and Wales, is now lost for about three quarters of Canadian speakers. The first pair are both /wɛt/, the second pair are both /wɪtʃ/ and the third, /weilz/, the overall score for /hw/ retention being only 23 percent as against 77 percent for its merger with /w/.

This change once again shows the typical stratification in terms of percentages from the oldest to the youngest for the retention of /hw/:

O:53   M:23   Y:9

This handful of phonological, grammatical, and lexical items is, of course, a very small sample of our SVEN data which is drawn from the responses of 300 informants to over 1000 questions, many with multiple subdivisions.

We are now looking forward to further investigations based on SVEN: Gaelan de Wolf's comparative study of the Ottawa and Vancouver Surveys, Erika Hasebe-Ludt's interdisciplinary research project involving the SVEN casual speech materials, Donna Richards' examination of the subjective attitudes of SVEN informants towards Canadian English and the question of a prestige form, and Dr. John Esling's fascinating electronic and computer analysis of the voice quality of Vancouver speakers based on SVEN recordings.

At the same time, Margaret Murdoch carries on with the herculean task of preparing all the SVEN data, the sets of computer printouts, the stacks of attendant documentation, etc., all of which are destined for the U.B.C. Library Archives.

REFERENCES

Gregg, R.J. (1981) General background to the Survey of Vancouver English (SVEN). Methods/Methodes IV, ed. H.J.Warkentyne, University of Victoria, Victoria, B.C., Canada, 41-47.

----------. (1983) Local lexical items in the sociodialectal Survey of Vancouver English. The Canadian Journal of Linguistics, 28:1, 17-23.

----------. (1984) Final Report to the Social Sciences and Humanities Research Council of Canada on an Urban Dialect Survey of the English Spoken in Vancouver (unpublished). Vancouver: Linguistics Department, University of B.C., 140 pp.

----------. (1985) The Vancouver Survey: analysis and measurement — Grammatical usage. Methods/Methodes V. ed. H.J.Warkentyne, (vide supra), 179-184.

Approximation of the Standard: A Form of Variability in Bilingual Speech

MIKLOS KONTRA & MARIA GOSY
Hungarian Academy of Sciences, Budapest

ABSTRACT

Analysis of Hungarian American speech tape recorded in formal interviews conducted by a high status speaker of Standard Hungarian shows numerous instances of modification from American Hungarian to Standard Hungarian forms.* Speech Accommodation Theory predicts such approximation of the standard. Recent investigations have mainly concentrated on the socio-psychological distance of interlocutors as an explanation for variable speech performance. It is claimed in this paper that there is also a temporal aspect in the adjustment of speakers' linguistic behavior: with the progression of time during a single interview more and more standard forms occur and more and more accommodation takes place.

1. APPROXIMATION OF THE STANDARD

In this paper the term **approximation of the standard** is taken from Susan Gal (1979:93) who has written the following about two of her German-Hungarian bilingual informants:

"[The informants] continued to pay attention to their speech. One indication of this is self correction of dialect forms. Another is the pauses made before the use of words that have both a dialect and a standard version (e.g. anyósom (standard), napam or svigermujderom (dialect) 'my mother-in-law'). In their speech they both continued to approximate the standard."

Such variability is not restricted to the lexical level. For instance, Seaman (1972:134) quotes an American-Greek sentence in which the word maksilári 'cushions' occurred three times — the first two utterances "contained English 'dark' [1] and the last was corrected to Greek 'clear' [1]." Of this informant Seaman says: "when she repeats the same word several times, the later Greek is more correct than the earlier" (ibid.).

In his remarks on the various national standards of English, Greenbaum (1985:31) seems to comment on the time factor in the change of speakers' listening performance:

"At the international level, the differences between the national standards of the 'inner circle' are relatively few, except for pronunciation. And even the pronunciation differences are not a major impediment, once speakers have tuned into each other's system of pronunciation."

Speakers of foreign languages (rather than those of second languages) all know the improvement in their speaking and listening performance when, after a span of time during which they have not used the foreign language, they start a conversation with a native speaker. In such a conversation one can literally feel the improvement in one's pronunciation and use of words and grammar. In other words one's performance approximates that of the native speaker. When the senior author of this paper taught at Indiana University-Bloomington for three years, he felt his English was always poor at 8 o'clock in the morning but it would become all right by about 10 o'clock. In a conversation before his first class of the day he would look for the right English word, use calques from Hungarian, and occasionally misunderstand what his colleagues and students said to him. After a linguistic warm-up, however, that is by the end of his first class, those imperfections of his English would tend to disappear.

In what follows **approximation of the standard** will be taken to mean variability whereby the use of non-standard (contact dialect) forms is followed by the use of standard forms as a result of the dialect speakers' accommodation to the speech of standard speakers.

2. THE DATA

The data are taken from about 80 hours of Hungarian speech tape recorded for the **Project on Hungarian-American Bilingualism in South Bend, Indiana**** in 1980 and 1981. The interviews were conducted by Miklós Kontra, whom his informants regarded as a friendly outsider, a visiting professor from Hungary.

As a rule American Hungarians are aware that their use of Hungarian is different from metropolitan Hungarian. Remarks on the linguistic differences abound in the interviews. Mixing E(nglish) and H(ungarian), i.e. code switching between these languages, is often termed "terrible" (cf. 3E5).***

South Bend Hungarians have a curious term, vadmagyar, one of the two meanings of which is 'a person that was born of Hungarian parents in America, and who does not speak Hungarian very well'. Such people, i.e. vadmagyarok, experienced difficulties in communicating with the newly-arrived refugees in 1956, as is shown by an excerpt from an interview with a woman born in South Bend:

"Well, we've always said we speak "debased Hungarian", but theirs was real Hungarian. You know, when I said én megnősütem 'I married a woman', they said én férjhö mentem 'I married a man', see, they corrected me, those who really spoke Hungarian." (Kontra & Nehler 1981:107)

The linguistic differences between American Hungarian (henceforth AH) and Standard Hungarian (SH, for short) have given rise to several AH jokes.****

With regard to each other's prestige AH is considered to be low, SH high.

In accordance with the aims of the South Bend project, the interviewer consciously used SH during the interviews. He also tried to act as SH listeners do, i.e. when an informant used a form which the interviewer thought a monolingual speaker of SH would not understand, he asked for clarification.

Thus the South Bend interviews are pointedly, deliberately conversations between speakers of a low-prestige contact dialect and a speaker of a high-prestige standard dialect. Within the social context of fieldwork, the interviewer clearly had a higher status than the informants. Upward linguistic convergence (cf. Giles & Powesland 1975:174) is to be expected in such a situation and we have indeed found several examples of it on several levels of speech.

3. EXAMPLES OF APPROXIMATION

When asked to characterize AH speech as opposed to SH, speakers of both dialects usually cite examples of accent and the use of loanwords from English. Thus pronunciation and vocabulary have the greatest psychological significance for speakers and listeners, but deviances from and approximations of SH occur on all levels of linguistic analysis.

3.1. Aspiration

Whereas SH has no aspirated stops, the word-initial voiceless stop sounds are typically aspirated in AH speech. When reading out word lists, South Bend Hungarians exhibit a large amount of variation both within and among idiolects (cf. Kontra 1986:54-56). In continuous AH speech two tendencies appear to regulate the occurrence/non-occurrence of aspirated stops.

First, as an AH speaker gets into an uninterrupted and easy-flowing narrative, so the aspiration of stops decreases. However, when the speaker is halted for lack of the appropriate expression or when he happens to use a H word that has an E cognate with an aspirated stop (e.g. tank 'tank'), aspiration often emerges in his speech again and then it decreases and often disappears altogether in about a minute.

Second, the SH speaker's use of a standard form often serves as a model which the dialect speaker attempts to follow. An AH speaker who uses strongly aspirated t's may decrease and stop aspiration after hearing 5 or 6 unaspirated t's in the speech of his interlocutor.

3.2. Geminate consonants

Consonant gemination is phonemic in SH, cf. hite 'his faith' and hitte 'he believed', kasza 'sycthe' and kassza 'cash register' etc. By means of a word-list test and a "same or different?" listening test we have shown that immigrants maintain the SH distinctions but about one-third of the 2nd/3rd-generation speakers do not acquire geminate consonants in their speech production and/or perception (cf. Kontra 1986:56 ff.).

In continuous speech we find variable use of non-geminate and geminate consonants where SH has the latter. Such variability in performance occurs in the speech of all the three categories of the South Bend informants (old-timers, refugees of 1956, and 2nd/3rd-generation speakers). Examples:

(1) Azé mégis nyernek egy ezer dolárt vagy kétezer dollárt.
    'They nevertheless win a thousand dollars or two
     thousand dollars.'   SB013A388***

(2) Fügetlen Templom and Független Templom
    'Independent Church'   SB013A130 and 134.

In (2) the word without and then with a geminate g occurs 12 seconds apart and the interviewer is silent during this period, thus self correction or the approximation of the SH norm is carried out by this old-timer unaided.

In a picture elicitation a 2nd-generation informant first pronounced the H word antenna 'antenna' with a single n (SB038A149), then she heard three instances of the word with a geminate n, and two and a half minutes later she pronounced the word according to SH rules (SB038A182). Acoustic measurements of this instance of convergence show a difference of 101.5 msec, cf. Figure 1.

3.3. Realizations of /l/

SH has only one (clear) l, AH has clear as well as dark l's. Speakers of AH are usually aware of the difference and they may make self corrections as in (3):

(3) Egy kis falu, Zemplén, Zemplén megyébe
    'A little village in Zemplén county'   SB041A011.

The l in the first Zemplén (the name of a northern Hungarian county) is audibly dark whereas in the second it is quite clear. The spectrogram shows a difference of 140 Hz in the first formants, cf. Figure 2.

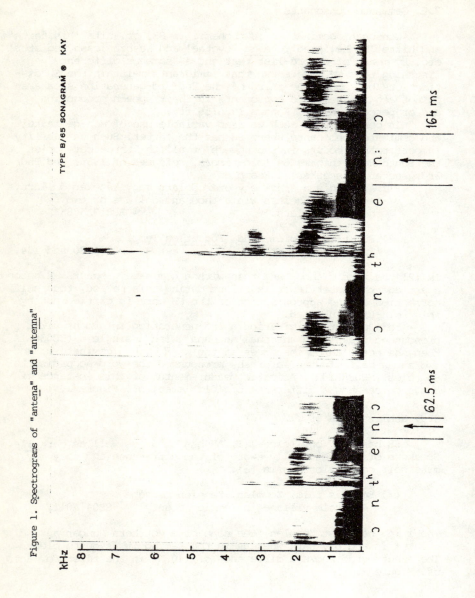

Figure 1. Spectrograms of "antena" and "antenna"

Figure 2. Spectrogram of "Zemplén" twice, with dark and clear [1]

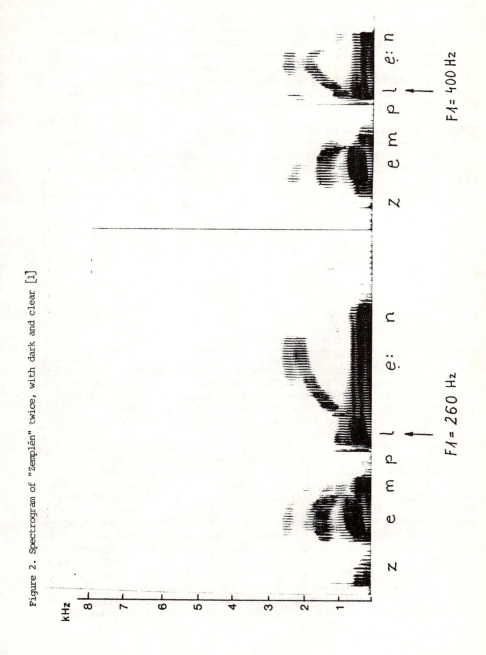

3.4. The rising question

In Kontra and Gósy (1987) we have shown that "the most conspicuous deviance from SH is the rising intonation of yes-no questions that would have a rise-fall in SH."

We have now examined one hour of tape recording for each of six informants, noting all occurrences of SH rise-fall and AH rising questions as well as the interviewer's SH rise-fall questions. The results are shown in Table 1.

Table 1. Questions with SH and AH intonation

Informants' identification No.	SH rise-fall questions	AH rise questions	Interviewer's SH rise-fall questions
1S141	11	4	34
1SX103	14	9	29
2SX33	4	6	55
2S134	3	2	52
3S23	2	30	21
3E5	0	9	27

In the table the first two informants are old-timers, the second two are refugees of 1956, and the last two are American-born. Informant 1S141 used 11 yes-no questions with the SH intonation and 4 with a rise (under the influence of English). On the other hand, the American-born Informant 3S23 used the rising intonation in 30 cases out of 32.

As regards the intonation of yes-no questions, at least in the six hours of recordings we have examined for this purpose, the pull effect towards SH cannot be shown. Questions with a SH rise-fall intonation, when they do occur, are not typically induced by the interviewer's model questions preceding the AH questions. Thus, approximation as we have defined it cannot be shown to operate here. However, the variability illustrated in Table 1 can be described as approximation in another sense of the word: as regards the rise-fall intonation of questions, Informant 1S141 approximates standard speech fairly well (producing 11 out of 15 questions with SH intonation), whereas Informant 3S23 does not approximate SH speech at all (since she uses only 2 SH questions out of 32).

An increase in a speaker's use of non-aspirated stops, geminate consonants, clear l's, and the rise-fall intonation of certain yes-no questions are all instances of convergence to and approximation of SH. The greater the increase in the use of these features, the better the approximation of the standard, that is the smaller the perceived accent of the speaker.*****

4. Morphology

The morphological structure of a H word is a great deal more complex than that of an E word due to the agglutinating character of Hungarian. American-born speakers of Hungarian often remark on their difficulties in putting the right endings at the end of H words. An example of interviewer-induced approximation is given in (4):

```
(4) Interviewer: De ezt tudod. Kával kezdődik.
                 'But you know this. It begins with a k.'
    Informant:   (:Uh:) ke... (:Oh:) kerek?******
    Interviewer: Na ugye. Ez melyik kerék? Az első kerék
                 vagy a hátsó kerék?
                 'See, I told you. Which wheel is this? The
                 front wheel or the rear wheel?'
    Informant:   Hátsó kerék.
                 'The rear wheel.'                3S38A181
```

The adjective kerek [kerek] 'round' and the noun kerék [kere:k] 'wheel' are etymologically related. The e [e]/é [e:] alternation is seen within the noun's paradigm as well: kerék (nominative singular) vs. kerekek (nominative plural) etc. In the above conversation quoted from a picture elicitation of vocabulary items, the American-born informant first used a morphologically non-standard form (kerek), then heard the standard form three times (kerék) and then used it herself.

Approximation also occurs without the interviewer's use of a standard form, as, for instance, in (5):

```
(5) Interviewer: Fájnak az én ...    (points to his fingers)
                 'My ... ache'
    Informant: Ujjamak.         Ujjamak.        Ujjaim.
               finger+my+pl     finger+my+pl    finger+pl+my
    Interviewer: Ujjaim.
    Informant:   (laughs)                       SB004B490-508.
```

In SH the stem ujj- is followed by the possessive number suffix -ai- and the possessive -m. The regular (i.e. non-possessive) plural morpheme /k/ does not occur in the possessive paradigms. In the above example the informant first used the regular /k/, then corrected himself and used the plural possessive morpheme /ai/ (cf. Vago 1980:104-105).

Finally, there are instances of non-convergence due to lack of "the necessary language skills" (Giles & Powesland 1975:161). Such an example is found in the interview with Informant 3S36,

where the interviewer wanted to elicit the verb meginnátok
'you pl would drink it'. Our informant went to considerable
trouble trying to build this wordform but he failed to do so
and finally admitted his failure:

(6) Megisz... megi... megisszá... megit...
Hogy van? Megi... issz... Ö megit...
'How is it?'
ó, nem tudom.
'Oh, I don't know.'   SB036B566-588.

5. Syntax

AH exhibits occasional syntactic differences from SH and
speakers may approximate SH constructions in their speech. Examples
will be drawn from the areas of word order and the use of definite
or indefinite conjugation.

(7) Szóval az csak volt, a rétes, az csak a dizört volt.
Vagy kompót, magyarul.
'Well, that was only the dessert. Or kompót in Hungarian.'
                                    SB102A186.

In (7) the word rétes and the loanword dizört (< dessert) both
mean the sweet food served at the end of a meal. The first clause

Szóval az csak volt, a rétes
well that only was the dessert

is modeled on English as far as word order is concerned (cf. That
was only the dessert), the second, however,

az csak a dizört volt
that only the dessert was

has SH word order with the subject complement (dizört) in focus
position before the verb (volt). A similar example is found in (8):

(8) megmondom miko én vótam (:uh... let's see:),
    I+tell+you when I was+I
    miko tizenegyéves vótam
    when eleven-year-old was+I   SB112A110-138.

Here again self correction resulted in the movement of the subject
complement (tizenegyéves) into the focus position before the verb
(vótam). Note also the non-use of én 'I' in the corrected clause,
which is also an instance of the approximation of SH. In the standard the pronoun én 'I' would not be used typically because the
ending of the verb voltam, i.e. -am, denotes 'I'. The overuse of
personal pronouns is characteristic of AH as compared with SH (cf.

Kontra 1986:108-109) — self correction in the above example eliminated this feature of the contact dialect.

Hungarian verbs have two basic conjugation patterns: definite and indefinite. The definite conjugation is used with explicit or implicit third person definite objects, the indefinite otherwise. This dual conjugation system is one of the greatest difficulties non-native speakers experience in learning Hungarian. Example (9) shows how an American-born speaker first uses the wrong form of a verb (the indefinite tudott instead of the definite tudta), and then corrects herself by (i) using a synonym with the required definite ending (értette), and (ii) selecting an infinitival object (beszélni angolul) which can pattern with an indefinite verb (tudott).

(9) itt volt nagyon sokáig, és tudott
here was+he very long and knew+he+indef
az angolt, értette az angolt,
the English understood+he+def the English
tudott beszélni angolul
he was able+indef to talk English+in

E004A100-122.

6. Vocabulary

It is probably the choice of words which a bilingual speaker uses that makes his speech conspicuously standard or non-standard as judged by various speakers. Comments on the right and wrong use of words, E words instead of H words, and non-standard H words instead of standard H words, are abundant in the interviews, especially in the picture elicitation tests (cf. Kontra 1982). Illustrative is the following exchange:

(10) Interviewer: Négyes?
'What's number four?'
Informant: Hát az Magyarországon cserép,
'Well, it's cserép 'shingles' in Hungary,
Amerikába singol.
and it's singol 'shingles' in America.'
Interviewer: Singol?
Informant: Singol. (laughs) SB033A122-142.

Lexical approximation has two major types. First, it is often the E word which comes first to a bilingual speaker's mind with its H equivalent following in the same sentence. That the language switching mechanism is in operation in such cases is shown by bilingual false starts, e.g.

(11) Interviewer: Hogyan szólítja a kisgyermek az
       'What does a child call his
       öreganyját?
       grandmother?'
  Informant: (:Gra...:) öregmama.
          'grandmother' SB141B615.

Oftentimes bilingual speakers go farther than false starts: they use the entire E word first and its H equivalent second, as in (12):

(12) Aszondom, úgy látszik, hogy (:twins:)-ek vagyunk.
   I+say that way seems that   plural are+we
   Mondtam, hogy úgy látszik, hogy ikrek vagyunk.
   said+I that that way seems that twins are+we

             SB104A067.

Such examples abound in the South Bend interviews: dōnétolni and adni 'donate', káré and autó or kocsi 'car', (:person:) and egyén 'person', virágbakszi and virágláda 'flower box', óderoz and rendel 'order', fölmúvoz and fölmegy 'move', kroátok and horvátok 'Croats' etc.
 Second, the choice may be between two H words as in (13):

(13) odaadja (:uh free:)-n, úgy mondva,
   he+give   for so to speak
   szabad   vagy ingyen   ugye a kutyát
   not in prison or without payment I mean the dog+acc.

            SB130B815-829.

Here the E word (free) is used with a H adverbial suffix in an otherwise H sentence, then two possible translation equivalents are used of which the first (szabad 'not in prison') is discarded in favor of the second (ingyen 'without payment') which fits the context of giving away dogs. Similar examples include self corrections of erő 'power' to áram 'electric power', iroda 'office' to rendelő 'doctor's office', and vigyáz 'to watch (e.g. TV)' to néz 'look at'.
 Use of the standard word or expression after the use of the contact dialect form does not always occur within the same sentence. In a continuous narrative an informant attempted to use the H expression nagy súlyt fektet valamire 'lay stress upon something' but used folytat 'continue' instead of fektet 'lay' (SB032A181) and finally finished his sentence in a clearly non-standard way. However, three minutes later he managed to recall the SH phrase and used it correctly (SB032A223). The interviewer did not use the phrase in question during those three minutes, thus here the convergent use of language did not occur in imitation of a SH form. Rather, we should assume that a complex lexical unit did not come

to the speaker's mind when he first attempted to use it but he successfully recalled it three minutes after the first attempt.

In their eagerness to avoid loanwords or mixing languages when speaking to a standard speaker, bilingual speakers use many loan translations. They may or may not be aware of calques and they may not know the SH equivalent of a calque they have just coined or used. Sometimes hypercorrections occur, i.e. an etymologically H phrase where SH uses a long-established E loan, e.g. AH ötven--ötven 'fifty-fifty' in place of SH fifty-fifty (SB145B496).

7. SUMMARY

Approximation of the standard or upward linguistic convergence has been shown to operate on all levels of American Hungarian speech in an interview situation where the interviewer was a high status speaker of Standard Hungarian. Beebe & Zuengler (1983) have demonstrated that the social and psychological distance of interlocutors can explain the variable linguistic performance of second language speakers. In this study such differences were largely controlled, yet variability was considerable. The variable performance of bilingual speakers within an interview seems to be a function of the speakers' more and more successful accommodation to the interviewer's speech as the interview progresses in time.

NOTES

* We are indebted to Susan Gal (Rutgers University) and Balázs Wacha (Budapest) for reading and commenting on the original draft of this paper.

** The South Bend Hungarian corpus exists in typewritten form and on magnetic computer tape. In both versions deviances from SH are marked for phonology (e.g. vowel harmony, word- and sentence-stress), grammar (e.g. word order, case endings), vocabulary (e.g. loanwords and loanshifts) and pragmatics (e.g. cases of misunderstanding between informants and the interviewer). Thus it is a trivial matter to have the computer search for and print in context and with loci all cases of, say, deviant intonation in the corpus. The entire corpus is over 2,500,000 characters in length. Informants include 14 old-timers, 10 refugees of 1956, and 16 2nd/3rd-generation speakers. — The project has been sponsored by Indiana University-Bloomington, Tulipános Láda, the Treasure Chest of Hungarian Culture, Inc., Chicago, and the Hungarian Academy of Sciences. We would like to thank Harold B. Allen, Michael D. Linn (both of the University of Minnesota) and Jenő Kiss (Eötvös Loránd University, Budapest) for their encouragement and professional advice throughout this project.

*** Loci are of two kinds: (i) when details are unwarranted, we quote only the identification number of an informant, e.g. 3E5, and (ii) when precise documentation is in order, a full locus is given, e.g. SB013A388, which is to be read as follows: the example is found on cassette SB013 in the South Bend archive, on side A, at 388 on the counter of a Sanyo M2502U cassette tape recorder.

**** A widely known example is based on the incidental homonymy of an AH word and a SH word. It goes like this: An AH man invites his mother, an old peasant woman, to the US. After landing in an airport in New York, she asks her son:

Fiam, hol van az utazókosaram?
'Son, where is my trunk?'

The reply goes:

Basznak   a tetején.
SH fuck+they the top+its+on 'Some people are fucking on its top.'
AH bus+of   the top+its+on 'On top of the bus.'

Upon which the surprised mother says:

A ménkü üssön beléjük! Nem találtak más helyet?
'What the hell! Can't they find some other place?'

One might think that such a conversation can only occur in jokes, not in real life. Far from it! Several of the South Bend informants, old immigrant women among them, used in the interviews the word basz with the intended meaning 'bus' without ever realizing that it was the most frequent four-letter word in SH.

***** Other characteristics such as the use of [w]'s instead of [v]'s, the use of the retroflex approximant [ɻ] instead of the SH dental trill [r], misplaced word-stress etc. also contribute to the American accent of AH speakers.

****** In the examples quoted material between (: and :) is English (code switched) speech in an otherwise Hungarian sentence.

REFERENCES

Beebe, L. M. & Zuengler, J. (1983) Accommodation theory: an explanation for style shifting in second language dialects. Wolfson, N. & Judd, E. (eds.) Sociolinguistics and Language Acquisition, 195-213. Rowley, Mass.: Newbury House.
Gal, S. (1979) Language Shift. New York: Academic Press.
Giles, H. & Powesland, P. F. (1975) Speech Style and Social Evaluation. London: Academic Press.
Greenbaum, S. (1985) Comments on "Standards, codification and sociolinguistic realism" by Braj B. Kachru. Quirk, R. & Widdowson, H. G. (eds.) English in the World, 31-32. Cambridge: University Press.
Kontra, M. (1982) The relation of L1 vocabulary to L2: a study of Hungarian-Americans. Gutwinski, W. & Jolly, G. (eds.) The Eighth LACUS Forum 1981, 523-540. Columbia, S.C.: Hornbeam Press.
------ (1986) Fejezetek egy amerikai magyar közösség magyar nyelvhasználatából. Unpublished dissertation (=kandidátusi értekezés), Budapest.
Kontra, M. & Gósy, M. (1987) Interference in intonation: notes on Hungarian-Americans. Forthcoming in Fleming, I. (ed.) The Thirteenth LACUS Forum 1986. Columbia, S.C.: Hornbeam Press.
Kontra, M. & Nehler, G. L. (1981) Ethnic designations used by Hungarain-Americans in South Bend, Indiana. Ural-Altaische Jahrbücher, 53, 105-111.
Seaman, P. D. (1972) Modern Greek and American English in Contact. The Hague: Mouton.
Vago, R. (1980) The Sound Pattern of Hungarian. Washington: Georgetown University Press.

A Microsociolinguistic Study of the Dialect of Ayr

RONALD K.S. MACAULAY
Pitzer College

The publication of Labov's New York study (Labov 1966) marked a major advance in the sociolinguistic investigation of language. In the replications of Labov's work there have been refinements to his methods but the underlying assumptions have prevailed in most subsequent sociolinguistic surveys. Three aspects of Labov's approach seem to have been particularly influential: (1) an emphasis on random sampling, (2) an interest in linguistic change, and (3) a preoccupation with stylistic variation. Each of these deserves careful evaluation.

Both traditional traditional dialect surveys (e.g. Orton 1962; Mather and Speitel 1975-86) and sociolinguistic surveys (e.g.,Trudgill 1974; Macaulay 1977) have been concerned about the breadth and representativeness of their sampling. The rationale for such a procedure is to justify extrapolating from the sample to the whole population. Recently Romaine (1980, p.170) has questioned the adequacy of such sampling methods and expressed the doubt that 'random sampling in its strictest sense is even a possible,let alone realistic, goal' for sociolinguistic research. But even if the selection of the sample can be achieved satisfactorily,there remains the problem of obtaining comparable samples of speech from each of the respondents. Traditional dialect surveys achieved this by the use of questionnaires to elicit citation forms. This provides comparable samples at the cost of information on the use of language in continuous speech. In tape-recorded interviews based on a strategy for 'the sociolinguistic interview' (Labov 1981), the comparability of speech samples is taken for granted although it is obvious that an interview with a voluble, willing respondent produces not only more but also qualitatively different speech from one with a reluctant, nervous, or tongue-tied respondent. This is a problem that has not received much attention in sociolinguistic research except from those (e.g., Wolfson 1976 and Milroy and Milroy 1977) who have adversely criticised the quality of speech obtained in interviews. However, under the right conditions, interviews can provide good samples of speech (Macaulay 1984); it would be unfortunate if such a fruitful source of information were to be neglected just because of the variability that occurs in survey interviews. The use of network contacts may significantly increase the chances of obtaining good examples of speech (Milroy 1980) but reduces the randomness of the sample. This trade-off is more than justified if the aim is to deal with more than a small number of phonological and morphological variables, since extended examples of continuous speech are necessary for the investigation of syntactic and discourse features.

It is somewhat paradoxical that most of the speech in sociolinguistic surveys remains unanalysed. Investigators have followed Labov's lead in concentrating on a few variables and ignoring the greater part of the speech recorded. Labov's motivation has always been clear since his primary interest is in linguistic change. In the preface to the New York study he expresses his hope that sociolinguistics will not result in 'a long series of purely descriptive studies' (1966,p.v). Labov's fears have certainly not materialised. Largely,no doubt, due to his example, sociolinguistic studies have been principally focussed on theoretical issues based on the analysis of a small number of key variables and little concerned with description of the wider linguistic context in which these variables occur. Viereck probably did not have sociolinguists in mind when he wryly pointed out a few years ago that 'even today data is the most obscene of the four-letter words for many linguists' (1979,p.16), but it is surprising how little sociolingustic DESCRIPTION has resulted from the empirical work of the past twenty years. As a result, sociolinguistic surveys have provided little information on most aspects of the language used by those whose language was sampled.

It is one of the few unchallenged generalizations in linguistics that languages are in a constant process of change, and this is hardly surprising since the world itself is constantly changing and language inevitably must change with it if it is to perform its function adequately. Yet perhaps more remarkable is the fact that most features of a language do not change, or at least do not change sufficiently for the differences to be noticeable within a single lifetime. The most salient changes are in vocabulary, but this is the aspect of linguistic change least studied by sociolinguists. Languages are, in fact, remarkably stable organisms, transmitting their essential characteristics from one generation to the next. This stability is all the more remarkable given the variability in children's language learning (e.g., Brown 1973; Chomsky 1969; Nelson 1973). If children from similar backgrounds show such differences in rates of language development, one might expect the language of adults to show a great many unpredictable features, but this is not the case. The process of socialization produces speakers who are clearly identifiable as members of a particular speech community, complying with the norms of speech for that variety. In a community where the number of outsiders is small, there is no reason why these norms should change rapidly or perhaps even at all, unless there is pressure from outside in some other form (e.g., educational policy, or the influence of the mass media). Sociolinguists have responded readily to the challenge of describing and explaining linguistic change but there has been surprisingly little interest in what may be equally remarkable, the failure of widespread changes to affect all communities similarly. Anyone familiar with Scottish English in its basilectal varieties will be struck by the number of conservative forms that remain, in comparison with most other varieties of English.

The focus on linguistic change in sociolinguistic research has also concentrated attention on those variables that show stylistic variation ('markers' in Labov's terminology). Labov has argued that the contrast in the use of a variable between monitored and unmonitored speech is one of the best indications of a linguistic change in progress. He has investigated these differences by examining speech in different contexts, from the informal to the formal. Unfortunately, style has proved to be a more complex phenomenon than Labov's early operational model (Labov 1966) suggested. Hymes 1972, Irvine 1979, and Traugott and Romaine 1982, among others, have pointed out the complexity of the situation. Moreover, attempts to control the stylistic context run into the basic problem that 'the context of situation' (Malinowski 1935) is not a physical reality but a mental one. As Glassie has observed:

> 'What matters is not what chances to surround performance in the world, but what effectively surrounds performance in the mind and influences the creation of texts. That is context.'
> [1982,p.521]

The attempt to isolate styles and label identifying features of a particular style (Milroy and Milroy 1977; Wolfson 1978) may lead to excessively rigid positions in which some forms of speech are downgraded in the search for a chimerical 'pure' style (see Macaulay in press for a more detailed discussion of this point). It is ironical that some sociolinguists, who of all people ought to be open-minded about any language variety, seem to be prejudiced in favour of studying certain forms of speech and indifferent to others.

In this paper I wish to report on a microsociolinguistic study of the dialect of Ayr, a town of approximately 50,000 inhabitants in south west Scotland, with a charter going back to the thirteenth century. The sample consists of interviews with 12 speakers recorded in 1978 and 1979. These interviews come from an aborted comparative study of urban speech in Scotland that I was unable to complete. Six of the speakers are middle-class and six lower-class. The interviews vary in length and quality, ranging from just over 4,000 words to 21,000 words, some containing no narratives and others having numerous narrratives that make up a substantial portion of the interview. The interviews clearly do not equally represent the everyday language of the speakers but by treating this variation as problematic it is possible to chart the dynamics of each interview, showing the effect of such factors as topic, genre, and the interview situation on the language recorded. The resulting profile of the speech event is independent of any subjective estimate of style and thus can be used as an objective correlative of any impressionistic views of the interview. Rather than assuming that the interviews are equivalent, the procedure provides a way to examine the significance of individual differences. Moreover, since the sample of speakers is socially diverse and there is considerable variation in the use of certain phonological, morphological, syntactic, and discourse features, it is possible to show which features are sensitive to social variation without the need to claim that the average use of any feature by the group sampled is representative of the population in general. The aim is to show the value of an approach that focusses on all the data collected rather than on variables taken out of context.

The interviews with the twelve respondents were transcribed in their totality in a modified orthography to show certain dialect pronunciation features and stored on 3.5" floppy disks using a Toshiba 1100 Plus micro-computer and WordPerfect 4.1 word processing software. The interviews were also coded to show major syntactic features as shown in (1):

(1)
CA coordinate clause introduced by _and_
CAO coordinate clause introduced by _and_ with no surface subject
CAV coordinate clause introduced by _and_ with no finite verb
CB coordinate clause introduced by _but_

```
CBO   coordinate clause introduced by but with no surface subject
CBV   coordinate clause introduced bu but with no finite verb
CO    coordinate clause introduced by or
COO   coordinate clause introduced by or with no surface subject
COV   coordinate clause introduced by or with no finite verb
CS    coordinate clause introduced by so
CSO   coordinate clause introduced by so with no surface subject
CSV   coordinate clause introduced by so with no finite verb
DS    quoted direct speech
FR    fragment in response to interviewer's question or comment
GE    gerund
IM    imperative
IN    infinitive
MA    main clause beginning with subject
MC    main clause with it-clefting
MD    main clause with demonstrative focussing
MF    main clause with adverbial first
ML    main clause with left dislocation
MO    main clause without subject
MP    main clause in paratactic construction
MR    main clause with right dislocation
MT    main clause introduced by there
MV    main clause without a finite verb
MY    main clause with Y-movement
NW    noun clause introduced by WH-form
PP    present participle
QU    interrogative clause
RN    nonrestrictive relative clause
RO    restrictive relative clause with 0 relative marker
RS    nonrestrictive sentence relative clause
RT    restrictive relative clause with that
RW    restrictive relative clause with WH- relative marker
SA    subordinate comparative clause introduced by as
SB    subordinate clause of reason
SC    subordinate clause of concession
SD    subordinate clause of comparison introduced by than
SI    subordinate conditional clause
SM    subordinate clause of manner
SN    subordinate noun clause
SP    subordinate clause of place
SQ    embedded question
SR    subordinate clause of result
SS    subordinate clause of purpose
ST    subordinate clause of time
SW    subordinate clause of reason
```

This coding allows the sorting procedure in the word processing programme to group together all the clauses of a particular type for tabulation and further analysis. Since the programme also provides a word count, the average length of clause and the frequency of a particular structure can easily be calculated. The clauses are numbered sequentially so that it is possible to observe the distribution of each structure throughout the interview. The procedure is simple and does not require any knowledge of programming. An example of the transcription, taken from the interview with Hugh Gemmill, a former farm labourer, is shown in (2):

(2)
```
z       (Did you get any holidays)
fr 411  oh aye aye but aye
ma 412  well the thing aboot the holidays is
si 413  as long as you werenae mairrit
ma 414  you were right enough for holidays
ma 415  it was the poor man
rt 416  that was married
ma 417  he got nae holidays
nw 418  well what he got
ma 419  was this
ma 420  the feeing fair was aye on a Tuesday the second Tuesday
ma 421   in October and the second Tuesday in -- eh -- April
ca 422  and
si 423  if you went to the fair
ca 424   you didnae get to Ayr Cattle Show
cb 425  but the single man he --
ma 426  it didnae maiter
sq 427  whether he was staying in the place
ro 428  he was in
sq 429   or shifting
ma 430  he got a week's holidays
ca 431  and -- eh --
nw 432  what a lot o them did
ma 433   they got a week's holidays
ca 434  and they didnae go to their place
ca 435  and the Tuesday after the fair -- after the --
ma 436  well the twenty-eichth of Mey was the term
ma 437  well the following Tuesday efter that date was
nw 438  what they caw'd "Duds Day"
ma 439  that's
st 440  when you went
in 441  to buy your claes for the next six month
in 442  to keep you
ca 443  and of coorse they got twaw or three days holiday again
ge 444  through daeing these things
ma 445  that's the kind
rt 446  that's oot for
rt 447  that didnae want
in 448  to work really
```

Space limitations prevent more than two token illustrations of the results. A full account will be provided in a forthcoming monograph (Macaulay in prep.). Table 1 shows that all the lower class speakers use a monophthong (a high rounded vowel which ranges from back to fairly front) in words such as down, out, and house, but the proportion varies from speaker to speaker.

Table 1
The variable (au)

	monophthong		diphthong	
	%	(n)	%	(n)
Sinclair	31	(112)	69	(249)
Ritchie	39	(31)	61	(49)
Laidlaw	48	(96)	52	(103)
Rae	83	(68)	17	(14)
Gemmill	85	(191)	15	(34)
Lang	87	(217)	13	(31)
All lower-class	60	(715)	40	(480)

For some speakers the frequency also varies as the interview progresses (Table 2), suggesting a degree of relaxation as the interview proceeds.

Table 2
The variable (au)

	monophthongal forms	
	1st half	2nd half
Sinclair	26%	36%
Ritchie	31%	52%
Laidlaw	38%	51%
Rae	73%	97%
Gemmill	89%	81%
Lang	88%	86%

For two speakers there is a much higher proportion of monophthongal forms in narratives dealing with early childhood experiences (Table 3), even though these narratives occur relatively early in the interviews. What is affecting the frequency here is clearly genre and not adaptation to the interview situation.

Table 3
The variable (au)

	monophthongal forms	
	narrative	elsewhere
Sinclair	82%	29%
Laidlaw	71%	46%

There are also lexical factors that affect the choice of monophthong or diphthong, with the latter being more probable in rarer words and in some idomatic uses.

The analysis shows that all the lower-class speakers have available to them diphthongal and monophthongal forms for the variable (au) and that the use of one or other represents a stylistic choice not available to the middle-class speakers. The factors that influence that choice cannot be fully determined from dyadic interviews but clearly include accomodation to the interlocutor, genre, and lexical specification.

The second example concerns the frequency of major types of clause in the interviews. Table 4 shows the clause distribution for the twelve speakers. The major difference between the two social class groups is that the middle-class speakers use more subordinate clauses but there is overlap between the two groups and considerable variation within each group. In particular, Sinclair has an unusually high proportion of subordinate clauses in the lower-class group. There are many other features in which the language of Sinclair's interview is closer to that of the middle-class interviews than the other lower-class speakers' and the explanation presumably lies in Sinclair's greater experience of the world outside of Ayr during the second world war. Without Sinclair's interview, the proportion of subordinate clauses in the lower-class group is 20.9%, significantly lower than the 30.4% in the midle-class interviews.

Table 4
Clause distribution: lower-class speakers

	Main		Coordinate		Subordinate	
	%	(n)	%	(n)	%	(n)
Rae	65.6	438	18.7	125	15.7	105
Lang	50.0	940	31.6	594	18.4	345
Ritchie	57.0	367	22.2	143	20.8	134
Laidlaw	54.7	1098	22.8	458	22.5	453
Gemmill	41.1	627	34.6	528	24.3	370
Sinclair	36.3	961	28.2	747	35.5	941
All LC	47.3	4431	27.7	2595	25.0	2348

Clause-distribution: middle-class speakers

	Main		Coordinate		Subordinate	
	%	(n)	%	(n)	%	(n)
Nicoll	41.3	811	36.0	706	22.7	446
Menzies	50.8	392	25.0	193	24.2	187
MacGregor	37.5	351	32.9	308	29.5	276
Gibson	41.9	485	26.1	302	32.0	371
Muir	45.0	327	22.6	164	32.5	236
MacDougall	28.6	337	26.4	312	45.0	531
All MC	40.1	2703	29.5	1985	30.4	2047

The figures in Table 4 suggest that greater use of subordinate clauses is characteristic of middle-class speech and this may be linked to education, since MacDougall, who has the highest proportion of subordinate clauses, is by the far the best educated. There are also, however, several differences between the two social class groups in the kinds of subordinate clauses used, with the middle-class speakers using more noun clauses, embedded questions, conditional clauses, and subordinate clauses of reason and concession, whereas the lower-class speakers use more adverbial clauses of place, time, and comparison. There are also differences in the use of infinitives, relative clauses, negation, and discourse markers.

It is important to emphasise, however, that it is not only differences that are interesting. The fact, for example, that the average length of finite clauses (6.2 words) is the same for both social class groups may say something about language processing which is more fundamental than the kinds of factors that show up as social class differences. The absence of comparative figures from other sociolinguistic investigations makes it difficult to know whether this conclusion would be supported elsewhere.

The portable tape-recorder transformed data-collection; the micro-computer could have at least as powerful an impact upon data analysis. All it takes is time and effort, and more time and more effort. It is to be hoped, however, that the time and effort will be devoted to describing all aspects of language and not only those that are thought to be in the process of changing.

References

Brown, R. (1973) _A first language: the early stages_. Cambridge, Mass.: Harvard University Press.
Chomsky, C. (1969) _The acquisition of syntax in children from 5 to 10_. Cambridge, Mass.: MIT Press.
Glassie, H. (1982) _Passing the time in Ballymenone_. Philadelphia: University of Pennsylvania Press.
Hymes, D.H. (1974) _Foundations in sociolinguistics_. Philadelphia: University of Pennsylvania Press.
Irvine, J. (1979) Formality and informality in speech events. Austin, Texas: _Texas Working Papers in Linguistics_, No.52.
Labov, W. (1966) _The social stratification of English in New York City_. Washington, D.C.: Center for Applied Linguistics.
_____(1981) Field methods of the project on linguistic change and variation. _Working Papers in Sociolinguistcs_, No. 81. Austin: Southwest Educational Development Laboratory.
Macaulay, R.K.S.(1977) _Language, social class, and education: a Glasgow study_. Edinburgh: Edinburgh University Press.
_____(1984) Chattering, nattering and blethering: informal interviews as speech events. In _Studies in linguistic ecology_, ed. by W.Enninger and L.Haynes, 51-64. Wiesbaden: Franz Steiner Verlag.
_____(In press) The rise and fall of the vernacular. In _On language: Rhetorica, Phonologica, Syntactica_, ed. by C.Duncan-Rose, J.Fisiak, and T.Vennemann. Beckenham: Croom Helm.
_____(In prep.) _The language of honest men and bonnie lassies: a microsociolinguistic study of the dialect of Ayr_.
Malinowski, B. (1935) _Coral gardens and their magic_. London: Allen and Unwin.
Mather, J.Y. and H-H.Speitel. 1975-86. _The linguistic atlas of Scotland: Scots section_, 3 vols. London: Croom Helm.
Milroy, J. and L.Milroy (1977) Speech and context in an urban setting. _Belfast Working Papers in Language and Linguistics_, 2:1,1-85.
Milroy, L. (1980) _Language and social networks_. Oxford: Blackwell.
Nelson, K. (1973) Structure and strategy in learning to talk, _Monographs of the Society for Research in Child Development_, 38, No.149.
Orton, H. (1962) _Survey of English dialects: introduction_. Leeds: Arnold.
Romaine, S. (1980) A critical overview of the methodology of urban British sociolinguistics. _English World-Wide_, 1, 163-98.
Traugott, E. and S.Romaine (1982) Style in sociohistorical linguistics. Ms.
Trudgill, P. (1974) _The social differentiation of English in Norwich City_.Cambridge: Cambridge University Press.
Viereck, W. (1979) Social dialectology: a plea for more data. _Studia Anglia Posnaniensa_, 11, 15-25.
Wolfson, N. (1976) Speech events and natural speech: some implications for sociolinguistic methodology. _Language in Society_, 5,189-211.
_____(1978) A feature of performed narrative: the conversational historical present. _Language in Society_, 7, 215-39.

Ransacking Linguistic Survey Data with a Number Cruncher

MICHAEL I. MILLER
Chicago State University

Though computer-driven data analyses are fashionable, the acid test of any post-mortem statistical analysis must be whether it can help produce linguistic insights that could not be obtained in the slide-rule days of twenty-five years ago. In this paper, I would like to illustrate how statistical packages can handle both qualitative and quantitative linguistic data. For these purposes, I will describe one frequency table, two contingency tables, and one linear regression example. My data are from a paper on black speech that Lee Pederson published after he completed his sociolinguistic survey of Chicago in 1964. This sample provides a good illustration for data-processing techniques in social dialectology because it is small, easily defined, and easily "crunched." Of course, the real potential of computerized analyses can be realized only with large data-bases of the types accumulated for the major linguistic atlases, but this example will illustrate some of the possibilities. All of my data-processing examples are from SPSSX (Statistical Package for the Social Sciences), but I have run most of them as well on SAS (Statistical Analysis System), and with some differences in detail, the packages are virtually interchangeable. Both packages have now migrated to the micro environment.

DATA MATRICES AND DESCRIPTIVE STATISTICS

At their best, linguists produce data arrays that look like Table 1, based on Pederson's 1965 article. Pederson included informant data on sex, age, community area, education, family background, occupation, years in Chicago, and sociolinguistic type, a modified Warner-type social-status index. The second half of the table shows how Pederson displayed the data on tautosyllabic /r/ after stressed vowels in twelve words. In additional tables he presented data on the phones of the first member of the /aI/ diphthong for eleven words, phones of the vowel of cut for twelve words, consonant loss in eighteen words, incidence of consonant phonemes in fourteen words, systematic alternation of stressed vowels in fourteen words, nonsystematic alternation of vowels in another fourteen words, lexical differences for ten semantic fields, and verb forms for ten irregular verbs, including both preterites and participles.

Table 2 presents frequency counts for each of the twelve words Pederson investigated under the rubric of tautosyllabic /-r/. Since he had dichotomized his data, these frequency counts are easy to get and dramatize the truth of Gillieron's famous aphorism that each word has its own history. Pederson tested the articulation of /-r/ following the three front vowels /I/, /E/ and /æ/, following the mid-central vowel in thirteen, furniture, and Birmingham, and after rounded back vowels in four, fourth, morning, mourning, horse, and hoarse. He concluded that assimilation of the regular Chicago pattern, which entails lateral tongue constriction, is well advanced for spread vowels, less so for rounded vowels. The frequency counts confirm this analysis and vary from nearly 70% assimilation of constricted -r in the case of beard to 16% for mourning

Though computerized and quantified, the presentation at this point differs only slightly from what Pederson published in 1964. Nevertheless, Pederson's data-presentation can be contrasted with, say, a count of the loss of post-vocalic /-r/ which does not take account of context but merely reports gross percentages derived from continuous stretches of speech. Pederson's approach is comparable among individuals, provides a broad view of speech habits, and displays the variation in specific phonological contexts (Kurath 1970).

For example, the frequency data show that by far the majority of black speakers use the unconstricted variant of fourth. But any analysis that failed to account for the sharp differences between words like beard and words like fourth or floor would tend to be skewed. Though black speech often differs, and differs sharply, from native Chicago white speech with respect to this single item, basing an analysis on the word fourth alone or failing to take into account word-to-word variation would obviously be a major mistake.

CONTINGENCY TABLES AND CHI SQUARE

Turning to critical or evaluative statistics, social dialectologists have been fond of using t-tests. However, if each word has its own history, then it seems obvious that the t-test as used by sociolinguists is often misleading. Regardless of the significance level of the t-test, the average amount of /-r/ in the uncontrolled speech of individuals aggregated into a group may be a meaningless statistic. On the other hand, since we can usually dichotomize linguistic data, contingency tables and chi-square are the method and the statistic of choice (Blalock 1970; Goodman 1969).

Table 3 shows a cross-tabulation based on Pederson's data. This is a classic 2X2 contingency table, with associated statistics. It presents an analysis of lateral constriction of /-r/ in beard crosstabulated with the variable Newer-versus-Older resident (i.e., persons who have lived in Chicago for twenty years or more versus relative newcomers). The cell values are the row percentages, which permits easy comparison of proportions between the two groups. However, the marginals--that is, the totals for both rows and columns--give both percentages and raw numbers, so it is easy for the reader to reconstruct the underlying N for each cell and avoid being misled by small values. The software also notes cells with small expected frequencies, which can affect the usefulness of chi-square. This method of data-presentation, recommended by Davis and Jacobs (1968), seldom appears in sociolinguistic literature, but it should. This table, for example, suggests that long-term black residents of Chicago use a constricted form of -r in beard more commonly than newer black residents.

NOMINAL ASSOCIATION AND CORRELATION

Among the statistics listed on the table, most software will produce the Pearson chi-square, which linguists commonly use, but the available packages also produce a variety of other statistics, most of which linguists use less often. Among these are chi-square-based measures, such as phi and the contingency coefficient, which, unlike chi-square itself, permit comparison across tables. Chi-square is a test for the existence of a relationship; statistics like phi and lambda are measures of the strength of a relationship once it has been established.

Using phi, it is possible to compare a table focussing on sex and another focussing on race and to determine from the value of phi which predicts the dependent variable better. For example, in the case of beard, the value of phi is .55 when the predictor variable is residence in Chicago, but it drops to .33 for sex (on a table not shown here), so if everything else is equal residence in Chicago is a more important factor than sex taken by itself in determining the pronunciation of beard. When dealing with nominal or qualitative variables, statistics like phi are analogous to regression with linear variables in the sense that they can identify the independent weight or importance of several variables. (I used these statistics in my 1984 paper "The City as a Cause of Morphophonemic Change". However, that paper contains several errors in the application of chi-square and numerous typographical errors in its final form.)

As the SPSSX Introductory Statistics manual points out (Norusis 1983), "common alternatives to chi-square-based measurements are those based on the idea of proportional reduction in error (PRE), introduced by Goodman and Kruskal (1954)" (p. 55). Among the most important of these is lambda, given in this case as .40. Lambda differs from chi-square in two significant ways: first, it measures degree of association between the two variables rather than testing for independence; second, one looks for a higher rather than a lower value in the statistic. In this case, lambda tells us that a 40% reduction in error is obtained when length of residence is used to predict articulation of tautosyllabic /-r/ in the word beard. Lambda is in this sense like phi, since it permits evaluation of the relative effectiveness of several predictor variables, like sex, education, or residence, used singly, and it permits comparison among several dependent linguistic variables as well. We can say, for example, that social status influences the pronunciation of thirteen more strongly than residence in Chicago influences the pronunciation of beard. Unlike phi, lambda is not restricted in its use to 2X2 tables.

ORDINAL CORRELATION

In a sense, Kendall's Tau b and Tau c, Goodman and Kruskal's Gamma, and Somers' D are useful statistics for this particular 2x2 table, but they are even more interesting in the interpretation of table 4 for thirteen cross-classified by social type. Each of these statistics approximates the Pearson correlation coefficient in cases like this that involve an ordinal rather than an interval scale. Mathematically, these represent a step up from purely nominal measures. They take advantage of the fact that concepts like lower, middle, and upper class represent scales of a sort and therefore differ significantly from concepts like male and female or black and white, for which it does not make sense to treat one as if it is in any sense greater or larger than the other. Gamma is the most useful for our purposes because it takes the greatest advantage of the PRE technique for the sorts of 2X3 tables commonly encountered in social dialectology. Detailed discussions can be found in any introductory statistics textbook (e.g., Blalock 1970).

The key features of this table, however, are not the test statistics but the frequencies recorded in the individual cells. The negative values of the statistics say that there is a negative correlation between social status and pronunciation. More importantly, however, the cell values show that the middle social group is more advanced in its adoption of the characteristic Chicago speaking pattern, while the lower group conservatively maintains the characteristic Southern pattern and the upper group seems to be following rather than leading the change. This is a good example of what has been called "hypercorrection by the middle class." (This phrase is of course a misnomer since it refers not to a phonological fact but to the relative or average _frequency_ of several phonological facts.)

In the analysis of categorical or qualitative variables, the next logical step is hierarchical log-linear analysis, which Professors Larmouth and Girard have discussed. The advantage of log-linear analysis is that it permits multiple correlation rather than the simpler independent correlation techniques we have been discussing. Other than the paper we heard earlier in this conference, the only paper I have seen in the sociolingusitic literature that mentions the log-linear concept is Professor Girard's contribution to the 1986 meeting of the Midwest Modern Language Association.

INDEXES

Blalock (1982) points out that correlation and regression analysis are treacherous fields, and he goes on to argue that in the social sciences, "unless dimensionality issues are seriously addressed, and unless our aspiration levels for measurement accuracy are considerably raised, it will remain virtually impossible to make progress in assessing comparability or in developing and testing theories of a reasonably general level" (p. 110). However, for linguists it is often difficult to organize data in interval scale terms. We can easily observe whether a specific individual produces a constricted variant of tautosyllabic /-r/ in _beard_, _thirteen_, or _fourth_; yet it seems strange to ask how much /-r/ occurs either in individual words or in someone's speech generally.

Several well-known solutions to this difficulty have been attempted, including the common method that I criticized earlier of aggregating data and reporting the "average" variation in the speech of a group without taking

into account contextual or individual variation. Another
approach, often useful in the social sciences, might involve
constructing indexes of the types several papers for this
conference have used. (I would exclude those that present
the "average" occurence of a selected linguistic feature in
uncontrolled text; these are not properly called indexes in
my terms.)

To illustrate this method for Pederson's data, I
constructed an r-index for each of Pederson's informants by
tallying each instance in which the informant used a
constricted /-r/ in one of these twelve words and dividing
that number by the total number of responses. This produced
a proportion for each informant; it is an interval scale,
but we do not know if it is the best possible scale because
we do not know for certain if these twelve words are the
best possible indicators. Short of sampling a person's
entire vocabulary, however, these twelve will do. I have
run tests of scale reliability, but this is a topic for
another paper. For now, I am reasonably certain that these
twelve items provide sufficient, sufficiently broad, and
linguistically significant data for a reliable scale.

LINEAR REGRESSION

Table 5 presents a multiple regression analysis for
three interval scales available for this sample: years
living in Chicago, social status, and the r index based on
the twelve words listed above. The r index is of course the
dependent variable.

The key features of this table are the R-square figure
of .28 and the significance of the F test at .01. The
analysis shows that when social status and years of living
in Chicago are both taken into account, these two factors
can predict the value of the r-index, though with a
relatively low degree of accuracy. Additional tables, not
shown here, demonstrate that years living in Chicago and
social status are not by themselves as accurate predictors
as the two combined; furthermore, and in my opinion
counter-intuitively, social status is a more important
predictor than years living in Chicago taken simply by
itself. (I have not considered the problem of covariation
between variables like years living in Chicago and age or
between social status and education for the purposes of this
example.)

Figure 1 is a scatterplot that shows the relationship
between the r index and Pederson's social status scale. The
values may seem to spread randomly over the plot, but in
fact there is a discernible slope from upper left to lower
right, expressed as the Pearson correlation coefficient of

-.46, but with an R-square of only .21. There is about one chance in a hundred that this negative slope is due to chance alone. And of course what the plot and associated statistics show is that r-ness and social status are positively related, since the higher the social-status score, the lower the status level. The exact locations of specific individuals are marked with letters that indicate their social status: lower, middle, or upper.

Put another way, the higher a black Chicagoan is on the social ladder, the more likely he is to use the typical Chicago pronunciation pattern for post-vocalic /-r/ across a reasonably wide vocabulary range. However, this generalization tells only part of the story. In a sense, the result shown here is not unlike the result we obtained for thirteen, which seemed to demonstrate hypercorrection by the middle class as compared with the upper group. Another look at this scatterplot, however, suggests exactly what hypercorrection might mean as an explanation for the pronunciation habits of Chicago blacks.

RESIDUALS

A significant detail is that several important outliers occur. An analysis of the residuals reveals that nearly all the significant outliers are caused by relatively new residents of Chicago. Further analysis reveals that several upper class people have unusually low r-index scores. In contrast, if we had taken a single item and placed it on a purely ordinal scale, such as we had in the case of thirteen, outliers like these on an interval scale would not be detectable. However, they would raise or lower the frequencies or average values on either end of the scale and thus make the middle group stand out. Of course, the middle group does differ from the upper and lower groups, but expressing that difference as a simple average would present a misleading picture.

In this case, it is obvious that there is a tight cluster of individuals with low social status and low r-index scores, regardless of the behavior of the outliers. Most of the correlation between social status and r index is explained by the behavior of this group, not by the behavior of the upper or middle groups. The middle group deviates from the norm both above and below the regression line. But far more important than hypercorrection by the middle class as a group, the black upper-middle-class in the sample includes several individuals who have obviously made little attempt to change their speech in the direction of the dominant, white Chicago pattern.

Some of these upper-class people are relative newcomers, but since this is the group with typically the highest level of contact with native white speakers, the phenomenon may have enormous social significance if it is verifiable. In any case, it may be good evidence for the thesis that black and white speech are developing independently, in at least some respects, in major northern American cities. This, incidentally, is a theory that Raven McDavid introduced at about the same time Pederson conducted this study under his supervision. McDavid liked to refer to the process as "neo-creolization." (Cf., Davis and McDavid 1972). Whether the theory can be substantiated by further research or not, the phenomena presented in this scatterplot obviously point to a need for more work in the field.

CONCLUSIONS

I have tried to show some ways in which easily available software can enhance the analysis of sociolinguistic data. In particular, I have attempted to show how Pederson's 1964 conclusion that front and back vowels have differing contextual effect on the adoption of constricted tautosyllabic /-r/ can be extended to include generalizations regarding the effects of social status and residence in Chicago. Devices available for these purposes include frequency tables, 2X2 contingency tables, ordinal contingency tables, indexes built on the frequency data, and both single and multiple regression analysis using the indexes. Using these devices for Chicago black speech, the analysis obviously must refer to the interaction effects of a broad range of social and linguistic variables.

More substantively, it appears that the social dynamics within Chicago's black community may be shaping certain linguistic values completely independent of the white community. Whether or not further field research substantiates this idea, it is a tribute to Pederson's techniques of data-gathering and data-presentation that almost twenty-five years later we can re-examine his work and find a solid base for new investigations in the same field.

I would like to thank my colleagues Virginia McDavid and Mark Wiljanen of Chicago State University for their comments on an earlier draft of this paper. This version incorporates suggestions by John Baugh, Joan Hall, Ron Butters, and Larry Davis during discussions at the conference. Errors are my own.

References

SOCIOLINGUISTIC METHOD

Davis, L.M. and McDavid, R.I., Jr. (1972) The Dialects of Negro Americans. In *Studies in Linguistics in Honor of George L. Trager* ed. by E. Smith, pp. 303-312. The Hague: Mouton.

Kurath, H. (1970) The Investigation of Urban Speech. *Publication of the American Dialect Society*, no. 49.

Miller, M.I. (1984) The City as a Cause of Morphophonemic Change *The SECOL Review*, 8, 28-59.

Pederson, L. (1965) Some Structural Differences in the Speech of Chicago Negroes. In *Social Dialects and Language Learning*, ed. by R.W. Shuy, pp. 28-51. Urbana, IL: National Council of Teachers of English.

STATISTICAL METHOD

Blalock, H.M., Jr. (1970) *Social Statistics* New York: McGraw-Hill.

_____ (1982) *Conceptualization and Measurement in the Social Sciences* Beverly Hills: Sage Publications.

Davis, J.A. and Jacobs, A.M. (1968) Tabular Presentation *The International Encyclopedia of the Social Sciences*. 15: 497-509. New York: MacMillan.

Girard, D. (1986) Statistical Methods in Dialectology: Review and Critique. Midwest American Dialect Society, Chicago.

Goodman, L. (1969) How to Ransack Social Mobility Tables and Other Kinds of Cross Classification Tables *American Journal of Sociology*, 75, 1-39.

Goodman, L.A. and Kruskal, W.H. (1954) Measures of Association for Cross-Classification *Journal of the American Statistical Association*, 49, 732-64.

SPSSX

Norusis, M.J. (1983) <u>SPSSX Introductory Statistics Guide</u>. Chicago: SPSS Inc.

―――― (1985) <u>SPSSX Advanced Statistics Guide</u>. New York: McGraw-Hill Book Company.

TABLE 1

INFORMANT AND TAUTOSYLLABIC R DATA

PEDERSON 1964 SAMPLE

N E W O L D	NO	S E X	A G E	C O M P E N	A M E D U C P	E D N T H P	Y R S C I T I E	E I T Y P E	T Y P E 2	T	R I N D E X	C A R B E L D S	T H U R N E M	F H I T T R R A U R H	M O F O R N G	M O U N G	H O A R S E
O	1	M	39	23	69	16	U	20	2	17	ABC	83	X X X X X X	X O	X O	X X
O	2	M	31	23	68	16	U	31	1	30	ABC	67	X X O X X O	O O	O O	O O
O	3	M	57	56	40	18	U	21	2	32	ABC	0	O O O O O O	O O	O A	O O
O	4	F	31	23	42	16	U	28	1	33	ABC	83	X X X X O X	X X	X O	X X
O	5	F	67	56	68	13	U	35	1	33	ABC	27	O O X O A O	X O	X O	X X
O	6	M	57	56	38	12	M	40	1	39	DE	83	X X X X X X	X O	O X	X X
O	7	M	60	56	39	10	M	60	1	41	DE	42	X O X X O X	X O	O O	O O
O	8	F	30	23	30	10	M	30	1	44	DE	75	X X X X O O	X X	X X	X X
O	9	M	55	56	67	12	M	28	1	44	DE	67	X X X O X O	X X	X X	X O
O	10	M	31	23	44	12	M	22	1	44	DE	42	X X X X O O	O O	O O	O O
O	11	F	46	40	69	10	M	25	1	47	DE	92	X X X X X X	X O	X X	X X
O	12	F	42	40	42	9	M	42	1	47	DE	9	X O O A O O	O O	O O	O O
O	13	F	42	40	68	10	M	37	1	49	DE	58	X X X O X O	O O	O X	O X
O	14	M	67	56	42	8	L	44	1	53	FG	50	X X O X X O	O O	O X	O O
O	15	F	27	23	42	10	M	21	2	54	FG	9	X O O O O O	O O	O A	O O
O	16	F	46	40	67	8	L	20	2	54	FG	25	O X X O O X	O O	O O	O O
O	17	F	50	56	67	7	L	24	1	55	FG	16	X O O O O X	O O	O O	O O
O	18	M	56	56	54	4	L	20	2	56	FG	8	X O O O O O	O O	O O	O O
O	19	M	40	40	80	6	L	23	1	60	FG	38	X O X A O X	A A	O A	O O
O	20	M	47	40	39	9	M	25	1	61	FG	27	X O X O O O	O O	O A	O O
N	21	F	48	40	73	16	U	12	2	21	ABC	36	O O X A X X	O O	O X	O O
N	22	F	43	40	49	16	U	11	2	25	ABC	83	X X X X X X	X X	X O	O X
N	23	M	32	23	35	16	U	2	2	35	ABC	16	O O X O X O	O O	O O	O O
N	24	M	45	40	42	11	M	17	2	52	DE	100	X X X X X X	X X	X A	X X
N	25	F	42	40	29	12	M	1	2	56	FG	25	X O X O X X	O O	O O	O O
N	26	F	35	23	80	9	M	1	2	57	FG	16	O O O X O X	O O	O O	O O
N	27	F	35	23	42	10	M	4	2	58	FG	16	O O O X O X	O O	O O	O O
N	28	F	36	23	42	10	M	8	2	59	FG	8	O O O O O O	O O	O O	O X
N	29	F	45	40	40	5	L	7	2	65	FG	8	O O O O O O	O O	X O	O O
N	30	F	27	23	42	7	L	7	2	65	FG	0	O A O O A O	O O	O A	O O

NUMBER OF CASES READ = 30   NUMBER OF CASES LISTED = 30

TABLE 2

ASSIMILATION OF TAUTOSYLLABIC -R IN CHICAGO BLACK SPEECH

FREQUENCY DATA

PEDERSON 1964 SAMPLE

WORD	VALID PERCENT	FREQUENCY	VALID CASES
FRONT VOWELS			
beard	66.7	20	30
Birmingham	62.1	18	29
chair	56.7	17	30
thirteen	55.6	15	27
careless	41.4	12	29
furniture	41.4	12	29
BACK VOWELS			
four	31.0	9	29
horse	31.0	9	29
morning	30.0	9	30
hoarse	30.0	9	30
fourth	17.2	5	29
mourning	16.0	4	25

TABLE 3

CROSSTABULATION OF <u>BEARD</u> BY LENGTH OF RESIDENCE

```
                          BEARD
           ROW PCT  I
                    I"LOSS"    ASSIMILA
                    IOF -R     TION OF R   ROW
                    IO         IX          TOTAL
NEWOLD             --------+--------+--------+
               N    I   70.0  I   30.0  I     10
      NEWER RESIDENT I        I        I    33.3
                    +--------+--------+
               O    I   15.0  I   85.0  I     20
      OLDER RESIDENT I        I        I    66.7
                    +--------+--------+
            COLUMN      10        20          30
             TOTAL     33.3      66.7       100.0
```

```
CHI-SQUARE       D.F.      SIGNIFICANCE        MIN E.F.        CELLS WITH E.F.< 5
----------       ----      ------------        --------        ------------------

  6.76875         1           .0093             3.333          1 OF    4 ( 25.0P)
  9.07500         1           .0026           ( BEFORE YATES CORRECTION )
```

```
                                                   WITH NEWOLD        WITH BEARD
        STATISTIC                 SYMMETRIC        DEPENDENT          DEPENDENT
        ---------                 ---------        ------------       ------------

LAMBDA                             .40000            .40000             .40000
UNCERTAINTY COEFFICIENT            .23737            .23737             .23737
SOMERS' D                          .55000            .55000             .55000
```

```
        STATISTIC                 VALUE            SIGNIFICANCE
        ---------                 -----            ------------

PHI                                .55000
CONTINGENCY COEFFICIENT            .48192
KENDALL'S TAU B                    .55000             .0015
KENDALL'S TAU C                    .48889             .0015
GAMMA                              .85938

NUMBER OF MISSING OBSERVATIONS =       0
```

TABLE 4

CROSSTABULATION OF <u>THIRTEEN</u> BY SOCIAL STATUS

```
            THIRTEEN
   ROW PCT I
          I"LOSS"   ASSIMILA  ROW
          IOF -R   TION OF R  TOTAL
          IO       IX       I
TYPE2     --------+--------+--------+
      ABC I  28.6 I  71.4  I    7
 UPPER    I       I        I   25.9
          +--------+--------+
      DE  I  12.5 I  87.5  I    8
 MIDDLE   I       I        I   29.6
          +--------+--------+
      FG  I  75.0 I  25.0  I   12
 LOWER    I       I        I   44.4
          +--------+--------+
      COLUMN   12      15      27
       TOTAL  44.4    55.6   100.0
```

CHI-SQUARE	D.F.	SIGNIFICANCE	MIN E.F.	CELLS WITH E.F.< 5
8.55804	2	.0139	3.111	4 OF 6 (66.7P)

STATISTIC	SYMMETRIC	WITH TYPE2 DEPENDENT	WITH THIRTEE DEPENDENT
LAMBDA	.37037	.26667	.50000
UNCERTAINTY COEFFICIENT	.19376	.15903	.24789
SOMERS' D	-.43269	-.50000	-.38136

STATISTIC	VALUE	SIGNIFICANCE
CRAMER'S V	.56300	
CONTINGENCY COEFFICIENT	.49059	
KENDALL'S TAU B	-.43667	.0093
KENDALL'S TAU C	-.49383	.0093
GAMMA	-.66176	

NUMBER OF MISSING OBSERVATIONS =   3

TABLE 5

* * * * M U L T I P L E   R E G R E S S I O N * * * *

VARIABLE LIST NUMBER 1   LISTWISE DELETION OF MISSING DATA
EQUATION NUMBER 1 DEPENDENT VARIABLE.. RINDEX POSTVOCALIC -R
BEGINNING BLOCK NUMBER 1. METHOD: ENTER   TYPE   LOGYRS

VARIABLE(S) ENTERED ON STEP NUMBER 1. LOGYRS LOG OF YEARS
    IN CHICAGO
                                     2. TYPE   SOCIAL INDEX
      SCORE

```
MULTIPLE R              .53231
R SQUARE                .28335
ADJUSTED R SQUARE       .23027
STANDARD ERROR        27.24155
  ANALYSIS OF VARIANCE
                DF      SUM OF SQUARES      MEAN SQUARE
  REGRESSION     2         7922.20928        3961.1046
  RESIDUAL      27        20036.75738         742.10213

     F =      5.33768         SIGNIF F =    .0111
```

------------------ VARIABLES IN THE EQUATION --------------

```
VARIABLE         B          SE B        BETA         T    SIG T

LOGYRS       18.73548    11.44517      .27568     1.637  .1132
TYPE          -.97457      .41989     -.39087    -2.321  .0281
(CONSTANT)   63.29844    27.01053                 2.343  .0267
```

FOR BLOCK NUMBER 1   ALL REQUESTED VARIABLES ENTERED.

FIGURE 1

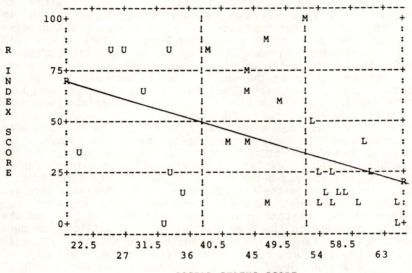

```
               R INDEX AND SOCIAL STATUS INDEX
       ----+----+----+----+----+----+----+----+----+----+---
  100+ :                   !           M           !        +
       :                   !                       !        :
R      :    U  U      U    !M         M            !        :
       :                   !                       !        :
I   75+--------------------!-------M---------------!--------+
N      R                   !                       !        :
D      :         U         !       M               !        :
E      :                   !            M          !        :
X      :                   !                       !        :
    50+--------------------!-----------------------!L-------+
S      :                   !                       !        :
C      :                   !  M   M                !     L  :
O      : U                 !                       !        :
R      :                   !                       !        :
E   25+-----------------U--!-----------------------!-L-L----L---+
       :                   !                       !         R
       :           U       !         M             !L L   L  :
       :                   !                       !L L   L L:
       :                   !                       !        :
    0+             U       !                       !       L+
       ----+----+----+----+----+----+----+----+----+----+---
          22.5     31.5       40.5      49.5      58.5
              27       36       45        54        63

                      SOCIAL STATUS SCORE

       30 CASES PLOTTED. REGRESSION STATISTICS OF RINDEX ON TYPE:
       CORRELATION -.46068  R SQUARED  .21223  S.E. OF EST  28.04675
       2-TAILED SIG.  .0104
       INTERCEPT(S.E.) 93.81564( 20.12329) SLOPE(S.E.) -1.14862(.41821)
       U:UPPER     M:MIDDLE    L:LOWER     $:MULTIPLE OCCURRENCE
```

The Roots of Appalachian English[1]

MICHAEL MONTGOMERY
University of South Carolina

For decades, researchers and collectors have prowled the hills of Southern Appalachia in order to study the diffusion of Scottish, Irish, and English cultural traits and to capture the echoes of early American immigrants in song, in story, and in voice. One thinks, for instance, of Cecil Sharpe tracking down Child ballads in the hills of eastern Kentucky in 1916 and 1917 and of the folklorist Richard Chase several decades later prospecting for Jack tales in the valleys of North Carolina. Henry Glassie has documented for us the similarities between Appalachian and Scottish cabins, and Joseph Earl Dabney has shown us how Appalachian traditions of moonshining for corn whiskey can be traced back to King James' Ulster Plantation.

This paper proposes a systematic investigation into how much the language of the Scotch-Irish, specifically the grammar, has influenced twentieth-century Southern Appalachian English in the United States, and it explains the rationale of a project and an approach to isolate and describe the influence. The term "Scotch-Irish", little used in the British Isles, is the American term for settlers from the north of Ireland who had originally come from Scotland in the Plantation of Ulster beginning in 1610 and who began to immigrate to the American colony in significant numbers about a century later, in the second decade of the eighteenth century. The term has had currency from the earliest days of immigration and was used by Queen Elizabeth I as early as 1573 (Hudson, 1984). But it did not become widespread until the mid-nineteenth century, when descendants of Protestant Irish from the north wished to clearly differentiate themselves from the Catholic Irish from the south who had begun to arrive in the United States in the 1830s by the hundreds of thousands. For the purposes of this paper, "Scotch-Irish English" will be used inclusively to refer to the features of the English language used in northern areas of Ireland and in Lowland Scotland. Combining the insights of both quantitative and qualitative paradigms, this study will compare a number of grammatical features, in particular features of the verb phrase, in these two general varieties of English.

NEED FOR RESEARCH

For more than half a century, research has progressed into substratal influences on the grammatical patterns of American black speech, as to whether those patterns have been influenced by West African languages (e.g. Turner, 1949; Dalby, 1972; Alleyne, 1980), by Caribbean varieties of Pidgin or Creole English, or by dialects of English in the British Isles such as Hiberno-English (e.g. Davis 1969, p. 335; Hill, 1975; Bailey, 1982; Rickford, 1986).

But comparable work on Appalachian English has hardly begun. The lack of such work is somewhat surprising for three reasons. First, it is surprising because the earliest and the predominant group to settle Southern Appalachia were the people whom we call the Scotch-Irish (Campbell, 1921, pp. 50-89; Leyburn, 1962; Dickson, 1966). The usual estimate is that approximately 500,000 settlers from the northern reaches of the island came to the Amercan colony in the six decades beginning in 1717. The ongoing controversy over how "Scottish" (i.e., descending from Lowland Scots) and how "Irish" these people were will not be entered into here; it remains a lively debate, fueled by contemporary ethnic rivalry, and is probably in the end unresolvable. Eid (1986, p. 213), the latest entrant in the discussion, says the "paucity of documentation of any kind" prevents the disproof of even the extreme views.

We know that the great majority of these immigrants landed in northern Delaware or southeastern Pennsylvania and migrated west across Pennsylvania and then southwestward across Virginia, reaching the Appalachian mountains in North Carolina, Kentucky, and Tennessee within two generations. What we are not so sure about is the details of the variety of English spoken by these Scotch-Irish immigrants and the prevalence of Gaelic among the population (in other words, the precise extent of the substratum to consider). Answers to these latter questions will be sought in this study.

The second reason why the lack of research is surprising is the longtime impression that Appalachian speech has preserved more and older elements from the British Isles than other varieties of American English. To be sure, anecdotal commentaries and wordlists comparing Appalachian forms with older forms of British English have been plentiful. The second edition of the <u>Annotated Bibliography of Southern American English</u>, now in its final editing, lists more than fifty published efforts to document archaisms in mountain speech, usually by pointing out Chaucerianisms, Shakespearianisms, Spenserianisms, and in some cases Old English forms (e.g. the third-person singular neuter pronoun <u>hit</u>); cf. Brown (1889, 1894, 1897). The reason why Southern mountain speech is very often called "Elizabethan" in the United States is that sixteenth-century literary forms, especially from Shakespeare, are the only points of reference Americans have at hand to compare mountain speech with, the only "data" they are familiar with.

At least one more sophisticated attempt has recently been made by Crozier (1984), who uses dialect dictionaries and publications of the linguistic atlas projects to determine the lexical influences of Scotch-Irish English on thirty-three terms in American speech. But the publications from larger-scale studies of both Scotch-Irish and Appalachian English, including linguistic atlas-type investigations, have concentrated on individual phonological features and lexical items, rather than grammar, and thus give us little idea of the workings of such grammatical systems of tense, aspect, and modality (which language contact studies have shown us are fruitful areas to detect substratal influences).

The shortage of research on Scotch-Irish grammatical features in Appalachian English is perhaps understandable. Research on varieties of Irish English until very recently has been preoccupied with the Gaelic substratum question (an exception to this is Braidwood, 1964) and the data for comparison have not been available. In addition, students of Appalachian English have been unaware of the few descriptions published. Yet this lack of comparison has left unanswered several key questions about the relationships between regional and nonstandard varieties of English in the sixteenth, seventeenth, and eighteenth centuries and in the present day.

THE "MISSING LINK" HYPOTHESIS

This brings us to the third reason why it is somewhat surprising that our research question has not been investigated heretofore. Recently Bliss (1972), Guilfoyle (1983), and Harris (1986) have contended that the habitual use of finite be, prevalent in Northern Irish speech today, was also common in the seventeenth and eighteenth centuries, i.e., when most "Irish" who came to the American colony from the north of the island. Hill (1975), Bailey (1982), and especially Rickford (1986) argue that this form was most likely influenced by, and was quite possibly the source for, the forms of habitual finite be, usually called "invariant be, in American Vernacular Black English. Rickford goes on to argue that habitual forms like doz, and duh attested in Caribbean English Creoles and in Gullah, may derive from does + nonfinite be prevalent in Southern Ireland, through contact Irish immigrants from the south of the island had with blacks beginning in the seventeenth century. (Rickford thus suggests different sources for Vernacular Black English and Caribbean Creole English habitual forms.)

Now let us remember that most of the Scotch-Irish immigrants in the eighteenth century eventually settled in Appalachia. Thus, the validity of Rickford's arguments seems to rest in part on finding evidence for finite be in present-day or earlier varieties of Appalachian speech. In other words, for Rickford to be correct, the language of Scotch-Irish settlers, particularly the early residents of Appalachia, needs to provide the "missing link" between Hiberno-English habitual forms and invariant be in modern-day American black speech. As yet no evidence for invariant or even unmarked be has shown up in any study of late twentieth-century patterns of the region's speech (e.g. in Wolfram and Christian's (1976) study in West Virginia, or in Montgomery's (1979) study in East Tennessee. This absence justifies investigation of earlier stages of Appalachian speech, but it is something of a puzzle that interviews with older, old-fashioned speakers from remote parts of the mountains have no trace of the form. After all, inflected be is plentifully attested in Scottish English of earlier centuries (Craigie, 1973, vol. I, p. 207), and present-day white speakers in the Deep South in Mississippi and Alabama living in communities with little historical contact with blacks are known to use the form (Bailey and Bassett, 1986).

A possible answer to the puzzle comes from another field. Scholars in history (e.g. Leyburn, 1962; Mercer, 1984) have concluded that the Scotch-Irish largely lost their distinctive cultural traits, their ethnicity, during their first hundred years in this country. Leyburn (1962, p. vi), the standard work in the field, says that even by the time of the Revolution, "the Scotch-Irish were no longer a separate national stock" (this view is disputed in several respects by Evans 1969, pp. 69-86). If this is true for their language, the linguistic question may be whether there was a large-scale relexification of the English of the early Scotch-Irish. In any case, by analyzing data from seventeenth- and eighteenth-century, taken from documents from the earliest days of Scotch-Irish immigration into the country, as outlined below, the present study will address the question of the extent to which the speech of Southern Appalachia has changed over the past three centuries. It will thus overcome the handicap of using only twentieth-century evidence for comparison. The degree to which we discover patterns of finite be in early Appalachian English will tell us much about the linguistic acculturation of Scotch-Irish speakers, as well as about which form is the source for VBE habitual be.

Only in recent years have the grammatical features of either Scotch-Irish or Appalachian English been investigated in more than the brief and anecdotal fashion, and only more recently has the methodology which would permit quantitative comparisons between the two varieties been developed. This project is the first to use computer-based methodology to undertake the large-scale explorations of relationships between the two grammatical systems.

LINES OF INVESTIGATION

Scotch-Irish English

Such a project as the one described here entails four major lines of investigation. One line involves establishing as a descriptive base the grammatical patterns of Scotch-Irish English in the early eighteenth century, when the large migrations of Scots from Ulster began. Reconstructing this stage is necessary because the literature lacks a description for the features we will consider here, since almost all discussion on Scotch-Irish English focuses only twnetieth-century patterns. It is crucial to establish these patterns because a considerable leveling of the features of both Appalachian and Scotch-Irish English has clearly taken place over the past two to three centuries, and the two varieties are not so clearly related to one another.

It appears that plentiful documentary material will be available (Brock, 1982). Examining early Scotch-Irish English will be done by analyzing evidence from informal writing (the type of writing closest to speech), specifically, collections of letters and other documents such as the emigrant letters at the Public Record Office of Northern Ireland in Belfast (mentioned in Green, 1969). There are extensive collections of such documents at the Scottish Record Office and at the National Library of Scotland, both in Edinburgh. One of the major challenges in this part of the research is to establish guidelines for which kinds of data from which kinds of writers to include to insure both its validity and its comparability.

A second line of exploration involves determining the relevant grammatical patterns of twentieth-century Scotch-Irish English. In addition to consulting the literature in the field, this will involve analyzing tape recordings and transcripts of speakers from the north of Ireland, most likely from the Tape-Recorded Survey of Hiberno-English Speech archive at Queen's University, Belfast, and tape recordings and field records of the Linguistic Atlas of Scotland at the University of Edinburgh, in Edinburgh, Scotland.

Appalachian English

With regard to Appalachian English, this project will establish the grammatical patterns of certain features from the comparable time periods. The third line of investigation is to study Appalachian English in the eighteenth and nineteenth centuries by examining manuscript collections, especially of letters, principally at three libraries: the W. D. Weatherford Library at Berea College, Berea, Kentucky (perhaps the best library on Southern Appalachia), the Caroliniana Library at the University of South Carolina at Columbia, and the Southern Historical Collection at the University of North Carolina at Chapel Hill.

The fourth line of study will involve the description of twentieth-century Appalachian English through reviewing the scholarly studies (approximately 300 items, identified from Montgomery and McMillan forthcoming) and through examination of tape-recorded data collected over the past fifty years. This will be done by using the following five collections:

1) Field records and taped interviews of approximately 150

informants from East Tennessee and North Georgia, interviewed by the Linguistic Atlas of the Gulf States project at Emory University, Atlanta, Georgia;

    2) Transcripts (and taped interviews where necessary) from the Appalachian Oral History Project, housed at Alice Lloyd College, Pippa Passes, Kentucky, and at Appalachian State University, Boone, North Carolina;

    3) Tape recordings of interviews (and their transcripts) made by Joseph S. Hall in the 1940s and 1950s of residents of the Gatlinburg, Tennessee, area, these records presently housed at the Sugarlands Visitors Center, Great Smoky Mountain National Park, Gatlinburg;

    4) Transcripts (and taped interviews where necessary) of West Virginia speakers interviewed for the Wolfram-Christian <u>Appalachian Speech</u> project;

    5) A set of tape recordings, made by this writer himself, of 40 speakers in White Pine, Tennessee, in 1977 and 1978.

To handle large amounts of data and to explore such general comparative questions, this project will focus on grammatical features only and will use, where possible, quantitative analysis. Among other approaches, it will employ the variable rule computer program developed by William Labov at the University of Pennsylvania and David Sankoff at the University of Montreal. Variable rule methodology is useful because it has the potential of identifying and confirming the subtleties of substratal influence proposed by qualitative analysis. This is because the variable rule program does not presuppose that the data for comparison will be homogeneous (i.e., it assumes that eighteenth-century Scotch-Irish English, or twentieth-century Appalachian English, is not uniform socially or geographically, as either surely is not) and it does not require datasets of equal size. It is thus able to isolate the relationships between linguistic features in a statistically reliable way. This methodology relies on Labov's "principle of accountability," which involves analyzing large corpora of data and comparing not counts of raw frequency, but counts of relative frequency (percentages of occurrence) of a feature in a well-defined and frequently-occurring syntactic context.

FEATURES BEING INVESTIGATED

A survey of the Scotch-Irish and Appalachian English literature (most specifically, Harris, 1987) suggests several areas for comparative investigation. Among the grammatical features occurring in both varieties that are good candidates are those in the following list. (In order to achieve the widest possible view, this list will ignore in the early stages of investigation distinctions between Scottish English and all varieties of English spoken in Ireland--the latter called "Irish English" collectively here; I ask the indulgence of those who carefully distinguish them):

1) Use of <u>anymore</u> as the equivalent of <u>nowadays</u> in affirmative sentences (cited by Crozier, 1984, p. 318, for both Scotland and Ireland and claimed to have a Gaelic source; it is widely documented from the throughout the Midland dialect area of United States (Montgomery (1979) found 35 examples from East Tennessee).

2) Occurrence of the <u>a</u>- prefix on present participles after verbs and on other structures, particularly after verbs of activity, as in <u>He went a-huntin'</u>. In the United States, this form is most productive in Appalachian speech, documented by Wolfram and Christian (1976. pp. 69-76). In Irish English it is also prevalent, where it is usually considered to be influenced by the Gaelic verbal noun construction (Majewicz, 1984, p. 47).

3) Omission of a subject relative pronoun, as in <u>Who is this 0 was telling me</u> . . . . This is identified by <u>Miller and Brown</u> (1980, pp. 16-17) in Scottish English and by Garvin (1978, 111) and Harris (1984b, p. 131) for Irish English. This author has found approximately 300 instances of this feature in his dissertation corpus (Montgomery, 1979). Other relative pronoun features are suggested by Romaine (1982) and by Aitken (1979, p. 105), who cites the Scots preference for <u>that</u> over <u>wh</u>-forms, a strong preference for which exists as well in Appalachian speech (Montgomery and Lee, 1987).

Verb Phrase Features

It appears, though, that the most fruitful area of research for comparison will be verbal auxiliaries, particularly with reference to the tense-aspect-modality systems of the two varieties of English. At this point, it is envisaged that eight features will be investigated.

4) Use of auxiliary verb <u>do</u> in affirmative declarative sentences, as in <u>I do think he's right</u> and especially with <u>be</u>, as to whether such forms are a) habitual, b) emphatic, or c) neither (Harris, 1986, pp. 176-77). Harris (1986), Henry (1957), Barry (1983, p. 109), Garvin (1977, p. 111), Kallen (1985), and Sullivan (1976, pp. 121-23) cite the form for southern Ireland; Harris (1984b, p. 133) indicates that the <u>do</u> + infinitive pattern occurs in the north as well.

5) Use of finite <u>be</u>, especially to mark present habitual aspect. Hill (1975), Bailey (1982), Guilfoyle (1983), and Harris (1984b, p. 133) cite this in Ireland, as in <u>They be shooting and fishing out at the forestry lake</u>; Aitken (1984, p. 105) cites it for Scottish English. As indicated earlier, there is no direct evidence in the literature for this feature in Appalachia, yet its occurrence/nonoccurrence is crucial to our ability to make statements about the source of American VBE habitual <u>be</u>.

6) Use of the past habitual marker <u>used to</u>, especially its cooccurrence with other auxiliaries (Miller and Brown (1980, p.

12) cite He used to would drink black coffee late at night in Scotland; identical patterns occur in Appalachian English). Other aspects to examine include the optional preposing of the habitual marker, as in Used to it was so unheard of, documented in Appalachian speech, and the used + infinitive pattern (without to), as in He used be sick often, cited for Ireland by Sullivan (1976, pp. 120-21) and Harris (1986, p. 175).

7) The tense-aspect system as revealed by the cooccurrence of verb forms and temporal adverbs. This includes the use of whenever with the simple past in sentences My husband died whenever I was living in the New Lodge Road (Harris, 1984b, p. 132) from the north part of Ireland; similar sentences occur in East Tennessee. It also involves constraints on occurrence of the present perfect vs. the simple past (Sabban, 1985, p. 128 mentions this as a common feature of Hebridean syntax). In Appalachian speech there are several patterns in which the present perfect is often used where other varieties of American English use the past tense, e.g. the use of ago with present perfect forms, as in That's been seven years ago (14 instances of which occur in Montgomery (1979)).

8) Patterns of subject-verb concord with third-person plural subjects. Wolfram-Christian (1976, pp. 76-79) note that a plural noun often takes is, was, or has as its verb, while a plural pronoun takes are, were, or have; this is confirmed for Appalachian English in Montgomery (1979). Policansky (1982) has found (as reported in Harris (1984b, p. 132) that "the morphological distinction between singular and plural in subject-verb concord is neutralized in many types of northern Hiberno-English: the singular marker -s appears on verbs with either a singular or a plural subject (unless the latter is a personal pronoun)". For Scottish English, Wilson (1915, p. 118) has noted that -s is "often used in all persons of the plural unless the verb follows immediately after a single pronoun," and the additional constraint that "when the subject is any other word or words than these pronouns standing alone, the plural of the verb generally takes the sibilant that marks the third person singular" (pp. 119-20). With a compound pronominal verb (e.g. me and him) the -s is also used. A related issue is the occurrence of -s on verbs other than third-person singular, as to whether the suffix is used in a) a habitual sense, b) a narrative sense, or c) neither.

9) Patterning of auxiliary verb contraction with the negative not, to determine a) whether not contracts, b) whether an auxiliary verb contracts with the subject of the clause (e.g. I'll not believe him), or c) whether an auxiliary verb contracts with not (e.g. I won't believe him); Aitken (1984, pp. 106-07) mentions that "in negative constructions Scots often reduces the operator [i.e., the auxiliary] rather than the negative, and prefers to do so with will and, especially, be"; Nicholas (1977) has noted the same phenomena in Western North Carolina.

10) Occurrence of multiple-modal patterns such as might

could and may can (Traugott, 1972, pp. 115-16; Miller and Brown, 1980, pp. 12-13; Aitken, 1979, p. 105) cites "double auxiliary" structures such as They'll can see to it or I'd could have done it in Scotland. Coleman (1975) shows their greater productivity in the mountain region of North Carolina, although Wolfram and Christian (1976, p. 90) and Montgomery (1979) found very few instances of them. Aitken (1979, p. 105) cites Scots preference for He'll maybe come later over He may come later, possibly a related pattern.

11) Progressivization of certain verbs, especially verbs of perception, such as He wasn't seeing too well and The people were having plenty of potatoes (Sabban, 1984, pp. 22-25). Aitken (1979, p. 105) cites I am hoping to be present in Scotland.

In this study the features that will be examined in terms of a specified syntactic context in the sense of adhering to Labov's "principle of accountability" are 4, 6, 8, and 9 above (in other words, they are tentatively defined as "syntactic variables"). Other features in addition to the ones enumerated may be observed during the progress of this study.

Previous attempts to connect the archaism of Appalachian English, particularly its vocabulary and morphology, to Scotch-Irish English have been smallscale, unsystematic, and tentative. The present study will examine large corpora of data, using variable rule and other anayltical procedures, in exploring the degree of similarity in the grammatical systems between the two varieties of English. The findings from this study will be of interest not only to linguists, but also to cultural geographers, historians, folklorists, and other scholars concerned with the diffusion of Old World patterns into the New World. As a result of this project, we may finally be able to say how "Elizabethan" or "Scottish" Appalachian English in fact is.

Note

1. I am indebted to many colleagues for their advice on the ideas of this paper, perhaps most strongly to an early mentor, Alan Thomas of University College of North Wales, who first suggested the project to me in a graduate seminar in 1974. The responsibility for its design are, however, entirely my own.

References

Aitken, A. J. (1984) Scottish accents and dialects. In Peter Trudgill (ed), Language in the British Isles. New York: Cambridge University Press.
Alleyne, M. (1980) Comparative Afro-American. Ann Arbor, Mich.: Karoma Press.

Bailey, C.-J. N. (1982) Irish English and Caribbean English: another rejoinder. American Speech, 57, 237-39.
Bailey, G., and Bassett, M. (1986) Invariant 'be' in the lower South. In Michael Montgomery and Guy Bailey (eds), Language Variety in the South: Perspectives in Black and White. Tuscaloosa: University of Alabama Press.
Barry, M. V. (1983) The English language in Ireland. In Richard W. Bailey and Manfred Gorlach (eds), English as a World Language. Ann Arbor, Mich.: University of Michigan Press.
Braidwood, J. (1964) Ulster and Elizabethan English. In G. B. Adams (ed), Ulster Dialects: an Introductory Symposium. Belfast: Ulster Folk Museum.
Brock, W. R. (1982) Scotus Americanus: a Survey of the Sources for Links between Scotland and America in the Eighteenth Century. Edinburgh: Edinburgh University Press.
Brown, C. S. (1889) Dialectal survivals in Tennessee. Modern Language Notes, 4, 205-09.
----- (1894) Dialectal survivals in Spenser. Dial, 16, 40.
----- (1897) Dialectal survivals in Chaucer. Dial, 22, 139-41.
Campbell, J. C. (1921) The Southern Highlander and His Homeland. Reprinted 1969. Lexington: University Press of Kentucky.
Chase, R. (comp) (1956) American Folk Tales and Songs and Other Examples of English-American Traditions as Preserved in the Appalachian Mountains and Elsewhere in the United States. New York: New American Library.
Coleman, W. (1975) Multiple Modals in Southern States English. Unpublished doctoral dissertation. Indiana University, Bloomington, Indiana.
Craigie, W. A. (1973) A Dictionary of the Older Scottish Tongue from the Twelfth Century to the End of the Seventeenth. Chicago: University of Chicago Press.
Crozier, A. (1984) The Scotch-Irish Influence on American English. American Speech, 60, 310-31.
Dabney, J. E. (1974) A Chronicle of Corn Whiskey from King James' Ulster Plantation to America's Appalachians and the Moonshine Life. New York: Scribner's.
Dalby, D. (1972) The African element in American English. In Thomas Kochman (ed), Rappin' and Stylin' Out: Communication in Urban Black America. Urbana: University of Illinois Press.
Davis, L. M. (1971) Dialect research: mythology and reality. Orbis, 18, 332-37.
Dickson, R. J. (1966) Ulster Emigration to Colonial America 1718-1775. London: Routledge and Kegan Paul.
Eid, L. V. (1986) Irish, Scotch and Scotch-Irish, a reconsideration. American Presbyterians: Journal of Presbyterian History, 64, 211-25.
Evans, E. E. (1969) The Scotch-Irish: their cultural adaptation and heritage in the American old west. In E. R. R. Green (ed), Essays in Scotch-Irish History. London: Routledge and Kegan Paul.

Garvin, J. (1977) The Anglo-Irish idiom in the works of major Irish writers. In Diarmaid O'Muirithe (ed), The English Language in Ireland,Dublin: Mercier.

Glassie, H. (1978) The types of the southern mountain cabin. The Study of American Folklore, by Jan H. Brunvand, 391-420. New York: Norton.

Green, E. R. R. (1969) Ulster emigrants' letters. In E. R. R. Green (ed), Essays in Scotch-Irish History. London: Routledge and Kegan Paul.

Guilfoyle, E. (1983) Habitual aspect in Hiberno English. McGill Working Papers in Linguistics, 1, 22-32.

Harris, J. (1984a) Syntactic variation and dialect divergence. Journal of Linguistics, 20, 303-27.

Harris, J. (1984b) English in the north of Ireland. In Peter Trudgill (ed), Language in the British Isles. New York: Cambridge University Press.

Harris, J. (1986) Expanding the superstrate: habitual aspect markers in Atlantic Englishes. English World-Wide, 7, 171-99.

Harris, J. (1987) English in Ireland. ESRC Pamphlet on Regional English Syntax.

Henry, P. L. (1957) An Anglo-Irish dialect of North Roscommon. Zurich: Aschmann and Scheller.

Hill, A. (1975) The habituative aspect of verbs in Black English, Irish English, and standard English. American Speech, 50, 323-24.

Hudson, T. F. (1984) Source of the term Scotch-Irish. In Jack W. Weaver (ed), Selected Proceedings of Scotch-Irish Heritage Festival, II at Winthrop College. Baton Rouge, La.: VAAPR.

Kallen, J. L. (1985) The co-occurrence of 'do' and 'be' in Hiberno-English. Ms.

Leyburn, J. G. (1962) The Scotch-Irish: a Social History. Chapel Hill: University of North Carolina Press.

Majewicz, E. (1984) Celtic influences upon English and English influences upon Celtic languages. Studia Lingua Posnaniensis, 27, 45-50.

Mercer, S. (1984) The Scotch-Irish and their responsibility for their heritage. In Jack W. Weaver (ed), Selected Proceedings of Scotch-Irish Heritage Festival, II at Winthrop College. Baton Rouge, La.: VAAPR.

Miller, J., and Brown, K. (1980) Aspects of Scottish English Syntax. English World-Wide, 3, 3-17.

Montgomery, M. (1979) A Discourse Analysis of Expository East Tennessee English. Unpublished doctoral dissertation. University of Florida, Gainesville, Florida.

Montgomery, M. and Lee, C. A. (1987) Relative clauses in written and spoken English. Paper delivered at 1987 University of North Carolina Linguistics Colloquium, to be published in proceedings.

Montgomery, M. and McMillan, J. B. (eds) Forthcoming (1988) Annotated Bibliography of Southern American English. Tuscaloosa:

University of Alabama Press.
Nicholas, J. K. (1977) I'll not say I won't do it. Paper presented at the South Atlantic Modern Language Association meeting, Washington.
Policansky, L. (1982) Grammatical variation in Belfast English. Belfast Working Papers in Language and Linguistics, 6, 37-66.
Rickford, J. R. (1986) Social contact and linguistic diffusion. Language, 62, 245-90.
Romaine, S. (1982) Socio-historical linguistics: its Status and Methodology. New York: Oxford University Press.
Sabban, A. (1984) Investigations into the syntax of Hebridean English. Scottish Language: an Annual Review, 3, 5-32.
Sharp, C. J. and Karpeles, M. (collectors) (1968) Eighty English Folk Songs from the Southern Appalachians. Cambridge, MA: M.I.T. Press.
Sullivan, J. P. (1976) The Genesis of Hiberno-English: a Socio-historical Account. Unpublished doctoral dissertation. Yeshiva University, New York, New York.
Taniguchi, J. (1972) A Grammatical Analysis of Artistic Representation of Irish English with a Brief Discussion of Sounds and Spellings. Tokyo, Japan: Shinozaki Shorin.
Traugott, E. C. (1972) A History of English Syntax. New York: Holt, Rinehart and Winston.
Turner, L. D. (1949) Africanisms in the Gullah Dialect. Ann Arbor: University of Michigan Press.
Van Hamel, A. G. (1912) On Anglo-Irish syntax. Englische Studien, 45, 272-92.
Wilson, Sir J. (1915) Lowland Scotch as Spoken in the Lower Strathearn District of Perthshire. London: Oxford University Press.
Wolfram, W. and Christian, D. (1976) Appalachian Speech. Arlington, Vir.: Center for Applied Linguistics.

The Dialectology of Scots: The Use of Dramatic Texts

JOHN M. KIRK
The Queen's University of Belfast

The methodology with which this paper is concerned is the use of dramatic texts in dialectology. By way of summary, I'm for it!

This use has not always been popular and the case against it is comprehensively summed up by Ives (1971: 177), in the conclusion that dramatic texts were 'a poor substitute for adequate fieldwork by a competent phonetician'. Ives's case, which is overwhelmingly concerned with phonology, is based on the categorical difference of medium between dramatic texts and speech, and, therefore, the inherent unreliability of written language, especially orthography, as a guide to phonology. By this method, he felt, an investigation into spoken dialect proceeds at best indirectly, by inference only.

The case against dramatic texts, however, is not simply their difference of medium, for it also concerns their status. Far from being accurate transcriptions or any other kind of scientific recreation, as accurate in every way as the substance of the alien medium allows, they are created with fresh literary intentions, with quite separate functional goals (e.g. a recognisable portrayal of social characteristics in the medium of the theatre, and so, for instance, comedy). As a result, Ives argues, dramatic texts necessarily present an artificial picture of speech. On the basis of orthographic evidence as well as its value as an indication of the dialect phonology, Ives's paper amounts to a substantial account of the dramatist's creative method – essentially selection (and so, by implication, also exclusion), regularisation (sometimes referred to as 'generalisation'), and exaggeration (the implicit foregrounding of the nonstandard) – i.e. of the divergence between actual forms and their literary protrayal, or, more abstractly, of the nonisomorphism between actual speech and its literary portrayal.

No doubt Ives's position reflected the prevailing climate of 1950 <1>. When attention becomes focussed on syntax and semantics, however, medium incompatibility is no longer relevant, for syntax and semantics are common and so independent of medium. While the dramatist remains dependent on selection, regularisation and exaggeration, his text is neither linguistically fictitious nor formed in an alien medium but is as substantively present as in actual speech. Although variable in their medium distributions, syntax and semantics may be said to be (to use the cliches) 'a common language' or to offer 'unity in diversity'.

The value of Sullivan's (1980) study is its demonstration that even a partial reproduction of Hiberno-English syntax, which is at once accurate, reliable, and realistic, is entirely possible from dramatic texts.

Not all dialects are so well endowed with a dramatic literature like Hiberno-English or Scots. Scotland possesses a literature in Scots - the so-called vernacular literature - which, according to Aitken (1984: 35), 'incomparably outstrips any other of the dialect literature of English for antiquity, for number of works and for distinction' <2>. This paper is offered as a defence of the position that dramatic texts are a valuable source of data for the study of syntax and semantics and of dialect status in general. Nowhere is this value more clearly shown than in the syntactic and semantic behaviour of primary and modal auxiliary verbs.

The empirical evidence comes from a corpus <3> representing two different styles of Scots available to the present-day writer, labelled respectively 'Traditional Scots' (Tr. Sc.) represented by Jamie the Saxt (McLellan 1970) <4> and 'Glasgow Scots' represented by five plays by Bill Bryden, John Byrne and Billy Connolly <5>.

HAVE got

Having dealt with BE recently elsewhere (cf. Kirk 1978a and 1987b) my first example is of the primary auxiliary HAVE. Especially in British English, it is claimed in Quirk et al. (A Comprehensive Grammar of the English Language: par. 3.34) that the HAVE got construction expressing Health, Possession and Relation (which, although perfective in form, is nonperfective in meaning) is 'informal' and is preferred in speech as an alternative to the use of stative lexical HAVE. In these senses, there are 119 occurrences of HAVE compared with 148 of HAVE got in the G.Sc. subcorpus. In Tr. Sc., by comparison, there are no occurrences of the HAVE got construction. These figures are presented in Table 1.

Table 1: G.Sc. - Lexical HAVE and HAVE got Forms - Occurrences and Percentages (from Kirk, 1986: Table 2.59)

	n.	%
Stative HAVE	119	44.6
HAVE got	148	55.4
Totals	267	100.0

In its presentation of the percentage distributions of the Health, Possession, and Relation senses of stative HAVE in comparison with the equivalent use of the HAVE got construction, Table 1 shows that the speech preference in favour of HAVE got forms is 55.4%. A G.Sc. example of the HAVE got construction is [1] (see Illustrative Appendix). The copiousness of the tokens reveals that all characters use the HAVE got construction, including the middle-class characters, as in [2]. Quirk et al.'s claim that the HAVE got construction is particularly common in negative and interrogative clauses is also confirmed by the G.Sc. subcorpus, as Table 2 shows:

Table 2: G.Sc. - Lexical HAVE and HAVE got - Occurrences (from Kirk, 1986: Table 2.60).

	Negatived Declaratives n.	Interrogatives n.	Negatived Interrogatives n.	Totals n.
HAVE got	13	14	0	27
Lexical HAVE	6	4	0	10
Totals	19	18	0	37

In these two constructions alone, HAVE got is more than twice as frequent as the HAVE construction. An example of a negative declarative is [3], and an example of an interrogative is [4]. Considered overall (cf. Table 1), HAVE got is half as frequent again as the HAVE construction. There are only five examples of the latter (e.g. [5]).

In an investigation of Edinburgh speech, elicited from schoolchildren in both the state and private sectors, sometimes referred to as Miller and Brown's corpus of Edinburgh speech, the HAVE got construction is between two-and-a-half and three times as frequent as stative HAVE (Miller 1982a). The distribution of these two HAVE constructions thus matches up to the formality represented in each subcorpus.

MUST

A second example concerns the distribution of senses expressed by the modal verb MUST. Table 3 compares Tr. Sc., G.Sc. and Standard English (St.E.). The latter is represented by the London-Lund Corpus (Lund), which comprises informal conversations in spoken Standard English (cf. Svartvik and Quirk 1980), and the Lancaster-Oslo/Bergen Corpus, which comprises written texts in British St. E., representing four principal registers: journalese, nonfictional prose, learned and scientific prose, and fiction (cf. Johansson et al. 1978).

Table 3: MUST Meanings – Percentages – Inter-corpus Comparisons (from Kirk, 1986: Table 5.13) <6>

	Lund %	G.Sc. %	Tr.Sc. %	LOB %
Root MUST	53.0	26.8	30.0	64.8
Epistemic MUST	46.0	73.2	70.0	31.4
Indeterminate	1.0	0.0	0.0	3.8
Totals	100.0	100.0	100.0	100.0

Table 3 shows that the distribution of MUST senses in Scots is the reverse of that in St.E.. In Scots, Epistemic MUST (expressing Prediction) predominates; in St.E., it is Root MUST (expressing Obligation). These figures are confirmed by the Edinburgh speech corpus. Miller (1982c) found that MUST was mainly Epistemic: 79 out of 85 occurrences (or 92.9%) in the private school data, and 65 out of 71 occurrences (or 91.5%) in the state school data. Two G.Sc. examples of Root MUST (one in the first, the other in the second, person) are [6], and two similar Tr.Sc. examples of Root MUST, realised as maun, are [7]. A G.Sc. example of Epistemic MUST is [8], and a Tr.Sc. exaple is [9].

Miller (1982c and 1982c) further argues that there is no Root MUST in the spoken Scots of his informants – the St.E. meaning of MUST of 'Obligation and Necessity' being expressed in Scots by HAVE TO, HAVE got TO, GET TO, and NEED. When the corpus of dramatic texts is compared with Miller and Brown's findings on the one hand and St.E. on the other, it is tempting to conclude that the dramatic texts go some way towards representing the situation in Scots speech, but perhaps the failure to exclude Root meanings completely may be due once again to the influence of written St.E. Just as Sullivan (1980) demonstrates in the case of Hiberno-English, however, the status of G.Sc. as a decidedly Scottish style is in no way diminished by the copresence of St.E. variants.

PERMISSION

A third example concerns the modal verb of Permission which is shown in Table 4.

Table 4: Tr.Sc. and G.Sc. - The Expression of Permission - Occurrences and Percentages.

	Tr.Sc. n.	G.Sc. n.	Tr.Sc. %	G.Sc. %
MAY	8	1	53.3	3.7
CAN	7	20	46.7	74.0
GET TO	0	6	0.0	22.3
Totals	15	27	100.0	100.0

The source of Permission varies, ranging from the one of the speakers present, to absent individuals, and finally on to regulations and other impersonal but binding authorities. Permission GET TO is identified as a clear feature of spoken Scots, and this is reflected in its frequency distribution both within the paradigm occupied by Permission modal verbs, and between Tr.Sc. and G.Sc. At the same time, G.Sc. avoids May, which, according to Quirk, et al. (CGEL: par. 4.53), is more formal and less common as a Permission modal than CAN. In Miller's (1982b) investigation of Edinburgh speech, MAY is extremely rare ('either completely absent or peripheral'). The only G.Sc. example (which is [10]) of Permission MAY is formulaic of politeness. Two examples of Permission MAY in Tr.Sc. are [11]. G.Sc. examples of Permission CAN are [12] and an example of Permission CAN in Tr.Sc. is [13]. Finally, the six examples of GET TO meaning Permission include [14] (GET TO, incidentally, can also mean Obligation).

The evidence of Table 4 reinforces the very strong Tr.Sc. conformity to, as well as the simplification of, the norms of formal, written St.E., and its equally strong avoidance of the reflection of the patterns of spoken norms, unlike G.Sc., in which the situation in actual speech is reflected.

DARE AND NEED

A further difference between the Tr.Sc. and G.Sc. subcorpuses concerns the categorisation of the Marginal Modals, DARE and NEED. These behave differently in each subcorpus and in St.E. According to Quirk et al. (CGEL: par. 3.42), DARE and NEED can be constructed either as main verbs or as modal verbs, but the former is more common. As modal verbs they are restricted to nonassertive contexts (i.e. negative and interrogative contexts). In Tr.Sc. both verbs function universally as full central modal verbs, as [15] (the first negatived, and the second interrogative). Examples of NEED include [16].

In G.Sc., however, DARE only functions as a central modal in affirmative and rhetorical interrogative sentences, as in [17], compared with its function as a main verb interrogative and negative sentences, as in [18].

NEED, however, functions as a central modal only in interrogatives and some negative sentences, as in [19]. In affirmative sentences NEED occurs as the main verb NEED TO, as in [20]. In G.Sc., in other words, DARE and NEED display quite opposite syntactic patterns and thus also reflect the variation described by Quirk et al.

In addition, NEED TO, as a main verb, also occurs in negative sentences, as in [21].

By contrast, in Miller's Edinburgh investigation, all occurrences of NEED are main verbs. Tr.Sc., however, operates a simplified system which is not only furthest removed from actual speech practice but in which the norms of written St.E. are once again simplified and generalised.

As the above examples show (and there are a great many more I could have given (cf. Kirk 1986)), the evidence for this demonstration comes from frequency distributions which reflect a range of syntactic and semantic distributions, whether at the surface level of form, of mood or of polarity realisation, or at an underlying level consisting purely of meaning. It is this evidence from such a variety of contexts which vindicates the use of dramatic texts; for the elicitation of such evidence would be impossible for traditional dialect questionnaires, particularly of the onomasiological variety which typically ask 'What is the name of the heavenly body which gives light during the day?' Even personal narratives, including 'danger of death' stories, as I argued in Kirk (1985), are limited in their value as evidence for meanings conventionally associated with the operator, including negation and interrogation, tense and aspect, mood and modality. Few structured observations could elicit so many second person examples (as indicated) or so many appeals to the hearer (by way of requests or commands) as dramatic texts, and all the evidence currently available from speech, notably the spoken texts of the Survey of English Usage (i.e. the London-Lund Corpus), is in St.E.

Compared with both Tr.Sc. and St.E., G.Sc. appears most distinctive in its semantics (i.e. the relationship between lexical categories and their meanings - whether mono - or polysemeous, and between meanings and their realisation, the diversity of which marks some stylistically) <7>. G.Sc. has its own, more complex system of semantic structures, as, for instance, the comparison of Possessive HAVE and HAVE got (above), or the range of verbs used to express 'Obligation and Necessity', or the tendency, which is realistic for speech, for modal meanings to be ambiguous between semantic categories. In Tr.Sc., by contrast, the categories of meaning are always quite unambiguous, no doubt the result of carefully considered authorial planning.

Despite such differences, however, the semantic systems are overwhelmingly shared by Tr.Sc., G.Sc. and St.E., and the structure of semantic agreement is shown quite emphatically by the very high degree of distributional agreement between the most frequent senses of the modal verbs, expressed as percentages of sense distributions within individual modal verbs, and represented in Table 5.

Table 5: Tr.Sc. and G.Sc. – Central Modal Verbs – Most Common Senses – Percentage Distributions (Inter-corpus Comparisons) (from Kirk, 1986: Table 5.22) <6>

	Lund %	G.Sc. %	Tr.Sc. %	LOB %
Epistemic WOULD	82.5	49.0	75.6	58.0
Epistemic WILL	57.5	59.5	66.9	71.4
Root Possibility and Ability CAN	95.0	81.9	70.1	88.7
Root Possibility and Ability COULD	90.9	82.4	88.2	90.0
Epistemic MIGHT	78.5	88.9	65.7	60.0

These investigations have demonstrated, I think quite clearly, that Tr.Sc. and G.Sc. differ in their speech implications. As two literary styles, the principal internal differences between Tr.Sc. and G.Sc. amount to differences of exponence in individual syntactic and semantic paradigms, i.e. of systemic heterogeneity (or diversity), these differences also being shared with St.E. At the same time, the syntactic and semantic functions inherent in these syntactic forms are identical, so that Tr.Sc. and G.Sc. also share with St.E. a homogeneity of dialect.

What the use of dramatic texts has been able to demonstrate is that none of these patterns of similarities and differences or of homogeneity and heterogeneity indicate that there are differences in terms of the abstract or typological categorisation or classification of their syntactic and semantic features. In other words, there is no autonomy, for Tr.Sc., G.Sc. and St.E. all share the same 'grammar', and so the same identity. Thus, insofar as syntax and semantics are concerned, the identity and status of

Scots, of whatever variety, as Kirk (1987c) shows, is heteronomous with St.E., being bound up and inextricably influenced by St.E., the two differing only in name. All are subject-verb-object dialects, in which the sentence has the same set of constituents and the same principles and patterns of ordering and embedding these constituents. Comparisons with CGEL and other studies of English syntax (e.g. Miller 1984) reinforce the mutual applicability of the abstract categories associated with the description of auxiliary verbs. Not one of these patterns is qualified to substantiate the claim, made by popular as well as academic commentators and reviewed disbelievingly by Aitken (1981) on external grounds, and now by myself on internal grounds, for the autonomy of Scots <8>.

The debate between Ives and Sullivan can thus be rehearsed between the two subcorpuses. Tr.Sc. substantiates Ives's worst fears. Its popularity in the theatre cannot be attributed to its dialect realism – to what one critic calls the artificiality of dictionary Scots (Bold, 1983: 292) – but to the consummate skill of its author (McLellan) who, according to one fellow playwright (Campbell 1986: 37), was 'a superb lyric poet who happened to have the additional gift of a theatrical imagination', whose work for the stage must be seen in the context of a popular Scottish audience, and who may thus be genuinely called a 'comic artist'. On the other hand, G.Sc. represents genuine and genuinely informal speech behaviour, its language discriminating between variants which in their accumulation are regionally and/or socially significant (spoken Glaswegian being a sociolect as well as a regional dialect), and also between the exponents of the informality conventionally associated with spontaneous speech and now most fully described in CGEL. G.Sc., it is true, also proceeds on the basis of selectivity, only with the difference that it is demonstrably accurate in its speech realism <9>. At the same time, it has, of course, demonstrable exclusions, such as the infinitive use of COULD in a double modal construction (e.g. I won't can afford it or I might could do it) or after the semi-auxiliary USED TO I used to could do it, or the Permission GET + Gerund construction (e.g. do I get keeping it?) <10> clearly indicative of the limitations of speech realism which are constantly subject to the norms of writing and no doubt also the standardising prescriptions of good taste, G.Sc. playwright remaining artists of the written medium rather than photographers of the spoken. In its subscription to the principle of total accountability (cf. Quirk and Svartvik 1979 and Johansson 1985), one of the values of an exhaustive study of frequency distributions is its ability always to discriminate between its data and, thus, from within its own resources, to evaluate any disproportionate foregrounding whether, on the one hand, of the nonstandard, which was such a worry to Ives, but which may have stylistic significance, or, on the other, of the influence of the written standard.

When Ives (1971: 150) considered dialects to be corpuses of implicitly agreed speech habits, composites or combinations of features which each had an individual distribution but which were found in any one limited area in a particular combination, Ives was right – while he was thinking of phonology, I have demonstrated it for syntax and semantics. We have seen from other papers at this conference how individual traits found here occur elsewhere but nowhere else in exactly the same combination.

At the same time, the degree of consistency between dramatic G.Sc. and Miller's spoken Edinburgh Scots seems to offer a useful challenge to three of Ives's impressionistic and actually unquantified claims. These concern, firstly, a dramatist's tendency to ignore or exclude distinctive characteristics of the spoken dialect, for the obvious and conspicuous characteristics do all appear to be represented; secondly, his tendency to make variants more regular than the actual speech represented (certainly true of Tr.Sc.); and, thirdly, his tendency to exaggerate the frequency of dialectal features, for speech realism has been shown to be not just a question of the presence or absence of features but also of their relative frequency, and certain frequencies may also have a stylistic function (cf. note 7).

Finally, the use of frequencies has also challenged Ives's claim about the derivation of information from dramatic texts by inference, for it has shown, as Sullivan (1980) does, too, that genuine, nonfictitious information about dialects at different levels can indeed be fully demonstrated. The use of dramatic texts in dialectology, you ask? In the case of Scots, I'm certainly for it!

Illustrative Appendix

This illustrative appendix is referred to in the text. The citation references are explained in Note 3.

[1] TH SA 6374 See that bugger I've got.

[2] SB AL 3475 I've got a young brother who's earning that and he's only sixteen.

[3] SB HE 5745 Ah'll be gaun wi' Wullie ... he husnae got a ticket.

[4] SB SA 3889 Noo, hus yese aw goat yur tickets fur the Staff Dance?

[5] TH LU 5977 Have you such a thing as a comb with soft teeth you could lend us?

[6] BL ST 1418 You must wait for the photo, Doctor.
TH MW 8054 Still, we mustn't dwell on these things, must we?

[7] JS BM 10603 Weill, Mistress Edward, ye'll ken fine, yer guid man bein a Bailie himsell, that I maun gaird aye my tongue weill in maitters that affect the Toun.
JS ME 10622 Ye maun sit doun, Bailie, and I'll licht a wheen maur caunles, for the gloamin's weirin on.

[8] LE JE 228 The neighbours must think yer a right nosey bugger.

[9] JS ME 10879 I canna richt mk oot, wi the wind blawn at the links, but Nicholl maun hae tummlet in a moss-hole. He's thick wi glaur.

[10] SA JA 9218 ... hi Lucille .. that's a very nice outfit, if I may say so.

[11] JS BM 10610 The Provost's at Leith for the horse-racin, and it's a maitter that the Toun Gaird couldna settle. It micht, I may tell ye, mean a cry at the Cross for the haill Toun to rise.
JS MV 12367 (King): Is it a bairn? (Melville): Yer Grace, ye may lippen for an heir in the coorse o the comin year.

[12] SB LU 5757 Sure you can get your Dad's MG the night, handsome?
SL PH 10563 You can work right up till your eighth month, you know.

[13] JS KI 11755 Afore a man can claim authority in speeritual maitters he maun ae thing yer Moderator hasna! He maun hae the pouer by Divine Richt to enforce his decrees!

[14] TH PH 6888 Listen, ... tails you <u>get</u> <u>to</u> talk to her first ... heads, I do ...
SL SP 8154 Jesus ... did you <u>get</u> <u>to</u> have a look?

[15] JS AT 10862 (logie): There's as muckle gowd in Papist Spain as there is in Protestant England.
(Atholl): But he <u>daurna</u> touch the Spanish gowd!
JS MA 11165 We f<u>in</u> <u>oot</u> that a man's a fause-hairtit traitor, thick as a thief wi ane that has time and again tried to take the life o the King, but <u>daur</u> we bring him to his trial? Na, Na, his friends at Coort <u>wad</u> stop us!

[16] JS LO 10792 Come come nou, Bailie, ye <u>needna</u> tak it
JS OC 11557 Yer Grace, they <u>needna</u> ken ye were threatent!

[17] SB CU 5888 How <u>dare</u> you shoot your mouth off like that. How <u>dare</u> you!
SL LU 6231 Don't you <u>dare</u> give this address if you get knocked down.

[19] LE JO 174 Well, if it's that yer lookin fur, ye'd <u>needny</u> look any further than across the Atlantic.
TH CU 6277 Farrell, would you remove this carrier bag, please? I <u>needn't</u> ask it it's yours.

[20] LE AG 755 Here Jean, A <u>need</u> <u>tae</u> go a place – where's the key?
BL ST 1405 Puggy, ye'll <u>need</u> <u>to</u> look after 'im!

Notes

1. Cf. the introductory editorial remarks to Ives (1971) by Williamson and Burke.

2. Recent studies of twentieth-century Scottish drama include Bold (1983) and Hutchison (1977).

3. The texts in question are Robert McLellan's <u>Jamie the Saxt</u> (JS) (McLellan 1970), Billy Connolly's <u>An Me Wi Ma Bad Leg Tae</u> (LE) (Connolly, ms. [first performance 1976]), Bill Bryden's <u>Benny Lynch</u> (BL) (Bryden 1975) and John Byrne's trilogy <u>Paisley Patterns</u> (PP) comprising <u>The Slab Boys</u> (SB) (Byrne 1981), <u>Threads</u> (TH) (Byrne 1980) and <u>Still Life</u> (SL) (Byrne 1982). Citation references, which follow below, consist of three elements: a two-letter reference to the play (by abbreviation, just indicated), a two-letter reference by character, and a line number, to the corpus of the six tests, in machine-readable form. The abbreviated character references are: AG Agnes (LE); AL Alan (PP); AT Atholl (JS); BM Bailie Morison (JS); CU Curry (PP); HE Hector (PP); JA Jack (PP); JE Jean (LE); JO John (LE); KI King (JS); LO Logie (JS); LU Lucille (PP); ME Mrs. Edward (JS); MV Melville (JS); MW Miss Walkinshaw (PP); OC Ochiltree (JS); PH Phil (PP); SA Sadie (PP); ST Stoorie (BL). The speeches of the Queen (in Pidgin Scots), Sir Robert Bowes and the Stranger (in English), in JS, are excluded.

4. As a variety Tr.Sc. is ahistorical, being contemporary neither with the events of the play nor with the author's own day; it follows a technique much deployed in Scottish literature and exploited, for instance, by Walter Scott (in <u>The Abbott</u> or <u>The Monastery</u>). In regional terms, Tr.Sc. is delocalised. It happens that McLellan came from, and spent his life within, the West Central Scots dialect area, but his literary dialect is essentially metropolitan Scots, by intention representative of the entire Lowland Scots speaking area. For his purposes, McLellan believed that it was sufficiently localised as Scots (i.e. not St.E.) and the question of greater local realism was irrelevant insofar as his intentions were not documentary or realistic but purely literary. In social terms, <u>Jamie the Saxt</u> distinguishes the dialect of the Scots-speaking characters from that of the St.E. -speaking characters (Sir Robert Bowes and the Stranger), and the Pidgin-Scots of the Danish-born Queen. But no further distinction is made in the Scots to reflect social differences between characters (between, for instance, the King and Mistress Edward, wife of Bailie Nicholl Edward, an Edinburgh cloth merchant, with whom the King lodges). In this respect, Tr.Sc. may be said to be 'asocial'.

Literary, selective and extremely regularised though Tr.Sc. is, although not exaggerated in the sense of an active foregrounding of the nonstandard, it has some basis in actual speech. The basis usually cited is the rural Scots typified by Buchan, the Black Isle and parts of the Borders. There is thus a link between conservative, rural, largely working-class and uneducated Scots speech and the conservative, metropolitan, delocalised literary Scots (perhaps most comprehensively set out by Murison 1977 and confirmed in general by Aitken 1981). The appeal of Jamie the Saxt, as vivid in performance in 1937 as it still is in the 1980's, is thus attributable to McLellan's ability to suggest that rural conservative Scots speech could have been spoken throughout the whole of Scottish society, including the Monarch himself; and at the same time to suggest, conversely, that even the King himself can be imaginatively shown to have the qualities of mind and character usually associated with rural conservative speech of its ordinary speakers ('the countrified, blunt-spoken quality, of the earth earthy, traditionally associated with Scots speech', according to Buthlay, 1982: 29). McLellan's achievement was the generic extension of literary Tr.Sc. from its uses in poetry and prose fiction to its use in drama.

Here is a brief extract from a discussion in the King's private chambers between the King himself, who happens to be deshabille, some of his noble lords:

BOTHWEL: Gin ye dinnae gie in I'll cairry ye ower to the winnock juist as ye are!
THE KING: (Almost in tears) Aa richt. I'll gie in the nou. But by God wait!
BOTHWELL: (To Atholl): Whaur are his breeks?
THE KING: They're in the closet.
BOTHWELL: Fetch his breeks, Lennox.
LENNOX: (indignantly) My Lord ye forget yersell.
OCHILTREE: I'll fetch them ... (coming in from the closet) This is the only pair I can fin.
BOTHWELL: They'll dae. Help him into them.
(from McLellan 1970: 55)

5. Since the early 1970's, a new literary dialect has emerged, based on Glasgow speech. In historical terms, Glasgow Scots is contemporary with the events of the five plays and nearly contemporary with the dte of writing and first performance. All the variables point to a fairly homogeneous historical dialect of the mid-twentieth century. It is the intention of the dramatist, as interviews with Bryden (e.g. Bold 1974) and Byrne (e.g. McMillan 1982) indicate, to represent the actual speech that the characters are assumed to have spoken in their supposed real life. In regional terms, G.Sc. is localised within the Scots-speaking area to that of West Central Scots which centres on Glasgow. The representation of local speech is also part of what these plays are about, for their intention is to extend the range of the dialect, from its purely vernacular use, to its use as a literary

(and specifically dramatic) vehicle. In social terms, G.Sc. also differentiates between those characters who are presented as though they were speaking in the vernaculr and conforming wholly (or predominantly) to its norms, and those, usually middle-class, characters who are presented as though they had let themselves be influenced by St.E. (such as the Doctor in BL or Miss Walkinshaw in PP.

Here is an extract from Connolly's play (<u>An Me Wi Ma Bad Leg Tae</u> in which, after a year in the army, Peter arrives home to his parents Bob and Jean and his brother John:

BOB: Och it's yersell, nice tae have ye hame again son, come away in. Here, gie's that case, ye must be sick lookin at it.
PETER: God aye, yer no kiddin there faither, ma back's near broke.
JOHN: Whit have ye got that's so heavy in there Peter? Yer wages, is it?
PETER: Aye, that'll be right.
JOHN: How's it goin'?
PETER: No bad.
JEAN: Aw, ma wee son, wid ye look at ye. Tae think o' ma wee boy.
JOHN: Aw, come on, gie's a wee look at 'im.
JEAN: A think ye've lost a bit o' weight son, whit are they dae'in tae ye?
JOHN: Have they cut ye doon tae six plates o' mince a day Peter, eh?
PETER: Och, it's the exercise, Maw, ah'm as fit as a fiddle. A've only lost yon kite A hid wi' the beer, an A wis glad tae see the back o' it A might add. Hey ... (he winks at John) ... y're lookin no bad yersell auld yin.
JEAN: Away an gie's yersell peace you. Aye, an less o' this auld yin stuff by the way.
(from Connolly ms.: 3-4)

The descriptive categories conventional in dialectology are thus more readily valid for G.Sc. In these terms, Tr. Sc. is not realistic - it might be called 'bourgeois' or 'gentrified' or even 'anachronistic'. By contrast, as a literary dialect, G.Sc. represents nothing short of a shift of medium, creating on the basis of speech a written form or overall register which previously did not exist. It lacks the simplified formality of the written language and bears many of the characteristics of 'informality' associated with conversational speech.

6. LOB and Lund statistics are from Coates (1983).

7. There are also a number of syntactic differences in the auxiliary form paradigm which makes G.Sc. distinctive. These include, for instance, the generalisation of <u>in't</u> (but not <u>ain't</u>

forms, common in England and in the United States, and found in G.Sc. only in imitations of American speakers) and also the extension of the paradigm to include the Perfective BE after Verb-ing construction. In PP, this has a stylistic function in the characterisation of Glasgow Catholics (as distinct from Glasgow Protestants), especially the character Phil (as in: TH PH 6896 You're just after sayin (heads), but it is used by other characters too.

8. Cf. 'The Heteronomy of Scots with Standard English' (Kirk, 1987c).

9. The G.Sc. texts are also realistic in other ways not present in Tr.Sc. and these include the presence of what Bolinger (1957) calls 'verbalised intonation' (specifically the tag particle eh) and the representation of some prosodic features, of hesitation phenomena, of incomplete and even interrupted utterances, of simultanerous (actually unison) speaking, and so on. The informality of G.Sc. is also represented as pantimime-like 'patter' and 'banter' - the abuseful humour which abounds throughout these texts, much of it face-threatening.

10. Cf. Brown and Millar 1978: 174; Macafee, 1983; 50; and Kirk 1986: 338ff.

References

Aitken, A.J. (1981) 'The Good Old Scots Tongue: Does Scots Have an Identity?', in Haugen, E., McClure, J.D. and D. Thomson (eds.) Minority Languages Today (Edinburgh University Press, Edinburgh) pp. 72-90

Aitken, A.J. (1984) 'What's So Special About Scots?', in Northern Ireland Speech and Language Forum Journal no. 10, pp. 27-44

Bold, A. (1974) 'Bryden Meets Bold' [Interview], in Scots Review no. 8, pp. 9-16

Bold, A. (1983) Modern Scottish Literature (Longman, London)

Bolinger, D.L. (1957) Interrogative Structures of American English (The Direct Question) (Alabama University Press, University) Publications of the American Dialect Society, vol. 28

Brown, K. and M. Millar (1978) 'Auxiliary Verbs in Edinburgh Speech', in Work in Progress vol. 11, Department of Linguistics, University of Edinburgh, pp. 146-184

Bryden, B. (1975) Benny Lynch (Southside, Edinburgh)

Buthlay, K. (1982) Hugh Macdiarmid (C.M. Grieve) (Scottish Academic Press, Edinburgh) Scottish Writers Series, vol. 2

Byrne, J. (1980) 'Threads', in A Decade's Drama: Six Scortsh Plays (Woodhouse Books, Todmorden) pp. 145-191

Byrne, J. (1981) The Slab Boys (Scottish Society of Playwrights, Glasgow)

Byrne, J. (1982) Still Life (The Salamander Press, Edinburgh) The Traverse Plays, no. 4

Campbell, D. (1986) 'A Sense of Community - Robert McLellan: An Appreciation', in Chapman no. 43-44, pp. 35-41

Coates, J. (1983) The Semantics of Auxiliary Verbs (Croom Helm, London)

Connolly, B. (ms. [first performance in 1976]) An Me Wi Ma Bad Leg Tae) (Borderline Theatre Company, Irvine)

Hutchinson, D. (1977) The Modern Scottish Theatre (The Molendinar Press, Glasgow)

Ives, S. (1971) 'A Theory of Literary Dialect', in Williamson, J.V. and V.M. Burke (eds.) A Various Language: Perspectives on

American Dialects (Holt, Rinehart and Winston, New York) pp. 145-177

Johansson, S. (1985) 'Grammatical Tagging and Total Accountability' in Backlund, I. and G. Kjellmer (eds.) Papers in Language and Literature (Acta Universitatis Gothoburgensis, University of Gothenburg) Gothenburg Studies in English, vol. 60, pp. 208-220

Johansson, S., Leech, G.N. and H. Goodluck (1978) Manual of Information to Accompany the Lancaster-Oslo/Bergen Corpus of British English, for Use with Digital Computers (Department of English, University of Oslo)

Kirk, J.M. (1985) 'Linguistic Atlasses and Grammar: The Investigation and Description of Regional Variation in English Syntax', in Kirk, J.M. et al. (eds.) Studies in Linguistic Geography (Croom Helm, London) pp. 130-156.

Kirk, J.M. (1986) Aspects of the Grammar in a Corpus of Dramatic Texts in Scots PhD Thesis, University of Sheffield

Kirk, J.M. (1987a) 'Auxiliary Verbs, Frequencies, and the Identity of Scots', in Journal of Multilingual and Multicultural Development vol. 8, pp. 159-171

Kirk, J.M. (1987b) 'Inter-corpus Comparisons: The Primary Auxiliary Verb BE', in Proceedings of the XIII ALLC Conference (Slatkine, Geneva)

Kirk, J.M. (1987c) 'The Heteronomy of Scots with Standard English', in Macafee, C. and I. Macleod (eds.) The Nuttis Schell (Aberdeen University Press, Aberdeen)

Macafee, C. (1983) Glasgow (John Benjamins, Amsterdam) Varieties of English Around the World, Text Series, vol. 3

McLellan, R. (1970) Jamie the Saxt edited by I. Campbell and R.D.S. Jack (Calder and Boyars, London)

McMillan, J. (1982) 'John Byrne' [Interview], in Scottish Theatre News June 1982, pp. 2-6

Miller, J. (1982a) 'GET in a Corpus of Spoken Scottish English' SSRC Grant no. 5152 Working Paper

Miller, J. (1982b) 'The Expression of Obligation and Necessity in Scottish English' SSRC Grant no. 5152 Working Paper

Miller, J. (1982c) 'The Expression of Obligation and Necessity in Scottish English' SSRC Grant no. 5152 Working Paper
Miller, J. (1984) 'Discourse Patterns in Spoken English', in

Sheffield Working Papers in Language and Linguistis no. 1, pp. 10-39

Murison, D.D. (1977) The Guid Scots Tongue (Blackwood, Edinburgh)

Quirk, R. and J. Svartvik (1979) 'A Corpus of Modern English', in Bergenholtz, H. and B. Schaeder (eds.) Empirische Textwissenschaft: Aufbau und Auswertung von Text-Corpora (Scriptor, Konigstein) pp. 204-218

Quirk, R., Greenbaum, S., Leech, G. and J. Svartvik (1985) A Comprehensive Grammar of the English Language (Longman, London)

Sullivan, J.P. (1980) 'The Validity of Literary Dialect: Evidence from the Theatrical Portrayal of Hiberno-English Forms', in Language and Society vol. 9, pp. 195-219

Svartvik, J. and R. Quirk (1980) A Corpus of English Conversation (CWK Gleerup, Lund) Lund Studies in English, vol. 56

Locating Minority Language Informants: A Network Approach to Fieldwork

PETER WYNN THOMAS
University College, Cardiff

INTRODUCTION

The general ethnographical orientation of traditional dialect surveys has meant that informant sampling has usually been crucially bound to location sampling with the fieldworker tending to assume a key role in the final selection of both informants and sampling points. The importance of the sampling stage of linguistic fieldwork cannot be overemphasised for, as Gauchat stressed at the beginning of the century (1905:186), more time is necessary for finding a good informant than for the interview itself. This is particularly the case when a researcher is attempting to locate the few remaining speakers of a linguistic variety.

Certain researarchers - e.g. Gardette (1968:54), Wright and Rohrer (1968:8) - have tried to alleviate some of the inevitable initial tension which may accompany the elicitation procedure may by being introduced to an informant as a friend of a friend rather than through the medium of local officials. The importance of approaching potential informants through the medium of a gatekeeper who knows the target group intimately is eminently exemplified by Pée's experiences in Flanders (Pop 1950:822-3). Initially Pée had enlisted informants without the services of an intermediary and had met with little success. Later, with the assistance of the priest and the diocesan missionary, who had acquaintances throughout the region and the mention of whose name was a sufficient passport in itself, Pée found that where he had previously been greeted with suspicion he was received with open arms so that he was able to extend his informant network throughout the study area.

Fieldworkers investigaing varieties whose speakers are relatively plentiful - e.g. those of the AIS (Pop 1950:574) and the SED (Orton 1962:15) - have been able to modify the composition of their location samples in their search for 'ideal' informants. In the case of surveys of minority varieties, however, the actual elicitation may be prefaced by exhaustive and exhausting searches for suitable informants so that it is frequently the case that a researcher does not have the option of moving camp to the next settlement if the informants she finds prove to be less than 'ideal'. Bourcelot (1966:Avant-propos), for example, testifies to having to visit all the settlements in certain cantons of his study area in order to find a few valuable informants and Gardette (1968:68,77,78) and Séguy (1973:I) similarly note that in several places they were recording the responses of the last surviving speakers of particular linguistic varieties. The survey of Irish presents an extreme example of the near total inability of the researcher to control the identity of sampling points or informants: the locations featured in the atlas were almost exclusively determined by the availability of the last few remaining speakers (Wagner 1958:x).

THE *LINGUISTIC GEOGRAPHY OF WALES* AND SOUTH-EAST WALES

The data for the LGW (A. Thomas 1973) were gathered by means of postal questionnaires. Implicit in the indirect postal method is that the survey director is unlikely to have personal contact with his informants. Rather, the data collection stage typically involves third parties who undertake to select informants and to mediate between them and the project director. In general the method seems to have worked well in Wales and to have produced reliable data.

The social and industrial history of the south-east, however, make the area unique in Wales. During the nineteenth century in particular the south-east witnessed general social upheaval as a consequence of industrialisation and mass immigration. The resultant social changes introduced various complications into the traditional dialect areas. The south-eastern LGW responses appear to reflect this variation for in comparison with those from the rest of the country they exhibit little cohesion.

In spite of the LGW results, fieldwork experience in the south-east and the testimony of several research theses suggested that data elicited in the same area from members of the least geographically and socially mobile element, the agricultural community, might pattern in a coherent manner. A resurvey of the area which expressly concentrated on the farmers has indeed revealed regular distribution patterns and it may be argued that the LGW results for the south-east are attributable to the majority of the questionnaires being completed by immigrants or the immediate descendants of immigrants (P. Thomas 1982, 1984).

LOCATING MINORITY LANGUAGE INFORMANTS IN SOUTH-EAST WALES

One of the major methodological problems encountered in the second south-eastern study was locating the informants. Apart from the fact that in such an industrialised area the agricultural community is a small minority, in 1981 Welsh was spoken by only 10% of the total population in the study area[1]. Identifying the target population was further hampered by the retirement and removal of most of the individuals of interest to private houses. Farms which had typically been in the same family for generations had often been taken over by non-Welsh-speaking immigrants or had been incorporated into larger agricultural units or forestry plantations. As with other minorities, retired Welsh-speaking farmers are not listed or enumerated by censuses or other surveys so that it was impossible to accurately define the membership of the group and attempt to obtain a representative sample. There was not even any certainty that informants could be found in all areas.

Fig 1a summarises the problem: it was hoped that there existed an unditentified but nearly drained reservoir of potential informants to whom I had no direct access. The goal was to identify these persons, to obtain access to them, to motivate them to participate in the project, and to elicit information from them in as relaxed and informal an atmosphere as possible. At the end of the fieldwork I hoped that I would not only have forged direct links with the maximum possible number of informants (as shown in Fig 1b) and to have established an informal researcher/friend-informant/friend relationship with them - this is a minimal requirement of any dialectologist's sampling and fieldwork strategies - but that I would also have enumerated and collected preliminary basic information about the potential informant population which might be mobilised during further projects.

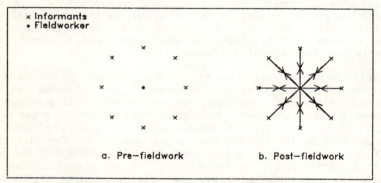

Fig 1: **A simplification of the fieldworker's task**

Fieldwork experiences in two industrial valleys had already taught me that traditional channels of introduction to potential informants, such as clergymen and other local inhabitants not themselves members of the target community, were not likely to prove fruitful (P Thomas 1982). A network approach was therefore eventually adopted as a matter of expediency rather than initial design.

Access to the farming network was achieved by means of chain referral or snowball sampling. The attraction of the method derives from the premise that any one individual can, at least in theory, get in touch with every other person (Boissevain 1974:24). The technique therefore offers a means not only of locating and contacting minority language speakers but of accomplishing the goal with the minimum of formality.

Farmers have until recently formed a tightly knit brotherhood: various forms of social contact and movement such as marriage, migration, and mutual self help have tended to take place within comparatively confined and well defined geographical and social spaces. Regular contact is also maintained between the men, at least, at markets and sales. It might therefore be expected that once access had been gained to the farming network each Welsh-speaking farmer contacted would experience little difficulty in naming other persons who would satisfy the selection criteria.

Since the goal was to approach any prospective informant as a friend of a friend, and I myself knew no farmers nor, indeed, in which particular villages there might still be Welsh-speaking farmers, the first step in the procedure was to mobilise members of my family, friends and colleagues who might serve as gatekeepers to the farming network. This exercise resulted in several successful introductions to informants via two links, the minimal number between the fieldworker and a target, i.e.:

Fieldworker ---> Gatekeeper ---> Informant

This situation was most frequently found in the westernmost part of the study area where Welsh speakers are numerous and Welsh is typically the natural and habitual vehicle of communication. Comparatively little difficulty was experienced in contacting farmers from all the settlements of interest in the west and once the network had been entered it was possible to systematically and almost effortlessly work through the area from farmer to farmer.

Information about potential informants would be routinely sought at the end of each elicitation session when I would ask if there were other Welsh speakers in the vicinity and in neighbouring localities who might be prepared to help with the project; the names would be instantly forthcoming. A careful note was kept of all names and addresses and the person or persons who had given them. When a prospective informant was later approached the mere mention of the people who had nominated him or her would serve as a passport for gaining entrance. In many cases, however, it would not be necessary for me to establish my credentials: the local grapevine would already have announced my presence in the area and I would not infrequently be greeted with a potted version of my life history and a chronicle of my recent movements and encounters.

In the east of the study area, on the other hand, Welsh is no longer
the habitual medium of communication for the few remaining Welsh-
speaking farmers and contacting these individuals and obtaining
representatives from as many communities as possible was no easy
matter.

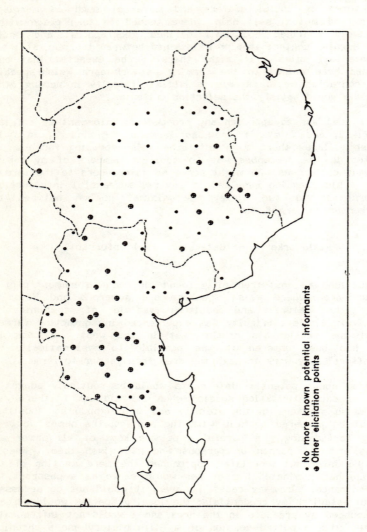

Fig 2: **The distribution of informant resources in the study-area**

As Fig 2 illustrates, the east contrasts with the west in that for most of the locations in the east I could discover no more potential informants other than those actually contacted and interviewed. This situation will occasion little surprise to those familiar with the linguistic history of the south-east. The erosion of Welsh in the study area is a process which is being halted only by the availability to younger generations of Welsh-medium education; further east is the county of Gwent which forms an anglicised buffer zone between the rest of south-east Wales and England.

Snowballing relies primarily on the fact that people know each other. The simple fact of knowing a person does, however, tell us nothing about the nature or extent of the acquaintance; in particular, it conveys nothing about the language a person uses or is able to use. In the west of the study area such considerations were of little consequence: it could be taken for granted that Welsh would be the usual medium of communication between farmers and the information received about any individual's family and his movements would be accurate to the finest detail. There was evidence, also, of western informants having intimate knowledge of the life histories of individuals whom they had never met. In one farmhouse, for example, I mentioned that I had not yet been given any names in a certain village. I was immediately told that a woman from that village lived in a farm some miles away and although the informant had never met the woman she nonetheless proceeded to telephone her. Having introduced herself she outlined the nature of the project and suggested that a joint elicitation session would provide an admirable occasion for them to meet. The young man from Cardiff would call for her! When the two women met for the first time they greeted each other like old friends, exchanged lengthy biographies and then began a memorable data collection exercise which lasted well into the night.

In the more anglicised and industrialised valleys of the east, on the other hand, it soon became apparent that such experiences would be unlikely. In the west information was almost unfailingly accurate and participants in the sampling process could be clearly categorised as either (a) gatekeepers, (b) contacts, (c) native Welsh speakers, or (d) non-contacted potential informants. In the east, on the other hand, these categories were joined by two others: non-native Welsh speakers - i.e. immigrants to the area - and, more problematically, individuals who could not or would not speak Welsh to me.

FIELDWORK IN TWO EASTERN VALLEYS: SOME SALIENT FEATURES

Fig 3 is a representation of the referral chain which resulted from fieldwork in two neighbouring eastern valleys. The primary status of each of the 34 individuals named or involved is conveyed by a symbol;

the direction of the referral (i.e. from or to any person) is indicated by the arrows linking certain nodes.

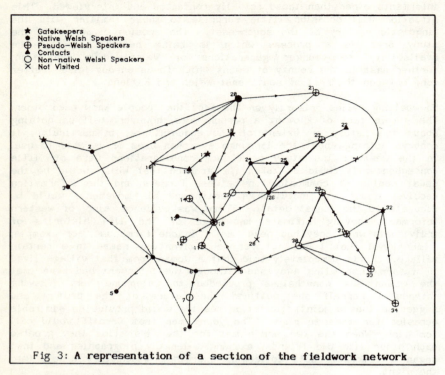

Fig 3: **A representation of a section of the fieldwork network**

The contributions of the individual gatekeepers

Access to the eastern network was via 5 gatekeepers. The contribution of each of these to the success of the referral strategy may be assessed by examining the shortest paths – or geodesics – between each of them and the 11 informants.

Table 1: **Geodesics between gatekeepers and informants**

Gate-keepers	Informants										
	25	24	26	20	6	4	8	5	2	3	13
9	4	3	2		1	2	1	3	3	3	2
32	7	6	5		4	5	4	6	6	6	5
19	5	4	4	1	7	8	7	9	3	3	3
12	5	4	3		7	8	7	9	9	9	3
1								1	1		

Table 1: **Geodesics between gatekeepers and informants**

Gate-keepers	\multicolumn{11}{c}{Informants}										
	25	24	26	20	6	4	8	5	2	3	13
9	4	3	2		1	2	1	3	3	3	2
32	7	6	5		4	5	4	6	6	6	5
19	5	4	4	1	7	8	7	9	3	3	3
12	5	4	3		7	8	7	9	9	9	3
1								1	1		

As Table 1 shows, geodesics between gatekeepers and informants vary in length from 1, indicating that access was direct, to a much longer 9-link path. The only gatekeeper to initiate paths which eventually led to all the informants was 19; gatekeeper 1, on the other hand, initiated paths to only two other persons. It is tempting to conclude, therefore, that the contribution of 19 was greater than that of the other initiators and that 1 was less valuable than the others. A factor which must also be considered, however, is the length of the geodesics between each gatekeeper and the informants.

The paths from 19 to the informants are typically long: four can be reached only via at least 7 links. The paths initiated by 12 are also long. From 9, on the other hand, access to informants is much easier: all but one may be reached, and this in 4 or fewer links. In this context it is instructive to refer to some of the defining characteristics of the gatekeepers. In order of contact they were:

- 32 A well-intentioned academic who, at the beginning of the project cascaded me with the names of potential informants. His advice proved to be generally misleading and ill-informed (see further below).

- 9 A farmer whom I did not previously know. Frustrated at my lack of success in the area at the time, I had gone to his farm (which I happened to be passing) and asked for help.

- 12 A friend, the son of a former minister of religion in the area.

- 19 A friend who had been brought up on a farm in another area where her family still lived.

- 1 A local historian contacted towards the end of the fieldwork in an attempt to ensure that the sampling had been as thorough as possible.

Had time been a more constraining factor on the length of the fieldwork period, it would undoubtedly have been advisable to have attempted to enter the network by such an integral and integrated person as 9 and to have avoided the allures of 32.

On the other hand, while the paths from all the gatekeepers except 9 to all the informants except 13 are in one sense redundant, these links are not without value. When a researcher is desperately searching for the last speakers of a linguistic variety the knowledge that all paths lead to the same informants is a welcome reassurance that he has investigated all leads as thoroughly as resources allow.

This does not mean to say, of course, that all potential informants have been named: there will always be the occasional individual who is not remembered perhaps because he has moved from the area, or whom people for reasons best known to themselves care not to mention.

Non-naming

A particularly salient feature of the referral process was the reciprocity of the naming:

   i   reciprocal: A named B and B named A
                         e.g. 7 ↔ 8; 24 ↔ 25; 30 ↔ 31; or

   ii non-reciprocal: A named B but B did not name A
                         e.g. 20 → 2; 20 → 3; 20 → 21

The first example of reciprocal naming between pairs of individuals occurred during my initial visits to one of the valleys where I had been sent by the academic, 32. As I visited the individuals suggested by him it became apparent that his information was deficient in one crucial detail: none of his nominees would - or could - speak Welsh to me! Working my way through the referral chains to individuals 29, 30, 31, 33, and 34, I found that only 30 was a Welsh speaker, but she was an immigrant to the area. The misapprehension about the others' ability to speak Welsh was not confined to the instigator of the chain, 32. As the symmetric relations on Fig 3 show, 29, 30, and 31 named each other as being Welsh speakers. Like 33 and 34, these 3 persons admitted to speaking English together but since 29 and 31 were the offspring of Welsh-speaking parents and attended Welsh chapels each assumed that the others could speak Welsh. Their general reactions to my questions left me with no suspicion that they might be misleading me. By the time I had exhausted the resources at my disposal in these valleys it transpired that 10 individuals could be classed as pseudo-Welsh-speakers.

The comparative rarity of reciprocal naming between pairs of native Welsh speakers - it occurred only between individuals 24 and 25, and 4 and 6 - is not immediately surprising. It may be thought that the individual members of the two groups of native Welsh speakers (2-3-4-5-6-8-20, and 24-25-26) would be aware from my reports that I had already been in contact with the other members of the group and they would therefore see no point in naming someone whom I had already seen. Such, indeed, appeared to be the case in the western valley, where reciprocal naming did not occur. Further east, on the other hand, reciprocal naming was common: here individuals were intensely aware that they were the last speakers of their particular varieties and would sadly name the members of the Welsh-speaking cliques of which they were members. They would invariably include themselves in the naming process. Given that there were so few Welsh-speakers in the particular valley under discussion, I would have expected 2, 3, 4, 5, 6 and 8 to have engaged in a clique enumeration exercise. Instead of so doing, however, they seemed to have little interest either in the project, or in clique description. Non-naming assumes additional interest when the temporal aspect of the fieldwork is considered.

With the exception of individual 20, all the members of the larger of the two groups were related.

1   Access to the first of the family group, 6 and 8, who were husband and wife, was achieved via the minimal two-link path. They could not name any potential informants.

2   Returning to 6 and 8 on a subsequent occasion, I mentioned that I had read an early description of the dialect by someone who shared the informants' surname. I was proudly told that the scholar - 7 on Fig 3 - was 8's brother and that he was coming to stay the following week. I was invited to tea to meet him.

3   The following week, during conversation with the dialectologist, 7, at which 6 and 8 were also present, 7 stressed the importance of my project and 6 was inspired to suggest that I should visit her cousin, 4.

4   Gatekeeper 1 sent me to see 2 and 3, who were brothers living on neighbouring farms. When asked for the names of other potential informants they could name no-one.

5   I visited number 4, who was captivated by the idea of the survey and seemed honoured that I should wish to record her. When asked for further names she mentioned - in addition to 6 and 8, whom she knew that I had already met

> – three other members of her family: 5 (an aunt of 4 and 6), and 2 and 3 whom I had also met, but who, she told me to my astonishment, were brothers of 6!

Non-naming of near relatives is a phenomenon found in several other areas and two explanations are possible. In the first place informants from all parts of the study area were typically surprised when I asked if there were any other members of their family whom I might visit: there appeared to be a common belief that there was little to be gained from interviewing more than one person from the same family, the implication being that they would naturally speak identical varieties.

On the other hand, occasional comments made after I had become better acquainted with some contacts and informants throughout the study area suggested that there might be in certain cases a deliberate strategy of kin-naming- and neighbour-naming-evasion. The motivation for such avoidance seemed to stem from a desire on the part of an informant to safeguard the prestige which had apparently accrued to him from being interviewed by a university lecturer and it was clearly important to several informants that they should not have to share this doubtful honour with anyone else from the neighbourhood! The importance which might be attached to this is well encapsulated by the reaction of one woman. Accompanying me to the gate as I left her home, she noticed that I had arrived in the Welsh Language Research Unit's van which bore on its sides the college crest and the name of the Unit in gold letters. The van had been parked outside the house on the main road for some two hours or so and had doubtless been spotted by at least half the population from both sides of their net curtains. 'Oh!' she exclaimed admiringly, 'Do call again! Soon!'

It may be, of course, that similar conditions were operating in the eastern valley. Growing familiarity with the informants suggested, however, that their reticence to name neighbours and other members of their families could be attributed not to their particular assumed status in relation to the project but, rather, to the status of Welsh in their experience.

During the childhood of most of these farmers Welsh was the medium of communication with their elders. Now their ability to speak Welsh is rarely activated so that the language has little contemporary relevance to them. All the members of the large family group in Fig 3 are fluent Welsh speakers and they all have fluent Welsh-speaking spouses but their home language has now shifted with that of the wider society to English. Proof of the language naturally used by spouses was frequently forthcoming during conversations: husband and wife would often apologise to me for addressing each other in English, admitting that they knew they should not do so, but that

that was their custom. The dialectologist, 7, was also aware of this for he once remarked to me about 6 and 8, 'They're speaking Welsh while we're here. But when we've gone, it'll be back to English'. It may be, then, that the non-naming in the case of this family may be attributed to a general feeling of apathy towards the language and, by extension, towards the project.

CONCLUSIONS

Networking through minority language communities is not without its problems. The method does, however, provide a framework for describing chain referral fieldwork. Entrance to networks proved most successful when the gatekeeper was himself a core member of the network. Relying on only one gatekeeper would, however, probably have resulted in failure to gain access to all the informants eventually discovered. More importantly, not resorting to multiple entrances would have entailed failing to uncover some of the detail about the nature of the links between various members of the target population; this in turn would have impoverished the understanding of the nature of the social and linguistic structure of the communities studied.

References

Atichison, J. and Carter, H. (1985) *The Welsh Language 1961-1981: An Interpretative Atlas*. Cardiff: University of Wales Press.

Boissevain, J. (1974) *Friends of Friends: Networks, Manipulators and Coalitions*. Oxford: Basil Blackwell.

Bourcelot, H (1966) *Atlas linguistique et ethnographique de la Champagne et de la Brie*. Paris: CNRS.

Gardette, P. *(1968) Atlas linguistique et ethnographique du lyonnais, IV: Exposé methodologique et Tables*. Paris: CNRS.

Gauchat, L. (1905) L'unité phonétique dans le patois d'une commune. *Festschrift Heinrich Morf (Aus romanischen Sprachen und Literaturen)*, 175-232. Halle: D.S. Niemeyer.

Orton, H. (1962) *Survey of English Dialects: Introduction*. Leeds: E.J. Arnold & Son.

Pop, S. (1950) *La Dialectologie: Aperçue historique et méthodes d'enquêtes linguistiques*. Louvain.

Séguy, J. (1973) *Atlas linguistique de la Gascogne*. Toulouse: Institut d'études méridionales de la faculté des lettres

Thomas, A. R. (1973) *The Linguistic Geography of Wales: A contribution to Welsh dialectology*. Cardiff: University of Wales Press.

Thomas, P. W. (1982) Putting Glamorgan on the Map. *Cardiff Working Papers in Welsh Linguistics*, 2, 73-101.

------ (1984) Glamorgan revisited: Progress report and some emerging distribution patterns. *Cardiff Working Papers in Welsh Linguistics*, 3, 119-45.

Wagner, H. (1958) *Linguistic Atlas and Survey of Irish Dialects*. Dublin: Dublin Institute for Advanced Studies.

Wright, P. & Rohrer, F. (1968) Early Work for the Survey of English Dialects: The Academic and Human Sides. *Leeds Studies in English*, New Series 2, 7-13.

Footnote

1 An insightful analysis of the recent history and contemporary distribution patterns of the Welsh language may be found in Aitchison and Carter (1985).

The Computerisation and Quantification of Linguistic Data: Dialectometrical Methods

WOLFGANG VIERECK
University of Bamberg, West Germany

In 1972, when I had the honour of delivering the keynote address at Methods 1 on Prince Edward Island, I ended my paper (Viereck, 1973) with a brief remark on those pioneers who beginning in the 1960s demonstrated the effective use of the computer in English dialectology. It turns out that I can continue now where I left off 15 years ago. In 1984, Schneider and I published a research report describing 30 research projects in American, Canadian and British English dialectology and sociolinguistics, all of which used the computer in various ways. Since the research of others is presented in that publication, I may perhaps be permitted to deal with my own now. My research is concerned with the computerisation of the data in Harold Orton's *Survey of English Dialects*, a project well-known to this audience. Computerisation of his data was attempted twice in the 1970s, but unfortunately nothing has come of these various efforts. Our computerisation of the Leeds materials has been underway at the University of Bamberg for several years now; progress has depended on the financial support available. Both key and conventions followed in the project have appeared in print (Viereck, 1985a). In the course of our work, we have encountered many problems, which I will not go into now (cf. Viereck, 1987a). The basic decision taken was not to deal with phonetics. This means that a certain type of question cannot be asked. This will no doubt be deplored by some. But in view of the fact that a dictionary and a quantification of the data were envisaged, phonetic transcriptions had to be transformed into normal orthography anyhow. Notwithstanding the difficulties, the project reached an advanced stage last year so that the German Research Foundation (DFG) saw it possible to provide financial support. The project will now be carried out in close cooperation with the "Abteilung für Linguistische Informatik" of the "Forschungsinstitut für deutsche Sprache - Deutscher Sprachatlas" at the University of Marburg/Lahn. Professor Putschke, Mrs. Hoffmann and Mr. Händler are experts in handling large amounts of computerized linguistic data. We owe the computer-produced maps of the *Atlas Linguarum Europae,* the *Kleiner Deutscher Sprachatlas,* the *Hessischer Flurnamenatlas* and the *Wortgeographie städtischer Alltagssprache in Hessen* to them; my atlas will be the fifth to be produced at Marburg. We plan to publish symbol maps of all rewarding items, especially marking conversational items, suggested words as well as informants'/fieldworkers' remarks on the status of words,

Methods in Dialectology 525

such as 'older', 'preferred' etc. and thus to allow statements on language change. Also, in a second phase, this project will go beyond what is already available, and that is interpretation. Orton and Wright's *Word Geography of England* (1975) is not a word geography as it fails to summarize and analyze the vocabulary of the various regions of England. Moreover, a quantitative analysis of the complete material will be provided. Each of the three linguistic levels will be analyzed separately and several statistical techniques will be tested to measure linguistic similarity and distance.

Maps 1 and 3 are the first symbol maps that I received from Marburg. Let me comment briefly on these maps. The final base map will show the pre-1974 county borders plus a few cities and rivers. On both maps, an attempt was made to integrate informants' remarks and fieldworkers' remarks into the symbolisation. Altogether there are - at present - two basic status categories:
1. recent, current forms and 2. older, rare forms.
With regard to the first category, responses with no remarks represent normal usage; the remarks "usually", "familiarly" emphasize the usage form as such. The third subgroup consists of the informants' opinions "modern" and "newer". The second category is subdivided into 3 groups, too. The first includes "older" and "obsolete", i.e. statements regarding the age of the forms. The second subgroup consists of the remarks "rare", "occasionally" and "less common", i.e. informants' views on the restricted frequency of usage. And finally, "(strong) pressure" and "suggested word" signal extremely restricted frequency of occurrence. The label "preferred" is treated together with "modern" and "newer", however diagonal shading inside the symbol indicates that a word may also be preferred because it is considered dialectal. The symbols of the first category denoting recent, current forms are thicker, whereas the symbols belonging to the second category denoting older and less common forms show straight shading inside. Older forms ("old, older, very old") have vertical shading, forms considered "less common" and "rare" horizontal shading. "(Strong) pressure" is indicated with diagonal shading down to the left, a "suggested word" with diagonal shading to the right. The symbolisation thus allows the combination of two statements. Dots denote that a word was excerpted from incidental material and a small square with a cross signals "no response".

This is one way of symbolising the important additional information provided by the informants and the fieldworkers in the *Survey of English Dialects,* information that has been absent from previous cartographic works based on that *Survey.*

Without going into detail, Maps 1 and 3 show a remarkable internal consistency with regard to the status labels and thus render the information very valid. North of the Humber the Scandinavian loan-

Map 1

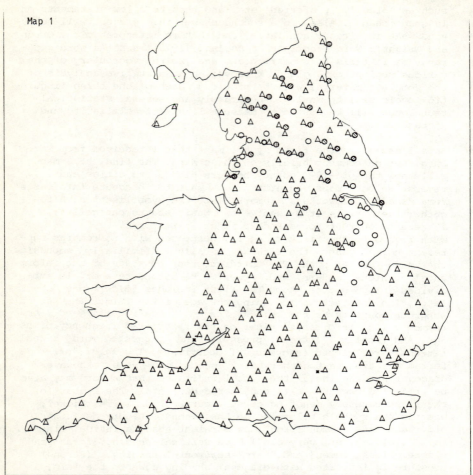

Methods in Dialectology

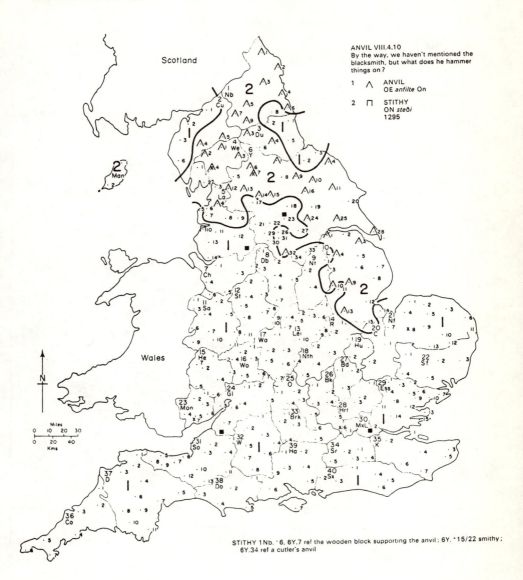

Map 2: Orton - Wright 1975:61

528   *Methods in Dialectology*

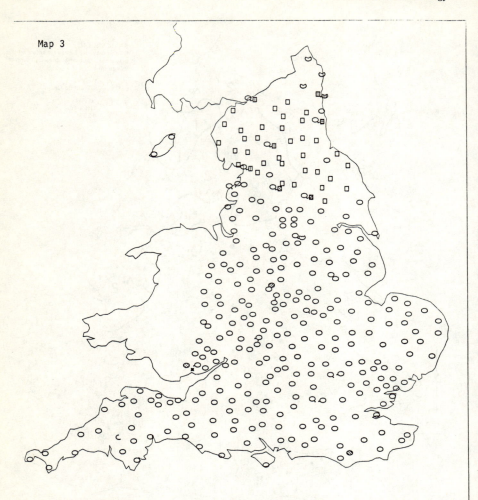

Map 3

• 4 616 Gander. •
○ gander (274)
ʊ gainer (4)
ʊ gandy (1)
□ steg (41)

no response 194

Methods in Dialectology

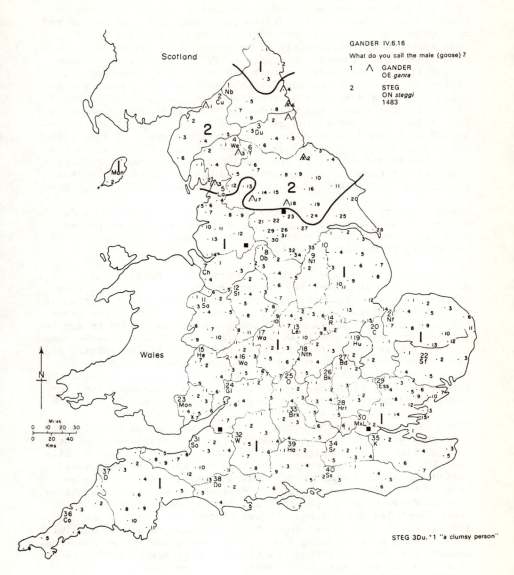

Map 4: Orton - Wright 1975:271

word *stithy,* realised as *stiddy,* is threatened much more than in Lincolnshire where the Standard English term *anvil* had not gained much ground around the middle of this century. Map 1 reveals also that *stithy* was recorded only three times. Although Wright's *English Dialect Dictionary* has a main entry for *stiddy,* Orton and Wright (1975, p. 61) unfortunately map only *stithy* (see Map 2). Without discussing Orton and Wright's mapping techniques, a comparison of Maps 3 and 4 also shows undue simplification on Map 4. As Map 3 makes clear, the response in Northumberland is not *gander* but *gainer.* The latter also has a main entry in Wright's dictionary. Maps 1 and 3 clearly show that varying degrees of competition between words - in these cases between words of Scandinavian and of native origin - must be distinguished. Of the two Scandinavian loanwords in competition with Standard English terms in the North of England, *stiddy* will no doubt be ousted much earlier than *steg.*

Another important feature of the computerised maps is the information on the frequency of occurrence of the various responses. This leads to the projected quantitative analysis of the data in the *Survey of English Dialects.*

The aim towards which quantitative research is carried out is to discover an areal patterning of dialects or dialect forms. This aim has been with dialectology, of course, since its inception as a scientific discipline in the last century, and dialectologists used a qualitative and a restricted quantitative method to achieve this aim as best as possible. Isoglosses, or heteroglosses - sometimes a single one - still serve as indicators for delimiting dialect areas today, so do bundles of heteroglosses, which are sometimes counted precisely. As we all know, these methods have their strengths and weaknesses, but they all allow an insight into their qualitative basis, which is a very important point.

Dissatisfaction with the state of the art was voiced occasionally - it grew with the growing number of linguistic atlases that became available: why collect so much data and only analyse so little? The sample of the sample analysed was sometimes very small indeed. Thus the slogan «dictionnaire - cimetière», said to go back to Gilliéron, was inevitably followed by «atlas linguistique - cimetière». As Séguy put it: "... les riches collections que constituent les atlas linguistiques restent sous-exploitées ..." (1973a, p. 3). And it was Jean Séguy who showed a way to deal with this dilemma by developing and applying new quantitative numerical methods for which he coined the term *dialectométrie* (1973a, p. 1) in full accordance with other *-metries* of our time[1].

The tasks of numerical classification can be defined in the following way: "a quantity of n objects that are characterized by m features are to be grouped into disjunct classes in such a way that the objects forming a class are as similar as possible with regard to all m features" (Vogel, 1975, p. 347; my translation). Such are also the aims of traditional dialectology. What is new then is not the objective, but only the terminology and the methodology.

What are Séguy's attempts at classification? He abandons the idea of the isogloss entirely, in favour of plotting the linguistic distance between all pairs of contiguous localities across the dialect area in question. "The concept is a simple one: using as large a number of items as the survey data supply, the responses from two neighboring localities are compared and the number of items in which they disagree is counted. When this number is reduced to a percentage of the total number of items considered, the result is the linguistic distance between those two localities. Once the process has been repeated for all possible contiguous pairs within the network, it is possible to prepare a map such as Map /5/, which is Séguy's summarizing map of his territory of Gascony (Séguy, 1973b, Map 2524). The map (here very much reduced) is based on 426 items from the ALG /Atlas Linguistique de la Gascogne/ ..." (Francis, 1983, p. 142).

Francis comments on this map in the following way: "The advantage of maps of this sort is that they show objectively and quantitatively the changing degrees of linguistic variation across an area while avoiding the misleading implications which too often arise from isoglosses, whether single or in bundles. It is easy to see, without benefit of boundary lines, that there is an area of high homogeneity (hence low linguistic distance) in the west central part of the Gascon area, where the linguistic distance between contiguous localities ranges between 11 per cent and 15 per cent. In contrast, the south central area shows much higher variation, ranging between 18 per cent and 28 per cent" (1983, p. 142).

A number of maps in vol. VI of Séguy's ALG look similar to those of traditional dialectology. Thus, Map 6 is entitled "Frontières dialectales du Gascon" and Map 7 is titled "Tracé des frontières". But the maps only appear similar at first sight. Séguy states: "... the 'dialect areas' which the boundaries of the map appear to surround are only false areas. If, taking two points not contiguous in the interior of one of these fallacious areas, we calculate their linguistic distance, it turns out that this distance equals or very often exceeds that of the boundary" (translation in Francis, 1983, p. 158). "A 'boundary' like line 1 merely indicates that the area contained is set off from the surrounding areas by a transition area of relatively strong contrast, though the actual features constituting the contrast vary from point to point along the line" (Francis, 1983, p. 158).

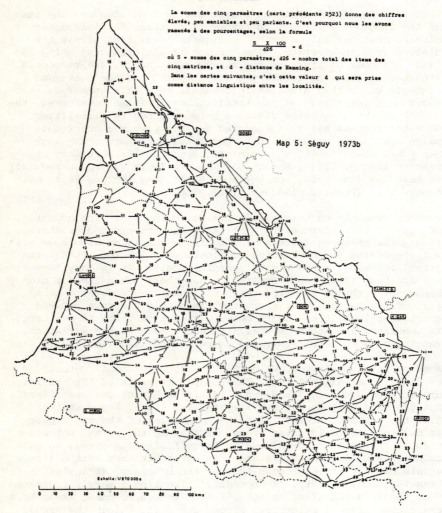

Map 5: Séguy 1973b

Methods in Dialectology 533

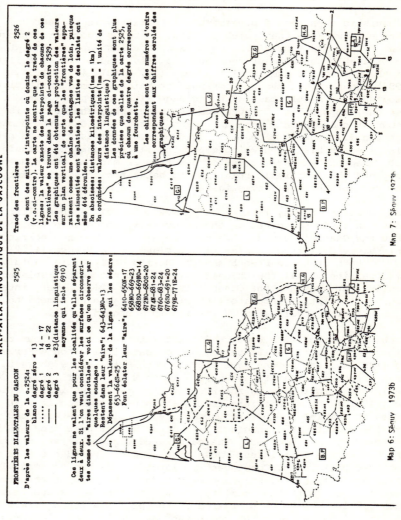

Map 6: Séguy 1973b

Map 7: Séguy 1973b

It must be said that while the methods are new, the insights are not. They confirm former statements by Gaston Paris and Louis Gauchat on the non-existence of clear-cut dialect areas and on the non-uniformity of geo-linguistic variation.

Linguistic maps should present the information in a clear and obvious way. From that point of view, there is room for improvement of Séguy's summarizing maps. Hans Goebl's maps represent a considerable advancement over Séguy's. Also, Goebl makes full use of the methods of numerical taxonomy (cf. Goebl, 1982, 1984, 1987). He borrowed the cartographic technique from quantitative geography - in this case a new coinage with -*metry* is, for obvious reasons, impossible. In quantitative geography, the method is known as choroplethic maps and based on the fact that the human eye can distinguish 6 to 8 colour depths. Goebl uses 6, and often his maps are black and white employing various shading techniques. Map 8 reproduced here is one of a series of maps on which Goebl presents the linguistic relationship between a chosen locality and the rest of the area investigated.

The locality chosen, Trinity on Jersey, Channel Islands (left white on the map), gives me the opportunity to deplore the fact that the Channel Islands have been regarded as Romance territory only since Gilliéron's *Atlas Linguistique de la France* (1902-1910). Both Standard French and the Norman dialect are rapidly disappearing on all the Channel Islands and are being replaced by English. At present, the Channel Islands are still a very interesting linguistics laboratory showing comparable phenomena to the - more recent - diffusion of Italian in Southern Tyrol.

Goebl has worked with Romance dialect material from various regions. I subjected a limited amount of data from Orton's *Survey of English Dialects* to the same test as Goebl did. Map 9 shows to what extent a point of departure - in this case a village in Cornwall - is identical with the rest of the area investigated (Viereck, 1985b). My map differs from Goebl's presentation in that it tries to combine the precise aspects - the figures - with the less precise aspects (the shadings), in other words: precision and visual clarity are combined.² The calculated figures refer only to the respective localities. These figures alone would not show any possible patterning. Consequently, larger areas had to be devised which are, of course, only approximations. The size of the area, here a circle with the locality dot as its centre, is arbitrary. Such circles are to be preferred to the presentation of fields of varying sizes covering the whole map, as used in Goebl's works and in my dialectometric analysis of Lowman's southern English data (Viereck, 1987b). The circles contribute in a new way to the evaluation of the *Survey of English Dialects* as a whole in that they show quite considerable areas not covered by the survey. Areas of varying sizes covering the whole map do not suggest this at all.

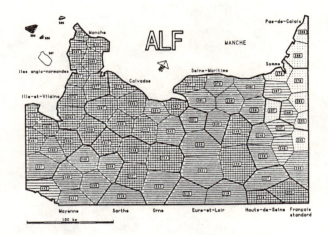

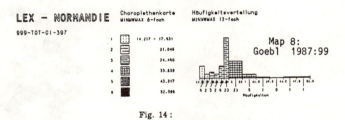

Fig. 14 :

Carte choroplèthe de la distribution de similarité (selon IPI(1)$_{jk}$) relative au point de référence 397 (La Trinité, Jersey).
Algorithme d'intervallisation : MINMWMAX à 6 intervalles.

536 Methods in Dialectology

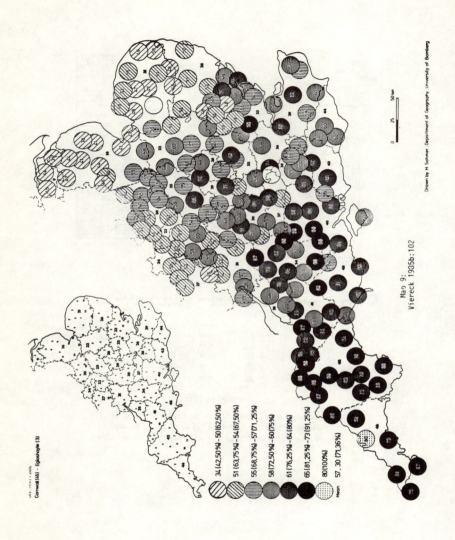

Map 9:
Viereck 1935b:102

In her paper "A new technique for dialectometry", Sheila Embleton has this to say: "One obvious disadvantage of Goebl's method is that it requires one map per locale, and even by computer these take a certain amount of time to construct. Examining the maps is still too much like leafing through a dialect atlas, map after map after map. As with Séguy's method, this method does not integrate all the information in an immediate and obvious way" (1985, p. 4). Two things must be said in this connection: first, it is not necessary, indeed it would not be sensible, to have an identity map for every locality. The linguistic continuum that Maps 8 and 9 clearly show also explains why such a procedure would be unnecessary. What is needed is an identity map for a few well-chosen localities, their exact number depending on the size of the area investigated and on possible peculiarities found in the area. The second point is that Embleton does not mention a second test to which Goebl and I subject our data. This is the so-called coherency test (see Map 10, Viereck, 1985b). The instruction for this test is: "Given a point P_1 on the atlas, calculate from a certain number of maps the average size of the surface area to which other points typical of P_1 belong". For this process, the commonalities of one locality with the other 184 had to be checked for each of the eighty lexical maps examined. The total number of identical forms found with regard to all localities and maps yielded the absolute coherency value for a locality. This procedure was adopted for all the sampling points. Then the absolute coherency value was divided by the number of maps to yield the absolute coherency mean for a locality. The proportion of that score compared with the number of localities investigated in the whole area, expressed as a percentage, is called the Relative Coherency Mean (RCM). These RCM scores, in turn, are presented on maps and provide a picture of the patterning of a dialectal area: regions with high RCM values are focal areas, those with low RCM scores relic areas.

When we look at Map 10 that shows the RCM for lexis, we see that the area with the highest RCM score, i.e. the highest level of identity, is in the Home Counties around London. This fact has sociolinguistic implications in this case. Here, high RCM scores point to a close proximity to the Standard language, whereas in investigations excluding the linguistic centre, areas with high RCM scores simply show a considerable linguistic homogeneity in the areas in question. No sociolinguistic conclusions should then be drawn.

Maps such as Map 10 show the various levels of identity of linguistic varieties. Among the related statistical techniques - sometimes also subsumed under the cover term of dialectometry -, cluster analysis and multidimensional scaling should be mentioned[3]. Embleton maintains that "multidimensional scaling has been applied in the case of different languages (as an alternative to trees) by Paul Black /1975-/1976 ... with reasonable suc-

538 Methods in Dialectology

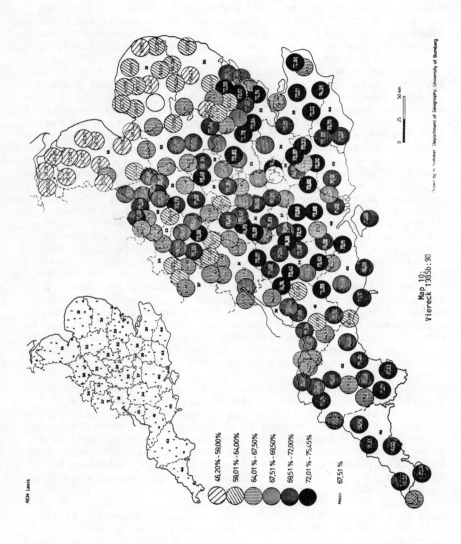

Map 10:
Viereck 1385b: 93

cess, but not so far to dialects" (1985, p. 4). This last statement is not correct since Black 1975-1976 who is concerned with Bikol, notes: "Bikol is a Malayo-Polynesian language spoken in the Philippines on the southern peninsula of Luzon and on several smaller, adjacent islands. Like any other widely spoken language, Bikol is far from homogeneous and shows considerable dialectal differentiation throughout the area in which it is spoken" (p. 45). "The hypothesis that the Bikol varieties belong to a single language, or more precisely a linguistic 'cline' or language or dialect 'chain', 'cluster', or 'continuum', characterized by more or less continuous variation throughout a geographical area, leads to the expectation that the percentages should conform to a structure capable of being represented in two-dimensional space" (Black, 1975-1976, p. 52). What Black comes up with is shown in Figure and Map 11. Figure 11 is the two-dimensional spatial representation of the Bikol relationships which has been superimposed on Map 11 "and lines have been drawn to connect the scaling locations, marked by crosses, with the geographical locations, marked by dots" (Black, 1975-1976, p. 55). The two greatest shifts in position involve Naga and Pandan. "Naga and Legaspi have moved closer together because they share 88%, the highest percentage of all pairs of varieties; not only are they both 'coastal' dialects as opposed to the neighboring 'mountain' dialects, but their surprisingly great linguistic similarity is well-known to Bikol speakers as well" (Black, 1975-1976, p. 55).

The results, stemming from this method, do not always seem to be mappable in a sensible way. This is in contrast to the RCM-Map discussed above, which shows linguistic relationships between varieties quite clearly, with the localities left in their geographical position. With multidimensional scaling, on the other hand, it is the discrepancies between the geographical map and the linguistic map that are of special interest. Embleton (1985) tested this method with some *Survey of English Dialects* data. She chose 18 localities with 128 lexical items in Orton and Wright's *Word Geography of England*, calculated lexical distances and produced a two-dimensional map of linguistic distance. The geographical position of the 18 localities is shown on Map 12a, and the linguistic map on Map 12b. Embleton comments on both in the following way: "Compared to the geographical map, locales 1 to 7, locales 8 to 10, and locales 11 to 18 cluster more tightly; these three clusters represent northern, midland, and southern respectively. The resultant extra space between the clusters corresponds then to some traditionally established isogloss bundles. Note also that within the southern group, 14 and 18 cluster together, as do 15, 16, and 17, and to a lesser extent 11, 12, and 13. Locale 18 has been pulled a considerable distance from its geographical position. This seems to be related to the death of Cornish, and the fact that dialects from further east (even as far east as the London area) were 'imported' to replace Cornish within the last sev-

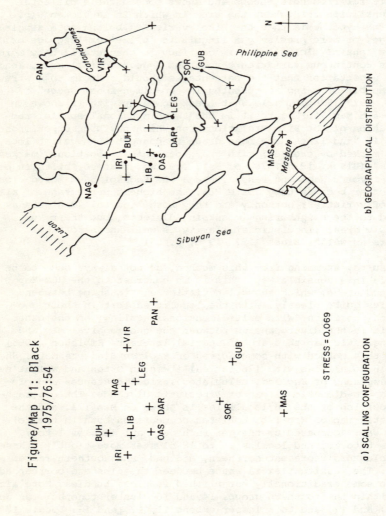

Figure/Map 11: Black
1975/76:54

BIKOL: TWO DIMENSIONAL SCALING VERSUS GEOGRAPHICAL DISTRIBUTION

Methods in Dialectology 541

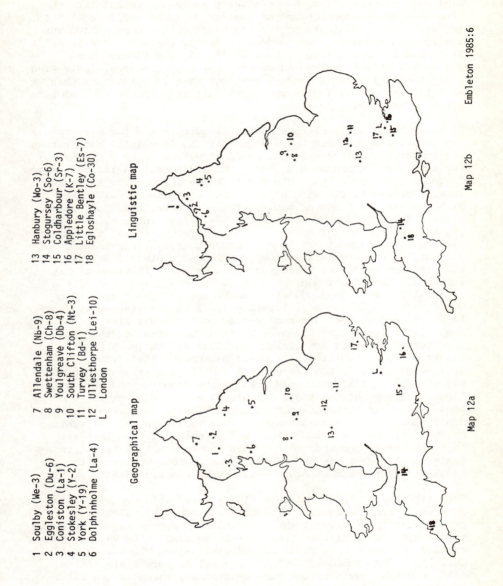

eral hundred years (i.e. comparatively recently, considering the time-span of the development of English dialects ...). Locales 15, 16, and 17, all dialects of the south-east, have been pulled into a very tight cluster near London, evidently through the extreme influence of London itself. Locales 11, 12, and 13 have been pulled slightly together and somewhat nearer to London, indicating again the influence of London, although to a lesser extent than with 15, 16, and 17 (which were after all much nearer to London to start with)" (1985, p. 7).

It seems that constructing a single linguistic map for more than a few localities in which the distance is the linguistic rather than the geographic distance is not possible without either divine intervention or suppression of data. Three dialects having the same distance from one another can easily be represented by an equilateral triangle. But what happens when there is a fourth variety with the same distance as the first three? Then, one would obtain a pyramid and no longer a figure in the plane. In fact, what is to prevent us from having more than four dialects, all at the same distance from each other? Such a figure cannot be represented accurately in three-dimensional space. In fact, given four dialects with randomly assigned distances for each pair, it seems highly improbable that their map can be drawn in the plane. One of the difficulties with mapping must also be seen in the fact that on Embleton's linguistic map, locality no. 1 is transferred to Scotland, which does not make much sense. Embleton was wise in choosing only 18 localities all over England. She remarks "that further testing of this new dialectometrical method (*perhaps* on a larger set of localities ...) would be appropriate" (1985, p. 7; italics mine). I cannot see how all the 313 localities of the *Survey of English Dialects* could possibly be incorporated on a single linguistic map showing their linguistic distance precisely and sensibly and am therefore not in a position to subscribe to Embleton's view that "the advantages of this multi-dimensional scaling method over the methods of Séguy and of Goebl ... are that the maps are easily constructed and that the information is all integrated onto one map in an immediate and obvious way, with the isogloss bundles and rapprochements shown clearly" (1985, p. 5).

Shaw (1974) and Morgan and Shaw (1982) have subjected some data from the *Survey of English Dialects* to a cluster analysis. They tried to group or cluster the localities in such a way as to bring together those localities that have large similarity values. "The simplest of these methods is called single-link cluster analysis (SLCA) ... The *method* of SLCA has several different *algorithms*, each of which result in the same *dendrogram,* which is the illustrative end-product of SLCA" (Morgan and Shaw, 1982, p. 16). Without going into detail regarding how clusters are formed - several methods exist here with different rules - the resulting hierarchy of clusters can also be represented on a map. The two maps reproduced here – Maps 13 and 14 – compare Shaw's results from 1974 with those of Morgan and Shaw (1982) in the East Midlands; each time the single-link technique was used. In 1974, fourteen localities were chosen; in 1982 their number had risen to twenty-five. Shaw summarizes his 1974 findings in the following way: "The illustrations show the three major clusters which were revealed by the dendrogram for one of the sets of data. The two southern clusters subsequently join to form one large cluster. One can see here a basic north-south division in the East Midlands dialect, with the southern group itself splitting into a northern and a southern subgroup" (1974, p. 176). Morgan and Shaw (1982, p. 19) have this to say: "Figure a reveals a North-South dichotomy ... while Figure b provides some more detail on this dichotomy, in particular pinpointing relatively isolated villages. Finding Hu 1 and C 1 in different clusters in Figure a may seem a little strange on account of their physical proximity, but, as reflected by Figure b, both these villages are among the most isolated of the 25".

The differences on both maps are striking. They are due, inter alia, to the different cut-off levels. The 1974 map shows the clusters at 53% similarity, while that of 1982 indicates clusters at the similarity level of 57.5%. In the first case, Hu 1 and C 1 form, together with two other localities, the southern subcluster, whereas in the second case C 1 belongs to the basic northern cluster and Hu 1 to the basic southern cluster. Also, the three isolated adjacent villages in the northern cluster do not cluster in my understanding of the term. The conclusion to be drawn from this discrepancy is that the computer alone would come up with all kinds of (strange) results. It is the dialectologist who has to adjust the numerical criteria experimentally to his personal classificatory expectations[4]. Thus, the dialectologist who knows that there are important isoglosses running from the Wash in a westerly direction, such as the one denoting the southern limit of /ɒ/ in *some* or the southern limit of /a/ in *chaff* would find Morgan and Shaw's 1982 clusters a bit odd.

It is a long way from the atlas data to a quantifying map, of whatever kind, in the course of which subjective decisions must be taken by the researcher. The quantifying method depends on standard sampling at all locality points. If this does not occur, then the dialectometric method cannot be applied optimally. On Map 10, my "RCM lexis" map, two sampling points (one in Norfolk and one in Berkshire) are left blank because they yielded an insufficient amount of data: the latter showed 69 zero entries and the former 26. The actual number of localities taken into consideration for the calculation of the arithmetic mean is therefore 183. Goebl (1977a) discusses the not infrequent zero entries in linguistic atlases. He solves the problem by calculating the identity values for every locality, not on the basis of the total number of maps

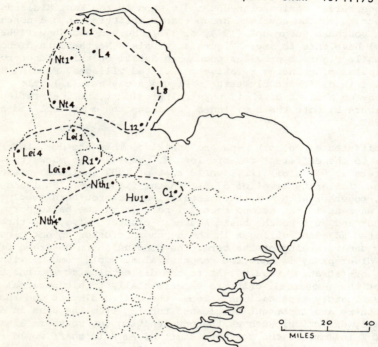

Map 13: Shaw 1974:175

Single Link cluster at 53 percent similarity.

Methods in Dialectology

Map 14: Morgan/Shaw 1982:18

Two sets of single link clusters, obtained from taking sections of the dendrogram illustrating the similarities between twenty five East Midland villages.
(a)——— indicates clusters at the similarity level 57.5%.
(b)- - - - - indicates clusters at the similarity level 60.5%.

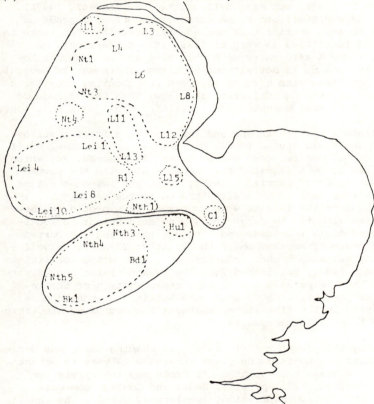

used but on the basis of the number of maps without zero entries for the locality in question. The obvious disadvantages of this procedure are that the number of maps on which the values are based varies from locality to locality and that the absolute values are no longer comparable.

There are other possibilities to deal with zero entries. One could accept a small number of zero entries as unavoidable as I did in quantifying Lowman's southern English data (cf. Viereck, 1987b). This may create distortions whose extent, of course, depends on the number of zero entries that one admits. Assuming that usage in neighbouring localities is very similar, if not identical, one might substitute a zero entry with the value for the nearest locality. This, again, is not without problems. There may be several adjacent localities with zero entries and neighbouring localities of the same distance but differing in usage. Then the average of the values of several neighbouring localities could be a solution.

Also, multiple responses in one and the same localities require decisions. One could try to reduce the numbers of responses until the ideal state, one response per locality, is reached. But which responses are to be eliminated then? What I did with the Lowman material was to count partial identity, i.e. one response out of two or more responses in a locality had to be the same in the locality with which the results were compared. This procedure, however, carries with it the danger of giving more weight to localities with multiple responses and, indeed, this danger occurred in the southeast of England where the Relative Identity Value for one locality was much higher than for the neighbouring localities (cf. Viereck, 1987b, pp. 16 and 20). The reason(s) for such divergence must then be pointed out in the interpretation of the results. Other possibilities to deal with multiple responses have been suggested in the literature. Whatever the decisions are, they are likely to effect the results.

In presenting the dialectometric values on shading maps, the decision regarding how to form the class intervals is very important since "in this stage the map-maker controls map interpretation" (Jenks and Coulson, 1963, p. 119). Jenks and Coulson comment: "Evidently intuition, inspiration, revelation, mystical hunches, prejudice, legerdemain and pre-determined ideas of what the class intervals should be have characterized the work of most map-makers" (1963, p. 120). Goebl has developed three algorithms for scaling his data: MINMWMAX, which he uses most often (see also Map 8), MEDMW and MED^5.

I think I have presented a sufficient number of problems the dialectologist cum statistician faces at various stages of his/her work. It is the dialectologist, however, who comes first; his or her foreknowledge of the area to be investigated is called upon at various stages of the investigation. Dialectometry is a true child of our technology-dominated time. Since the classification of dialects is only one task of the dialectologist, dialectometry will be able to complement traditional dialectology in this respect but cannot replace it. For dialectologists who would like to know what the features are that define a certain dialect area, a quantifying procedure would be unsatisfactory since much of the qualitative information contained in a linguistic atlas is lost through the counting process (cf. also Morgan and Shaw, 1982, p. 16). In addition, dialectometry is, as Francis (1983, p. 165) explains, "completely item-centered ... so that the method does not directly indicate structural similarity or distance". Yet this objection is not valid for those linguistic levels where a structural weighting of items would be impossible or arbitrary.

I subjected Lowman's southern English data both to a traditional analysis, counting a limited number of heteroglosses (Viereck, 1980) and to a dialectometric analysis, using the coherency test and the identity test (as described) and arrived at the same results. This testifies to the effectiveness of traditional methods. With regard to the data in the *Survey of English Dialects,* I am not yet satisfied with the results achieved with the various quantitative methods. This may be due to the fact that only a limited amount of data was used. What we need then are more analyses of comparable data using related techniques in order to really judge the true merits of the new approach.

Notes

1. In all fairness, it must be said that such polythetic procedures had been developed by others before Séguy. In their paper "Correlation methods of comparing idiolects in a transition area" (1952), Reed and Spicer enter linguistic similarity for each locality on the map, with reference to the main reference point where distance is zero and then draw "isogrades" (their term), i.e. join the localities with the same similarity values (coefficient Q_c). In 1967, Charles Houck described "A computerized statistical methodology for linguistic geography" without, however, mapping his results. In the early 1970s, Henri Guiter developed original dialectometric procedures, independent of Séguy (cf. Guiter, 1974, 1979, 1987).
2. Goebl separates the two aspects. In addition to the choroplethic maps, he publishes accompanying numerical maps.
3. Linn/Regal and Philps reported on their research involving cluster analysis at Methods 5 in 1984. Attention should also be drawn to dialectometric work carried out, e.g. by W. Möhlig, on African languages (cf. Guarisma and Platiel,1980) and, e.g. by S. Murumets, at the Academy of Sciences of the Estonian SSR in Tallinn.
4. In his important study on Welsh, Alan Thomas notes with regard to his procedure adopted for identifying continua that the permitted tolerances allowed in the process of determining site clusters (80% - 120%) evade statistical precision: "The precise degree of tolerance allowed in the matching procedure must be a matter of trial and error: it can be assessed *only on the plausibility of the results* which are produced in specific cases" (1980, p. 9; my italics).
5. On all three, see Goebl, 1977b, pp. 342ff.

References

Black, P. (1975-1976) Multidimensional scaling applied to linguistic relationships. *Cahiers de l'Institut de Linguistique de Louvain,* 3, 43-92.
Embleton, S.M. (1985) A new technique for dialectometry. Paper read at the Ling. Assn. of Can. and the US - Forum. Saskatoon.
Francis, W.N. (1983) *Dialectology: An Introduction.* London: Longman.
Goebl, H. (1977a) Rätoromanisch versus Hochitalienisch versus Oberitalienisch: Dialektometrische Beobachtungen innerhalb eines Diasystems. *Ladinia,* 1, 39-71.
—— (1977b) Zu Methoden und Problemen einiger dialektometrischer Meßverfahren. In W. Putschke (ed.), *Automatische Sprachkartographie. Germanistische Linguistik,* 3-4, 335-56.
—— (1982) *Dialektometrie. Prinzipien und Methoden des Einsatzes der Numerischen Taxonomie im Bereich der Dialektgeographie.* Wien: Verlag der Österreichischen Akademie der Wissenschaften.
—— (1984) *Dialektometrische Studien. Anhand italoromanischer, rätoromanischer und galloromanischer Sprachmaterialien aus AIS und ALF,* 3 vols. Tübingen: Niemeyer.
—— (1987) Points chauds de l'analyse dialectométrique: *Pondération* et *visualisation. Revue de Linguistique Romane,* 51, 63-118.
Guarisma, G. and Platiel, S. (eds) (1980) *Dialectologie et Comparatisme en Afrique Noire.* Paris: Société d'Etudes Linguistiques et Anthropologiques de France.
Guiter, H. (1974) Une vérification de loi linguistique par corrélation. *Revue de Linguistique Romane,* 38, 253-64.
—— (1979) Critique et limites d'une méthode. *Mélanges à la Mémoire de Louis Michel.* Montpellier: Université de Montpellier. 261-72.
—— (1987) Etalonnage d'une méthode géolinguistique. *Revue de Linguistique Romane,* 51, 55-62.
Houck, C. (1967) A computerized statistical methodology for linguistic geography: a pilot study. *Folia Linguistica,* 1, 80-95.
Jenks, G.F. and Coulson, M.R.C. (1963) Class intervals for statistical maps. *Internationales Jahrbuch für Kartographie,* 3, 119-34.
Linn, M.D. and Regal, R.R. (1984) Numerical taxonomy as a tool in dialect research. Paper read at the 5th International Conference on Methods in Dialectology, University of Victoria, British Columbia. July.
Morgan, B.J.T. and Shaw, D.J. (1982) Graphical methods for illustrating data in the Survey of English Dialects. *Lore and Language,* 3, 14-29.
Orton, H. et al. (1962-1971) *Survey of English Dialects (B): The Basic Material,* 4 vols., each in 3 parts. Leeds: E.J. Arnold.
—— and Wright, N. (1975) *A Word Geography of England.* London: Seminar Press.
Philps, D. (1984) The structure of dialect space. Paper read at the 5th International Conference on Methods in Dialectology, Uni-

versity of Victoria, British Columbia. July.
Reed, D.W. and Spicer,J.L. (1952) Correlation methods of comparing idiolects in a transition area. *Language,* 28, 348-59.
Schneider, E.W. and Viereck, W. (1984) The use of the computer in American, Canadian and British English dialectology and sociolinguistics. In H. Goebl (ed.), *Dialectology.* Bochum: N. Brockmeyer. 15-60.
Séguy, J. (1973a) La dialectométrie dans l'*Atlas Linguistique de la Gascogne. Revue de Linguistique Romane,* 37, 1-24.
—— (1973b) *Atlas Linguistique de la Gascogne,* vol. VI. Paris: Centre National de la Recherche Scientifique.
Shaw, D. (1974) Statistical analysis of dialectal boundaries. *Computer and the Humanities,* 8, 173-7.
Thomas, A.R. (1980) *Areal Analysis of Dialect Data by Computer. A Welsh Example.* Cardiff: University of Wales Press.
Viereck, W. (1973) The growth of dialectology. *Journal of English Linguistics,* 7, 69-86.
—— (1980) The dialectal structure of British English: Lowman's evidence. *English World-Wide,* 1, 25-44.
—— (1985a) The data of the *Survey of English Dialects* computerised: key and conventions. In W. Viereck (ed.), *Focus on: England and Wales.* Amsterdam, Philadelphia: John Benjamins. 235-46.
—— (1985b) Linguistic atlases and dialectometry: The Survey of English Dialects. In J.M. Kirk, S. Sanderson and J.D.A. Widdowson (eds), *Studies in Linguistic Geography. The Dialects of English in Britain and Ireland.* London: Croom Helm. 94-112.
—— (1987a) The data of the *Survey of English Dialects* computerized - problems and applications. Paper read on the Eighth International Conference on English Language Research on Computerized Data. Hanasaari/Hanaholmen. May.
—— (1987b) Lowman's southern English dialectal data and dialectometry. *English World-Wide,* 8, 11-23.
Vogel, F. (1975) *Probleme und Verfahren der numerischen Klassifikation.* Göttingen: Vandenhoeck and Ruprecht.
Wright, J. (1898-1905) *The English Dialect Dictionary,* 6 vols. London: Henry Frowde.

Linguistic Atlasses of German. A Study of Computer-Aided Projects

WERNER H. VEITH
University of Mainz

1.0 AREAS COVERED BY THE ATLASSES

The long tradition of German dialectology has produced many linguistic atlasses, such as, the "Deutscher Sprachatlas" (DSA) and the "Deutscher Wortatlas" (DWA), dealing with the phonological, morphological and lexicological variation of the German dialects in Central Europe. In addition, many so-called regional atlasses cover restricted areas. Several of those projects were brought to a close long before computer science had been developed, others were planned without the assistance of this modern technology. The projects which I would like to bring to your attention are all computer-aided.

Currently, there are ten such projects of which eight are localized in the hatched area of the map (following page). Two more burst the map's geographical limitation. Three of the atlasses cover an extended geographical are:
(1) The "Kleiner Deutscher Sprachatlas" KDSA ("Concise Linguistic Atlas of German") by Werner H. Veith and Wolfgang Putschke is based on data collected before 1933 in Central Europe, i.e., in Germany (within the borders of that time), in Austria, Switzerland, Liechtenstein, Eastern France, Luxemburg, Northern Italy, Northern Yugoslavia, Czecho-Slovakia and Poland.
(2) The area of the "Wortatlas der kontinentalgermanischen Winzerterminologie" WAKWT ("Atlas of the Continental-Germanic Terminology of Viticulture") by Wolfgang Kleiber depends a) upon the distribution of the viticulture and b) upon whether the terminology is German or, rather, was German around 1930. Besides the areas listed under no. (1), also parts of Hungary, Rumania, and the Soviet Union are included.
(3) The "Fraenkischer Sprachatlas" FSA ("Franconian Linguistic Atlas") by Jan Goossens. The precise title translated is: "Linguistic Atlas of the Northern Rhineland and the Southeast Netherland". This title reveals that the South of the Netherlands and the Northeast of Belgium are included plus the neighbouring parts of Germany as far south as Koblenz and as far east as Muenster.

The authors of seven more atlasses want to analyse and describe the peculiarity of the dialect varieties in small regions - a tradition which was founded by Wenker's "Sprach-Atlas der Rheinprovinz" in 1878. Consequently, those atlasses cover

restricted areas:
(4) The "Mittelrheinischer Sprachatlas" MRhSA by Gunter Bellmann is extended between Bonn and Karlsruhe, having the Rhine as the eastern and the French border as the southern and western limitations.
(5) The "Wortgeographie staedtischer Alltagssprache in Hessen" (Word geography of urban colloquial German in Hessia) by Hans Friebertshaeuser and Heinrich Dingeldein covers the territory of the state of Hessia.
(6) The "Hessischer Flurnamenatlas" (Hessian atlas of field-names) by Hans Ramge et al. also covers the territory of the state of Hessia.
(7) The extent of the "Sudwestdeutscher Sprachatlas" by Hugo Steger, Bernhard Kelle et al. is the area between Karlsruhe, Ulm and the Rhine valley.
(8) The "Sprachatlas von Bayerisch-Schwaben" by Werner Koenig borders on this atlas in the east and to the following projects in the west:
(9) The "Atlas lingistique et ethnographique de l'Alsace", vol. 11f. by Marthe Philipp (Atlas of the Alsace in Eastern France) and
(10) The "Atlas linguistique et ethnographique de la Lorraine germanophone" by Marthe Phillip (Atlas of Lorraine in Eastern France).

2 METHODS

As all of these atlasses are computer-aided, the methods of data-processing are corresponding, such as, data input, sorting, geographic localization of the data, and, finally, plotting. Those particular procedures, however, are not meant to be discussed here but rather the methodological differences occuring, e.g., in the data structure, in the geographical coverage, and in the cartographic presentation of the data. The basic linguistic data of the atlasses are in some cases predominantly handwritten in the orthography of a certain period, such as for no.s (1, 3, 6) but where the other projects are concerned, they are based on data in phonetic transcription, so that an additional time has to be scheduled to write the suitable programs.

In this connection, the data structure is not unimportant, i.e., whether sounds, affixes, stems, words, compounds, or texts are used as the input. When the project of the KDSA, no. (1), e.g., was started in the early seventies, then the capacity of the computers was still relatively small, so that the words which originally had been provided for the input, had to be broken down into their morphological elements. Not unimportant was the huge geographical coverage of the KDSA comprehending 5,892 localities. The WAKWT, no. (2), in comparison covers 420, and the regional atlas of Lorraine, no. (10), not more than 109 localities. Not the size of the pure linguistic data only, but also that of the geographic coverage has enormous consequences for different methods in feeding the computer, in data storage, retrieval, processing and plotting.

A further question is how to split up the input segments in order to receive smaller ones, e.g., morphemes instead of lexemes and phonemes instead of morphemes. Such a procedure is necessary in order to get phonological units on the maps of the KDSA with its morphological input. For a phonological atlas it is reasonable to let the computer read the consonants and the vowels separate from each other. This has changed the character of the tokens which in the KDSA have been received by compiling the identical records of each single locality. The phonological tokens are much less complex than the morphological ones with the consequence a) that the legend of a map with phonological entries is by far not as long as of maps with morphological entries and b) that the map itself is less complicated and clearly arranged. Each token meant for the legend is provided with an indicator a) of frequency referring to the number of records compiled and b) also of the phonological environment. Two or more tokens which can be considered as variants of the same phoneme or phonotactical sequence, respectively, are merged into one. If there are no variants, then, of course, the token is itself the type. To such a type the appropriate symbol which is meant for the map is assigned automatically, e.g., a triangle, a circle − even, if necessary, with diacritical marks. This symbol is taken out of a list of symbols referring, e.g., a) to the quality of a vowel and b) to its phonological environment (cf. sample chart on the following page).

The cartographic presentation of the atlasses differs quite much. First, the volume of the geographic information varies and it is in some atlasses rather scarce. Second, for eight atlasses geometric symbols, such as circles, triangles etc., were to be programmed and plotted whereas the Linguistic Atlas of the Alsace and also the one of Lorraine have been following a method applied to the French and other Romance atlasses − a method, namely, to plot textwords into the maps. This has the effect that the user cannot directly recognize the areas varying considered by the levels of linguistic description, because the regional variation in phonology is different from the one in lexicology.

This aspect raises the question of the different objectives of the atlasses. Some, as the two just mentioned, want to cover the fields of phonology, of morphology, and of lexicology, as well, while other projects aim at a phonological or lexicological description, respectively. Based on empirically collected data, most of the atlasses are synchronic, even if most projects furnish additional information to characterize the historical background of an item which is put on the map. In addition, the WAKWT, no. (2), and the two atlasses of German in France, no.s (9,10), provide information about the ethnographic background of a word being the subject of a map; this is not unimportant for the semantic interpretation of words. The following table is a synopsis.

OBJECTIVES OF THE TEN LINGUISTIC ATLASSES DISCUSSED

Atlas no	(1)	(2)	(3)	(4)	(5)	(6)	(7)	(8)	(9)	(10)
chronology										
synchronic	x	x	x	x	x	(x)	x	x	x	x
historic	(x)	(x)	(x)			x	x	x	(x)	(x)
description										
phonological	x			x			x	x	x	x
morphological							x	x	x	x
lexicological		x	x		x	x	x	x	x	x
ethnographic	x								x	x

References

Atlas linguistique et ethnographique de l'Alsace [Linguistic and ethnographic atlas of the Alsace]. Paris.
- Vol. 1 (1969) by Beyer, Ernest and Matzen, Raymond.
- Vol. 11 (1985) by Philipp, Marthe [et al.].
Atlas linguistique et ethnographique de la Lorraine germanophone [Linguistic and ethnographic atlas of Lorraine] by Philipp, Marthe. Paris.
- Vol. 1 (1977).
- Vol. 11 (1986).
Bellmann, Gunter (1979/1984). Mittelrheinischer Sprachatlas. Phonetisch-phonologischer und morphologischer Atlas. Fragebuch. Mainz.
Bellmann, Gunter (1982). Deskriptive Sprachgeographie in der Gegenwart. Zu Konzept and Praxis des mittelrheinischen Sprachatlasses. Rheinische Vierteli jahresblatter. 46, 271-287.
Bellmann, Gunter (1987). Areallinguistik und Soziolinguistik im Mittelrheinischen Sprachatlas. Beitrage zur Dialektologie am Mittelrhein.,
Bellmann, G. (ed.) Wiesbaden/Stuttgart.
Friebertshauser, Hans (1983). Die groBlandschaftlichen Worterbucher der deutschen Dialekte Areale und lexikologische Beschreibung. Dialektologie. Eir. Handbuch zur deutschen und allgemeinen Dialektforschung, Besch, Werner [et al.] (eds) Berlin/New York. Vol 2, 1283-1295.
Friebertshauser, Hans, Dingeldein, Heinrich J. (1985). Wortgeographie der stadtischen Alltagssprache. Ein Forschungsprojekt zum aktuellen Sprachgebrauch in Hessen. Zeitschrift fur Dialektologie und Linguistik, 52, 43-52.
Goossens, Jan (ed.) (1981a). Der Sprachatlas des nordlichen Rheinlands und des sudostlichen Niederlands "Frankischer Sprachatlas" (FSA). Ortsregister. Grundkarte. Marburg.
Goossens, Jan (1981b). De Taalatlas van het zuidoosten van het Nederlands taalgebied en het noorden van het Duitse Rijnland. Taal en Tongval 33, 45-160.
Goossens, Jan (1982). Der Sprachatlas des nordlichen Rheinlands und des sudostlichen Niederlands. Mit 3 Karten. Rheinische Vierteljahresblatter 46, 254-270.
Kelle, Bernhard (1977). Datenaufbereitung und automatische Kartierung beim Sudwestdeutschen Sprachatlas. Germanistische Linguistik [Hildesheim: Olms] 3/4, 89-105.
Kelle, Bernhard (1983). Der Sudwestdeutsche Sprachatlas., Wortschatzprobleme im Alemannischen, Haas, Walter/Naf, Anton (eds.) Freiburg/Schweiz, 281-294.
Kleiber, Wolfgang (1980). Zur sprachgeographischen Struktur der deutschen Winzerterminologie. Wiesbaden.
Kleiber, Wolfgang (1984). Zur Sprachgeographie der rumaniendeutschen Winzer- terminologie. Ein Bericht uber neue Forschungen. Forschungen zur Volks- und Landeskunde [Sibiu, Rumania], 27.2,89ff.

Konig, Werner (1975). Der Sudwestdeutsche Sprachatlas. Montfort, 27, 170-194.
Konig, Werner, Neureiter, Nicoline [et al.] (1984). Fragebuch zum Sprarchatlas von Bayerisch-Schwaben (BSA) nach dem Fragebuch zum Sudwestdeutscher, Sprachatlas Augsburg.
Ramge, Hans (1980). Die Erhebung der rezenten Flurnamenbestande in Hessen. Beitrage zur Namenforschung, 404-411.
Ramge, Hans (1985).. Hessische Flurnamengeographie. Methodische und praktische Probleme am Beispiel von Bezeichnungen fur Sonderland. GieBener Flurnamen-Kolloquium, Schutzeichel, Rudolf (ed.). Heidelberg, 660-693.
Veith, Werner H. (1982). Der Kleine Deutsche Sprachatlas als Arbeitsmittel. Tubingen.
Veith, Werner H. (1984). Kleiner Deutscher Sprachatlas (KDSA). Dialektologische Konzeption und Kartenfolge des Gesamtwerks. Zeitschrift fur Dialektologie und Linguistik, 51, 295-331.
Veith, Werner H. (1985). The Concise Linguistic Atlas of German (Kleiner Deutscher Sprachatlas). Journal of Historical Linguisticsa & Philology. II. 1 & 2., 26-39.
Veith, Werner H., Putschke, Wolfgang, Hummel, Lutz (collab.) (1984-). Kleiner Deutscher Sprachatlas. Tubingen.
Veith, Werner H., Putschke, Wolfgang (eds.) (1987). Sprachatlanten des Deutschen. Laufende Projekte. Tubingen.

Caught in the Web of Change

JOAN H. HALL
Dictionary of American Regional English

Although the Dictionary of American Regional English was conceived almost one hundred years ago with the founding of the American Dialect Society, it was not born until seventy-four years later with the appointment of Frederic G. Cassidy as Chief Editor. That long gestation period allowed for a fairly thorough course of prenatal care. It also coincided with decades of significant change in the world into which the project would be born.

In the realms of dialectology and lexicography, milestones during the period 1889-1963 included completion of the English Dialect Dictionary and the Oxford English Dictionary, the beginning of the Linguistic Atlas of the United States and Canada projects, and publication of the Dictionary of American English, the American Dialect Dictionary, and the Dictionary of Americanisms. During that period, fieldworkers toiling alone with bicycles and notebooks gave way to trained groups of investigators with cars and bulky wire recorders, who in turn yielded to large teams of fieldworkers with "word wagons" and lightweight, fairly sophisticated tape recorders. At a slower pace, files of handwritten 4X6-inch quotation slips would soon give way to stacks of printouts and computer-generated files. But as large as these changes were, in terms of the mechanics of dictionary-making those which have taken place since the birth of DARE in 1963 have been of even greater magnitude: the carefully laid plans of the 1960s have had to be reevaluated through the adolescence and into the prime of this major investigation into the speech of the American people. Of the many new electronic techniques of the 70s and 80s, which should be chosen? Which are really time savers, and which just flashy but practically useless gadgets?

Although K.M. Elisabeth Murrays's fine book about James Murray and the OED hadn't been written then, Frederic Cassidy was well aware in 1963 of the trials Murray had had to endure in making the "big dictionary" a reality, not as an "adequate" book that would satisfy the Delegates of the Press by its timely production, but as the thorough, minutely detailed and scholarly work on which we all now depend. In planning for DARE, Cassidy was mindful of the need for a well trained staff using the same methods and working all in the same place, of the problems of coordinating the work of well intentioned but not always well trained or reliable volunteers, and of the need for good relations with a supportive publisher. In the last regard, Cassidy has been much more fortunate than Murray, not having to plead for space or justify each line of text. Nor has the Harvard University Press tried to meddle with methods or content, as was true of some of the Delegates of the Oxford University Press. (On the other side of the coin, however, Harvard Press has subsidized the printing but not the writing of DARE, leaving the substantial problem of funding the project to its Chief Editor.) Cassidy was also conscious of the need for a systematic collection of oral as well as written data (Cassidy 1963, 1967), and aware that the amount of information collected could not be handled via the pigeon holes in a scriptorium.

By the 1960s, computers were the obvious choice when it came to dealing with the more than 2,300,000 responses collected by the fieldworkers. DARE's programmers arranged for the field data to be organized in various ways: they could be arranged alphabetically question by question; they could be organized by frequency of response for each question; and they could be indexed through the entire corpus. In addition, a mapping program was devised that would show, on a map adjusted to reflect the states' relative population densities, the location of every community studied. For any given response to a question, the program would outline the map, show where each Informant giving the response lived, and also give a statistical breakdown of five social variables for the Informants: age, sex, race, amount of education and community type (Henderson). These were fairly sophisticated manipulations for the time, and DARE staff and observers alike were excited by these innovations in traditional dialect work.

Although there was hope initially that the actual editing of the Dictionary could be done on-line, this hope had to be abandoned when it became obvious that the then-available programs allowed no easy way of handling both the field data and all the written materials that had been collected. So actual editing was begun in 1975 using traditional methods: entries were handwritten on 4X6 slips and stored in filing cabinets. As the entries were being prepared manually, however, procedures were being developed in the early 80s for the typing of the text into a mainframe computer with all of the typesetting codes added, so that the computer tape produced at DARE could be run directly by the Press's typographers. This avoided a retyping and proof-reading of the text, both steps which would have been tedious, time-consuming, and fraught with error given the complexities in style, type fonts, and type sizes (von Schneidemesser, 1983). To aid in our own catching of such errors, a checking program called "Proofer" was developed that would automatically check for such things as chronology of quotations, correct short-titles, unmatched brackets, or parentheses, etc. This was an extremely valuable aid.

Two basically different methods, then, worked in parallel streams during the period 1975-85, as Volume I was edited and produced: quote-taking, editing, and what we call "funnelling"--- the reading of entries by the Chief and Associate Editors--were done according to well established, traditional methods, while map-making, analysis of social features, and production of the text utilized new electronic methods.

From time to time as new developments occurred in computer technology, we were asked why we didn't switch to editing with computers. People who hd been "converted" to the electronic age could not understand why we didn't take the plunge. "Go ahead," they urged. "Time's awasting. The new methods are faster, more efficient, and perhaps even cheaper than the old. Buy the new machines. Have programs written exactly to your specifications. Train your staff (those who are eager will love it; the reluctant will learn to accept it). Take advantage of the marvels of a new age." "But wait," cautioned others. "Why be the first on a new machine? The first to find the bugs and to risk losing valuable data. The first to wait while the problems are ironed out at your expense. Finish this project first, and then start the next one when the new techniques have proven their value."

Was it possible to listen to both angels? Could it ever work to be a "social computer user"? To be like the "social drinker" who insists that he doesn't have to abstain, but can indulge when appropriate, and never get in over his head? We wondered. Surely some changes would be worth making. But every change brings an inevitable, if temporary, loss in productivity, and we had to get the dictionary published. How to weigh the claimed advantages of a new procedure over the suspected disadvantages?

The following observations reflect the point of view of a computer neophyte who wants to use the most effective techniques available but who is reluctant to give up the security of the tried-and-true. In John Shore's scheme, I am a Type 1 computer personality. Let me quote from his very readble book for computer novices, The Sachertorte Algorithm and Other Antidotes to Computer Anxiety:

> "Remember the distinction between Type A and Type B personalities? One was compulsive and driven, the other easygoing and relaxed. To classify people in terms of such distinctions is naive, but it can be instructive.
> I think there are two kinds of computer users; I'll call them Type 0 (zero) and Type 1. Type 0 personalities liked secret codes when they were children—many still do. They would rather solve a puzzle than read a novel, and they would rather fix or improve a tool than use it to help them with a job...Type 1 personalities are different–they dislike puzzles and jargon, and they're more interested in their jobs than they are in their tools. The Type 0 personality prefers a tool with lots of options and adjustments, knowing that flexibility is useful in honing the tool to fit a wide range of jobs. For the Type 1 personality, the additional flexibility is counterproductive" (Shore, 1985: 75).

The Type 0 personality, then, often brings to the job enthusiasm, creativity, and eagerness to try new ideas, while the Type 1 personality proceeds more cautiously, asking for tests, backups, and more time to think through the consequences of a change. DARE has been fortunate, I think, in having both Type 0's and Type 1's on the staff. While the competing viewpoints sometimes create sparks, the decision-making process benefits by hearing from both sides.

Back in the late 70s and early 80s, there were some very good reasons for caution and for the decision not to try to convert to an on-line editing system. To have put even our "Main File" (a collection of quotations from regional novels, diaries, newspapers, folklore journals, private collections of dialect materials, etc.) on-line would have meant having every quote rechecked and retyped, because the initial computerization of the material had been done with a program that did not allow both upper and lower case letters; thousands of quotations already copied onto 4X6 slips would have had to be entered and proof-read. Our bibliography of sources cited had grown to over six thousand items and showed no signs of slowing significantly. All in all, any attempt at complete conversion seemed utter folly. But did we have to go all the way? Would it be possible to use many of our traditional editing techniques, but employ them on the new-microcomputers? The possibilities were tantalizing. The equipment was expensive, though, and in the early 80s only a few staff members were well acquainted with home computers. We hesitated. We might have hesitated even longer had it not been for two catalytic events.

The first was the announcement in the summer of 1985 that the Madison Academic Computing Center would be shutting down their Univac 1100, the mainframe on which our maps were made, and with which we converted coded text into galleys. Although there was substantial advance warning (shutdown is slated for July 1, 1988), the announcement was alarming, for it meant completely rewriting the mapping program two years sooner than planned. Given the state of the art in 1975, the mapping program was very sophisticated. But by the standards of 1985, it was quite awkward. DARE's programmer/analyst immediately went to work to determine the best way to proceed: Should we convert to one of three other large computers at the Computing Center? Or rewrite the whole system for use on microcomputers in our own offices? (The option of simply finding another Univac in the area was not possible because too much code was based on local changes to the operating system.)

This decision-making period coincided with DARE's being granted a number of computers by the UW-Madison's College of Letters and Sciences, and later with our very fortunate inclusion in a project sponsored by IBM that provided computers for instructional and training purposes. DARE was given a substantial amount of equipment including three PC's, four XT's and an AT, the AT being large enough to handle the mapping program if the field data were condensed using an archiving program. All of a sudden, the option of having editors make their own maps from their desks whenever they needed them was a live possibility. We opted for an in-house mapping program.

The second catalytic event was a site visit made by a team of reviewers from the National Endowment for the Humanities in October of 1985. While the members of the team were unanimous in their appreciation of the quality of the first volume of DARE, which had been published only two months erlier, they were hopeful that they could provide some ideas for the streamlining of procedures that would increase productivity. Suggestions centered on ways we might eliminate some of the routine and tedious editorial tasks. "Wouldn't it be possible", they asked, as we ourselves had, "to write the entries on word processors? Changes could be made more easily, and the problem of legibility would be eliminated. Duplicate copies could be made with a flip of the wrist for quotes that needed library verification. Backup copies of all files would ensure the safety of the text."

Surely these features were attractive. But there were enough problems in terms of day-to-day procedures that the Type 1's among us wondered whether making the change would create more problems than it would solve. For example: handwritten copy allowed us to see the changes that were made in the processes of quotechecking, funnelling, and revising; each person's handwriting was recognizable, and the thinking process was traceable from one version to the next. That history would be lost if changes were simply made on the machines. Thousands of quotations were on slips in file drawers—how could they be integrated into the process? To retype them to incorporate them in an entry would not only waste time, but would also necessitate another proofreading. How would changes be made in the funnelling process? Would a funneller simply make the changes on the disk? If so, how would the editor be made aware of the changes and learn from the reviewing process? How could we keep track of late entries that were out of alphabetic order in another file? And if editors were typing their own entries, shouldn't they also add the coding so that nothing would have to be retyped for the typographers? Many questions needed to be answered.

One Type 0 editor felt that while the problems were real, they were surmountable. He accepted the challenge of devising programs and procedures that allowed editors to use computers to eliminate many repetitious tasks, but that integrated the new procedures with the established methods of reviewing and changing entries. Over the last year and a half, he, working with our programmer/analyst and production staff, has developed programs that allow an editor to call up the text of DARE questions for use in quotations from the DARE fieldwork; to retrieve automatically the appropriate dates for each Informant cited; to call up short-titles needed for citations; to keep track of all quotations sent out for verification; to make cross-reference slips for all variant forms cited; to index entries written; and, as an interim process before the primary mapping program is fully converted to micros, to make maps for relatively small numbers of Informants by typing in the Informant codes. This mapping program allows the editor to superimpose the outlines of particular regions on the map, and provides the percentage of Informants who fall within those regions. It is an especially useful tool in determining appropriate regional labels.

Using all of these techniques, this editor has been able to increase his productivity by approximately 25%. And, since the arrival of the IBM machines, he has taught the new procedures to five other editors. Each has been enthusiastic about the change, and has shown an increase in number of entries written after a period of training.

At the same time, however, every advantage seems to have its corresponding disadvantage. As Sidney Landau has discovered, "while the advantages of computer use are manifest,.. the drawbacks are often belittled or ignored" (Landau, 1984: 287). But once the hidden problems become apparent, they not only cannot be ignored, they seem to spawn more than their share of complications and frustrations.

For example, a simple decision about alphabetizing abbreviations resulted in a stream of unforeseeable problems. We decided that in the master short-title list, abbreviations such as AZ (for Arizona) would be placed alphabetically in their appropriate spelled-out positions, i.e., AZ would occur after Argosy and before Arlington. But the program we were using for sorting wouldn't accept that, so we changed the policy to place AZ at the beginning of the A's. That seemed acceptable. What we didn't realize was that in the short-title list developed for editors' use, the program searched for AZ only at its alphabetically spelled-out place. Changing that program was not difficult, but in moving the abbreviations around by hand, a few were missed. Months later an editor discovered the problem and the stray titles were rounded up. But in the meantime, editors who hadn't found particular short-titles on the list assumed that the titles were new and asked the bibliographer to make new bibliographic entries. If the new short-title matched the old, there was no real problem except for the duplication of work; if it didn't, new confusions were created. These were not problems for which any person or machine could be "blamed". They simply illustrate some of the inherent problems in trying to integrate differing systems and to anticipate and manage complexity.

Integration, in fact, is perhaps the biggest challenge in attempting to superimpose newfangled notions on the traditional and the tried-and-true. While a series of procedures might work well separately, it is not axiomatic that they will therefore work well together. One must also integrate machine methods with manual methods; machine requirements with human needs (e.g., temperatures cool enough for the machines but warm enough for a typist's fingers; or, a room dark enough to reduce screen glare for one person, but not so dark as to be claustrophobic for the office mate); one person's enthusiasm and natural ability with another's reluctance or computer anxiety; one individual's patience in proofing his own quotes with another's overconfidence in his typing ability; one's need to have quotations spread out on the desk with another's comfort in scrolling back and forth on the screen. Each individual's relationship to the machine is so personal and so important that it is crucial to try to be flexible and to accommodate human as well as equipment needs.

What we have found in trying to integrate the new with the old is that, while it has always been crucial to have good communication among staff members, it is more so now than we could ever have anticipated. And not only must ideas, plans, and actions be communicated, they must also be minutely documented, both with explanations for the reasons for changes, and detailed descriptions of the mechanisms of the changes. For, almost without fail, whatever one person does will affect someone else's work, in either minor or (sometimes) catastrophic ways. And what seems entirely clear to one person or even to a committee on one occasion is likely to be forgotten or remembered differently a few weeks later.

The kind of detailed prenatal care and planning that preceded the birth of DARE now has to be replicated with the introduction of each new process. There is no question that computers can do amazing things with the rearrangement and sorting of data. But they can only do these things if the data have been coded carefully and correctly in the beginning. So to predict in its infancy all the conceivable uses for a program in its maturity is one of the biggest challenges for both the user and the programmer.

DARE has recently confronted this challenge in the process of choosing, modifying, and using a bibliographic program. For years, we had indulged in speculative "what if's," with musings such as these: "What if we had the bibliography on-line and could not only get the full bibliographic data and the correct short-title, but could also find out which library housed the book, retrieve the call number for the quotation checkers, determine the time and the setting of the book's action, see if the book were part of a series, whether different volumes had different publication dates, whether different editions had been cited, and whether the author used a pseudonym? And furthermore, what if we could have all these features keyed in from the start, but only print those which would be useful to our readers?"

The wish list seemed very long, but our production editor and programmer/analyst combined forces to survey the market and see whether anything commercially available might be made to work, or whether the programming would have to be tailored to fit. Fortunately, enough years had elapsed since our first wishing and our actual implementation that one program, ProCite, now existed that did nearly all we wanted it to do. Although some compromises had to be made, they were definitely outweighed by our not having to do the programming in-house. Actual use of the program has required painstaking analysis of the data in order to use all the fields correctly, and has presented some minor unanticipated problems. But at this point it looks as though there is hope that the original planning was thoughtful enough to take us from infancy to maturity without too stressful an adolescence.

Having the new machines has meant, of course, that we are using them for many more tasks than had been anticipated. They were extremely useful in indexing the editorial handbook, a detailed style and policy manual that needs continuous revision. It cannot be said that the computer took all the drudgery out of this task, for each item to be indexed still had to be carefully coded; but once the coding was done, the creating and updating of the index proceeded quickly and smoothly.

Computers have also made it possible to search the text of Volume I to create indexes of all the regional and social labels used, both for in-house use and for readers of DARE. (These indexes will be published by the American Dialect Society). And we can search the text for up to thirty discrete character strings whenever we want to know, for instance, how many times we have used Polish in an etymology, or Gullah in a social label.

Further, it will be possible this fall, through an agreement with the University of Wisconsin–Madison libraries, for DARE's bibliographer to use a modem to access the On-line Computer Library Center system. This will greatly speed his bibliographic research.

Having made all these changes and adapted computers to so many of our procedures, have we at DARE avoided getting in over our heads? In particular, have we been able to maintain the quality of editing achieved for Volume I as we streamlined the editorial process for Volume II? In making changes, we have tried to keep Sidney Landau's practical advice in mind:

"Always, in evaluating whether or not it would be wise to add a particular program, the question is not Would it be helpful to have this program? The answer is invariably yes. The relevant question is, Does it make sense to take the time, hire the people, and pay the costs to perform this particular operation? ..One must weigh the cost—not just monetarily—of doing an operation oneself against that of having it done by computer. Most of all, one must think hard about how important each step of a project really is and decline to computerize steps that are relatively unimportant unless the programs for such steps are routine. An operation simply done by human beings may be extremely complicated to program for a computer" (Landau, 1984: 278).

This advice has been particularly relevant in our consideration of the possibility of writing a program that would take the editors' entries, automatically add the typesetting codes, and remove the intermediate step of having them retyped for the Press's typographers. Doubtless it would be possible to write such a program. But whether it could be written in anything like a reasonable length of time, and whether editors could adapt to its stringent requirements are two crucial questions.

Even if a program were automatically to convert text to italic and boldface type where appropriate, and to change point size for head sections, definitions, and quotations so that editors did not have to code for such changes, it still would not account for the intricate details of spacing in discrete parts of the entry. To ask editors to add the not inconsiderable details of compositing to their mastery of the already complex editorial format is to invite human overload. The informal "rule of seven", that says we can readily remember a seven-digit telephone number but would regularly stumble if it were nine digits, seems applicable. It is reasonable to require editors to know and apply the details of editorial format; it is unreasonable to require them to be compositors as well.

Our new computer capacity would allow us to do numerous other kinds of checks, searches, and rearrangements of data. For now, however, we have elected not to do all we are theoretically capable of doing. The computer mystique is a potent force in today's world, and to decline powers that are available seems to some a foolish stance. But if, as has been said, people using computers tend to make more radical decisions than otherwise (Braunstein, 1987), perhaps we're not wrong. What we want to avoid at all cost is the notion that our computers can eliminate the need for the painstaking care and thought that have always been required of lexicographers. In our short experience with editing on word processors, it has become apparent that "As the computer increases the freedom of writers, so does it increase the responsibility of readers" (Shore, 1985: 19) This is true not only because of the tendency for editors to make more radical statements knowing that they can be readily changed (and, incidentally, to make more typos than they did writing errors), but also because it is easy for funnelers to be less critical of entries that look clean and professional than those that are covered with hen scratchings.

Our experience with changing procedures well into the prime

of DARE has been both exhilarating and frustrating. We have been thrilled to see some tedious tasks eliminated and to witness some real increases in productivity. We have also felt like the character on a poster that hangs on our production office door: obviously having "had it" with computers, he stands with a mallet poised over his machine. The caption reads, "Hit any key to continue."

It is easy, in those moments, to become nostalgic over the thought of James Murray sitting alone in the quiet of the scriptorium, his beloved books at his side. It is easy, in those times, to forget that the scriptorium was cold in winter, hot in summer; that Murray wrote all his letters by hand, then copied them over in order to have a record. What we must try to remember is that it is his qualities of thoughtfulness, diligence, thoroughness and accuracy that must remain unchanged through the decades. If the means for achieving them improve, so much the better. We at DARE will try to be open to such means; but we will continue to reject any that tempt us to "transform elegant simplicity into baroque complexity" (Shore, 1985: 102).

Notes

1. Early programmers included Richard Veneszky, Tom Johnson, and Bill Woodson. The mapping program was the responsibility of Tom Johnson.

2. DARE's production editor, Luanne von Schneidemesser, is responsible for having planned, tested, and refined the processes of coding the text and shepherding Volume I through the production process.

3. "Proofer" was the inspiration and product of DARE's programmer/analyst, Jean W. Anderson, whose computer expertise and experience with the Dictionary of the Old Spanish Language project have been invaluable to DARE.

4. IBM and the University of Wisconsin-Madison have cooperated on a program called 'Trochos,' designed to develop innovative uses for microcomputers in instructional settings.

5. The site visit team included Dorothy Wartenberg (NEH), John Algeo (University of Georgia), John Nitti (University of Wisconsin-Madison), and David Richrdson (Cleveland State University). We appreciate their thoughtful suggestions.

6. DARE is indebted to editor Craig Carver for having the persistence to keep trying in the face of Type 1 hesitation, and the ingenuity to find solutions that others thought did not exist.

7. Jean Anderson's revision of the mapping program will allow access to the 2,309,569 responses from the fieldwork. Editors will type the questions and responses they wish to map, and the program will find those responses. Multiple responses and multiple questions may be combined. The big advantage of this program over the original one, in addition to its easy use by editors, is that we will be able to eliminate the step of going to an outside source to find the appropriate response code for each term to be mapped.

8. DARE is grateful to editor Edward Hill for his careful job in revising and maintaining the handbook, and in doing the tedious job of coding for the index.

References

Braunstein, Leslie. (1987) Move it! Computers put on the pressure. USA Today 8 June, 11/E.

Cassidy, Frederic G. (1963) The ADS Dictionary--How Soon? Publication of the American Dialect Society, 39, 1-7.

------ (1967) American Regionalism and the Harmless Drudge. Publications of the Modern Language Association, 82,3,12-19.

Henderson, Michael M.T. (1974) Processing Data for DARE--Current Practices. American Speech 49,119-122.

Landau, Sidney I. (1984) Dictionaries: The Art and Craft of Lexicography. New York: Scribner's.

Murray, K.M. Elisabeth. (1977) Caught in the Web of Words: James Murray and the Oxford English Dictionary. New Haven: Yale University Press.

Shore, John. (1985) The Sachertorte Algorithm and Other Antidotes to Computer Anxiety. New York: Viking.

von Schneidemesser, Luanne. (1983) The Dictionary of American Regional English: From Handwritten Copy to Final Galley. Burton, Sarah K. and Short, Douglas D. (eds) Proceedings fo the Sixth International Conference on Computers and the Humanities. Rockville, Maryland: Computer Science Press.

Creating Linguistic Databases From Machine-Readable Dialect Texts

OSSI IHALAINEN
University of Helsinki

WHY DIALECTOLOGISTS HAVE FOUGHT SHY OF SYNTAX

One striking thing about English dialectology is that there has been very little research on syntax. Two different reasons for this have been suggested. First, it has been claimed that there are no great differences in syntax between various dialects, the implication being that there cannot be much need for syntactic analysis either.[1] Second, it has been pointed out that the study of syntax requires larger quantities of linguistic material than are available today.[2]

While there is a lot to be said about the tenability of the first view, the second view seems to describe the present situation quite realistically. The purpose of my paper is to show what can be done about the problem of data. Or to be quite precise, the problem is not simply data. Even if we had vast quantities of transcripts at our disposal, it might take years to collect enough data on a specific syntactic point to study it in any detail. Fortunately, there are quite a few computer programs that will search the texts for us, so that the main difficulty at the moment would appear to be the lack of large machine-readable texts. To see where we stand, it is illuminating to compare the position of dialectologists with that of researchers working on Standard English.

MACHINE-READABLE CORPORA OF STANDARD ENGLISH AND SYNTACTIC ANALYSIS: AN ILLUSTRATION FROM THE BROWN CORPUS

Unlike students of Standard English, dialectologists do not have at their disposal grammatically tagged corpora like the Brown Corpus or the Lancaster-Oslo-Bergen Corpus. To get an idea of what can be done with Standard English, let us consider the following sentence from the Brown Corpus:

IN	IN	A01093007E1
THE	AT	A01093008E1
*BLUE	NP	A01093009E1
*RIDGE	NP	A01093010E1
MEETING	NN	A01093011E1
,	,	A01093012E1
THE	AT	A01094001E1

```
AUDIENCE            NN      A01094002E1
WAS                 BEDZ    A01094003E1
WARNED              VBN     A01094004E1
THAT                CS      A01094005E1
ENTERING            VBG     A01094006E1
A                   AT      A01094007E1
CANDIDATE           NN      A01094008E1
FOR                 IN      A01094009E1
GOVERNOR            NN      A01094010E1
WOULD               MD      A01094011E1
FORCE               VB      A01094012E1
IT                  PPO     A01095001E1
TO                  TO      A01095002E1
TAKE                VB      A01095003E1
PETITIONS           NNS     A01095004E1
OUT                 RP      A01095005E1
INTO                IN      A01095006E1
VOTING              VBG     A01095007E1
PRECINCTS           NNS     A01095008E1
TO                  TO      A01095009E1
OBTAIN              VB      A01095010E1
THE                 AT      A01095011E1
SIGNATURES          NNS     A01095012E1
OF                  IN      A01096001E1
REGISTERED          VBN     A01096002E1
VOTERS              NNS     A01096003E1
.                   .       A01096004E1
```

Each line of the text consists of a word, its grammatical tag and an address that can be used for reference.

Let us assume that we are particularly interested in the those accusative and infinitive constructions where the "accusative" is a pronoun. In other words, we are looking for sentences like "They expected her to give evidence." These sentences can be identified on the basis of the grammatical information given in the corpus. What we need is a computer program that will select those particular sentences from our corpus.

One package that will search the Brown Corpus for various linguistic patterns, whether defined in terms of morphemes or tags, is a program called BrownScan.[3] The following lines of code in FORTRAN are part of a BrownScan program, and they define the string to be searched for. That is, the machine is instructed to look for sentences containing the elements "pronoun" and "infinitive", which form a subset of the accusative and infinitive construction:

```
IF( JJFND .AND. TAG(1:2).EQ.'TO') FND=.TRUE.
IF( TAG(1:1).EQ.'P')THEN
```

```
        JJFND=.TRUE.
    ELSE
        JJFND=.FALSE.
    END IF
```

The search is based on the tags "TO" and "P", the symbols given in single quotes in the program fragment above. To demonstrate how the program works, I have chosen a short sample from the very beginning of the Brown Corpus. The output of this particular BrownScan run looks like the following:

```
A01093007E1      46        1     IN THE *BLUE *RIDGE MEETING ,
                                 THE AUDIENCE WAS WARNED THAT
                                 ENTERING A CANDIDATE FOR
                                 GOVERNOR WOULD FORCE IT
                                 TO***** TAKE PETITIONS OUT
                                 INTO VOTING PRECINCTS TO
                                 OBTAIN THE SIGNATURES OF
                                 REGISTERED VOTERS .
A01162003E1      75        2     BUT HE ADDED THAT NONE OF
                                 *GEORGIA'S CONGRESSMEN
                                 SPECIFICALLY ASKED HIM TO*****
                                 OFFER THE RESOLUTION .
```

```
GENRE=A

            SENT.    WORDS    REC.
INPUT         88      1907    2077
HEADL          6        13      13

OUTPUT         2        47      50
HEADL          0         0       0

        LINES PRINTED:    12
```

Following the list of sentences is a list of statistics. For example, in this particular case 1907 words (88 sentences) from Genre A (Journalese) of the Brown Corpus were read. Two sentences with the property defined by the program were found.

THE HELSINKI CORPUS OF BRITISH ENGLISH DIALECTS

Although the BrownScan program was originally written for the study of the Brown Corpus, there is no reason why it could not be used to study other machine-readable texts as well, once they have been converted to the Brown format. And dialect texts, of course, are no exception.

At the University of Helsinki we are compiling a large machine-readable corpus of dialectal British English, which we hope to be able to tag automatically.[4] The texts that are being computerized in Helsinki are transcripts of interviews with elderly speakers of rural British English dialects. The recordings date from the 1970's. Generally speaking, the informants are of the type and age used for the Survey of English Dialects. The data gathering method, however, was quite different. Our purpose was to gather spontaneous speech as much as possible without any particular linguistic point in mind at the recording stage. The following regions were covered: Devon, Somerset, Cambridgeshire, Suffolk, and Yorkshire. Recently we have also added interviews with speakers of Irish English.

The tape-recordings have been transcribed orthographically and stored on diskettes and computer tape. We have at the moment some three hundred thousand words on tape and we are aiming at about half a million words. There is much more data available, but we do not have the means to store it all.[5]

In the remainder of this paper I would like to show what can be done with our computerized texts now, and how the corpus could be further developed. The following is a sentence from an interview stored in the Brown format:

Farmer	NN0
said	VBD
to	IN
me	PPO
one	ABX
night	RN
at	IN
Lowtrow	PN0
Cross	PN
,	,
he	PPS
said	VBD
,	,
Thee	PPS2
's	DOZ
had	HVN
me	PPG
rabbits	NNS
,	,
he	PPS
said	VBD
.	.
I	PPS
looked	VBD

up	RP
to	IN
n	PPO
.	.
I	PPS
said	VBD
,	,
What	WPO
's	PPS20+DOZ
say	VB
?	.
I	PPS
had	HVN0
thee	PPG2
rabbits	NNS
?	.
I	PPS
han't	HVZ*
had	HVN
thee	PPG2
rabbits	NNS
,	,
I	PPS
says	VBZ
.	.
I	PPS
shall	MD
have	HV
em	PPO
next	JJ
year	RN
.	.
And	CC
so	S
I	PPS
did	DODS
.	.

The tags are slightly different from the tags found in the Brown sample above. This is because dialects show grammatical categories and syntactic structures that are not found in Standard English. For instance, in the above sample there are some second person singular forms. The zeroes in the tags indicate omission. Thus, in the sentence What's say? the subject pronoun thee has been omitted.

Below we have an example of a BrownScan run on one of the dialect texts. The program searches a text called Milton for the occurrence of tags beginning with "PPS2"; that is, the program looks for sentences with a second person singular subject, whether expressed or omitted. The sentences found are stored in a data file, where the material can be further studied and processed.

```
IF( TAG(1:4).EQ.'PPS2') FND=.TRUE.
```

390	1	Farmer said to me one night at Lowtrow Cross , he said , Thee***** 's had me rabbits , he said .
392	2	I said , What 's***** say ?

GENRE=MILTON

	SENT.	WORDS	REC.
INPUT	595	4665	5611
HEADL	0	0	0
OUTPUT	2	23	29
HEADL	0	0	0

LINES PRINTED: 5

As the listing shows, the second person subject form is <u>thee</u>, the same as the object form. Furthermore, the subject may be totally omitted in questions. That the Somerset dialect has a unified <u>thee</u> for all grammatical functions is shown by the following search, which is based on the word <u>thee</u> itself rather than on its tag:

```
IF(WORD(1:4).EQ.'thee'.OR.WORD(1:4).EQ.'Thee')FND=.TRUE.
```

347	1	I had thee***** rabbits ?
348	2	I han't had thee***** rabbits , I says .
463	3	I said , I wish thee***** 's come over and kill a pig for me , Jim , I says , he's bad .
470	4	Thee 's kill n theeself***** , he says .
472	5	Oh , he said , I'll let thee***** have some tools , so said .
488	6	Boss wants for thee***** to kill these pigs and lambs .
493	7	Read the letter theeself***** !
495	8	He says if thee***** 's make a mistake , he'd put up with it .

GENRE=MILTON

	SENT.	WORDS	REC.
INPUT	656	6401	7749
HEADL	0	0	0
OUTPUT	8	75	93
HEADL	0	0	0

LINES PRINTED: 18

Here the Somerset dialect is in sharp contrast with dialects where second person subject, object and possessive forms are differentiated. In Somerset the single form <u>thee</u> has all these functions.

USING DIALECTAL MATERIAL STORED IN DBASE FILES

Not all linguists, of course, have at their disposal a mainframe computer, and even if they did, they might not have the time to learn all the intricacies of its use. However, today there are quite a few packages for microcomputers that are easy to use but still powerful enough to be used as research tools. In the following I shall show how to use a program called dBase III in syntactic research.

When one wants to create a database from a running text, the first thing to decide is what the basic linguistic unit or units are. In the case of syntax, the basic unit would seem to be a sentence. I am not pretending that this concept is unproblematic when one deals with spoken material, but nevertheless I have decided to use sentences rather than, say, tone units because in syntax grammatical relations hold across tone unit boundaries. Let us assume then that we would like to store sentences in the database field that holds the primary language material.

In order to be able to do this, we have to transform our material into a sentence-per-line text. This is a trivial task and can be done automatically. At the University of Helsinki we use a small program written in Snobol4 to do this, but similar programs can be written in any other programming language. Once we have a sentence-per-line text, sentences can be appended from it into a dBase file automatically.

To illustrate how dBase files can be used in research, let us look at an area that might look quite confusing and uninteresting at first, but turns out to be theoretically interesting on closer scrutiny. I shall look at a short random sample drawn from interviews with eight Somerset informants. The sample is 6400 words long, and the individual passages in it are about 800 words on average. The problem that we want to look at is the distribution of forms like was and were. Personally, I am interested in speakers that show both forms, that is, speakers who say both I was and I were. This kind of variation is particularly interesting because it might show us something about the way standard forms enter into dialect.

Having loaded the program and opened a data file, we can start searching for the patterns we are interested in. That is, we shall start looking for the strings I was and I were. The line preceded by a dot is a command that instructs the computer to list all speakers who say "I were".

. display speaker for "I were"$ sentence

Record§	speaker
95	Frost
98	Frost
100	Frost
110	Frost
230	Spencer

Having located the speakers who say "I were", we can search the file again to see if there are speakers who also say "I was".

. display speaker for "I was"$ sentence

Record§	speaker
33	Vowels
78	Frost
163	Chillcot
236	Spencer
257	Spencer
299	Norman
342	Milton
343	Milton
358	Milton
376	Milton
434	Milton
436	Milton
448	Milton
546	Jury
547	Jury

As can be seen from the lists, there are two speakers (Frost and Spencer) who show the "I was/I were" alternation. In the following I shall concentrate on the speech of Frost. In other words, we shall be using only part of the database. This can be achieved by the "set filter" command.

. set filter to "Frost"$ speaker

Having restricted the database to the speech of Frost, we shall look at all the past tense forms to get a general picture of the situation. In the following all the sentences with <u>was</u> or <u>were</u> are listed.

. report form listse for "was"$ sentence .or. "were"$ sentence

	Sentence	Speaker
1.	Thik fish couldn't get out after they were in there.	Frost
2.	They were boiled, ehm.	Frost
3.	Oh, just cook em ordinary, like I was saying, you know.	Frost
4.	Piece or two each for a... they** that were in the family and you had a good meal.	Frost
5.	My father used to knit the nets and... be* night when we were in house, you know, done work.	Frost
6.	And another job he did do was make spars for thatching ricks.	Frost
7.	Out on the black ground that was.	Frost
8.	And we... I were out there playing wi a biggish girl, you know, running up and down the ditch.	Frost
9.	't were a dry ditch and they had thease big hole dug where they took water out of and I fell in there and I very near got drowned.	Frost
10.	They thought I were gone, yeah, honest.	Frost
11.	I had me teeth and that and...	Frost

pinched them right together and me*
tongue was showing, like.

12. I were near gone.   Frost

13. And they got the water out — 't   Frost
were the water, see done it.

14. I can mind that were a man... shook   Frost
me up well.

15. They were out to work somewhere.   Frost

16. I were there playing about with   Frost
thease girl, you know, running
away.

17. Just a bit (of) order, you know   Frost
what I mean, out'n the moor, out
there in (the) heath, out on the
black peat ground that was.

18. We children would be out there to   Frost
help em... as we were growing up.

19. These turfs, they were all laid out   Frost
over the ground all the summer to
dry.

20. Then when that were done, they did   Frost
dry up in... dry in these stacks
and we used (to) put em in a big
rick, all the lot, put em in a big
rick and stand.

The above list shows some interesting cases of variation. For example, there are instances of both <u>that</u> <u>was</u> and <u>that</u> <u>were</u>. Since <u>that</u> occurs with <u>was</u> and <u>were</u>, we might want to look at the two syntagms separately to see if any kind of pattern emerges. The new groupings are given below:

. report form listse for "that was"$ sentence

   Sentence   Speaker

21. Out on the black ground that was.   Frost

22. Just a bit (of) order, you know   Frost

Methods in Dialectology 579

```
        what I mean, out'n the moor, out
        there in (the) heath, out on the
        black peat ground that was.
```

. report form listse for "that were"$ sentence

```
    Sentence                              Speaker


23. Piece or two each for a... they**    Frost
    that were in the family and you had
    a good meal.

24. I can mind that were a man... shook  Frost
    me up well.

25. Then when that were done, they did   Frost
    dry up in... dry in these stacks
    and we used (to) put em in a big
    rick, all the lot, put em in a big
    rick and stand.
```

The sentences listed above suggest that the syntagms that was and that were might be partly mutually exclusive, so that only that was occurs in sentence final position. This of course is simply a hypothesis that will be confirmed or disconfirmed by further data. What is significant here is that even this 900 word sample has made it possible to formulate a hypothesis that makes sense in the light of what is known about the distribution of variants in British English dialects.[6]

AUTOMATIC TAGGING OF TEXTS

Although a lot of information can be extracted from running texts, tagging would greatly enhance their use in research. However, even if the money and skilled workers were available, analysing thousands of sentences manually would take a prohibitively long time. On the other hand, if the analysis could be done automatically, the task could be carried out in a reasonable time.

Fortunately, there are quite a few natural language parsers available. All of these have been designed for Standard English and it is not quite clear how well they could handle non-standard English. But even if they required extensive modification, the time and energy spent on modifying these programs would not be wasted.

Also, writing rules for the parser would show us a lot about dialectal syntax. For example, consider the following sentences showing a common type of ellipsis in South-Western British English:

Wadn no lorries in they days.
Wadn very many keeped on in they days.
Wadn no weighing em in they days.
Wadn no lorries in they days, you see.
Wadn no machines back'n my days.
Oh, wadn no skittle alley then.
It was easy because __ was no cars then, you see.
We used to drive em because __ wadn no lorries in they days.
-- because __ was so much dust you could hardly see anything.

These sentences show ellipsis of the existential <u>there</u>. This particular pattern is only one instance of "verb-initial" syntax in South-Western British English and an adequate parser would have to recognize the general trend rather than a number of isolated instances.[7] Thus, the task of writing rules for the parser would compel us to try hard to capture all the generalizations there are. Also, comparison of the rules that handle verb-initial structures in Standard English and in various dialects would show us a lot about dialectal syntax.

There are several parsers for the analysis of Standard English that produce quite satisfactory syntactic and word class analyses. At the moment we do not know how well these could handle non-standard speech. In Helsinki we have made plans to process our material by using the TESS parser developed at the University of Lund.[8] We are experimenting with this particular parser because it was specifically designed to handle spoken English. Even if it could code, say, only 75 per cent of the material, producing a tagged dialectal corpus would become feasible.

CONCLUSION

I would like to conclude this paper by repeating the main points. The study of dialectal syntax must necessarily be based on large amounts of tape-recorded speech. The only way of coping with this material is to store one's transcripts in machine-readable form. When this has been done, the material can be tagged grammatically and searched efficiently by using various query programs designed for syntactic research.

A dialect text, either grammatically tagged or untagged, can be stored in a database file and studied by using a microcomputer and a program like dBASE III. Getting running texts into a database file is not difficult. A text that has been made into a sentence-per-line file can be read directly into a database file, after which a researcher can search his text for specific patterns, count occurrences and sort his data in various ways to show underlying regularities. Also, sets of data can be easily generated and stored for further study by using the program's report generating facilities.

Sets of data extracted from running text will almost certainly reveal several patterns of dialectal syntax that have gone unnoticed. They will also allow us to test the accuracy of generalizations that have circulated in the literature but were incapable of verification because of the lack of empirical data.

NOTES

1. For example, Wakelin (1977, p. 125) comments as follows:

> "On the whole, few contrasts with Standard English or between different dialects are found on the syntactical level, since there appears to be in general an underlying identity of syntactical patternings in all forms of English."

Wakelin's discussion of syntax covers less than a page, but even the few points that are discussed suggest that the author's view about the extent of syntactic variation should be taken with a pinch of salt.

A good idea of what syntactic points there might be to study can be obtained from Wakelin (1987), which is an excellent collection of short but suggestive passages of tape-recorded South-Western British English speech. However, it is my impression that in order to be able to study individual grammars in any detail one needs about three hours of speech per informant. And even then, some of the patterns that one frequently hears used do not necessarily appear -- unless one records spontaneous conversation between two or more informants. The problem of obtaining good data for syntactic analysis has worried me since my first paper on dialectal syntax (Ihalainen 1976), and it still does (Ihalainen 1981, 1987). We are very far from the day when one feels comfortable about syntactic data.

2. The present situation is aptly described in Francis (1983, p. 41):

> "... most significant syntactic variation requires larger samples of a language than it has been convenient or even possible to collect by the usual methods. Usually a complete sentence, often a quite long one, is needed to display a variant syntactic construction. The field-worker collecting material with notebook and pencil finds it very difficult to record long sentences without asking

the informant to repeat what he has said, a procedure which is difficult and unsatisfactory for both. As a result, the syntactic material which has been collected more or less systematically is limited to those variations which can be displayed in a short sample. Among these are such matters as subject-verb agreement, the formation of negatives, pronoun reference and case, and question formation. The systematic study of larger forms of syntactic variation is only now becoming possible because of the accumulation of larger samples of speech by tape-recording. This is one of the challenging areas of dialectology today."

How difficult the problem of obtaining good data is, can be seen from the fact that William Labov had assessed the situation in almost identical terms thirteen years earlier ("The Study of Language in its Social Context," Studium Generale, Vol. 23, 1970, 33-87).

3. The BrownScan program was written by Visa Rauste at the University of Helsinki particularly for the study of the Brown Corpus. However, it has been extensively used to retrieve information from all kinds of texts. The present version is written in Fortran77 and should run on most mainframe computers.

4. This corpus is described in some detail in Ihalainen (1985c, p. 14) and Ihalainen, Kytö and Rissanen (1987, pp. 25-29).

5. The texts are keyed in manually and stored both on diskettes and on computer tape. The machine-readable texts thus created are of high quality. However, entering data manually is both expensive and slow. Given the rate at which data processing technology is advancing, one can envisage a time when tape-recorded speech can be converted into writing automatically. However, this piece of futurology does not help us in our present situation.

6. For a discussion of the complex of factors conditioning grammatical variation in the type of language analysed in this paper, see Ihalainen (1985a, 1985b, 1986, 1987).

8. For a description of this program, see Eeg-Olofsson (1987, pp. 45-47).

7. Among other verb-initial patterns, which of course have nothing to do with sentences showing subject ellipsis except that they too have an initial verb, are for instance sentences like Tasted it, have ee?, Got a youngish wife, he have.

REFERENCES

Eeg-Olofsson, Mats. (1987) "Assigning New Tags to Old Texts -- An Experiment in Automatic Word Class Tagging," in Corpus Linguistics and Beyond, Proceedings of the Seventh International Conference on English Language Research on Computerized Corpora, ed. Willem Meijs. Amsterdam: Rodopi, 45-47.

Francis, Nelson. (1983) Dialectology: An Introduction. Longman: London.

Ihalainen, Ossi. (1976) "Periphrastic 'Do' in Affirmative Sentences in the Dialect of East Somerset." Neuphilologische Mitteilungen, 67, 608-622.

---- (1981) "A Note on Eliciting Data in Dialectology: the Case of Periphrastic 'Do'. Neuphilologische Mitteilungen, 82, 25-27.

---- (1985a) "He took the bottle and put 'n in his pocket: The Object Pronoun he in Present-Day Somerset," in Varieties of English Around the World, General Series, Volume 4, Focus on: England and Wales, ed. Wolfgang Viereck (Amsterdam: John Benjamins, 1985), pp. 153-161.

---- (1985b) "Synchronic Variation and Linguistic Change: Evidence from British English Dialects." Papers from the 4th International Conference on English Historical Linguistics. Amsterdam Studies in the Theory and History of Linguistic Science, Vol. 41. Ed. Roger Eaton, Olga Fischer, Willem Koopman, and Frederike van der Leek. Amsterdam: John Benjamins Publishing Company, 61-72.

---- (1985c) "A Corpus of Dialectal British English." ICAME NEWS. Newsletter for the International Computer Archive of Modern English. No. 9., 14.

---- (1986) "An Inquiry into the Nature of Mixed Grammars: Two Cases of Grammatical Variation in Dialectal British English." Dieter Kastovsky and Aleksander Szwedek, eds., Linguistics Across Historical and Geographical Boundaries: In Honour of Jacek Fisiak on the Occasion of his Fiftieth Birthday, Volume 1, Linguistic Theory and Historical Linguistics. Berlin-New York-Amsterdam: Mouton de Gruyter, pp. 371-379.

---- (1987) "Towards a Grammar of the Somerset Dialect: A Case Study of the Language of J.M." Neophilologica Fennica. Modern Language Society 100 Years. Memoires de la Societe Neophilologique de Helsinki, Tome XLV. Helsinki, Modern Language Society, 71-86.

Ihalainen, Ossi, Merja Kytö and Matti Rissanen. 1987. "The Helsinki Corpus of English Texts: Diachronic and Dialectal. Report on Work in Progress." Willem Meijs, ed. Corpus Linguistics and Beyond. Amsterdam: Rodopi, 21-32.

Meijs, Willem, ed. 1987. Corpus Linguistics and Beyond. Proceedings of the Seventh International Conference on English Language Research on Computerized Corpora.

Amsterdam: Rodopi.

Ojanen, Anna-Liisa. "Use and Non-Use of Prepositions in Spatial Expressions in the Dialect of Cambridgeshire." Wolfgang Viereck, ed. Focus on: England and Wales, Varieties of English Around the World, General Series, Volume 4. Amsterdam: John Benjamins Publishing Company ,179-210.

Orton, Harold and Martyn Wakelin. 1967. Survey of English Dialects. The Southern Counties. Leeds: Arnold.

Rogers, Norman. 1979. The Wessex Dialect. Bradford-on-Avon: Moonraker Press.

Wakelin, Martyn. 1977. English Dialects: An Introduction. London: Athalone Press.

---- (1987) The Southwest of England. Varieties of English Around the World. Text Series 5. Amsterdam: John Benjamins Publishing Company.

The Automatic Computation of Linguistic Maps with the Aid of Cluster Analysis

BERNHARD KELLE
Universität Freiburg, West Germany

ABSTRACT

The information contained in 17 maps taken from the first installment of the Southwest German Dialect Atlas (SGDA) has been synthesized with the help of clusteranalytic techniques. The results condense the information taken from these maps into a single linguistic map in which the area under study is subdivided into linguistically homogenous regions. The quality of the results can be substantiated by comparison with the 17 individual maps.
We discuss how to evaluate the varying results emerging from the different methods used. Cluster-analytically generated maps could constitute a valuable addition to the atlas, in that they can summarize whole groups of maps which are thematically related.

1. DATA BASIS

The data for the Southwest German Dialect Atlas (SGDA) were collected from 1972 to 1986. The material was collected in interviews on locality. The answers to a questionnaire were phonetically transcribed by trained fieldworkers. Since 1975 the data has been prepared for computer processing. The research area (cf. map 1) is situated between the cities of Basel and Lindau in the south and between Karlsruhe and Ulm in the north.
The first part of the atlas comprises 50 linguistic maps[2]. Approximately a third of them constitute the data basis for this paper. These maps characterize the phonology of our research area. The main subject of these phonological maps is the description of short vowels. The first part of the atlas also comprises eight lexical maps centred on the subject of "human beings and human community".

2. COMPUTATION OF THE MAPS

2.1. Cluster analysis

Cluster analysis consists of grouping objects into homogeneous classes or clusters on the basis of a similarity criterion. The clusters generated in this paper were obtained from start classifications, which were either formed "by chance", i.e. arbitrarily, or originated from a particular computation. The final aim is to reduce the number of clusters, i.e. to fuse the most similar clusters, in order to achieve an efficient classification.

2.2. Data matrix

The data matrix for the cluster analysis is generated from the data contained in the thematic maps of our atlas. A symbol, descibing a certain linguistic item, is assigned to each locality (e.g. a circle, dash or triangle) in a map. There are no localities without data nor localities with more than one datum. In order for the data organized in this manner to be incorporated into the data matrix a transformation is required.
The first step in this transformation is to assign a value to each symbol, thereby creating a file for every map. Within these files, numerals are used instead of symbols.

E.g.:

Code of locality	Co-ordinate	Numeral (instead of symbol)
A-110	293	002
B-022	318	004
F-002	022	001
.		
.		

Since the numerals do not represent continous variables but rather are nominally scaled, they must be prepared for computation with the aid of a second transformation. For this purpose we must note how many different data symbols appear on each map. Each type of symbol is assigned a number valid for all the maps. The data matrix thus obtained appears as follows:

Map	1				2			3			...17
Attribute	01	02	03	04	05	06	07	08	09	10	...
Loc. A	-	-	+	-	+	-	-	-	-	+	

Methods in Dialectology 587

```
Loc. B   | + | - | - | - | - | + | - | - | - | + |
Loc. C   | - | - | + | - | - | - | + | + | - | - |
Loc. D   | - | + | - | - | + | - | - | - | + | - |
  .
  .
```

Because each locality on a map carries only one symbol (in order to characterize the type), only one feature is coded positive per map and locality. In this way a vector of binary attributes is established for the 'cases' (=localities). Thus binary attributes on a nominal scale are available for further computation. The data matrix we used includes 579 cases (=localities) and 17 attributes (=17 maps).

2.3. The computation method

The computations were executed with the aid of a cluster-analytic programme called CLUSTAN. CLUSTAN consists of different modules, intended, for example, for data input and output, for computation of correlation matrices with different coefficients, and for 'clusteranalytic' procedures in a stricter sense. From these, the procedure 'RELOCATE' was the one we used initially, because it permitts the iterative relocation of cases followed by cluster fusion for the generation of a local optimum solution. A major advantage of this procedure consists in the fact that it is also able to handle a large number of cases.
First we start with random classifications and then introduce two different coefficients (average distance, shape difference) to obtain two suboptimal classifications with 10 clusters each. Subsequently, these two suboptimal results are used as start-classifications for a cluster fusion, the number of clusters is gradually reduced to a minimum of two clusters. These two runs, which are the basis for the computation of maps, make use of the coefficient 'error sum of squares' (dissimilarity type, cf. maps 2 and 3).
Starting from another random start-classification, we then computed two other clusters with a third procedure (search for a global optimum, cf. map 4) in order to check the result of the two previous computations. As far as the fourth computation is concerned, we used the procedure 'RELOCATE' as a hierarchical fusion process, which boils down to a computation according to Ward's method (cf. map 5, cf. WISHART 1984, xy).
We then transformed the list of results into a map. Every cluster is assigned a symbol on the map. As soon as the automatically plotted maps were available, we were able to check whether a geographic cluster pattern could be identified. We intentionally decided not to present the results in the form of a dendrogram, since the one and only relevant criterion for the valuation of clusters from the point of view of linguistic geography is whether the analysis exposes spatial connections, i.e. whether a

structure becomes visible by including the parameter 'coordinate in space'. In a sense, this transformation of cluster analysis into a space represents a 'significance test'.

3. THE RESULTS

3.1. The formation of linguistic areas

All classifications were reduced until two clusters were obtained. For each step in the reduction process a map was produced.
We compared the results for the number of six clusters [3]. All four classifications have the following areas in common:

Southern and central Rhine valley,
Central and Upper Swabia,
Region around Ehingen,
Northeast of Black Forest.

Varying classifications are obtained for the northern Rhine Valley, the Black Forest, the Neckar region and the upper Danubian region. With regard to maps 3, 4 and 5 it is worth mentioning that the classifications are nearly identical. In order to compare the computed results, we examine two significant maps which yield representative explanations for our findings: map 6, topic "gesoffen" (drunk), map 7, topic "essen" (to eat).
On map 7 the structure of the area may be easily identified as the product of the classifications represented on maps 3, 4 and 5. On map 6, however, the area east of the river Wiese (southern Black Forest) corresponds to the area on map 2. On map 2 we also notice a belt, running from the northern Rhine region to the southern Black Forest which might be explained by some maps in our sample which deal with the vowel "a".

3.2. The valuation of the results

The results must be considered as a synopsis of the different maps as well as an attempt to render linguistic areas visible. As shown in map 7 ("to eat"), the structure of different areas can be clearly seen. Regarding the "germanic e", several maps were used in order to generate the data matrix. Thus we can conclude that the result of our computations should be seen as a combination map referring to a certain topic. It indicates the main areas and gives solutions for borders and transition belts. These solutions, especially, distinguish it from traditional combination maps, since the later always require one to decide on the place of the transition. Used in this way, the data matrix should exclusively comprise maps which relate to one topic.

In judging the relevance of the linguistic area we computed, caution is necessary. The combination of only 17 maps does not provide enough material in order to establish areas which are generally valid. We also concentrated our work on a certain topic, i.e. short vowels, in accordance with the purpose of the first installment of the atlas. The outcome is likely to improve as soon as more maps and a variety of topics are included.
We must, however, point out that the potential capacity of this method is limited by the software, since it can only handle a certain number of variables and cases. In the case of restricted capacities the selection of maps is especially important because different methods of selection may be used: a random choice from a great range of maps is likely to indicate dialect areas.
In cases where stress is put on special topics, however, we find that the result corresponds more to the principle of combination maps.
Concerning the combination of map groups dealing with certain topics of lexical geography, the results of GOEBL's studies are now available (cf. GOEBL 1984). It will be interesting to see if his methods can be verified on the basis of the material in the SGDA (cf. ALTMANN 1985).

4. FINAL OBSERVATIONS ON AUTOMATICALLY COMPUTED MAPS

The method presented here for the production of linguistic maps applies the techniques that were introduced by SHAW 1974, VAN HOUT 1980, JONES-SARGENT 1983, GOEBL 1983, 1984a, PHILPS 1984 and others [4].
The computation of dialectometric maps - taken in the widest sense - requires even more so, than in the case of conventionally produced linguistic maps, that we ask whether
- the spacial patterns that can be identified open up possibilities for interpretation. These patterns generally reflect diachronic processes that can be analysed synchronically. Thus it is not enough to render these spatial images visible, but rather we must try to explain them. Otherwise it would be mere decription and lag behind conventional dialect geography.
- computed spacial patterns do not result from "the language", as it is often suggested, but they develop and change within linguistic communities and thus must be traced back to individual speakers. Nevertheless linguistic areas are not "communication areas" that have certain forms of communication within their borders. From a geographic point of view, real communication between individual speakers and groups of speakers is limited to the community (cf. STEGER 1983, STEGER/JAKOB 1983).
- The results that are obtainable with the aid of numeric-

taxonomic methods can be favorably compared with those gained by conventional methods.
On the one hand, results that correspond to traditional findings confirm the usefulness of taxonomic methods. On the other hand, structures that do not reproduce any of the known patterns remain contestable as long as they do not yield clues for interpretation. From the point of view of the taxonomist it is indeed correct and necessary to suggest that this might be due to connections not yet discovered with other parameters, e.g. social ones, but this is insufficient for the judgement of a non-taxonomist. Therefore we must not only look for new coefficents, new laws and computation methods but for new ways of interpretation as well.

REFERENCES:

ALTMANN, Gabriel (1985) Die Entstehung diatopischer Varianten. Ein stochastisches Modell. Zeitschrift für Sprachwissenschaft, 4, 139-155.

GOEBL, Hans (1983) "Stammbaum" und "Welle". Vergleichende Betrachtungen aus numerisch-taxonomischer Sicht. Zeitschrift für Sprachwissenschaft 2, 3-44.
---- (1984a) Dialektometrische Studien. Anhand italoromanischer, rätoromanischer und galloromanischer Sprachmaterialien aus AIS und ALF. (Beihefte zur Zeitschrift für romanische Philologie 191-193). 3 vol. Tübingen.
---- (ed.) (1984b) Dialectology. (Quantitative Linguistics 21). Bochum.

GOEMAN, Antonie, C. M. (1986) Alleged unreliability of european continental dialect geography. A statistical appraisal. SCHöNE, Albrecht (ed.) (1986) Kontroversen, alte und neue. Akten des VII. internationalen Germanisten-Kongresses Göttingen 1985. Vol. 4, Tübingen, 305-318.

GOEMAN, Antonie, C. M. and REENEN, P. Th. van (1985) Word-final t-deletion in Dutch dialects: The roles of conceptual prominence, articulatory complexity, paradigmatic properties, token frequency and geographical distribution. (Vrije Universiteit Working Papers in Linguistics 16). Amsterdam.

HOUT, R. van (1980) Is een mathematisch-statistische dialectgeografie mogelijk? KRUIJSEN, J. (ed.) (1980) Liber amicorum Weijnen. Assen, 146-158.

JAKOB, Karlheinz (1985) Dialekt und Regionalsprache im Raum Heilbronn. Zur Klassifikation von Dialektmerkmalen in einer geographischen Übergangslandschaft. (Studien zur Dialektologie in Südwestdeutschland 3). 2 vol., Marburg.

JONES-SARGENT, Valerie (1983) Tyne-Bytes: A computerised sociolinguistic study of Tyneside. (Bamberger Beiträge zur englischen Sprachwissenschaft 11). Frankfurt.

KELLE, Bernhard (1986) Die typologische Raumgliederung von Mundarten. Eine quantitative Analyse ausgewählter Daten des Südwestdeutschen Sprachatlasses. (Studien zur Dialektologie in Südwestdeutschland 2). Marburg.

KÖNIG, Werner (1988) Atlas zur Aussprache des Deutschen. München, forthcoming.

NAUMANN, Carl Ludwig (1976) Grundzüge der Sprachkartographie und ihrer Automatisierung (Germanistische Linguistik 1-2). Hildesheim.

NORTH, David (1985) Spatial aspects of linguistic change in Surrey, Kent and Sussex. VIERECK, Wolfgang (ed.) (1985) Focus on: England and Wales. (Varieties of English around the world 4). Amsterdam, Philadelphia, 79-96.

PHILPS, Dennis (1984) Dialectometrie automatique. GOEBL, Hans (ed.) (1984) Dialectology. (Quantitative Linguistics 21). Bochum, 275-296.

SCHNEIDER, Edgar, W. and VIERECK, Wolfgang (1984) The use of the computer in American, Canadian and British english dialectology and sociolinguistics. GOEBL, Hans (ed.) (1984) Dialectology. (Quantitative Linguistics 21). Bochum, 15-60.

SHAW, David (1974) Statistical analysis of dialect boundaries. Computers and the Humanities 8, 173-177.

STEGER, Hugo (1983) Konzeptionelle und methodische Anforderungen an einen rehionalen Sprachatlas. Forschungsbericht "Südwestdeutscher Sprachatlas" Mit Beiträgen von E. GABRIEL et al. (Studien zur Dialektologie in Südwestdeutschland 1). Marburg, 1-15.

STEGER, Hugo and JAKOB, Karlheinz (1983) Raumgliederung der Mundarten. Vorstudien zur Sprachkontinuität in deutschen Südwesten. Stuttgart.

STEINHAUSEN, Detlef and LANGER, Klaus (1977) Clusteranalyse. Einführung in Methoden und Verfahren der automatischen Klassifikation. Berlin.

THOMAS, Alan, R. (1977) A cumulative matching technique for computer determination of speech-areas. Germanistische Linguistik 3/4, 275-288.
---- (1980) Computer analysis of a dialectal transition belt. Computers and the Humanities 14, 241-251.

VIERECK, Wolfgang (1984) Der Einsatz des Computers in der amerikanisch-englischen und britisch-englischen Dialektologie und Soziolinguistik. Zeitschrift für Dialektologie und Linguistik 51, 6-30.

WISHART, David (1984) Clustan. Benutzerhandbuch (3. Ausgabe). Stuttgart, New York.

ENDNOTES:

1. I would like to take the opportunity to thank B. Günter , G. Sheldon and J. Svitek for their help in the preparation of this paper.

2. The installment comprises 48 maps which are subdivided into four introductory maps and 44 thematic maps. In addition the first installment includes a foil that specifies the localities.
3. Concerning extension and number of the clusters which we obtain from computations cf. STEINHAUSEN/LANGER 1977, 169, 171.
4. The development of linguistic geography and its special application in the field of numeric taxonomy is described in e.g. NAUMANN 1976, KELLE 1986; important articles and descriptions of projects are collected in GOEBL 1984b, SCHNEIDER/VIERECK 1984, VIERECK 1984. For other related studies, consult THOMAS 1977, 1980, GOEMAN/VAN REENEN 1985, JAKOB 1985, NORTH 1985, GOEMAN 1986, KÖNIG 1988.

Methods in Dialectology

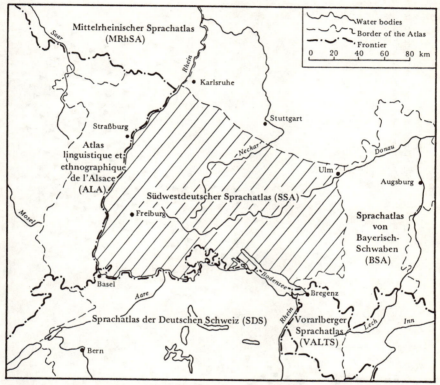

Map 1:   The investigation area of the Southwest German Dialect Atlas   (=SSA)

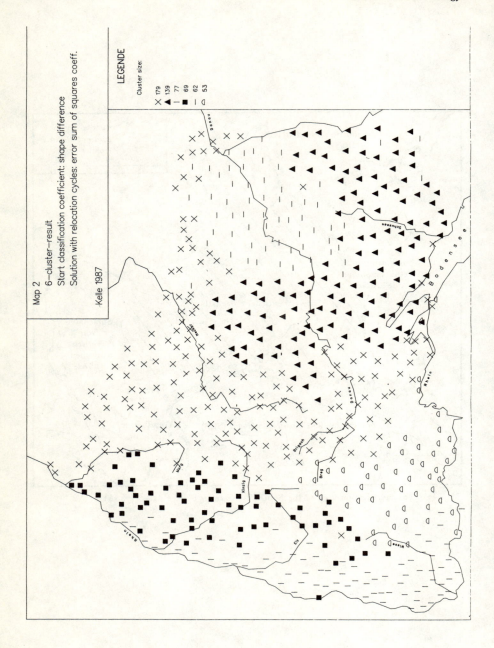

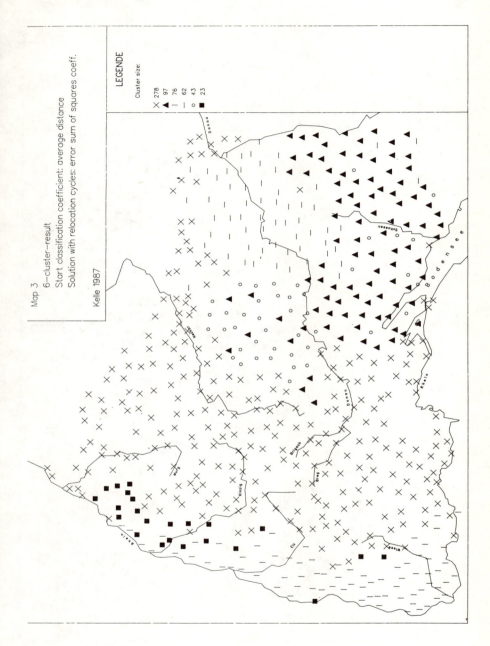

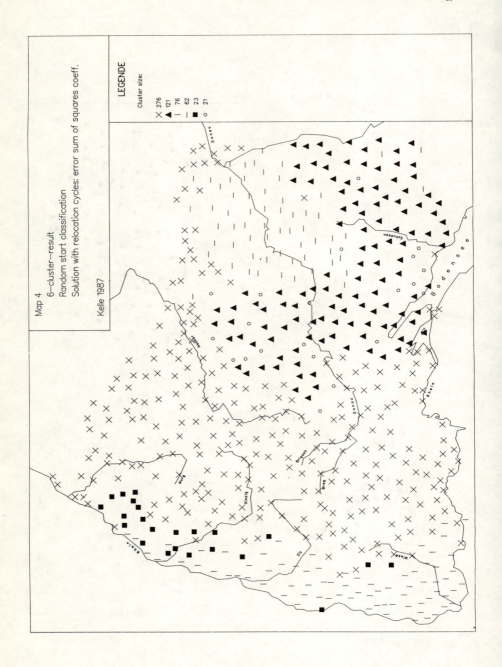

Methods in Dialectology

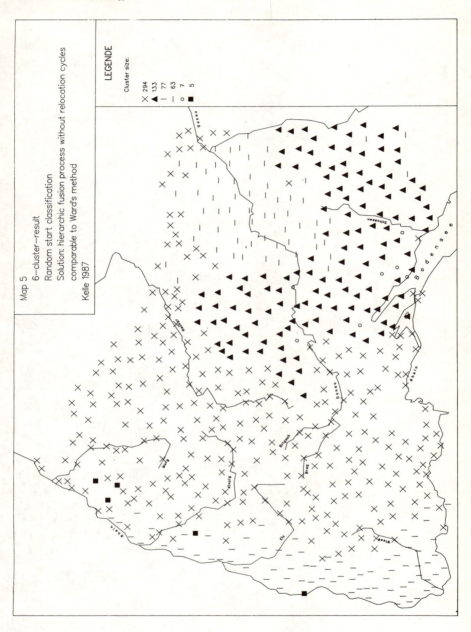

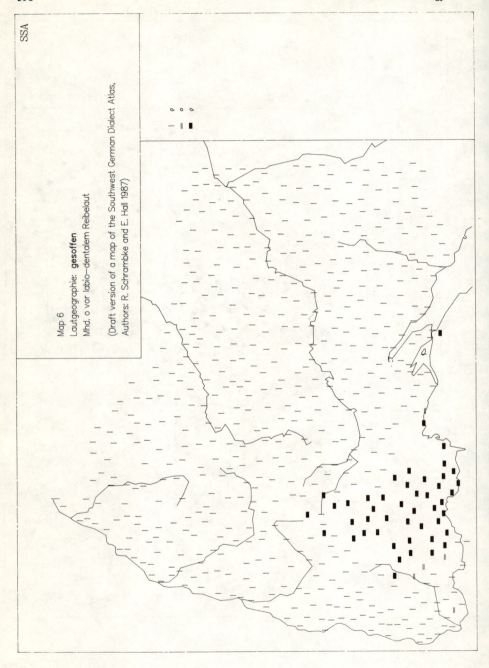

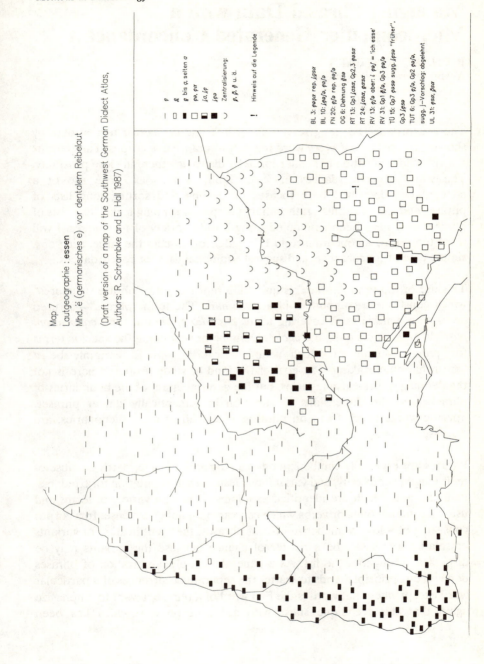

Map 7
Lautgeographie: essen
Mhd. ë (germanisches e) vor dentalem Reibelaut

(Draft version of a map of the Southwest German Dialect Atlas,
Authors: R. Schrambke and E. Hall 1987)

Managing Phrasal Data with a Microcomputer Generated Concordance

RICHARD A. SPEARS
Northwestern University

The concordance has long served as an indexing device for textual data by showing the context of every word in every utterance in a corpus. This permits the visual identification of similar forms by displaying them in close proximity. The value of concordances in lexicography is obvious.[1] The use of a concordance described here focuses on editing and sorting long lists of phrases and their variants—rather than a corpus of running text. These lists of phrases may have been assembled using a wide variety of techniques. I will show the use of a concordance in this endeavor, discuss the structuring of a simple type of concordance, and suggest additional uses for concordances.

This use of the term "phrase" is quite different from the "phrase structures" which constitute a component of a grammar. The term "phrase"—as used here—is a generic term covering terms like *idiom, phrasal verb, collocation, proverb, multilexical unit,* and *cliché*. Defining or redefining the specific terms for phrases—many of which seem to overlap—would certainly be a worthwhile undertaking. The goal of the kind of study proposed here is not the defining of pre-existing terms, but the determination of the boundaries of phrases and the dimensions of variation in semantically similar phrases. Specific works which focus on phrases, nearly all of them dictionaries, are discussed below.

Phrases are especially cumbersome to catalog and manage, partly because of their length, complexity, and variability. Despite their reputation for fixedness, many phrases which are identified as idioms occur in a variety of forms and usually contain nouns or verbs which can vary in number or tense. In a corpus consisting of a long alphabetized list of phrases, the identification of variants or related forms can be a matter of chance because the variants may be dispersed throughout the list. As a general rule, alphabetization of phrases done on *any* principle tends to scatter the separate occurrences of a particular word except when that word is the first word of a phrase. I want to emphasize again that this technique starts with a list of phrases which has been assembled by a variety of means. This process is not intended to automate the discovery of phrases.

When a simple concordance is used as a research tool, phrases can be edited and spelling or other irregularities can be regularized. Duplicates can be removed and variants can be linked to one another. For instance, **lay something aside, put something aside** and **set something aside** would be quite distant from one another in an alphabetized list and may not be recognized as related variants unless the researcher is reminded of one by the other. They are brought into close proximity in the concordance at a common element, the word **aside**. Similarly with **went round the bend** which can be eliminated as a variant of **go round the bend.** The synonymous phrases **tread on someone's toes** and **step on someone's toes** will be seen together at the concordance entry **toes.** The variants **go off the deep end** and **jump off the deep end** will be found at **end.** The phrases **not able to help something** and **can't help something** would be found at **help.** Whole and partial tokens of the same phrase can be recognized, for instance **to make a long story short** and **long story short** will be found both at **story** and **short.** This scheme can also provide confirmation of patterns, as for instance the many variants beginning with **get, have,** and **give** as in **get a grasp of something, have a grasp of something,** and **give someone a grasp of something.** The potential relationship between the members of these sets could not have been recognized in a long alphabetized list.

Mainframe computers provide the memory necessary to make enormous concordances, but they require programmers, and one has to be able to program or be able to communicate with programmers—both of which can be difficult tasks. Certainly a mainframe computer is the only possible way to produce a concordance of a massive corpus, but more modest projects can be carried out with more modest equipment. Those who cannot afford either mainframe use or programers, or those who are not required to deal with multi-million word corpora can manage with a microcomputer and a suite of off-the-shelf software.

Regardless of the hardware and software used, there are three important considerations in the creating of concordances on a computer. (1) Problems with computer alphabetization. (2) The logistics of producing a list of the words which are to be displayed by the concordance. (3) Adjusting the many variables available in the procedure to the researcher's specific goals. These are covered in the discussion below. It should be emphasized that this process is not designed to reveal phonological variants.

A major problem in any type of computer sorting has to do with the computer's notion of alphabetical order. Upper and lower case characters have different computer codes. A simple sorting routine uses an alphabetical order wherein all the capital letters, A-Z, precede all the lower-case letters, a-z. More complex sorters can be told to ignore case, but even the best alphabetization principle will not serve the purpose of bringing structurally similar material into the same location without some forethought. A more serious problem is that the typical computer sorter program does not ignore punctuation. Symbols which a human would ignore in alphabetizing such as commas, spaces, or hyphens have specific places in the sorting order and serve to create considerable chaos. The three forms **gold digger** [2 words], **golddigger** [1 word], and **gold-digger** [hyphenated] can appear at very different places in a large sorted corpus.

A concordance produced by this scheme has a very simple structure. The word preceding the colon is the search word, and the phrase following the colon is the data phrase.

>ASIDE: aside from someone or something
>ASIDE: lay something aside
>ASIDE: laying a finger aside of his nose
>ASIDE: put something aside
>ASIDE: set something aside
>ASIDE: utter an aside
>ASIDE: whisper an aside

A list of search words is derived from the list of data phrases—that is to say, the corpus—and the entire data list is searched for any occurrence of the search word. Each time the search word is found in a data phrase, the search word *and* the data phrase are appended to a new list which is the concordance. The list of search words could be made by hand, but it is easier to automate the procedure.[2]

First, a data list of the phrasal material, one phrase to a line, is created on a word processor. Here is a sample data list:

> Keep on trucking!
> play by ear
> fed up to here with something
> set something aside
> can't help something

The next step is to create a search list from the data list. A small program named *Dictsort* which comes as part of a spelling checker program called *The Word Plus* will put all the words in the data list into one long, alphabetical list, eliminating duplicates in the process. At the same time, the words will be put into upper case letters, ignoring all punctuation except the apostrophe.[3]

This is a sample of a search list made from the data list shown above. In the actual computer file, there can be only one word on each line, and no commas.

ASIDE, BY, CAN'T, EAR, FED, HELP, HERE, KEEP, ON, PLAY, SET, SOMETHING, TO, TRUCKING, UP, WITH

A text editor is used to place an ampersand (or some other symbol which does not occur in the data list) before and after each word in the search list. The results should look like this list. Again, only one word per line, and no commas.

&ASIDE&, &BY&, &CAN'T&, &EAR&, &FED&, &HELP&, &HERE&, &KEEP&, &ON&, &PLAY&, &SET&, &SOMETHING&, &TO&, &TRUCKING&, &UP&, &WITH&

Then each line in the data list is altered by placing an ampersand at the beginning and end. Replace each space with two ampersands, and surround each hyphen, period, comma, and other punctuation, except apostrophes, with ampersands. The results will look like this:

> &Keep&&on&&trucking&!&
> &play&&by&&ear&
> &fed&&up&&to&&here&&with...
> ...&&something&
> &set&&something&&aside&
> &can't&&help&&something&

The ampersands assure that there will be no matches between **thin** and **some**thing or **lay** and **play**. The form of the search word which will hunt for **thin** is actually spelled **&THIN&** making a match with **&something&** impossible. Any concordance-building program which does not take this into consideration will create only chaos. Of course, these ampersands will be removed at the end of the process.

There are a number of ways of processing these files into a concordance. One alternative to writing a program from scratch utilizes a word processor and the software which comes with the DOS operating system. A second approach utilizes more software: (1) A word processor capable of finding and replacing control characters. (2) A data base program such as *dBase II*. (3) A version of *The Word Plus* which has the program *Dictsort*. (4) A sorting program such as *Super-Sort*. A hard disk drive is essential for handling large files. All of these programs have been offered at no charge with the purchase of various microcomputers, and all are available for CP/M and MS-DOS operating systems. The concordance may take hours to complete depending on the speed of your computer, hard disk access time, and the sizes of the lists. Using a large RAM disk will speed up the process enormously.

The first approach will work only if the words in the data list and the search list are identical in case. Using only the operating system and a word processor, a simple concordance (with no search word displayed) can be created with the MS-DOS FIND command: FIND "&WORD&" DLIST >>CONCORD. The file DLIST holds the data list. CONCORD is the name of the file which will receive the concordance. A word processor can be used to create a batch file having one FIND command of this type for each item on the search list. File redirection in the first FIND command should take the form: >CONCORD.

In the second approach, a data base program provides considerable flexibility. Such a program requires the creation of three data base files: [using dBase, for example] search.dbf, data.dbf, and concord.dbf. Search.dbf has one field (called "finder1") long enough to hold the longest item in the search list. Data.dbf has one field (called "phrase") long enough to hold the longest item in the data list. Concord.dbf has two fields, ("finder2" and "phrase"). The first is identical in size to the "finder1" field in search.dbf and the second is identical in size to the "phrase" field in data.dbf.

The search list and the data list are converted to data base files, and a third data base file is created to hold the concordance. A command file uses each item in the search list to go through the entire data list looking for exact matches. For each match, the search word and the phrase in which the match is found are added to the concordance file. Here is a typical set of commands written for dBase II which will produce a concordance:

```
CLEAR
SET TALK OFF
SET ECHO OFF
SELECT PRIMARY
USE CONCORD
APPEND BLANK
SELECT SECONDARY
USE SEARCH
GO BOTTOM
STORE # TO END
STORE 1 TO COUNT
DO WHILE .NOT.EOF.
GO COUNT
STORE TRIM(FINDER1) TO PRY
STORE COUNT + 1 TO COUNT
ERASE
? 'SEARCHING FOR ',PRY
SELECT PRIMARY
STORE # TO LINENUM
APPEND FROM DATA FOR PRY $ !(PHRASE)
GO LINENUM+1
DO WHILE .NOT.EOF.
REPLACE FINDER2 WITH PRY
SKIP
ENDDO
SELECT SECONDARY
IF #=END
USE
SELECT PRIMARY
USE
ERASE
```

? 'FINISHED'
CANCEL
ENDIF
ENDDO[4]

With some data base programs one can browse quickly through the concordance file and reduce the search words to lemmas by hand as one sees fit. One of the important elements of this process is the flexibility offered to the researcher at this point. Various words in the search column of the concordance can be edited to change the results of a subsequent sorting. Contractions could be made into two records. For instance, **can't** could be replaced by two records each having the same data phrase: one for **can** and one for **not**. Compounds could be broken up into two records. For instance **golddigger** is replaced by two records each having the same data phrase: one for **gold** and one for **digger** or even **dig**. Verbs can be put into the present tense, and plurals can be converted to singulars. The phrases of the concordance can also be edited and regularized in the same way. Also at this point, duplicates resulting from this editing procedure can be deleted.

To complete the procedure, the concordance data base file is converted to a non-data base file, and a word processor is used to replace each sequence of two ampersands with a space and to delete the remaining ampersands. At this point other typographical changes can be made, such as adding the colon seen in the sample concordance shown earlier. A sorting program is used to sort the concordance, ignoring the difference between upper and lower case, into its final form.

There is a use for simple concordances in the presentation of data, also. Disciplines which concentrate on words, such as lexicology, lexicography, and dialectology tend to deal with phrases as exceptions, and these exceptions have been handled in a variety of ways. Whereas standard alphabetical orderings are suitable for individual words, putting phrases where they can be found in a dictionary is a special problem. A concordance can aid in the determination of a suitable entry head. The same concordance can also be useful in creating and enriching cross-referencing, or making it more efficient. The two typical solutions to forming an entry head for phrasal material in dictionaries are (1) to include the phrase at the entry head for the "key word" of the phrase or (2) to make a unique entry head in what Paul Beale has called "quartermaster English". The term refers to a quartermaster's typical inventory-listing style. Beale used this term in the introduction to his editing of Partridge's *Dictionary of Slang and Unconventional English* (1984). I don't know if he made it up, but is it a useful expression. An example of quartermaster English is **fix, in a** for **in a fix**, where the "key word" is made the first word of an entry head. Both solutions assume that the user of the dictionary has the same notion of "key word" that the dictionary maker has. These two solutions do not serve well when working with data which is all phrases.

There are more phrasal entries in dictionaries than one might imagine. Eric Partridge's *Dictionary of Clichés* (in various editions, 1948-78) is composed entirely of phrasal entries as is his *Dictionary of Catch Phrases* (1977). Both Oxford and Longman have published dictionaries of phrases. The *Phrases and Idioms Index*, Urdang (1983) has over 400,000 phrasal entries, many of which are the various quartermaster English versions of the same phrase. This three-volume set combines the entries from a number of different reference works and indicates in which work each entry phrase can be found. Its great size attests to four important points. First, it demonstrates the enormous amount of phrasal material which has drawn the attention of lexicologists and lexicographers. Second, it shows the high variability of many of these phrases. Third, it shows the popularity of quartermaster English as a listing device. Fourth, it reveals a lack of agreement as to where a phrase should be broken in the quartermastering process, or stated another way, what the "key word" of a phrase is.

It is possible to use a combination of devices to direct a dictionary user to a particular entry. The new Chapman *Dictionary of American Slang* (1986) includes numerous phrasal entries and contains a very high proportion of "router entries" whose sole purpose is to direct the user to the proper entry. In some cases, all the possible quartermaster versions of one phrase are found in their appropriate alphabetical locations, and a single key word—possibly extracted from a concordance—directs the user to a whole cluster of entries containing the key word. The latter device is also used in *A Dictionary of American Idioms*, Boatner (1966). *The Kenkyusha Dictionary of Current English Idioms*, Ichikawa (1964) uses quartermastering, but includes an index to some of the major non-initial words. In effect, these dictionaries use a small subset of a simple concordance to direct users to the various entries containing a "key word". Most of them assume that the "key word" is known to both the dictionary compiler and the user.

A complete concordance-based index to the entry heads of a dictionary offers a viable alternative to the "key word" based listing devices described above. In dictionaries or glossaries of phrases, so-called idioms, clichés, proverbs, etc., a separate concordance can be used as an index to the phrasal entries. In essence, every word can become a "key word". This allows the user to find the suitable phrasal entry from *any* of its component words. In practice, however, function words of the highest frequency are too numerous to serve as "key words." How might one decide what the "key word" is in a sequence like **A bird in the hand is worth two in the bush**? Using a concordance as an index, this proverb could be located by looking up **bird, hand, worth, two,** or **bush.** This kind of index was prepared for *NTC's American Idioms Dictionary*, Spears (1987). The dictionary's entry heads appear in the compiler's notion of what the entry head ought to be with no quartermastering at all. Users who cannot find what they want in the dictionary on the first try are encouraged to use the concordance (called a **Phrase Finder Index**), which shows the form of the phrase used in this particular dictionary. Virtually all the routing is handled by the **Phrase Finder Index**. Here is a sample showing the word **sick** from this index:

SICK
☐ get sick ☐ sick and tired of someone or something ☐ sick as a dog ☐ sick in bed
☐ sick to death of someone or something
☐ take sick

The concordance reduces the number of "router entries" and the amount of cross-referencing for routing purposes. This approach to listing phrases is especially useful in learners' dictionaries where different cultural backgrounds may interfere with the recognition of a "key word", and where the user may have caught only a snatch of a phrase or cannot identify the boundaries of a phrase. Unlike selective indexes, a concordance provides a simple way of searching through all the various collocations containing a specific word.

A more theoretical use for a concordance has to do with the designing of research which would benefit dictionary users and which might shed some light on the nature of phrases in language. What are the boundaries of phrases? Or, do all phrases have fixed boundaries? What are the variants of specific phrases, and how are they recognized as variants by speakers of a specific language? Are they learned and stored as units or generated from scratch every time they are used? What is the role of phrases in languages other than English? The answers to these questions will not come from a concordance—if indeed they will come from anything at all—but a concordance can organize phrasal data in such a way that the basis for these and other questions will be made apparent, and a concordance can point to specific data which can be incorporated into testing instruments.

In summary, I want to emphasize that I am not suggesting that this particular concordance-building scheme is superior to, or even equal to custom-made or commercially written products. This is an alternate approach which—because of its low cost and flexibility—may appeal to researchers with limited needs and limited means. The real issue here is what can be done with a concordance. Lexicography, lexicology, and dialectology have focused on both words and phrases. Concordances can serve these disciplines as powerful research tools in the study of phrases. The ability to make concordances easily may encourage researchers to pursue answers to some of the questions posed above.

Notes

1. A concordance was used in the production of *The New York Times Everyday Dictionary*, Paikeday (1982). See also the new *Collins/COBUILD Dictionary of the English Language*, Sinclair (1987), which is based on a concordance.

2. This involves using a word processor to remove punctuation, and put each word on one line. The duplicate and unwanted words must be removed by hand, and the entire list alphabetized.

3. A very long data list may have to be broken up into smaller files to be processed by *Dictsort*. If this is necessary, the resulting search lists should be combined and run through *Dictsort* again for the final search list. The search list can be edited to eliminate unwanted words such as articles, some or all prepositions, proper names, and so forth.

4. A documented version of this list of dBase II commands is available from the author. The same programming strategy can be used with other commercial data base applications programs. A large corpus will require many hours to process.

References

Chapman, R.L. (1986) *New Dictionary of American Slang.* New York: Harper and Row.

Courtney, R. (1983) *Longman Dictionary of Phrasal Verbs.* Harlow, Essex, England: Longman.

Cowie, A.P., Mackin, R., and McCaig I.R. (1975-1983) *Oxford Dictionary of Current Idiomatic English.* (2 vols.) London: Oxford.

Boatner, M.T., Gates, J.E., and Makkai, A. (1975) *A Dictionary of American Idioms.* Woodbury, New York: Barron's Educational Series.

Ichikawa, S. (ed.) *The Kenkyusha Dictionary of Current English Idioms.* Tokyo: Kenkyusha.

Long, T.H. (ed.) (1979) *Longman Dictionary of English Idioms.* Harlow, Essex, England: Longman.

Paikeday, T.M., (1982) *The New York Times Everyday Dictionary.* New York: Times Books.

Partridge, E. (1977) *Dictionary of Catch Phrases.* New York: Stein and Day.

—————. (1978) *A Dictionary of Clichés.* (5th ed.) London: Routledge and Kegan Paul.

—————. (1984) *A Dictionary of Slang and Unconventional English.* New York: Macmillan.

Sinclair, J. (ed.) (1987) *The Collins COBUILD English Language Dictionary.* London: Collins.

Spears, R.A. (1987) *NTC's American Idioms Dictionary.* Lincolnwood, Illinois: National Textbook Co.

Urdang, L. (ed.) (1983) *Idioms and Phrases Index.* Detroit, Mich.: Gale Research.

Aitken's Context in Northumberland, Cumberland and Durham: a Computer-assisted Analysis of Material from the Survey of English Dialects (SED)

BEAT GLAUSER
Anglistisches Seminar, Heidelberg

According to the Atlas of English Sounds (AES) words of the type dry, Friday, iron, ivy, knife, lice, mice, miser, shy, white, .. tend to have two characteristic vowel reflexes in Northumberland, North Cumberland and North Durham, namely the RP equivalent [aɪ] and a diphthong with a slightly higher and sometimes more central first component (Kolb et alii, 1979:1). Typical narrow transcriptions are [ɛɪ], [ɛ̆ɪ], [ɘ̈ɪ], [ɘɪ]. AES uses sixteen words to document this phenomenon and is very precise with regard to geographical spread, less so when it comes to defining possible context restrictions. [aɪ] appears to be present in open syllables (exception: hive); the diphthong with the higher first component occurs everywhere else (exception: Friday). Towards the south of the area in question ai gets more frequent at the expense of the ei sound. In some of these localities the group of words normally favouring ei has this sound in fewer than 75% of all cases, which is the limit below which AES does not map values as categorical.

AES and its statement depend on the SED's Basic Material (Orton et alii, 1962-71), which is known to be much richer than any of the parts that have been interpreted so far. Unfortunately, its organisation makes working with it very awkward when we have to look for certain phonetic forms that we wish to excerpt in large numbers. The answers to every questionnaire item are listed village by village, the whole material filling twelve volumes, which means going through all the questions separately to assemble the data for any individual locality. Several scholars have suggested that computers should be used to facilitate access, but the narrowness of the phonetic transcription used, perhaps in conjunction with the fact that nobody really knows just how rich the material is, has so far frustrated all attempts at coding.

For the present analysis all the forms from the nine Northumbrian localities, from two villages in Cumberland and three in Durham were fed into fourteen SUPERBASE data files (one per village, with between 70 and 150 entries each) which were run on a COMMODORE 64 (In connection with a Heidelberg research project called PROTEXT, we now have access to an ORACLE database on our IBM PC and on the mainframe computer of the Heidelberg RECHENZENTRUM. This promises that we shall soon be able to handle larger and more difficult

```
         + Nb 1 + + + + + + + + + + + + + + + + +
         +                                       +
         + WORD <eh L E-cc^ii v            >      first stage
         +                                       +  feeding in the
         + MEANING <ALIVE                  >      basic information
         +                                       +
         + NUMBER <04.08.06.00 >                 +
         +                                       +
         + INFORMANT <1>                         +
         +                                       +                second stage
         + CONTEXT P <L    >   CONTEXT F <v  >    filling in the
         +                                       +  redundant fields
         + SOUND <11>                            +  with the help of
         +                                       +  BASIC programmes
         + + + + + + + + + + + + + + + + + + + +
         08 E-cc-hi^ii    I   08 09 10 11 12 30 tot    third stage
         09 E-hi^ii       1      1  4  9 25 15  54    adding the
         10 E^ii          2   2     6  9 25 19  61    inventory in the
         11 E-cc^ii       3            2  6  3  11    file-card format
         12 E-cc-lo^ii        2  1 10 20 56 37 126
         30 a^ii

         Fig. 1: Sample Computer File-card for
                 Lowick (Nb 1)
```

problems. The phonetic notation was coded according to a system suggested by MacWhinney+Marengo (1986), where the Cardinal Vowels are allotted up to two letters and diacritics add to the length of a segment (cf. Fig. 1). Additional fields were used for meaning, and questionnaire and informant numbers. To achieve faster access, secondary fields containing a numerical code for the diphthongs as well as information concerning the preceding and following segments were added later. However, this new and redundant information was derived from the original fields via BASIC programmes, and therefore did not substantially increase the coding work. Finally, it proved very practical to have to hand a summary and a key of the available forms, so this information was added in the format of the file-card. 08 stands for a diphthong with a centralised first component slightly higher than Cardinal Vowel No. 3 and a second component [ɪ]. 09 represents [ɛɪ], 10 [εɪ], 11 [ɛ̆ɪ], 12 [ɇɪ], and 30 [aɪ]. Obviously a COMMODORE 64 has neither the storage nor the processing capacity to handle the Basic Material as a whole, but the data to be viewed in the light of Aitken's context (some 1,500 forms) can be interpreted with ease, and the exercise provides experience with projects of this kind. Secondly, we shall also be able to see whether working with all the material SED has to offer on a given phonological problem really does lead to more precise statements or whether the law of diminishing return comes into operation.

loc.	eɪ	ëɪ	e̤ɪ	ɛ̤ɪ	çɪ	ɛɪ	ɛ̈ɪ	ɛ̤ɪ	çɪ	ɐɪ	æɪ	ɑɪ	aɪ	total
Nb 1				2	1	10	20	56					37	126
Nb 2			1		2	14	26	47	6			3	33	132
Nb 3					1	15	43	28	2			3	40	132
Nb 4						70	5		5				31	111
Nb 5	1	1	5			10	26	55	3		1		42	144
Nb 6						16	5	1	1			12	42	77
Nb 7	8	1	1			22	16	48	1		1		34	132
Nb 8	2	2	2			9	14	46			1		38	114
Nb 9						49	2						29	80
Cu 1					1	55			1		1	1	51	110
Cu 2						48	9	2	1				37	97
Du 1						11	2	6		1	27		41	88
Du 2						19	20	19			2		46	106
Du 3			1			28	10				3		55	97
	11	4	9	3	5	376	198	308	20	1	36	19	556	1,546

Fig. 2: Total Inventory of Phonetic Forms

Fig. 2 shows the total inventory of the vowel reflexes we are interested in. Altogether there are 1,546 forms extant, which means that, besides those 36 words that occur practically everywhere, between 70 and 100 additional tokens are available per village. We can also see that what was described in terms of a bipartite structure earlier on is much more complex, at least on the phonetic level. Stanley Ellis, the SED field worker for this area, took down thirteen different vowel reflexes, ranging from [eɪ] to [aɪ], the individual values being distributed very unevenly across the various localities.

At Allendale (Nb 9) there are only three phonetic variants, [ɛɪ], [ɛ̈ɪ] and [aɪ]. The second one is so rare (two instances) that we are certainly justified in grouping it with [ɛɪ] and analysing the data in terms of two realisations. The most complex situation, at Haltwhistle (Nb 7), involves nine different reflexes, and even if we neglect [ëɪ], [e̤ɪ], [çɪ] and [æɪ] (one instance each), there are still five major phonetic variants to be dealt with.

Some of the 'minor' sounds are typical of certain localities. The diphthongs with a [+ high] and [+ mid] first component, for instance, can be found only at Wark (Nb 5), Haltwhistle (Nb 7) and Heddon-on-the-Wall (Nb 8). Moreover, of the 36 instances of [æɪ] 27 occur at Washington (Du 1), while 12 of the 19 [ɑɪ] come from Earsdon (Nb 6).

In a first attempt to group these phonetic values, the shaded rectangular area on the diagram has been excluded. This seems more reasonable at this stage than arbitrarily attributing the reflexes to either of the two main groups. With the exception of Washington (Du 1), where 28 instances of [ɑɪ] are somewhere in between ei and ai, only small numbers of doubtful cases emerge.

In Wark (Nb 5), Haltwhistle (Nb 7) and Heddon-on-the-Wall (Nb 8), there may be a tripartite division. A look at the words involved suggests that we should treat the shaded semi-circle separately as well. At Nb 5 [ë̞ɪ] occurs in flea, free, sight, three, tree (3 instances); at Nb 7 in blea-berry 'bilberry', flea/fly, knee, pea (2), sea/see, tea (2) and at Nb 8 in fly (2), knee, see (2), tree. Apart from one instance of sight, this sound type only occurs in word-final position. This links it with Southern Scots, where [i:] has been diphthongised in this same position (Zai 1942:70+76). Mather+Speitel (1976:159-69) find traces of this phenomenon in Liddesdale and South-East Dumfriesshire only.

locality	ei	ai	tot	% ei	% ei individual informants	
Nb 2	96	36	132	72.7	(76 71)	
Nb 4	80	31	111	72.1	(73 65)	
Nb 7	87	34	121	71.9	(65 85)	
Nb 1	89	37	126	70.6	(72 69 73)	
Nb 5	94	42	136	69.1	(70 64)	
Nb 3	89	43	132	67.4	(65 67 72 63)	+ 66
Nb 8	69	38	107	64.5	(62 74 33)	
Nb 9	51	29	80	63.8	(75 69 50 58)	
Cu 2	60	37	97	61.9	(62 66 33)	+ 57
Du 2	58	46	104	55.8	(81 72 14 42)	
Cu 1	57	52	109	52.3	(52 47 50 67)	+ 48
Du 3	39	55	94	41.5	(10 48 48)	+ 39
Du 1	19	41	60	31.7	(34 26)	
Nb 6	23	54	77	29.9	(30 30)	+ 30
	911	575	1,486	61.3		

Fig. 3: ei and ai in Northumberland, Durham and Cumberland: implicational arrangement according to percentage of ei

Fig. 3 (omitting the shaded areas from Fig. 2) concentrates on the two major sounds ei and ai, giving the number of tokens of each, the totals and the occurrences of ei as percentages of the totals. There is impressive stratification, from 72.7% at Ellington (Nb 2) to a mere 29.9% at Earsdon (Nb 6).

Methods in Dialectology

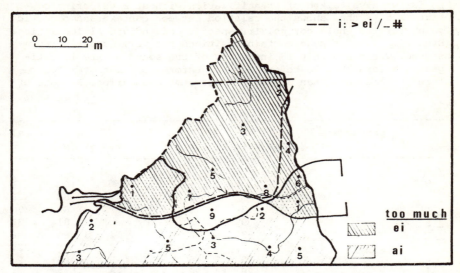

Map 1: Percentage Values for ei in Northernmost England

Mapping these values (Map 1) suggests that the figures make sense geographically. To the south ei is a rare sound, occurring only in words like eight, neighbour, straight, weigh, .. (Kolb et alii, 1979:118). The lines show how our area is structured according to the implicationally greatest divergencies between two localities as indicated in Fig. 3. Rural Northumberland seems to form a unit. Five of the Northumbrian localities have values above 66%. The remaining lines form a girdle reaching from Cumberland to Tyneside, Tyneside having by far the lowest values. Abbeytown (Cu 2) is irregular in that the percentage of ei sounds is higher than in more northern Longtown (Cu 1).

Looking at the figrues for the individual informants (Fig. 3) we see that four values fit badly: informant 3 at Heddon-on-the-Wall (Nb 8), informant 3 at Abbeytown (Cu 2) and informant 1 at Wearhead (Du 3) have massively lower percentages of ei than what seems to be the norm in their respective localities.

Among the forty informants interviewed in the 14 villages, 23 produce ei-values that range between 61% and 81%. The fewer items the corpora contain, the more frequent do deviations from the norm become. The two extreme values can be found where the number of items is under 20. There are no deviations greater than 30% in corpora with more than 40 forms, and with over 60 forms the greatest divergence is 20%.

So far we have talked of stratification without considering context. Fig. 4 thus shows the relation between context and phonetic value for the whole corpus, irrespective of individual localities. Even with 1,500 tokens certain positions are very scantily represented. There are only 13 instances of the sound we are investigating before /b/, 20 before /ð/, 26 before /z/, but over 200 before /t/ and more than 300 before morpheme boundaries. Because of

	percentage												total
	eɪ	ëɪ	ẽɪ	ɛ̈ɪ	ɛɪ	ɛɪ	Ëɪ	ɛ̃ɪ	ɛ̣ɪ	ᴁɪ	æɪ	ɑɪ	aɪ	n
_θ												100	1
_z					4		8					88	26
_r					5	3	3	1			3	84	70
_ə					9	3	3				3	81	32
_v					3	5	8			2	1	80	86
_≠	3	1	3		7	3	5	1		2	1	75	327
_ð					15	5	5	5		5		65	20
_l					28	14	26	2		4		28	51
_p					42	9	18				3	27	33
_d					29	18	29	2		1	3	17	158
_n					33	20	27	1		3	1	16	178
_s			1		32	21	28			3	1	14	72
_t			1	2	39	15	31	1	0	3		8	275
_m					25	28	35			1	3	8	75
_k					50	11	23	5		5		5	74
_f					25	35	31	5			2	2	55
_b					46	8	15			31			13
	0	0	0	0	0	24	13	20	1	0	2	1	36	1,546

Fig. 4: Percentage Indices of Phonetic forms per Context
(-- context expectation for intermediate sounds)

this uneven distribution the values in the respective columns are given as percentage indices. This means that for instance in 4% of all /z/ contexts the vowel is [ɛɪ], in 5% of all /r/ contexts the same thing is true. The /r/ phoneme includes a number of different phonetic realisations, rolled [r] and flapped [ɾ] in Cumberland, frictionless continuant [ɹ] at Wearhead (Du 3), the 'burr' in Northumberland (except Nb 9) and at Washington (Du 1) and Ebchester (Du 2); and where [ə] has r-colouring or appears as a back vowel [ɔ] because of the 'burr', it has been grouped with /r/ as well. This means that the context [ə] includes only such cases as have no following /r/, the most frequent word being dandelion.

Methods in Dialectology

[aɪ] seems to be favoured before /z/, /r/, /ə/, /v/, in word-final position and before /ð/ (between 88% and 65%). Then there is a gap of 37%, and the contexts preferring the other vowel sounds follow with between 28% and 0% [aɪ]. If we are ready to accept exceptions of up to 30%, this is the same context as in 'Aitken's Law': [aɪ] before voiced fricatives, before /r/ and in word-final position, a diphthong with a higher and sometimes centralised first component everywhere else (Aitken 1981).

Having identified the contexts that favour ei as being the same as in Scotland, i.e. everywhere expect in word-final position, before /r/ and before voiced fricatives, we can now do three things to interpret our percentage indices more meaningfully. First of all, let us compare the observed percentages from Fig. 4 with the ones we would expect if Aitken's context was observed categorically (the first two columns of Fig. 5). Even with corpora as large as ours there is still too much fluctuation to allow comparisons of overall percentage values. The contexts that should produce the highest percentage of ei (69.7%) occur at Thropton (Nb 3). At Earsdon (Nb 6) they are strikingly different. There should not be more than 51.9% ei to start with, which means that Map 1 may appear coherent, but is the result of figures that cannot be compared.

The deviant values of individual informants are, on the whole, the result of context. One exception comes out clearly, however. Informant 1 at Wearhead (Du 3) does not treat (ai) as a variable at all. His one form with [eɪ] in a word with RP /i:/ is typical of South Durham usage according to the SED material from Du 4 to Du 6. In continuing our computations we shall exclude these data.

Secondly, the shaded rectangle of intermediate values in Fig. 3 can now be judged with regard to context. The overwhelming majority of these sounds occurs in ei-contexts. The same thing holds for [aɪ]. As soon as we draw the line between the RP value ai and all the other reflexes there is a much better fit. This would suggest that the phonological boundary has to be drawn between the RP value ai and everything else, which indicates that, psychologically speaking, everything not exactly RP is felt to be substandard. It also testifies to an attempt on the part of the informants to adapt their speech in the direction of RP, especially on Tyneside.

Continuing our computations with a bipartite structure of [aɪ] versus all the articulations with a closer first component may seem risky with regard to the word-final [ëɪ]-sounds. The problem is that all the villages which show diphthongisation of RP /i:/ in word-final position also have more open articulations in this context, so that any separation into two values is difficult to maintain with the limited material at hand.

loc.	% of ei tentative	expected	adapted	difference		% of ei for ai	% of ai for ei
Nb 7	71.9	59.8	75.0	+	15.2	16.7	1.5
Nb 2	72.7	64.4	72.7	+	8.3	12.8	4.5
Nb 4	72.1	65.8	72.1	+	6.3	9.0	2.7
Nb 5	69.1	65.3	70.8	+	5.5	7.7	2.2
Nb 1	70.6	65.1	70.6	+	5.5	7.9	2.4
Nb 3	67.4	69.7	69.7		0.0	6.8	6.8
Nb 8	64.5	64.9	66.7	+	1.8	7.9	6.1
Nb 9	63.8	63.8	63.8		0.0	1.3	1.3
Cu 2	61.9	68.0	61.9	./.	6.1	3.1	9.2
Du 2	55.8	62.3	56.6	./.	5.8	5.5	11.3
Cu 1	52.3	63.6	53.6	./.	10.0	9.1	19.1
Du 1	31.7	60.2	53.4	./.	6.8	10.2	17.0
Du 3	41.5	62.3	51.9	./.	10.4	3.9	14.3
Nb 6	29.9	51.9	45.5	./.	6.4	6.6	13.0
∅	61.3	63.8	64.6	+	0.8	8.1	7.3

Fig. 5: Expected and Observed Percentages of ei and ai in Accordance with 'Aitken's Law' (ai / _ ≠, r, voiceless fricatives)

Column 3 of Fig. 5 gives the new percentages. Here ei stands for all the diphthongs apart from RP [aɪ] (and the words from informant 1 at Wearhead (Du 3) have been neglected). On the whole there is little change, but the localities in the south of our area are now integrated slightly better than when the intermediate sounds were excluded.

Thirdly, let us concentrate on the exceptions (columns 4 - 6). Only at Thropton (Nb 3) and Allendale (Nb 9) does Aitken's context appear to exert its influence fairly categorically: there is no difference between the values we expect and those we observe. A closer look reveals, however, that too much ei tends to occur side by side with too much ai. Generally, high ei values (in contexts where there should be ai) correspond with low ai values (for ei) in Rural Northumberland. In Cumberland, Durham and at Earsdon (Nb 6) the situation is the other way round.

Map 2 is an attempt to separate the two phenomena. Entering only those values that are higher than 7%, we have a northern area with ei versus a southern one with ai, but at Longtown (Cu 1), Earsdon (Nb 6) and Washington (Du 1) the two phenomena overlap. At Allendale (Nb 9) they are absent altogether.

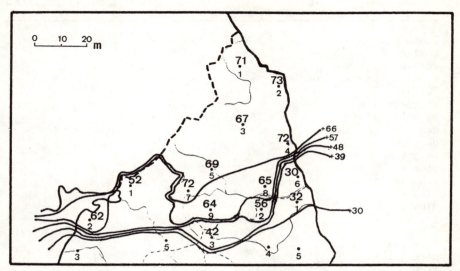

Map 2: Too much ei (more than 7%) in the North; too much ai (more than 7% in the South)

So far we have found a context that is observed in one village fairly categorically, in the others more or less so, the deviations producing a systematic geographical pattern. Fig. 6 tabulates the 112 words extant with ai, where Aitken's context would suggest ei. This arrangement shows the SED material at its worst. Limited geographical distributions (thine does not occur in Northumberland) and 'incidental' material (six words can only be found in one village) produce a very uneven picture, and the results are rather poor. Among the more frequent forms only spider and wright seem to justify some kind of exceptional status.

Heslop (1892) has two spellings for 'the insect that spins a web', spidert and spyther. The second one could imply a voiced dental fricative, which is a context asking for ai. However, spyther occurs at Wearhead (Du 3) exclusively, and its vowel reflex is ei. Wright was asked for directly by the SED field worker ('What do you mean by wright?'). This may be responsible for the many articulations with the RP vowel. Other frequent 'exceptions', e.g. boil, Friday, side, time, write, .. occur even more frequently in the form we would expect them to take.

Among all these forms, voiced contexts are notably more frequent than voiceless ones (73 tokens as opposed to 39). The 'exceptions' before /m/, /n/, /b/, /d/, /g/, /l/ amount to 14% as against only

Word	Nb 1	2	3	4	5	6	7	8	9	Cu 1	Du 2	1	2	3	total dev.
black-kite n	–	–	–	–	–	–	–	–	–	–	1	–	–	–	1
boil n	1	–	1	1			1			1			–		5
coil n										–	–	1	–	–	1
flipe n	–	–	–	–	–	1	–	–		–	–	–			1
Friday			1							2			2		5
frightened a						1				–	–	–		–	1
ga(b)le-end n	–	–	–	–	–	–	–	–	–		1	–	–	–	1
grind v		–		–	–	–	–	1	–						1
gripe n	–	–	–	–	–	–		1	–		1				2
height n								1	–		–	–	–		1
hide v		1	–							1		1			2
hike (+ing)	–	–	–	–	–	1	–	–	–	–					1
hind n		–			–	1		–	–	1	–				2
hipe v	–	–	–	–	–	–	–	–	–	–	–	–	1	–	1
ice n	1					2					–	1			4
like		–	–			–					–		–	1	1
lice (pl.)										1					1
mice (pl.)		1									1				2
might								1	1					–	2
mind v		1								2			1		4
mine					1					1		1	1	1	5
nine											2	1			3
rein (+ pl.)	–	–	–	–	–	–	–	–	–	1	–	–	–	–	1
ride v		–	–	–	1	–	–	–	–	–	–	–	–	–	1
rime n	–	–	–	–	–	–	–	–	–	–	1	–	–	2	3
rind n v						1		–		2	–		1	–	4
scyth(e) n	–	–	–	–	–	–	–	–	–	–	–	–	1	–	1
side n v		1				1	1			2	3			1	9
sight n		1	–			–				–	1	–			2
sile v		1			1					1	–		1		4
slice n	–					–	–	–	–	–	–	1	–		1
spice n	–	–	1							–	1	–			2
spider n	1	1	1	1		1				1	1	1			7
stile n						–		1		1	1				3
stine n	–	–	–	–	–	–	–	–	–	1	–	–	–		1
strike v	–	–	–		1	–	–	–	–				–		1
thine	–	–	–			–				1		1	1	1	4
time n										2				1	3
twine v	–		2			–				1			–		3
white a v		2												1	3
wind-pipe n	–	–	–								1	–	–		1
wipe v						–	–		–				1	1	2
wright n			1	1		1			–		2		1		6
write v							1				1		1		3
	3	6	9	3	3	10	2	7	1	20	10	15	12	11	112

Fig. 6: ai Where Aitken's Context Predicts ei (blank = ai)

word	Nb 1	2	3	4	5	6	7	8	9	Cu 1	2	Du 1	2	3	total	dev.
weigh v	1	1	1	1	-	1	1	-	-	1	1	1	1	-	10	
neigh v	-	-	-	-	-	-	-	-	-	-	-	1	-	-	1	11
blea-berry n	-	-	-	-	-	1	-	-	-	-	-	-	-	-	1	
do v	-	1	-	-	-	-	-	-	-	-	-	-	-	-	1	
flea/fly n	-	2	1	-	1	-	2	2	-	1	-	-	-	-	9	
free-stone n	-	-	-	1	-	-	-	-	-	-	-	-	-	-	1	
he	-	-	-	-	1	-	-	-	-	-	-	-	-	-	1	
-kneed a	-	-	-	-	-	-	1	1	-	-	-	-	-	-	2	
pea n	-	-	-	-	-	-	2	-	-	2	-	-	-	-	4	
sea n	-	-	-	-	-	-	1	2	-	-	-	-	-	-	3	
see v	-	2	2	-	-	-	1	1	-	-	-	-	-	-	6	
sway n	-	1	-	-	-	-	-	-	-	-	-	-	-	-	1	
tea n	-	-	-	-	-	-	2	-	-	2	-	-	-	1	5	
three	-	-	1	-	1	-	-	-	-	1	-	-	-	-	3	
three n	-	2	-	-	3	-	-	1	-	-	-	-	-	-	6	53
eye n		3	1												4	
high a	-	-	-	-	-	-	-	-	-	2	-	-	-	-	2	
thigh n	1	1	-	-	-	2	-	-	1	-	-	-	-	-	5	11
aye							2			-					2	
byre n					1								2	-	3	
cry v	1	-	-		1	-				-				-	2	
dry a										1					1	
either	-	1	-	-	1	-	1		1	-	-	1		-	5	
fire n				2								2			4	
five	2			2	2		2					2			10	
hive n			1							1		1			3	
near a	-	-	-	-	-	-	-	-	-	-	-	-	-	1	1	
nigh	-	-	-	2	-	-	-	-	-	-	-	-	-	-	2	
scythe n						-						1	-		1	
sky n	1	1					-								2	
spidher n	-	-	-	-	-	-	-	-	-	-	-	-	1	-	1	
stye n		1								-		-			1	
thy	-	-	-	-	-	-	1	-	-	-	-	-	-	-	1	
try v n	1		1												2	
tyre n	-	-	-	-	-	-	-	-	-	-	-	-	1	-	1	
why	-	-	-	-	-	3	-	-	-	-	1	-			4	
wye	-	-	-	-	-	-	-	-	-	1	-	-	-	-	1	47
	7	16	7	8	11	2	22	7	1	10	3	9	6	3	112	

Fig. 7: ei Where Aitken's Context Predicts ai (blank = ei)

7% before /p/, /t/, /k/, /f/, /θ/, /s/. When Aitken's context expands, it seems to embrace first of all /l/, then the nasals and the voiced plosives. At Longtown (Cu 1) this new constraint is observed almost categorically.

Fig. 7 is a tabulation of ei where ai would be expected. The following four groups can be tentatively distinguished:

(a) Weigh and neigh belong to a small set of words with ME /x/ that regularly have ei in the whole North of England (cf. Kolb et alii, 1979:118). /x/ was lost late in this area. Heslop (1892: xvii) mentions the presence of this sound in northern Northumberland. Between Northern Middle English e and /x/ a palatal glide seems to have developed before the fricative was deleted, which led to forms like [wɛɪ] 'weigh' and [nɛɪ] 'neigh'. This now word-final diphthong has not undergone any subsequent change. For some reason Aitken's context does not apply here.

(b) ei in words like blea-berry, flea, free, he, .. documents a phenomenon that is typical of the Southern Counties of Scotland. Here old /i:/ and /u:/ were diphthongised in word-final position. Zai (1942) has [ɛ̆ɪ] in words with RP word-final /i:/, but [ɑ·ɪ] in those from RP /ai/. This diphthongisation covers Nb 2, Nb 3, Nb 5, Nb 7, Nb 8 and Cu 1 (cf. Map 2). The SED field worker characterised some of the words from this set with a more closed transcription, but as he did not do so regularly, the two groups are treated under ei

(c) Eye, high, thigh could derive from /i:/ (cf. Kolb et alii, 1979:9-15), so that ei in these words might also be the regular result of diphthongisation in word-final position.

(d) All this accounting for 'exceptions' must not be allowed to hide the existence of a fourth group for which there is no obvious explanation. In this context it is interesting to see that for Morebattle in Roxburghshire Zai (1942) has [ɑ·ɪ] only in word-final position and characterises all additional words with this sound as influenced by RP. If this statement is not too simplistic, the variable (ai) has gradually been insinuating itself into Aitken's context. Some of our 'exceptions' may be errors, some of them old forms. Our two areas on Map 2 could now be interpreted as expansion towards Aitken's context in the north, expansion beyond in the south.

In a summary of this analysis covering all the material SED has to offer on a given phonological problem, the following points should be stressed:

1. The initial suspicion that the variable (ai) in Northumberland, Cumberland and Durham has a purely geographical distribution (the

Methods in Dialectology 623

more rural, the more ei) appears at first sight to be confirmed by Map 1. A more detailed analysis reveals, however, that context matters.

2. The context, ai in word-final position, before /r/ and before voiced fricatives, is the same as in Scotland ('Aitken's Law'), but it takes a less prominent position. On the one hand Scots innovations seem to have reached as far south as Tyneside and North Durham, and on the other hand Aitken's context exerts its influence on only a marginal part of the northern English phonological systems: it is responsible for a more open articulation of the variable (ai).

3. ai where we would expect ei, shows a tendency towards context generalisation. In Longtown (Cu 1) ai occurs fairly regularly before voiced segments, whereas voiceless ones favour ei. Indications of this development can be traced throughout the southern area, however.

4. What appears at first sight to be too much ei is partly the regular result of a Southern Scots development, viz. the diphthongisation of /i:/ in word-final position. This phenomenon is restricted to Longtown (Cu 1) and Rural Northumberland and does not reach as far down as Tyneside. Too much ei there would have to be explained differently.

5. If we accept Zai's analysis of the Southern Scots dialect of Morebattle as a conservative basis for our findings, Aitken's context must have acquired the variable (ai) fairly recently. Too much ei in the north of our area could mean that the context has not been completely implemented yet, too much ai on Tyneside, at Longtown (Cu 1) and in Durham might show a tendency to expand Aitken's context to embrace all voiced segments.

6. These results were arrived at with the help of the complete material SED has to offer on this phenomenon (1,546 forms). Tables 6 and 7 reveal, however, that the data base is still too restricted as soon as we start looking for specific contexts. All in all it is surprising to what extent phonological processes can be documented on the basis of this material once it has become more readily accessible. In order to learn more about the details of an ongoing change, however, we will have to start from here, form new hypotheses and gather new and comparable data.

References

Aitken, A.J. (1981) The Scottish vowel-length rule. In M. Benskin and M.L. Samuels (eds) So meny people longages and tonges. Philological Essays in Scots and Mediaeval English Presented to Angus McIntosh. Edinburgh. 131-57.

Heslop, O. (1892) Northumberland Words. A Glossary of Words Used in the County of Northumberland and on the Tyneside. London: Englist Dialect Society.

Kolb, E. et alii (1979) Atlas of English Sounds. Berne: Francke.

Mather, J.Y and Speitel, H.H. (1986) The Linguistic Atlas of Scotland, Scots Section, Volume 3, Phonology. London: Croom Helm

MacWhinney, B. and Marengo K. (1986) MULTIBET 1.0: A proposal for an ASCII translation and a set of names for extended IPA notation. Transcript Analysis 3, 83-99.

Orton, H. et alii (1962-71) The Survey of English Dialects. (B) The Basic Material. Four volumes. Leeds: Arnold & Son.

Zai, R. (1942) The Phonology of the Morebattle Dialect (East Roxburghshire). Lucerne: Räber & Co.

The Verisimilitude of the Gullah Dialect in Francis Griswold's *A Sea Island Lady*

MAILANDE CHENEY SLEDGE
Marion Military Institute Marion, U.S.A.

INTRODUCTION

To add realism to works of literature, writers through the ages have attempted to represent folk speech by using literary dialect. Perhaps the best-known American black literary dialect, according to George Philip Krapp (1925:248), is the Middle Georgia black dialect of Joel Chandler Harris's Uncle Remus stories. Krapp (1925:254) contends, however, that "the barbarous Gullah was the customary form of negro dialect for use in literature until after the middle of the nineteenth century." Gullah or Geechee, an English-based creole with Scottish, African, and other influences, is the dialect of the slaves and their descendants near the coast and on the islands of South Carolina and Georgia.[1]

Because works containing Gullah representations by Ambrose Gonzales, DuBose Heyward, Julia Peterkin, and other regional writers of the 1920s and 1930s were well received, Francis Griswold expected his regional readers to be familiar with his representation in A Sea Island Lady (1939).[2] Writing for a national audience, however, he had to represent the dialect in such a way that his readers would not be impeded by it and, hopefully, would even appreciate the realistic contribution it made to his work. Griswold was thus as careful in his handling of the dialect as he was in his development of plot and character, recording of historical events, and description of natural settings.

METHODS

All the available scholarship on American dialects, Negro dialects, Black English, the Gullah dialect, and literary dialects as well as all the available literary works containing Gullah-influenced dialect was reviewed. Then in June 1978 I visited the South Carolina-Low Country area of Beaufort, Colleton, and Charleston Counties and made tape recordings of interviews with both Type III and Type I informants--Type III informants being educated and culturally oriented and Type I informants being not educated or with very little education.[3] These tapes included two Type III informants from Beaufort and five Type I informants from Walterboro, St. Helena Island, Lady's Island, and Bluff Plantation on the Combahee River, South Carolina. All of these tapes were helpful, but the only one cited in the study was the one of an interview with a seventy-eight-year-old man on Bluff Plantation.

A year later, in August 1979, I examined the South Carolina field records of the Linguistic Atlas of the Middle and South Atlantic States (LAMSAS) and of Lorenzo Dow Turner made for his study Africanisms in the Gullah Dialect (1949), at that time at the University of South Carolina, and obtained photocopies of the records most nearly corresponding to the speech of the authors and the dialect of the Gullah characters in the works I was considering for my study. The records obtained were of one Type III, three Type II, and five Type I informants from South Carolina. After studying these records, I restricted my subject to Griswold's ASIL. Because Griswold was born and reared in Albany, New York, in May 1984 I obtained an additional LAMSAS field record of a Type III informant from Albany. This record was chosen as most nearly representative of Griswold's "standard" speech type, and the Type III field record from Beaufort as most nearly representative of the "standard" speech of the area represented in the novel, the speech Griswold heard during the ten years he spent in the area while writing the novel.

The comparison of these two field records and their synopses in Kurath and McDavid's Pronunciation of English in the Atlantic States (1961) showed very little phonemic difference, the variations being allophonic rather than phonemic. With these slight differences being considered, I compiled a phonemic inventory of the vowels and consonants of Griswold's speech type with which to compare the phonemes his respellings suggested.

The geographical area of ASIL is limited mostly to Beaufort and St. Helena Island, or Beaufort County, in the heart of the Low Country-Gullah area of South Carolina. The choice of Griswold's work was made, in part, because of the availability of the LAMSAS and Turner field records from this area by which to verify the phonological aspects of the dialect. In addition, the time of the recording of the interviews (1933, 1934, 1946-48) was near enough to that of the writing of the dialect representation (1928-38) to make a comparison and verification even more valid than it would have been for a work written, for instance, in the 1800s.[4] Another reason for choosing Griswold's work was that, of the novel's 964 pages, he includes Gullah-influenced dialect on approximately one hundred pages, thus giving sufficient material for a substantial analysis.

The next step was to organize a framework for the analysis and then to copy each unconventionally spelled word and each unusual, variant, or characteristically regional lexical item and to list representative or significant grammatical features used by Griswold to represent the Gullah dialect. Selected phonological and grammatical features have been chosen to illustrate Griswold's handling of the Gullah dialect.

PHONOLOGY

For the phonology Griswold's respellings were arranged into four sections: (1) substitution of phonemes, (2) omission of phonemes, (3) addition of phonemes, and (4) transposition of phonemes. In the substitution of phonemes, the respellings were grouped according to phoneme under stressed vowels, unstressed vowels, and consonants. They were then divided according to the phoneme represented by the respelling and the phoneme it replaced. Sometimes, especially in the analysis of the consonants, the respellngs were further grouped according to position, such as initial, medial, or final.

With the discussion of each vowel phoneme was included statistical information from the study Phoneme-Grapheme Correspondences as Cues to Spelling Improvement (1966) by Paul R. Hanna et al., a study relating to the phoneme-grapheme correspondence for that particular phoneme or complex phoneme and the frequency of its occurrence to represent that phoneme in American English. After determining the pronunciations suggested by Griswold's respellings, I searched for pronunciations of each different respelled word in the Type III LAMSAS field records from Albany and Beaufort and in the five Type I LAMSAS and Turner field records representing the dialect of the Gullah characters. When available, I included the phonological information from the field records; from Turner's AGD and two articles in the Publication of the American Dialect Society (1945, 1948); from other Linguistic Atlas-based studies, such as ones by Sumner Ives (1954) and Ann Sullivan Haskell (1964) and PEAS; and from various dictionaries, word lists, and glossaries. On many occasions items were found on the personal tape already mentioned.

Substitution of Phonemes

Stressed Vowels. Griswold respelled to represent every vowel phoneme usually used in "standard" American English except two not usually found or seldom heard in Gullah and the complex phoneme /aw/ as in out or down.[5] For the vowels not found in Gullah, Griswold respelled to suggest the ones the Gullahs use. Furthermore, the analysis in the study shows that most of Griswold's approximately two-hundred-forty respellings to show vowel substitutions are supported by the Atlas or Turner field records, Turner's AGD, Atlas-based studies, or Webster's Third New International Dictionary.

/i/ as in bit

Examples of his respellings to show the substitution of the phoneme /i/ as in bit are /i/ for /e/ and /ə/ in yistiddy (yesterday) 176, /i/ for /e/ in Dimmycrack (Democratic) 238, and /i/ for /u/ in pit (put) 121.

/e/ as in bet

Respellings to represent the phoneme /e/ as in bet occur in such substitutions as /e/ for /i/ in ef (if) 141; /e/ for /ə/ in Jestish (Justice) 131; /e/ for /ey/ in tek (take) 5 and mek (make) 497; and /e/ for /iə/ or /ɜ/ in yeddy (Gullah hear or heard) 131, 140. The personal tape has over twenty words giving the substitution of /e/ for /ey/, including gravy, Mr. Jacocks, plantation, and Savior.

/æ/ as in bat (Turner's a [a])

Instead of /æ/, the low front lax vowel of glass or bat, one very common in American English but not so in British English and not present in Gullah, the Gullahs use a vowel that I am calling Turner's a [a]. In Turner's discussion of this vowel in AGD (1949:16) he states:

> [a]--Gullah and most African languages have only one a-vowel. In Gullah, [a] is the low front vowel closely resembling the French vowel in la. . . . It is the sound used regularly in positions where in General American [æ] and [ɑ] are usually heard.

Some of the respellings Griswold uses to represent the Gullah low front vowel are Turner's a [a] for /i/ in wag'rous (vigorous) 788, for /e/ in planty (plenty) 788, for /ɜ/ in Hakmuh (Herkimer) 75 and Hacklus (Hercules) 140, and for /a/ in crap (crop) 728 and drap (drop) 514.

Turner's a [a] also occurs in a large group of words respelled with the doubled grapheme <aa>, which seems to show the lengthening of the vowel [a:] with no /ə/ glide or r-coloring. Some of these words are maa'sh (marsh) 202, paa'don (pardon) 509, gyaa'den (garden) 599, cyaa'tin' (carting) 577, Chaa'son (Charleston) 10, and Gaa'baldi (Garibaldi) 223, in which Griswold uses the apostrophe to show the omission of only the phoneme /r/ or /r/ before the consonant /l/ or in the unstressed syllable /rɨ/ or /rə/. Other examples with the doubled grapheme <aa> suggesting the lengthened vowel [a:] without the phoneme /r/ are paa (pa, father) 506 and gran'paa 160.

/a/ as in pot (Gullah [ɒ])

The other vowel showing variance is the American-English low central to low back vowel /a/ of calm or crop that in Gullah is more like the British checked vowel [ɒ]. About this vowel, Turner (1949:18) states:

> [ɒ]--A low back vowel having the sound of [ɒ] in the British word not. . . . In Gullah, [ɒ] is heard

regularly in such words as law, all, brought, etc., as well as in body, pot, dollar, etc. Among many Gullahs [ɒ] is heard also in such words as bundle, ugly, young, etc. . . .

Some of the respellings Griswold uses to represent the Gullah low back vowel are [ɒ] for /i/ in onsult (insult) 498, [ɒ] for /æ/ in glod (glad) 131 and woccination (vaccination) 181, [ɒ] for /ə/ in ogly (ugly) 165 and hosban' (husband) 203, and [ɒ] for /ow/ in 'oman (woman) 165. In various contexts and in the phrase ogly 'oman, the Gullah [ɒ] in 'oman would give a harmony of sound with the [ɒ] in the other words.

/iy/ as in beet

The complex phoneme /iy/ as in beet occurs in such respellings as /iy/ for /e/ in deestruction (destruction) 182, showing a shift in stress, and /iy/ for /ey/ in green (grain) 509 in the phrase "'one good green of sanse.'"

/aw/ as in out

Griswold has the complex phoneme /aw/ in such dialectal spellings as 'bout (about) 469 and groun' (ground) 151; in merged words such as howcome 176 and nohow 131; and in hyphenated words such as all-about 497. Most of these words suggest dialect and also quickened tempo without impeding the reader as too many respellings might do.

Vowels Under Weak Stress. In the respelling of weak or unstressed vowels, Griswold generally uses one of three orthographic symbols--⟨i⟩, ⟨y⟩, or ⟨u⟩, but he also uses ⟨ie⟩ in tittie (sister) 5, ⟨e⟩ in uppety (uppity) 498, and ⟨a⟩ in Maussa (master) 11. Except for the one use of the grapheme ⟨e⟩ for the phoneme /e/ or perhaps /ə/ in uppety, Griswold respells to represent only the phonemes /i/ and /ə/ in unstressed vowels.

Consonants. The substitution of one consonant for another in literary dialect is easier to represent and to interpret than is the substitution of one vowel for another. Like Harris in his Uncle Remus stories (Ives 1954:38) Griswold substitutes initial /d/ for /ð/ in dese (these) 61 and dat (that) 60 and /n/ for /ŋ/ in lookin' 10 and tellin' 172. Unlike Harris (Ives 154:38), who substitutes final /f/ for /θ/ in Uncle Remus's pronunciations of bofe (both) and mouf (mouth), Griswold substitutes /t/ for /θ/ to represent his Gullah characters' pronunciations of bat' (bath) 469 and mout' (mouth) 498.

/b/ as in bat (Gullah [β])

Griswold respells with the grapheme ⟨b⟩ for the grapheme ⟨v⟩ in such words as berry (very) 203 and bittle (victuals) 164, Debble (devil) 176 and Sabeyuh (Savior) 509, and b'liebe (believe) 238 and t'ribe (thrive) 728. Instead of the voiced bilabial stop /b/, as in bat, however, in many instances he may be attempting to represent the voiced bilabial fricative [β], about which Turner states in AGD (1949:24, 241):

> [β] occurs in Gullah in positions where [v] and [w] would be used in G[eneral] A[merican] [25].
> The Gullah speaker seldom uses the labio-dental ... voiced fricative ... [v] and the voiced labio-velar semivowel [w], but substitutes ... for [v] and [w] the voiced bilabial fricative [β] or the voiced frictionless continuant [ʍ] ... [241].

Griswold substitutes the grapheme ⟨b⟩ for the grapheme ⟨w⟩ in bellden (well then) 153. The substitution of ⟨v⟩ for ⟨w⟩ occurs in such words as vaitin' (waiting) 6 and veek (week) 507 and ⟨w⟩ for ⟨v⟩ in such words as wag'rous (vigorous) 788, 'wantage (advantage) 577, and Sawannah (Savannah) 150. Griswold probably heard the voiced bilabial fricative [β] in most of these words, but he had to choose the grapheme ⟨b⟩, ⟨v⟩, or ⟨w⟩ to approximate and suggest that sound and, at the same time, keep his respellings in easily recognizable forms.

Other interesting substitutions are /t/ for /k/ in the last syllable of tiffity (certificate) 150, /d/ for /z/ in Jedus (Jesus) 788, /k/ for /f/ in phoskit (phosphate) 276, and /č/ for /k/ in pratchly (practically) 203. Turner (1949:270) has in Jesus in initial position the palatal plosive [ɟ]. In his discussion of [dʒ] Turner (1949:27) states, "Among the older Gullah speakers [dʒ] is seldom heard; they substitute for it the palatal plosive [ɟ]." Perhaps this initial sound [ɟ] influenced the consonant /z/ in the second syllable to produce a sound that many authors of Gullah literature represent by using the grapheme ⟨d⟩ in the second syllable of Jedus.

Omission of Phonemes

The material in this section was arranged according to phoneme or phonemes omitted and position in the word, such as omission of consonants in prevocalic or postvocalic clusters, omission of a single intervocalic consonant or a single vowel between consonants, or omission of a vowel with a preceding consonant or a vowel with a following consonant.

Sometimes Griswold simply respelled a word, such as in fum (from) 15, chillun (children) 131, shame (ashamed) 77, and Fairy (Pharaoh) 75.[6] At other times, he used the apostrophe to show omission of initial, medial, and/or final phonemes or syllables, such as initially in 'blige (obliged) 182 and medially and finally in Reb'ren' (Garibaldi) 223, and finally in Yan' Yaddy (Auntie Adelaide) 506. More complex omissions are represented in such respellings as shum (see him, her, them, it) 131, mo'n (more than)

121, f'um (for him) 788, le'm (let them) 122, tiffity (certificate) 150, and Chaa'son (Charleston) 10.

Addition of Phonemes

The material in this section was arranged in the subsections addition of phonemes in initial, medial, and final positions and addition of syllables. Examples of addition of phonemes in initial position are of the phoneme /d/ in druthuh (rather) 213; of the phoneme /s/ in skinfolks (kinfolks) 498, squalsome (quarrelsome) 499, and striflin' (trifling) 507; and of the phoneme /y/ in Yan' Yaddy (Auntie Adelaide) 506, yeddy (hear, heard) 131, 509, and yown yeye (own eye) 505. The addition of homorganic medial /b/ occurs in fambly (family) 160, of medial /s/ in meansly (meanly) 498, of medial /r/ in freemale (female) 577, and of medial /y/ in such words as cyan' (can't) 505, fi-yuh (fire) 21, gyaa'den (garden) 599, and hyuh (here) 60. The addition of phonemes in final position appears in the addition of final /s/ in such hyperinflected words as the conjunction whiles (while) 522, the adjective smalls (small), and the noun mens (men) 509 and in the addition of final unstressed /i/ in enty (ain't) 59, tiffity (certificate) 150, and yeddy (hear, heard) 131, 123.

Addition of syllables occurs in the addition of initial /ɨn/ or /en/ in endurin' (during) 853), initial /rɨ/ in replace (place) 131, and final /səm/ in proudsome (proud) 499.

Transposition of Phonemes

The transposition of phonemes is shown by the respellings of ax, ax'um, aksin' (asked, ask him, asking) 509, 150, 945, and less'n (unless) 507.

GRAMMATICAL FEATURES

The grammatical features were arranged under the sections verb forms, noun forms, pronoun forms, adjective forms, qualifiers, prepositions, conjunctions, interjections, subject-verb agreement, infinitives, negatives, double negatives, double comparisons, and omission of words. With examples of the features were included, when available, references to the LAMSAS and Turner field records, Turner's AGD, Atwood's A Survey of Verb Forms in the Eastern United States (1953), Wentworth's American Dialect Dictionary (1944), and other Atlas-based studies. Most of these features and forms are discussed in Turner's AGD in the chapters on "Syntactical Features," "Morphological Features," or "Some Word-Formations."

Verb Forms

Sixty-six verb forms, all uninflected, were listed in alphabetical order in the infinitive form followed by the form or forms used by Griswold with a citation from the novel including the form and information from the sources given above, as available. Following the list of verb forms is a subsection on personal forms in the indicative mood. These were subdivided into first, second, and third person with citations from the novel showing representative examples of dialectal variations in the present, past, and future tenses. Each list or discussion was followed by citations with similar construction, as available, from the Type I field records and Turner's AGD. This same procedure applies to all the other sections.

Noun Forms

Griswold's dialectal noun forms include ones with lack of inflection to show plurals or possessives, ones with hyperinflections, and ones with hyphenation to show gender or distinction. Representative examples are t'ree day 176, Isaac paa 506, mens 599, gal-chile 176, and gues'-folk 852.

Pronoun Forms

The pronoun section has representative examples of the dialectal forms used by Griswold in the nominative, possessive, objective, demonstrative, relative, and reflexive or intensive pronoun positions and examples of substitution of one gender for another. Some examples are, for the nominative, "'dem cyan' git credick'" 507; possessive, "'don' hu't he feelin''" 176; objective, "'Dey gwine pure eat we out'" 577; demonstrative, "'dem stockin''" 176; relative, "'a gemman what been bo'n'" 182; and reflexive, "'He ain' gib heself no res''" 469 (MCS emphasis).

Adjective Forms

In his chapter "Some Word-Formations," Turner (1949:232) states that one way that the Gullahs form words is by using groups of words for various parts of speech. Griswold uses hyphenated or merged words as nouns, sweet-talk 453; verbals, fuh straight-talk 452; adjectives, big-mout' 498 and dry-drought groun' 728; adverbs, might-be 452; and prepositions, 'pontop 131. Perhaps his best representation, however, is his adjectivals, which were grouped into hyphenated forms, dialectal forms, and "eb'ry" forms. Representative examples are in the phrases "'flat-foot blue-gum pusson'" 203, "'too ras'less and wag'rous'" 788, and "'eb'ry Gawdbless las' one of you'" 453.

Prepositions

The dialectal forms of prepositions include 'pontop 131, same like 78, 'scusin' (except) 131, and to (in, at) 176, 60-61.

Conjunctions

The dialectal forms of subordinating conjunctions include howcome (why) 76, less'n (unless) 507, and whiles 522.

Interjections

The only interjection that seems to be peculiar to Gullah is the word Ki 5, a form of greeting. Another similar form is the exclamation do 728, which is an entreating expression similar to the word please.

Infinitives

The infinitive form used most frequently by Griswold, some forty times in the novel, consists of the dialectal fuh (for) plus the infinitive form of the verb, such as in "'All I been need, Miss Em'ly, is somebody fuh straight-talk me like dat fuh gib me backbone fuh cuss dem nigguh out good'" 452 (MCS emphasis).

Double Comparisons

Griswold has one interesting use of the double superlative adjectival with a single comparative adverbial in the same speech--"'Mostes' place whuh I been at I done mek good money, but trouble is he go out mo' fas' dan he come in'" 497. He also has several uses of the double comparison with both adjectives and adverbs--"'I mus' get me some mo' bettuh moss'" 174 and "'Mens is a pain, an' de mo' bigguh dey come, de mo' haa'duh dey is fuh han'le'" 509 (MCS emphasis).

One passage from the novel should illustrate many of the features discussed above (728-29).

> Biggie shook his head over the situation. "Miss Em'ly, de 'omans is mos' fuh blame, 'cause he pit de mans up to goin', coaxin' an' sweet-talkin' an' plaguin' um till he got no good sense lef' an' don' know he own mine. An' seem-like de 'omans do pure t'ribe 'pon dat high city life, but de mans ain' wut in de city,--he do widduh-up same like cotton in haa'd dry-drought groun'. But mans an' 'omans, dey all-two come home fuh bury, I know dat! . . . My missie, I comin' frank wid you now. Vhen I been young I hod good privilege fuh run off an' all about, but time gone an' I ain' studyin' 'bout dat

no mo', ma'm. I could be in Sawannah right now, an' I could be to de Nort', an' I could be daid,--do Gawd. Naw'm, I ain't studyin' 'bout leabin' de oilan' like dem po' peoples dat ain' nebbuh been no place an' seen nutt'n. I gots too much wuk fuh do, makin' de noo crap, fuh study 'bout fool. An' de mo' dem crazy nigguh gone, de mo' my own two han' gots fuh t'ink 'bout, ma'm."

SUMMARY AND CONCLUSION

Because Griswold lived his early life in or near Albany, New York, and spent ten years in the Low Country of South Carolina, one can surmise that he wrote the dialect as it was filtered through his own idiolect and also through the "standard" speech he heard in the Beaufort, Charleston, and Low Country area while he was writing the novel. It is significant that Griswold was writing his representation either before or approximately at the same time that Turner and Lowman were doing their field work in the Low Country area and certainly before McDavid did his field work there. Griswold's representation, therefore, did not come from the linguistic materials, but, as he himself stated in a letter in reply to my inquiry, "My version of Gullah, such as it is, was derived from the island people themselves."[7] As one cannot recapture the phonology and other features of Griswold's speech at that time, one must rely on the transcriptions made of actual speech in Albany and in Beaufort in reconstructing the phonemics of Griswold's speech type by which to compare the speech of the Gullah characters.

As one may expect, many of the features found in Gullah are also found in other dialects, and, therefore, such respellings as git (get) 5, cheer (chair) 449, and Jedgmen' (Judgment) 371 may not seem significant or distinctive. At the same time, Griswold's handling of respellings to represent the Gullah low front vowel a [a] and the Gullah low back vowel [ɒ] and other vowels and consonants, including the Gullah voiced bilabial fricative [β] and the Gullah palatal plosive [ɟ], show his skill in representing dialect. Likewise, his inclusion of such features as omission of phonemes in final consonant clusters and of unstressed vowels, syllables, and words; lack of inflection in verb forms and in plural and possessive forms of nouns; substitution of one gender for another; and hyphenation and blending to form words add to the verisimilitude of his work.

The most important conclusion about the authenticity of Griswold's representation of the Gullah dialect is that although he did not have Turner's AGD to aid him in his task, he included in his work practically all of the features discussed by Turner in his book.

Finally, the inclusion of the representation of the Gullah dialect through the Gullah characters adds realism to the novel.

Like the oyster shells in the tabby construction in the Low Country, the Gullah dialect and the Gullah characters speaking it seem to be the cement that holds the novel together. Through a careful and accurate representation of the Gullah dialect, Griswold creates an atmosphere of verisimilitude such that the reader feels that he is hearing these characters speak, as Kurath (1949:44) states, "a unique type of English, . . . this Negro dialect, called Gullah. . . ." Thus, Francis Griswold's skillful handling of the Gullah dialect in A Sea Island Lady enriches the experience for the reader of the novel and enhances its linguistic and literary value.

Notes

[1] For other explanations, see Turner (1949:[xiii], 1); McDavid and McDavid (1951:6). See also Montgomery and Bailey (1986:24), who refer to the problem of "determining whether Gullah is a locally creolized variety, a product of the isolation and other demographic factors peculiar to that area, or whether it represents an extreme form of creolized English different only in degree from varieties of black speech farther inland." After the first reference, Turner's work is referred to as AGD.

[2] Page numbers in the body of this paper refer to the reprinted edition (1971. Beaufort, SC: Beaufort Book), hereafter referred to as ASIL.

[3] The initial contacts for these interviews were made by Dr. George E. H. Moore, veterinarian from Walterboro, SC, who is very familiar with the Low Country area and its people.

[4] Of the field records from South Carolina, three were recorded by Turner in 1933, one by Guy S. Lowman in 1934, and five by McDavid in 1946-48; the one from Albany was recorded by Lowman in 1940.

[5] With some modifications, the phonemic alphabet used here is the one developed by George L. Trager and Henry Lee Smith, Jr. (1951).

[6] Words italicized in the original are underlined twice in this paper.

[7] Griswold, letter to the author, 27 Oct. 1983.

References

Atwood, E. Bagby. 1953. A Survey of Verb Forms in the Eastern United States. Studies in American English 2. Ann Arbor: University of Michigan Press.
Griswold, Francis. 1939. A Sea Island Lady. New York: William Morrow.
Griswold, Francis. 1983. Letter to the author.
Hanna, Paul R., Jean S. Hanna, Richard E. Hodges, and Edwin H. Rudorf, Jr. 1966. Phoneme-Grapheme Correspondences as Cues to Spelling Improvement. OE-32008. Washington, DC: US Dept. of HEW.
Haskell, Ann Sullivan. 1964. "The Representation of Gullah-Influenced Dialect in Twentieth Century South Carolina Prose: 1922-30." Diss. University of Pennsylvania.
Ives, Sumner. 1954. The Phonology of the Uncle Remus Stories. Publication of the American Dialect Society 22:3-59.
Krapp, George Philip. 1925. The English Language in America. 2 vols. New York: Century, for MLA. Vol. I.
Kurath, Hans. 1949. Word Geography of the Eastern United States. Ann Arbor: University of Michigan Press.
Kurath, Hans. 1961. The Pronunciation of English in the Atlantic States. Ann Arbor: University of Michigan Press.
McDavid, Raven I., Jr., and Virginia G. McDavid. 1951. "The Relationship of the Speech of American Negroes to the Speech of Whites." American Speech 26:3-27.
McDavid, Raven I., Jr., Raymond K. O'Cain, and George T. Dorrill, eds. 1980- . Linguistic Atlas of the Middle and South Atlantic States. Chicago: University of Chicago Press.
Montgomery, Michael B., and Guy Bailey, eds. 1986. Language Variety in the South. University: University of Alabama Press.
Trager, George L., and Henry Lee Smith, Jr. 1951. Outline of English Structure. Norman, OK: Battenburg.
Turner, Lorenzo Dow. 1945. "Notes on the Sounds and Vocabulary of Gullah." Publication of the American Dialect Society 3:13-28.
Turner, Lorenzo Dow. 1948. "Problems Confronting the Investigator of Gullah." Publication of the American Dialect Society 9:74-84.
Turner, Lorenzo Dow. 1949. Africanisms in the Gullah Dialect. Chicago: University of Chicago Press.
Webster's Third New International Dictionary of the English Language Unabridged. 1961.
Wentworth, Harold. 1944. American Dialect Dictionary New York: Thomas Y. Crowell.

The Historical Present as Evidence of Black/White Convergence/Divergence

RONALD R. BUTTERS
Duke University

According to William Labov (1987, p. 5) "there is [at present] continued divergence of black and white vernaculars" in the United States--that is, the "speech pattern" of blacks "is developing in its own direction and becoming more different from the speech of whites in the same communities" (1985, p. 1). Labov cites a variety of differences between black and white English which support (or seem to support) the divergence hypothesis. In Philadelphia white vernacular, for example, [aw] is increasingly being fronted by younger speakers to [eɔ] in such words as out, house, about, and south. Blacks, however, are not participating in this change; they continue to use [ɑw] (Graff, Labov, and Harris 1986, pp. 45-47). Labov contends that racial segregation in large urban areas is a major factor in isolating black speakers from linguistic changes in the white community; the situation seems to be somewhat different in less-segregated communities. Thomas (1986, p. 4), for example, found that "of thirty-three responding informants" (both black and white) in his study of lower-middle and working-class high school students in Columbus, Ohio, "all but one, a white male with northern Ohio parents, had onsets of /aw/ more fronted than the onsets of /ay/." Apparently, blacks and whites are well enough integrated in East High School that blacks are participating in the ongoing linguistic changes of the majority community.[1]

While Guy Bailey (1987) has enthusiastically embraced Labov's position (indeed, Bailey and Maynor, 1985, arrived independently at a similar conclusion, based on their research in Texas), other scholars have been more sceptical.[2] Walt Wolfram, Fay Vaughn-Cooke, John R. Rickford, and Arthur K. Spears, in papers presented at the 1985 NWAV meeting at Georgetown University (published in the Spring 1987 issue of American Speech), and John Baugh (at the American Dialect Society meeting in New York in 1986), all call into question (with varying degrees of criticism) the divergence hypothesis. The paper I am now presenting is intended as a part of the continuing debate about black-white linguistic divergence. I want to look here at only one piece of evidence: Labov's claim that black vernacular English speakers, within the past generation or so, have reinterpreted the verbal -s morpheme of standard English, using it as a past-tense marker in narratives. This linguistic change, says Labov, is "the strongest piece of evidence that speakers of the Black English Vernacular in Philadelphia are developing their . . . [own] grammar" (1985, p. 3).

For those who are not familiar with Labov's arguments about

verbal -s, let me summarize them briefly. The following narrative, spoken by a young black male in Philadelphia, was recorded by Myhill and Harris (1986, p. 28):

> I was, you know, tryin' to be Jeff Slick, in a sense, you know what I mean, but I say, I figure if I can talk somebody out of some money, you know, everything is A-okay. So I started rappin' to this guy, and, um, the next thing I know, this dude, um, punched me in my face, an' I SWINGS aroun', he knock--he had hit me so hard, I SWINGS aroun', my hat FALLS off on his car, an' like when I did about face, I turnt roun', an' I hit him, boom, an' when I hit 'im, he fell down, an' I wen' on the car to pick my hat up, right? An' when I like was steppin' off, this guy RUNS behin' me, this white guy RUNS behin' me an' BEND down, SAY "Hold it!", an' you know, I just seen 'im bendin' down, I didn't even really see, I just seen somethin' in his han', I couldn't visualize it, you know, 'cause it was like on that little street, Ramstead Street. He had three other cops with 'im. They, like, just set me up, you know, then this other dude jumped out in the front, he SAY "Hold it!", an' um, I'm just standin' there, you know, like "What the hell's goin' on?", you know, then this other cop just RUNS up to me, man, GRAB both my hands an' RAM my head into the wall.

Labov notes that the use of the agreement morpheme here is not standard: it is not restricted to third person singular (e.g., line 4 I swings--though there are few instances of plural use, according to Myhill and Harris) and the meaning is clearly 'past-time indicator'. Labov argues that this must be a new use among Philadelphia blacks because he does not find such a use in narratives that he and his colleagues recorded in New York in the 1960s or in other, earlier VBE narratives. He argues that it cannot be a borrowing from other dialects of English because (a) the "rules" of use are slightly different and (b) because blacks in the urban ghetto are too isolated from whites and middle-class blacks to have learned a linguistic form from them.

I believe that each of these claims is open to serious challenge. Let us take, first of all, the claim that ghetto blacks are too isolated to have borrowed the narrative past -s morpheme from other vernacular dialects. As Wolfram (1987) points out, an almost identical phenomenon is prominent in the vernacular narratives of middle-class speakers, for example the following, from Shiffrin (1981, p. 46; note that, interestingly, this excerpt also does not use the -s morpheme with plurals):

> Then all of a sudden everybody GETS involved,

and they made a mess. So, uh . . . this lady SAYS
. . . this uh Bert, "Oh, my son'll make them. He's
an electrician." So he MAKES them, and he CHARGES
all the neighbors twenty dollars a set, and there I
paid three dollars. So I called her a crook. And
I called her son a crook. So they were really mad
at me.

The usage is so familiar a part of vernacular American English that I have yet to meet a native speaker who finds the example unusual. To argue that ghetto speakers are so isolated from mainstream vernacular English that such a construction "couldn't" be borrowed strikes me as unconvincing. There is something circular about arguing, as Labov does (1985, p. 3), that the linguistic evidence stands as an "independent and objective measure of . . . the dangerous drift of our society towards a permanent division between black and white," and then arguing that the "division" or isolation is an explanation of some aspect of the data.

Even if mainstream vernacular narrative past-time -s could be ruled out entirely as a source of ghetto narrative -s, the superculture vernacular could be looked to as a logical source of narrative VBE -s. Note the following:

   Smith takes the pass on the outside. He
   dribbles to mid-court, passes to James. James
   pauses, turns, drives--up to the basket, no good,
   Brown takes the rebound. . . .

The language of sportscasting, like that of the narratives which generally make use of narrative -s, is action narrative. Although Labov is certainly correct that there are speakers of VBE who, even in late adolescence (and perhaps adulthood) have no standard agreement morpheme, it makes sense that such speakers will nonetheless attempt to make SOME sort of sense of a form which they occasionally hear, whether their interpretation be that it is as fancy talk, emphatic, durative/iterative (all have been suggested)--or, on the model of the language of sportscasting, as a marker of action narrative. Ironically, of all the uses to which a reconstituted -s may have been put in BVE, the action narrative seems MOST likely to show evidence of influence from the superculture--if not from mainstream vernacular English (and Labov has not demonstrated that mainstream vernaculars must be ruled out, he has merely DECLARED that to be the case), then perhaps from the very familiar language of sportscasting.

It is worth pointing out in passing that Myhill and Harris's informant shares a number of other linguistic features with superculture English--some of them vernacular, some specialized. He uses the vernacular you know as a filler eight times and like three times. He also uses I was like in the mainstream vernacular sense of 'I was thinking'. He generalizes from -s to another present tense form, am. He uses this in the mainstream vernacular sense of 'a certain person or thing' (So I started rapping to this guy. . . .; The next thing I know, this dude. . . .), usually to introduce new ideas or entities not previously mentioned. He uses the peculiarly literary verb visualize, and he uses the military term about face. Of course, these features may well be regular parts of BVE. Some of them may even have originated there and spread to white speakers. But in any case they suggest that the speaker--and BVE speakers in particular--are not so isolated from the mainstream as Labov maintains.

Labov argues against borrowing in a second, rather novel, way: because the rule in BVE is slightly different from the rule in mainstream narrative, he reasons, it cannot have been borrowed at all. Note again the first item quoted above: This white guy runs behin' me and bend down, say. . . . See also runs, grab, and ram at the end of the passage. In a high number of cases in the narratives that Myhill and Harris reported, when two (or more) verbs are conjoined and the first gets an -s, the second does not. This is Labov's basis for maintaining that the differences are qualitative--hence, in his view, more significant--and not "merely" quantitative.

I think that Labov is making too much of this. In the first place, the strength of the supposed rule is by no means clear. In Myhill and Harris's sample given above, in fact, it is certainly not invariant. Thus in line 8 we get falls, not fall, and did, not does; in line 12, say gets no marker, yet, strictly speaking, it is not overtly conjoined with bend; in the sixth line from the end, say is the first conjoined verb, not the second. There may well be a strong TENDENCY here to eliminate the -s under conditions of conjoining, but it is clearly a quantitative tendency, NOT a categorical rule. Indeed, it is questionable that the mere elimination of redundant material should be called a "rule" at all, given the universal tendency in human language to eliminate repeated elements, for example, He went home and he went to bed becomes He went home and went to bed; I may get up tomorrow and I may go to Toledo becomes I may get up tomorrow and go to Toledo. The fact that speakers appear to be following a very natural tendency in human language is certainly no argument against borrowing.[3]

But even if we agree to call the -s + CONJ + ZERO tendency a linguistic "rule," this is scarcely an argument for divergence: "Which," Wolfram says (1987, p. 48) "is more different, a system which uses historical present with some -s marking realignment or one which shows no evidence of the historical present usage?" It seems odd indeed to say that two dialects are "diverging" with respect to a given feature if in fact they are becoming more alike.

It is also worth considering whether or not the use of narrative -s in current VBE in Philadelphia is truly an innovation. One cannot doubt that Labov has not found narrative -s in his earlier narratives in New York; he says he hasn't. However, the fact that he didn't find them doesn't mean that they were not THERE: ironically, one of the strong claims that he makes for the importance of the Myhill and Harris study is the supposed superiority of their data-collecting methods. But if their data is truly better than Labov's earlier data, might not that mean merely that narratives have been there all along, but only just now are being discovered? Arthur Spears noted (1987, 51-52) that one should begin the quest for the possible history of narrative -s by looking at English-based creoles. If we do so, I have discovered, the results are very interesting indeed. Note the following (from Holm, 1983, 112):

>It waz a ragid fishaman. I yuwsa layk fishing an evar dey hi gowz awt fishin an i kech fish an bring it an sel. Sow wan dey hi went awt fishin an hi didn' kech eniting. . .til hi kech a gowldn fish. An di fish sez tu him, i sez, "Trow mi bak intu di siy," i sey, "an ail giv yu a riwahrd." Sow wen i went howm hiz wayf sez tu him, i sey, "Wat yu kech?" I sez, "Owl leydi, ayz ownli kech a gowldn fish." "Sow way yu don wid it?" "Di fish towl mi tu trow im bak intu di siy an hi wil giv me a riwahrd." "An wat yuw aks for a riwahrd?" I sez, "Noting." Di owl leydi sez tu im, i sez, "Yuw now dat awr kotbowrd ar empti. Wi down hav a skromz av chiyz nar a piys av bred tu iyt. Gow bak an tel di fish dat wi down wahn awr kotbowrd ar empti." Di fishaman wen tu di siy. I sez, "Hed in di eyr an teyl in di siy: fish, fish, listen tu miy." Di fish kom op; i sez, "Wat du yu wahn?" I sez, "May wayf sez tu tel yu dat awr kotbowrd ar empti. Wi down hav a . . . skromz av chiyz nar a piys av bred." Di fish sez tu him, "Gow bak howm." Naw hi gowin bak diskorijin bika hi din get no riwahrd. Hi wen an di wey howm an i luk bot di wayf hapi, yu kno, so i kahl im in. So wel, di teybl waz wel set so dey sit dawn an enjay derself. Fyuw deyz afta di wayf kompleyn tu im. I sez, "A piys av chiyz an a piys av bred iz nat inof for a riwahrd." I sez, "Gow bak and tel di fish dat dis owl haws dat wi ar living intu iz notin mowr beta dan a pig pen."

There is little time here for more than a brief discussion; however, note even just the first five lines. The verb tense sequence is <u>was, used to, goes-and-catch-and-bring-and-sell, went-and-didn't-catch, sez, sez, say, take-and-throw</u>. These are exactly the same patterns that Myhill and Harris found in Philadelphia--here in Nicaraguan Miskito Coast Creole, mesolectal variety. One should of course be cautious about inferring that what we have here are two different ends of the post-creole continuum. But we do have two quite DIFFERENT points in linguistic space and time showing evidence of exactly the same linguistic feature. If a linguistic rule is involved here, one is tempted to see some sort of historical connection. If, on the other hand, what we are observing is a universal linguistic tendency, then one might well say that there is nothing particularly unique about the way in which speakers of Philadelphia VBE use narrative -s.

The possibility of a historical connection can be clarified further by looking at narratives from closer to home. When I look at my Wilmington, North Carolina data (dating from 1973) I find a large number of narratives like the following (the beginning of a lengthy description of a movie plot; the speaker is a black male, age 17):

> It was a movie called "The Black Caesar." It was real good and a man, a black man, was running, you know he got beat up by this white cop and the white people always run him around and so on and--so when he got, you know, he got out of prison, they set him up. Well, he went in the prison for about five years. And when he came out, well, he got back at all of them but this white cop, and he remember beating him on the head and took him in the alley and just beat, broke him all up.

The amazing thing about this and many other of the Wilmington BVE narratives is that they are told almost entirely in the past tense--only one uninflected verb, remember, is to be found in this whole paragraph (assuming that run is a nonstandard preterite). Either our elicitation techniques did not elicit narrative past -s (a very likely conjecture) or else it wasn't there for this particular speaker.[4] This is virtually the same as the situation with Labov's data from the 1960s. Even narratives of personal experience and action frequently are told in the past tense, though as speaker involvment increases the number of totally uninflected forms increases.

Happily (at least for my argument), however, narrative past -s does occur occasionally in narratives in my Wilmington data. Note the following two narratives, both spoken by the same black adolescent male in 1973:

> We had a white lifeguard name was Matt. Y'know, . . . I'm a tell, tell how cool he is. Mack, Mack get up--we would sit on the church steps, y'know, an' Mack comes over there--I was talkin' to this girl, uh, Gwen. An' I thought sure I was just

blowin' her mind decent. An Mack comes up there
an' Mack say, "Hey, what about Yolanda, man?" I
say, "Shut up, Mack, shut up!" He breaks her name
all across--and that girl ain't spoken to me since.
An' then he's over there laughin' about it. . . .

On the Fourth of July or somethin', there's
nothin' but blacks up there at Topsail Beach. An'
there's a lot of black guys who don't dig whites
period. An' uh, Mack goes up there all cool, calm,
go up there 'n' shoot the pinball machine 'n' stuff
like that, plays foosball, he don' care. An' I'm
sittin' there lookin' at this nut actin' all funny
an' stuff, I'm right ready to get out there. . . .
I don't want no action to start, you know, and I'm
up there whuppin' heads around there and me gettin'
my head whupped. And so he ends up jus' messin'
around. And he ain't scared to talk to no black
girl. . . . And he doesn't get in trouble.

Shoo, I went in a redneck joint there one--I
went in one one night downtown there. Me an' about
five other dudes, y'know, we gonna be cool, y'know,
go in there. Dude look at us, you know--shoot a
little pool. An' they ain't had nothin' on they
jukebox excep' ol' country and western stuff, you
know. . . . So I gets up there y'know, "Hey, man,
that's all you got in that music is a ol' redneck
thing, songs right here?" All loud 'n all, y'know.
And I'm moving back behind the machines, tryin' to
duck out the way. An' this guy comes up--bottle
stuff, an, talkin' much junk, he say, "Reggie, you
in this with us, man?" I said, "Leave me outta
this." He say, "Come on, man, I'm a start it
knockin'." "You gonna end it, too, cause I'm 'onna
leave." So you know, the guys just looked at us as
we walked out. You shoulda seen me boogeyin'
around the corner. I coulda won the hundred
meters, man.

In both narratives, -s alternates with zero forms and past tense forms, just as in Myhill and Harris's data. Furthermore, the speaker exhibits a high use of say instead of sez--again just as in Myhill and Harris's example. Finally, there is at least some tendency towards the loss of the second -s on a conjunct.

I'm not at all sure what to conclude from this. Obviously, Philadelphia blacks in the 1980s share the use of narrative past -s with Wilmington blacks of the 1970s and Holm's Creole speaker. One cannot argue conclusively for a historical connection, but one certainly can't rule it out. Only Labov's assertion that no such examples existed in New York in the 1960s is problematical (see n.

4). I do feel, however, that in the light of such examples it is impossible to maintain that narrative -s is strong evidence for divergence.

In an interesting paper on Samaná (the English of an enclave of elderly black speakers in the Dominican Republic, whose ancestors--ex-slaves--moved there from the United States in 1824) Tagliamonte and Poplack conclude that the paper can be viewed as "lending support . . . to the divergence hypothesis" (1986, p. 23). Because Samaná has been relatively isolated from other varieties of English, it has had no opportunity for decreolization. Yet Samaná is much closer to standard English than are most creoles. Assuming that the original immigrants spoke basilectal black English, Tagliamonte and Poplack conclude that the state of basilectal English in the United States in 1824 was much closer to standard English than is black vernacular English today.

One of the features that they examine is the use of verbal -s. They find (p. 25) that "58% of the -s inflections in the Philadelphia corpus [of Myhill and Harris] were found in narrative clauses, as opposed to 8% in non-narrative clauses"; for Samaná the "proportions are just the reverse: 4% and 51% respectively." Therefore, they reason, with respect to the -s feature, today's vernacular black English is less like standard English than slave language was. To accept this view, one must be persuaded that Samaná is representative of the English of American slaves.[5] One must furthermore accept the assumption that, like Labov in New York in the 1960s, Tagliamonte and Poplack did not find narrative -s because it did not exist, and not because they were simply unable to elicit it from their informants (see n. 4). Finally, one must assume that the Philadelphia speakers could not have learned the use of narrative -s from some form of standard English--whether vernacular narratives or sportscasting--but rather invented it totally on their own (a dubious assumption, as I hope I have shown). Again, given the (possibly) universal tendencies in human language towards narrative presents (see n. 3), one cannot argue that young Philadelphia black vernacular speakers could not have created their own narrative presents; universalist arguments, however, would also tend to support the view that narrative presents were there all along--just not discovered by the researchers. In the end, I have to come back to paraphrase Wolfram's words, quoted earlier: which is more divergent from white vernacular English, a system like Samaná which may not use narrative presents, or a system like that of young Philadelphia black vernacular speakers, which uses virtually the same narrative present as white vernacular English? If anything, the supposed change in -s seems to me to support CONvergence, not divergence.

NOTES

1. See also Butters (1986) for further discussion of linguistic convergence of black and white vernaculars in a smaller, more racially integrated community--Wilmington, North Carolina.

2. See Butters (forthcoming) for some discussion of Bailey and Maynor's claims.

3. Universality creates a further difficulty for using narative -s to support divergence claims: many languages other than English make use of similar present-for-past forms. See, for example, the following Colombian Spanish narrative (collected for me last fall in New York City by Angel Soto):

> Pues, voy a hablar de mi primer "date" o mi primera experiencia con sallendo con un muchacho. . . . Pues, cuando llegué todo el mundo me recibe como la prima gringa . . . y todo el mundo pensaba que yo era ciento por ciento americana. Entonces, por fin conocí a unos muchachos que eran amigos de mi prima que ya habián vivido en los Etados Unidos. . . Entonces, se me acerca y me dice "Can you dance?" Entonces, yo me muerto de la risa y de la pena tambien y le digo, "No claro que si," que, en español le digo que sí, que no, pues que bailemos, y me pusé, pues, penisima porque todo el mundo pensando que yo era ciento por ciento gringa que no tenía nada de tipo latina. . . . Todos el mundo tomaba, (creo) que se llamaba "Boones Farm Wine" que era una marca gringa, pero todo el mundo lo compra alla porque es tan barato. Entonces, estamos tomando toda la noche y en claro los muchachos tomando aguardiente. Pero el muchacho con quien yo estaba, Andres, no está mu' tomando.

I have circled all the present-tense items in the narrative and underlined all the past-tense ones. We see here the same alternation, then, between present and past forms that marked the English narratives. We see here, also, although not under exactly the same circumstances, the deletion of repeated morphological material (los muchachos tomando aguardiente). I suppose a "historical" connection is possible here, in the sense that Maria is bilingual, is speaking to an American bilingual, and may therefore have "borrowed" the gringo practice of using present tense forms in past-time narratives. On the other hand, the presence of present-for-past in the very different kinds of narratives that we have seen in this paper strongly suggests that some kind of universalist tendencies are at work.

4. Although we followed Labov's methodology from the 1960s for making our interviews as informal as possible, the inherent artificiality of the interview situation to some extent at least surely kept our informants from speaking as they would have if there had been no interviewer present. Like Labov in the 1960s, I was a good deal older than my subjects; I was white, they were black; they knew I was a university English professor. It may well be, then, that, under the circumstances, many of our informants eschewed the less-formal historical present even though they were familiar with it. The same considerations may well explain why Labov in the 1960s did not get historical present narratives from his ghetto subjects. For an example of the latest in interviewing techniques, see Viv Edwards' splendid book (1986).

5. Opponents of the view that American slave language was not on the whole a good deal more creolized than vernacular black English today must explain (or explain away) the highly creolized nature of Gullah. (For recent work on Gullah, see Nichols, 1983; Rickford, 1985; Mufwene, 1986; Mufwene and Gilman, 1987; and the references therein.) The very existence of Gullah is strong evidence that, at least at some point, slaves in the United States spoke creole. Tagliamonte and Poplack might want to argue that this stage was a good deal prior to 1824. See Poplack and Sankoff (1987) for arguments that "the diverse geographic and social origins of the [Samaná] settlers . . . suggest . . . that their language could not have been limited to a specific regional or class variety [i.e., it could not have been an acrolectal variety]" (Tagliamonte and Poplack, 1986, p. 2). While Poplack and Sankoff argue persuasively, the evidence, as Tagliamonte and Poplack note (1986, p. 1) is in the end "unfortunately rather sparse."

Tagliamonte and Poplack regretably have not consulted an important source of information about nineteenth-century American black English: the Slave Narratives (Rawick, 1972), which record (in written form) the speech of the last generation of slaves, who were young people at the time of Emancipation in the 1860s. Schneider (1983, p. 105) notes that verbal -s was widely used in the Slave Narratives with all nouns and pronouns (not just third singular), and that "two different inflectional systems which have a clear regional distribution" existed. Moreover, "the social evidence indicates that within the ex-slaves' sociolect verbal -s seems to be the lower stratum variant in use more freely with field hands, uneducated informants, and males, whereas the uninflected verb form displays a bias toward being used as something like a prestige form in all grammatical persons, including the third singular" (p. 107). The decreased use of non-narrative -s in twentieth-century black vernacular English cannot be viewed as "decreolization" because creoles in general lack -s entirely. Insofar as -s disappears in our century on grammatical persons other than third singular it can be viewed as movement towards standard English, that is, towards convergence. Schneider does caution us (p. 100), however, that the frequently heard claims that verbal -s does not exist in vernacular black English (e.g., Labov et al. 1968, I: 164) are subject to serious challenge. (See also Butters, 1973.) Unfortunately, Schneider's article and his book (1981) do not distinguish narrative and non-narrative uses of verbal -s.

REFERENCES

Bailey, G. (1987) Are black and white dialects diverging? Papers from the NWAVE XIV panel discussion. American Speech, 62, 32-40.

Bailey, G. and Maynor, L. (1985) Decreolization? Paper presented at the International Linguistic Association Annual Meeting. To appear in Language in Society.

Baugh, J. (1986) Linguistic divergence or linguistic innovation: A review of suffix /-s/ variation in vernacular black English. Paper presented at the American Dialect Society Annual Meeting.

Butters, R. R. (1973) Black English -Z--Some theoretical implications. American Speech, 48, 37-45.

--- (1986) Linguistic convergence in a North Carolina community. Paper presented at the Fifteenth Annual Conference on New Ways of Analyzing Variation.

--- (Forthcoming) The Death of Black English: Linguistic Convergence and Divergence in American English.

Edwards, V. (1986) Language in a Black Community. Clevedon: Multilingual Matters Ltd.

Graff, D., Labov, W. and Harris, W. A. (1986) Testing listeners' reactions to phonological markers of ethnic identity: A new method for sociolinguistic research. In D. Sankoff (ed.), Diversity and Diachrony. Amsterdam/Philadelphia: Benjamins. pp. 45-58.

Holm, J. (ed.) (1983) *Central American English*. Heidelberg: Groos.

Labov, W. (1985) The increasing divergence of black and white vernaculars: Introduction to the research reports. Unpublished manuscript, University of Pennsylvania.

--- (1987) Are black and white dialects diverging? Papers from the NWAV XIV panel discussion. *American Speech*, 62, 5-12.

Labov, W., Cohen P., Robins, C. and Lewis, J. (1968) *A Study of the Non-Standard English of Negro and Puerto-Rican Speakers in New York City. Report on Cooperative Research Project 3288*. Philadelphia: U.S. Regional Survey.

Mufwene, S. S. (1986) Number delimitation in Gullah. *American Speech*, 61, 33-60.

Mufwene, S. S. and Gilman, C. (1987). How African is Gullah, and why? *American Speech*, 62, 120-39.

Myhill, J. and Harris, W. (1986) The use of verbal -s inflection in BEV. In D. Sankoff (ed.), *Diversity and Diachrony*. Amsterdam/Philadelphia: Benjamins. pp. 25-32.

Nichols, P. (1983) Black and white speaking in the rural South: Difference in the pronominal system. *American Speech*, 58, 201-15.

Poplack, S. and Sankoff, D. (1987) The Philadelphia story in the Spanish Caribbean. *American Speech*, 62, 291-311.

Rawick, G. P. (ed.) (1972) *The American Slave: A Composite Autobiography*. Westport, CT: Greenwood.

Rickford, J. R. (1985) Ethnicity as a sociolinguistic boundary. *American Speech*, 60, 99-125.

--- (1987) Are black and white dialects diverging? Papers from the NWAV XIV panel discussion. *American Speech*, 62, 5-12.

Schneider, E. W. (1981) *Morphologische und syntaktische Variablen im amerikanischen Early Black English*.

Frankfurt am Main: Lang.

——— (1983) The origin of the verbal -s in black English. American Speech, 58, 99-113.

Shiffrin, D. (1981) Tense variation in narrative. Language, 57, 45-62.

Spears, A. K. (1987) Are black and white dialects diverging? Papers from the NWAV XIV panel discussion. American Speech, 62, 48-55.

Tagliamonte, S. and Poplack, S. (1986) How black English past got to the present: Evidence from Samaná. Unpublished paper, University of Ottawa.

Thomas, E. (1986) Vowel changes in Columbus, Ohio. Unpublished paper, Duke University.

Vaughn-Cooke, F. B. (1987) Are black and white dialects diverging? Papers from the NWAV XIV panel discussion. American Speech, 62, 12-32.

Wolfram, W. (1987) Are black and white dialects diverging? Papers from the NWAV XIV panel discussion. American Speech, 62, 40-48.

Acquisition of Phonological Variants

J.K. CHAMBERS
University of Toronto

This report presents the first results from a developmental study of dialect acquisition. The subjects are six Canadian-born youngsters whose families emigrated to Oxfordshire in southern England in 1983 and 1984. They are identified below by code-names comprised of a pseudonymous given name and sociolinguistic surnames:

<u>Family X</u>   <u>Family Y</u>
Max 9Xm   Dan 13Ym
Hal 13Xm   Sam 14Ym
Pam 15Xf   Ken 17Ym

In the surname, the number encodes the age of the subjects in 1985, when I interviewed them the first time; the upper-case letter (X or Y) indicates the family; and the lower-case letter (m or f) indicates the gender. Thus, Dan 13Ym is a 13-year-old boy in family Y, the younger brother of Sam and Ken.

In 1985, family X had been in England two years and family Y one. This difference in the subjects' exposure to the new dialect they are acquiring is seldom significant in the results. While Max 9Xm and Hal 13Xm are the most advanced acquirers of the dialect among the subjects, both Dan 13Ym and Sam 14Ym are more advanced than Pam 15Xf, suggesting that other factors are more determinant than exposure time in the first year or two of dialect acquisition.

This paper deals only with the results for the acquisition of phonological features at the earliest stage of dialect acquisition. This is only one aspect of the whole study, which also quantifies the acquisition of lexical and pronunciation variants, correlates acquisition rates with the independent variables of age, gender, attitudes, social integration, and responses to stigmatization, and reanalyses these linguistic and social factors for the same subjects at a later stage based on real-time data from a second round of interviews, completed in July 1987, exactly two years after the first.

In the first round, I also interviewed six Oxfordshire natives who match the Canadian subjects in age and gender. These youngsters are referred to below as 'controls' and identified by these code-names:

<u>Age/Gender-mates for X</u>   <u>Age/Gender-mates for Y</u>
Rob 9Cm   Nat 13Cm
Rik 13Cm   Pip 14Cm
Tab 15Cf   Jon 17Cm

Methods in Dialectology

The surnames encode the same information as for the subjects, except that the upper-case letter (C) identifies them as controls.

The quantification of the phonological features is based on the reading of the following list of 28 phrases during the interview:

spring and summer	Cuba and France	birthday greetings
north and south	Don and Dawn	strawberry blond
urban and rural	Lisa and Daniel	forty brass monkeys
city and country		a naughty tot
	hot water bottle	caught in a knot
metal and plaster	bubble bath	automatic transmission
sofa and couch	a lawn cot	rotten, raw eggs
painting and drawing	the branch of a plant	lots of hawks
reading and writing	a partridge in a pear tree	the prettiest girl in the class
laughing and dancing	jolly St. Paul	the slaughter of the Scots

Although the free conversation and spontaneous responses to other tasks in the interview gave ample opportunity to observe phonological variants in the speech of the subjects and controls, the phrase list, with identical tokens in the same contextual style, provides the best data for comparing the progress of dialect acquisition among the individuals.

1. THE PHONOLOGICAL FEATURES

Among the 28 phrases of the phrase list are several tokens which reveal the presence or absence of rule-governed or systematic phonological differences between Canadian English (CE) and southern English English (SEE). These tokens can be categorized as instances of five general features: absence of t-Voicing (§1.1), absence of low vowel merger (§1.2), presence of vowel backing (§1.3), presence of r-lessness (§1.4), and presence of intrusive [r](§1.5). This rather cumbersome terminology in terms of 'presence' or 'absence' is necessitated by the different status of the processes in the phonologies of the dialects. The first two in the list above are general features of CE which do not occur in SEE, and thus it is their absence in the speech of the Canadian youngsters that indicates the acquisition of a dialect feature. The last three are general features of the middle-class speech of southern England which do not occur in Canada, and it is their presence in the speech of the Canadian youngsters that indicates the acquisition of a dialect feature. The list includes ten instances of the first four features and five of the last one.

The evidence for each of the features is distributed irregularly throughout the phrase list. The list was organized, as indicated above, mainly by semantic similarities. For instance, <u>hot water bottle</u> precedes <u>bubble bath</u>; the former phrase was transcribed for instances of t-Voicing, vowel merger and r-lessness, and the latter for an instance of vowel backing. The list was also organized partly by syntactic similarities, with, for example, Cuba and France, Don and Dawn and Lisa and Daniel in sequence; the first was transcribed for instances of vowel backing and intrusive [r], the second for vowel merger, and the third for intrusive [r]. None of the subjects or controls had a clue about the purpose of the reading exercise, but, as we shall see below, the results on intrusive [r] are skewed in such a way as to suggest that some of the English youngsters were 'correcting' their speech for this stigmatized feature.

In the following discussion, the processes are outlined in turn, with the instances elicited in the interview listed and the results indicated both textually and graphically.

1.1. Absence of t-Voicing.

The rule of t-Voicing is a general feature not only of Canadian English but of most varieties of North American English. Medial /t/ voices when it follows a vowel or [r] and precedes an unstressed vowel. (For a detailed formulation, including special cases in which [l] and [n] can occur in the preceding environment, see Kahn 1976: 56-61.) In CE, the /t/ occurs as [d] most of the time but may also occur as tap [ɾ] in fast speech for some speakers and may perhaps occur as a 'voiced fortis' stop in fairly careful speech. In ordinary speech, however, /t/ becomes [d] in this environment (and it is not a significant "oversimplification" to call it that as Wells [1982: 248-52] claims, in his review of the literature). As a result, numerous pairs of words are homophones in CE, including kitty:kiddie, putting:pudding, petal:pedal, hearty:hardy, (Minne)sota:soda, and so on. In southern England, such pairs are distinguished, of course, by the voiceless-voiced contrast. The instances on the phrase list are as follows:

city	naughty	water
writing	prettiest	forty
greetings	metal	automatic (both /t/s)

As expected, the English youngsters had no voiced alveolars in any of these forms. As Fig. 1 shows, the Canadian youngsters have made considerable progress in eliminating t-Voicing from their phonologies, with the youngest, Max 9Xm, at 100%, the same score as the English group. Two others are nearly categorical, at 90% and 80%, and the other three all score 20%.

The results thus split the sample population into two distinct groups, those with low scores (20%) and those with high scores (80-100%), with no one in the intermediate sixty percentiles. The significance of this split is discussed below (§2.3).

The word-by-word results suggest that not all lexemes are equally susceptible to losing their t-Voicing: Sam 14Ym failed to voice all /t/s except the second one in automatic, and Hal 13Xm failed to voice all but that one and the one in water. Both, that is, said [ú:tʰəmædɪk], leaving the first alveolar unvoiced but voicing the second one, which is the only one on the list that occurs after

non-primary stress.
Similarly, not all lexemes are as susceptible to retaining their t-Voicing. For the three speakers clustered at 20%, one of the two

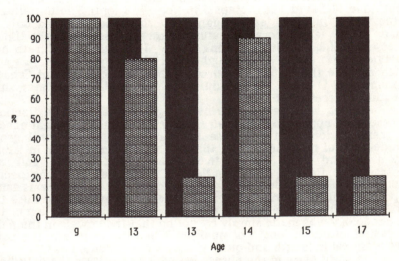

Fig. 1--Absence of t-Voicing in the speech of 6 Canado-English speakers, from youngest to oldest. In background, the scores for their English age/gender mates

instances in which /t/ was unvoiced was naughty, which means that none of the Canadians voiced this alveolar. The most likely explanation is that this word is much more frequent in England than in Canada--when it is heard in Canada, it has an Old-World quaintness--and it may well have been learned (or, more likely, become part of their active vocabulary) by all these youngsters only after they emigrated. But that explanation fails to explain why two of the three in the low-scoring group also failed to voice the /t/ in metal.

1.2. Absence of low vowel merger.

Standard CE has one fewer vowel phoneme than most other standard varieties due to the merger of two low back vowels. The merger makes homophones of such pairs as dotter:daughter, bobble:bauble, tot:taught, rot:wrought, and offal:awful. In other standard North American varieties, these pairs are usually distinguished by unrounded and rounded vowels, /ɑ/ and /ɔ/, respectively. In RP and other standard British varieties they are usually distinguished by a pair of rounded vowels, /ɒ/ and /ɔː/. The vowel in both words in CE is typically unrounded /ɑ/, although there is some allophonic variation (Woods 1979) and some western Canadians typically have rounded /ɒ/ (or perhaps /ɔ/, as reported by Walker [1975]). The Canadian unrounding of the vowel in dotter, rot, and so on, is a typical feature of North American English (see Trudgill and Hannah 1982: 32-34, 37; Kurath and McDavid 1961: Maps 136 [fog], 138 [on]). The unrounding of the vowel in daughter, wrought, and so on, is standard only in Canada, but it is a venerable feature of certain regions in the United States, including the Susquehanna Valley, Pennsylvania (Kurath and McDavid 1961: Maps 129 [daughter], 132 [sausage], 134 [water]), which may be the historical source of the feature in inland Canada. This merger is now widely diffused in the United States, and spreading (Terrell 1976).

In non-RP speech in southern England, the vowel distinctions in these pairs appear to be less straightforward than one might expect. My transcriptions of the phrase list for the English control group include several notes indicating that the vowels may differ in length only (/ɔ/ and /ɔː/), rather than quality and length, and my transcriptions for one speaker, Nat 13Cm, include two unexpected occurrences of unrounded [ɑ], in water and cot. These variations cause no problems in comparing the two populations, however, because the words are paired in the elicited phrases, and the determination of the SEE phonology was made simply by noting that the vowels in the pairs contrasted, either in length or quality. When the vowels in the pairs were identical in length and quality, they were classified as CE.

The word pairs in the phrase list which constitute the data-base for the absence of vowel merger are listed here according to their RP phoneme:

RP /ɒ/	RP /ɔː/
Don	Dawn
hot	water
cot	lawn
jolly	Paul
blond	strawberry
tot	naughty
knot	caught
rotten	raw
lots	hawks
Scots	slaughter

The English subjects, as expected, distinguished the vowels of all pairs. The Canadians showed almost no consistency as a group, as Fig. 2 indicates. Two of the youngest scored very high (90% and 80%), indicating considerable progress in the acquisition of the contrast, but neither of them rounded either vowel in the phrase jolly St. Paul. Two of the others kept the vowels apart in only one phrase: Dan 13Ym said

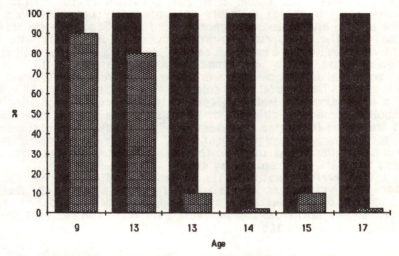

Fig. 2 --Absence of low back vowel merger in the speech of 6 Canado-English speakers. In background, the scores for their English age/gender-mates.

strawberry blond with [ɑ] and [ɒ], respectively, and Pam 15Xf said Don and Dawn with [ɑ] and [ɔ], respectively. The other two, Sam 14Ym and Ken 17Ym, have apparently not yet begun to split the merged vowel of their first dialect.

1.3. Presence of vowel backing.

One of the most noticeable differences between North American and southern English dialects is the contrast between the vowels [æ] and [ɑ] in two lexical sets which are phonologically-defined but may or may not be phonologically-conditioned. The modern variants are the reflexes of Middle English ă in two environments: before voiceless fricatives as in daft, bath, and grass, and before clusters of nasal and obstruent as in chant, demand and chance. This difference between the English of North America and southern England arose as an innovation in London English to lengthen the vowel in these environments near the end of the seventeenth century, apparently too late to affect North American speech and too minor to diffuse much beyond the south of England. (On both the origins and the diffusion, see Chambers and Trudgill 1980: 127-29.) In RP and southern English varieties, the long vowel in these positions became back, and the distinctive feature is qualitative rather than quantitative.

There are a couple of good reasons for inferring that vowel backing is lexicalized rather than rule-governed in SEE. First, the environments in which it occurs are apparently never derived, so there are no alternations between [ɑ] and [æ]. Second, some lexical items with the appropriate environments occur invariably with the front vowel in RP, not back, such as anvil, cafeteria, classic and (Roman Catholic) Mass. The only good reason for inferring that it is rule-governed is that several words vary between the two vowels even in RP, where variation is relatively rare. (See Wells 1982: 135 for a list.) One plausible explanation for the variation is that the phonology includes a rule of vowel backing with several exceptions, and the unsettled forms represent the two available generalizations by speakers: graph, plastic, transport, and the other words with variant pronunciations undergo the rule for some speakers but are added to the list of exceptions by others.

Whatever its status in the phonologies of the native dialect speakers, vowel backing affects mainly frequent words in the lexicon and offers dialect learners ample opportunity to infer a rule (spuriously or not) from the available evidence. The relevant words on the phrase list are these:

plaster	dancing
laughing	France
bath	branch
brass	plant
class	transmission

The English youngsters scored either 100% or 90%, depending upon their treatment of transmission, the only word on the phrase list which can vary in SEE. Two of the controls had a back vowel in transmission and the other four had the close front vowel [æ]. A couple of mild discrepancies in the transcription suggest that this feature is not as firmly fixed in the dialect as most accounts suggest. One of the controls, Nat 13Cm, varied the vowel from back to front (open): in the ten words, he had [ɑ] three times, [ɑ‹] five times (including transmission), and [aˑ] twice. The youngest member of the control group, Rob 9Cm, actually corrected his pronunciation from a front vowel to back, saying "[pʰlas]...[pʰlɑstə]" for plaster, the first word from this group on the list.

For the Canadian group, this feature marks a sharp division between the youngest speaker and all the others, as Fig. 3 shows. Max 9Xm scores 100%, backing the vowel in all the words (including transmission) and, ironically, outscoring his English age/gender-mate. All the other subjects have very low scores. Hal 13Xm backs the vowel in laughing, Dan 13Ym fudges the vowel in plaster to [a‹], and Sam 14Ym fudges the vowels in both plaster and laughing ([a] and [aˑ], respectively). The other two show no response at all for this feature.

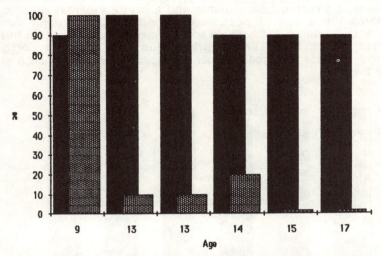

Fig. 3 -- Presence of back vowels in words such as 'bath' and 'branch' in the speech of 6 Canado-English speakers. In background, the scores of their English age/gender-mates.

1.4. Presence of r-lessness.

No phonological feature divides England and (inland) North America more decisively than the deletion of postvocalic /r/ in such words as girl, pear and summer. In England, the rule is ubiquitous among middle-class speakers. In North America, the rule never made headway beyond the Atlantic seaboard.
 The feature also divides the sample populations of this study quite decisively. The tokens on the phrase list are as follows:

<pre>
summer   north
plaster   urban
water   partridge
pear   birthday
forty   girl
</pre>

 The responses of the English control group held no surprises at all. Everyone scored 100%. The Canadian youngsters have made very little progress in acquiring this feature of SEE, as Fig. 4 shows. No one scores more than 30%, and the pattern shows no hint of age-grading or any other coherent social correlate. Linguistic correlates are also impossible to find. Sam 14Ym, whose score gives some shape to Fig. 4, deletes the /r/ in summer, pear and forty, that is, in an unstressed final syllable, a stressed final syllable and a preconsonantal syllable, thus running the gamut of possible environments. The other two speakers who delete an /r/ both do so in preconsonantal position but in different words: Max 9Xm in urban, and Dan 13Ym in north. Obviously, r-lessness has made almost no impact upon their speech at this early stage.

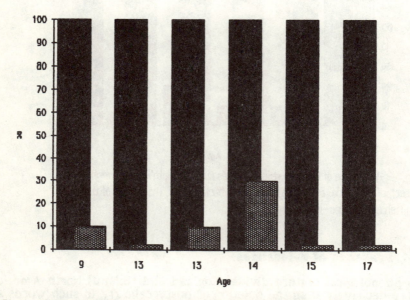

Fig. 4--Presence of r-lessness in the speech of 6 Canado-English speakers. In background, the scores of their English age/gender-mates.

1.5. Presence of intrusive [r].

The rule inserting [r] epenthetically where no lexical /r/ exists is a concomitant of r-lessness, and should be inconspicuous in dialects where r-lessness has not become established. Intrusive [r] develops as a natural extension of r-lessness (Wells 1982: 222-27, Trudgill and Hannah 1982: 13-15). In r-less accents, final /r/ is lost across word boundaries when it precedes a consonant, as in pear tree, but retained when it precedes a vowel, as in pear and apple. This linking [r] then generalizes into a transitional consonant between vowel-final words preceding vowels, as in Cuba[r] and France, and ultimately word-internally between vowel sequences, as in draw[r]ing. Because these [r]s cannot be underlying, the process must be an epenthesis rule.

In England, the intrusive [r] rule is variable rather than categorical, perhaps partly because it is stigmatized, but it appears to be almost impossible for speakers to suppress completely. It occurs occasionally in RP (although the speaker is likely to deny it if one brings an instance to his or her attention) and in the speech of English actors who are otherwise capable of very convincing and sustained imitations of American speech. The five instances on the phrase list are as follows:

 sofa[r] and couch
 painting and draw[r]ing
 Cuba[r] and France
 Lisa[r] and Daniel
 rotten, raw[r] eggs

The variability of the rule is reflected in the performances of the English controls, as shown in Fig. 5, with scores ranging from 100% to 20%. Only one of the Canadian subjects, Max 9Xm, participates at all, scoring 40%. Max and all the members of the control group insert the intrusive [r] word-internally into drawing, the only word-internal instance in the list. This result should be surprising in view of the way the rule develops, with word-internal epenthesis as an extension of linking [r]. In fact, it is the only instance of intrusive [r] in the elicited speech of Tab 15Cf. The others, again including Max, also insert the [r] in sofa and couch, so that the two subjects who score 40%, Max and Rik 13Cm, attain their score in identical ways, with intrusions into drawing and sofa and couch and nowhere else. This result should perhaps be surprising because sofa and couch has the same phonetic environment as Cuba and France and Lisa and Daniel, where they fail to insert it. In fact, Lisa and Daniel is one of the two phrases which occurs without intrusive [r] for most speakers, along with rotten, raw eggs.

Linguistically, then, these results do not seem to make sense. The explanation for them apparently does not lie in the linguistic properties of the phrases at all. The best correlation for intrusive [r] is the order in which the items were elicited, as shown in Table 1. If the token was one of the first three of its type on the list that the subjects were reading, the chances of its occurring with an intrusive [r] were greatly enhanced: on the list of 28 phrases, sofa and couch came up sixth, drawing seventh, and Cuba and France tenth, but Lisa and Daniel came up twelfth and rotten, raw eggs twenty-fifth.

The correlation between the order of elicitation and the actual occurrences of intrusive [r] suggests that, for Max and the SEE speakers, self-monitoring became more vigilant after the first instances of intrusive [r] were elicited. Most of them succeeded in suppressing it after two or three instances. The impression that

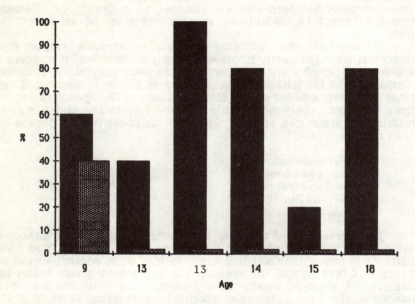

Fig. 5--Presence of intrusive [r] in the speech of 6 Canado-English speakers. In background, the scores of their English age/gender-mates.

monitoring affected the results is reinforced by Pip's response during the interview. When he first encountered <u>Cuba and France</u> on the phrase list, he inserted the [r] but garbled his pronunciation of <u>France</u>. On repeating the phrase, he eliminated the intrusive [r].

Speaker	Order of elicitation				
	sofa and..	drawing	Cuba and...	Lisa and...	...raw eggs
Nat 13Cm	+	+	+	+	+
Jon 17Cm	+	+	+	+	o
Pip 14Cm	+	+	+	o	+
Rob 9Cm	+	+	o	o	o
Rik 13Cm	+	+	o	o	o
Max 9Xm	+	+	o	o	o
Tab 15Cf	o	+	o	o	o

Table 1--Presence (+) or absence (o) of intrusive [r] for all speakers, in the order in which the data was elicited. Speakers are ordered in left column by the number of instances, from most to least.

The Canadian youngsters' responses on intrusive [r] are even flatter than they were for r-lessness. That result follows quite naturally, of course, from the relationship between these two rules. Since intrusive [r] is a concomitant of r-lessness, instances of it should begin to appear in the new dialect only after r-lessness has become established in it. In this early stage of acquisition, the only wrinkle in the development is Max 9Xm, who scores higher on intrusive [r] than he does on r-lessness.

2. LINGUISTIC DETERMINANTS

2.1. Order of acquisition of phonological variants.

If one looks selectively at the Canadian youngsters' responses to the various phonological features, two different observations are apparent.

On the one hand, analysis of the first three phonological variants clearly shows that the individual subjects differ markedly from one another in their receptiveness to these features. The basic pattern of the first three graphs presented above is peaks and valleys.

On the other hand, their analysis also shows a consistent group response with respect to these features. Generally, if the youngest member of the sample is highly receptive, the others are receptive to some degree, and vice-versa. If the youngest member shows little or no response, the older ones also show no response. The basic pattern of the last two graphs is prairie-like.

The Canadian youngsters are obviously not acquiring these SEE phonological features randomly or sporadically. Instead, there appears to be a hierarchy of receptiveness to them. The hierarchy is reflected in Table 2 by the group scores, derived by combining the individual scores for each feature.

Phonological feature	Group Score
Absence of t-Voicing	55 %
Absence of vowel merger	31.6
Presence of vowel backing	23.3
Presence of r-lessness	8.3
Presence of intrusive [r]	6.6

Table 2--Hierarchy of receptiveness to the phonological variants by the Canado-English group.

2.4. Linguistic principles of dialect acquisition.

Looking back at the patterns discovered in the acquisition of phonological features, some principles emerge.

First, two of the phonological features show similar patterns. Both absence of vowel merger (Fig. 2) and presence of back vowels

(Fig. 3) show precipitous declines from the youngest speakers to the older ones, who all score low. In this respect, the acquisition of these two phonological features resembles the pattern found in pronunciation replacements in this study (but not reported in this article). Absence of vowel merger involves the acquisition of a vowel phoneme. Presence of back vowels, if it is rule-governed, involves the acquisition of a rule of considerable complexity: it has two unrelated environments (before fricatives, and before nasal + obstruent clusters), several variant forms, and some exceptions. (If it is not rule-governed, the data for it should be classified as further instances of pronunciation replacements, and the similarities between them are tautologous.) It is reasonable to consider any rule with two (or more) conditioning factors or opaque outputs (variants or exceptions) as a complex rule. **Acquisition of new phonemes and complex rules split the population into early acquirers and late acquirers** in the first stage of dialect acquisition. The split is age-graded, with early acquirers identifiable as the younger members of the Canadian sample.

Second, the hierarchical order of phonological acquisitions summarized in Table 2 shows that features characterized by their absence precede those characterized by their presence. Assuming this result does not follow from accidental properties of the particular features chosen for analysis, the conclusion seems clear: **Eliminating rules of the old dialect progresses faster than acquiring rules of the new dialect.** Intuitively, this principle seems almost obvious.

Third, comparing the subjects' responses with respect to eliminating t-Voicing and acquiring r-lessness, the two non-complex (as defined above) phonological rules in the survey, the discrepancy appears even greater than one might expect from the preceding principle. In addition to the absence-presence distinction, these two processes are diametrically opposed in another respect. The elimination of t-Voicing gives rise to pronunciations that are not only heard in the new dialect area but are also reinforced by the orthographical representations of the data. Words such as city, greetings and forty are orthographically transparent in the sense that they are spelled with ‹t›, not ‹d›, and pronounced [t], not [d], in England. The acquisition of r-lessness gives rise to pronunciations that are heard in the new dialect area but are contradicted by the orthographical representations of the data. Words such as summer, four and forty are orthographically opaque in the sense that they are spelled with ‹r›, pronounced [r] in Canada but deleted (or realized obliquely in vowel modifications) in England. All the subjects are literate, as is typical in studies of dialect acquisition but not in first-language acquisition and often not in second-language acquisition. In the early stage of dialect acquisition, **features which are orthographically transparent progress faster than features which are orthographically opaque**. It remains to be seen whether orthographically opaque features can ever be completely mastered by learners who are literate. Such features may exist in dialects (and languages) only because first-language learners are invariably illiterate.

2.3. Phonological acquisition as lexical diffusion.

The five features selected for study do not have the same phonological status, and the differences to some extent determine the nature of the results. Two of them are the result of categorical rules, t-Voicing in CE and r-lessness in SEE, and another, vowel merger, is the result of different phonemic inventories in the two dialects. These differences should (and do) result in categoricity (100%) in the responses of the English control group and either absence (0) or variability (1-99%) in the responses of the Canadian subjects. Another of the features, intrusive [r], is the result of a variable rule in SEE, susceptible particularly to stylistic variation, and the other one, vowel backing, may not be rule-governed at all but may be the (partly variable) lexicalization of an old rule (or rules). The evidence for these should (and does) result in variability in the responses of the English control group and either absence or variability (presumably with a lower frequency at this early stage) in the speech of the Canadian subjects.

These results are consistent with a particular hypothesis about dialect acquisition and, more generally, about phonological change, namely, lexical diffusion, which maintains that **phonological innovations are actuated by the acquisition of instances of the new rule or phoneme** and only become rule-governed or systematized (if ever, in the first generation of acquirers) after a critical mass of instances has been acquired.

In other words, the mechanism for the acquisition of systematic phonology in its first stage is identical to the acquisition of pronunciation variants. The two are only separable in later stages, when generalization from instances is appropriate for phonology but mistaken for pronunciations. For example, a Canadian in Oxfordshire who acquires the SEE pronunciations of tomato and charade with [ɑ] in place of his native [ey] must at some point discern that he or she cannot therefore generalize that CE [ey] becomes SEE [ɑ] because of other instances where [ey] occurs in both dialects, as in lemonade, radiator, potato, and so on. But at some point he or she must also discern that the deletion of [r] in forty and four is applicable to all instances.

The evidence of phonological acquisition by the Canadian youngsters in this early stage strongly supports both crucial aspects of the lexical diffusion hypothesis.

First, phonological features occur originally in the speech of the acquirer as pronunciation variants of specific lexical items. Thus Max 9Xm scores higher on intrusive [r] with 40% than he does on r-lessness with 10%. Viewed in terms of the systematic phonology of the target dialect, this result is ludicrous, because intrusive [r] occurs as a concomitant of r-lessness, and because it is a variable rule and r-lessness is a categorical rule. It is inconceivable that any native speaker of SEE could have more instances of intrusive [r] than of r-lessness, and, of course, none of the controls do. But Max 9Xm apparently does not have these rules integrated into a phonological system. At this early stage, the instances of both are pronunciation variants, and they are too few or too infrequent to provide the basis for inferring the rules.

Second, the critical mass required as the basis for phonological generalizations appears to be about 20% of all instances. This approximation is proving remarkably robust in variation studies, with numerous changes in diverse languages confirming slow progress for the first 20% and then a rapid rise to about 80%, resulting in the familiar S-curve (Wang and Cheng 1970, Bailey 1973:77, Bickerton 1975:65, Chambers and Trudgill 1980:179). The three phonological changes which are reasonably well established for the Canadian subjects show this pattern. For absence of t-voicing (Fig. 1), three speakers score 20% and three score 80% or more. For absence of back vowel merger (Fig. 2), four score under 20% and two score 80% or more. For presence of vowel backing (Fig. 3), five score 20% or less and one scores 100%. For none of these is any speaker caught in the interval from 20-80%.

The division is age-graded. The high scores belong to the younger subjects and the low scores to the older ones.

As the acquisition of the new dialect continues, we would expect the older subjects to participate more fully, and in ways that are now predictable. Their acquisitions should be selective, involving the more accessible features—eliminating rules of the old dialect, and acquiring orthographically transparent ones—and their progress should conform to the thresholds of the S-curve. For the younger subjects, the next phase is not predictable.

References

Bailey, Charles-James N. (1973) *Variation and Linguistic Theory*. Virginia: Center for Applied Linguistics.

Bickerton, Derek (1975) *Dynamics of a Creole System*. Cambridge University Press.

Chambers, J.K., and Peter Trudgill (1980) *Dialectology*. Cambridge University Press.

Kahn, Daniel (1976) *Syllable-Based Generalizations in English Phonology*. Bloomington: Indiana University Linguistics Club.

Kurath, Hans, and Raven I. McDavid, Jr. (1961) *The Pronunciation of English in the Atlantic States*. Ann Arbor: University of Michigan Press.

Terrell, Tracy D. (1976) "Some theoretical considerations on the merger of the low vowel phonemes in American English." *Proceedings of the Second Annual Meeting of the Berkeley Linguistics Society*. 350-59.

Trudgill, Peter, and Jean Hannah (1982) *International English*. London: Edward Arnold.

Walker, Douglas C. (1975) "Another Edmonton idiolect: Comments on an article by Professor Avis". In *Canadian English: Origins and Structures*, ed. J.K. Chambers. Toronto: Methuen. 129-32.

Wang, William S-Y, and Chin-chuan Cheng (1970) "Implementation of phonological change: the Shûang-fêng Chinese case." *Papers from the Sixth Regional Meeting of the Chicago Linguistics Society*. 552-57.

Wells, J.C. (1982) *The Accents of English: An Introduction* [Vol. 1]. Cambridge University Press.

Woods, Howard B. (1979) *A Socio-dialectal Survey of the English Spoken in Ottawa*. Ph.D. thesis. University of British Columbia.

Dialects as Stepping Stones to a Language

EINAR HAUGEN
Harvard University

In this paper I shall use the term "dialect" to refer to spoken vernaculars, while "language" will be limited to standardized written forms.

The relation of dialects to languages can be reduced to two major types: (1) in which the dialects are subordinated to a closely related language, as the dialects of England, France and Germany are related to English, French and German; and (2) in which the dialects are dominated by an unrelated or only remotely related language, as the Bantu languages of Tanzania to English or those of Zaire to French. The former type is normal with languages that have long been standardized by central governments for the use of speakers of various dialects. The latter is common in countries that have recently been liberated from colonial rule, where the language of the colonizing power has remained in common use even after liberation, while the local vernaculars are still competing for recognition and status as languages of government and literature.

My topic today will be to present some aspects of the linguistic development in a country that falls between the two types. Norway's relatively unique position in the modern world is due to its sharing characteristics from both types of linguistic development. In 1814, Norway emerged from four centuries of domination by Denmark; during this time it had lost its Old Norwegian language and acquired that of the closely related Danish.

By this time Danish was a well-developed standard language, in whose recent development Danish and Norwegian authors had shared. The governing bureaucratic class of the restored monarchy saw no reason to abandon Danish, considering the situation to be of type one. But the spirit and the letter of the new constitution was imbued with romantic nationalism in the wake of the French and American revolutions and the Napoleonic era. Within the first generation reformers arose who proclaimed that this was a case of type two. As a free nation Norway had to have a language of its own, different from tha of its recent masters. In this search for the restoration of old glories the dialects became a prime resource. They have won a status that is unknown in any other western country within my knowledge.

While a consensus gradually developed that something must be done about an independent language, and that the dialects were a valuable resource, the experts split on the concrete proposals. Roughly speaking, there grew up three distinct points of view: a conservative view that dialects were interesting but irrelevant; a radical view that a new language must be developed on the basis of the most 'genuine' dialects; and a moderate view that one could make do with traditional Danish when properly modified in line with the most important dialects. These views were expressed by leading scholars: the conservative spokesman was the historian Peter Andreas Munch, the radical was the linguist Ivar Aasen, and the moderate was the educator Knud Knudsen.

Munch saw the Danish period as an undeniable part of Norwegian history. Aasen rejected it in favor of a language that he would call 'Landsmål', tying the present to the past by selecting elements from the 'oldest' living dialects and comparison with Old Norwegian. Knudsen advocated a gradual modification of Danish to approximate it to the living dialects of the urban upper classes.

These scholarly proposals were quickly embodied in political parties. Munch's party came to known as the 'Right' (Hoire), while the Aasen and Knudsen views were housed within the 'Left' (Venstre). In 1884 the Left managed to capture a majority in the Parliament (Stortinget). A year later the Parliament voted to give what they called 'the Norwegian Folk Language' equal official status with what they called 'the Usual Book Language.' The terminology was deliberately vague as between Aasen's and Knudsen's line; the main point was that from now on Norwegian was going to be written differently from Danish. Just what the language would be was left to the future. A system of local option was instituted, and the nature of the Norwegian language became a political issue of succeeding generations.

MODERN REFORMS

Bitter battles ensued, and the first major break did not come until the early twentieth century, thanks to the enthusiasm born with Norway's release from the dynastic union with Sweden in 1905. In 1907 a greatly modified version of Dano-Norwegian was adopted and widely acclaimed. This new form of Dano-Norwegian early received the name of Riksmål, 'Language of the Realm' and from now on the battle was joined between Riksmål and Landsmål.

The orthography of 1907 restored the postvocalic voiceless stops (p t k) of Norwegian, which had become voiced (b d g) in Danish: ape 'ape' for abe, ut 'out' for ud, kake 'cake' for kage. But it took into account those urban dialects that still retained some spelling pronunciations of Danish, e.g. viden 'knowledge' beside vite 'know', sagforer 'lawyer' beside sak 'law case'. The orthographic changes included a number of morphological changes, e.g. plurals in -er and zero, as in sanger 'songs' for sange, hus 'houses' for huse; preterites in -dde, -t and -et, as in bodde 'lived' for boede, kastet 'threw' for kastede; pronominal forms like nogen 'some' for nogle, dere 'you pl.' for I. Meanwhile the Landsmål language was winning adherents in the West Norwegian countryside, and it became necessary to establish organizations in defence of Riksmål.

In 1917 an effort was made to bring Riksmål still further into line with the advancing Landsmål in a new orthographic change. In these years many thinkers were proposing an amalgamation of the two languages, a fusion that would both eliminate the archaic features of Landsmål and the exlusively urban features of Riksmål. The orthography of 1917 expanded the idea of alternative forms. This developed from the exclusions permitted in 1907 on behalf of conservative urban forms.

The major required change in 1917 was the gemination of long consonants, making takk 'thanks' out of tak, topp 'top' out of top, and dugg 'dew' out of dug. We need not stop with other, minor changes, but go right on to the problem of optional versus obligatory forms.

A number of rather striking differences between Norwegian and Danish tradition consisted of phonetic and morphological features that reflected a somewhat more dialectal and conservative state of Norwegian. It now became optional to introduce these relatively rural forms into Riksmål, which had previously rejected them. In the Parliament they were carried by a margin of only one vote, after long and bitter debates. We may list the most important of them:

(1) Norwegian diphthongs vs. Danish monophthongs, e.g. hauk 'hawk' (Danish høg), einer 'juniper' for ener, røis 'rock pile' for røs.
(2) Consonantal differences, e. g. g for v in farge 'color', hage 'garden' for farve, have; kv for hv in kvit 'white', kvile 'rest' for hvit, hvile.
(3) Noun declensions in -a, e.g. in the sg. def. feminine sola 'the sun', visa 'the ballad' for solen, visen; in the def. plur. neuter taka 'the roofs', husa 'the houses' for takene (Danish tagene), husene.
(4) Verb conjugations in -a (the weak preterite), e.g. kasta 'threw' for kastet (Danish kastede).

The significant aspect of these changes was that they departed radically from the Riksmål tradition (and in some respects from the Landsmål tradition by adopting -a for the def. sg. nouns instead of Aasen's -i, e.g. soli 'the sun'). They reflected a fusionist view of the language situation, the hope of some reformers that they would lead the way to complete amalgamation and the creation of a single Norwegian language, to be called 'samnorsk', united Norwegian. In preparation for such a consummation the politicians rebaptized the languages in what proved to be a typical politician's solution. Landsmål was now to be called Nynorsk 'New Norwegian', while Riksmål was saddled with the inept Bokmål 'Book Language.' It became common to refer to them not as 'languages' (språk) but as 'language forms' (målformer).

WARTIME OCCUPATION

So far the impetus of Norwegian independence had carried the reform movements ahead; but in 1940 the German invasion brought to a sudden end all the attempts to make a single Norwegian language out of two. By this time Nynorsk had still only captured those parts of the country whose dialects approached Aasen's ideal most closely, i.e. the picturesque western fjords and the Midland valleys. All the cities remained in the Riksmål or Bokmål camp along with most of eastern and northern Norway. What the reformers had overlooked was that in the meanwhile the nature of Norwegian society had been radically changed. Beginning in the early 1900's the country changed from a primarily rural to an urban industrial economy. Water power furnished abundant electricity, and modern industry got a foothold that made the country only to a small extent a country of farmers and fishermen. From having at one time won nearly half the rural population, the Nynorsk percentage slipped to sixteen percent and remained concentrated in its own part of the country. But in 1938 the Labor Government adopted a new orthography in which the optional forms became largely obligatory.

During the German occupation the Norwegian people were welded together as never before. The old slogans that called the adherents of Riksmål 'un-Norwegian' and 'pro-Danish' fell into disuse. The young people of the cities proved to be every bit as patriotic as those in the country. So when the Government proceeded after the war to introduce again the reforms of 1938, a new kind of opposition rose. The adherents of Riksmål formed new organizations under the banner of their old name. They made a distinction between the Bokmål as the new government-imposed version and the good old Riksmål of 1917. They refused to join the newly appointed Norwegian Language Committee (Norsk Språknemnd) because it was committed to the 1938 reform and, as they saw it, would discriminate against them. They created an academy of their own and agitated in public and in Parliament in favor of their point of view.

POSTWAR DEVELOPMENTS

The result was that for the first time since 1884 the

reformers met a genuine reverse. The government agreed that the time had come to appoint a new committee that would "protect" the wealth that exists in our written languages and in our dialects in town and country." In 1964 the committee was appointed under the leadership of the distinguished linguist Hans Vogt. Two years later it proposed the creation of a new language body with a less rigidly reformist mandate. Under the name of the Norwegian Language Council (<u>Norsk Språkråd</u>) this highly representative organ came into existence in 1973 and has since functioned admirably as a common forum for all the various language factions. Even the Riksmal activists have their representation.

In 1981 the Council was finally ready to present a new orthography for Bokmål. An elaborate system had been devised that made it possible to write Bokmål in a variety of ways. The Riksmål forms that were rejected in 1938 were now reinstated as optional alternatives, e.g. <u>frem/fram</u> 'forward', <u>hvass/kvass</u> 'sharp', <u>syd/sør</u> 'south'. Most striking is the reinstatement of the Dano-Norwegian monophthongs for Norwegian diphthongs, e.g. ben/bein 'straight', <u>grøt/graut</u> 'porridge', or such pairs as <u>bro/bru</u> 'bridge'.

Feminine singulars may now end in either <u>-a</u> or <u>-en</u>, and plural neuters in <u>-a</u> or <u>-ene</u>. Weak preterites may end in either <u>-a</u> or <u>-et</u>. But exception is made for words that refer to peculiarly Norwegian phenomena, usually rural; these must have the Nynorsk form, e.g. <u>krøttera</u> 'the cattle', <u>bygda</u> ''the farm community', <u>beina</u> 'the legs', <u>barna</u> 'the children'. Most of the exceptions are already a natural part of daily urban speech. The committee report states that the changes affect the spelling of some 150 words and the inflection of five hundred neuter nouns, 1100 feminine nouns, and about 240 weak verbs. The choice is a bit more limited in textbooks than in the pupils' own writing, which may move widely across the spectrum. As Professor Eyvind Halvorsen said in summing up the activity of the Language Council in 1981: "The spelling of 1917 in fact represented the extreme limits of the Riksmål when its norm was fixed on about the same lines as Danish and Swedish." As a matter of fact, most leading newspapers have never gone much beyond it.

Once the new norm was established, the Language Council could issue its long-awaited desk dictionaries, one each for Bokmål and Nynorsk. They appeared in 1986 and embody the varieties of the norm. Here all the rival, optional forms are listed under each head, e.g. <u>graut</u> and <u>grøt</u> are both listed, with appropriate cross references. Well before this time the Riksmål people had issued their own Riksmål Dictionary in 1977, which was and is followed by most private presses.

THE DIALECT WAVE

The Nynorsk partisans had remained very much in the shade during the conflict between the Bokmål and the Riksmål people. They had not made any new advances since the war, and their support was dwindling, even as they had secured a firm foothold as equal partners on the Language Council. They took renewed heart on seeing that the Norwegian people rejected membership in the European Economic Community (EEC). They detected an ethnic revival in the rural communities. In the 1970's they launched a campaign to encourage dialect speakers to maintain their dialects. They smuggled their own language into a popular slogan: "Speak Dialect and Write Nynorsk." While it is too early to judge how effective this propaganda ploy will be, we can only say that dialects are well and alive in modern Norway; they are not discriminated against to the extent that they are in Denmark and Sweden. At the same time there is no doubt that rural dialects are losing ground against the urban varieties.

The campaign on behalf of dialects has a long tradition in Norwegian life, and it has been reinforced by a fear of Anglo-American influence. Young people today are overwhelmed by the English-speaking media, from pop music and rock groups to paperbacks, radio programs, video discs, and TV shows. The major influence on the language today is predominantly Anglo-American, with Swedish a distant second. Dialects may be retained as linguistic structures, but they are increasingly being diluted by English loans. Counter measures have been launched by the Language Council, and only the future can tell us how successful these are.

We may sum up the message of this paper by saying that in Norway dialects are honored because they are felt to embody the national spirit. Against this fact stands a realization that for four centuries Danish was the language of Norway. The country is at once a West European country with a language that is in constant modernization and a post-colonial country in which a language is being created with roots in the local dialects. Because the people have been unable to resolve this conflict, they continue to be linguistically divided. Any complete understanding of the Norwegian language requires at least two dictionaries, two grammars, and two handbooks. Yet it would not be correct to call the country bilingual; at most it may be said to have a dual identity, in which the dialects form the cement that holds it together.

References

Guttu, T. et al. (1977) Riksmålsordboken. Oslo: Kunnskapsforlaget.
Haugen, E. (1966) Riksspråk og folkemål. Oslo: Universitetsforlaget (tr. D. Gundersen)
Norsk språk i dag: Rapport frå ein konferanse på Lysbu, 9/-10. november 1981. Oslo: Norsk språkråd.
Rettskrivningsvedtak i 1985. Språknytt 1986, 14.2.1-4 Oslo: Norsk språkråd.
Dictionaries: Bokmålsodboka (1986) Oslo: Universitetsforlaget.
Nynorskordboka (1986) Oslo: Det norske samlaget.

Projects of linguistic atlasses of German in the FRG and in neighbouring countries (computer-aided projects are hatched, but add the *KDSA* and the *HAKWT*)

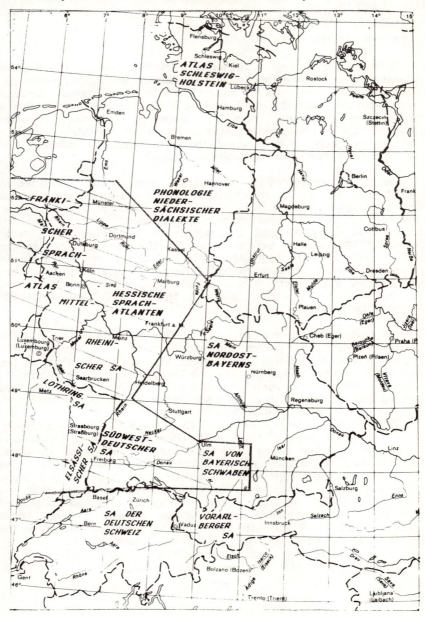

Variation in the Plural Reflexive in Spoken English: Preliminary Evidence for Merger

JOHN J. STACZEK
Georgetown University

A subset of a larger corpus of variation data on the English reflexive reveals some preliminary evidence for linguistic change. Consistency in the data of plural reflexives in spoken America English reveals that the **-self/-selves** distinction is merging into a single form consistent with the paradigm for the singular. Although the forms are sometimes found in varieties of non-standard English, it is argued that the variation extends into educated conversational varieties of English.

For the purposes of this discussion, **merger** will be defined as a mechanism of change in which two forms coalesce into a single form (Lehmann 1962, p.156). Lehmann's use of the term was generally applied to phonological rearrangement. I have extended the use to morphological rearrangement consistent with what Crystal (1980, p.225) refers to as "...the coming together (or CONVERGENCE) of linguistic UNITS which were originally distinguishable." Analogous terms from historical linguistics are **coalescence, syncretism,** and **neutralization**, all of which refer to "...the merging of forms following the loss of INFLECTIONS" (Crystal 1980, p.225).

In 1979 I first began to notice, certainly without looking for the phenomenon, a spoken and sometimes written usage of the English reflexive that was inconsistent with the formal rules of the grammar. In other research (Staczek 1983, 1985, and forthcoming), I have explored the variation data of reflexives and suggested various interpretations for the modification of reflexive rules.

During the collection of data I also began to observe a change in the use of the form of the plural reflexive, the topic I expect to comment on in this paper. Quite vividly I can recall the first token of data as I sat acutely attentive in the dentist's chair. The conversational exchange with the senior dental student in a large university dental clinic made me take notice of a usage that has since been found repeated spontaneously in other settings and under different circumstances. In the domain of casual chat between dentist and patient, the following brief exchange on the matter of the casting of a gold onlay took place in 1985:
1. Patient: Yes, and who does the casting?
    Dentist: Oh, we do the casting ourself.

My purpose in asking the question was more naivete than a conscious effort to try to elicit a reflexive. As the form surfaced, I was already intimately aware of more than casual variation in the use of the reflexive. Moreover, as a linguist interested in variation, I too had heard and, of course, read about reductions of the type [s f] for 'self' or [s v] for 'selves' in other varieties of American English. Once tuned to the possibility with the first person plural, it was not difficult to observe other similar changes in the pattern with regard to other plural pronouns.

Motivation for the reflexive is well-documented in the current transformational literature (Culicover 1982; Harris 1973a, 1973b; Jackendoff 1972; Lakoff 1971; Langacker 1969; Leech and Svartvik 1975; Lees and Klima 1963; Postal 1966, 1974; and, Ross 1970). Moreover, in recent work by Staczek (1983, 1985, and forthcoming), I have proposed an interpretation for reflexive variation on the basis of interclausal and discoursal features, accounting for data such as the following:

(2) Realities are created by humanity ourselves.

(3) I believe that studying economics and business in Germany is the best way to prepare myself for this profession.

(4) You were there when it happened. And, since these matters have previously been discussed with yourself and the arresting officer...

(5) I'd like to remind ourselves.

(6) This is so atypical for myself.

(7) Between ourselves and Mark we should get started on the proposal.

(8) You're the best in the country; let's hear it for yourself.

(9) We're trying to check on gold medals, for O'Brien and myself.

Returning to the variation in question and the possibility of merger, in Staczek (forthcoming) I introduced two other pieces of data:

(10) We just arrived ourself.
(11) We built it ourself.

and offered the following explanation:

> ...these are simply incorrect applications of the reflexive rule that deals with agreement [in which] there may also be a case for an analogy with the second person pair of 'yourself/yourselves'...that a second person singular reflexive appears in many contexts even when the plural form may be called for. The plural form may be undergoing replacement. Of course, its antecedent is unmarked morphologically for number but semantically marked given the context, which may explain this phenomenon. By artificial or false analogy, the first person plural subject then generates the morphologically simple form. Further hypothesizing, the frequency of **-self** as compared to **-selves** is probably much higher and thereby causes a merger and eventual loss of the plural reflexive form.

On the analogy of the process of sound change whereby the "...sounds change so completely that they fall together with the sounds of another phoneme" (Lehmann 1973, pp.159-160), a morphological merger, in conversational varieties of English, seems to be occurring. Evidence such as the following suggests a merger:

(12) We were both wondering ourself who made this mess.

(13) We were afraid not to show ourself to anyone.

(14) How we portray ourself influences the way we behave.

(15) We discourage that quality in ourself.

(16) Who do we owe it (national debt) to? Ourself?

(17) Let's look a little more closely and ask ourself some questions.

(18) Often as not we do it ourself.

(19) We ask ourself if it's worth it.

(20) We don't quite understand it ourself.

(21) Me and my daughter were home by ourself.

The use of **ourself** with the first person plural subject is quite consistent in the above conversational tokens. While (12) represents the reflexive used as intensifier (interest), (13-21) are clause mate reflexives. They follow the regular rule that generates the reflexive; they do not however copy the number of the clause-mate antecedent.

In the following second person plural tokens, plurality is clearly expressed in (22-24):

(22) There is a lot of inspiration that all of you can get for yourself.

(23) You guys better quit doin' this. You're gonna hurt yourself one of these days.

(24) I'm sure many of you have played this headgame with yourself.

The subjects--'all of you', 'you guys', and 'many of you'--would regularly generate a plural reflexive. However, because of the lack of a singular/plural distinction in the second person subject pronoun, a singular reflexive replaces the plural. The plural markers for the subject appear not to motivate a plural reflexive.

Another interesting second person token is found in (25)

(25) Speaker [addressing a group]: You can see for yourself it's a complex matter.

In this case, it is difficult to determine the intent of the speaker, that is, whether the speaker is addressing each member of the audience individually or together as a plural set. The speaker may very well have only one form of the pronoun subject and reflexive for singular and plural addressees.

Regarding the third person plural, sentences as (26-32) demonstrate the use of a plural subject generating singular reflexive:

(26) We hope that the people (AIDS victims) will take care of themself.

(27) Just when they've convinced themself, the kids will decide not to go.

(28) You think they're painting too benign a picture of themself.

(29) ...people who carve out a place for themself in a department...

(30) They can't help but enjoy themself.

(31) ...hoping that they'll be looking at themself...

(32) They have to see a harmony between themself and what they want in life.

Sentences (12-32) represent the three plural pronouns and demonstrate the consistency of the potential for simplification or merger of two forms into one in contemporary spoken English. However, a consideration of some historical rules and changes reveals that the forms are not unknown in the development of English. Flom (1930, p.70), in a brief reference to the reflexive pronouns, describes the state of affairs in Old English, namely, that "OE no longer possessed a distinctive reflexive form....to express the reflexive idea the word **self** was sometimes added." In a later description of the reflexive pronouns, Curme (1935, p.10) refers to the rule that accounts for the generation of the reflexive and to the changing development of the forms:

> ...In the seventeenth and eighteenth centuries **its self** was sometimes used instead of **itself**. In early Modern English, the older plural forms **our self**, **your self**, **them self** were still lingering, but were a little later replaced by **ourselves**, **yourselves**, **themselves**.

Thus, where historically there existed a single form **self** that combined with the singular and plural subject pronouns, an analogical split occurred to produce, in late Modern English, the **selves** form with the plural pronoun. The historical evidence suggests, as Flom pointed out earlier, that changes take place at different times, in different ways, at different rates, and within and beyond dialects.

While there is historical evidence to suggest a type of analogical pattern congruity, the new evidence relates somewhat to a confusion, or even morphological merger, with the free morpheme **self** as shown in the data from Staczek (1983, 1985, and forthcoming):

(33) Allow me to introduce my marvelous self.

(34) Just look at your skinny little self.

(35) Peter is not his same old self.

(36) Bring your thirsty self right here.
[American beer commercial]

In sentences (33-36) the matter of primary and secondary stress needs to be taken into account. The forms, however, are morphologically similar. Traugott (1972, p.127) proposes an interesting interpretation from sources in Old English, Middle English, and Modern English to account for the usages found in sentences (33-36):

> ...Reflexive -**self** forms did, however, come to be used more and more during the ME and ENE [Modern English] periods...Even when **self** does occur in ME and ENE it rarely seems to function as the empty element it is now. As in OE it is usually emphatic and has many of the characteristics of the noun **self**; often it seems equivalent to expressions like **my jolly body**, **my proper person**, which are frequently found in ME but become less common during ENE.

Related to Traugott's analysis is a sentence like (37):

(37) We like ourself very much, don't we?

This token comes from a Church Chat skit on the American television program, **Saturday Night Live**, for which a script is prepared but, since the program is broadcast live, there is undoubtedly room for some adlibbing. It is further an example of the condescending 'we' form that replaces 'you' or the 'we' form of respectful address. In this case, the addressee is singular and a plural reflexive would sound somewhat awkward.

Unrelated to the evidence that suggests a merger of two forms into the morphologically simple singular, there are additional data on the reflexive that require further observation and analysis:

(38) You have to be so careful about how you position yourselfs.

(39) Do yourselfs a favor!

In sentences (38) and (39), the use of **yourselfs** may be a simple speaker error in which the speaker is addressing a group by indicating an -s plural that does not follow the regular **self** >

selves final voicing rule; or the use may represent a systematic change of some other unspecified type. The evidence does not warrant an absolute conclusion. Sentence (40) may also represent speaker error.

(40) One locked themselves in a room.

Or, (40) might come from a sentence like (41):

(41) One of them locked themselves in a room.

the clause mate for which is not 'one' but 'them'. This too could be (a) a speaker misperformance or (b) a case of a plural feature to the left of the verb generating a plural to the right in the reflexive.

In sentence (42), there comes into play the problem of nonspecific gender of 'anyone'. This may account for the **them-**morpheme of the reflexive, on the analogy of the usage in (43)

(42) Did anyone see themselves in the mirror?

(43) Did anyone forget their books?

'Anyone', as a singular form, may explain the analogical occurrence of the singular -**selves** form because of the choice in usage to avoid specifying gender for a clause mate whose antecedent is genderless. A similar case may be made for (44):

(44) Each person put down an evaluation for the faculty including themselves.

'Themselves', according to usage, is grammatically, though not morphologically, an appropriate form.

In sentences (45-46), principles similar to those in (42) and (43) obtain, yet there is a suggestion about the speaker's inclusion of self in the reflexive. In (45) the form is merged into a singular; in (46) it follows the regular pattern for the plural with 'our'.

(45) Alert me so I can defend ourself.

(46) I'm proud of ourselves.

In sentences (47-48) there appears to be no superficial clause mate to generate a reflexive:

(47) It can be used to recapture the growth

that occurs naturally in ourself.

(48) It's nice to remind ourself.

In both cases there might be reason to suggest the influence of what Ross (1970) calls a performative verb hierarchy, in other words, a cross-clausal generation of the reflexive on the basis of discoursal features (Staczek, in press).

In the final set of tokens, sentences (49-50), we have the case of the collective noun 'people' generating a plural pronominal segment and a singular reflexive:

(49) What we encourage people to do is give themself credit for the labor in remodeling.

(50) They feel the repression of the people themself.

Sentence (50) could, of course, be structurally ambiguous because of the placement of the reflexive: it could have a clause mate in 'they' or one in 'people'. Whichever the case, the merged form of the plural reflexive surfaces.

In summary, while I do not believe that fifty tokens from a larger corpus represent decisive evidence for a formal merger, they are certainly compelling and suggestive as preliminary evidence for such a merger in conversational varieties of American English.

REFERENCES

Bloomfield, M.W. and Newmark, L. (1963) A Linguistic Introduction to the History of English. New York: Alfred A. Knopf.

Culicover, P.W. (1982) Syntax. New York: Academic Press.

Crystal, D. (1980) A First Dictionary of Linguistics and Phonetics. London: Andre Deutsch.

Curme, G. (1935) A Grammar of the English Language. Volumes 1 and 2. Essex, CT: Verbatim. (Original work published 1935).

Dinneen, F.P. (ed) (1966) 17th Annual Round Table Meeting on Linguistics and Language Studies. Washington: Georgetown University Press.

Fasold, R.W. (ed) (1983) Variation in the Form and Use of Language. Washington: Georgetown University Press.

Fasold, R.W., Schiffrin, D. and Lowenberg, P. (eds) (in press) Language Variation and Change. Amsterdam: John Benjamins.

Fasold, R.W. and Shuy, R.W. (eds) (1977) Studies in Language Variation: Semantics, Syntax, Phonology, Pragmatics, Social Situations, Ethnographic Approaches. Washington: Georgetown University Press.

Flom, G.T. (1930) Introductory Old English Grammar and Reader. Boston: D. C. Heath and Company.

Harris, F.W. (1973a) Reflexivization I. In: McCawley, J. (ed).

_____ (1973b). Reflexivization II. In: McCawley, J. (ed).

Jackendoff, R. (1972) Semantic Interpretation in Generative Grammar. Cambridge: Cambridge University Press.

Lakoff, G. (1971) Irregularity in Syntax. New York: Holt, Rinehart and Winston.

Langacker, R. (1969) On pronominalization and the chain of command. In: Reibel, D. and Schane, S. (eds).

Leech, G. and Svartvik, J. (1975) A Communicative Grammar of English. London: Longman.

Lees, R. and Klima, E. (1963) Rules for English pronominal-pronominalization. <u>Language</u> 39. 17-28.

Lehmann, W.P. (1973) Historical Linguistics: An Introduction (2nd ed.). New York: Holt, Rinehart and Winston.

McCawley, J. (ed) (1973) Syntax and Semantics: Notes from the Linguistic Underground. New York: Academic Press.

Postal, P. (1974) On Raising: One Rule of English Grammar and Its Theoretical Implications. Cambridge, Massachusetts: MIT Press.

_____ (1966) On so-called 'pronouns' in English". In: Dinneen, F.P. (ed).

Reibel, D.A. and Schane, S. (eds) (1969). Modern Studies in English. Englewood Cliffs: Prentice-Hall.

Ross, J.R. (1970). On declarative sentences. In: Jacobs, R.A. Rosenbaum, P.S. (eds) Readings in English Transformational

Grammar. Waltham, Massachusetts: Ginn and Company.

Staczek, J.J. (forthcoming). Sentential and discoursal variation in the English reflexive. In: Fasold, R.W., Schiffrin, D. and Löwenberg, P. (eds) Language Variation and Change. Amsterdam: John Benjamins, BV.

____ (forthcoming). The English pronominal reflexive: An aspect of usage variation. <u>Studia Anglica Posnaniensia</u>.

____ (1985). Reflexive variation: L1/L2 speaker's acceptability and grammaticality judgments. Paper presented at the 19th annual TESOL Convention, New York, New York.

____ (1983). Pronominal self-abuse: Variation in the use of reflexives. Paper presented at the XXVIII SECOL Conference, College Park, Maryland.

____ (1982). Self-abuse: variation in the use of reflexives. Paper presented at the Second Mid-West Regional TESOL Conference, Purdue University, West Lafayette, Indiana.

Traugott, E.C. (1972) The History of English Syntax. New York: Holt, Rinehart, and Winston.

Visser, F.Th. (1963) An Historical Syntax of the English Language (Vol. 5, part 1). Leiden: E. J. Brill.

Linguistic Variation in the Non-Stratified Social Context

SANDRA CLARK
Memorial University of Newfoundland

ABSTRACT. This paper discusses an application of Labovian sociolinguistic methodology to a context which does not exhibit socio-economic stratification, a tiny rural American Indian community. Several of the major problems associated with the extension of the methodology to this type of context are outlined, among them stylistic manipulation, sample selection and determination of the optimal social correlates of linguistic variation. It is shown, nonetheless, that variation methodology can prove highly successful outside the urban context for which it was developed, and that linguistic behaviour in such settings may display heretofore unnoted parallels with language use in more socio-economically complex contexts.

INTRODUCTION

Over the past twenty years, the quantitative study of linguistic variation in particular speech communities has tended to focus on urban contexts which display a clear socio-economic hierarchy. It is by now a commonplace observation that social class stratification is extremely important not only in clarifying patterns of synchronic linguistic variation in individual speech communities, but also in identifying variables that are involved in various stages of language change.

Since Labov's pioneering New York City investigation, the study of linguistic variation has of course been extended to a number of contexts which do not display the same complexities of social class stratification that would be found in major urban centres of North America and Europe. Among these are investigations that have applied the variationist paradigm to rural settings involving much smaller populations; Canadian examples include King (1983) and Flikeid (1984) on Acadian French, as well as Colbourne (1982) and Pringle and Padolsky (1983) on rural dialects of English. In spite of the broadening of the Labovian approach to linguistic variation which these studies have entailed, they nonetheless deal with contexts in which language use co-varies to some degree with socio-economic stratification. Further, in all of these rural studies, the speech variety representing the prestige norm, to which the upwardly mobile of a particular speech community aspire, is quite easily identifiable.

There appear, however, to be few, if any, investigations which have applied quantitative sociolinguistic methodology to speech communities which display no overt socio-economic stratification. A context of this type is precisely the focus of this paper. The speech community to be discussed is a tiny Amerindian village of fewer than 600 inhabitants, located in Labrador, or in the extreme north-eastern portion of the North American continent. The village in question is Sheshatshiu, whose residents are speakers of Montagnais, an Algonquian dialect closely related to the Cree dialects spoken farther to the west. By North American standards, most of the residents of the community live in quite abject poverty. Their housing is substandard, often lacking water and sewage facilities, and perhaps even electricity; there is little steady employment, and extensive reliance on government financial assistance. While some families seem slightly better off than others, objective social class measures would undoubtedly result in the allocation of virtually all community members to one and the same social class.

The question of course immediately arises as to what interest such a context would hold for a sociolinguistic researcher working within a variationist paradigm. The village of Sheshatshiu offers definite proof that considerable language variation may exist even within a tiny, rural, overtly unstratified setting. For the settlement represents an extremely interesting situation of dialect mixing. Sheshatshiu is a relatively new community, created as a permanent residence site only some 30 years ago; prior to this, it constituted merely a summer gathering ground for nomadic Montagnais groups who spent the rest of the year hunting and trapping in the interior. The Montagnais who were forced to abandon their traditional way of life in order to obtain the supposed educational and economic benefits that would result from fixed settlement brought to the new community a number of regionally- or geographically-differentiated dialects. These are what constitute the essence of the variation to be found in the present-day community, although, as will be demonstrated, the linguistic situation within this tiny community is in fact fairly complex.

PROBLEMS WITH EXISTING METHODOLOGY

In dealing with a context of the type proposed in this paper from a variationist perspective, a number of problems arise. There are in fact three principal areas in which difficulties may be identified in the application of existing methodology:

1. The elicitation of a range of styles or registers

The collection of data from various stylistic levels has of course been a basic tenet of variationist methodology, one that has provided considerable insight not only into the social organization of the community, but also into ongoing linguistic change. A population which is largely illiterate, however, offers major obstacles to the implementation of the usual techniques of stylistic data gathering.

2. Selection of a representative sample of community residents
and
3. Determination of the optimal social correlates of language variability in the community

In a context which exhibits no overt socio-economic stratification, and in which the precise social correlates of linguistic variation are by no means clear, the ideal technique of stratified random sampling is extremely difficult to implement.

In the following sections, each of these problems will be discussed in some detail.

Stylistic Manipulation

In marked opposition to traditional studies on regional linguistic variation, Labovian methodology offers a mechanism designed to capture an entire range of linguistic styles or registers. This mechanism, of course, involves the manipulation of a number of reading tasks, each of which is designed to elicit a different degree of formality within a subject's verbal repertoire. While the literature has indicated certain weaknesses with aspects of reading task methodology (e.g. Milroy, 1980; Davis, 1983), our concern here is considerably more fundamental. For Sheshatshiu represents a context in which stylistic elicitation strategies involving reading tasks would be doomed to failure, since most residents of the community - like many inhabitants of less developed areas - are not literate in their mother tongue.

Several sociolinguistic investigations involving rural settings have been faced with a similar dilemma, and have attempted to solve it in different ways. In a genuinely bilingual context, of course, a 'translation from the majority language' approach could be adopted, as, for example, in the Acadian French study of King (1983). In many less developed areas, however, the average individual will have had little majority language contact; consequently, a translation method would fare little better than a reading task. This would certainly be the case in Sheshatshiu, whose oldest residents are monolingual in the native language.

One study, at least, has used a creative two-tiered interview technique which dispenses with the necessity of reliance on either translation or reading (Flikeid 1984). In this approach, casual and formal speech styles are obtained through variation in the interviewer: casual style via an interviewer internal to the community, who speaks a local, non-standard dialect, and formal style by means of an interviewer from outside the area, who uses a more standard speech variety. It is a variant of this two-tier technique which the Sheshatshiu investigation attempted to implement. A fairly casual speech style was elicited through the recording of everyday conversation; where possible, a local native interviewer was involved, although in a setting of this nature it is often difficult to find a person with the necessary expertise to assume sole responsibility for such a task. A formal style, on the contrary, was obtained through the use of outside, non-native interviewers fluent in a related dialect of Montagnais. However, to ensure that the formal interviews would elicit an adequate number of tokens of the linguistic features under investigation, they were not structured around conversation. Rather, the non-native interviewers used a formal word list, and presented, in their related dialect, stimulus items equivalent to the lexical items they were attempting to elicit. In addition to its efficiency, this method had the advantage of avoiding the forced and artificial setting of formal conversational interaction with a partial stranger, a situation undesirable in a Montagnais cultural context.

There is considerable evidence from the Sheshatshiu study that the two-tiered interview approach proved highly successful, and yielded a much better understanding of language variation in this context than would an interview technique involving a single style. This is a very interesting observation, in light of the fact that the study dealt with a largely illiterate population with no clearly recognizable 'standard' speech variety. Some of the variables investigated nonetheless exhibited marked style shifting of the type to be found in urban socio-economically stratified settings. An example of this phenomenon is provided in Figure 1, which displays the use of an innovative or fairly recently attested [h] variant of the consonant phoneme (s), on the part of the three age groups by which the sample was eventually stratified. As can be seen, there is a considerable increase in the use of the innovative [h] pronunciation in casual speech style by all the age groups, which suggests a degree of awareness of this feature within the community of Sheshatshiu that is characteristic of a social marker. Nonetheless, the style shifting exhibited by this particular variable stands in marked contrast to the pattern which emerged for most of the phonological variables investigated, since most displayed a lack of stylistic stratification characteristic of a social indicator. This finding is also an interesting one, since it suggests that in the overtly unstratified community of Sheshatshiu phonological differences which mark the various regional dialects brought to the new settlement are not in general perceived by its residents. Indeed, direct observation and questioning reveal that with respect to intracommunity differences, lexical and grammatical features are considerably more salient to community members. Yet, as we will be seeing later, there *is* a clear direction of phonological change in the community, in favour of one of these regional dialects.

Sample Selection

In sociolinguistic variation studies, the usual sampling procedure is that of stratified random sampling, whereby the population is divided into a number of social strata, within each of which random sampling techniques are applied. Obviously, this approach is impossible if researchers are not thoroughly familiar with the social structure of the community, and not fully aware of the principal social factors - apart of course from the expected variables of age and sex - which underlie linguistic variability within it. As Linn (1983:236) puts it, 'Preselection of informants in stratified sampling is dependent upon knowing to which stratum each informant will belong before the interview.' However, owing to an absence of sufficient information on the hierarchical structure of the community, he notes that 'For most sociolinguistic studies, stratification must be performed after selection.'

A lack of thorough documentation of Sheshatshiu social structure led in the present investigation to the selection of a very large sample by comparison to that of the usual sociolinguistic variation study: 87 subjects, or 29% of the available over-14 population (which numbered some 300 if one excludes those who were absent from the community, or who exhibited speech and hearing defects). This occurred in spite of the fact that the three co-investigators were acknowledged experts on Montagnais, from both the anthropological and linguistic perspectives. Nonetheless, they were to discover that the community of Sheshatshiu differed socially in a number of ways from the related Montagnais communities with which they were more familiar.

Quite apart from the difficulties involved with the determination of appropriate stratificational parameters, the problems associated with the application of random sampling techniques also proved considerable in the Sheshatshiu context. Since certain community members continue to exhibit migratory behaviour, a random sample would have included names of individuals who were simply inaccessible during the six-month data collection period. In addition, such a sample would not have guaranteed the inclusion of representatives of the different generations of individual family groups, and hence made difficult the cross-generational comparison desirable in a situation in which considerable language change appears to be in progress. As a result, the decision was made to opt for a quota rather than a random sampling approach.

Even quota sampling proved difficult to implement in the context under investigation. While the factors which rendered difficult the selection of subjects in the Montagnais seting may not be identical to problems to be encountered in other non-socio-economically stratified contexts, they will give some idea of the range of potential difficulty. The Sheshatshiu study was hampered by the existence of an extremely complex naming system, as a result of which names routinely used by the community to identify its members often did not coincide with the names by which such individuals were officially recognized; in addition, siblings on occasion might not share the same surname. Further, the extensive adoption practices of this Indian group made it impossible to assume that siblings possessed a common social or linguistic background. The obvious conclusion is that variationist studies are extremely difficult to conduct in contexts outside the normal western setting, since such contexts are often poorly documented from the social perspective. Researchers must therefore be prepared to devote an extensive period to background research in the community prior to actual sociolinguistic investigation.

Determination of the Social Correlates of Linguistic Variation

As mentioned above, considerable evidence of regional linguistic diversity is to be found among the dialects spoken by the oldest residents of the settlement of Sheshatshiu. These differ one from another with respect to lexical, grammatical and phonological features to a much greater extent than do the speech varieties found among the youth of the community, where a more focused, community-wide dialect is emerging - among whom, in other words, dialect convergence is taking place. Nonetheless, the actual geographical and/or social correlates of linguistic variation proved quite difficult to pinpoint even among the oldest members of the community.

It was earlier noted that non-stratified contexts whose inhabitants are closely related ethnically do not necessarily display the same type of social organization. In the present instance, the investigators' general familiarity with the various Montagnais groups inhabiting the Quebec-Labrador peninsula had led to the hypothesis that the major social divisions in the community would reflect traditional hunting group affiliations; indeed, a study conducted on Sheshatshiu Montagnais land use and occupancy (Tanner 1978) had suggested that present-day community residents belonged to six territorial hunting groups. Further investigation revealed, however, that the Montagnais of Quebec/Labrador have through their nomadic existence displayed considerable geographical mobility, allying themselves, for a number of reasons, with different hunting groups in different hunting seasons. The Sheshatshiu Montagnais represent what may in fact be an extreme case, since every resident of the present-day community exhibits ties with almost every other resident (whether through co-residence patterns for hunting purposes, marriage, kinship, or adoption).

A period of extensive fieldwork in the village revealed that the community itself could provide the key to its social organization.

It emerged that there was in ready use within the settlement a system of folk group membership; this was defined largely in territorial terms, and proved to be a less narrow classificational system than had the original hypothesis of hunting group affiliation. Three basic groups were identified (see Figure 2). Although each group is recognized by a traditional name, it is here represented in terms of the geographical area over which it ranged, relative to the present-day community: northern, southwestern and southern.

A classification scheme based primarily on subjects' opinions and intuitions, however, can hardly be conceived of as ideal. Sociolinguistic variation studies have revealed that subjects' self-perceptions are not to be taken at face value, since they correlate considerably more with desired social identity than with actual social and linguistic reality. Consequently, the community classificatory system in use in Sheshatshiu can only be considered a starting point; while it is clear that the three folk groups identified by the community are firmly grounded in reality, it is not unusual to find a lack of consistency between subject's self-identification in terms of folk group, and others' identification of them.

As in urban variability studies which rely on objective quantitative measures of SES, the solution to the problem involved the development of objective measures of community group membership. This was accomplished through extensive genealogical research, in both the community and the archival records. It included the collection of data on origins, place of birth, and territorial backgrounds of subjects' grandparents and parents, in addition to those of their spouses, as well as considerable information on the migration patterns of subjects' families in the years prior to permanent settlement. Once all such details were assembled, it proved a fairly straightforward task to assign subjects to one of the three basic groups; this task was facilitated by a marked tendency to endogamous marriage among earlier generations. In the remainder of this paper, the social variable which represents the objective assignment of sample members to the three groups will be referred to as territorial group membership.

It is of course the case that this objectively-derived social construct shares certain similarities with the concept of social network - a concept that has enjoyed considerable popularity in the recent sociolinguistic literature, following its development and application by Lesley Milroy (1980) in her working-class Belfast variation study. In a tiny rural community such as Sheshatshiu, social networks may be expected to be quite dense as well as multiplex. The community is sufficiently small that every inhabitant knows every other; subgroups of community residents interact closely through ties of kinship, friendship, mutual assistance in home and hunting-related tasks, and so on. Close observation of the community revealed, however, that the chief interactional unit was not the broad territorial group, but rather the immediate family, whether consanguineal or affinal. Further, in the absence of complex economic and occupationally-related transactions of the type common in a community whose primary stratification is socio-economic, the elaboration of a Network Strength Scale such as is found in the Milroy study was not deemed a viable enterprise. Nonetheless, the considerable amount of background data collected for every subject in the Sheshatshiu sample is enabling the construction, for every individual, of a scale of integration into each one of the three main territorial groups. In conjunction with the variable of territorial group membership, which assigns each sample member to his or her dominant territorial group, these group membership scales will aid in comprehending the extensive linguistic variation that characterizes the community.

CONCLUSION

Following our brief discussion of the primary difficulties associated with the application of variationist methodology in an overtly unstratified context, some assessment is in order of its ability to deal with this type of context. This is particularly true with respect to the social construct of territorial group membership, which is being advanced in the Sheshatshiu study as a primary correlate of linguistic variation in the community. The remainder of this paper will attempt to demonstrate that a variationist-based methodology can reveal extremely interesting insights into the social dynamics of a community such as Sheshatshiu. Indeed, it will be shown briefly that this methodology indicates that overtly unstratified speech communities may display remarkable sociolinguistic parallels with the clearly stratified settings that are the usual focus of investigation.

The Sheshatshiu study has to date examined 18 different phonological variables; grammatical variables still await analysis. In all cases, the relative frequencies of use of members of the 87 subject sample - that is, the proportion that they used a particular variant of a given phonological variable, by comparison to their usage of all variants of this same variable - were compared via the statistical test known as analysis of variance, using the three independent social variables of territorial group membership, age and sex. The precise sample design is provided in Table 1, where the southwestern group is stratified according to its two main subdivisions. Of the 18 phonological variables examined, all but one proved to display significant differences in usage among the three basic territorial groups. In other words, the variable of territorial group membership has proven to be a very powerful factor in clarifying linguistic variation in the new community of Sheshatshiu, second only to the factor of age, for which significant differences in usage emerged, in at least one speech style, for all 18 of the phonological features examined.

As might be expected, however, the significance of the social variable of territorial group membership cannot be fully understood in a community of this nature independently of age, since, given the apparent dialect convergence among younger community residents, linguistic markers of territorial group appear much more in evidence among older residents of the community than among its younger members. Statistical analysis does indeed confirm this impression: for a number of the phonological features examined, there are significant interactions between territorial group membership and age. An example is provided in Table 2, which represents the use in casual speech style of the pre-aspirated sequence (ht) by both age and territorial group. While Tables 2A and 2B reveal there to be significant overall differences in usage among, respectively, the three territorial groups and the three age groups, Table 2C indicates the reason for this, namely, highly significant differences in usage among the oldest speakers of the sample, based on their territorial group affiliation. Pre-aspiration in the sequence (ht) is clearly linked to the oldest or 46+ group of <u>northern</u>-affiliated subjects, and in casual speech style is scarcely used by any other subgroup, least of all by any speakers under the age of 45.

The revised variationist paradigm outlined in this paper has, then, indeed proven successful in clarifying intracommunity linguistic variation in an apparently unstratified setting. Yet can the paradigm reveal anything further than the expected, that is, beyond the establishment of a linking of language use with territorial group and age? Can it yield any insight into the social organization of the settlement, particularly with respect to the possible existence of a subtle social hierarchy? Given the fact that a more homogeneous, community-wide dialect is emerging among the youth, one very fruitful line of investigation offered by the apparent time dimension of this study is the direction of phonological change. That is, if language change in the community clearly favours the adoption of variants which are markers of membership in one particular territorial group, rather than the other two, this would provide some indication as to the existence of a territorial group hierarchy.

Of the 18 phonological features examined, 14 clearly involve an increase in use of a variant characterizing one of the three territorial groups, at the expense of variants associated with the speech of the other two. As Table 3 demonstrates, there is an obviously favoured direction of change, namely, a tendency among younger generations to adopt linguistic markers characterizing southwestern group membership.

Let us examine one of these cases a little more closely. Table 4 represents the apparent time and territorial group profiles associated with the deletion of word-initial short (i). Deletion of word-initial short vowels is a southwestern territorial group marker, as the over 46 age usage in both formal and casual speech styles suggests. From the linguistic behaviour of the oldest group, it is clear that initial (i) deletion is _not_ a feature of southern speech; yet in formal speech style, it is precisely the under 45 groups of _southern_ speakers who use it the most, while in casual style, the teenage group of southern speakers uses the deleted variant in 61% of its occurrences, that is, considerably more than do the other two teenage territorial groups. These observations indicate a hypercorrect linguistic behaviour on the part of younger southern speakers, a behaviour not unlike that exhibited by lower middle class speakers in many urban variability studies. This in turn suggests the existence of a prestige hierarchy within the community, one in which those with southwestern territorial group affiliations occupy the uppermost position.

There are numerous pieces of evidence to support such a hypothesis. Several of the other phonological variables examined behave in exactly the same way, exhibiting hypercorrection on the part of southern youth in favour of a southwestern-affiliated variant. As in urban contexts, it is Sheshatshiu females rather than males who display greater sensitivity to (presumably more prestigious) southwestern variants. Confirmation also comes from the examination of a broader geographical area. Drapeau (1986) shows that linguistic change among the Montagnais groups of the entire Quebec-Labrador peninsula favours the adoption of variants associated with what we are here calling the southwestern territorial group, the reason for this being the earlier contact of this group with white European society, and hence its earlier acculturation. Finally, close examination of certain highly comparable individuals in the sample suggests that language is indeed an important measure of social status. For example, northern subjects who marry into the more prestigious southwestern group seem to preserve their non-southwestern territorial speech markers much more so than northern-affiliated subjects who have married within their own group; these latter individuals seem to feel some subconscious need to adopt prestige linguistic markers. While space does not permit further development of these points, nor to provide an indication as to how marriage patterns within the community confirm the existence of a status hierarchy, more details are to be found in Clarke (1986).

In conclusion, I hope to have shown that, even though its application remains largely confined to urban western social settings, sociolinguistic variation methodology has much to offer the study of language use in other contexts as well. In spite of their size, speech communities numbering in the hundreds rather than the tens of thousands may display considerable linguistic variability. Since, however, such variability may not possess strong links with social class, as it does in the more familiar and better documented urban settings, the greatest difficulty faced by the researcher is the determination of the optimal social correlates of observable language variation in the context under investigation. One of the findings of the Sheshatshiu study is that a speech community which displays no overt social hierarchy may nonetheless be hierarchically stratified, and that linguistic behaviour in such settings may display heretofore unnoticed parallels with language use in more socio-economically complex contexts. It is to be hoped that further variationist work in speech communities of the Sheshatshiu type will indicate the extent to which such findings may be generalized.

ACKNOWLEDGEMENTS

The project reported on in this paper was made possible by a team research grant from the Institute for Social and Economic Research, Memorial University of Newfoundland. Other members of the team were Marguerite MacKenzie, Jose Mailhot and Adrian Tanner. Since MacKenzie and Mailhot were responsible for all of the fieldwork, and provided much of the needed expertise on Montagnais social organization, my debt to them is extensive, and is gratefully acknowledged. Thanks must also be extended to John Porter, who was responsible for all the phonetic transcription.

REFERENCES

Clarke, Sandra. (1986) Dialect mixing and linguistic variation in a non-overtly stratified society. Paper presented at the 14th annual conference on New Ways of Analyzing Variation (NWAV), Stanford University, California. To appear in the conference proceedings.

Colbourne, B. Wade. (1982) _A Sociolinguistic Study of Long Island, Notre Dame Bay, Newfoundland_. Unpublished M.A. thesis, Memorial University of Newfoundland.

Davis, Lawrence M. (1983) The elicitation of contextual styles in language: a reassessment. _Journal of English Linguistics_, 16, 18-26.

Drapeau, Lynn. (1986) Innovations in Montagnais. Paper presented at the conference on Linguistic Variation on the Northern Plains, University of Manitoba, Winnipeg.

Flikeid, Karin. (1984) A comparative study of Acadian French: report on the first phase. Paper presented at the 12th annual NWAV conference, University of Pennsylvania, Philadelphia.

King, Ruth. (1983) _Variation and Change in Newfoundland French: A Sociolinguistic Study of Clitic Pronouns_. Unpublished Ph.D. thesis, Memorial University of Newfoundland.

Linn, Michael D. (1983) Informant selection in dialectology. _American Speech_, 58,3, 225-43.

Milroy, Lesley. (1980) _Language and Social Networks._ Oxford: Basil Blackwell.

Pringle, Ian and Padolsky, Enoch. (1983) The linguistic survey of the Ottawa valley. _American Speech_, 58,4, 325-44.

Tanner, Adrian. (1978) Land Use and Occupancy among the Indians of North-West River, Labrador. Mimeo, St. John's, Newfoundland.

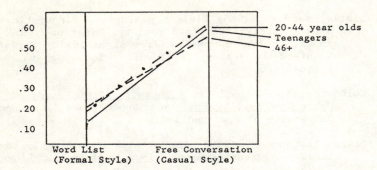

Figure 1. <u>Style shifting by three age groups in the use of an innovative [h] variant of the (š) variable</u> (number of tokens = 10064 in formal style, 8055 in casual style)

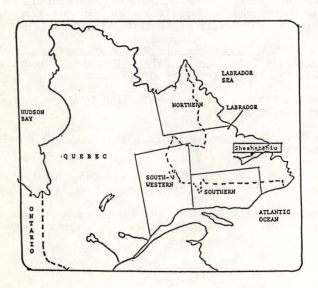

Figure 2. <u>Distribution of Montagnais dialects in the Quebec-Labrador peninsula in terms of traditional territories</u>

	TERRITORIAL GROUP							
AGE	Northern (Mushuau)		Southern (Maskuanu)		Southwestern			
					(Uashau)		(McKenzie)	
	Male	Female	Male	Female	Male	Female	Male	Female
14-19	4	4	1	2	1	2	5	3
21-44	8	6	3	4	4	4	3	4
46+	3	3	4	3	4	6	2	4
Totals	15	13	8	9	9	12	10	11

Table 1. The 87-subject Sheshatshiu sample

14-19 year olds: formal schooling, fluent in English, "community" orientation
21-44 year olds: some schooling, some knowledge of English, "mixed" orientation
46 year olds and over: no schooling, little knowledge of English, "bush" orientation

	SOUTHWESTERN VARIANTS	OTHER VARIANTS (i.e., NORTHERN AND SOUTHERN)	TOTAL
Usage increasing among younger generations	5	2	7
Usage stable or decreasing among younger generations	2	5	7

Table 3. Direction of phonological change in the Sheshatshiu speech community

TABLE 2. Relative frequency of usage of the
pre-aspirated sequence (ht), casual speech style
(number of tokens = 1720)

TERRITORIAL GROUP	AGE					
	FORMAL STYLE			CASUAL STYLE		
	14-19	21-44	46+	14-19	21-44	46+
Northern	.33	.28	.13	.31	.35	.18
Southwestern	.27	.25	.25	.28	.19	.20
Southern	.38	.49	.14	.61	.16	.09

(F=2.45, p=.05, df=4/69)   (Trend: p=.11)

TABLE 4. Relative frequency of use in two speech styles
of a deleted, 'southwestern' variant of initial (i),
in terms of age and territorial group membership
(number of tokens = 1186 in formal style,
736 in casual style)

GROUP	
Northern	.06
Southern	.01
Southwestern	.03

TABLE 2A. <u>Relative frequency of usage by the three territorial groups</u>
(F=6.78, p<.01, df=2/69)

AGE	
14-19	.00
21-44	.01
46+	.09

TABLE 2B. <u>Relative frequency of usage by the three age groups</u>
(F=22.45, p<.001, df=2/69)

GROUP	AGE		
	15-19	21-44	46+
Northern	.00	.01	.24
Southern	.00	.01	.03
Southwestern	.00	.01	.06

TABLE 2C. <u>Relative frequency of usage by both age and territorial group</u>
(F=8.84, p<.001, df=4/69)

Author Index

Arthurs, J. 155
Awbery, G. M. 164
Babitch, R. M. 121
Ball, M. J. 1
Baugh, J. 175
Bellin, W. 67
Bennett, J. 428
Butler, G. R. 11
Butters, R. R. 637
Cassidy, F. G. 326
Chambers, J. K. 650
Ching, M. K. L. 20
Cichocki, W. 187
Clark, S. 684
Cunningham, I. A. E. 46
Davis, L. M. 225
de Wolf, G. D. 55
Dürmüller, U. 278
Evans, R. 241
Flikeid, K. 79
Frazer, T. C. 89
Girard, D. 251
Glauser, B. 611
Gosy, M. 442
Gregg, R. J. 434
Hall, J. H. 557
Hasebe-Ludt, E. 55
Haugen, E. 666

Hausmann, R. B. 285
Ihalainen, O. 569
Ikemiya, T. 306
Kelle, B. 585
King, R. 95
Kontra, M. 442
Kretzschmar, W. A. Jr. 200
Larmouth, D. 251
Linn, M. D. 138
Macaulay, R. K. S. 456
Maynor, N. 109
McDavid, V. G. 333
McGregor, G. 362
Miller, M. I. 464
Montgomery, M. 480
Kirk, J. M. 492
Preston, D. R. 373
Regal, R. R. 138
Ryan, R. 95
Schneider, E. W. 396
Sledge, M. C. 625
Spears, R. A. 600
Staczek, J. J. 674
Thomas, P. W. 510
Underwood, G. N. 406
Veith, W. H. 551
Viereck, W. 524